The Handbook of
SPIRITUAL DEVELOPMENT
in CHILDHOOD
and ADOLESCENCE

The SAGE Program on Applied Developmental Science

Consulting Editor

Richard M. Lerner

The field of Applied Developmental Science has advanced the use of cutting-edge developmental systems models of human development, fostered strength-based approaches to understanding and promoting positive development across the life span, and served as a frame for collaborations among researchers and practitioners, including policymakers, seeking to enhance the life chances of diverse young people, their families, and communities. The **SAGE Program on Applied Developmental Science** both integrates and extends this scholarship by publishing innovative and cutting-edge contributions.

The Handbook of
SPIRITUAL
DEVELOPMENT
in CHILDHOOD
and ADOLESCENCE

Editors

Eugene C. Roehlkepartain, *Search Institute*

Pamela Ebstyne King, *Fuller Theological Seminary*

Linda Wagener, *Fuller Theological Seminary*

Peter L. Benson, *Search Institute*

SAGE Publications

Thousand Oaks ▪ London ▪ New Delhi

For information:

Sage Publications, Inc.
2455 Teller Road
Thousand Oaks, California 91320
E-mail: order@sagepub.com

Sage Publications Ltd.
1 Oliver's Yard
55 City Road
London EC1Y 1SP
United Kingdom

Sage Publications India Pvt. Ltd.
B-42, Panchsheel Enclave
Post Box 4109
New Delhi 110 017 India

Printed in the United States of America on acid-free paper.

Library of Congress Cataloging-in-Publication Data

The handbook of spiritual development in childhood and adolescence / editors, Eugene C. Roehlkepartain . . . [et al.].
    p. cm. — (The Sage program on applied developmental science)
Includes bibliographical references and index.
ISBN 0-7619-3078-7 (hardcover)
    1. Youth—Religious life—Handbooks, manuals, etc. 2. Faith development—Handbooks, manuals, etc. 3. Youth psychology—Handbooks, manuals, etc. I. Roehlkepartain, Eugene C., 1962- II. Title. III. Series.

BV4571.3.H36 2005
200'.83--dc22

                                                           2005012703

05   06   07   08   09   10   9   8   7   6   5   4   3   2   1

Acquiring Editor:	Jim Brace-Thompson
Editorial Assistant:	Karen Ehrmann
Production Editor:	Sanford Robinson
Typesetter:	C&M Digitals (P) Ltd.
Indexer:	Kathy Paparchontis

For our cherished children and grandchildren

Micah and Linnea
Aidan
Jack, Ella, Reed, and Zane
Liv, Kai, and Ryder

CONTENTS

FOREWORD

ROBERT COLES

In 1956, I was a young physician in training at the Massachusetts General Hospital in Boston. I was planning to be a psychiatrist and was also pursuing an interest in pediatrics. The clinical work was demanding—enough so that I had little time for the kind of reading I'd once enjoyed as an English major much taken with George Eliot's novels and those of the Russian masters Tolstoy and Dostoevsky, on both of whom I wrote long essays in my senior year.

One day while I was on duty in the emergency ward, a 16-year-old high schooler arrived accompanied by his parents. He had suddenly lost the full use of his legs, in the midst of what had seemed to be a mild upper respiratory infection. The more I spoke with him in taking the usual clinical history, the more I was given pause by what he had to relate, apart from his description of the onset of a paralytic illness. To this day, I can hear him saying these words (which I tape-recorded as part of a hospital research project that I was then doing, eventually published in the *American Journal of Psychiatry* as "Neuropsychiatric Aspects of Acute Poliomyelitis"):

My friends come to see me [he was a hockey player] and they get so upset, I have to calm them down! Look, it's no picnic, being this sick, but I have plenty of time to stop and think about what's really important. I didn't choose this [illness], but I figure I can do the best I can to beat it—and meanwhile I try to keep my spirits up. My folks, my brothers, and my sisters come here a lot, and they're great—they're rooting for me. The priest comes every day, and he's sure for me, praying a lot that I get better. Now I think of the Bible the way I never used to. I look hard at what Jesus Christ went through: a lot worse than this polio! I guess it took getting sick for me to have a deeper religious life. That's what my girlfriend said, and you know, she has a point. You get sick like this, and you're stopped in your tracks. My legs aren't working right, but my head is all-alive with thoughts. The priest said I'm beginning to talk like they do in religion classes, or philosophy classes. I laugh and say: "Go tell that to my teachers; maybe they'll boost my grades!" Actually, I was thinking the other morning about Thoreau. We read him in class, and now, here in the hospital, I thought of him. He'd be upset if he got polio so that he couldn't walk around that Walden Pond of his, but probably he'd make sure something good came out of it; he'd get deeper into life—what it all means—and that's a big trip, and there's a payoff to it, he told us. You become deeper yourself, that way. Sure you're paying a stiff price, but good things don't always come easy—that's what you learn reading the Bible, and from reading good books by people who want you, the one reading their words, to stop and think with them about what's it all about, being here for a while.

In a sense, that young person's realizations belong in this volume, which is dedicated to expanding our understanding of spiritual development in childhood and adolescence.

Indeed, the youth whose words grace my effort to respond to the following pages would eventually recover enough to walk (with crutches at first) and then return to school. He became a lawyer, and one day he told me: "I owe to polio a big part of my thinking, feeling life—and for sure, my spiritual life. The Lord lets us know, doesn't he, that if you're going to think about what really matters in life, you've got to be tapped on the shoulder. Something happens that asks you to go below the surface of things, that asks you to wonder about what it's all about—life's lessons, its purposes."

Yes, indeed, I recall thinking—and thought yet again as I explored the chapters ahead: the reflections of a range of essayists (observers of their fellow human beings) who want to address young people such as the one I have described, children and teenagers who are trying to find their bearings in life, and who do so psychologically, morally, spiritually, in the hope that their time here will really count. It's no small challenge, and yet it's such an affirming one: life's very reasons, ideals, and purposes, pursued and given expression—an invaluable achievement.

PREFACE

his inaugural edition of *The Handbook of Spiritual Development in Childhood and Adolescence* is being published as part of a new burgeoning of scholarly interest in child and adolescent spiritual development. Around the world, scholars have formed interest groups and convened conferences to explore these issues. Special issues of academic journals in psychology, sociology, medicine, anthropology, education, and other fields have been published.

Yet this area of inquiry lacks a cohesive, established base of foundational theory or research. Scholars tend to work within their own discipline and in relative isolation, disconnected from each other and lacking easy access to theory and research in other disciplines, traditions, and cultures. Study in this domain has lacked the visibility, integration, and research strength needed to give it prominence and broad acceptance in the academy as an integral theme in human development. Also missing has been the synthesis needed to set the stage for future research, as well as encourage the use of available research in policy and practice.

By assembling leading scholars from multiple disciplines and four continents, it is our hope here to offer a comprehensive review of current scientific knowledge and to propose directions for the future. Drawing on psychology, sociology, anthropology, educational philosophy, and related disciplines, this handbook offers a kaleidoscope of current research. Furthermore, in the emerging tradition of applied developmental science (Lerner, Fisher, & Weinberg, 2000), it establishes the need for a dynamic interaction between knowledge generation and application wherein research informs practice, and, just as important, the realities, issues, and insights of practice inform research questions and approaches.

The volume emerged initially from conversations among scholars, particularly at Search Institute, Fuller Theological Seminary, Tufts University, and Stanford University, who have engaged in a long-term project on thriving in adolescence, and its intersection with spiritual development. Then, in 2003, Search Institute received a grant from the John Templeton Foundation, which provided support for this volume as well as a companion work in religious studies that synthesizes how the world's religious traditions understand spirituality in childhood and adolescence (see Yust, Johnson, Sasso, & Roehlkepartain, in press). At the same time, scholars at Tufts University have compiled another complementary volume, *An Encyclopedia of Religious and Spiritual Development in Childhood and Adolescence,* also published by Sage (Dowling & Scarlett, in press). Together, these seminal works (along with the growing number of journals and conferences on these topics) are poised to move this field of inquiry and practice to new levels.

REFERENCES

Dowling, E., and Scarlett, G. (Eds.). (in press). *An encyclopedia of religious and spiritual development in childhood and adolescence.* Thousand Oaks, CA: Sage.

Lerner, R. M., Fisher, C. B., & Weinberg, R. A. (2000). Toward a science for and of the people: Promoting civil society through the application of developmental science. *Child Development, 71,* 11–20.

Yust, K.-M., Johnson, A. N., Sasso, S. E., & Roehlkepartain, E. C. (Eds.). (in preparation). *Nurturing child and adolescent spirituality: Perspectives from the world's religious traditions.* Lanham, MD: Rowman and Littlefield.

ACKNOWLEDGMENTS

I f any kind of publication merits extensive acknowledgments, it is a handbook such as this one. To produce a work of this size, scope, and quality requires investments and commitments from many, many people and institutions. We particularly acknowledge Richard M. Lerner, a friend and colleague, who not only contributed and served as an adviser but also gave tremendous encouragement and guidance in the early stages of conceptualizing this book. It is likely that it would not have happened without his mentoring and encouragement.

First, and most important, our sincerest thanks and appreciation go to the 67 scholars who have contributed to this volume as authors. Coming from many disciplines, perspectives, and nations, they invested tremendous energy in writing within the demanding expectations and exacting parameters that are necessary to create a cohesive volume. We applaud their patience with multiple layers of feedback and review, the nagging e-mails, and the aggressive schedule. We are proud to be associated with you through this volume.

In addition to the authors, capturing the rich diversity and scope of scholarship in spiritual development requires engaging multiple perspectives and relationship networks in order to ensure that the volume adequately represents the field. Fourteen scholars from around the world served as editorial advisers, assisting the editors in shaping the scope of the volume, recommending authors, and reviewing chapters. In many cases, these leading scholars have also contributed chapters to the book. These advisers are:

Hanan A. Alexander, Ph.D., Center for Jewish Education, University of Haifa*

Chris J. Boyatzis, Ph.D., Department of Psychology, Bucknell University

Jacquelynne S. Eccles, Ph.D., Institute for Social Research, University of Michigan

James W. Fowler, Ph.D., Candler School of Theology, Emory University

Edwin I. Hernandez, Ph.D., Center for the Study of Latino Religion, University of Notre Dame

Ariela Keysar, Ph.D., Center for the study of Religion in Society and Culture, Brooklyn College, City University of New York

Shiva Khalili, Ph.D., National Research Center for Medical Sciences, Tehran, Iran

Richard M. Lerner, Ph.D., Eliot-Pearson Department of Child Development, Tufts University

---

*Affiliations listed for identification purposes only.

Rebecca M. Nye, Ph.D., Divinity School, University of Cambridge

Kenneth I. Pargament, Ph.D., Department of Psychology, Bowling Green State University

F. Helmut Reich, Ph.D., Th.D., Departement Erziehungswissenschaften, University of Fribourg, Switzerland

Christian Smith, Ph.D., Department of Sociology, University of North Carolina at Chapel Hill

Margaret Beale Spencer, Ph.D., Graduate School of Education, University of Pennsylvania

James E. Youniss, Ph.D., Department of Psychology, The Catholic University of America

In addition to these advisers, several other scholars offered careful peer reviews of the chapters in this volume, asking tough questions, offering sound advice, and adding immeasurably to the quality of the book. These reviewers were Chris J. Boyatzis, Bucknell University; John Calhoun, National Crime Prevention Council (retired); Mari Clements, Fuller Theological Seminary; W. Andrew Collins, University of Minnesota; Joseph Erickson, Augsburg College; Leslie J. Frances, University of Wales, Bangor; Hayim Herring, Synagogues: Transformation and Renewal; Cameron Lee, Fuller Theological Seminary; Robert London, California State University, San Bernardino; Mark Regnerus, University of Texas; Hope Straughan, Wheelock College; and Froma Walsh, University of Chicago.

Primary financial support for compiling and editing this handbook was provided by the John Templeton Foundation, Philadelphia, Pennsylvania, through its support of Search Institute's initiative to map the state of spiritual development in the social sciences. Particular thanks to Arthur Schwartz, who understood the need and affirmed the vision. In addition, we thank the Thrive Foundation for Youth for its support of early work that led to the development of this book.

We also wish to thank our work colleagues at Search Institute and Fuller Theological Seminary, who tolerated our preoccupied minds, closed doors, and puzzled questions. However, we single out colleagues who directly contributed to the development of this book. At Search Institute, particular thanks goes to Mary Byers, who guided the manuscript through copyediting; Sandra Longfellow, who assisted with library work, literature searches, and bibliographies; Brent Bolstrom and Katie Streit, who provided research assistance; and Susan Herman, who not only provided administrative support but helped protect time for writing and editing.

To our colleagues at Sage Publications, Jim Brace-Thompson and Karen Ehrmann: Thank you for believing in this project, for keeping on the pressure so that this project maintained its rightful priority amid competing demands, and for the careful attention you have given it throughout the process to ensure that this handbook is of highest quality.

Finally, we particularly appreciate our families for their support, encouragement, and patience throughout the process of developing this book: Jolene, Micah, and Linnea Roehlkepartain; Brad and Aidan King; Jay, Jack, Ella, Reed, and Zane Wagener; and Tunie Munson-Benson, and Liv, Kai, Brad, and Ryder. Through it all, you eased our stresses and nurtured our spirits. Our deepest thanks.

1

Spiritual Development in Childhood and Adolescence: Moving to the Scientific Mainstream

Eugene C. Roehlkepartain

Peter L. Benson

Pamela Ebstyne King

Linda M. Wagener

Around the world, there appears to be a growing concern with spirituality in the general public as well as among scholars. Whether one looks at the list of best-selling books, searches the Web, watches contemporary movies or TV shows, or reads general-interest magazines, one quickly finds evidence of this trend. And one sees religion and spirituality (mixed with nationalism and ethnic tensions) playing defining roles in most major geopolitical conflicts in a world that is becoming both smaller and more fragmented.

While spirituality in general has considerable currency, there is additional focus on the spiritual development of children and adolescents. The source of this interest varies considerably. For example, some people—particularly those within religious communities—worry that the beliefs, narratives, and commitments of the world's religious traditions are not adequately taking root in young people's lives (e.g., Lindner, 2004). As Wuthnow (1998) puts it, "When the sacred no longer has a single address, people worry that it may disappear entirely" (p. 10). Other observers contend that the world's religious heritage is "tainted by an incriminating record of injustice, tribalism, violence, and the violation of fundamental human rights" (King, 2001, p. 2). Instead, they say, the urgent need is to engage young people in new ways of seeing, knowing, and discovering, since "a simple return to or retrieval of past spiritualities is no longer enough to meet urgent contemporary social and personal needs" (King,

2001, p. 2). Still others note that children are, too often, at the center of major conflicts, terrorism, and the trauma of war, all of which point toward spiritual pathology or pain (see Wagener & Malony, chapter 10, this volume). Finally— and perhaps most germane to this handbook— there is an emerging sense among developmental scholars that something has been missing in the scholarship, and that domain is spiritual development (Benson, chapter 34, this volume; Coles, 1990; Lerner, Alberts, Anderson, & Dowling, chapter 5, this volume).

Although this appears to be a "moment" in the public imagination when things spiritual have gained attention, there has been little consensus in the scientific community about the nature and scope of this dimension of life. To be sure, there are consistent strands in the social sciences, such as the subfields of psychology and sociology of religion, that have, for more than a century, built a growing knowledge base of theory and research. To this point, however, most of this knowledge base has been dispersed into textbooks, journals, conferences, and interest groups focused in a particular discipline, geographic area, or religious tradition, with little overlapping scholarship or dialogue. Much of the work finds its "home" in the psychology of religion. This field interfaces more with social psychology and personality than it does with developmental psychology (Spilka, Hood, Hunsberger, & Gorsuch, 2004). Furthermore, the psychology of religion is quite insulated from anthropology and sociology. Spiritual development cannot be understood without significant conversations across these and other fields.

For the first time, this handbook draws together leading social scientists in the world from multiple disciplines to articulate what is known and needs to be known about spiritual development in childhood and adolescence. In doing so, this volume presents a rich and diverse array of theory, qualitative and quantitative research, and proposals for the future that are designed to move spiritual development from a sidelight in the academy to become a mainstream, accepted, and sustained field of inquiry and learning.

The editors of this volume share two goals, one short term and one long term. The short-term goal is to synthesize the research on spiritual development in a way that encourages and guides additional scholarship. The long-term goal is to help position spiritual development as a central and mainstream issue in the social sciences, including psychology, sociology, and anthropology, which have had a tenuous relationship with this domain. The lack of full engagement with this domain in the mainstream social sciences has limited our capacity to fully understand the person in its entirety at all points in the life span and within its multiple social, cultural, and national contexts. This volume is an effort to fill this gap.

To set a context for the book, this introductory chapter first examines some of the history of how the mainstream social sciences have neglected this area of inquiry; then it highlights some of the challenges and approaches to defining spiritual development. Next, the chapter looks at the major theoretical traditions that have informed and shaped the current scientific understanding of spiritual development, particularly in developmental psychology and the psychology of religion. Growing out of those theoretical underpinnings, we then articulate several themes and assumptions that guided the development of the handbook.

MARGINALIZATION IN THE SOCIAL SCIENCES

Although pioneers in the social sciences such as William James, G. Stanley Hall, J. H. Leuba, Edwin Starbuck, Max Weber, and Emile Durkheim considered religiousness and spirituality to be integral to their fields, the study was marginalized throughout much of the 20th century. Through the years, many scholars have documented the relative lack of attention to issues of religion and spirituality in the social sciences in general (Davie, 2003; Gorsuch, 1988; Paloutzian, 1996; Weaver et al., 1998; Weaver et al., 2000) and, more specifically, in the study of adolescence (Benson, Donahue, & Erickson, 1989; Bridges & Moore, 2002; Donelson, 1999; Kerestes & Youniss, 2003; Markstrom, 1999; Wallace & Forman, 1998) and childhood (Hay, Nye, & Murphy, 1996; Nye, 1999). The scientific study of religion began reemerging in the 1960s and, by the new millennium, Hill et al.

(2000) concluded that "the state of the discipline today can be characterized as sufficiently developed but still overlooked, if not bypassed, by the whole of psychology" (p. 51). Today, this subfield of psychology of religion is struggling with how it relates to notions of "spirituality," with some arguing that the subdiscipline should be renamed "psychology of religion and spirituality" (Emmons & Paloutzian, 2003; Pargament, 1999).

The inattentiveness to spiritual development in the mainstream social sciences can be graphically illustrated in the study of developmental psychology. Benson, Roehlkepartain, and Rude (2003) searched six leading developmental psychology journals *(Child Development, Developmental Psychology, International Journal of Behavioral Development, Journal of Adolescent Research, Journal of Early Adolescence,* and the *Journal of Research on Adolescence)* to ascertain the frequency of citations to religion, religious development, spirituality, or spiritual development. Of 3,123 articles published between 1990 and July 2002 having to do with children or adolescents, only 27 (0.9%) referenced one or more of these key words. And only one article explored issues of spirituality in childhood and adolescence. Content analyses of other journals and publications have reached similar conclusions, though some have documented somewhat higher proportions based on other search criteria (Weaver et al., 1998; Weaver et al., 2000).

A variety of explanations have been given for the historic marginalization of religion and spirituality in the social sciences. Almost all have to do with the academy's biases about religion. And because religious and spiritual development share conceptual space, the former has affected the reputation of the latter. Wulff (1997) identifies some of the more prominent obstacles. Among them is the pervasive personal rejection of religion by social scientists, a fact supported by several studies of academics' attitudes toward religion (Bergin, 1991; Campbell, 1971; Larson & Witham, 1998; Shafranske, 1996). Another is the view that religion, like art or music or politics, is a discretionary human activity and not a core, fundamental dynamic of human life. The area may also be shied away from because it is "politically sensitive and philosophically difficult" (McCrae, 1999, p. 1211).

In addition, Smith (2003) documents reductionist thinking among sociologists that dismisses religious or spiritual phenomena as expressions of something else. "What appears to be divine or spiritual or transcendent or pious or sacred are *really only* about social class, race, gender, ethnicity, nationalism, solidarity, social control, and so on" (p. 19, italics in original; see also Wuthnow, 2003). And, although there are exceptions, many anthropologists have concluded that religion or spirituality is "a by-product of cognitive adaptations selected for 'more mundane' survival functions" (Alcorta & Sosis, in press; see also Atran, 2002).

Recent years, however, have seen a marked growth in scholarship related to spirituality and spiritual development. A number of reviews of the literature in child and adolescent religion and spirituality provide access to the knowledge base in multiple disciplines (see, for example, Benson, Donahue, & Erickson, 1989; Benson & King, in press; Benson et al., 2003; Bridges & Moore, 2002; Donahue & Benson, 1995; Donelson, 1999; Hay et al., 1996; Kerestes & Youniss, 2003; Markstrom, 1999; and Smith, 2003). In addition, several special issues of peer-reviewed journals have been published that address spirituality or spiritual development, including *Annals of Behavioral Medicine, Review of Religious Research, Journal of Health Psychology, Journal of Personality,* and *American Psychologist* (special section). Mills (2002) documents a substantial increase in medical journal articles that address religion or spirituality and health (also see Thoresen, 1999). Though the word *spirituality* did not even appear in the MedLine database until the 1980s, "in recent years, every major medical, psychiatric, and behavioral medicine journal has published on the topic" (Mills, 2002, p. 1), fueled, in part, by the pioneering work of Harold G. Koenig and the late David B. Larson (e.g., Koenig, McCullough, & Larson, 2001). This work has not focused specifically on children and adolescents, but it has generated significant attention in the public and media to this domain of life.

In addition to this growing attention to the broad domain of spirituality, a number of recent contributions in mainstream developmental science publications have also focused specifically on children and adolescents. Reich, Oser, and Scarlett (1999) have compiled a volume titled *Psychological Studies on Spiritual and Religious Development,* uniquely featuring European scholars. A major article on spiritual development appeared in *Developmental Psychology* in 2004 (King & Furrow, 2004). The *Journal of Adolescence* published an issue focused on adolescents and religion (1999), and a special issue of *Applied Developmental Science* on spiritual development was published in 2003. For the first time since it began publication in 1946, the *Handbook of Child Psychology* includes a chapter on spiritual development in its sixth edition (Oser, Scarlett, & Bucher, in press). And, in addition to this volume, Sage Publications has released the *Encyclopedia of Religious and Spiritual Development in Childhood and Adolescence* (Dowling & Scarlett, in press), which offers brief introductions to hundreds of topics.

DEFINITIONAL ISSUES

Although there is evidence of increased attention to this domain, there is no consensus about what "this domain" really is. Indeed, a fundamental challenge in compiling scholarship on "spiritual development" is a definitional issue, knowing that how the subject is defined not only sets boundaries on the areas of scholarship but also influences whether it is deemed legitimate in the academy. What is meant by spiritual development? How is it different from spirituality? And how it is it different from religious development—the domain with which it has been most closely associated? Despite a number of helpful explorations of these definitional issues (see, for example, Hill et al., 2000; King, 2001; MacDonald, 2000; Marler & Hadaway, 2002; Oser et al., in press; Reich, 2001; Slater, Hall, & Edwards, 2001; Stifoss-Hanssen, 1999; Wuthnow, 1998; Zinnbauer et al., 1997; and Zinnbauer, Pargament, & Scott, 1999), there has yet to emerge any consensus. As Zinnbauer and colleagues (1997) write: "The ways in which the words [religiousness and spirituality] are conceptualized and used are often inconsistent in the research literature. Despite the great volume of work that has been done, little consensus has

been reached about what the terms actually mean" (p. 549).

There are several ways to think about the terms *spirituality* and *spiritual development,* all of which are reflected in various contributions to this handbook. First, they have been described by many scholars as a particular dimension of the religious experience. Wulff (1997) has suggested that this situation has been necessitated by a change in the use and meaning of the term *religion.* William James (1902/1958), he notes, recognized that religion had several intertwined dimensions. There are both institutional aspects to religion, including belief systems and rituals that one inherits when choosing to be part of a religious tradition. At the same time, there is an experiential dimension, which is more direct and immediate.

In Wulff's view, the meaning of religion has evolved to focus more on the first of these two, with religion "becoming reified into a fixed system of ideas or ideological commitments" (p. 46). This has led to the use of the term spirituality to convey the more subjective and experiential aspects of religion. According to Zinnbauer and colleagues (1997): "Spirituality is now commonly regarded as an individual phenomenon and identified with such things as personal transcendence, supra consciousness sensitivity, and meaningfulness. . . . Religiousness, in contrast, is now often described narrowly as formally structured and identified with religious institutions and prescribed theology and rituals" (p. 551). In fact, some models now subsume religiousness as a category within spirituality (see, for example, MacDonald, 2000).

This bifurcation of religion and spirituality has both proponents and detractors. For some, these are artificial lines of demarcation, blurring the fact that belief and tradition are dynamically intertwined with the experiential (Wuthnow, 1998). Another concern voiced by some scholars is that the split between religion and spirituality unnecessarily fuels the idea that one is bad (i.e., religion) and the other is good (i.e., spirituality). (See, for example, Hill et al., 2000; Pargament, 1999.) Such evaluations are likely to emerge in postmodern societies in which social institutions are viewed with suspicion and individual development is held as a primary value. In these cases, individuals may seek to know, relate to, and respond to the sacred without the perceived trappings and constrictions of traditional religious doctrine, ritual, and institutional engagement. Still others argue that the debate is really a Western—even North American—one in that it ignores how these terms are experienced and used in non-Western and developing societies (see, for example, Mbiti, 1969; Stifoss-Hanssen, 1999).

A relatively new wave of definitions is predicated on finding a common denominator that can bind religion and spirituality together and at the same time demarcate their differences. This anchor point is the concept of the sacred. Pargament (1997) suggests that examples of the sacred include the concepts of God, divinity, transcendence, and ultimate reality. Accordingly, spirituality can be defined as "a search for the sacred, a process through which people seek to discourse, hold on to and, when necessary, transform whatever they hold sacred in their lives" (Hill & Pargament, 2003). Similarly, Miller and Thoresen (2003) suggest that spirituality refers to one's engagement with that which she or he considers holy, divine, or beyond the material world. Religion also seeks the sacred, creating the doctrine, beliefs, and rituals that bind believers to it and to each other.

A second recent effort seeks to define spirituality without explicit reference to a sacred or transcendent realm. Beck (1992), for example, refocuses the concept of spirituality on a set of human qualities rather than a search for the sacred or transcendent. These qualities, he suggests, can be developed by either religious or nonreligious persons. Among these are insight and understanding; an awareness of the interconnections among and between persons and other life forms; an experience of mystery and awe; and a posture of generosity and gratitude. Roof (1993) puts it this way: Spirituality "gives expression to the being that is in us; it has to do with feelings, with the power that comes from within, with knowing our deepest selves" (p. 64).

A new line of theory and research introduces a third perspective. This work suggests that there is a core and universal dynamic in human development that deserves to be moved to center stage in the developmental sciences, alongside and integrated with the other well-known streams of development: cognitive, social, emotional, and moral. The name commonly given to this dimension is spiritual development. And it is hypothesized to be a developmental wellspring out of which emerges the pursuit of meaning, connectedness to others and the sacred, purpose, and contributions, each and all of which can be addressed by religion or other systems of ideas and belief.

One way to think about this core developmental dimension is to focus on the human capacity (and inclination) to create a narrative about who one is in the context of space and time. Persons are active participants in creating this narrative, working with "source" material that comes from and is handed down by family and social groups, but superimposing on this material a great deal that emerges from personal experience and personal history. This process of constructing the self in social and historical context is universal, transhistorical, and transcultural.

A variety of theoretical perspectives can be brought to bear on this narrative-shaping journey. Building on the neo-Freudian ideas in Rizzuto's *The Birth of the Living God* (1979), Robert Coles grounds spirituality in the deepest of human needs (without pathologizing this dimension of life, as did Freud). In Coles's (1990) words:

> We are the creatures who recognize ourselves as "adrift" or as "trapped" or as "stranded" or as being in some precarious relationship to this world; and as users of language, we are the ones who not only take in the world's "objects" but build them up in our minds, and use them (through thoughts and fantasies) to keep from feeling alone, and to gain for ourselves a sense of where we came from and where we are and where we're going. (p. 8)

In this vein, a second definition of spiritual development—which was used as a starting point for shaping this volume—also focuses on the person as actively constructing a view of the self-in-context:

> Spiritual development is the process of growing the intrinsic human capacity for self-transcendence, in which the self is embedded in something greater than the self, including the sacred. It is the

developmental "engine" that propels the search for connectedness, meaning, purpose and contribution. It is shaped both within and outside of religious traditions, beliefs and practices. (Benson et al., 2003, pp. 205–206)

Given the emergent nature of this area of inquiry, it is premature—and potentially counterproductive—to propose that a single definition could adequately capture the richness, complexity, and multidimensional nature of spiritual development. As Nye (1999) writes: "Attempts to define [spirituality] closely, and derive an adequate 'operational definition' can be sure of one thing: misrepresenting spirituality's complexity, depth and fluidity. Spirituality is like the wind—though it might be experienced, observed and described, it cannot be 'captured'—we delude ourselves to think otherwise, either in the design of research or in analytical conclusions" (p. 58). Furthermore, without further field exploration, this approach risks being another "ungrounded theory" that does not reflect human realities in different cultures, contexts, and traditions (see Pargament, 1999). Thus, while the preceding definition has been offered as a starting point for shaping this volume, all authors have been encouraged to articulate their own approach and assumptions, in hopes that the resulting diversity enriches the dialogue and understanding.

RESEARCH TRADITIONS THAT INFORM THIS FIELD

Although this emerging field of child and adolescent spiritual development is relatively new in the social sciences, there is an extensive literature that can inform this area of inquiry. Several major works have synthesized various aspects of the domain. Three works in the psychology of religion are particularly noteworthy. Wulff's (1997) monumental text reviews the contributions of some of psychology's most influential thinkers, including James, Hall, Freud, Jung, Erickson, Allport, Fromm, and Maslow. In addition, Spilka and colleagues (2003) have produced a third edition of their extensive synthesis of the scientific literature in the psychology of religion. Similarly, Oser, Scarlett, and Bucher (in press) have examined

and synthesized these themes. And Strommen (1971) produced an important edited volume synthesizing the research on religious development. That 1971 volume is, to a certain extent, a forerunner to this volume.

Throughout the history of the social sciences, noted scholars have examined the intersection of religious or spiritual development with personality, society, and/or human development. Although their view of religion (and, by extension, spirituality) has not always been favorable, religion has been acknowledged as either a helpful or a hindering force in the developmental process. Several strands of this ongoing theory building and research have informed current understandings of child and adolescent spiritual development, including psychoanalytic theories, stage theories, and systems-oriented approaches to psychological development.

Psychoanalytic Theories

As noted, religion and spirituality were initially maligned by psychoanalysts, particularly by Freud (1961), who referred to "religion as a universal obsessional neurosis," a mere illusion derived from infantile human wishes (p. 43). However, a number of prominent psychoanalysts have proposed meaningful and productive ways in which spirituality or, in most cases, religion can function in the developmental process.

Although Carl Jung saw religion as a delusion, he recognized its value in providing assurance and strength, allowing humankind to transcend the instinctive stage of the unconscious into the heights of great moral and cultural achievements (Wulff, 1997). He noted that religion was "incontestably one of the earliest and most universal expressions of the human mind" (Jung, 1938, p. 5) and that religion was not only a sociological and historical phenomenon, but also something of considerable personal concern to a great number of individuals.

From the object-relations tradition, Ana-Maria Rizzuto (1979) argued that representations of God are an inevitable universal outcome of the child's relationships with the parents and other caretakers along with the child's growing interest in causal events. Whether or not the individual believes in the representation as a divine entity remains a potentiality throughout life. For Rizzuto, these God images serve as an illusory transitional object, bringing comfort and meaning to the individual. She also found that God images develop at every life stage, leading her to conclude that "each new phase in the identity cycle brings with it a specific religious cycle" (p. 52).

As a self-identified psychoanalyst turned fieldworker, Robert Coles (1990) broke new ground by articulating the natural, complex, and adaptive function that spirituality played in the lives of children. In his 30-year project on the inner life of children, Coles and his wife, Jane Coles, gathered data from interviews and drawings from children around the world. He recalls that it was not until years into the project that he began to take note of the spiritual lives of children. As a classically trained analyst, Coles was initially concerned with the illusionary quality of religion, but over time his conceptualizations were transformed as he noted with surprise the positive and sometimes life-changing quality of children's spirituality. After witnessing how children's religious beliefs and experiences helped them cope with racial discrimination and transform civic culture during the civil rights era in the South, he wrote, "whether our emphasis is sociological or psychological or theological, . . . even the most private 'illusions' can become part of a decidedly public event" (Coles, 1990, p. 20). His phenomenological approach to understanding child spirituality brought a deep quality of respect and illumination to the complex spiritual lives of children.

Stage Theories

Stemming from the psychoanalytic tradition, Erik Erikson's epigenetic theory of development introduced stage theory to the psychology of religion. In addition, Erikson gave unprecedented attention to the potential role of religion and spirituality in development. For example, he suggested that the successful resolution of the first stage of development brings about the virtue of hope, which "is the enduring belief in the attainability of fervent wishes" (1964, p. 118). Hopefulness over time is transformed into mature faith, allowing one to believe without evidence that the universe is trustworthy. Erikson acknowledged that religion is the institutional

confirmation of hope and can serve throughout the life span as a source of hope. And he asserted that religion not only provides a transcendent worldview, moral beliefs, and behavioral norms, but religious traditions also embody these ideological norms in a community of believers (Erikson, 1968).

Erikson's stage theory greatly contributed to the faith development theory of James Fowler (1981; also see Fowler & Dell, chapter 3, this volume). For Fowler, faith is universal and can exist within and outside of religious traditions. It's a person's way of responding to transcendent value and power in such a way that the trust in and loyalty to the source of transcendence integrate our identity and give our lives unity and meaning (Fowler, 1981). Although stage theories such as Fowler's have been criticized for their strong cognitive basis and for suggesting that children are limited to less mature faith (e.g., Balswick, King, & Reimer, 2005; Day, 2001; Loder, 1998; Streib, 2001), they have been invaluable in allowing the study of the transcendent domains of religion, spirituality, and faith to gain more serious consideration.

The research of Fritz Oser and Paul Gmünder (1991) has produced the "European school" of cognitive-psychological religious stage theory. Although the stages are related to the work of Fowler, these stages specifically focus on religious judgment. Their work concentrates on the nature and structure of religious thinking, elucidating how persons interpret their personal experiences both of self and the world in life of the Ultimate (God, transcendent other). Oser and Gmünder argue for a sphere of knowing that is distinctively religious. Although related to moral cognition, this religious intellect is independent of moral knowledge and other forms of cognition.

There are strong similarities between the theories of Fowler (1981) and Oser and Gmünder (1991). Both are indebted to genetic structuralism and describe a development that leads from the particular to the universal and from heteronomy to autonomy. Both approaches establish significant age trends, and the stages from both theories, to a certain extent, parallel one another. Notwithstanding these similarities, there are differences (see Oser et al., in press; Fowler, Nipkow, & Schweitzer, 1991). Primarily, Fowler incorporates into his scheme of stages many different psychological elements, including moral, social, and cognitive development; identity; and comprehension of symbols. In contrast, Oser and Gmünder concentrate on religious judgment. Fowler addresses faith in a very general sense; in contrast, Oser and Gmünder speak of religious judgment for establishing control and regulating the relationship between oneself and an Absolute. Whereas Fowler's approach may be more suitable for raising questions related to life history and existential themes, Oser and Gmünder's approach elucidates the transformation dynamics of cognitive structures.

Developmental Systems Theories

Increasing attention has been given to understanding the role of context in spiritual development. Developmental systems theories shift the focus to transactions between individuals and their various embedded contexts (see Lerner et al., chapter 5, this volume). Developmental process is located in the ongoing transactions between the person and her or his multilayered contexts. From a developmental systems perspective, the goodness of fit between person and environment is of primary concern. Oser and colleagues (in press) point out that in the current literature, religiousness and spirituality are of interest insofar as they provide opportunities to foster a better fit.

ASSUMPTIONS GUIDING THE HANDBOOK

Each of these research and theoretical traditions, among others, has brought important insights and accents to the science of child and adolescent spiritual development. Reviewing these various approaches and the current research, the editors of this handbook identified a series of theoretical assumptions that have guided the process of structuring this handbook. Each of these core assumptions is woven into Benson's (chapter 34, this volume) thinking about an architecture for a theory of spiritual development.

Spiritual Development as a Universal Human Process

Throughout history and across all societies, forms of spirituality have become part of human experience, and it has remained a robust force in life for both individuals and societies, despite numerous predictions of its demise. To be sure, such a conclusion is not readily apparent through available survey research on religion among youth and adults. For example, Norris and Inglehart (2004) document two countervailing dynamics. First, they document an ongoing decline in the influence of religious institutions in affluent societies (with a public that remains more traditionally religious, the United States is a notable outlier among industrialized nations). This secularization trend is counterbalanced in poorer, nonindustrialized societies by a *growing* proportion of the world's total population being traditionally religious (owing to the comparably higher population growth in these societies).

As noted, the United States (where much of the scholarship on spiritual development and religion has occurred) remains a unique case. Although there has been growing attention to those adult populations who are "spiritual, but not religious" (Fuller, 2001) and although that percentage may be rising, Marler and Hadaway (2002) document that only about one in five U.S. adults places her- or himself in this category, with the majority of American adults (64%) currently describing themselves as spiritual *and* religious (9% describe themselves as religious only and 8% indicate that they are neither religious nor spiritual). Lippman and Keith (chapter 8, this volume) report similar findings among adolescents in the United States (see also Smith, 2005), but they also document the uniqueness of these American patterns in a broader global context.

These various forms of survey research on religious participation or belief are helpful as proxies for spiritual development in countries such as the United States with a relatively high overlap between religiosity and spirituality. They are inadequate, however, for understanding spiritual development, in its many diverse forms, as a universal process. For example, a growing, though still limited, body of scientific evidence suggests that spirituality or religiosity has biological or physiological roots (e.g., Brown, Murphy, & Malony, 1998; d'Aquili & Newberg, 1999; D'Onofrio, Eaves, Murrelle, Maes, & Spilka, 1999; Hay, Reich, & Utsch, chapter 4, this volume; Newberg & Newberg, chapter 13, this volume).

Although the evidence is incomplete, the editors hypothesize that spiritual development is a dimension of human life and experience as significant as cognitive development, emotional development, or social development. All of these dimensions of development are interrelated. It is the spiritual dimension that is most involved in a person's effort to integrate the many aspects of development. As a core process of development involving the creation of a life narrative (in which the self is connected to larger constructs of values, tradition, space, and/or time), spiritual development cannot be reduced to merely human need or desire.

The narrative-building and self-transcending tasks of spiritual development can, but do not necessarily have to, be about the divine or the sacred. While it is commonplace for persons to draw religious imagery, doctrine, symbol, and tradition into this developmental "work"—particularly in cultures and social contexts grounded in such perspectives—notions of divinity, God, or gods are not essential for spiritual development.

It is problematic, however, that the vast majority of published scholarship in well-established journals presumes a North American context with a primary focus on the majority population (Caucasian and Judeo-Christian). And, as multiple chapters in this volume document, this lack of cross-cultural research and understanding has greatly limited advancements in the field, not only because its relevance to the majority of the world's population is untested, but also because it carries with it a set of assumptions about the dynamics and processes of spiritual development that are not universal and may, in fact, be anomalies. Several chapters in this volume (notably Gottlieb, chapter 11; Lippman and Keith, chapter 8; Mattis, Ahluwalia, Cowie, & Kirkland-Harris, chapter 20; Verma and Sta. Maria, chapter 9) make important contributions to closing this gap.

A Multidimensional Domain

The vast majority of researchers in the field agree that spirituality has multiple domains (e.g., Gorsuch & Walker, chapter 7, this volume; Hill & Hood, 1999; Lerner et al., chapter 5, this volume). For example, MacDonald (2000) analyzed 20 measures of spirituality, identifying five "robust dimensions of spirituality" (p. 185): cognitive orientation; experiential/phenomenological dimension; existential well-being; paranormal beliefs; and religiousness. These examples point to the many accents that surface in this field. They reinforce the understanding of spirituality and spiritual development as complex, multidimensional phenomena and processes that require sophisticated theory, measurement, and analysis across diverse populations, cultures, and traditions.

However, much of the current research (including many, though not all, contributions to this volume) relies primarily on relatively superficial measures of spirituality or—perhaps more common—on measures of religious commitment, belief, or participation as proxies for spirituality or spiritual development (Benson, Scales, Sesma, & Roehlkepartain, 2005). This gap holds true, despite the abundance of available scales that measure dimensions of religiosity and, increasingly, spirituality (Gorsuch, 1984; Gorsuch & Walker, chapter 7, this volume; Hill & Hood, 1999; Tsang & McCullough, 2003). The contrast between the call for deep, multidimensional theoretical frameworks and the "shallow" measures most often used in this domain represents one of the major challenges for the future of research in child and adolescent spiritual development.

Spiritual Development as a Process

The notion of spiritual *development* adds an important dimension in its emphasis on process. Spiritual development introduces questions about the nature of spiritual change, transformation, growth, or maturation as well as life phases and stages. For example, Wink and Dillon (2002) argue that spiritual development "demands not only an increase in the depth of a person's awareness of, and search for, spiritual meaning over time, but it also requires an expanded and deeper commitment to engagement in actual spiritual practices" (p. 80; see also Scarlett, chapter 2, this volume).

Through most of the 20th century, spiritual (or, more often, religious) development was viewed through stage theory (e.g., Fowler, 1981) or was dominated by nondevelopmental approaches (see Oser & Scarlett, 1991). In the same way that developmental psychology has moved beyond stage theory as a primary frame (e.g., Overton, 1998), spiritual development must also move beyond an overreliance on stage theory, which "implies a certain amount of discontinuity in religious [and spiritual] development, whereas it may actually be a reasonably continuous process" (Hood, Spilka, Hunsberger, & Gorsuch, 1996, p. 55).

The emphasis on process also grows out of an emphasis on the developmental trajectory across time (instead of emphasizing distinct, predictable, and often disconnected developmental stages). This approach highlights development as a continuous process in which early experiences and opportunities shape (though do not predetermine) future experiences and choices (Rutter, 1983; Scales, Sesma, & Bolstrom, 2004). Hence, understanding the continuity of development through childhood and adolescence is as vital to understanding spiritual development as it is to recognizing the phases and stages that are also part of that process.

It is important to acknowledge that to some, however, the term *development* implies growth from less to more, which is incongruent with some religious and philosophical understandings that spirituality is fully formed in a newborn and is too often suppressed, not nurtured, in society (see Yust, Johnson, Sasso, & Roehlkepartain, in press). Others note that spirituality is more mystical, relational, and divinely gifted than is suggested by the use of the word development, which can imply a sort of inevitability to the process. Coming to terms with the language to suggest both the reality of process as well as these related issues remains an important area for dialogue and discovery.

Interaction Between Person and Context

Many conceptualizations of spirituality, particularly in the West, have been highly focused on individual experience and impact. Mattis and Jagers (2001) note that the vast majority of conceptualization and research in the area of spirituality has emphasized the individual "quest," rather than the social and relational context of spiritual development. However, their research in the African American community and tradition consistently finds that interpersonal relationships (with family, peers, etc.) play a vital role in cultivating and shaping the spiritual development of children and adolescents. (See also Gottlieb, chapter 11, this volume; Mattis et al., chapter 20, this volume; Schwartz, Bukowski, and Aoki, chapter 22, this volume.)

Their perspective is consistent with developmental systems theories that emphasize the interaction between person and context, in which the child or adolescent is embedded within multiple contexts or ecologies (including culture, family, school, faith community, neighborhood, community, nation; see part IV) that shape the young person's developmental path (Bronfenbrenner, 1979; Lerner, 1998, 2002; Lerner et al., chapter 5, this volume). This perspective would suggest that spirituality is not only an individual quest but also a communal experience and phenomenon.

Just as important as recognizing the ways in which various contexts shape young people's spiritual pathway is to see this influence as bidirectional, with children and adolescents also affecting the people and places that are part of their lives. This interaction speaks to the importance of "goodness of fit" between the young person and her or his ecological contexts (Pearce & Haynie, 2004), as well as emphasizes personal agency in shaping one's own spiritual pathway. This perspective challenges widespread practices of emphasizing "passing down" traditions and beliefs that effectively "erode the perception of children as agents within society" (Lindner, 2004, p. 57). Lindner goes on to note that, despite the burgeoning research on religion and spirituality, "scant attention has been given to children's own views of religion and their spiritual life" (p. 60). Multiple chapters in this handbook (most notably, Hart, chapter 12) emphasize this theme.

Spirituality as a Life-Shaping Force

The preponderance of available research suggests that spirituality has a powerful effect in life. As documented in part V of this handbook, spirituality has been found to be inversely related to numerous negative outcomes and positively associated with numerous positive outcomes.

Indeed, in the realm of spiritual development, the area of scholarship that perhaps has generated the most scientific study is the exploration of spirituality and religion and their developmental correlates. It is arguable that the consistent positive relationships between religion and developmental benefits have captured the attention of the public and the academy.

It is important, though, to note that spirituality, like religion, can have both positive and negative expressions and outcomes. Some scholars have found, for example, that certain forms of religiousness may be more pathological, including a strictly utilitarian or extrinsic religion or spirituality, a conflict-ridden, fragmented religion or spirituality, an impoverished authoritarian religion or spirituality, and a defense mechanism that allows people to deny and retreat from reality (summarized in Hill et al., 2000; also see Wagener & Malony, chapter 10, this volume). Although psychology in the 20th century too often emphasized the pathological outcomes of spiritual commitment (e.g., Ellis, 1980), the recent openness to spirituality tends toward recognizing only its positive aspects and impact. It is important that this trend not lead to defining spiritual development as only a positive process; nonetheless, the growing recognition of the positive contribution that spirituality can make in the lives of children and adolescents bodes well for continued attention to and examination of this pivotal dimension of life.

CONCLUSIONS

Spiritual development may be at a "tipping point" for becoming a major theme in child and adolescent development. A growing number of scholars in various disciplines have invested themselves in this field. The public imagination appears to be ready in numerous cultures, traditions, and contexts, all of which are struggling with social changes that threaten to undermine the spiritual lives of young people.

It is impossible to know whether the current popular interest in spirituality is a passing fad or a long-term trend. Perhaps this interest will be eclipsed by other crises or concerns. Perhaps it will just fade from public consciousness. Or perhaps we are only at the beginning of a major, lasting resurgence in things spiritual that will be sustained for decades.

In some senses, it hardly matters. As documented by the contributors to this handbook, the evidence is growing that spiritual development is a vital process and resource in young people's developmental journey from birth through adolescence. Indeed, when human development marginalizes spiritual development, it does a great disservice to itself and to young people. Without accounting for the spiritual dimension, human development builds theories, research endeavors, and, by extension, practices on an incomplete understanding of our humanness.

Just as important, the developmental sciences add too little to vital questions of our time if they do not apply themselves to these complex issues. As Benson et al. (2003) write: "Spiritual development is likely a wellspring for the best of human life (e.g., generosity, unity, sacrifice, altruism, social justice) as well as for our darkest side (e.g., genocide, terrorism, slavery). Using social science to examine this potent force in society and individual lives of young people has been neglected for too long" (p. 210). *The Handbook of Spiritual Development in Childhood and Adolescence* seeks to ensure that this oversight does not persist.

REFERENCES

Alcorta, C. S., & Sosis, R. (in press). Ritual, emotion, and sacred symbols: The evolution of religion as an adaptive complex. *Human Nature.*

Atran, S. (2002). *In gods we trust: The evolutionary landscape of religion.* Oxford, UK: Oxford University Press.

Balswick, J. O., King, P. E., & Reimer K. S. (2005). *The reciprocating self: A theological perspective of development.* Downers Grove, IL: InterVarsity Press.

Beck, U. (1992). *Risk society: Towards a new modernity.* London: Sage.

Benson, P. L., Donahue, M. J., & Erickson, J. A. (1989). Adolescence and religion: A review of the literature from 1970 to 1986. *Research in the Social Scientific Study of Religion, 1,* 153–181.

Benson, P. L., & King, P. E. (in press). Religion and adolescent development. In H. R. Ebaugh (Ed.), *Handbook on religion and social institutions.* New York: Springer Science + Business Media.

Benson, P. L., Roehlkepartain, E. C., & Rude, S. P. (2003). Spiritual development in childhood and adolescence: Toward a field of inquiry. *Applied Developmental Science, 7,* 204–212.

Benson, P. L., Scales, P. C., Sesma, A., Jr., & Roehlkepartain, E. C. (2005). Adolescent spirituality. In K. A. Moore & L. H. Lippman (Eds.), *What do children need to flourish? Conceptualizing and measuring indicators of positive development* (pp. 25–40). New York: Springer Science + Business Media.

Bergin, A. E. (1991). Values and religious issues in psychotherapy and mental health. *American Psychologist, 46,* 394–403.

Bridges, L. J., & Moore, K. A. (2002). *Religion and spirituality in childhood and adolescence.* Washington, DC: Child Trends.

Bronfenbrenner, U. (1979). *The ecology of human development.* Cambridge, MA: Harvard University Press.

Brown, W., Murphy, N., & Malony, H. N. (1998). *Whatever happened to the soul? Scientific and theological portraits of human nature.* Minneapolis, MN: Fortress.

Campbell, C. (1971). *Toward a sociology of irreligion.* London: Macmillan.

Coles, R. (1990). *The spiritual life of children.* Boston: Houghton Mifflin.

d'Aquili, E. G., & Newberg, A. B. (1999). *The mystical mind: Probing the biology of religious experience.* Minneapolis, MN: Fortress.

Davie, G. (2003). The evolution of the sociology of religion: Theme and variations. In M. Dillon, *Handbook of the sociology of religion* (pp. 61–75). Cambridge, UK: Cambridge University Press.

Day, J. M. (2001). From structuralism to eternity? Re-imagining the psychology of religious development after the cognitive-developmental paradigm. *International Journal for the Psychology of Religion, 11,* 173–183.

Donahue, M. J., & Benson, P. L. (1995). Religion and the well-being of adolescents. *Journal of Social Issues, 51,* 145–160.

Donelson, E. (1999). Psychology of religion and adolescents in the United States: Past to present. *Journal of Adolescence, 22,* 187–204.

D'Onofrio, B. M., Eaves, L. J., Murrelle, L., Maes, H. H., & Spilka, B. (1999). Understanding biological and social influences on religious affiliation, attitudes, and behaviors: A behavior genetic perspective. *Journal of Personality, 67,* 953–984.

Dowling, E. M., & Scarlett, W. G. (in press). *Encyclopedia of religious and spiritual development in childhood and adolescence.* Thousand Oaks, CA: Sage.

Ellis, A. (1980). Psychotherapy and atheistic values: A response to A. E. Bergin's "Psychotherapy and religious values." *Journal of Consulting and Clinical Psychology, 48,* 635–639.

Emmons, R. A., & Paloutzian, R. F. (2003). The psychology of religion. *Annual Review of Psychology, 54,* 377–402.

Erikson, E. H. (1964). *Insight and responsibility.* New York: Norton.

Erikson, E. H. (1968). *Identity: Youth and crisis.* New York: Norton.

Fowler, J. W. (1981). *Stages of faith: The psychology of human development and the quest for meaning.* San Francisco: HarperCollins.

Fowler, J. W., Nipkow, K. E., & Schweitzer, F. (Eds.). (1991). *Stages of faith and religious development.* New York: Crossroad.

Freud, S. (1961). *The future of an illusion.* London: Hogarth Press and the Institute of Psycho-Analysis.

Fuller, R. C. (2001). *Spiritual, but not religious: Understanding unchurched America.* New York: Oxford University Press.

Gorsuch, R. L. (1984). The boon and bane of investigating religion. *American Psychologist, 39,* 228–236.

Gorsuch, R. L. (1988). The psychology of religion. *Annual Review of Psychology, 39,* 201–221.

Hay, D., Nye, R., & Murphy, R. (1996). Thinking about childhood spirituality: Review of research and current directions. In L. J. Francis, W. K. Kay, & W. S. Campbell (Eds.), *Research in religious education* (pp. 47–71). Macon, GA: Smyth & Helwys.

Hill, P. C., & Hood, R. W. (1999). *Measures of religiosity.* Birmingham, AL: Religious Education Press.

Hill, P. C., & Pargament, K. I. (2003). Advances in the conceptualization and measurement of religion and spirituality: Implications for physical and mental health research. *American Psychologist, 58,* 64–74.

Hill, P. C., Pargament, K. I., Hood, R. W., McCullough, M. E., Swyers, J. P., Larson, D. B., et al. (2000). Conceptualizing religion and spirituality: Points of commonality, points of departure. *Journal for the Theory of Social Behavior, 30,* 52–77.

Hood, R. W., Spilka, B., Hunsberger, B., & Gorsuch, R. (1996). *The psychology of religion: An empirical approach* (2nd ed.). New York: Guilford.

James, W. (1958). *The varieties of religious experience: A study in human nature.* Cambridge, MA: Harvard University Press. (Original work published 1902)

Jung, C. (1938). *Psychology and religion.* New Haven, CT: Yale University Press.

Kerestes, M., & Youniss, J. E. (2003). Rediscovering the importance of religion in adolescent development. In R. M. Lerner, F. Jacobs, & D. Wertlieb (Eds.), *Handbook of applied developmental science: Vol. 1. Applying developmental science for youth and families—Historical and theoretical foundations* (pp. 165–184). Thousand Oaks, CA: Sage.

King, P. E., & Furrow, J. L. (2004). Religion as a resource for positive youth development: Religion, social capital, and moral outcomes. *Developmental Psychology, 40,* 703–713.

King, U. (2001). Introduction: Spirituality, society, and the millennium—Wasteland, wilderness, or new vision? In U. King (Ed.), *Spirituality and society in the new millennium* (pp. 1–13). Brighton, UK: Sussex Academic Press.

Koenig, H. G., McCullough, M. E., & Larson, D. B. (2001). *Handbook of religion and health.* Oxford, UK: Oxford University Press.

Larson, E. J., & Witham, L. (1998, July). Leading scientists still reject God. *Nature, 394,* 313.

Lerner, R. M. (1998). Theories of human development: Contemporary perspectives. In W. Damon & R. M. Lerner (Eds.), *Handbook of child psychology: Vol. 1. Theoretical models of human development* (5th ed., pp. 1–24). New York: Wiley.

Lerner, R. M. (2002). *Concepts and theories of human development* (3rd ed.). Mahwah, NJ: Erlbaum.

Lindner, E. W. (2004). Children as theologians. In R. B. Pufall & R. P. Unsworth (Eds.), *Rethinking childhood* (pp. 54–68). New Brunswick, NJ: Rutgers University Press.

Loder, J. (1998). *The logic of the spirit: Human development in theological perspective.* San Francisco: Jossey-Bass.

MacDonald, D. A. (2000). Spirituality: Description, measurement, and relation to the five factor model of personality. *Journal of Personality, 68,* 157–197.

Markstrom, C. A. (1999). Religious involvement and adolescent psychosocial development. *Journal of Adolescence, 22,* 205–221.

Marler, P. L., & Hadaway, C. K. (2002). "Being religious" or "being spiritual" in America: A zero-sum proposition. *Journal for the Scientific Study of Religion, 41,* 288–300.

Mattis, J. S., & Jagers, R. J. (2001). A relational framework for the study of religiosity and spirituality in the lives of African Americans. *Journal of Community Psychology 29,* 519–539.

Mbiti, J. S. (1989). *African religions and philosophy* (2nd ed.). Oxford, UK: Heinemann Educational Publishers. (Original work published 1969)

McCrae, R. R. (1999). Mainstream personality psychology and the study of religion. *Journal of Personality, 67,* 1209–1218.

Miller, W. R., & Thoresen, C. E. (2003). Spirituality, religion, and health: An emerging research field. *American Psychologist, 58,* 24–35.

Mills, P. J. (2002). Spirituality, religiousness, and health: From research to clinical practice. *Annals of Behavioral Medicine, 24,* 1–2.

Norris, P., & Inglehart, R. (2004). *Sacred and secular: Religion and politics worldwide.* Cambridge, UK: Cambridge University Press.

Nye, R. M. (1999). Relational consciousness and the spiritual lives of children: Convergence with children's theory of mind. In K. H. Reich, F. K. Oser, & W. G. Scarlett (Eds.), *Psychological studies on spiritual and religious development: Vol. 2. Being human: The case of religion* (pp. 57–82). Lengerich, Germany: Pabst Science.

Oser, F. K., & Gmünder, P. (1991). *Religious judgment: A developmental approach.* Birmingham, AL: Religious Education Press.

Oser, F., & Scarlett W. G. (1991). *Religious development in childhood and adolescence.* San Francisco: Jossey-Bass.

Oser, F. K., Scarlett, W. G., & Bucher, A. (in press). Religious and spiritual development throughout the life span. In W. Damon & R. M. Lerner (Eds.), *Handbook of child psychology: Vol. 1.*

Theoretical models of human development (6th ed.). Hoboken, NJ: Wiley.

Overton, W. F. (1998). Developmental psychology: Philosophy, concepts, and methodology. In W. Damon & R. M. Lerner (Eds.), *Handbook of child psychology: Vol. 1. Theoretical models of development* (5th ed., pp. 107–188). New York: Wiley.

Paloutzian, R. F. (1996). *Invitation to the psychology of religion* (2nd ed.). Needham Heights, MA: Allyn & Bacon.

Pargament, K. I. (1997). *The psychology of religion and coping: Theory, research, practice.* New York: Guilford.

Pargament, K. I. (1999). The psychology of religion and spirituality? Yes and no. *International Journal for the Psychology of Religion, 9,* 3–16.

Pearce, L. D., & Haynie, D. L. (2004). Intergenerational religious dynamics and adolescent delinquency. *Social Forces, 82,* 1553–1572.

Reich, K. H. (2001, April). *Fostering spiritual development: Theory, practice, measurement.* Paper presented at the International Conference on Religion and Mental Health, Teheran, Iran.

Reich, K. H., Oser, F. K., & Scarlett, W. G. (Eds.). (1999). *Psychological studies on spiritual and religious development: Vol. 2. Being human: The case of religion.* Lengerich, Germany: Pabst Science.

Rizzuto, A.-M. (1979). *The birth of the living God: A psychoanalytic study.* Chicago: University of Chicago Press.

Roof, W. C. (1993). *A generation of seekers.* San Francisco: HarperCollins.

Rutter, M. (1983). Continuities and discontinuities in socio-emotional development: Empirical and conceptual perspectives. In R. N. Emde & R. J. Harmon (Eds.), *Continuities and discontinuities in development* (pp. 41–68). New York: Plenum.

Scales, P. C., Sesma, A., Jr., & Bolstrom, B. (2004). *Coming into their own: How developmental assets promote positive growth in middle childhood.* Minneapolis, MN: Search Institute.

Shafranske, E. P. (Ed.). (1996). *Religion and the clinical practice of psychology.* Washington, DC: American Psychological Association.

Slater, W., Hall, T. W., & Edwards, K. J. (2001). Measuring religion and spirituality: Where are we and where are we going? *Journal of Psychology and Theology, 29,* 4–21.

Smith, C. (2003). Theorizing religious effects among American adolescents. *Journal for the Scientific Study of Religion, 42,* 17–30.

Smith, C. (with Denton, M. L.). (2005). *Soul searching: The religious and spiritual lives of American teenagers.* New York: Oxford University Press.

Spilka, B., Hood, R. W., Hunsberger, B., & Gorsuch, R. (2003). *Psychology of religion: An empirical approach* (3rd ed.). New York: Guilford.

Stifoss-Hanssen, H. (1999). Religion and spirituality: What a European ear hears. *International Journal for the Psychology of Religion, 9,* 25–33.

Strieb, H. (2001). Faith development theory revisited: The religious styles perspective. *International Journal for the Psychology of Religion, 11,* 143–158.

Strommen, M. P. (1971). *Research on religious development: A comprehensive handbook.* New York: Hawthorn.

Thoresen, C. E. (1999). Spirituality and health: Is there a relationship? *Journal of Health Psychology 4,* 291–300.

Tsang, J.-A., & McCullough, M. E. (2003). Measuring religious constructs: A hierarchical approach to construct organization and scale selection. In S. J. Lopez & C. R. Snyder (Eds.), *Positive psychological assessments: A handbook of models and measures* (pp. 345–360). Washington, DC: American Psychological Association.

Wallace, J. M., & Forman, T. A. (1998). Religion's role in promoting health and reducing risk among American youth. *Health Education and Behavior, 25,* 721–741.

Weaver, A. J., Kline, A. E., Samford, J. A., Lucas, L. A., Larson, D. B., & Gorsuch, R. L. (1998). Is religion taboo in psychology? A systematic analysis of research on religion in seven major American Psychological Association journals: 1991–1994. *Journal of Psychology and Christianity, 17,* 220–232.

Weaver, A. J., Samford, J. A., Morgan, V. J., Lichton, A. I., Larson, D. B., & Garbarino, J. (2000). Research on religious variables in five major adolescent research journals: 1992–1996. *Journal of Nervous and Mental Disease, 188,* 36–44.

Wink, P., & Dillon, M. (2002). Spiritual development across the adult life course: Findings from a longitudinal study. *Journal of Adult Development, 9,* 79–94.

Wulff, D. M. (1997). *Psychology of religion: Classic and contemporary.* New York: John Wiley.

Wuthnow, R. (1998). *After heaven: Spirituality in America since the 1950s.* Berkeley and Los Angeles: University of California Press.

Wuthnow, R. (2003). Studying religion, making it sociological. In M. Dillon (Ed.). *Handbook of the sociology of religion* (pp.17–30). Cambridge, UK: Cambridge University Press.

Yust, K.-M., Johnson, A. N., Sasso, S. E., & Roehlkepartain, E. C. (Eds.). (in press). *Nurturing child and adolescent spirituality: Perspectives from the worlds religious traditions.* Lanham, MD: Rowman and Littlefield

Zinnbauer, B. J., Pargament, K. I., Cole, B., Rye, M. S., Butter, E. M., Belavich, T. G., et al. (1997). Religion and spirituality: Unfuzzying the fuzzy. *Journal for the Scientific Study of Religion, 36,* 549–564.

Zinnbauer, B. J., Pargament, K. I., & Scott, A. B. (1999). The emerging meanings of religiousness and spirituality: Problems and prospects. *Journal of Personality, 67,* 889–919.

Part I

FOUNDATIONS FOR THE SCIENTIFIC STUDY OF SPIRITUAL DEVELOPMENT IN CHILDHOOD AND ADOLESCENCE

Introduction to Part I

W hat is spiritual development? How does it relate to other constructs, such as religious development and faith development? What theories undergird this emerging field? What methodological and measurement issues come into play in examining this domain of life in childhood and adolescence?

These foundational chapters provide diverse perspectives on such theoretical, definitional, and measurement questions. W. George Scarlett leads with an analysis of current approaches to spiritual and religious development, highlighting key distinctions that need to be addressed (e.g., development vs. change over time, domain-based vs. person-based, structural vs. content analysis, and faith vs. belief). He then critiques current ways of viewing and investigating spiritual development, challenging scholars to integrative approaches that take seriously both sides of those distinctions.

The next four chapters each present distinct theoretical frameworks for examining spiritual development. James W. Fowler and Mary Lynn Dell present the history of Fowler's pioneering faith development theory, review the stages of faith development, and articulate the rationale behind the approach. They then introduce major scholarly efforts to examine this theoretical work, calling for new research that is grounded in contemporary issues of globalization that take into account both increased secularization on the one hand and, paradoxically, the growth of fundamentalist and conservative faith practices, on the other.

Next, David Hay, K. Helmut Reich, and Michael Utsch seek to disentangle the relationship between religious and spiritual development. They present an overview of religious development theory, focusing particularly on stage theories of religious development. The empirical approach they take to spiritual development leads them to conclude that spiritual awareness is biologically structured in the human species. It is expressed through a culture's language, rituals, and doctrines, an idea that presents important challenges and opportunities in cultures with many languages, rituals, and doctrines—not all of them religious—through which spirituality can find expression.

Whereas Hay, Reich, and Utsch distinguish between religion and spirituality through theoretical analysis, Richard M. Lerner, Amy E. Alberts, Pamela M. Anderson, and Elizabeth M. Dowling do so empirically, basing their work on developmental systems theories that stress the mutual influence between the developing person and her or his multiple contexts and developmental systems. They conclude by presenting their empirical findings that suggest that spirituality constitutes an important component of positive functioning over and above the contribution of religiosity alone.

In their philosophical treatise, Hanan A. Alexander and David Carr note that philosophers are not concerned with collecting empirical evidence but rather with breaking open the meaning of concepts and attending to their consistency and coherence. After looking at the complex definitional issues (and arguing that "spiritual education" is a more helpful construct than "spiritual development"), they examine the place of spiritual education in liberal democracies as well as the settings for spiritual education, particularly schools.

The complexity and multidimensionality of spiritual development—combined with the practical issues of conducting research with children and adolescents—make research design and measurement complex issues in understanding this dimension of life. Richard L. Gorsuch and Donald Walker review issues in measurement and research design, highlighting the importance of distinguishing between belief, motivation, behaviors, and experiences. They also discuss design and analysis issues in both cross-sectional and longitudinal research, concluding with a caution to recognize the limitations of scientific analysis in this domain.

Even this brief overview highlights that these authors clearly are not of one mind. They formulate and answer the critical questions differently, drawing on their own disciplinary field. For example, Lerner and Scarlett (along with their colleagues) approach these issues from a developmental psychology perspective on child and adolescent development. In contrast, Fowler and Gorsuch, each leading scholars in the psychology of religion, bring those lenses and that literature to the discussion. Hay, Reich, and Utsch examine the issues primarily through the lens of biological and physical sciences, whereas Alexander and Carr offer a philosophical perspective that both challenges and enriches the others. And if the section also included sociologists, anthropologists, historians, and theologians (to name a few), the discussion would be even more complex! Adding to the wealth of their ideas and stances, the authors work within different geopolitical contexts: North America, Europe, and the Middle East (which obviously leaves out important perspectives from many other parts of the world). Rather than reflecting primarily a weakness in the field, we suggest that this diversity of approaches, opinions, and contexts expands our understanding of this complex domain of life. The challenge is to foster mutual learning and cross-pollination across disciplines and contexts, rather than simply creating parallel streams of theory and research, each of which offers important, but incomplete, knowledge regarding the nature and processes of spiritual development in childhood and adolescence.

2

TOWARD A DEVELOPMENTAL ANALYSIS OF RELIGIOUS AND SPIRITUAL DEVELOPMENT

W. GEORGE SCARLETT

N o scientific study of religious and spiritual development is possible without adequate definition of the phenomenon to be studied.[1] But what should we mean by "adequate definition"—a dictionary definition that specifies some essence, or something else? The thesis here is that we need something else and that that something is a time-free definition of religious and spiritual development, one that is normative in positing ideal end points and approximations of ideal end points, one that attends to the development of persons and not just to domains, one that allows for a developmental analysis of modes of imagining, and, most important, one that describes the development of faith.

DISTINCTIONS FOR DEFINING RELIGIOUS AND SPIRITUAL DEVELOPMENT

There are signs that the study of religious and spiritual development is taking shape to become a recognized field (Benson, Roehlkepartain, & Rude, 2003). Recently, however, both the rejection of stage models and attention to culture have retarded progress in defining religious and spiritual development by discouraging our making explicit those norms needed to define what we should mean by religious and spiritual development. Later on, an examination of alternative approaches will make this point clear. But before discussing alternative approaches several distinctions are needed so as to adequately frame our discussion.

Development Versus Change Over Time

Everything turns on what meaning we give to the concept of development. Most often, development has referred to change over time in separate processes occurring within persons. Recently, development has been relocated—as in non-universal theory's relocating development in domains of knowledge and skill (Feldman, 1985) and as in developmental systems theory's relocating development in ongoing transactions between persons and society (Lerner, Dowling, & Anderson, 2003). However, these recent relocations retain the meaning of development as change over time. In contrast, the meaning of development that frames the rest of this discussion distinguishes development from change over time. Here, the meaning of development is captured in Bernard Kaplan's (1983) defining development as "movement towards perfection, as variously as that idea may be constructed" (p. 57).

The phrase "as variously as that idea may be constructed" points to the obvious challenge of defining development normatively, as movement toward perfection. The challenge is to define perfection in light of multiple notions of perfection. We need to consider the various notions of perfection among representatives from different cultures and faith traditions. The challenge, then, is to define development (the vertical) with an understanding of individual and group differences (the horizontal) in how perfection is conceived. This is a tall order indeed.

Domains Versus Persons

The second distinction is between development within *domains* related to overall religious and spiritual development and development of *persons* into spiritual exemplars.[2] Measuring development within relevant domains is an easier task than is measuring development of persons. It is the second kind of development that is the more important, however. A simple illustration will show how this distinction works and, at the same time, how development within relevant domains does not automatically translate into development of persons.

For members of many faith traditions, one relevant domain is the moral theology or moral philosophy that partially defines a tradition. Religious and spiritual development can, therefore, be logically related to knowledge of the moral theology or moral philosophy of a faith tradition. Furthermore, and in keeping with the traditional emphasis on structural development, knowledge need not refer to rote memory of articles of faith or creeds. It can and should refer to knowledge of the deep structure or hidden logic that makes any theology or philosophy systematic. An example is Roman Catholic moral theology, which is complex and systematic because it has evolved over thousands of

years. Any cursory glance at a modern-day papal encyclical will reveal this much.

However, few Roman Catholics read papal encyclicals, and many have a poor grasp of the underlying logic of the church's positions on moral issues. So, for example, it is not uncommon to find a Roman Catholic passionately opposing abortion while also passionately supporting capital punishment—without feeling any contradiction. This last phrase, *without feeling any contradiction,* points to a principal symptom of an undeveloped knowledge of Roman Catholic moral theology, for Roman Catholic moral theology sees abortion and capital punishment not as unrelated but as tied to the greater issue of how we should define and value human life.

This is but one of a great many examples of domain-specific knowledge in religious and spiritual development. There are counterparts in the collective experience of every faith tradition, both religious and secular. Furthermore, domains need not refer to knowledge or ideas. They may also refer to skills and religious practices. For many faith traditions, the central domains are not about ideas but about actions such as a ritual dance or a sacred ceremony (Smith, 1998). In each domain, there is something to be learned if one is to develop with respect to a particular faith tradition.

However, what is special about spiritual development—or rather the meaning we give to spiritual development—is that the concept refers to two separate considerations. On the one hand, it refers to the acquisition of domain-specific knowledge or skills. On the other hand, it refers to the development of perfection in persons.

This domain–person distinction is at the heart of our experience of religious and spiritual development. It is, for example, intelligible to say that Martin Luther was a genius with respect to his theology. After all, it was Luther's theology that changed the course of Western history. At the same time, it is equally intelligible to say that Luther's fits of rage and mean-spirited prejudices disqualified him as a spiritual exemplar.

Or take a different configuration that brings out this same domain–person distinction. In his small classic, *The Death of Ivan Ilyich* (1886/2004), Tolstoy depicts in the servant

Gerasim a spiritual exemplar, someone who attends to the needs of others in a simple, honest, straightforward, and cheerful way, even when the tasks are disgusting. However, nothing about Gerasim or any of Tolstoy's other peasant spiritual exemplars indicates that they are exceptional with respect to domain-specific skill or knowledge. There are, it seems, only a few rare individuals who combine skill, knowledge, and overall spiritual maturity: Gandhi, Lincoln, Martin Luther King Jr., and His Holiness the Dalai Lama are examples. So too are the founders of many of the world's faith traditions.

Perception and Reason Versus Religious and Spiritual Imagining

Focus on imagining has not been the focus of most studies of religious and spiritual development. A more common focus has been on perception and reasoning (Oser, 1991). There are exceptions, however. Perhaps the best exceptions today are Kwilecki's case studies of highly religious individuals in southern Georgia, most of whom are extremely poor, poorly educated, and from historically oppressed minorities. She writes:

> Inside the church, society's flotsam and jetsam became intimates of the invisible, mysterious Creator and Ruler of the world. Surrounded by squalor, they nevertheless praised a munificent, unseen Sustainer and proclaimed themselves victors, not victims, in life. In many cases, I observed, the more wholeheartedly and uncritically a person lived this imaginative spiritual identity, the stronger he or she became, the more capable not merely of survival but of satisfaction and purposefulness. How could an orientation so oblivious to facts be so functional? (Kwilecki, 1999, p. 15)

And when discussing one man who had overcome enormous hardships and humiliations, she comments:

> Thus, destitute in an indifferent world, Charles invested his only resource—energy and time—toward ends accessible solely through imagination. He thereby survived the worst conditions—scarcity, futility, degradation—with the best

qualities—gentleness, hope, virtue. It made quite a picture, I thought: an adult absorbed in a realm with the same empirical status as Oz and ennobled by it! The religious, I surmised, were at once escapist and heroic, foolish and grand. (p. 16)

For our purpose of framing, these examples will suffice to establish the main point: that religious and spiritual development is about the development of a special kind of imagining, an imagining that responds to the symbols of faith traditions but in unique, often idiosyncratic ways.

Structural Versus Content Analysis

Structural criteria have long helped carry out developmental analyses. Furthermore, they have done so with respect to religious and spiritual development—as evidenced in the works of psychologists such as Goldman (1964), Oser (1991), and Oser and Gmünder (1991), as well as in the work of philosophers such as Cassirer (1944, 1955, 1960).

Cassirer's structural analyses are especially helpful in understanding imagining and religious and spiritual development. For Cassirer, at the lower stages of religious and spiritual development, individuals live in a mythopoetic world where symbol and referent are fused and where there is no distinction between meaning and existence, that is, where what is imagined is taken to be reality. Cassirer (1955) distinguishes between mythical and religious consciousness with the latter being more developed. However, he views myth (a tradition's imagination) and religion as inseparable:

> If we attempt to isolate and remove the basic mythical components from religious belief, we no longer have religion in its real, objectively historical manifestation; all that remains is a shadow of it, an empty abstraction. And yet, although the contents of myth and religion are inextricably interwoven, their form is not the same. And the particularity of the religious form is disclosed in the changed attitude which consciousness here assumes toward the mythical image world. It cannot do without this world, it cannot immediately reject it; but seen through the medium of the religious attitude this world gradually takes on a

new meaning. The new ideality, the new spiritual dimension, that is opened up through religion not only lends myth a new signification but actually introduces the opposition between "meaning" and "existence" into the realm of myth. Religion takes the decisive step that is essentially alien to myth: in its use of sensuous images and signs it recognizes them as such—a means of expression which, though they reveal a determinate meaning, must necessarily remain inadequate to it, which "point" to this meaning but never wholly exhaust it. (p. 239)

To develop religiously or spiritually is, then, to develop the dual capacity to imagine passionately while recognizing one's imagining as imagining. For example, the imaginative act of praying to gods, ancestors, or whatever means nothing if one cannot momentarily lose self-consciousness while praying and concentrate on feeling the imagined as real. As Fosdick (1931) put it:

Only to one who prays can God make himself vivid. . . . Men say that they do not pray because to them God is not real, but a truer statement generally would be that God is not real because they do not pray. Granted a belief that God is, the practice of prayer is necessary to make God not merely an idea held in the mind but a Presence recognized in the life. (p. 36)

However, prayer and praying develop to the extent that the person praying develops a self-consciousness about individual wishes and points of view—a self-consciousness that certain petitions may not be the right petitions and that the will of the gods, ancestors, or whatever might be quite different from the will of persons. In so developing, prayer becomes a self-conscious imaginative act shaped as much by a sense of one's own limitations as by belief in the absence of limitations in the Being being prayed to (Scarlett & Perriello, 1991).

The examples of Cassirer and of prayer might suggest that structure is all that matters, but this is not the case. Content matters as well. As the theologian H. Richard Niebuhr (1946) put it, "The heart must reason; the participating self cannot . . . make a choice between reason and imagination but only between reasoning on the basis of adequate images" (p. 108).

Here, we get ourselves into murky waters because the question of how to evaluate whether content is adequate seems without answers. But to be true to our experience of religious and spiritual development, we have no choice but to dive in, for our experience tells us that the content of religious and spiritual imagining matters. For example, intuitively, we understand that Mother Teresa's imagining the poor to be Christ in his terrible disguise matters and matters deeply.

Here is another example to show that the content of imagining matters. Paul Pruyser (1991) remembers his own early experience with religious imagining:

I attended a denominational school . . . that stood for much greater Calvinist orthodoxy than did my family. Thus, home and school presented me with two different religious and emotional worlds. The first was mellow, optimistic, and forgiving; the second strict, somber and punitive—both equally taking recourse to scripture. . . . There is nothing like such an upbringing to convince a young boy that religion is what you make it, that all of it is what I now call "illusionistic." Fortunately, home won over school, undoubtedly because of its deeper roots in my childhood practicing of the transitional sphere. The hand of God, much talked about in school, was closer to my mother's tender-and-firm hand than to the threatening and often slapping extremities of my teachers. (p. 180)

In other words, for Pruyser, a decisive step in his own religious and spiritual development was his choosing between alternative imaginings. For Pruyser, the truth or value of imagining lies not so much in its structure as in the value of its content for supporting healthy development. The gentler, nurturing, more compassionate and loving imagery that was promoted in Pruyser's home life seemed healthier and more spiritual than the more punitive imagery promoted in his school life. In the next example, we see even more clearly how religious and spiritual development is tied to the content and not just to the structure of imagining.

After the death of his child, Rabbi Harold Kushner (1981) changed his image of God from that of an all-powerful but not so compassionate God to a totally compassionate but not all-powerful God. He did so not to make the world unrealistically "nice" and not to soothe his troubled feelings. He did so to adjust his image of God in the light of his discovering something true about compassion and living a moral life. Furthermore, his new understanding came not from his looking to the heavens but from his looking all around him—to those who did not know how to be compassionate and to those who did. Furthermore, for Kushner, a totally compassionate God was more than powerful enough.

Faith Versus Belief

What do spiritual exemplars, both great and small, have in common? If one looks at their beliefs, one finds that the differences outweigh the similarities. Lincoln's belief in a Calvinist God has no counterpart in the Dalai Lama's belief in nirvana. But what Lincoln, the Dalai Lama, and all spiritual exemplars have in common is a strong and powerful faith that works for good.

But what is faith if not belief? Wilfred Cantwell Smith, the historian and longtime dean of comparative religious studies, has argued that faith is a universal quality of *persons,* that it is a quality difficult if not impossible to measure, and that it refers to a person's involvement in the symbols of a faith tradition rather than to the symbols themselves. Faith, then, is more a verb than a noun. It is more about action and living a certain way than it is about something static such as a dogma, belief, or symbol. Smith (1998) points out that this meaning of faith is much older than the newer meaning of faith as belief. Before the Enlightenment, one might readily have admitted believing in the Devil but at the same time been adamant about having faith only in God.

It was the Enlightenment, then, that fostered the newer meaning and reduced religion to matters of belief or to its alternative, feeling. The picture Smith paints of faith-filled lives emphasizes how individuals, by responding to the symbols of their faith traditions, have been transformed, "saved," if you will, or at least developed:

> To live religiously is not merely to live in the presence of certain symbols, but to be involved with them or through them in a quite special way, a

way that may lead far beyond the symbols, that may demand of a person's response, and may affect one's relations not only to them but to everything else: to oneself, to one's neighbor and to the stars. (Smith, 1998, p. 3)

The point here is that faith is about involvement and response, not simply belief or feeling. "One does not believe a symbol. Rather, one responds to it" (p. 146).

But what is meant by response to a symbol? Obviously, responses vary considerably and include common spiritual practices: prayers, ritual dances, meditation, hymn singing, and so forth, as well as reading sacred texts. In reality, however, almost any act can take on spiritual meaning and become a response to a faith tradition's symbols. For example, Shakers turned the mundane act of crafting chairs into a form of worship as they imagined themselves making chairs good enough so that angels passing by might want to sit on them (Andrews, 1963).

The consequences of conflating faith and belief have been to marginalize religion and to dismiss spirituality as something less than rational:

> Belief became . . . the category of thought by which skeptics, reducing others' faith to manageability, translated that faith into mundane terms. They substituted for an interest in it as faith an interest rather in the exotic mental processes and conceptual framework of those whose lives had been sustained and enriched by it. . . . What had been a relation between the human and something external and higher . . . was transformed by the new thinking into a self-subsistent, mundane operation of the mind. . . . To imagine that religious persons "believe" this or that is a way of dominating intellectually, and comfortably, what in fact one does not truly discern. (Smith, 1998, p. 144)

Smith is right. Certainly, in the scientific study of religious and spiritual development we have often focused on something other than faith, on beliefs in particular, but also on feelings. In so doing, we have said interesting things about individuals and groups but not enough about what is most important, namely, faith and its development. For now, it is enough to establish that faith, not belief or feeling, should be the central focus for the study of religious and spiritual development.

One last point with regard to the faith–belief distinction: Faith need not refer to religious faith. Faith as involvement in a symbol system, a system meant to define and support the good life, can be entirely secular. For example, one legacy of classical Greece and Rome has been a secular faith, which is, says Smith, "a living tradition with its own metaphysical underpinning, its own great champions and even martyrs, its own institutions, its own apprehension of or by transcendence, and . . . its own type of faith" (1998, p. 134).

Having provided a framework for thinking about religious and spiritual development, we can move on to evaluating current empirical approaches in the light of this framework. Since this framework has to do with norms for defining the maturing of faith and persons, the discussion of current approaches will be in terms of their not being about persons, or faith, or development defined by norms.

CURRENT APPROACHES

Is religious and spiritual development to be conceived of as a march toward a single, albeit complex and universal, end point, thus following norms that push, pull, or define where individuals are to head if they are to develop? Or is religious and spiritual development to be conceived of as water flooding a hillside, or as a branching bush, or as some other metaphor that characterizes development in terms of multiple pathways leading to multiple end points?

Development conceived of as an upward climb toward perfection is development defined by approximations to perfection. Development conceived of as multidirectional pathways leading to multiple end points is development defined by what happens to individuals as they react to unexpected moments and as they participate in particular contexts and cultures.

These two conceptions of development lead to quite different goals for the social scientist bent on explaining religious and spiritual development. Using a normative conception of development, explanation tends to be about the structural development that underlies or defines *lower* and *higher, immature* and *mature*—and about universals. Using a nonnormative conception of

development, explanation tends to be closer to describing change over time, not just or mainly in the individual, but also in the individual's transactions and participation in contexts and cultures so as to function and adapt.

Here we look at four quite different approaches that share a common understanding that religious and spiritual development need not, in fact, should not, be thought of in terms of stages and universal end points. Each criticizes normative, stage-structural models for failing to explain the nonlinear changes that often occur in how religiousness and spirituality get expressed from birth to death. Each also criticizes stage-structural models for not capturing the diverse ways that individuals express themselves religiously and spiritually, for being overoptimistic about the fruits of structural development, and for putting Western, liberal values above all others. David Wulff (1993) sums up these criticisms this way:

> The positing of religious development, especially in the form of progressive and irreversible stages, requires the assumption of religion-specific dispositions or structures as well as of particular end-states representing the fullest realization of the inborn potential. It is difficult to say, however, of what these rarely observed end-states consist. Furthermore, the construction of these states requires the imposition of certain philosophical and theological views, thus undermining any claims for universality. (p. 182)

Here, then, we review the contributions of these current approaches to religious and spiritual development and their specific, as well as general, criticisms of normative, stage-structural theories. We begin with the contributions and criticisms of Susan Kwilecki's substantive-functional approach (1999), which follows in the tradition of religious studies.

Kwilecki's Substantive-Functional Approach

Kwilecki's work is with adults, not children, because, in her view, "childhood is not the period of consummate religious expression" (1999, p. 264). She is, therefore, critical of current research on religious and spiritual development, which she says, "meticulously explains the differences in . . . the religious conceptualization of a five and a nine year old, but does not address the spectacular variety of adult religious perspectives" (p. 264). Because of this variety, Kwilecki defines religious and spiritual development in terms of quantitative measures: "Growth or development in personal religion occurs . . . when ideas and experiences of the supernatural become increasingly salient and functional to the individual. . . . My criterion of religious development—the scope, depth, and pervasiveness of supernaturalism in life—is essentially quantitative" (pp. 32–33).

For Kwilecki, what grows or develops has to do with imagination more than with perception and reason:

> Becoming religious . . . means realizing, and increasingly acting upon the realization, that ultimately our fate lies with forces that transcend our generally most effective tools of adaptation—the senses and reason. Attempting to monitor critical but elusive powers, the religious are daily thrown upon the imagination, a faculty difficult to discipline and trust. Ongoing negotiations with unseen beings strain even the hominid capacity for symbolization. Not everyone becomes religious to the same degree. (p. 31)

As lives lived imaginatively, the religious, for Kwilecki, are not to be evaluated using the cognitive developmental schemes derived from Piaget and Kohlberg.

With respect to defining religious and spiritual development, Kwilecki's work reminds us that the focus needs to be on whole persons functioning in complex and ever-changing circumstances. To capture religious and spiritual development, then, we cannot rely solely on general description systems such as those found in stage-structural theories. We need to know the details of individuals' lives, the challenges they face as well as their inner thoughts, fantasies, and feelings.

Kwilecki's work also shows us the value of certain forms of thinking and behaving that often are explicitly or implicitly denigrated by stage-structural theories. For example, in her case study of "Jack McCullers," a mechanic who reported he once received a divine command to purchase a head gasket for a Toyota, when he did not own a Toyota or know anybody who did. Kwilecki's response to the religious imaginings of McCullers was: "What could be sillier than thinking that the ruler of the universe would waste time on interventions and messages such as these? What could be lovelier than thinking that the ruler of the universe is so intimate and playful?"(personal communication). In short, in Kwilecki's approach we see the inherent ambiguity in religious imagining, ambiguity that is often missing in normative, stage-structural approaches.

Kwilecki's approach, then, corrects deficiencies found in normative, stage-structural approaches. But is her way of defining development entirely quantitative and without norms? In her writing, we can occasionally detect a normative and qualitative definition of development, one that seems sensible if not inevitable. Throughout her writing, Kwilecki goes back and forth between describing the ordinary individuals who are the focus of her case studies and extraordinary religious and spiritual exemplars. In her admiration of ordinary examples of faith, but especially in her admiration of exemplars, one can detect an implicit developmental approach defined in terms of qualitative differences. Whether writing about Mother Teresa, Black Elk, or the Zen nun Satori Myods, Kwilecki admires the faithful's ability to pursue noble purposes, especially in the face of adversity—and always she is taken with the faithful's ability to imagine realities beyond appearances, their ability to remain optimistic, and their ability to use imagination to adapt. Her person-centered approach can, therefore, lay the foundation for a normative developmental approach that is sensitive to culture, circumstances, and individual personalities.

Kwilecki's work focuses on adults because she believes that it is in the adult years that faith takes on its varied and sometimes magnificent forms. In the next example of a current approach, the focus is on children, because children's rich and varied spiritual experience has been overlooked by stage-structural models. Kwilecki's approach is nonnormative in the way she defines religious and spiritual development in quantitative terms, as faith gaining strength. Her approach gives us development without explicit norms. The next approach gives us norms for assessing children's spirituality but without development.

The Spiritual Child Movement

In recent years, a number of psychologists and educators have been writing about "the spiritual child" (Hart, chapter 12, this volume; Hay, 1998; Reimer & Furrow, 2001), so many that one can discern a "spiritual child" movement. The spiritual child movement is, in part, a reaction to stage-structural theories of religious and spiritual development, which are generally seen as following along the lines set down by Goldman. As such, one of the main criticisms put forth by this group is that stage-structural theories are too cognitive. For example, Hay (1998) writes:

[T]he cumulative feeling I am left with after reviewing what we know about childhood spirituality is an uneasiness about the adequacy of developmental theory (meaning stage-structural theories) to give an account of it. . . . The major problem (with stage theories) is their narrowness, coming near to dissolving religion into reason and therefore childhood spirituality into nothing more than a form of immaturity or inadequacy. (pp. 50, 51)

The idea that children are spiritual is not new. Throughout history, faith traditions have, at some time or another, found an innate spirituality in children—as demonstrated in the passage from Mark 10:15: "Whosoever shall not receive the kingdom of God as a little child, he shall not enter therein"; in the reincarnation beliefs surrounding the search for a new Dalai Lama (Thurman, 1991); and in the treatment of babies by the Beng of Ivory Coast (Gottlieb, chapter 11, this volume). At various times, then, children have been seen as having a natural and uncritical faith, a natural wisdom and capacity for discerning "the way things really are," and a spirituality that comes from being "old souls." Therefore, what is new in the current spiritual child movement is not the idea of children being spiritual but the arguments attacking stage-structural theories for being too cognitive.

The spiritual child movement is, then, based on the idea that spirituality is rooted in personal experience, feeling, and biology. Those leading the movement do, of course, acknowledge that there is a cognitive element in what they refer to as spiritual experience. To experience spiritually requires at least the cognitive ability to step back and "be aware"—of the larger picture, of the mystery of life, of there being something more than what is given by the senses. But this ability is present at very young ages, as young as 4 by some accounts, but certainly by 6.

The capacity for spiritual awareness is present at young ages because, says this group, humans have evolved in ways that provide for this capacity (Hart, chapter 12, this volume; Hay, 1998). Spiritual capacity is, thus, inherited capacity, a product of brain development. It is given to children by biology rather than by parents, teachers, or culture—though for spirituality to develop, children need lots of encouragement and support. In sum, the spiritual child movement is bent on getting across one main idea, namely, that children have the capacity for rich and varied spiritual experiences that form (or should form through being encouraged and supported) the foundation of their religious, ethical, and spiritual development.

What is the evidence supporting this claim that children have the capacity for experiences that are essentially spiritual? The evidence there is comes from interview studies of children, from retrospective paper-and-pencil studies of adults, and from collections of anecdotes. Members of this group have been the first to point out that their methods and the available evidence do not meet rigorous scientific standards. Even with regard to the issue of how to define children's spirituality, this group admits that it is difficult at best and perhaps impossible to pin down children's spirituality by means of definition. There is, says this group, an inevitable subjectivity to discerning children's spirituality. For example, Rebecca Nye (Hay & Nye, 1998; Nye, 1999) writes that what she observed as moments when the children she interviewed were relating their spiritual experiences were not captured by the words appearing in transcripts. Those moments were singled out because, during them, children seemed to "shift into another gear" when speaking about their experiences.

Given current evidence and methods, it might be easy to dismiss this movement on the grounds that it is not based in solid scientific research. However, doing so ignores the real phenomena being discussed. The main question is, then, not whether the phenomena discussed are real but whether they warrant the designation *spiritual*. Other terms, used by the leaders of this movement themselves, work equally well: words such as *wonder, awe, wisdom,* and *relational consciousness*. Adding the term *spiritual* runs the risk of adding a gratuitous interpretation.

Furthermore, by calling attention to children's "spiritual experiences," the group promoting the spiritual child movement has self-consciously de-emphasized the role of judgment and reasoning and thinking in general to the point of sometimes adopting an opposite extreme to that of Goldman. The previous quote by Hay might well serve as an example.

Finally, this group's approach may be questioned for how development is conceived (or not conceived, as the case may be). It is one thing to point out moments of awe, wonder, and wisdom in the lives of children and another to define faith and its development. Of the two enterprises, the second seems more significant. Moments of awe, wonder, wisdom, and relational consciousness are not likely to shoulder much of the work of establishing a foundation for religious and spiritual development. At least, research has yet to show they do. And even if it is not the moments themselves that are important, but rather the innate capacities they point to, we are still left with the question of how these innate capacities develop into mature patterns of faith. Granted that what develops has to do with wonder, awe, and wisdom, we are left still with the task of figuring out the qualitative differences between the wonder, awe, and wisdom of a child and that of, say, John Muir speaking of mountains as "God's cathedrals" (Cronon, 1997) and Gandhi demonstrating the wisdom of the Gujarati precept, "Return good for evil" (Gandhi, 1927–1929/1993).

In the discussion of the next approach, we also find an appreciation for how much children understand, as well as an appreciation for the influence of elders and culture. However, unlike the previous two approaches, the next approach is grounded in experimental research done within post-Piagetian and postrationalist, cognitive

developmental psychology—with its focus on domain-specific development and cultural diversity.

Cognitive-Cultural Theories

Stage-structural theories posit universals, which make such theories susceptible to overlooking cultural diversity. The wealth of information now obtained from new disciplines such as cognitive anthropology suggests that no stage-structural theory can do justice to the rich variety of thinking and acting that is found in and among cultures. Rather than adopt the stairway to maturity model, today's cognitive developmental psychologists, like Darwin before them, have adopted the model of an ever-branching bush. Who is to say which branch is better?

Current cognitive-cultural theories (see Johnson & Boyatzis, chapter 15, this volume) search for competencies specific to nonuniversal domains rather than only for competencies that cut across domains (e.g., object permanence). This search has provided a more nuanced view of intellectual development. The word *domain* can have as its reference something quite broad, such as the domain of physics and physical causality, or something quite narrow, such as the domain of baseball or knock-knock jokes (Feldman, 1985). It is the broad sense of domain that is used in current cognitive studies, and three broad domains in particular have been the focus of research on children's cognitive development, namely, the physical, biological, and psychological (theory of mind) domains. Throughout their early years, children are seen as developing intuitive knowledge in these three domains so that by age 4, most have a fairly well developed intuitive ontology (Boyer & Walker, 2000; Harris, 2000).

This view of young children having a fairly well developed intuitive ontology directly contradicts the older Piagetian view, which characterizes young children's thinking as being irrational and prelogical. In this newer view, young children come off as neither rational nor irrational. Rather, they come off as adept at handling different systems of thinking about reality. For our purposes, two systems in particular are central.

The first system is for thinking about everyday events. This is the default system. It rests on direct observation and on an innate push to find patterns and causal connections. It is not a system that looks for magic and the counterintuitive. On the contrary, it is thoroughly empirical. Preschoolers may pretend, but in doing so, they call their pretense make-believe. And when not pretending, if their causal inferences seem irrational, it is more because they lack information and experience than because their thought processes are inherently irrational.

The other system is for thinking about the counterintuitive. It comes into play more because of culture and the testimony of trusted caregivers than it does because of children's reflections on reality. Early on, children are exposed to counterintuitive ideas and counterintuitive worlds that make up their culture's religious heritage, and, remarkably, they have little difficulty taking on these ideas and worlds and making them their own (Harris, 2003).

They do so for a number of reasons. First, they trust their caregivers and mentors—those giving testimony to the reality of the counterintuitive (Harris, 2000). Second, because religious ideas are often both counterintuitive and presented as true, children find them arresting and memorable (Atran & Norenzayan, in press). Third, children are able to keep a kind of double booking—with intuitive ontology employed most of the time, and their newly acquired counterintuitive ontology employed when the occasion fits (Harris, 2003). Fourth, even when assimilating counterintuitive religious belief systems, children borrow from their intuitive ontology, making it possible to draw inferences from the counterintuitive world to the everyday, and vice versa (Harris, 2000).

As can be seen in this account, the questions here are about the development of distinctions and boundaries between separate domains. They are not questions about stages leading in a particular direction. Furthermore, children older than 4 are characterized as being much more similar to adults in their basic thought patterns than the older Piagetian characterizations lead us to believe. Finally, culture, not simply organismic development, explains age changes in what children believe.

What does this mean for the study and understanding of religious and spiritual development?

For one thing, it means rejecting theologically influenced developmental models in favor of descriptions grounded in cross-cultural field research. For another thing, it means that religious development is not a separate cognitive domain but rather a domain that draws on the cognitive achievements designed originally for mundane tasks. Finally, it means religious thinking is neither more primitive nor more mature than other kinds of thinking. It is simply different. And this relativity extends to distinctions between religious traditions themselves so long as individuals within any given tradition develop basic intuitive ontologies (physical, biological, psychological) and so long as the counterintuitive religious agents and worlds serve the usual adaptive functions of fostering moral (communal) commitment and relieving existential anxiety (Atran & Norenzayan, in press).

This is a composite view of current thinking about religious development from a cognitive-cultural perspective. What are we to make of it? What are its strengths and weaknesses? The main strength in this approach is its providing a better account of how religious beliefs are acquired. The main weakness is the approach's conflating belief and faith—so much so that, at times, the subject investigated seems to be something other than religious and spiritual development. For example, the approach fails to distinguish differences between children's questions such as "Why don't angels fall down to earth" (Harris, 2000), and adults' questions such as "Why do bad things happen to good people?" (Kushner, 1981). The first question lacks moral significance. The second question forces thinking about what kind of universe we live in and how we ought to face injustice and adversity. While there may be disagreement about whether both kinds of questions fall within the domain of religious and spiritual development, it seems clear that the second kind of question has more to do with what has previously been defined as questions of faith.

Developmental Systems Theories

Developmental systems theories shift the focus from individuals to transactions between individuals and their various embedded contexts (Lerner et al., 2003). The main assumption here is about plasticity being a fundamental feature of human development. With respect to religious and spiritual development, the focus is on faith-based communities and their role in helping youth develop positively (Benson et al., 2003; King & Boyatzis, 2004; Roehlkepartain, 1995). A study by Regnerus and Elder (2003) will serve as the main example.

This study illustrates the developmental systems approach in several ways, first by its speaking about involvement in a faith-based community as a potential "resilient pathway." The term *resilient pathway* reveals the approach's main assumption about plasticity. The results of this study show that in high-risk communities, church attendance functions as a protective mechanism "stimulating resilience in the lives of at-risk youth"—as shown by church attendance correlating positively with staying "on track" in school.

However, it is in Regnerus and Elder's explanation of the results, rather than the results themselves, that we see the main features of the developmental systems approach:

> The ritual action of attending worship services or ceremonies, in contrast with theological differences that mark distinct religious affiliations and beliefs, appears to be a process that operates independently of particular belief systems and organizational affiliations. Church attendance may constitute—even if by accident—a form of social integration that has the consequence of reinforcing values conducive to educational achievement and goal setting. . . . [In addition] . . . church attendance and doing well in school require commitment, diligence, and routine. The ritual practice of rising and going to church or mass, and so forth—whether compelled by one's own faith or one's parents' demands—commits a youth to a practice and routine, a skill that translates into tools needed for academic success. (p. 646)

In other words, for the study's at-risk youth, going to church regularly meant they were exposed to values and good routines that could be transferred to school.

Obviously, studies such as Regnerus and Elder's are much needed, especially for understanding how to support at-risk youth. But are they studies of religious and spiritual development,

or are they simply studies of positive development defined broadly? I think they are the latter because they skirt the task of charting and explaining faith and its development. While these studies often acknowledge that faith is a unique and important variable, they do not explain how faith develops. And in not explaining how faith develops, they leave out the inner workings that define and explain religious and spiritual development.

CONCLUSIONS

As discussed, current approaches have much to offer by way of correcting deficiencies in previous stage-structural accounts of religious and spiritual development. As also discussed, however, current approaches do not adequately define religious and spiritual development—in part because in dispensing with the concept of stage, current approaches have dispensed with an essential aspect of defining religious and spiritual development. The next phase of research needs, then, to combine the strengths of stage-structural approaches with the strengths of current approaches.

How might this be accomplished? In addition to calling attention to stage theories being insensitive to cultural diversity, post-Piagetian critics have criticized stage theory for (1) not providing an adequate account of variability and (2) not accounting for transition processes. However, recently, a number of theorists have answered the critics and in so doing have revitalized stage theory. Feldman's discussion (in press) bears special mention.

After outlining each of the main criticisms of Piaget's stage theory, Feldman proposes ways to answer the criticisms. The first major criticism of stage theories such as Piaget's is that they do not account for the wide variation in behavior one finds within any given stage. Feldman answers this criticism by suggesting that we think of a stage as consisting of two substages— with the first devoted to constructing the stage and the second devoted to extending and applying the stage's system as widely as possible. Stages are marked, then, by their midpoints.

The second major criticism of stage theories is that they do not provide adequate accounts of transition mechanisms. In the case of Piaget's stage theory, equilibration as a transition mechanism bears too much of the burden for explaining transitions. Feldman answers this criticism by suggesting that we keep Piaget's equilibration mechanism but give more emphasis to other mechanisms to explain transitions, including learning. That is, there need not be any contradiction between developing a stage theory and providing explanations such as those offered by cognitive-cultural theorists focused on how children acquire counterintuitive beliefs about supernatural agencies. In sum, suggestions such as Feldman's allow us to hold on to the concept of stage so as to better define religious and spiritual development without becoming culturally insensitive. Once again, we find there is no reason to throw out the baby with the bathwater.

The next phase of research needs, then, to provide a more differentiated concept of stage in order to define religious and spiritual development normatively—as movement toward "perfection." It needs also to describe and explain the development of persons and not just domain-specific achievements. It needs to describe and explain the development of religious and spiritual imagining and not just reasoning, and it needs to provide ways to evaluate content and not just structure. But most of all, it needs to focus on faith, not just belief, and faith's development.

NOTES

1. The term *religious and spiritual development* is used throughout with the understanding that religiousness and spirituality are distinct though overlapping phenomena.

2. For a clear, insightful discussion of domains and development analyses, see Feldman (1985).

REFERENCES

Andrews, E. (1963). *The people called Shakers.* New York: Dover.

Atran, S., & Norenzayan, A. (in press). Religion's evolutionary landscape: Counterintuition, commitment, compassion, communion. *Behavioral and Brain Sciences.*

Benson, P. L., Roehlkepartain, E. C., & Rude, S. P. (2003). Spiritual development in childhood and adolescence: Toward a field of inquiry. *Applied Developmental Science, 7*(3), 205–213.

Boyer, P., & Walker, S. (2000). Intuitive ontology and cultural input in the acquisition of religious concepts. In K. S. Rosengren, C. N. Johnson, & P. L. Harris (Eds.), *Imagining the impossible: Magical, scientific, and religious thinking in children* (pp. 130–156). Cambridge, UK: Cambridge University Press.

Cassirer, E. (1944). *An essay on man.* New Haven, CT: Yale University Press.

Cassirer, E. (1955). *The philosophy of symbolic forms: Vol. 2. Mythical thought.* New Haven, CT: Yale University Press.

Cassirer, E. (1960). *The logic of the humanities.* New Haven, CT: Yale University Press.

Cronon, W. (Ed.). (1997). *John Muir: Nature writings.* New York: Penguin Putnam.

Feldman, D. H. (1985). *Beyond universals in cognitive development.* Norwood, NJ: Ablex.

Feldman, D. H. (in press). Piaget's stages: The unfinished symphony of cognitive development. *New Ideas in Psychology.*

Fosdick, H. E. (1931). *The meaning of prayer.* New York: Association Press.

Gandhi, M. K. (1993). *Gandhi: An autobiography. The story of my experiments with truth.* Boston: Beacon Press. (Original work published 1927–1929)

Goldman, R. (1964). *Religious thinking from childhood to adolescence.* New York: Seabury.

Harris, P. L. (2000). On not falling down to earth: Children's metaphysical questions. In K. S. Rosengren, C. N. Johnson, & P. L. Harris (Eds.), *Imagining the impossible: Magical, scientific, and religious thinking in children* (pp. 157–178). Cambridge, UK: Cambridge University Press.

Harris, P. L. (2003). Les dieux, les ancêtres et les enfants [Gods, ancestors and children]. *Terrain, 40,* 81–98.

Hay, D., & Nye, R. (1998). *The spirit of the child.* London: Fount.

Kaplan, B. (1983). Genetic-dramatism: Old wine in new bottles. In B. Kaplan, *Toward a holistic developmental psychology* (pp. 53–75). Hillsdale, NJ: Erlbaum.

King, P. E., & Boyatzis, C. J. (2004). Exploring adolescent spiritual and religious development: Current and future theoretical and empirical perspectives. *Applied Developmental Science, 8*(1), 2–6.

Kushner, H. (1981). *When bad things happen to good people.* New York: Avon.

Kwilecki, S. (1999). *Becoming religious.* Cranbury, NJ: Associated University Press.

Lerner, R. M., Dowling, E. M., & Anderson, P. M. (2003). Positive youth development: Thriving as the basis of personhood and civil society. *Applied Developmental Science, 7*(3), 172–180.

Niebuhr, H. R. (1946). *The meaning of revelation.* New York: Macmillan.

Nye, R. (1999). Relational consciousness and the spiritual lives of children: Convergence with children's theory of mind? In H. Reich, F. K. Oser, & W. G. Scarlett (Eds.), *Psychological studies on spiritual and religious development* (pp. 57–83). Lengerich, Germany: Pabst.

Oser, F. (1991). The development of religious judgment. In F. Oser & W. G. Scarlett (Eds.), *Religious development in childhood and adolescence* (pp. 5–27). San Francisco: Jossey-Bass.

Oser, F., & Gmünder, P. (1991). *Religious judgement: A developmental approach.* Birmingham, AL: Religious Education Press.

Pruyser, P. (1991). Forms and functions of the imagination in religion. In H. N. Malony & B. Spilka (Eds.), *Religion in psychodynamic perspective: The contributions of Paul W. Pruyser* (pp. 170–191). New York: Oxford University Press.

Regnerus, M., & Elder, G. (2003). Staying on track in school: Religious influences in high- and low-risk settings. *Journal for the Scientific Study of Religion, 42*(4), 633–649.

Reimer, K. S., & Furrow, J. L. (2001). A qualitative exploration of relational consciousness in Christian children. *International Journal of children's spirituality, 6,* 7–23.

Roehlkepartain, E. C. (1995). *Youth development in congregations: An exploration of the potential and barriers.* Minneapolis, MN: Search Institute.

Scarlett, W. G., & Perriello, L. (1991). The development of prayer in adolescence. In F. Oser & W. G. Scarlett (Eds.), *Religious development in childhood and adolescence* (pp. 63–67). San Francisco: Jossey-Bass.

Smith, W. C. (1998). *Faith and belief: The difference between them.* Oxford, UK: Oneworld.

Thurman, R. (1991). *Wisdom and compassion: The sacred art of Tibet.* New York: Thames and Hudson.

Tolstoy, L. (2004). *The death of Ivan Ilyich.* New York: Bantam Classics. (Original work published 1886)

Wulff, D. (1993). On the origins and goals of religious development. *International Journal for the Psychology of Religion, 3*(3), 181–186.

3

Stages of Faith From Infancy Through Adolescence: Reflections on Three Decades of Faith Development Theory

James W. Fowler

Mary Lynn Dell

Faith development theory was pioneered originally in the 1970s (Fowler, 1974) and 1980s (Fowler, 1981) as a framework for understanding the evolution of how human beings conceptualize God, or a Higher Being, and how the influence of that Higher Being has an impact on core values, beliefs, and meanings in their personal lives and in their relationships with others. Because of the formative influence of this theoretical work in both religious and spiritual development (including multiple references in this volume), it merits full articulation and a recounting of its origins. This chapter gives the early history of the author's faith development theory and introduces readers to its key concepts, with special emphasis on those stages most commonly seen in children and adolescents. It also reviews some of the critical and constructive assessments of faith development theory by scholars in the field, through the lenses of several volumes of collected articles.

The Birth and Nurture of Faith Development Studies

Harvard Divinity School in 1968 was a place where a diverse community of students studied

---

AUTHORS' NOTE: Portions of this chapter are adapted from Fowler, J. W. (2004). Faith development at 30: Naming the challenges of faith in a new millennium. *Religious Education, 99,* 405–421, used by permission of the Religious Education Association; and from Fowler, J. W., and Dell, M. L. (2004). Stages of faith and identity: Birth to teens. *Child and Adolescent Psychiatric Clinics of North America, 13,* 17–34, used by permission of Elsevier.

theology in the context of the bitterly dividing struggle in the United States over the Vietnam War. It was also a time when polarization in the civil rights movement had intensified. Against those backgrounds, I developed my first course for master's of divinity students out of my experiences at a retreat center called Interpreter's House (after the place in *Pilgrim's Progress*), and my interest in the kind of practical theology that attends to and expresses the human experiences of growth and of awakening to faith. I wanted students to honor the dynamics of doubt, as well as the formative faith experiences in their families and faith communities. I called that first course "Theology as the Symbolization of Experience." H. Richard Niebuhr and Paul Tillich provided theological starting points, which I correlated with readings from Erik Erikson, Robert Bellah, and a number of other social scientific sources. With a class of 40, I supplemented the twice-weekly class sessions by meeting with my students each week in four separate discussion groups of 10. In these weekly small gatherings, candid sharing among students took place, with me and each other, and in their wrestling with the texts we read. Many of them were deeply engaged by the moral challenges of the war in Vietnam, with the struggle for full civil rights for African Americans, and other pressing social justice issues.

Early in my teaching, students began to ask whether I knew the work of then new Harvard professor Lawrence Kohlberg. At Harvard's Graduate School of Education, Kohlberg was just establishing the Center for Moral Development, building on his research and development of the stage theory of moral development. I soon sought out Kohlberg's unpublished writings. Through our students, he and I met. His use of Jean Piaget's theory of cognitive development, along with his interview research and theory of moral development, complemented the work of Erikson and the theological figures I was teaching.

Under the influence of coming to know Kohlberg and the stimulating circle of younger investigators around him, in a year or two, I began to have my students conduct what we came to call faith development interviews. Using a questionnaire that we constructed, and eventually, a set of interpretation and analysis

guidelines, we began to form the baseline data that would result in the construction and validation of what came to be known as faith development theory.

Among the blessings to my life and work in that period was the presence, in the early 1970s, of three Jesuits in their tertianship year in one of my courses. They sensed that my faith at this point was very cognitively oriented, and that my deeper needs for prayer and spirituality might not be being met. They introduced me to the Spiritual Exercises of Saint Ignatius. Eventually this led to my participating in a fruitful Nineteenth Annotation guided retreat, in the Ignatian tradition, under the leadership of Fr. Robert Doherty, S. J.

In the meantime, my ties to Kohlberg's circle at the Harvard Graduate School of Education grew and deepened. Carol Gilligan, Robert Selman, and eventually, Robert Kegan, and theologian educator Sharon Parks—along with many others—were formative in a rich environment of structural developmental studies. When the Joseph P. Kennedy, Jr. Foundation provided a substantial fund for faith development research, I formed a team of graduate students from theology and developmental psychology. For 3 years, along with my students, we conducted and analyzed the 359 interviews on which the stages of faith are based.

The growing influence of Kohlberg's theory of moral development and its pedagogical implications found strong acceptance in many Catholic schools across the nation and, indeed, the world. The educators who had claimed the structural development theory of Kohlberg, seeing its kinship to the natural law tradition, were primed to engage the emerging research and theory of faith development. This interest led to an invitation that would draw me into a 10-year relation with Boston College's Summer Institute for Religious Education and Pastoral Ministries, a program that drew hundreds of nuns, priests, and lay Catholic educators each year from the United States and across the world. The refinement, adoption, and dissemination of the emerging faith development theory greatly expanded through these Boston College connections. The invitation to write what became *Stages of Faith* and to publish it with Harper came in 1979, and was partly the result of my summer students copying and sending the notes and handouts for the course to colleagues all over the world. In 1977, I had moved to Emory University's Candler School of Theology to teach and do research. There, with strong support for the faith development enterprise, I was able to complete *Stages of Faith,* which was published in 1981. The book is now in its 40th printing, if you count both the hardback and paperback editions.

AN OVERVIEW OF FAITH DEVELOPMENT THEORY

Faith development theory and research have focused on a generic understanding of faith that sees it as foundational to social relations, to personal identity, and to the making of personal and cultural meanings (Dell, 2000; Fowler, 1980, 1981, 1986a, 1986b, 1987, 1989, 1991, 1996). Like many dimensions of our lives, faith seems to have a broadly recognizable pattern of development. This unfolding pattern can be characterized in terms of developing emotional, cognitive, and moral interpretations and responses. Our ways of imagining and committing in faith correlate significantly with our ways of knowing and valuing more generally. We are asking you to think of faith in a more inclusive sense than Christian, Buddhist, Islamic, or Judaic faith. Faith, in the sense used here, even extends beyond religious faith. Understood in this more inclusive sense, faith may be characterized as an integral, centering process, underlying the formation of the beliefs, values, and meanings that:

1. Give coherence and direction to persons' lives;

2. Link them in shared trusts and loyalties with others;

3. Ground their personal stances and communal loyalties in a sense of relatedness to a larger frame of reference; and

4. Enable them to face and deal with the challenges of human life and death, relying on that which has the quality of ultimacy in their lives.

Faith, taken in this broad sense, is a common feature of human beings. In the language of child psychiatrist Erik Erikson, faith begins with basic trust, as the child forms bonds with the mother and other intimate caregivers. As the child matures, physically and emotionally, faith accommodates the development of an expanding range of object relations, and exposure to religious symbols and practices may nurture a sense of relatedness to the transcendent. We will draw on research, theory, and clinical observations that provide more detailed perspectives on the emergence and development of faith, understood in this broader sense, from birth through the teen years.

STAGES OF FAITH: AN OVERVIEW

In the following descriptions of the faith stages and the changes they bring, we acknowledge the complex interplay of factors that must be taken into account if we are to begin to understand faith development. These include biological maturation, emotional and cognitive development, psychosocial experience, and the role of religiocultural symbols, meanings, and practices. This complexity is increased if we consider gender and race, which we try to do in this account. Because development in faith involves all of these aspects, human development—movement from one stage to another—is not automatic or assured. Persons may reach chronological and biological adulthood while remaining best described by a structural stage of faith that would most commonly be associated with early or middle childhood, or adolescence. By the same token, contexts of spiritual nurture and practice, coupled with a person's spiritual aptitude and discipline, may lead some children to a deeper and more rapid development in faith.

Primal Faith (Infancy to Age 2)

More physical and neurological growth and development occurs in the first year of life than during any other life stage. Assuming a relatively uncomplicated pregnancy and delivery and a healthy neonate, parents can expect the birth weight to double by 5 months of age and triple by the first birthday. Length at birth will increase by 50% during the first year. By the second birthday the brain will attain 70% of its full adult weight, its neurons sprouting millions of dendrites. By 3 months of age infants can attend to visual and auditory stimuli for at least 3 to 5 seconds. By 16 weeks they can hold up their heads, and by 5 months they have developed characteristic arm and leg movements for contented and angry states. At 9 months, babies can gesture intentionally for desired objects or to be picked up. At 12 months, females are able to walk with support, with African American and other ethnicities mastering these gross motor skills earlier than many infants of European backgrounds. Females often achieve these physical milestones slightly earlier than males. By her first birthday she attains object permanence, the knowledge that an object continues to exist even when it is out of her immediate sight (Dell & Dulcan, 1998; Zuckerman, Frank, & Augustyn, 1999).

Attachment between the infant and her or his parent/caregiver is a process with important implications for the child's future relationships. Attachment refers to the emotional bond—begun at birth and nurtured for months thereafter—that is enduring, specific to the individual adult and infant combination, and that both stimulates, and is stimulated by, physical closeness. After the first successful attachment to the primary caregiver(s), the infant can generalize the ability to attach emotionally to select others. The first year is crucial in shaping the young child's ability to make healthy attachments in other relationships. For too many individuals, male and female, inadequate caregiving, abuse, and neglect adversely affect this vital process. In Erikson's framework, the developmental task of this time period is characterized as the development of a sense of basic trust (Erickson, 1963; Zuckerman et al., 1999).

In this first stage a prelanguage disposition of trust forms in the mutuality of one's relationships with parents and other caregivers. This sense of trust offsets the inevitable anxiety and mistrust that result from the succession of cognitive and emotional experiences of separation and self-differentiation, which occur during infant development. Experiences combining to form this trusting disposition include body contact and care; vocal and visual interplay; ritualized interactions associated with early play, feeding, and tending; and the development of interpersonal affective attunement in the infant's relations with caregivers. Factors such as these activate prepotentiated capacities for finding coherence and reliability in self and primal

others, for forming bonds of attachment with them, and for shaping a disposition to trust the larger value and meaning commitments conveyed in parental care. Anxiety and mistrust have their own developmental pattern of emergence that caregivers' consistency and dependability help to offset (Erickson, 1963; Fowler, 1989, 1996; Stern, 1985).

Intuitive-Projective Faith (Toddlerhood and Early Childhood)

In young children, gross motor, fine motor, and cognitive development are intertwined processes related to the maturation timetables of the central and peripheral nervous systems. Neurons are migrating, proliferating, and making more complex connections. Children become capable of more sophisticated communications with the production of neurotransmitters. Myelination, the sheathing of neurons in protective layers of fatty and protein substances, increases the rate of neuronal firing and facilitates faster, more complex signals between brain cells and from the brain to the rest of the body. Good nutrition is crucial to these physiological processes, and early educational stimulation is increasingly appreciated for its role in activating certain neural pathways that might otherwise remain dormant or understimulated. The toddler and preschool periods are times of monumental brain development, continuing a young girl's or boy's susceptibility to physical and emotional neglect and abuse (Krug & Mikus, 1999; Zigler & Gilman, 1998).

Cognitively, the toddler is in transition between Piagetian stages. The last phase of the sensorimotor stage occurs in the first part of the 2nd year. Piaget's preoperational stage emerges in the 3rd year as she tries out symbolic thought and representational play. Toddlers are curious about other children, and progress from individual, solitary play (parallel play) to doing the same thing side by side, without significant interaction with each other (associative play). For Erikson, the fundamental issue of this stage is autonomy versus shame and doubt, and, if all goes well, the desired outcomes are the positive qualities of self-control and willpower (Dell & Dulcan, 1998; Erickson, 1963; Krug & Mikus, 1999; Lewis, 1997; Piaget, 1970, 1976).

From the time children begin to use language to communicate about self and objects in the world, we see the emergence of a style of meaning making based on an emotional and perceptual ordering of experience. Imagination, not yet disciplined by consistent logical operations, responds to story, symbol, dream, and experience. Children attempt to form images that can hold and order the mixture of feelings and impressions evoked by their encounters with the newness of both everyday reality and the penumbra of mystery that surrounds and pervades it. Death becomes a conscious focus as a source of danger and mystery. Experiences of power and powerlessness orient children to a frequently deep existential concern about questions of security, safety, and the power of those on whom they rely for protection. Owing to naive cognitive egocentrism, children do not consistently differentiate their perspectives from those of others. Lacking simple perspective taking and the ability to reverse operations, young children may not understand cause-and-effect relations well. They construct and reconstruct events in episodic fashion. Fantasy and make-believe are not distinguished from factuality. Constructions of faith are drawn to symbols and images of visible power and size. Stories that represent the powers of good and evil in unambiguous fashion are prized; they make it possible for children to symbolize and acknowledge the threatening urges and impulses that both fascinate and disturb them, while providing an identification with the vicarious triumphs of good over evil that such stories as fairy tales can provide (Bettelheim, 1977). There is in this stage the possibility of aligning powerful religious symbols and images with deep feelings of terror and guilt, as well as of love and companionship. Such possibilities give this stage the potential for forming deep and long-lasting emotional and imaginal orientations—both for good and for ill (Fowler, 1976).

Mythic-Literal Faith (Middle Childhood and Beyond)

By the 7th year, the brain has reached 90% of its adult weight, and the process of myelination is largely complete. Fine motor-adaptive skills and small-muscle control are refined as well, permitting elementary school children to tie their shoes easily, snap their fingers, and whistle. Girls and boys are close to the same height and weight until approximately age 10, with girls tending to experience the onset of pubertal changes an average of 2 years earlier than boys (Dell & Dulcan, 1998).

Melvin Levine (1990) has outlined 12 "developmental missions" for a young person in middle childhood: (1) to sustain self-esteem; (2) to find social acceptance, primarily with peers; (3) to "reconcile individuality with conformity"; (4) to identify and emulate role models; (5) to examine values; (6) to feel successful in the family; (7) to explore the freedom and limits of autonomy; (8) to grow in knowledge and skill; (9) to become reconciled to his or her own body; (10) to handle fears; (11) to limit and control appetites and drives, including food, sexual drives, material wants, the seeking of attention; and (12) to "know thyself," or to develop self-awareness.

Although the emotive and imaginal funding of the previous stage is still operative in this newly emerging stage, concrete operational thinking (Piaget) makes possible more stable forms of conscious interpretation and shaping of experience and meanings. Operations of thought can now be reversed, which means that cause-and-effect relations are more clearly understood. Simple perspective taking emerges, which ensures that the differentiation of one's own experiences and perspectives from those of others becomes a dependable acquisition. The young person constructs the world in terms of a new "linearity" and predictability. Although still a potent source of feelings, the previous stage's store of images may get "sealed over," and the episodic, intuitive forms of knowing that marked earlier childhood are subordinated to the use of capacities for more logical and prosaic modes of thinking (Piaget, 1970, 1976).

In the *mythic-literal* stage, the child, adolescent, or adult does not yet construct the interiority—the feelings, attitudes, and internal guiding processes—of the self or others. That is to say, 10-year-olds do not yet reliably have their feelings. They are involved in the process of learning to recognize, interpret, and manage strong feelings and impulses. Similarly, they do not construct God in particularly personal terms, or attribute to God highly differentiated internal emotions and interpersonal sensitivities. In making sense of the larger order of things, therefore, this stage typically structures the ultimate environment—the cosmic pattern of God's rule or control of the universe—along the lines of simple fairness and moral reciprocity. God is often constructed on the model of a consistent and caring, but just, ruler or parent. In this stage one often sees a sense of cosmic fairness at work: The child believes that goodness is rewarded and badness is punished.

In shaping meanings the mythic-literal child primarily employs narrative. In this respect, this stage provides a permanent contribution to meaning making. Stories are as close as the mythic-literal stage comes to reflective synthesis. Neither children nor adolescents (or adults) of this stage carry out extensive analytic or synthetic reflection on their stories. They offer narratives from the middle of the flowing streams of their lives. They do not "step out on the banks" to reflect on where the streams have come from, where they are going, or on what larger meanings might give connection and integrated intelligibility to their collection of experiences and stories. In this stage the use of symbols and concepts remains largely concrete and literal.

The mythic-literal stage begins to wane with the discovery that ours is not a "quick-payoff universe"; that is, evil or bad persons do not necessarily suffer for their transgressions, at least in the short run. And often, "bad things happen to good people." We have coined the term "11-year-old atheists" for children who, in having this latter experience, temporarily or permanently give up belief in a God built along the lines of simple cosmic moral retribution.

The mythic-literal stage initiates and develops the beginnings of reflection on the feelings and ideas of faith. It may be that girls, whom Carol Gilligan and others see as having an earlier and more developed interest in and vocabulary for interpersonal relatedness, progress more rapidly in an awareness of the emotions and skills of interpersonal relatedness. This can mean that girls may give attention to the dynamics of relationships earlier than do boys, bringing both greater sensitivity, on the one hand, and more ease in both managing and manipulating interpersonal relations, on the other (Gilligan, 1982).

Synthetic-Conventional Faith (Adolescence and Beyond)

Puberty (for girls) brings accelerated growth in height and weight, an increase in the percentage of overall body fat, and the emergence of secondary sexual characteristics. In addition it brings the menarche, usually beginning between 8 and 13 years of age. The average age for menarche in the United States among girls of European American ancestry is 12.9 years; among girls of African American descent it is slightly more than half a year earlier at 12.2 years (with a standard deviation of 1.2 years for both groups) (Ford & Coleman, 1990; Neinstein, 1990; Offer, Schonert-Reichl, & Boxer, 1996). For boys, on average, the comparable patterns of the onset of the bodily and emotional transformations of adolescence come a year or so later.

Accompanying the exploding physical, glandular, and sexual changes brought on by adolescence, the *synthetic-conventional* era also brings revolutions in cognitive functioning and interpersonal perspective taking. With the emergence of early formal operational thinking (Piaget), a young person's thought and reasoning take wings. Capable of using and appreciating abstract concepts, young persons begin to think about their own thinking, to reflect upon their stories, and to name and synthesize their meanings (Piaget, 1970, 1976).

In this period we see the emergence of mutual interpersonal perspective taking (Selman, 1974, 1976): "I see you seeing me; I see the me I think you see." And the obverse can also be appreciated: "You see you according to me; you see the you you think I see." This capacity can make youths acutely sensitive to the meanings they seem to have for others, and the evaluations those meanings imply. The lack of "third person" perspective taking, however, often makes the young teen overdependent on the responses and mirroring responses and evaluations of significant others. Identity and personal interiority—one's own and others'—become absorbing concerns.

Personality, both as style and substance, becomes a conscious issue. From within this stage youth construct the ultimate environment in terms of the personal. God representations can be populated with personal qualities of accepting love, understanding, loyalty, and support during times of crisis. During this stage youths develop attachments to beliefs, values, and elements of personal style that link them in con-forming (forming-with) relations with the most significant others among their peers, family, and other nonfamily adults. Identity, beliefs, and values are strongly felt, even when they contain contradictory elements. They tend, however, to be espoused in tacit, rather than explicit, formulations. At this stage one's ideology or worldview is lived and asserted; only gradually does it become a matter of critical and reflective articulation.

Where earlier deficits in the self and in one's patterns of object relations have not been worked through and healed, they become factors that can inhibit the use of cognitive abilities in the tasks of identity and ideology construction in adolescence. Frequently we see splits between the emotional and cognitive functioning of adolescents or adults that are directly attributable to such unresolved issues and relations from early childhood. Sometimes the potential of God as a constructive self-object must be jettisoned because God can only be emotionally populated with the shaming or narcissistic qualities growing out of our experiences with our earliest and most salient object relations.

One decisive limit of the synthetic-conventional stage is its lack yet of third-person perspective taking—a lack of the capacity to construct and work from a perspective that holds both self and other in the same frame, and provides a basis for growing objectivity regarding interpersonal relationships. This means that in its dependence on significant others for confirmation and clarity about one's identity and meaning to them, the synthetic-conventional self does not yet have a third-person perspective from which it can see and evaluate self–other relations from a viewpoint outside themselves. In the synthetic-conventional stage the young person or adult can remain trapped in the "Tyranny of the They"—that is, an overdependence on the mirroring and evaluations of influential significant others.

The Later Stages of Faith

In order to place faith stages typically encountered in childhood and adolescence in context with the trajectory of growth that may be experienced in young, middle, and older adulthood, readers may find somewhat less detailed explanations of the final three stages of faith development theory helpful. In addition, we recognize that many professionals not only work with parents and other adults significant in the lives of children, but continue clinical work with adult patients and thus may be interested in the entire theory from birth through the end of life.

As one considers faith development theory in general, and especially the final three stages, it is important to bear in mind three points.

First, by determining which stage an individual may be operating from at any given time, we are in no way assigning a grade to or judgment about the validity, sincerity, value, or effectiveness of that individual's relationship to the deity of his or her faith. To identify a person's stage or stage transition does not imply that his or her spiritual life is better, more faithful, or desirable than anyone else's, whether in that stage or another. Faith development theory is not intended to be used, nor should it ever be used, as a measure of "how good a Christian," "how good a Jew," "how good a Muslim," or "how good" anyone of any faith tradition may be. Making such judgments constitutes a major abuse of this theory. We are not putting a value judgment on the contents of a person's faith and religious/spiritual identity. We are attempting to describe patterns of knowing and relating through assessing cognitive, moral, and other forms of development that constitute a person's relationship to the transcendent or the Higher Being of a particular religious tradition and relationships with other humans, both inside and outside a person's particular faith community.

Second, with each successive stage comes a series of qualitatively distinguishable patterns of thought, realizations, and behaviors, and in each stage qualitatively new and more complex operations and capacities are added to those of the preceding stage(s).

Third, transition from one stage to another is not inevitable or assumed. For instance, although many elementary school–age children are best described by the mythic-literal stage, so are many adolescents and some adults. While there are no upper age limits to these stages, there are minimum ages below which the later stages are not normally found. For instance, it is unlikely for an individual to meet the description of the synthetic-conventional stage before the early teens or early adolescent years, and it is rare to see someone fully grounded in the individuative-reflective stage prior to the early

20s. On the other hand, one can see individuals much older than the minimum ages experiencing transitioning into a next stage. And it is not unusual for many not to reach the later stages. Again, this does not constitute a value judgment on the maturity, sincerity, or worth of any individual's religious faith (Fowler, 1981, 1987).

Individuative-Reflective Faith

Two significant indicators mark the *individuative-reflective* stage. First, one must develop the ability to reflect critically on the values, beliefs, and commitments one subscribed to as part of constructing the previous stage, the synthetic-conventional. This reexamination of deeply held beliefs can be a painful process. Second, one must struggle with developing a self-identity and self-worth capable of independent judgment in relation to the individuals, institutions, and worldview that anchored one's sense of being up until that time. Questions representative of this stage include: Who am I when I am not defined primarily as someone's daughter, son, or spouse? Who am I apart from my educational, occupational, or professional identity? Who am I beyond my circle of friends or familiar community? In constructing the individuative-reflective position, inherited or familiar symbols, creeds, beliefs, traditions, and religious trappings are scrutinized, and those of other faiths and traditions may be evaluated for what they might have to offer. This testing applies, as well, to secular value systems, worldviews, and the circles that espouse them. In the end, the familiar and traditional beliefs and practices may not be rejected or discarded, but if they are retained, they are held with more self-aware clarity and intentional choice (Fowler, 1981, 1987).

Conjunctive Faith

The *conjunctive* stage is characteristic of a reflective adult thinker who recognizes that truths of all kinds can be approached from multiple perspectives and that faith must balance and maintain the tensions between those multiple perspectives. This stage makes sense out of paradoxes. In Christianity, for instance, God is seen as all-powerful and yet God limits the divine expression of power in granting humans agency and freedom. And though the sovereign of history, God took on the humble and lowly form of a human man who permitted himself to be put to death at the hands of other humans. This knowledge and faith build on necessary paradox and tensional, complex trust and commitment.

Individuals in the conjunctive stage express a principled interest in and openness to truths of other cultural and religious traditions, and believe that dialogue with those different others may lead to deepened understandings and new insights into their own traditions and beliefs. Other paradoxes that are dealt with in this stage include the realities that one is both old and young, with both masculine and feminine qualities, conscious and unconscious, and intentionally constructive and well meaning while at the same time being unintentionally destructive in some aspects of life and community membership. One is both singular and individuated, yet has an increased awareness of being dependent on and in interdependent solidarity with both friends and strangers. This results in the desire for new ways to relate to God, others, and self (Fowler, 1981, 1987).

Universalizing Faith

In this review of faith stages, we note that the circle of "people who count" has in each stage expanded, so that by the time one reaches the *universalizing* stage, one is concerned about creation and being as a whole, regardless of nationality, social class, gender, age, race, political ideology, and religious tradition. In this ultimate stage of faith, the self is drawn out of its own self-limits into a groundedness and participation in one's understanding of the Holy. Those once seen as enemies may be understood also to be children of God and deserving of unconditional love. Evil of all kinds is opposed nonviolently, leading to activism that attempts to change adverse social conditions as an expression of that universal regard for all life that emanates from God's love and justice.

While persons of universalizing faith continue to be human, with common shortcomings and inconsistencies, they are exceptional in the strength of their passion that all creation should manifest God's goodness and that all humanity be one in peace. In their boldness to live out the convictions of their faith, they are both freeing and threatening to the rest of us. Relatively few individuals claim this level of vision and faith-related action. Among those exceptional figures most would agree manifested or manifest the universalizing stage are Mohandas Gandhi, Mother Teresa, the Reverend Dr. Martin Luther King Jr., and, perhaps some would say, former U.S. president Jimmy Carter, Archbishop Desmond Tutu, and anti–death penalty activist Sister Helen Prejean (Fowler, 1981, 1987).

Stages of Faith: The Effort to Be Inclusive

Faith development theory bridges the categories of specific religions. Wilfred Cantwell Smith (1979), a great scholar in the interpretations of the world's religious traditions, set forth a succinct characterization of faith:

> Faith, then, is a quality of human living. At its best it has taken the form of serenity and courage and loyalty and service: a quiet confidence and joy which enable one to feel at home in the universe, and to find meaning in the world and in one's own life, a meaning that is profound and ultimate, and is stable no matter what may happen to oneself at the level of immediate event. Men and women of this kind of faith face catastrophe and confusion, affluence and sorrow, unperturbed; face opportunity with conviction and drive; and face others with cheerful charity. (p. 12)

Smith contrasts faith with other terms that are frequently used as synonyms for faith: religion and belief. He finds that, closely studied, most of the major world traditions see faith not just as a matter of believing or of adhering to the teachings of a religious tradition. Rather, he says, "faith involves an alignment of the heart or will, a commitment of loyalty and trust" (p. 11). His explication of the Hindu term for faith, *sraddha,* puts it best: "It means, almost without equivocation, 'to set one's heart on.' To set one's heart on someone or something requires that one has 'seen' or 'sees the point of' that to which one is loyal" (p. 11). Faith is a resting of the heart, the investing of trust in and loyalty to a Reality or Being or Power (Fowler, 1981). Smith points out that the Hebrew (*aman he'min,*

munah), the Greek (*pistuo, Pistis*), and the Latin (*credo, credere*) words for faith parallel those from the Buddhist, Muslim, and Hindu sources (Fowler, 1981; Selman, 1976).

SIGNIFICANT DISCUSSIONS OF FAITH DEVELOPMENT THEORY AND RESEARCH

There have been four collections of writings in which commentators and critics of faith development research and theory have written on the topic.[1] The first appeared in 1980 and was initiated by Dr. Christiane Brusselmans, a religious educator from the Catholic University of Leuven, Belgium. She, with her colleagues at Leuven, and with the Harvard developmentalists Lawrence Kohlberg, James Fowler, and Robert Kegan, convened a conference in the 12th-century Cistercian Abbaye d'Senanque in the south of France in 1979. This conference brought together an international group of scholars, principally from Belgium, Switzerland, Ireland, and the United States. It included Protestants, Catholics, and Jews. The collection of essays from that fruitful conference was published as *Toward Moral and Religious Maturity* (Brusselmans, 1980).

The second collection of writings was edited by Professor Craig Dykstra, then on the faculty of Princeton Theological Seminary, and Dr. Sharon Daloz Parks, then a professor at Harvard Divinity School. With the support and hospitality of President Barbara Wheeler of the Auburn Theological Seminary in New York, Professors Dykstra and Parks convened a group of 13 professors of theology, psychology, and religious education in New York to present papers that provided constructive criticism and suggestions in critical engagement with faith development theory and research. A striking theme in this conference grew out of the intentional inclusion of feminist voices in commenting and proposing alternatives to faith development theory, based on gender studies and women's theological voices. The conference took place in 1982; its proceedings were published in 1986 as *Faith Development and Fowler* (Dykstra & Parks, 1986).

A third collection of writings that critically engaged with faith development theory took form under the editorship of Dr. Jeff Astley of the North of England Institute for Christian Education and Dr. Leslie Francis of Trinity College, Carmarthen, Wales. Unlike its predecessors, this volume did not result from a conference. Rather, the editors drew together a set of Fowler's writings along with commentaries and critical articles on faith development by other authors from the United States and the United Kingdom, many of which had been published previously in journals. The majority of the authors were religious educators and scholars from developmental studies (Astley & Francis, 1992).

The fourth volume of critical commentary was primarily prepared by and for European scholars, though it was translated for English-speaking readers as well. Edited by Karl Ernst Nipkow and Friedrich Schweitzer of the University of Tübingen, the essays in this volume placed faith development theory alongside the work on religious development of the Swiss scholar Fritz K. Oser, whose research in the structural developmental tradition of Jean Piaget has strong empirical grounding, particularly in relation to the study of children and youth. Oser wrote to inform the teaching of religion in Swiss and other European schools (Fowler, Nipkow, & Schweitzer, 1991). Both Fowler and Oser owe debts of gratitude to Lawrence Kohlberg as well as Jean Piaget. In this volume, some of the most penetrating commentary on the background and criticism of structural developmental theories comes from Nipkow and Schweitzer, from Clark Power of the University of Notre Dame, and from Nicola Slee of Rohampton Institute, Whitelands College, England. From the standpoint of religious education, Gloria Durka of Fordham University, Gabriel Moran of New York University, and John W. Hull of the University of Birmingham (England) provided trenchant insights.

A CRITICAL ISSUE IN THE DISCUSSION OF FAITH DEVELOPMENT THEORY

The most central divider between those who endorse faith development with few reservations and those who have some strong critical resistance lies, I believe, in the effort of faith development theory to define faith in a functional and structural form that can be inclusive of the dynamics of faith in many traditions, and even for some persons or groups who hold secular ideologies. Those who embrace the use of structural developmental trajectories, with their focus on different levels of cognitive, moral, and emotional operations, generally find the research and stage theory helpful in addressing questions of readiness and of matching educational methods. They find that the scaffolding the theory offers is also helpful in shaping the educational aims involved in teaching and exploring faith traditions. They acknowledge and assert—as I do—that the substantive contents of faith traditions, with their scriptures, liturgies, ethical teachings, and visions of the Holy, do provide strong, distinctive, and unique elements for religious formation. The "structuring power" of the substantive contents of faith makes a tremendous impact on the perceptions, motives, visions, and actions of believers. The stage theory makes its contribution, however, by helping to match the competences of each stage—and the operations of mind and emotion that characterize them—with ways of teaching and with the symbols, practices, and contents of faith at different levels of reflective inquiry and complexity. Educators of this mind-set find faith development theory helpful for preparing persons to teach at different age and stage levels, and to match their methods and communicative practices with the groups' probable stage or range of stages.

On the other hand, there are those who, for theological reasons, hold faith to be unique and particular to the Christian or to another specific religious tradition. For them, faith is not generic, and it is not definable apart from the contents and the practices of particular traditions. In his first article in the volume *Faith Development and Fowler* (Dykstra & Parks, 1986), Dykstra (1986a) engages in a close argument in which he objects to distinguishing the structuring and functioning of faith from the substance, content, and practices of Christian faith. It pleases me, however, that later in that same volume, Dykstra (1986b) provides a strong and clear account of the usefulness of the stage theory for helping to guide and check the appropriate levels of teaching and curriculum for persons based on their structural stage—if the structuring power of the contents of a faith tradition is not excluded or treated as interchangeable with that of other traditions or secular orientations.

This issue is an important one, and it should be made clear that the structuring power of the contents of religious faith traditions—the teachings, scriptures, practices, and ethical orientations, with their substance and power—is never to be ignored in the use of faith development theory. It should never be the primary goal of religious education simply to precipitate and encourage stage advancement. Rather, paying attention to stage and stage advancement is important in helping us shape our teaching and involvement with members of religious traditions. Movement in stage development, properly understood, is a by-product of teaching the substance and the practices of faith.

CONCLUSIONS

In closing, some of the strengths, limitations, and criticisms of faith development theory need to be acknowledged. Fortunately, the formative sample of 359 interviews was almost equally balanced at 50% from each gender. In the original sample Protestants made up 45% of the interviewees, Catholics represented 36.5%, 11.2% were Jews, and 3.6% were Orthodox Christians. A remaining 3.6% were "other." Given the growth in the numbers of adherents to other major traditions in the United States, interview research needs to be conducted to widen the sample to include Muslim, Buddhist, and secular respondents. Interviewees have not been studied longitudinally.

Further, most of the foundational research was conducted in the 1970s and 1980s. Subsequent research in the early 1990s largely confirmed the theory. Professor Heinz Streib of the University of Bielefeld is presently conducting the most significant research in the faith development tradition. The research he and his colleagues are carrying out in Europe and in the United States promises to yield considerable tangible new data and insights into these issues.

A new major round of faith development interviews could shed light on the impacts on people's faith of "globalization" and of the features of experience that have come to be called the "postmodern condition." Both of these phenomena reflect patterns of radical secularization and the erosion of religious and moral authority, on the one hand, and, paradoxically, the worldwide growth of fundamentalist and conservative faith practices, on the other. Add to these factors the rise in interest of many "nonreligious" persons in "spirituality," and one begins to grasp the richness and diversity that faith development research encounters today.

NOTE

1. A recent, thoughtful collection of essays by international authors critically engaging this author's work in faith development and practical theology is Osmer and Schweitzer (2003).

REFERENCES

Astley, J., & Francis, L. (Eds.). (1992). *Christian perspectives on faith development*. Leominster, UK: Gracewing; Grand Rapids, MI: Eerdmans.

Bettelheim, B. (1977). *The uses of enchantment: The meaning and importance of fairy tales*. New York: Vintage.

Brusselmans, C. (Ed.). (1980). *Toward moral and religious maturity*. Morristown, NJ: Silver Burdett.

Dell, M. L. (2000). She grows in wisdom, stature, and favor with God: Female development from infancy through menarche. In J. Stevenson-Moessner (Ed.), *In her own time* (pp. 117–143). Minneapolis, MN: Fortress.

Dell, M. L., & Dulcan, M. K. (1998). Childhood and adolescent development. In A. Stoudemire (Ed.), *Human behavior: An introduction for medical students* (3rd ed., pp. 261–317). Philadelphia: Lippincott-Raven.

Dykstra, C. (1986a). What is faith? An experiment in the hypothetical mode. In C. Dykstra & S. D. Parks (Eds.), *Faith development and Fowler* (pp. 45–64). Birmingham, AL: Religious Education Press.

Dykstra, C. (1986b). Faith development and religious education. In C. Dykstra & S. D. Parks (Eds.), *Faith development and Fowler* (pp. 251–271). Birmingham, AL: Religious Education Press.

Dykstra, C., & Parks, S. D. (Eds.). (1986). *Faith development and Fowler*. Birmingham, AL: Religious Education Press.

Erikson, E. H. (1963). *Childhood and society* (2nd ed.). New York: Norton.

Ford, C. A., & Coleman, W. L. (1990). Adolescent development and behavior: Implications for the primary care physician. In M. D. Levine, W. B. Carey, & A. C. Crocker (Eds.), *Developmental and behavioral pediatrics* (3rd ed., pp. 71–72). Philadelphia: Saunders.

Fowler, J. W. (1974). Agenda toward a developmental perspective on faith. *Religious Education, 69,* 209–219.

Fowler, J. (1980). Faith and the structuring of meaning. In C. Brussel mans (Ed.), *Toward moral and religious maturity* (pp. 58–81). Morristown, NJ: Silver Burdett.

Fowler, J. W. (1981). *Stages of faith.* New York: HarperCollins.

Fowler, J. W. (1984). *Becoming adult, becoming Christian: Adult development and Christian faith.* San Francisco: Harper and Row. (Revised edition published by Jossey-Bass, 2000)

Fowler, J. W. (1986a). Faith and the structuring of meaning. In C. Dykstra and S. D. Parks (Eds.), *Faith development and Fowler* (pp. 15–42). Birmingham, AL: Religious Education Press.

Fowler, J. W. (1986b). Dialogue toward a future in faith development studies. In C. Dykstra and S. D. Parks (Eds.), *Faith development and Fowler* (pp. 275–301). Birmingham, AL: Religious Education Press.

Fowler, J. W. (1987). *Faith development and pastoral care.* Philadelphia: Fortress Press.

Fowler, J. W. (1989). Strength for the journey: Early childhood development in selfhood and faith. In D. Blazer (Ed.), *Early childhood and the development of faith* (pp. 1–36). Kansas City, MO: Sheed and Ward.

Fowler, J. W. (1991). *Weaving the new creation: Stages of faith and the public church.* New York: HarperCollins.

Fowler, J. W. (1996). *Faithful change: The personal and public challenges of postmodern life.* Nashville, TN: Abingdon.

Fowler, J. W., Nipkow, K. E., & Schweitzer, F. (Eds.). (1991). *Stages of faith and religious development.* New York: Crossroad.

Gilligan, C. (1982). *In a different voice.* Cambridge, MA: Harvard University Press.

Krug, E. F., & Mikus, K. C. (1999). The preschool years. In M. D. Levine, W. B. Carey, & A. C. Crocker (Eds.), *Developmental and behavioral pediatrics* (3rd ed., pp. 38–50). Philadelphia: Saunders.

Levine, M. D. (1990). Middle childhood. In M. D. Levine, W. B. Carey, & A. C. Crocker (Eds.), *Developmental and behavioral pediatrics* (3rd ed., pp. 51–67). Philadelphia: Saunders.

Lewis, M. (1997). Overview of infant, child, and adolescent development. In J. M. Wiener (Ed.), *Textbook of child and adolescent psychiatry* (2nd ed., pp. 44–56). Washington, DC: American Psychiatric Press.

Neinstein, L. S. (1990). Menstrual problems in adolescents. *Medical Clinics of North America, 74,* 1181–1182.

Offer, D., Schonert-Reichl, K. A., & Boxer, A. M. (1996). Normal adolescent development: Empirical research findings. In M. Lewis (Ed.), *Child and adolescent psychiatry: A comprehensive textbook* (2nd ed., p. 280). Baltimore: Williams and Wilkins.

Osmer, R. R., & Schweitzer, F. L. (Eds.). (2003). *Developing a public faith: New directions in practical theology.* St. Louis, MO: Chalice Press.

Piaget, J. (1970). Piaget's theory. In P. Mussen (Ed.), *Carmichael's manual of child psychology* (3rd ed., vol. 1). New York: John Wiley and Sons.

Piaget, J. (1976). *The child and reality.* New York: Penguin.

Selman, R. L. (1974). *The developmental conceptions of interpersonal relations.* Boston: Harvard-Judge Baker Social Reasoning Project.

Selman, R. L. (1976). Social-cognitive understanding: A guide to educational and clinical practice. In T. Lickona (Ed.), *Moral development and behavior* (pp. 299–316). New York: Holt, Rinehart and Winston.

Smith, W. C. (1979). *Faith and belief.* Princeton, NJ: Princeton University Press.

Stern, D. N. (1985). *The interpersonal world of the infant.* New York: Basic Books.

Zigler, E. F., & Gilman, E. D. (1998). Day care and early childhood settings. *Child and Adolescent Psychiatric Clinics of North America, 7,* 483–498.

Zuckerman, B. S., Frank, D. A., & Augustyn, M. (1999). Infancy and toddler years. In M. D. Levine, W. B. Carey, and A. C. Crocker (Eds.), *Developmental and behavioral pediatrics* (3rd ed., pp. 24–36). Philadelphia: Saunders.

4

Spiritual Development: Intersections and Divergence With Religious Development

David Hay

K. Helmut Reich

Michael Utsch

Our intent in this chapter is to clarify the basic nature of spirituality and its development, as well as the complex and partly disputed relation between spiritual development and religious development, and to draw some conclusions from these clarifications. To make this task manageable, we focus primarily on forms of spirituality that have a referent shared with traditional religion.

In restricting our investigation in this way, we are aware that spirituality has many varieties extending beyond formal religion (e.g., Demerath, 2000), such as new age pursuits, participation in great sport or music festivals, being in the service of life, and on to Marxist spirituality (Page, 1993). Similarly, religion can be understood more broadly, for instance as *ultimate concern,* which may be about nature, its beauty and/or its preservation, improving the lives of the underprivileged, and so on.

As to the controversial relation between religious and spiritual development (e.g.,

Zinnbauer et al., 1997; Zinnbauer, Pargament, & Scott, 1999), we do not espouse the following two views: (1) "Religion involves creeds and catechisms. Spirituality involves feelings and experiences that transcend mere words. Religion is imitative and comes from without; religion is 'so I've been taught.' Spirituality comes from within; spirituality comes from 'my strength, hope and experience'" (paraphrased by Vaillant, 2002, p. 260). Rather, we take the view that outstanding spiritual leaders developed most religions, but because human nature is fallible, their followers and successors "corrupted" their teaching to some degree and even misused it to support power politics, racism, sexism, and other aims. Nevertheless, some spiritual core remains in all religions (which, however, also have other preoccupations). We therefore take it that religions overlap with the spiritual domain (e.g., Benson, Roehlkepartain, & Rude, 2003, p. 209; Stifford-Hansen, 1999). (2) Religion is said to be acquired in childhood and youth, and, if all goes well, empathy, the appreciation of context, and dialogue with others later lead to spiritual maturity (cf. Vaillant, 2002, p. 262). In contrast, along with other researchers (e.g., Coles, 1990) we posit that spirituality is an inbuilt feature of the human species that develops from the beginning of an individual's life (or not), depending on the conditions to be discussed shortly.

Being open-minded and convinced of the need to accept and to learn from other cultures and religions to ensure a peaceful and fruitful life in the global village, we would have liked this chapter to be all-inclusive. Unfortunately, the bias for Judeo-Christian concepts is unavoidable, since almost all of the research has been done on populations that are, culturally speaking, Christian. Nevertheless, as will become clear later in this chapter, universality is implied by our central contention that spiritual awareness is biologically inbuilt in the human species. On the basis of the data we cannot go much beyond that.

WORKING DEFINITIONS AND THEIR ELABORATION

No generally agreed definition exists either for religion and religiosity or for spirituality, both of which are complex and multidimensional concepts. To fix the ideas here, the following definitions are used.

Religion is (a) an evolved system of thought, feeling, and actions shared by a group as members' response to an object of devotion; (b) a code of ethics governing personal and social conduct; (c) a frame of reference relating individuals to their group and the universe. Usually, religion concerns itself with what transcends the known, the natural, or the expected; it is an acknowledgment of the extraordinary, the mysterious, and the preternatural (adapted from *The Columbia Electronic Encyclopedia,* sixth edition, 2001). Religious development is the process through which a person's basic selection of parts of an institutionalized religion, together with his or her own religious ideas and concepts, becomes a mature religiosity. Points (a) and (b) indicate that religion is a form of life, and point (c) that it enables a human discourse, an

interindividual exchange about "where we came from," "where we will go," "who we are," and "how everything relates to everything else." It is this relative comprehensiveness that made us choose this particular definition (without denying that there exist other equally valid ones).

What is underemphasized in these definitions of religion and religiosity is the potentially life-transforming aspect of religious faith. Intense, genuine interaction with a Higher Being is real because it yields real effects (lifestyle, energy balance, health, relations with self and others, etc.).

Although each religion claims to fit all situations and to answer universal needs, the translation from an abstract doctrine to a personally accepted "truth" and experiential base has to be worked out by each person for him- or herself. "Universal, pure religion" cannot exist within the reality of human nature and existence. Religious effects only become visible in personally recognized shapes and individually determined forms. If a religion's "offers" are not matched to personal needs, religiosity freezes and dies (e.g., Forman, 2004, pp. 118–122). Moreover, if religions are to provide helpful "tools" for coping with everyday life, they must correspond to specific needs at different developmental stages. At least in the Western world there are signs that traditional religions are perceived as having shortcomings, and the search is on for alternatives.

For instance, more and more people participate in event-centered workshops of the new age movement and/or espouse transpersonal psychology. A significant number of (European) Christians no longer believe in the transforming power of confession, absolution, and prayer. For them, subjective psychological interpretations drawn from the secular realm seem to be more relevant as guidance for behavior than Christian ethics. But does psychology possess the competence to offer existential guidance and transcendent connectedness, or do humanistic approaches instead promote a cult of self-worship (Barnard, 2001; Vitz, 1994)? It is certain that religions have to face the fundamental changes in Western culture often referred to as secularization, individualization, and globalization. At this juncture, psychology can help transform a dogmatic religious truth into an individual spiritual experience (Tan, 2003).

And now to *spiritual* development. The task of exploring the relationship between spiritual development and the development of religious faith is both multifaceted and controversial, not least because of the complexity of meaning of all the major terms employed (Hill et al., 2000; Zinnbauer et al., 1997). Most people take spirituality to be connected with religion—prayer, meditation, and the devotional life in general. Occasionally this shade of meaning can imply something dramatic, a lifetime of ascetic renunciation and contemplative prayer leading to ecstatic union with the Godhead. Extending the tradition of structural theories of human development, Helminiak (1987) conceptualizes spiritual development as human development characterized by four factors: integrity or wholeness, openness, self-responsibility, and authentic self-transcendence. He has described five distinct developmental stages. Without going into details, the challenge for a mature identity is to adapt spirituality personally—to integrate the human spiritual principle into the very structures of the personality.

On the other hand, a person who reads poetry, enjoys string quartets, and fits the exemplar of the sensitive aesthete is often referred to as spiritual. In still more radical contrast, Karl Marx (1844/1957) wrote of religion as "the spirit of a spiritless situation"; in other words, from his point of view religion represents a false spirituality. Here the term *spirit* carries implications of what it means to be fully aware of our indissoluble membership of the human collective or, as Marx put it, to discover oneself as a "species-being" (Bancroft, 1993).

For a definition we use the following:

> Spiritual development is the process of growing the intrinsic human capacity for self-transcendence, in which the self is imbedded in something greater than the self, including the sacred. It is the developmental "engine" that propels the search for connectedness, meaning, purpose, and contribution. It is shaped both within and outside of religious transitions, beliefs, and practices. (Benson et al., 2003, p. 205)

This definition is consistent with what has already been said, except that the transformational power of spirituality should be emphasized even more, for instance, toward leading a simpler, more frugal life, that is, a reduction in striving for material possessions.

With these clarifications in place, we now turn to the discussion of religious development, spiritual development, and their intersections and divergences.

RELIGIOUS DEVELOPMENT

The fact of (religious) development and its importance were recognized by Paul of Tarsus, who wrote, "When I was a child, I spoke like a child, I thought like a child, I reasoned like a child; when I became an adult, I put an end to my childish ways" (1 Corinthians 13:11 New Revised Standard Version). Research done 2,000 years later (e.g., Hyde, 1990) has basically confirmed Paul's statement, yet has elaborated it considerably. In addition to speaking, thinking, and reasoning, children also feel and act, conceive of God in their own ways (e.g., Fetz, Reich, & Valentin, 2001; Rizutto, 2001), build up their own religiosity and worldview, have families and friends, go to school, and interact with these human and other environments. And all these competencies evolve, as children become adolescents. Although each individual is unique, the development of religiosity and faith, or at least some aspects of them in children and adolescents, is to a degree comparable for many persons in these age groups (e.g., Subbotsky, 2000). This fact makes it possible to understand the development of religious knowing broadly in terms of stage theories such as those of Goldman (1964) and Elkind (1964), that of faith development according to the stage theory of Fowler (1981, 1987, 1996), and religious development in terms of Oser and Gmünder's theory (1991; Oser & Reich, 1996; see Zondag & Belzen, 1999, for the range of this theory). Given that these theories have been presented and discussed frequently in the secondary literature (e.g., Reich, 1992, 1993a; Spilka, Hood, Hunsberger, & Gorsuch, 2003, pp. 82–86), they will not be taken up in any detail here.

Why Favor Stage Theories of Religious Development?

Religion can be defined either by its content or by its function. In the working definition presented earlier, points (a) and (b) are essentially abstractions from its content, and point (c) refers mainly to the function of religion. Given the multifaceted and partly heterogeneous contents of various religions, and even more so of individuals' religiosity, there is little hope of covering all aspects of their content with a single, practically useful, universally valid theory. This realization does not invalidate research aimed at finding commonalities of religious content, such as a concern for beings that at the level of naive physics or biology may be considered counterintuitive, commonalities that nevertheless exhibit standard psychological properties such as those described by the theory of mind (e.g., Boyer & Walker, 2000). There is a better chance for identifying "universality" arising from concentrating on the function. By their very nature, structuralist stage theories such as those already cited are not primarily geared to content but rather more to function.

However, this position brings with it the following difficulties. First, the structure of a person's religiosity cannot be measured directly; it has to be elucidated through the current expression of that person's religiosity, and the argumentation and justifications used in that connection by the individual in question (Huber, Reich, & Schenker, 2003). Neither are *all* of human thought, affect, and volition understandable in terms of psychic structure, nor is the elucidation of all structures equally easy or difficult. Technically speaking, there are hard stages and soft stages (Reich, 1993a). The "easiest" case is no doubt that of logico-mathematical thinking stages in Piaget's sense (hard stages). Take transitivity: If $A > B$, and $B > C$, then, necessarily, $A > C$. Now consider the following situation: a young person is invited to compare A with B and B with C (whatever A, B, C stand for). The question "Is C larger or smaller than A?" could yield one of three prototypical answers: (1) "I do not know," (2) "I first have to compare the two," and (3) "$A > C$." From these answers, the intimation is that respondent (1) argues at the preoperational level, respondent (2) at the level of concrete operations, and respondent (3) at that of formal operations. The latter two involve a (tacit) reference to a mental structural system, the underlying logic of which applies to all possible contents. This kind of approach is much more difficult—and perhaps not possible—if, for instance, "stages" of

religious experiences (rather soft stages) are concerned (Paloutzian, Corveleyn, & O'Connor, 2001). This is so notably because of the diversity of what is grouped under the notion of religious experience. The difficulty with stages of religious and faith development falls somewhere between the two aforementioned cases. The development of religious knowing (Elkind, 1964; Goldman, 1964), being closer to Piagetian stages, is an easier case than that of Oser and Gmünder's (1991; see also Oser & Reich, 1996) theory of religious judgment or Fowler's (1981, 1987, 1996) faith development theory. Whereas a system built on formal binary logic (where it is applicable) can claim universal validity, the two last-mentioned stage schemes are variously critiqued (e.g., Fowler, Nipkow, & Schweitzer, 1988/1991; Streib, Corveleyn, & Paloutzian, 2001) and are not fully confirmed experimentally, especially when we consider the very small number of respondents who scored at the highest stage. Nevertheless, stage schemes are useful, especially in religious education and pastoral counseling.

Blind Spots of Present Stage Theories of Religious and Faith Development

Apart from lacking a more detailed description or explanation of the mechanism for changes in religiosity and faith (e.g., Reich, 1993b, 2003a), and being limited to a stage *progression* (i.e., dealing explicitly neither with conversion nor with deconversion), the theories we are discussing do not fully take into account the difference between phenomenalistic perception and rationalistic understanding (Subbotsky, 2000), that is, between a religious ontology of divine beings and their interpretation in terms of everyday expectations (Boyer & Walker, 2000), or between the implicational and the propositional levels (Watts, 2003, pp. 208–212). These conceptual pairs are not synonymous, but express differently the fact that humans have at least two approaches to "reality" and its representation.

SPIRITUAL DEVELOPMENT

An Empirical Approach to Spirituality

In the face of the protean complexity in the meaning of spirituality and its development referred to earlier, at the core of our argument we offer an empirical approach that comprehends this family of meanings of spirituality and helps us understand their relation to religious development. We view spiritual development as based on a self-transcending awareness that is biologically structured into the human species. According to Sperry (2001, pp. 38ff.), self-transcendence is the most basic and encompassing of all human drives, and is the source of everything that is uniquely human. On this interpretation, spirituality is a universal, found in all human beings whatever their formal religious beliefs, or lack of them. To accommodate this emerging understanding we will henceforth use terms such as *spiritual awareness, spiritual experience,* or *spirituality* in a generic sense, the relation with religion being as stated above.

No doubt the notion of spiritual awareness as common to humankind is implicit in all the great monotheisms (including Judaism, Christianity, and Islam) and perhaps almost any traditional system of religion. For instance, it constitutes the essence of Buddhism. In Christianity it was fostered from the early desert fathers and Augustine to Bonaventure, Meister Eckehart, Ignatius of Loyola, John of the Cross, and Teresa of Ávila, to name a few. But the plausibility of this assumption began to become dubious within Western culture at the time of the European Enlightenment, when members of the intelligentsia started questioning the rationality of religious belief per se. Consequently, the defense of religious faith increasingly turned away from the practical experience of transcendence toward an apologetic based on the philosophical reasonableness of religion (Buckley, 1987).

At the intellectual level the reassertion of the importance of personal experience emerged as part of the Romantic movement at the end of the 18th century. The young Friedrich Schleiermacher published *On Religion: Speeches to Its Cultured Despisers* (1799/1996) and shifted the grounds of the argument away from rationalism by claiming that religion is ultimately based on feeling; in his famous phrase, the "feeling of absolute dependence." The term *feeling* is highly ambiguous, but Schleiermacher appears to have had in mind the connotation of "perception" or "awareness" rather than simply "emotion." The nature of our existential condition,

coming to an awareness of ourselves in the midst of a mysterious and infinite universe, more or less guarantees that such an awareness of dependence is potentially present in all human beings.

Due to this hidden capacity of spiritual awareness, in highly industrialized countries there exists a remarkable search for direction in existential questions and a striving for inner enlightenment. While traditional meaning systems are increasingly perceived as old and "dried up," Western societies have opened themselves to exotic techniques to extend their "impoverished rationalistic" thinking: Shamanistic rituals, neo-Hindu satsangs, intensive meditation practices, and other ways to enter a trance state of consciousness became common (cf. Forman, 2004, pp. 83–107). Parapsychological and transpersonal phenomena are used as an empirical proof for the existence of the spiritual reality parallel to psychic life (Lorimer, 2001; Sheldrake, 2003). Still, the drive to handle and control existential forces by using a "spiritual technique" produces a dilemma: Through which technical method can the spiritual dimension be managed? There is some evidence that the spiritual dimension follows paradoxical rules contrary to the normal assumptions of rational insight. Concepts of a "spiritual intelligence" (Emmons, 2000) or of "spiritual transcendence" (Piedmont, 1999) offer a new way of description to account for the paradoxical nature of spirituality.

Several strands of the subsequent evolution toward an empirical understanding of spiritual awareness (Hay, in press) can be identified, all leading to the conclusion that we are looking at a human universal. They include prominently:

(a) William James's Gifford Lectures at Edinburgh University, published as *The Varieties of Religious Experience* (1902/1985). James drew together a large body of data from many different religious cultures under the heading of "religious experience," some would say illegitimately (see, e.g., Strout, 1971). Nevertheless James's espousal of the doctrine of psychophysical parallelism (the claim that corresponding to every psychological event there is a parallel physiological event) allowed him to state as his concluding conjecture that such experience is "the subconscious continuation of our conscious life" (1902, p. 512; 1985, p. 403). James offered what continues to be a highly influential naturalistic account of *religious* experience, at least the humanly receptive side of it. In doing so, he implicitly extended the concept beyond any specific religion to something wider, a *More,* common to all humanity and perhaps more appropriately described as "spirituality."

(b) Rudolf Otto's (1917/1950) exposition of the term *numinous,* which he coined to evoke the experience of being in the presence of the sacred or holy, or as he described it, the *mysterium tremendum et fascinans* (overwhelming and fascinating mystery). His intention was to correct what he saw as a limitation in Schleiermacher's phenomenology of religious experience. Although writing from the perspective of a Christian theologian, Otto freely referred to the experience of the numinous both in so-called primitive societies and in other world religions. In discussing Buddhism, for example, he asserted that "the 'void' of the Eastern, like the 'nothing' of the Western mystic, is a numinous ideogram of the wholly other" (Otto, 1917/1950, p. 30). Like Schleiermacher's, Otto's view implies universality and in this sense can be seen as in tune with James's understanding.

(c) The zoologist Alister Hardy's Gifford Lectures given at Aberdeen University and published as *The Living Stream* (1965) and *The Divine Flame* (1966). In these and subsequent publications (1975, 1979, 1984), Hardy suggested that the biological basis of spiritual awareness in the species *Homo sapiens* emerged as the result of organic evolution. In other words, it evolved through the process of natural selection because it has survival value. Included in his supporting argument was testimony drawn from social anthropologists, psychologists, ethologists, and, more controversially, students of parapsychology, that the function of such awareness is to give strength, particularly in times of existential crisis. It is important to add that while making this claim for a naturalistic basis for spirituality, Hardy did not see it in mechanistic terms and emphasized the importance of freely chosen *behavior* as a selective force. He also insisted that his hypothesis explicitly affirmed a positive attitude toward

religion (these matters are discussed in greater detail in Hay, 2004).

It is significant that these "movers" come from a Protestant Christian background. Until relatively recently almost everyone engaged in the scientific study of religious experience shared this upbringing (Hutch, 1982). Their religious commitment, combined with their independence from the traditional authority structure of Catholicism, in itself motivated their desire to identify a universally valid basis for spirituality. But in so doing they simultaneously opened the possibility of an understanding of spiritual awareness as biologically inbuilt, that is (as Otto proposed) analogous to a Kantian a priori and not dependent on social construction, though of course its expression is always mediated by a culture.

The evolutionary perspective in the psychology of religion is growing in influence (see Boyer, 2001; Boyer et al., 2000; Buss, 2002; Kirkpatrick, 1999), and clearly it is one with which we have considerable sympathy, but it has to be seen as complementary to other disciplines (e.g., D. S. Wilson, 1999). Our version of the biological argument asserts the existence of an embodied spiritual awareness or "relational consciousness" that is antecedent to both religious and ethical beliefs (Hay & Nye, 1998). The embodied nature of this precursor of religion means that the latter cannot be dismissed as "nothing but" social construction. Many of the proponents of evolutionary psychology fail to clarify the relationship between spiritual awareness as a natural phenomenon and religion as a belief system, leading them to take up a reductionist and deterministic stance toward the latter. In our view this is a non sequitur based on unsupported skeptical assumptions drawn from the Enlightenment tradition.

There is a growing body of empirical evidence supporting the plausibility of Hardy's proposal (reviewed in Hay & Morisy, 1978; Hay, 1994). His hypothesis is naturalistic, but he also has a positive view of the importance of religion. He is therefore in radical conflict with all the currently dominant naturalistic explanations of religious experience, which at least in their origins were attempts to account for religion, seen as a mistaken social construction (cf. Feuerbach, 1841/1989). Thus, as representatives of the Enlightenment skeptical tradition, Marx, Durkheim, and Freud have each had a dominant influence, not only on contemporary presuppositions about religious phenomena, but also in channeling and directing the conventions of research in religious studies. It is therefore significant that their hypotheses generate testable predictions that are not supported by recent empirical research (Hay, 1994).

The biological rootedness of spiritual awareness emphasized by Hardy has more recently been given added plausibility from two further directions. The so-called neurotheologians (Joseph, 2003; Newberg, d'Aquili, & Rause, 2002; Persinger, 1997; Ramachandran & Blakeslee, 1998) have offered a variety of hypotheses on the site of spiritual awareness in the brain. The usefulness of this work for the psychology of religion has been reviewed critically by Reich (2004), but there is no doubting the seriousness with which this neurobiological perspective is now being taken. Also, Robert Torrance (1996, pp. 265–268) draws upon Prigogine's and Stenger's (1984) arguments for a creatively indeterminate universe and for the essential continuity of the organic and inorganic realms, to situate spirituality squarely in that indeterminate and creative dimension of physical reality. For Torrance the spiritual quest thus has a direct and literal relationship to our emerging understanding of cosmology. We are not human beings, but human becomings. These factors, along with the increasing cross-cultural links between members of the major religions during the 20th century, have encouraged the view that spirituality is not the prerogative of any one religion, or even of religion in general. A major contemporary legacy is the increasingly common opinion that, currently, spirituality and religion do not have a *necessary* connection (Schneiders, 2000; Zinnbauer et al., 1997).

Perhaps associated with this disjunction, spiritual experience, or at least the willingness to admit to it, appears to be on the increase in the Western world. Positive response rates for a series of national surveys of spiritual experience conducted in the United States, Britain, and Australia, and published between 1962 and 2000, show an increasing frequency of report over time (Hay, 1994; Hay & Hunt, 2000).

Inspection shows that the positive response rates vary from 20.5% in the case of the earliest national survey in the United States in 1962 (Back & Bourque, 1970) to 76% in the Millennium survey carried out in Britain (Hay & Hunt, 2000). Most tellingly, within the same country Hay and Heald's 1987 survey and Hay and Hunt's 2000 survey showed an increased positive response over 13 years from 48% to 76% of the national sample. In contrast, over approximately the same period regular church attendance in Britain fell by 20% (Brierley, 2000). Small-scale surveys conducted by Tacey (2003) suggest that an almost identical pattern of institutional collapse combined with increasing enthusiasm for spiritual experience is taking shape in Australia. Lambert (2003), studying data from the sequence of surveys across nine European countries sponsored by the European Study of Values, concludes that there is a detectable increase in interest in spirituality among young people who declare themselves to have no religion.

The Nature of Spiritual Development and Its Relation to Religious Development

Given the multiple facets of spirituality and its development, a classical stage scheme cannot fully capture it. The changes implied in our working definition may come about more continually or more abruptly; they may be temporary or "permanent"; they may be fully perceived or remain undetected. A mature spirituality translates into inner peace and harmony, into the certainty of having made the right basic choices, into the ability to dedicate one's thoughts, feelings, and efforts in a balanced, "stress-free" way to both devotion to the sacred and the execution of one's daily chores, into a sharing of joyful giving and receiving in relation to one's human and physical environment (Carter, 1992).

The data we have been examining suggest that the major reductionist hypotheses on the nature of spiritual experience are mistaken, while the suggestion of a biological basis for the spiritual quest has so far proved less vulnerable to empirical test. For instance, Hamer (2004) is led to explain this quest by a brain mechanism linked to several genes, in particular to VMAT2, even if, as often is the case in this type of research, these findings involve correlations, not proofs, for a causal relationship. All the same, we have also seen that significant numbers of people in the Western populations surveyed either do not recognize or refuse to admit personal awareness of this dimension of experience in themselves. Given the traditional link between religion and spirituality, *we suggest that the natural spiritual awareness common to all human beings has, during the course of European history, become overlaid by a socially constructed secularist critique that denies its reality.* As Durham has shown in his book *Coevolution* (1991), social evolution can at times clash with organic evolution, and this is what we suggest has happened, not only as demonstrated in the social evolution of secularism in Europe, but also as reflected currently in individual biographies (e.g., Fetz et al., 2001, pp. 238–246). In certain respects this inverts Feuerbach's (1841/1989) assertion that religion is a humanly invented construction overlying the natural secularity of the species. Students of secularization (Brown, 2001; Bruce, 2002; Chadwick, 1975; Preus, 1987; B. R. Wilson, 1966) and atheism (Berman 1990; Buckley, 1987; Thrower, 1999) have explored the sources of this latter construction in great detail, and in effect they provide striking evidence in support of our thesis.

Intersections and Divergences

Given this overlay, and the close historical links between spirituality and religion (even today many people see them as synonymous despite contradictory data), there is a likelihood that when religion is rejected, spiritual intuitions will also come to be suppressed or perhaps even repressed.

On the other hand, religiousness may be used to cover personal flaws. Psychological explorations can help us identify inadequate forms of personal spirituality associated with certain forms of religion (Godin, 1985). Spirituality offers the ability to trust, hope, and love. The approach of positive psychology offers new ways of understanding how religious insights can be fruitfully transformed into spiritual experience (Snyder & Lopez, 2002).

In writing these two paragraphs, we also have in mind the "dark" side of religion (Appleby, 2000) and "sick" spirituality. Morris

Cohen (1946, pp. 337–361) characterizes that dark side as follows: (a) Religion strengthens superstition and hinders science and the spirit of truth-seeking. (b) Religion is an antimoral force. (c) Religion stifles emotional life. Space restrictions prohibit going into the many examples Cohen discusses. Briefly, they illustrate his three points and can serve as a warning and a call to vigilance to avoid such perversions. If one applies our working definition of spirituality to an ideology such as Hitler's National Socialism, one realizes that formally it might be called a spirituality of sorts. But of course, it is sick to the core, specifically because its form of relationship replaces love with coercive power.

Although a less extreme issue, it needs to be said that a "normal" spiritual development not infrequently involves difficulties and tribulations on the way (see, e.g., Scharfetter et al., 1991). This raises the question of the appropriate "setting" for one's spiritual development. (a) In an era of do-it-yourself, relying basically just on oneself is a "natural" choice. (b) However, given the risks involved, others may opt for a spiritual counselor. (c) A compromise would be to become a member of a like-minded group.

Resulting Suggestions

Foundational Findings

The taboo about "outing" one's religious experiences, we suggest, has led to the suppression and at times repression of both religious belief and spiritual awareness, making them implicit rather than explicit (Hay, 2003). One corollary of this conjecture is the expectation that the most likely place to find openly admitted spiritual awareness is in young children, since they have not yet assimilated the cultural critique of such awareness. The recent work of Rebecca Nye (see Hay & Nye, 1998; Nye, 1999), in which she explored the spirituality of 6- and 10-year-old children in two industrial cities in England, demonstrated this to be so. She did not find any child to be lacking in spiritual awareness, although it was often expressed in terms remote from formal religion and with a restricted and impoverished vocabulary.

Reflection on what has gone before in this chapter leads us to make the following four hypotheses and suggestions regarding the nature of spiritual development. Taken cumulatively, they imply a major change of perspective of religious and spiritual education away from a didactic approach and toward an exploration:

- Spiritual *awareness* is biologically structured into the human species. Inasmuch as it resembles the physical senses, it does not undergo development beyond the natural maturing that is a feature of all physical aspects of the body. Hence it is prior to all discursive reasoning, whether scientific, philosophical, or theological.
- Spirituality is primarily *expressed* through the mediation provided by the language, rituals (including facial and bodily expressions), and doctrines of a culture, and these are always acquired socially through either formal or informal education.
- The dialectic between spiritual awareness (or "relational consciousness," as Nye refers to it) and culture needs to be borne in mind by educators (see also Endean, 2001; Kelly, 2002). Children cannot be taught spiritual awareness; it is built in to their physiology. However, it bears fostering (Yust, 2003). Teachers can direct children's attention to their awareness and offer them language with which to articulate it.
- In a divided culture many alternative languages, not all of them religious, may be available through which spirituality can be expressed. Those concerned with both religious and spiritual education need to become aware of the skills necessary to cross these cultural boundaries (Yoshikawa, 1987).

Living as we do in a scientifico-technical age, and science to some degree still being in the grip of logical positivism (especially in neurobiology), the tendency in bringing up the young is to discourage phenomenalistic perception and a religious ontology of divine beings as well as the implicational level of understanding. Instead, privilege is given to rationalistic understanding, religious interpretation by noncounterintuitive, everyday expectations as well as the propositional level of understanding. This is not helpful for religious development and may be deadly for spiritual development.

What Parents, Educators, Clergy, and Researchers Interested in Religious and Spiritual Development Should Know

While it is useful and good for parents, educators, clergy, and personally concerned individuals to know about certain cognitive presuppositions for religious development (e.g., Barnes, 2000; Reich, 2003b), there is more to it, especially when it comes to spiritual development.

What counts in this connection from early childhood onward is *ontological* development. Ontological development concerns the (perceived) existence or nonexistence of various entities and their predicates, or more precisely the material categories needed to discuss those predicates. Relevant issues include, "Do fairies, quarks, or unicorns exist or not?" "Is that kind person who gives me presents really my uncle or not?" "Are clouds alive or dead?" (Reich, 2002, p. 28). The path leading to satisfactory answers is often rather lengthy. Children distinguish three worlds: (1) that of experienced reality; (2) the realm of the imagination, where the individual conjures up beings, objects, and events; and (3) the world of fantasy and of fiction, found in fairy tales, cartoons, and so on (Boyer & Walker, 2000, p. 145). To illustrate: A girl in fourth grade was talking excitedly about the angels and their beautiful starry crowns, which they always keep shiny, when all of a sudden she switched worlds: "But in reality heaven does not exist. Up there is only air and water" (quoted in Fetz, Reich, & Valentin, 2001, p. 68).

What is the outcome of these considerations? As regards psychological research with children and adolescents, a major issue may be to disentangle what they genuinely consider "real" (and what therefore influences their actions) from what they have been taught in religious education—in other words, what they say because they have been told that it is theologically correct.

From the perspective of fostering and supporting religious and, even more so, spiritual development of children, the central issue is to get spirituality ontologically into world (1), and hence experienced as reality. It may of course be that the route to world (1) passes through world (2), as explained, for instance, by Winnicott's (1971) version of object relations theory. The main point is that world (3) is hardly a good road to spiritual maturity. The danger of adults employing references to that world and thereby blocking children's spiritual development is at least twofold. Suppose an eight-year-old explained that if God disappeared, the world would return to its original state of darkness and chaos (Fetz et al., 2001, pp. 200–201). One way to deal with such a view would be to put it into world (3) and never to take it seriously. Another possibility is to put it into world (1) and to argue against it, either from the perspective of physics or from that of a fundamental religion for which God is eternal. In contrast, a supporting response would be to enter into the child's world (2), to understand how the child came to that view, what it means to the child, and perhaps build bridges to world (1).

Future Research

Given the strong renewed interest in spirituality, research will no doubt be intensified and cover various aspects, including those not thematized here. We would advocate investigating specifically two areas crucial to an understanding of spirituality, namely, neurobiology (e.g., Reich, 2004) and ethics, as arising from relational consciousness (Etzioni, 1993; Putnam, 2000; Selznick, 1992; D. S. Wilson, 2002). Our reasons are twofold. On the one hand, research in these areas is likely to further insights into the deep nature of spirituality and spiritual development and thereby facilitate it. On the other hand, these are areas in which spirituality has determined adversaries (at least in practical terms), and better insights might lead to a more fruitful dialogue.

CONCLUDING REMARKS

We have attempted to disentangle the relations between spiritual development and religious development, and to bring out the implications for the individual concerned, his or her human and physical environment, and related research.

Spirituality is not just a private "hobby," an object of academic study, but is of social importance (Forman, 2004; Howard & Welbourn, 2004). Observers of the social situation in many Western countries note increased strife and

mounting difficulties in coming to mutual agreements, both privately (partnerships, marriages) and publicly (e.g., reform of social systems, environmental issues). They ascribe these difficulties notably to the diversity of values favored in a pluralistic society (with secularism, consumerism, and multiculturalism high on the list), and to an exaggerated, narcissistic individualism, which does not hesitate to go for its satisfactions even at the expense of others. Clearly, getting the world's 6 billion human beings to a U.S. standard of living would mean ecological breakdown (Laszlo, 2001). What is needed is voluntary simplicity, solidarity, and family planning, all of which are all likely to be facilitated by a deeper spirituality.

REFERENCES

Appleby, R. S. (2000). *The ambivalence of the sacred: Religion, violence and reconciliation.* Lanham, MD: Rowman & Littlefield.

Back, K., & Bourque, L. B. (1970). Can feelings be enumerated? *Behavioral Science, 15,* 487–496.

Bancroft, N. (1993). Spirituality in Marxism: A communist view. In B. B. Page (Ed.), *Marxism and spirituality: An international anthology* (pp. 83–91). Westport, CT: Bergin & Garvey.

Barnard, G. W. (2001). Diving into the depths: Reflections on psychology as religion. In D. Jonte-Pace & W. B. Parsons (Eds.), *Religion and psychology: Mapping the terrain* (pp. 297–318). New York: Routledge.

Barnes, M. H. (2000). *Stages of thought: The co-evolution of religious thought and science.* Oxford, UK: Oxford University Press.

Benson, P. L., Roehlkepartain, E. C., & Rude, S. P. (2003). Spiritual development in childhood and adolescence: Toward a field of inquiry. *Applied Developmental Science, 7*(3), 205–213.

Berman, D. (1990). *A history of atheism in Britain: From Hobbes to Russell.* London: Routledge.

Boyer, P. (2001). *Religion explained: The human instincts that fashion gods, spirits and ancestors.* London: Heinemann.

Boyer, P., & Walker, S. (2000). Intuitive ontology and cultural input in the acquisition of religious concepts. In K. S. Rosengren, C. N. Johnson, & P. L. Harris (Eds.), *Imagining the impossible: Magical, scientific, and religious thinking in children* (pp. 130–156). Cambridge, UK: Cambridge University Press.

Brierley, P. (2000). *UK Christian handbook: Religious trends.* Carlisle: Paternoster.

Brown, C. G. (2001). *The death of Christian Britain.* London: Routledge.

Bruce, S. (2002). *God is dead: Secularization in the West.* Oxford, UK: Blackwell.

Buckley, M. (1987). *At the origins of modern atheism.* New Haven, CT: Yale University Press.

Buss, D. M. (2002). Sex, marriage, and religion: What adaptive problems do religious phenomena solve? *Psychological Inquiry, 13*(3), 201–204.

Chadwick, O. (1975). *The secularization of the European mind in the nineteenth century.* Cambridge, UK: Cambridge University Press.

Carter, N. C. (1992). *Martha, Mary, and Jesus: Weaving action and contemplation in daily life.* Collegeville, MN: Liturgical Press.

Cohen, M. R. (1946). *The faith of a liberal.* New York: Holt.

Coles, R. (1990). *The spiritual life of children.* Boston: Houghton Mifflin.

Columbia electronic encyclopedia, The (6th ed.). (2001–2004). *Religion.* Retrieved January 12, 2005, from http://www.bartleby.com/65/re/religion.html

Demerath, N. J., III. (2000). The varieties of sacred experience: Finding the sacred in a secular grove. *Journal for the Scientific Study of Religion, 39,* 1–11.

Durham, W. H. (1991). *Coevolution: Genes, culture, and human diversity.* Palo Alto, CA: Stanford University Press.

Elkind, D. (1964). The child's conception of his religious identity. *Lumen Vitae* (English ed.), *19,* 635–646.

Emmons, R. A. (2000). Is spirituality an intelligence? Motivation, cognition, and the psychology of ultimate concern. *International Journal for the Psychology of Religion, 10*(1), 3–26.

Endean, P. (2001). *Karl Rahner and Ignatian spirituality.* Oxford, UK: Oxford University Press.

Etzioni, A. (1993). *The spirit of community: Rights, responsibilities and the communitarian agenda.* London: HarperCollins.

Fetz, R. L., Reich. K. H., & Valentin, P. (2001). *Weltbildentwicklung und Schöpfungsverständnis: Eine strukturgenetische Untersuchung bei Kindern und Jugendlichen* [A structure-genetic investigation of children's and adolescents' worldview development and understanding of God's creation]. Stuttgart, Germany: Kohlhammer.

Feuerbach, L. (1989). *The essence of Christianity* (G. Eliot, Trans.). Amherst, NY: Prometheus Books. (Original work published 1841)

Forman, R. (2004). *Grassroots spirituality: What it is, why it is here, where it is going.* Charlottesville, VA: Imprint Academic Philosophy Documentation Center.

Fowler, J. W. (1981). *Stages of faith: The psychology of human development and the quest for meaning.* New York: Harper & Row.

Fowler, J. W. (1987). *Faith development and pastoral care.* Philadelphia: Fortress Press.

Fowler, J. W. (1996). *Faithful change: The personal and public challenges of postmodern life.* Nashville, TN: Abington Press.

Fowler, J. W., Nipkow, K. E., & Schweitzer (Eds.). (1991). *Stages of faith and religious development: Implications for church, education and society.* New York: Crossroad. (Original work published 1988)

Godin, A. (1985). *The psychological dynamics of religious experience.* Birmingham, AL: Religious Education Press.

Goldman, R. (1964). *Religious thinking from childhood to adolescence.* London: Routledge & Kegan Paul.

Hamer, D. H. (2004). *The God gene: How faith is hardwired into our genes.* New York: Doubleday.

Hardy, A. (1965). *The living stream.* London: Collins.

Hardy, A. (1966). *The divine flame.* London: Collins.

Hardy, A. (1975). *The biology of God.* London: Jonathan Cape.

Hardy, A. (1979). *The spiritual nature of man.* Oxford, UK: Clarendon Press.

Hardy, A. (1984). *Darwin and the spirit of man.* London: Collins.

Hay, D. (1994). "The biology of God": What is the current status of Hardy's hypothesis? *International Journal for the Psychology of Religion, 4*(1), 1–23.

Hay, D. (2003). Why is implicit religion implicit? *Implicit Religion, 6*(1), 17–41.

Hay, D. (2004). A biologist of God: Alister Hardy in Aberdeen. *Aberdeen University Review, 9*(3), 209–223.

Hay, D. (in press). Experience. In A. Holder (Ed.), *Companion to Christian spirituality.* Oxford, UK: Blackwells.

Hay, D., & Heald, G. (1987, April 17). Religion is good for you. *New Society,* 20–22.

Hay, D., & Hunt, K. (2000). *The spirituality of people who don't go to church* (Final report, Adult Spirituality Project). Nottingham, UK: Nottingham University, Centre for the Study of Human Relations.

Hay, D., & Morisy, A. (1978). Reports of ecstatic, paranormal or religious experience in Great Britain and the United States: A comparison of trends. *Journal for the Scientific Study of Religion, 17,* 255–277.

Hay, D., & Nye, R. (1998). *The spirit of the child.* London: HarperCollins.

Helminiak, D. (1987). *Spiritual development: An interdisciplinary study.* Chicago: Loyola University Press.

Hill, P. C., Pargament, K. I., Wood. R. W., Jr., McCullough, M. E., Swyers, J. P., Larson, D. B., et al. (2000). Conceptualizing religion and spirituality. *Journal for the Theory of Social Behaviour, 30*(1), 51–77.

Howard, S., & Welbourn, D. (2004). *The Spirit at work phenomenon.* London: Azure.

Huber, S., Reich, K. H., & Schenker, D. (2003). Studying empirically religious development: Interview, repertory grid, and specific questionnaire techniques. *Archiv für Religionspsychologie, 24,* 180–201.

Hutch, R. (1982). Are psychological studies of religion on the right track? *Religion, 12,* 277–299.

Hyde, K. E. (1990). *Religion in childhood and adolescence: A comprehensive review of the research.* Birmingham, AL: Religious Education Press.

James, W. (1985). *The varieties of religious experience.* Cambridge, MA: Harvard University Press, 1985. (Original work published 1902)

Joseph, R. (2003). *NeuroTheology: Brain, science, spirituality, religious experience.* San Jose, CA: University Press.

Kelly, T. M. (2002). *Theology at the void: The retrieval of experience.* Notre Dame, IN: University of Notre Dame Press.

Kirkpatrick, L. A. (1999). Toward an evolutionary psychology of religion and personality. *Journal of Personality, 67,* 921–952.

Lambert, Y. (2004). A turning point in religious evolution in Europe. *Journal of Contemporary Religion, 19*(1), 29–45.

Laszlo, E. (2001). *Macroshift: Navigating the transformation to a sustainable world.* San Francisco: Berrett-Koehler.

Lorimer, D. (Ed.). (2001). *Thinking beyond the brain: A wider science of consciousness.* New York: Floris.

Marx, K. (1957). Introduction to the contribution to the critique of Hegel's philosophy of right. In K. Marx & F. Engels, *On religion* (pp. 37–52). Moscow: Progress Publishers. (Original work published 1844)

Newberg, A., d'Aquili, E., & Rause, V. (2001). *Why God won't go away: Brain science and the biology of belief.* New York: Ballantine.

Nye, R. (1999). Relational consciousness and the spiritual lives of children: Convergence with children's theory of mind. In K. H. Reich, F. K. Oser, & W. G. Scarlett (Eds.), *Psychological studies on spiritual and religious development: Vol. 2. The case of religion* (pp. 57–82). Lengerich, Germany: Pabst.

Oser, F. K., & Gmünder, P. (1991). *Religious judgement. A developmental approach* (N. F. Hahn, Trans.). Birmingham, AL: Religious Education Press. (Original work published 1984)

Oser, F. K., & Reich, K. H. (1996). Religious development from a psychological perspective. *World Psychology, 2*(3–4), 365–396.

Otto, R. (1950). *The idea of the holy* (2nd ed.) (J. W. Harvey, Trans.). Oxford, UK: Oxford University Press. (Original work published 1917)

Page, B. B. (Ed.). (1993). *Marxism and spirituality: An international anthology.* Westport, CT: Bergin & Garvey.

Paloutzian, R. F., Corveleyn, J., & O'Connor, K. V. (Eds). (2001). Stage models of religious experiences [Special issue]. *International Journal for the Psychology of Religion, 11*(4).

Persinger, M. A. (1997). *Neuropsychological bases of God beliefs.* New York: Praeger.

Piedmont, R. L. (1999). Does spirituality represent the sixth factor of personality? Spiritual transcendence and the five-factor model. *Journal of Personality, 67,* 985–1014.

Prigogine, I., & Stenger, I. (1984). *Order out of chaos: Man's new dialogue with nature.* New York: Bantam.

Preus, S. (1987). *Explaining religion: Criticism and theory from Bodin to Freud.* New Haven, CT: Yale University Press.

Putnam, R. (2000). *Bowling alone: The collapse and revival of American community.* New York: Simon & Schuster.

Ramachandran, V. S., & Blakeslee, S. (1998). *Phantoms of the brain: Probing the mysteries of the human mind.* New York: Morrow.

Reich, K. H. (1992). Religious development across the life span: Conventional and cognitive developmental approaches. In D. L. Featherman, R. M. Lerner, & M. Perlmutter (Eds.), *Life-span development and behavior* (Vol. 11, pp. 145–188). Hillsdale, NJ: Erlbaum.

Reich, K. H. (1993a). Cognitive-developmental approaches to religiousness: Which version for which purpose? *International Journal for the Psychology of Religion, 3*(3), 145–171.

Reich, K. H. (1993b). Integrating differing theories: The case of religious development. *Journal of Empirical Theology, 6*(1), 39–49.

Reich, K. H. (2002). *Developing the horizons of the mind: Relational and contextual reasoning and the resolution of cognitive conflict.* Cambridge, UK: Cambridge University Press.

Reich, K. H. (2003a). The person–God relationship: A dynamic model. *International Journal for the Psychology of Religion, 13*(4), 229–247.

Reich, K. H. (2003b). Cognitive preconditions for religious development. *Research in the Social Scientific Study of Religion, 14,* 1–32.

Reich, K. H. (2004). Psychology of religion and neurobiology: Which relationship? *Archiv für Religionspsychologie, 26,* 117–133.

Rizzuto, A.-M. (2001). Religious development beyond the modern paradigm discussion: The psychoanalytic point of view. *International Journal for the Psychology of Religion, 11*(3), 201–214.

Scharfetter, C. (with Falconi, R. M., Hollenstein, M., Jacobowitz, S., Rhyner, B., & Soni, L.). (1991). *Der spirituelle Weg und seine Gefahren: Eine Übersicht für Berater und Psychotherapeuten* [The spiritual path and its dangers: An overview for counselors and psychotherapists]. Stuttgart, Germany: Enke.

Schleiermacher, F. (1996). *On religion: Speeches to its cultured despisers* (R. Crouter, Ed. and Trans.). Cambridge, UK: Cambridge University Press. (Original work published 1799)

Schneiders, S. (2000). Religion and spirituality: Strangers, rivals, or partners? *Santa Clara Lectures, 6*(2), 1–26.

Selznick, P. (1992). *The moral commonwealth: Social theory and the promise of community.* Berkeley and Los Angeles: University of California Press.

Sheldrake, R. (2003). *The sense of being stared at.* London: Crown.

Snyder, C. R., & Lopez, S. J. (Eds.). (2002). *Handbook of positive psychology.* New York: Oxford University Press.

Sperry, L. (2001). *Spirituality in clinical practice: Incorporating the spiritual dimension in psychotherapy and counseling.* Philadelphia: Brunner-Routledge.

Spilka, B., Hood, R. W., Jr., Hunsberger, B., & Gorsuch, R. (2003). *The psychology of religion: An empirical approach* (3rd ed.). New York: Guilford.

Stiffoss-Hansen, H. (1999). Religion and spirituality: What a European ear hears. *International, Journal for the Psychology of Religion, 9*(1), 25–34.

Streib, H., Corveleyn, J., & Paloutzian, R. F. (Eds.). (2001). Faith developmental theory and the modern paradigm [Special issue]. *International Journal for the Psychology of Religion, 11*(3).

Strout, C. (1971). The pluralistic identity of William James. *American Quarterly, 23*(2), 135–152.

Subbotsky, E. (2000). Phenomenalistic perception and rational understanding in the mind of an individual: A fight for dominance. In K. S. Rosengren, C. N. Johnson, & P. L. Harris (Eds.), *Imagining the impossible: Magical, scientific, and religious thinking in children* (pp. 35–74). Cambridge, UK: Cambridge University Press.

Tacey, D. (2003). *The spirituality revolution.* Sydney, Australia: HarperCollins.

Tan, S.-Y. (2003). Integrating spiritual direction into psychotherapy: Ethical issues and guidelines. *Journal of Psychology and Theology, 31*(1), 17–25.

Thrower, J. (1999). *Religion: The classical theories.* Edinburgh, UK: Edinburgh University Press.

Torrance, R. M. (1996). *The spiritual quest: Transcendence in myth, religion, and science.* Berkeley and Los Angeles: University of California Press.

Vaillant, G. E. (2002). *Aging well.* Boston: Little, Brown.

Vitz, P. (1994). *Psychology as religion: The cult of self-worship.* Grand Rapids, MI: Eerdmans.

Watts, F. (2003). Interacting cognitive subsystems and religious meanings. In R. Joseph (Ed.), *NeuroTheology: Brain, science, spirituality, religious experience* (pp. 207–214). San Jose, CA: University Press.

Wilson, B. R. (1966). *Religion in secular society: A sociological comment.* London: Watts.

Wilson, D. S. (1999). Tasty slice—but what is in the rest of the pie? *Evolution and Human Behavior, 20,* 279–287.

Wilson, D. S. (2002). *Darwin's cathedral: Evolution, religion, and the nature of society.* Chicago: University of Chicago Press.

Winnicott, D. W. (1971). *Playing and reality.* London: Tavistock.

Yoshikawa, M. J. (1987). The double swing model of intercultural communication between the East and the West. In D. L. Kincaid (Ed.), *Communication theory: Eastern and western perspectives* (pp. 319–329). San Diego, CA: Academic Press.

Yust, K. M. (2003). Toddler spiritual formation and the faith community. *International Journal of Children's Spirituality, 8*(2), 133–149.

Zinnbauer, B. J., Pargament, K., Cole, B., Rye, M. S., Butter, E. M., Belavich, T. G., et al. (1997). Religion and spirituality: Unfuzzying the fuzzy. *Journal for the Scientific Study of Religion, 76*(4), 549–564.

Zinnbauer, B. J., Pargament, K. I., & Scott, A. B. (1999). The emerging meanings of religiousness and spirituality: Problems with prospects. *Journal of Personality, 67,* 889–919.

Zondag, H. J., & Belzen J. A. (1999). Between reduction of uncertainty and reflection: The range and dynamics of religious judgment. *International Journal for the Psychology of Religion, 9*(1), 63–81.

5

On Making Humans Human: Spirituality and the Promotion of Positive Youth Development

Richard M. Lerner

Amy E. Alberts

Pamela M. Anderson

Elizabeth M. Dowling

Arguably, spirituality and religiosity are the only mental and behavioral characteristics that are distinctly associated with human beings. For instance, characteristics of functioning, such as love, hate, language, caring, cognition, temperament, personality, and purpose, can be found or operationalized in other species. However, the commitment to ideas or institutions that transcend the self in time and place is the essence of spirituality. Reich, Oser, and Scarlett (1999), for instance, operationalize spirituality as viewing life in new and better ways, adopting some conception as transcendent or of great value, and defining oneself and one's relation to others in a manner that goes beyond provincialism or materialism to express authentic concerns about others. In turn, the subordination of self to institutions that are believed to have relations to the divine is the essence of religiosity. Reich et al. (1999) operationalize religiosity as involving a relationship with a particular institutionalized doctrine about a supernatural power, a relationship that occurs through affiliation with an organized faith and participation in its prescribed rituals.

We believe that spirituality and religiosity may be singularly human characteristics. Nevertheless, the cognitive, emotional, and behavioral characteristics that operationalize spirituality and religiosity are not present in the newborn. These characteristics *develop* across the life span. In other words, these two facets of human functioning, which together mark what is uniquely human about humans, emerge over the course of life.

AUTHORS' NOTE: The preparation of this chapter was supported by grants from the National 4-H Council and the William T. Grant Foundation.

Although theoretically and empirically identifiable as important influences on human development across much of the life span (e.g., Koenig & Lawson, 2004), both spirituality and religiosity, as developmental phenomena, are transformed in personal and adaptive salience and cognitive conceptualization across the course of life. This transformation is a key feature of the adolescent period.

In adolescence, spirituality is significant for the healthy, positive development of a person's sense of self—his or her identity—and for enabling identity to frame the individual's pursuit of a life path eventuating in idealized adulthood, that is, an adulthood involving mutually beneficial relations between the individual and his or her social world. We argue that such an adulthood maintains and advances humanity.

Accordingly, in this chapter we argue that spirituality may play a key role in creating in people the defining characteristics of their humanity *and* in energizing the positive development of the person at a key portion of the life span—adolescence—that is critical for ensuring both healthy individual development across the life span and the perpetuation of the species. We believe that spirituality may foster an integrated moral and civic identity within a young person and lead the individual along a path to becoming an adult contributing integratively to self, family, community, and civil society. The argument we present will be linked to data that suggest that the process of exemplary positive development among youth—a process we label as "thriving"—involves both the direct effects of spirituality on positive development and the mediation of religiosity between spirituality and thriving. We believe, and will conclude our presentation by suggesting, that the spirituality–thriving relation has significant implications for policies and programs aimed at promoting positive youth development among diverse youth.

THEORETICAL BASES FOR UNDERSTANDING THE RELATION BETWEEN SPIRITUAL DEVELOPMENT AND THRIVING AMONG YOUTH

Across the past quarter century, human developmental scientists have increasingly eschewed both mechanistic and organismic models of individual development (Lerner, 2002), in that the splits (Overton, 1998) between nature- and nurture-based variables associated with such conceptions have proved to be theoretically limited, logically problematic, and empirically counterfactual. These models have been replaced by integrative, fused, or relational theories, conceptions that stress the mutually influential connections among all levels of the development system, ranging from genes through society, culture, the designed and natural ecology, and ultimately history (e.g., see Baltes, Lindenberger, & Staudinger, 1998; Bronfenbrenner & Morris, 1998; Elder, 1998; Ford & Lerner, 1992; Lerner, 2002; Magnusson & Stattin, 1998; Thelen & Smith, 1998). Accordingly, in developmental systems theories, the mutual influence between the developing person and his or her complex and changing context may be represented as individual ⬅ ➔ context relations.

The ideas of developmental systems theory (Lerner, 2002) are a useful frame for formulating a model of exemplary positive youth development, of thriving, and of the role of spiritual development in enhancing the adolescents' contributions to the society within which they develop. Two features of developmental systems theories are important to stress in order to understand their use for conceptualizing positive youth development: relative plasticity and developmental regulation.

The relation described within developmental systems theory of individual development to history means that change is a necessary feature of human life. However, change in individual ⬅ ➔ context relations is, of course, not limitless. Interlevel relations within the human developmental system both facilitate and constrain opportunities for change. For example, change (e.g., learning a new language with native-speaker fluency in adolescence or young adulthood) is constrained both by past developments (knowledge of one's native language) and by contemporary contextual conditions (the absence or presence of opportunities to immerse oneself in a new language and culture). As a consequence, contemporary developmental systems theories stress that only relative plasticity exists across life and that the magnitude of this plasticity may vary across ontogeny (Baltes et al., 1998; Lerner, 1984, 2002).

Nevertheless, relative plasticity legitimates an optimistic and proactive search for characteristics of individuals and of their ecologies that, together, can be arrayed to promote positive developmental change (Birkel, Lerner, & Smyer, 1989; Fisher & Lerner, 1994; Lerner, 2002; Lerner & Hood, 1986). Accordingly, the emphasis in developmental systems theory on relative plasticity provides a foundation for an applied developmental science aimed at enhancing human development through strengthening the linkages between developing individuals and their changing family and community settings. The mutual influence between individual and context regulates the course of development; when these bidirectional influences maintain or advance the health or well-being of both components of individual ← → context relations, they are termed adaptive developmental regulations. From an applied developmental science perspective, healthy development involves positive changes in the relation between a developing person—who is both able to contribute positively to self, family, and community and committed to doing so—and a community supporting the development of such citizens.

By our definition, a young person involved across time in such healthy, positive relations with his or her community, and on the path to an ideal adulthood, may be said to be *thriving*.

Developmental Regulation and Moral and Civic Identity

Mutually supportive individual ← → context relations in ontogeny reflect the phylogenetic requisites for the survival of humans and their contexts (Gould, 1977). Such relations involve the breadth of the developmental system, including brain, behavior, social relations, and the institutions of society (cf. Lerner, 2004). In other words, in human development, successful (adaptive, health-promoting) regulations at the level of individual functioning involve changing the self to support the context and altering the context to support the self. Such efforts require the individual to remain committed to contributing to the context and to possess, or to strive to develop, the skills for making such contributions.

Such a relation is the essence of adaptive developmental regulation. There are universal, structural, and cultural components of such regulations, as well as society-specific components. The universal components of the thriving process involve the *structure* of the regulatory connection between person and context. This context is composed of other people (e.g., peer groups, families) and of the institutions of society and culture. These institutions involve at least two components. There are cultural institutions, such as schools and religious institutions, and there are conceptual or ideological institutions, such as the values that exist in a society with regard to the desired features of human functioning.

A relation that subserves the maintenance and perpetuation of the developmental system is one in which the individual acts to support the institutions of society and, simultaneously, these institutions support the healthy and productive functioning and development of the individual (Elder, 1998; Ford & Lerner, 1992). In such a relation the actions of the individual on the context and the actions of the context on the individual are fused in the production of healthy outcomes for both the individual and the institutions (Elder, 1998).

As such, the key feature of the thriving process is one in which the regulation of individual← → context relations eventuates in positive outcomes at multiple levels of the developmental system, for example, the person, the family, and the community (Lerner, 2004). In fact, a key structural value of all societies is that individuals' regulation of their individual ← → context relations should make positive contributions to self, family, community, and society (Elder, 1998). In all societies, then, healthy and valued (or "idealized") personhood is seen as a period, or "stage," in which such generative developmental regulation is produced (Csikszentmihalyi & Rathunde, 1998; Erikson, 1959).

Ideally, then, a thriving youth will become an adult generating productive and culturally valued contributions to self, family, community, and civil society. These contributions will have an intergenerational impact. Idealized personhood maintains civil society by contributing to the current components of community, business, and civic life. It also perpetuates civil society by imbuing these components with assets for future adaptation to historical change. *Children are these assets.* Most important, then, a key facet of idealized personhood is socialization of the members of the next generation to become active agents of civil society—as parents, teachers, mentors, and so on.

Of course, in different societies there is variation in what a person must do to manifest the structural values of productive and healthy personhood. How a person must function to manifest structurally valued regulation will vary from social and cultural setting to setting and across historical (and ecological) conditions (Elder, Modell, & Parke, 1993; Erikson, 1959). For example, in the United States regulations that support individual freedom, equity, and democracy are highly valued. In other societies it may be that regulations that support interindividually invariant belief in and obedience to religious dictums are of superordinate value.

In all cases, however, each society will show variation within a given historical moment in what behaviors are judged as valuable in (consistent with) supporting the universal structural value of maintaining and perpetuating individual ← → context regulations that subserve mutually beneficial individual and institutional relations (Meyer, 1988). As a consequence, then, the indicators of what an individual must manifest as he or she develops from infancy to adult personhood may vary across place and time (Elder et al., 1993). There may be variation across different societies, and across points in time within the same society, in definitions of individual ← → context relations that comprise exemplary development, or thriving, and thus in the specific behaviors that move a young person along a life path wherein he or she will possess the functional values of society and attain structurally valued personhood.

Thriving, Liberty, and Moral Duty

Developmentally emergent and contextually mediated successful regulations of positive individual ← → context relations ensure that individuals will have the nurturance and support needed for healthy development. Simultaneously, such regulation provides society with people having the mental capacities and the behavioral skills— the inner and outer lives—requisite to maintain,

perpetuate, and enhance what a society defines as just, equitable, and democratic institutions (Lerner, 2004; Lerner, Freund, De Stefanis, & Habermas, 2001; Lerner & Spanier, 1980).

This mutual interdependency between person and context can foster thriving.

Such individuals are committed to contributing to social justice and equity for all individuals in society because society is committed to ensuring justice and equality of opportunity and treatment (equity) for them. Through civic engagement they enter a life path marked by the "five Cs" of positive youth development: competence, confidence, connection, character, and caring (or compassion). Such youth will pursue the noble purpose of becoming productive adult members of their community (Damon, Menon, & Bronk, 2003), developing the "sixth C" of contribution to self, family, others, and, ultimately, civil society. This type of developmental regulation—between thriving individuals and their civil society—is the essence of a system marked by liberty (Lerner, 2004). Figure 5.1 provides an illustration of the model of thriving that we have developed (e.g., Lerner, 2004; Lerner et al., 2003).

In short, adaptive developmental regulation results in the emergence among young people of an orientation to transcend self-interest and place value on, and commitments to, actions supportive of a social system promoting equity, democracy, social justice, and personal freedoms. This regulatory system is one that enables the individual and individual initiative to prosper. As such, it is this relation—between an individual engaged in support of a democratic system that, in turn, supports the individual—that is the essence of healthy developmental regulation. Moreover, a commitment to contribution rests on defining behavior in support of mutually beneficial individual ← → context exchanges as morally necessary. Individuals' moral duty to contribute exists because, as citizens receiving benefits from a social system supporting their individual functioning, it is necessary to be actively engaged in, at least, maintaining and, ideally, enhancing that social system (Youniss, McLellan, & Yates, 1999).

Thriving and Spiritual Development

The sense of transcendence of self and of zero-sum-game self-interest that accrues as

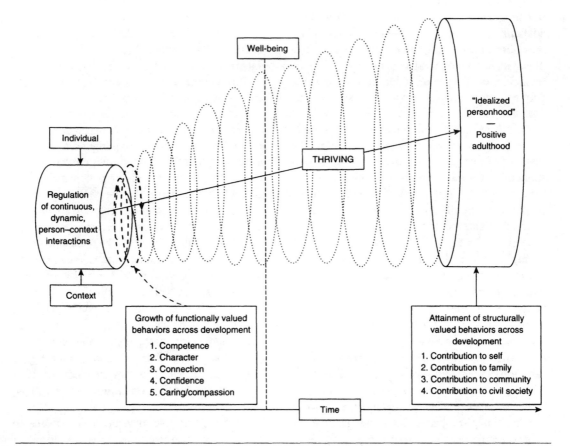

Figure 5.1 A Developmental Systems Model of the Thriving Process

integrated moral and civic self-definitions (identities) develop may be interpreted as a growing spiritual sense (Benson, 2003; Dowling, Gestsdottir, Anderson, von Eye, & Lerner, 2003; Dowling et al., 2004; Lerner, Dowling, & Anderson, 2003). Erikson (1959) discussed the emotional "virtues" that were coupled with successful resolution of each of the eight psychosocial crises he included in his theory of ego development. He specified that fidelity, defined as unflagging commitment to abstract ideas (e.g., ideologies) beyond the self, was the virtue associated with adaptive resolution of the identity crisis of adolescence, and thus with the attainment of a socially prescribed, positive role (cf. Youniss et al., 1999). Commitment to a role was regarded by Erikson (1959) as a means for the behaviors of youth to serve the maintenance and perpetuation of society; fidelity to an ideology coupled with a role meant that the young

person would gain emotional satisfaction—which to Erikson (1959) meant enhanced self-esteem—through contributing to society by the enactment of role behaviors (Lerner, 2002).

One need not focus only on crisis resolution to suggest that behaviors attained during adolescence in the service of identity development may be coupled with an ideological "virtue," that is, with a sensibility about the meaningfulness of abstract ideas that transcend the self (Youniss et al., 1999). From a perspective that focuses on adaptive developmental regulation within the developmental system, it is possible to suggest that spirituality is the transcendent virtue that is coupled with the behaviors (roles) reflecting an integrated moral and civic identity.

Contemporary researchers (e.g., Youniss et al., 1999) increasingly frame questions about the impact of community contributions and service activities on healthy identity development.

Erikson (1959) proposed that when young people identify with ideologies and histories of faith-based institutions, identities can be placed within a social-historical framework that connect youth to traditions and communities that transcend the immediate moment, thereby providing young people with a sense of continuity and coherence with the past, present, and future.

Consistent with Erikson's prescription, youth-service programs sponsored by faith-based institutions such as the Catholic Church are embedded in interpretive values and historical meaning. For example, a parish that sponsors a highway cleanup activity for its youth will likely rely on a moral and value-laden framework to explain its involvement, describing that involvement in religious traditions and stories (Youniss et al., 1999). Youth who take part in service activities are likely to "reflect on these justifications as potential meanings for their (own) actions. These established meanings, with their historical richness and picturing of an ideal future may readily be seen as nourishment for youths' identity development" (Youniss et al., 1999, p. 244).

As such, youth whose exchanges with their contexts (whose developmental regulations) are marked by functionally valued behaviors should develop integrated moral and civic identities and a transcendent, or spiritual, sensibility (Benson, 2003; Youniss et al., 1999). There is, in fact, evidence that adolescents' sense of spirituality is linked to thriving.

Thriving and Religiosity Among Adolescents

There are moderate to weak associations between youth religious practices and beliefs and both lower probabilities of problem behaviors (e.g., delinquency, drug and alcohol use and abuse, and sexual activity) and higher probabilities of positive behaviors (e.g., prosocial behaviors such as altruism, moral values, and mental health) (Bridges & Moore, 2002; Kerestes & Youniss, 2003). There are also weak to moderate associations between positive youth behaviors and parental involvement in religion (Bridges & Moore, 2002). For instance, Metz and Youniss (2003) found that high school students who identified themselves as religious were more likely to volunteer, participate in school organizations, and have higher grade point averages. In addition, religious students were more likely to have parents who had volunteered; these religious, volunteering students were also more likely to be female (Metz & Youniss, 2003).

Bridges and Moore (2002) note that these associations between religiosity and positive youth development are weakened owing to the low quality of measures of youth religiosity. In addition, they indicate that there is a lack of sufficient longitudinal data to chart the potentially changing role of religiosity in positive youth development (Bridges & Moore, 2002). Moreover, Kerestes and Youniss (2003) note that charting this role is complicated by the fact that "religion is a multidimensional phenomenon that cannot easily be segregated from the social context in which it is practiced" (p. 170).

In this regard, a promising advance in the measurement of religiosity and its link to positive youth development has been reported by King and Furrow (2004), who indexed religiosity multiple indicators that had sound measurement characteristics; they also assessed the social capital supporting religious development that was present in the social context of youth. In a cross-sectional sample of several hundred diverse urban youth, they found that religiously active adolescents who had high levels of social capital (measured by indicators of social interaction, trust, and shared vision) had higher levels of moral functioning.

To Reich et al. (1999) and others (e.g., Youniss et al., 1999), a young person's sense of religiosity may be an important source of positive development; however, religiosity may or may not be dependent on a young person's experiencing a sense of transcendence or spirituality when involved in the formal rites and institutions of an established faith tradition. In fact, according to Benson (1997), religion and spirituality may be regarded as orthogonal and important sources of thriving among youth.

In sum, then, contemporary scholars of adolescent development are pointing to the implications of religiosity and spirituality on positive youth development (see, e.g., King & Benson, chapter 27, this volume; Lerner, 2004; Youniss et al., 1999), but they conceptually differentiate the role of these constructs in such development. However, there have been few attempts to date psychometrically to operationalize and obtain support for these constructs within one data set pertinent to adolescence. For this reason, it is useful to discuss briefly some research in our laboratory that has been aimed at providing empirical tests of the purported links in adolescence among spirituality, religiosity, and thriving.

RESEARCH WITHIN THE INSTITUTE FOR APPLIED RESEARCH IN YOUTH DEVELOPMENT

One study we have conducted used one of the few data sets with an item pool potentially appropriate for rich psychometric analyses. Search Institute in Minneapolis, Minnesota, has several large data sets in its research archives that contain information pertinent to the constructs of religiosity, spirituality, and thriving during the adolescent period. Dowling et al. (2003) reported initial analyses of the *Young Adolescents and Their Parents* (YAP) data set (Search Institute, 1984). The YAP involves the responses of a cross-sectional sample that includes 8,165 youth, ranging from fifth through ninth grades (9 to 15 years of age), and 10,467 parents.

The YAP sample, which was gathered in 1982 and 1983, was drawn randomly from 13 national youth-serving organizations and religious organizations. The survey was administered in group settings in 953 locations. Focusing only on the youth data in the YAP, Dowling et al. (2003) drew a random sample of 1,000 youth from the overall sample. This smaller sample was composed of 472 boys (mean age = 12.2 years, *SD* = 1.5) and 528 girls (mean age = 12.1 years, *SD* = 1.4) and was representative of the demographic characteristics present in the larger YAP sample.

Of the 319 items in the youth survey, the participants responded to 91 questionnaire items that pertained to religiosity, spirituality, and positive youth development or thriving (e.g., social competence, self-esteem, and respect for diversity). Orthogonal, principal axes factor analyses were conducted for each of the three constructs

of interest, that is, religiosity, spirituality, and thriving. Varimax rotational procedures were used. A Root 1 criterion was followed for the extraction of factors. The resulting factor solution was confirmed through the use of structural equation modeling (SEM), using the LISREL 8.53 program (Jöreskog & Sörbom, 2002).

As shown in Table 5.1, four factors potentially associated with the construct of religiosity emerged, three factors potentially associated with the construct of spirituality emerged, and nine factors potentially associated with the construct of thriving emerged. Using LISREL 8.53, an attempt was made to confirm a model of the constructs (or latent variables) of religiosity, spirituality, and thriving, and, in turn, the factors and items associated with these constructs. As reported in Dowling et al. (2003), the hypothesized model involves three levels: (1) the three second order factors of religiosity, spirituality, and thriving; (2) the four first order factors associated with religiosity, the three first order factors associated with spirituality, and the nine first order factors associated with thriving; and (3) the manifest variables—the items—associated with each of the latent variables defined as the sets of first order factors.

Dowling et al. (2003) report that the results of the LISREL analysis, which employed maximum likelihood methods for estimation, indicated that the model fit the data well. Accordingly, the findings of this test of the overall model confirm the presence of three relatively independent constructs (religiosity, spirituality, and thriving). Figure 5.2 presents the first and second order factors confirmed by Dowling et al. (2003).

In short, the results of both the factor analysis and the SEM procedures converged in indicating that, within the YAP data set, the constructs of religiosity, spirituality, and thriving can be independently identified and confirmed, with each construct multivariate in its latent structure. The confirmation of the independent presence of these three constructs afforded a necessary condition to begin to explore theoretical ideas about the role of spirituality in exemplary positive youth behavior and development.

Accordingly, in a second study using the 1,000 adolescents from the YAP data set,

Table 5.1   Hypothesized Religiosity, Spirituality, and Thriving Factors and a Representative (High Loading) Item for Each Factor

Religiosity Factors	*Representative Item*
1. Impact of religious beliefs on self	Does your religion make you feel better when things don't go well?
2. Religious views	What is your view of God?
3. Religious restrictions of God on people	God has a lot of rules about how people should live their lives.
4. Role of a faith institution in one's life	How many years have you attended classes which teach about God and other religious things?
Spirituality Factors	
1. Orientation to do good work	Imagine you saw a little kid fall and get hurt on the playground. Would you run over and try to help?
2. Participation in self-interest activities	In the past 12 months, how many times have you been out on a date?
3. Orientation to help others	How many hours did you give help to people outside your family that have special needs during the last month without pay?
Thriving Factors	
1. Rules for youth presented by mother	Mom tries to help me see why rules are necessary and important.
2. Rules for youth presented by father	When I do something wrong, my father takes the time to help me see why it was wrong.
3. Presence of a moral compass	How wrong is it to lie to your parents?
4. Future orientation/path to a hopeful future	What do you want most in life (e.g., to have world without war)?
5. Search for positive identity	How much interest do you have in finding out what is special about you?
6. Personal values	What do you want most in life? To do whatever I want to do when I want to do it.
7. Engagement with school	How do you feel about going to school?
8. View of gender equity	I think women should have the same rights as men.
9. View of diversity	How right or wrong is racial discrimination?

Dowling et al. (2004) posed the following question: Does religiosity mediate the influence of spirituality on thriving? In other words, is the only pathway of spirituality to thriving through religiosity? While the literature would not support the complete absence of combined influences of spirituality and religiosity on thriving (e.g., Benson, 1997), we expected that there would nevertheless be some influence of the former construct on thriving that existed over and above any combined or mediated influence involving the latter construct.

To address this question, the second order factors of spirituality, religiosity, and thriving

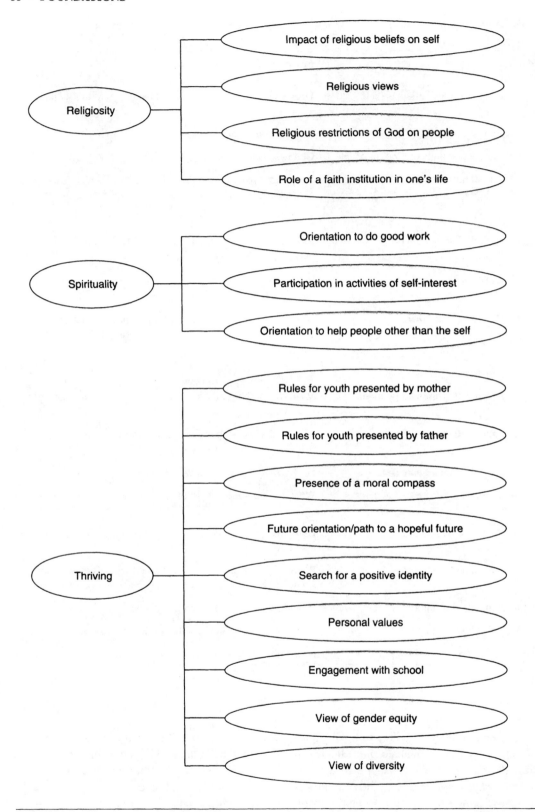

Figure 5.2   First and Second Order Factors Found by Dowling et al. (2003)

Model 1

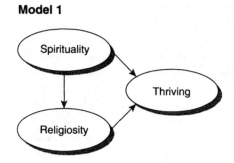

Model 2   **Model 3**

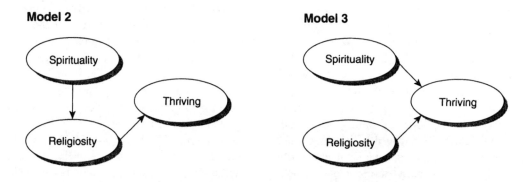

Figure 5.3   Three Models of Possible Structural Relations Among Spirituality, Religiosity, and Thriving

were operationalized without going through the respective sets of first order factors shown in Figure 5.2, but with the use of the same indicators. LISREL 8.53 was again employed to ascertain the structural relations that were hypothesized to exist among these three latent constructs. We anticipated that both spirituality and religiosity would be related to thriving. We also expected, however, that there would be an influence of spirituality on thriving that existed over and above any combined or mediated influence of religiosity on thriving. In other words, in the terms of Baron and Kenny (1986), we expected to find support for a fully mediated structural model.

To test this hypothesis, three models were estimated through the use of LISREL 8.53, employing maximum likelihood estimation methods. As shown in Figure 5.3, the first model

is that of complete mediation. This model includes the paths from spirituality to religiosity, from religiosity to thriving, and from spirituality to thriving. This fully mediated model reflects our key expectation that there would be an influence of spirituality on thriving that existed over and above any combined or mediated influence of religiosity on thriving. The second model is the mediation-only model. It includes only the paths from spirituality to religiosity and from religiosity to thriving. This second model is hierarchically subordinate to Model 1. The third model includes only the paths from religiosity to thriving and from spirituality to thriving, thus depriving religiosity of the role of a mediating entity. Model 3 is also hierarchically subordinate to Model 1.

Dowling et al. (2003) present data indicating that the first, complete mediation model depicted in Figure 5.3 corresponds well to the data. As such, we conclude that the fit of the comparison models was significantly worse than the fit of the complete mediation model. In other words, each of the comparison models performs significantly below the complete mediation model. As such, the model that includes a path from spirituality to thriving, as well as the path of spirituality through religiosity to thriving, best fits the data from the YAP subsample tested in this research.

Conclusions

The developmental systems view of human development (Lerner, 2002) posits that, as a consequence of the influence of plasticity and adaptive developmental regulation, there exists the potential in every young person for healthy and successful development. In this view, youth who are dynamically engaged in mutually beneficial ways with their contexts will contribute positively to the healthy development of both self and society (Lerner, 2004; Lerner, Brentano, Dowling, & Anderson, 2002). Although multiple relations between person and context have been the focus of study in positive youth development, we believe that the role of spirituality in thriving among young people merits further attention, especially because spirituality may fuel the adaptive individual ← → context relations that enable humans to contribute in productive ways to the healthy development of self, family, community, and civil society (Dowling et al., 2003, 2004; Lerner, 2004; Lerner et al., 2002; Youniss et al., 1999).

Interest in these ideas led to our use of the Search Institute (1984) data set *Young Adolescents and Their Parents* (YAP), and to our finding that, in adolescence, it appears that paths from spirituality to religiosity, from religiosity to thriving, and from spirituality to thriving are a better fit to the data set than are hierarchically related, reduced models that lack either the direct effect of spirituality on thriving or the mediating effect of spirituality on thriving through religiosity. Accordingly, our results to date, albeit limited by the ethnic, racial, and religious composition of the YAP sample, as well as by the historical era within which the YAP data were collected (and of course by the

measurement model and data analytic approaches used in our research), are nevertheless consistent with the idea that within the developmental system associated with exemplary positive development—that is, with thriving—among youth, spirituality constitutes an important component of such functioning and one that is not fully commensurate with other key dimensions of an adolescent's inner life, such as religiosity.

Indeed, in demonstrating that both spirituality and religiosity must be considered—and independently indexed—as important parts of the developmental system linked to thriving among adolescents, the present findings provide a basis for the design of measurement and structural models in future, longitudinal analyses aimed at understanding whether, when, and under what ecological conditions, and for what youth, spirituality and religiosity provide independent or combined sources of exemplary positive youth development.

The nature of the links among thriving, civic engagement, and moral development that mark adaptive developmental regulation makes it clear that a society interested in the maintenance and enhancement of liberty should develop policies to strengthen, in communities, the capacities of families to provide the individual and ecological assets—the personal and social "developmental nutrients" needed for thriving (Benson, 2003)—that are suggested by Search Institute (Benson, 2003; Lerner, 2004; Lerner, Fisher, & Weinberg, 2000). These assets are associated with positive youth development—and to an increased probability of thriving among young people (Scales, Benson, Leffert, & Blyth, 2000). Within such a policy context, asset-rich communities would enact activities (e.g., programs) that would provide young people with the resources needed to build and to pursue healthy lives that make productive contributions to self, family, and community.

Thriving will more likely emerge when youth develop in such a policy and community action/program context (Benson, 2003; Lerner et al., 2000; Pittman, Irby, & Ferber, 2001; Roth, Brooks-Gunn, Murray, & Foster, 1998). Competent, confident, connected, caring youth who also possess character will have the moral orientation and the civic allegiance to use their skills to enact in themselves and, when parents, promote in their children, behaviors that "level the playing field" for everyone. Committed—behaviorally, morally, and spiritually—to a better world beyond themselves, such individuals will act to sustain for future generations a society marked by social justice, equity, and democracy and a world in which all young people may thrive.

REFERENCES

Baltes, P. B., Lindenberger, U., & Staudinger, U. M. (1998). Life-span theory in developmental psychology. In W. Damon (Series Ed.) & R. M. Lerner (Vol. Ed.), *Handbook of child psychology: Vol. 1. Theoretical models of human development* (5th ed., pp. 1029–1144). New York: Wiley.

Baron, R. M., & Kenny, D. A. (1986). The moderator–mediator variable distinction in social psychological research: Conceptual, strategic, and statistical considerations. *Journal of Personality and Social Psychology, 51,* 1173–1182.

Benson, P. L. (1997). Spirituality and the adolescent journey. *Reclaiming Children and Youth, 5*(4), 206–209.

Benson, P. L. (2003). Developmental assets and asset-building community: Conceptual and empirical foundations. In R. M. Lerner & P. L. Benson (Eds.), *Developmental assets and asset-building communities: Implications for research, policy, and practice* (pp. 19–46). New York: Kluwer Academic/Plenum Publishers.

Birkel, R., Lerner, R. M., & Smyer, M. A. (1989). Applied developmental psychology as an implementation of a life-span view of human development. *Journal of Applied Developmental Psychology, 10,* 425–445.

Bridges, L. J., & Moore, K. A. (2002). *Religious involvement and children's well-being: What research tells us (and what it doesn't).* Washington, DC: Child Trends.

Bronfenbrenner, U., & Morris, P. A. (1998). The ecology of developmental process. In W. Damon (Series Ed.) & R. M. Lerner (Vol. Ed.), *Handbook of child psychology: Vol. 1. Theoretical models of human development* (5th ed., pp. 993–1028). New York: Wiley.

Csikszentmihalyi, M., & Rathunde, K. (1998). The development of the person: An experiential perspective on the ontogenesis of psychological complexity. In W. Damon (Series Ed.) & R. M. Lerner (Vol. Ed.), *Handbook of child psychology:*

Vol. 1. Theoretical models of human development (5th ed., pp. 635–684). New York: Wiley.

Damon, W., Menon, J., & Bronk, K. C. (2003). The development of purpose during adolescence. *Applied Developmental Science, 7,* 119–128.

Dowling, E. M., Gestsdottir, S., Anderson, P. M., von Eye, A., & Lerner, R. M. (2003). Spirituality, religiosity, and thriving among adolescents: Identification and confirmation of factor structures. *Applied Developmental Science, 7*(4), 253–260.

Dowling, E. M., Gestsdottir, S., Anderson, P. M., von Eye, A., Almerigi, J., & Lerner, R. M. (2004). Structural relations among spirituality, religiosity, and thriving in adolescence. *Applied Developmental Science, 8*(1), 7–16.

Elder, G. H., Jr. (1998). The life course and human development. In W. Damon (Series Ed.) & R. M. Lerner (Vol. Ed.), *Handbook of child psychology: Vol. 1. Theoretical models of human development* (5th ed., pp. 939–991). New York: Wiley.

Elder, G. H., Modell, J., & Parke, R. D. (1993). Studying children in a changing world. In G. H. Elder, J. Modell, & R. D. Parke (Eds.), *Children in time and place: Developmental and historical insights* (pp. 3–21). Cambridge, UK: Cambridge University Press.

Erikson, E. H. (1959). Identity and the life-cycle. *Psychological Issues, 1,* 18–164.

Fisher, C. B., & Lerner, R. M. (1994). Foundations of applied developmental psychology. In C. B. Fisher and R. M. Lerner (Eds.), *Applied developmental psychology* (pp. 3–20). New York: McGraw-Hill.

Ford, D. L., & Lerner, R. M. (1992). *Developmental systems theory: An integrative approach.* Newbury Park, CA: Sage.

Gould, S. J. (1977). *Ontogeny and phylogeny.* Cambridge, MA: Harvard University Press.

Jöreskog, K. G., & Sörbom, D. (2002). LISREL 8.53 [Computer software]. Lincolnwood, IL: Scientific Software International.

Kerestes, M., & Youniss, J. E. (2003). Rediscovering the importance of religion in adolescent development. In. R. M. Lerner, F. Jacobs, & D. Wertlieb (Eds.), *Handbook of applied developmental science: Promoting positive child, adolescent, and family development through research, policies, and programs: Vol. 1. Applying developmental science for youth and families: Historical and theoretical foundations* (pp. 165–184). Thousand Oaks, CA: Sage.

King, P. E., & Furrow, J. (2004). Religion as a resource for positive youth development: Religion, social capital, and moral outcomes. *Developmental Psychology, 40,* 703–713.

Koenig, H. G., & Lawson, D. M. (2004). *Faith in the future: Health care, aging, and the role of religion.* Philadelphia: Templeton Foundation Press.

Lerner, R. M. (1984). *On the nature of human plasticity.* Cambridge, UK: Cambridge University Press.

Lerner, R. M. (2002). *Concepts and theories of human development* (3rd ed.). Mahwah, NJ: Erlbaum.

Lerner, R. M. (2004). *Liberty: Thriving and civic engagement among America's youth.* Thousand Oaks, CA: Sage.

Lerner, R. M., Brentano, C., Dowling, E. M., & Anderson, P. M. (2002). Positive youth development: Thriving as a basis of personhood and civil society. In R. M. Lerner, C. S. Taylor, & A. von Eye (Eds.), *New directions for youth development: Theory, practice, research: No. 95. Pathways to positive youth development among gang and non-gang youth* (pp. 11–34). San Francisco: Jossey-Bass.

Lerner, R. M., Dowling, E. M., & Anderson, P. M. (2003). Positive youth development: Thriving as the basis of personhood and civil society. *Applied Developmental Science, 7*(3), 172–180.

Lerner, R. M., Fisher, C. B., & Weinberg, R. A. (2000). Toward a science for and of the people: Promoting civil society through the application of developmental science. *Child Development, 71,* 11–20.

Lerner, R. M., Freund, A. M., De Stefanis, I., & Habermas, T. (2001). Understanding developmental regulation in adolescence: The use of the selection, optimization, and compensation model. *Human Development, 44,* 29–50.

Lerner, R. M., & Hood, K. E. (1986). Plasticity in development: Concepts and issues for intervention. *Journal of Applied Developmental Psychology, 7,* 139–152.

Lerner, R. M., & Spanier, G. B. (1980). *Adolescent development: A life-span perspective.* New York: McGraw-Hill.

Magnusson, D., & Stattin, H. (1998). Person–context interaction theories. In W. Damon (Series Ed.) & R. M. Lerner (Vol. Ed.), *Handbook of child psychology: Vol. 1. Theoretical models of human development* (5th ed., pp. 685–759). New York: Wiley.

Metz, E., & Youniss, J. (2003). A demonstration that school-based required service does not deter—but heightens—volunteerism. *PS: Political Science and Politics, 36*(2), 281–286.

Meyer, J. W. (1988). The social constructs of the psychology of childhood: Some contemporary processes. In E. M. Hetherington, R. M. Lerner, & M. Perlmutter (Eds.), *Child development in life-span perspective* (pp. 47–65). Hillsdale, NJ: Erlbaum.

Overton, W. F. (1998). Developmental psychology: Philosophy, concepts, and methodology. In W. Damon (Series Ed.) & R. M. Lerner (Vol. Ed.), *Handbook of child psychology: Vol. 1. Theoretical models of human development* (5th ed., pp. 107–187). New York: Wiley.

Pittman, K., Irby, M., & Ferber, T. (2001). Unfinished business: Further reflections on a decade of promoting youth development. In P. L. Benson & K. J. Pittman (Eds.), *Trends in youth development: Visions, realities and challenges* (pp. 4–50). Boston: Kluwer Academic.

Reich, H., Oser, F., & Scarlett, W. G. (1999). Spiritual and religious development: Transcendence and transformations of the self. In K. H. Reich, F. K. Oser, & W. G. Scarlett (Eds.), *Psychological studies on spiritual and religious development: Vol. 2. Being human: The case of religion* (pp. 57–82). Scottsdale, AZ: Pabst Science.

Roth, J., Brooks-Gunn, J., Murray, L., & Foster, W. (1998). Promoting healthy adolescents: Synthesis of youth development program evaluations. *Journal of Research on Adolescence, 8,* 423–459.

Scales, P. C., Benson, P. L., Leffert, N., & Blyth, D. A. (2000). Contribution of developmental assets to the prediction of thriving among adolescents. *Applied Development Science, 4*(1), 27–46.

Search Institute. (1984). *Young adolescents and their parents* [Unpublished raw data archive]. Minneapolis, MN: Author.

Thelen, E., & Smith, L. B. (1998). Dynamic systems theories. In W. Damon (Series Ed.) & R. M. Lerner (Vol. Ed.), *Handbook of child psychology: Vol. 1. Theoretical models of human development* (5th ed., pp. 563–633). New York: Wiley.

Youniss, J., McLellan, J. A., & Yates, M. (1999). Religion, community service, and identity in American youth. *Journal of Adolescence, 22,* 243–253.

6

PHILOSOPHICAL ISSUES IN SPIRITUAL EDUCATION AND DEVELOPMENT

HANAN A. ALEXANDER

DAVID CARR

Our intent in this chapter is to map the conceptual terrain of spiritual education and development by addressing four key philosophical questions: What can it possibly mean to educate in spirituality? Does it make sense to construe spirituality as an innate quality that develops naturally in human beings? How is education in spirituality possible given the demand for rational autonomy or substantive choice in open, liberal, democratic societies? And in what institutional settings is spiritual education possible or desirable? We devote sections to each of these questions and conclude with some discussion of critical issues and opportunities for future research.

To say that the chapter addresses philosophical questions requires some clarification. Philosophers are not concerned with the sorts of queries that may be addressed by collecting empirical evidence concerning how things are in the world. They inquire rather about the meaning of the concepts we use in order to understand the significance of any such evidence. Grasping what it means to educate in spirituality, for example, or whether spirituality can in

any sense be regarded as a matter of natural development, does not require examining quantitative results of psychological experiments, or qualitative ("thick") descriptions of concrete cultural experiences, though such research methods may highlight philosophical issues in a number of significant ways. Rather, philosophical understanding of spirituality and spiritual education calls for attention to the logical grammar of received discourse about such matters, and to questions of the consistency and coherence of usage in different areas of that discourse. Although such analysis may not yield particular accounts or theories of spirituality, spiritual education, or spiritual development, it may well help us see what might possibly count as a coherent case of spiritual education or spiritual development by means of what Green (1999, p. x) called "unwrapping the ordinary"— the logical exploration of everyday speech to identify criteria of coherent usage. The first two sections of this chapter attempt to provide instances of such exploration with respect to the conceptual analysis of spiritual education and development.

In addition to being concerned with the conditions under which it makes sense to use concepts, philosophers are also interested in apparent tensions between claims to which many of us might want equally to subscribe. How, they ask, is it possible for us to hold that such and such a proposition is true, given that we also seem willing to subscribe to certain other, apparently opposed assumptions?

> How is it possible for us to have free will, supposing that all actions are causally determined? . . . How can there be stable meaning . . . given that everything in the world is changing? . . . How is evil possible, supposing the existence of an omnipotent, omniscient good God? (Nozick, 1981, p. 8)

Addressing questions such as these calls for what Nozick (1981) has dubbed a philosophical explanation, in which we search for deeper principles that remove the apparent conflict and try to bring our beliefs into alignment. Such tension would seem to be apparent between a number of leading accounts of spiritual education and the requirements for education in liberal democracies. How, we might ask, is it possible to educate for belief in the claims of particular religious or other spiritual traditions, given that liberal societies require democratic citizens capable of independent rational choice of belief? In the third and fourth sections, we address this question by examining two rather different accounts of how spiritual education is possible in democratic societies, and identifying four sorts of institutions in which it might be said to occur. Our recommendations for future research follow from these philosophical analyses and distinctions.

CONCEIVING SPIRITUAL EDUCATION

Recent philosophical writers on spirituality and spiritual education have invariably begun by observing the difficulty, if not impossibility, of defining the notion of spirituality. In this section we will comment on this difficulty before drawing a number of distinctions that enable us to map rival conceptions of spirituality and spiritual education, and—in the next section—to see what must be characteristic of such views to constitute accounts of spirituality and not something else.

The Difficulties of Defining Spirituality

At one level, of course, to observe the difficulty of defining such terms as spirituality is to offer little more than a philosophical banality. Aristotle (trans. 1925, pp. 2–3) recognized that beyond the realms of mathematics and logic few terms of ordinary usage have precise boundaries. Moreover, although he made this point specifically in relation to ethical discourse, Aristotle clearly did not believe that it raised any insurmountable theoretical or practical difficulties for the conduct of moral education. There is, to be sure, much controversy about what it means to be honest, just, temperate, courageous, and so on, but it is nonetheless fairly clear, at least in the Aristotelian view, that to exhibit moral character one would need to be, among other things, honest, just, temperate, and courageous.

Things would seem to be otherwise when it comes to concepts such as spirituality and spiritual education. Indeed, contemporary discussions of these matters may not have fully appreciated precisely why the notion of spirituality is resistant to definition. Such resistance is not merely a function of normative disagreement about what it might mean to be just or courageous in this or that circumstance. Moral agents could disagree about what is for the best, without disagreeing about what it is to be a moral agent—which would presumably entail, among other things, aiming to do broadly what is for the best. However, disagreements about spiritual life or conduct would not appear to be of this kind. What the growing contemporary literature of spiritual education and development seems to show is that the resistance to defining spirituality is symptomatic of more fundamental ontological uncertainty over the very nature, objects, or referents of spiritual discourse. *Spirituality* is difficult to define because of deep ambiguities of everyday usage that have encouraged educational theorists, policy makers, and practitioners to pursue diverse social, cultural, and political aims, agendas, and outcomes in the name of spiritual education.

This has brought a level of conceptual, theoretical, and practical complexity to the problem of curriculum planning for spiritual education that extends beyond any problems to which moral education may be prone. Although we may disagree—as devotees of cognitive developmentalism, ethics of care, or character education—over the extent to which moral education should be part of the explicit or the hidden curriculum, or about whether the cultivation of principled reflection, caring affect, or particular virtues lies at the heart of moral formation, the problem for the planner of the spiritual curriculum would seem often to be more that of accommodating quite different and possibly competing social and developmental agendas— if not also of mounting some principled opposition to some of these agendas.

Dimensions of Spiritual Education

What are some of the key agendas behind recent concern for spiritual education? They might best be characterized along six distinct but interrelated continua concerned with the extent to which spiritual education might be regarded as (1) confessional or nonconfessional; (2) religiously tethered or untethered; (3) theologically objectivist, collectivist, or subjectivist; (4) independent of or reducible to morality; (5) culturally thick or thin; and (6) pedagogically cognitive or affective. We have called these distinctions "continua" to emphasize that they are not dichotomies, "either-ors," or (what Dewey, 1963, would have called) dualisms, but rather opposite ends of spectra that crisscross the conceptual terrain of spiritual education and development. Most leading accounts of spiritual agenda are "situated" somewhere along each of these six axes.

Confessional or Phenomenological Spiritual Education. For many people spirituality is either synonymous with, or at least intimately connected to, religion. It is clear that some of the recent emphasis on spiritual education relates directly to contemporary issues and problems concerning the nature and place of religious formation in common or state schooling. Education systems across the world are heir to diverse traditions of association or disassociation between church and state embodying widely different

conceptions of the educational status and significance of religion. Leaving aside states that promote atheism on the one hand or theocracy on the other, there is a difference among liberal democracies between those that exclude religion from state education on constitutional grounds, such as the United States, and those in which religion was traditionally taught in state schools, such as Britain and other European countries. Clearly, many of those who regard spirituality as a significant human experience or quality may have problems with any state schooling that excludes religious instruction on the grounds that such exclusion fails to provide for an important aspect of human development. But what are the key spiritual educational issues for those educational traditions in which religious formation has always played a significant part?

The problems of regarding spirituality as an aspect of religious formation for culturally pluralist liberal democracies are complex. The most obvious of these is that the partisan identification of spirituality with one set of religious claims in contexts of religious plurality becomes problematic not only for those members of faith communities other than the culturally privileged or native one, but also for those professing no religious commitment whatsoever who might nevertheless lay claim to some degree of spiritual awareness or insight. The general response to this problem on the part of those who wish to preserve some element of religious instruction in common or state schools is to recast religious education in a form that is even-handedly respectful of a contextually appropriate range of key religious faiths, and that does not involve any partisan "confessional" initiation into some privileged faith (see, e.g., Noddings, 1993; Wilf, 1996; and the much earlier but still very relevant Dewey, 1960a). This has led to the development of a nonconfessional or "phenomenological" model of religious education. Although this orientation sometimes emphasizes what it takes to be the common moral content of diverse faiths, it mostly focuses on the academic study of different religions as more or less interesting human cultural practices (see Lovat, 1991). Even the relatively separate denominational (mainly Catholic and Anglican) sector of British schooling has not remained insulated from recent political pressure to adopt more neutral nonconfessional approaches to religious education. This said, the right of faith schools to engage in more systematic promotion of given modes of religious spirituality has also been generally respected.

Tethered or Untethered Spiritual Education. Related to these concerns is an important distinction drawn by Alexander and McLaughlin (2002) between the religiously "tethered" spirituality of denominational induction and the "untethered" spirituality of the nondenominational if not explicitly secular contexts of state schooling. "Tethered" spirituality, which corresponds roughly to the "traditional" spirituality that Carr (2003; see also 1994, 1996) has distinguished from "modern" and "postmodern" conceptions of spirituality, seems relatively unproblematic at least to the extent that what counts as spiritual education in, say, Roman Catholic schooling will amount more or less to acquiring the knowledge, understanding, and sensibilities of a devout Roman Catholic. Needless to say, this may well be problematic to those outside this faith who might regard any such initiation as no more than unwarranted indoctrination. What may seem more problematic is the issue of what could possibly count as untethered spirituality or spiritual education, especially in those nondenominational or secular educational contexts in which religious education has been largely reduced—by means of the phenomenological pedagogies mentioned above—to anthropology or cultural studies (see Jackson, 1997, 2004; Lovat, 1991). Indeed, one may be hard pressed to understand what drives the concern to introduce a spiritual dimension into any schooling uncoupled from confessional concern. All the same, many religious agnostics and atheists do appear to hold that there is an important dimension of human sensibility that they would refer to as spiritual, but which cannot be equated with religious knowledge or faith. But how precisely should we conceive any such a dimension?

Subjective, Collective, or Objective Spiritual Education. Clearly, no such spiritual dimension could be identified with an incorporeal (and perhaps immortal) spirit or soul, or with a transcendent deity as this has sometimes been conceived in such major world faiths as Christianity, Islam, and Hinduism, since secular or atheist advocates of spirituality are not likely to believe in any such entities. It might, however, be identified with a particular concern for or way of relating to the rest of nature, more naturalistically conceived, or indeed with some sense of oneness or continuity with that nature. In this light, spirituality might be identified more with attitudes or dispositions than with some "ghost in the machine" (Ryle, 1966), and a spiritual or "spiritually educated" person could be one who regarded the material world in a peculiarly noninstrumental way. That said, it is far from easy to give a clear sense or meaning to any such noninstrumental regard, and it seems prone to a number of rather different if not incompatible interpretations.

Alexander's (2001) distinction between subjective, collective (or intersubjective), and objective spirituality offers one approach to understanding such untethered orientations. The distinction is grounded in Taylor's (1989) account of the ways in which one might identify or "locate" a meaningful and purposeful life. First, subjective spirituality seeks spiritual fulfillment through the cultivation of inner wholeness or peace. Many of the secular, psychologically focused, or new age conceptions of spirituality mentioned earlier, and not a few mystical traditions, would seem to fit in this category (e.g., Marshak, 1997; Sloan, 1993; Wilber, Engler, & Brown, 1986). Second, collective or intersubjective spirituality focuses on solidarity with a particular community, fellowship, culture, or group. In this category we would find, for example, those spiritual educators who emphasize identification with the oppressed and downtrodden (Erricker, 2004; Gearon, 2001, 2004), or with a particular national, cultural, or ethnic group (Tamir, 1993). Third, objective spirituality is concerned with transcendent "realities" such as the divine as conceived and symbolized in traditional religious faiths (Rosenak, 1984, 1995). This orientation is "objective" in the sense that it focuses the spiritual quest outside the bounds of self and society—over and against our egocentric selves and the narrow communities in which we live.

Spiritual Education as Morally Reducible or Irreducible. Perhaps the simplest conception of an untethered spirituality for spiritual education might see it as essentially reducible to education in morality—and there is some reason to believe, on the basis of recent educational policy, that it often means little more than this. From this viewpoint, interest in spirituality and spiritual education is driven by concerns about contemporary emphases in the prescribed curricula of much state education on the economic benefits and vocational goals of schooling, and by a corresponding neglect of the wider emotional, moral, and social needs of the "whole child" (Erricker, 2004; Gearon, 2001, 2004; McLaughlin, 1996). The problem with prevailing curriculum trends, in this view, is that they are too focused (in the words of the poet Wordsworth) on "getting and spending" (Nichol Smith, 1921, p. 146) and in danger of producing generations of possessive individualists who care for little but themselves and their own material acquisitions.

The trouble now is that any concern to develop individual regard for others might seem largely reducible to the goals of promoting social obligation and responsibility that schools have pursued under the various headings of moral, personal, social, or citizenship education (Buckley & Erricker, 2004). In that case, what role might be played by spiritual education that is not already covered by such other curriculum areas? To be sure, although some advocates of spiritual education certainly have wanted to connect spirituality with moral sensibility or commitment, it would seem that many have also wished to reject any narrow identification of morality with the exclusively rational moral capacities of modern cognitive developmentalists (see, notably, Kohlberg, 1984; Piaget, 1932). From this viewpoint, the recognition that there is more to moral conduct and development than cognitive capacities might well reinforce the idea that what distinguishes spiritual from unspiritual persons is something more morally motivational than intellectual. In this light, a spiritual person would be a person of "spirit" and therefore to be judged by reference to such qualities of character as self-control, fortitude, resilience, persistence, steadfastness, and hope—as well as also perhaps in terms of such states of attachment as care, compassion, and concern.

Thick or Thin Spiritual Education. This consideration would also, of course, connect spiritual education to rather "thicker" conceptions of moral formation of the kind associated more with neo-Aristotelian virtue ethics (see, e.g., Geach, 1977; Hursthouse, 1999) and contemporary so-called character education (Lickona, 1992) than to "thinner" varieties of liberal moral education grounded in ethics of rights and duties. This observation is related to Michael Walzer's distinction between "thick" and "thin" moral traditions; between what he calls moral "maximalism" and "minimalism." We can distinguish, Walzer writes, between two different albeit interrelated kinds of moral argument: "a way of talking among ourselves, here at home, about the thickness of our own history and culture . . . and a way of talking to people abroad, across different cultures, about a thinner life we have in common. . . . There are the makings of a thin and universalistic morality inside every thick and particular morality" (Walzer, 1994, p. xi). A maximalist moral tradition, Walzer continues, will be "idiomatic in its language, particularist in its cultural references, and circumstantial in two senses of that word: historically dependent and factually detailed. Its principles and procedures will have been worked out over a long period of time through complex social interactions" (p. 21). Although some fairly explicit attempts have been made to link spiritual education to thicker virtue ethical conceptions, it may also be difficult to disconnect such qualities of character from more specific moral teleologies of the kind encountered in tethered conceptions of spiritual education in the interests of their more general educational development.

Cognitive or Affective Spiritual Education. Thicker conceptions of spiritual formation associated with virtue ethics and character development, which are more concerned with the cultivation of will than reason, focus on wider personal qualities rather than on narrow academic or instrumental concerns. On this view, spiritual education could not be reducible to the acquisition of religious knowledge or social skills, and would have to engage the agent's heart and soul in some ontologically deeper sense. Indeed, reflection along these lines, especially on the allegedly noninstrumental character of much human spirituality, has led many recent advocates of spiritual education to emphasize the affective dimension of human spiritual sensibility—namely, the extent to which it connects with feelings as much as, if not more than, with cognition and will (see Huebner, 1999). One trend evident in the recent theoretical and policy-related literature of spiritual education that reflects this perspective emphasizes the cultivation of an attitude of "awe and wonder" toward various aspects of human life and the natural environment (for relevant examples of British policy documentation, see National Curriculum Council, 1993; Office for Standards in Education, 1994; Schools Curriculum and Assessment Authority, 1995).

One of the clearest forms of such reflection on the nature of spiritual education would appear to focus directly on the aesthetic, emphasizing the need for attitudes of respect toward the natural environment and for cultivating a love of natural beauty for its own sake (see Cajete, 1994). However, other educational goals that seem to be run together (not entirely consistently) with this aesthetic emphasis include the promotion of a sense of awe at the unfathomable mystery of things, perhaps through contemplation of infinity in mathematics and eternity in cosmology, and a certain quality of unconditional regard for the sacred uniqueness of other human subjectivities (see Flier, 1995). Although none of this could be considered notably pellucid from either a conceptual or an educational viewpoint, there are nevertheless evident connections between these emphases on respect for others and the environment and what we have identified as the religious and moral elements in recent concerns for spiritual education.

SPIRITUALITY AND PSYCHOLOGICAL DEVELOPMENT

For those equally dissatisfied with any of these tethered or untethered conceptions of spirituality and spiritual education, another possibility for understanding spiritual life and education has appeared attractive: that of conceiving spiritual formation as a kind of general developmental process. On this view, one might seek to avoid both the Scylla of locally tethered spiritual community and the Charybdis of less tethered moral and aesthetic spiritual attitudes, by connecting spirituality to some notion of universal human development, more or less in the way that such modern cognitive developmentalists as Piaget (1932) and Kohlberg (1984) have tried to understand moral formation. In some such way, one might hope to discern a common or universal developmental structure or course for spiritual development amidst the wide diversity of its more particular and substantial cultural instantiations. Although Christian spirituality might be substantially different from Hindu spirituality—and these different in turn from humanist, Marxist, Freudian, existentialist, or feminist spiritualities—one might still suppose any mature spiritual sensibility to be the outcome of some more common developmental path. In a closely related vein, under the influence of Piaget and Kohlberg, the religious educationalist James Fowler (1981) has written of stages of faith marking a general human capacity to discover or construct meaning and purpose in life, and Goldman (1984) and Elkind (1961) have sought to identify similar developmental processes underlying the emergence of children's concepts of God.

Despite the intuitive appeal of this idea, which probably derives much of its authority from an all-pervasive climate of developmental thinking in latter-day educational theory, any such view clearly invites hard questions. One of these has to do with what the very idea of development might mean as applied to notions such as spirituality, and another relates to the very role of normative discourse and human agency in spiritual discourse.

What Is Spiritual Development the Development Of?

First, as Wilson (1980) once asked of the notion of moral development, what precisely might we hold spiritual development be the development of? Wilson pointed out that the idea of development as commonly applied to human growth is normally used to mark the progress of children or young people with respect to such powers as standing, walking, talking, reasoning, sexual reproduction, and so forth. While much of this concerns human physiological development, we may also suppose that some of it—for example, the development of linguistic capacities—has also a psychological aspect. Notwithstanding this, Wilson argued, it is hard to conceive what it could mean for morality to emerge in any such developmental way—not least in view of the variable normative content or substance of morality. From this viewpoint, moral development seems less like the passive development under causally optimal conditions of such natural or biological processes as learning to walk, talk, or reason, and more like the voluntary rational endorsement under human instruction of a particular evaluative, and very likely contestable, perspective.[1]

Given the inherent ambiguity of notions of spirituality, which we have previously observed to be more ontologically significant in the realms of spiritual than in other normative discourses, it is not at all easy to see what might count as the development of spirituality, at least in the sense in which we speak of physiological or linguistic development. In the case of a confessional, tethered, or thick account of spiritual life, for example, what might count as a uniquely developmental aspect of spirituality that could not be more clearly explained in terms of the rational and emotional capacities needed to grasp and embrace certain articles and practices of faith? On the other hand, in the case of more phenomenological, untethered, subjective, or intersubjective conceptions of spirituality—involving, perhaps, appreciation of nature or a sense of wholeness, or awe and wonder, or solidarity with humanity—do we not take these to be cultivated, nurtured, or acquired dispositions more than innately given traits that develop naturally as humans mature?

Spirituality as a Normative Category

Largely in this spirit, Carr (2002, 2004a) has criticized not just ideas of educational development in general, but those of moral and spiritual development in particular. He has held that attempts by Piaget, Kohlberg, and others to ground moral growth in quasi-natural processes are generally misguided, and that the normativity of so-called moral development goes "all the way down." From this viewpoint, for example, it would be an error to suppose that Kohlberg's account of moral cognitive development and Aristotelian virtue ethics are rival scientific hypotheses awaiting proof or disproof on the basis of empirical evidence. On the contrary, such "theories" reflect rival conceptions of ultimate human good or flourishing that are subject rather to normative evaluation. There is no question that one could educate children to be either effective Kohlbergian moral decision makers or virtuous Aristotelian characters; the question is which of these aims one should want to achieve if one cannot achieve both (which seems precluded by the apparent inconsistencies between these conceptions). Although susceptible to rational discussion and debate, this question is nevertheless a normative issue and is not therefore amenable to scientific or empirical evidential solution. Indeed, the normativity of moral discourse has been clearly recognized by moral philosophers from Aristotle (trans. 1925) to Kant (1967), who both distinguished, albeit in different ways, between theoretical (scientific) and practical (moral) reasoning.[2]

Carr's point regarding educational "developmentalism" in general and moral development in particular applies as much, if not more, to developmental conceptions of spiritual growth (Carr, 2001, 2004b). In this respect, we should be particularly skeptical of any and all attempts to link spiritual development to neurophysiological or brain function. Insofar as any attempt to show that a given brain process pertains to spiritual development by virtue of its association with this or that psychological experience, event, or property, it can hardly avoid assuming (rather than empirically proving) some controversial answer to the key question of what experiences, events, or properties spiritual experiences, events, or properties are. But this, once again, is a normative rather than a scientific question. In general, given the wide diversity of conceptions of human flourishing associated with spirituality and spiritual education, not only is it unclear what might be theoretically gained by conceiving spirituality as a kind of quasi-natural development that might occur independently of systematic educational initiation into some or other perspective on the good life, it is even more unclear how one might approach spiritual education from any such direction.

Indeed, the key problem of conceiving spiritual development as some sort of physiological or brain development is not dissimilar to that which latter-day critics of tethered spirituality have discerned in any tight identification of spiritual with local religious formation: It raises in an acute form the issue of free will versus determinism. Although relations between moral and spiritual discourse and development are vexed, and we have already questioned the viability of reducing the latter entirely to the former, it seems sensible to suppose that spirituality is no less inherently normative than morality and that there can be no progress in either sphere failing some measure of intellectual and practical freedom. It makes little sense to characterize a form of life or state of being as a moral or spiritual goal, or as something to which agents might freely aspire—or even as something for which they might be praised or blamed for aspiring or not aspiring to—unless they can also be meaningfully held to choose whether to aspire. If such "external" forces as society, chemistry, history, or the gods, rather than human beings themselves, are the causes of human action, then it is difficult to see how we might talk meaningfully of moral or spiritual achievement—still less perhaps of moral or spiritual education (see Alexander, 2001, pp. 45–46; Kant, 1785/2002, 1967; Smith, 2002, pp. 65–66; Taylor, 1985). From this viewpoint, the fear of traditional critics of religiously tethered conceptions of spiritual education, that such conceptions inevitably involve indoctrination into closed systems of thought that can seriously inhibit or disable human autonomy, may be simply recapitulated in modern scientific attempts to identify or even re-create the neurophysiological conditions of putative spiritual experience.

Moreover, while it is arguable that empirical scientific approaches to the investigation of spiritual life rest on little more than a category mistake—since spirituality is more properly conceived as a normative quality or dimension of human life and action than as a causally conditioned conscious state, process, or event—it should be recognized that the dangers present in the indoctrinatory potential of some social conditions and climates are very real indeed. Although the capacity for freedom needed for moral or spiritual engagement is a desirable human attribute, not every family, culture, religion, society, or educational system nurtures it in the same measure. There are those, in some homes and societies, who are raised or schooled to be quite oblivious to their right or potential to direct (even under the most adverse circumstances) the course of their lives. Indeed, some families, cultures, religions, and political systems appear to have deliberately set out to deny or suppress any realization of such possibilities of freedom from mental, social, or spiritual bondage.

Such considerations give rise to an important question about what kind of social or cultural conditions most conduce to the free—or at least noncoercive—cultivation of positive moral and spiritual values. But this question in turn brings fresh philosophical troubles. On the one hand, insofar as moral and spiritual values are normative, they would seem to be best cultivated in those conditions of thick or substantial cultural initiation that many would also regard as indoctrinatory. On the other hand, the freedom of choice presupposed to authentic attachment to moral and spiritual values would appear to be best promoted in those contexts of liberal democratic association that many would see as inimical to the required cultural rooting of such values. The purpose of the next section must now be to examine different possibilities of reconciling this apparent tension or contradiction.

SPIRITUAL EDUCATION IN LIBERAL DEMOCRACY

An especially crucial issue raised in the literature of spiritual education concerns its role in both common and private or independent schools in open liberal democratic polities. Views on this question are roughly divided as follows. One perspective focuses on the rights of parents to educate their children according to particular—tethered and untethered—spiritual traditions, and of this or that group to preserve through education its values or way of life across the generations even in plural liberal democratic contexts. A second approach focuses more on the requirement in liberal democracies for citizens of sufficiently robust moral or spiritual identity to be capable of bearing the weight and responsibilities of wider democratic citizenship.

Affiliated Liberalism

Walter Feinberg (1998; Feinberg & McDonough, 2003) captures the first sort of orientation in his notion of affiliated liberalism. According to this position, a broadly Rawlsian political liberalism that advocates minimal political restriction in order to allow a maximum diversity of value orientation, the rights of culturally or religiously affiliated parents and groups to raise their children in particular spiritual traditions ought to be guaranteed—even when these might be in tension with, or pose significant challenges to, such key liberal principles as tolerance of alternative values—provided that such parents or groups do not actively subvert or violate the democratic requirement to accord the same right to those of different or opposed persuasions (see Callan, 1997; Rawls, 1971). However, a tension arises for affiliated liberals between the rights of parents to initiate their children into particular spiritual traditions, or of groups to sustain themselves across the generations, and the rights of any children who may be so educated. On the one hand, if the rights of those on the receiving end of such education are only recognized at the age of legal majority (from 18 to 21), then they may by that point have already been denied the possibility of challenging or refusing the value perspectives to which they have been exposed. On the other hand, if the right of challenge or refusal is extended at an earlier age (adolescence, the age of reason, or the stage at which they become conscious of choice), then they may not have been sufficiently well exposed for full appreciation of the tradition they are challenging or refusing. In this regard, Schweitzer (2004) asserts that any consideration of children's educational rights should precisely take into account the right to be initiated into a substantial normative tradition that addresses life's most basic questions, such as why we find ourselves on this earth and what our mortal or immortal destiny might be.

Liberal Communitarianism

Alexander (2001, 2004) proposes a second general approach to these issues that he labels "liberal communitarianism," which seeks a reconciliation between liberal universalism and local particularism along the lines of Tamir's (1993) "liberal nationalism." According to this view, liberal society requires that citizens with robust visions of the good actively and substantially participate in democratic debates and discussions (Sandel, 1982). On this account, the quest for spiritual perspectives and values is driven or required by the failure of thin political liberalism of the sort advocated in the later work of Rawls (1993) to provide sufficiently substantial conceptions of the good to guide appropriate and significant life choices. As we have seen, Taylor (1989, pp. 25–52) observes that answers to Socrates' famous question about how one should live are to be found in our personal aspirations, in the cultural traditions and ideals into which we have been initiated as members of historical communities, or in terms of those "objective" values that may seem to transcend self and society—such as in traditional concepts of divinity. To be sure, exclusive emphasis on any one of these particular sources of value can lead to the quagmires of subjectivism, relativism, or dogmatism that precisely serve to impede or disable those capacities for human freedom needed for effective liberal democratic association and participation. For this reason, any sensible approach to spirituality and spiritual education should aim to steer a middle course between extremes of local cultural attachment and complete disengagement from any and all rooted values. Arguably, however, some such moral and spiritual middle way is a desideratum of liberal polity, insofar as such society precisely aims to foster the critical autonomy necessary for the demands of democratic citizenship without undermining the conditions for substantial identity formation that any society requires for the making of meaningful life choices.

Liberal communitarianism may be less tolerant of some extreme spiritual perspectives than affiliated liberalism on the grounds that such extremes threaten to undermine the rational conditions for effective liberal moral or spiritual discourse and debate. In this connection, another helpful distinction might be observed between open spiritual orientations that seek to engage positively with such liberal democratic assumptions as the right to choose one's own life path, and closed perspectives that regard such liberalism as a fundamental threat to their way of life, and so seek to insulate their followers from it. This distinction is also closely related to the one that Alexander (in press) has drawn between moral or spiritual ideologies that accept the need for reasonably open or critical moral or ethical reflection, and amoral or unethical ideologies that lean toward more closed or limited views of human destiny and purpose. To the extent that such latter ideologies endeavor to limit critical ethical reflection and impede the possibility of further moral and spiritual evolution or progress, they are clearly in some tension with the key requirements and assumptions of liberal democracy. In this regard, while affiliated liberals often seem more concerned with defending the rights of adherents of such closed perspectives—irrespective of their nonliberal credentials—liberal communitarians are more favorably disposed to politically open than closed spiritual orientations.

That said, one difficulty with the liberal communitarian position concerns the status of competing spiritual conceptions of the good in the common school, since such conceptions are by their very nature subject to controversy and disagreement. McLaughlin (2003) refers to views of this kind (after Gallie, 1955–1956) as "contested." Indeed, subscribing to a fairly extreme thesis of normative incommensurability, MacIntyre (1981, 1988, 1999) has claimed that since there is no neutral rational basis for preferring this vision of the good to that one, the very idea of a common school education in values needs to be called into question. On the other hand, Noddings (1993) seems to hold that the common school should set out to explore the various tensions and oppositions between diverse conceptions of the good with respect to such controversial issues as abortion, eugenics, or the possibility of afterlife, even where this might challenge or undermine the home faith traditions of pupils.

A second difficulty with liberal communitarianism concerns the extent to which the liberal state may require that religiously or culturally separate schools, dedicated to promoting distinct ethical or spiritual ideals, should include in their curriculum ideals, values, and knowledge compatible with more open or liberal democratic modes of association. Liberal democracies may allow their citizens to have "thick" identities,

but can "thickness" of this sort be taken too far from the perspective of open society—for example, when cultures or traditions dominate individuals so completely that they cannot meaningfully be said to be making the autonomous decisions that liberal democracy really requires? This is an especially significant problem in Israel, where the state does indeed fund (along with modern Orthodox, secular Jewish, and Arab sector schools that are more supportive of democratic ideals) ultra-Orthodox Jewish schools that do not see preparation for democratic citizenship as part of their mission. On this question, Alexander (2000) has argued that ultraconservative faith schools should be eligible for liberal democratic state funding only on the condition that they teach the basic skills and values required for effective democratic and economic participation in the wider context of religious and secular Israeli citizenship. In this view, ultra-Orthodox schools that deny the legitimacy of a democratic state in general, or of a democratic Israeli state in particular, should not be funded from the public purse.

SETTINGS OF SPIRITUAL EDUCATION

If democratic association requires citizens of thick spiritual identity to be capable of intelligent moral and political choices, what sorts of educational and other institutions would promote identities of this kind? It takes a village to raise a child, or so goes the adage, but what sort of village? In his now classic essay, "Toward an Ecology of Education," the historian Lawrence Cremin (1976) described the educational interdependence of school, home, and church in 19th-century "small town" America. In addition to these institutions, contemporary neo-Aristotelian and communitarian philosophers might want to emphasize the significance of community. In short, spiritual education might be said to be a function of the complex interplay of school, family, congregation, and community.

Spiritual Education in Schools

Schooling is more often associated with formal and disinterested pedagogical processes than with anything that might be regarded as spiritual nurture. Indeed, in some important respects, contemporary educational concern for the moral and spiritual development of young people may be viewed as a reaction against the overemphasis on academic study and vocational and other training of modern-day schooling. Over the course of the 20th century common schools, particularly in economically developed countries such as the United States and the United Kingdom, have increasingly fought shy of engagement with moral and spiritual aspects of development, regarding these as too controversial or as too close to the religious education banned in American public schools by the constitutional separation of church and state. Arguably, however, it does not follow from such separation that schools cannot be settings for spiritual education. Indeed, synagogues and churches have often traditionally relied on supplemental schooling— Sunday schools, Sabbath schools, Hebrew schools, religious or congregational schools—to assist the initiation of young people into religiously tethered spiritual traditions, and a trend toward faith schools (called in the United States "day schools") has emerged over the past two decades among those concerned to educate children in specific spiritual traditions. What, then, can we now say of the relation between spiritual formation and schooling?

The idea that contemporary schools are too much focused on the rational and vocational goals of modern market economy, and thereby neglect or deny the wider spiritual and other growth of young people, is not new to late 20th-century spiritual awakening. Drawing on Freudian and other psychoanalytic traditions (Freud, 1930/2002), and inspired by a renewed interest in Rousseau's romanticism (Rousseau, 1762/1979), the progressive educators of early 20th-century child-centered education argued that the task of schooling is to protect children from excessively intrusive adult and social interference in order to allow their natural goodness to emerge unscathed (Lane, 1954; Mason, 1974; Neill, 1968). In midcentury a humanistic educational movement emerged drawing on these themes as well as on such existentialist philosophers as Heidegger (1967) and Buber (2000), and such depth psychologists as Rogers (1969) and Fromm (1992). Humanistic educators argued that schools ought to pay greater attention to the

expression of feeling and the cultivation of "being-in-the-world" (Huebner, 1999). One example of such educational humanism can be seen in George Brown's notion of "confluent education," which sought to give as much room in the school curriculum to affective as to cognitive development (Brown, 1971). A second example may be found in Elliot Eisner's (1994) conception of education as a "fine art" concerned to assist youngsters with expressing their inner feelings through a variety of aesthetic and scientific forms of signification and representation. A third instance of educational humanism focused on the inner life of the child may be found in the feminist ethic of care pioneered by Nel Noddings (1984) and Carol Gilligan (1982). This view holds that the prime concern of schools and teachers should be to foster caring classroom structures and climates that may enable young people to realize their potential as morally engaged beings.

Again, the critical and postmodern pedagogies of such educational theorists as Michael Apple (1990), Peter McLaren (2002), and Stanley Aronowitz and Henry Giroux (1993) may represent yet another late 20th-century humanistic perspective conducive to the current spiritual turn. In this view, the task of schooling is to promote student awareness of the inequalities of power, to afford some insight into the false myths of opportunity and merit, and to foster an awareness of the pervasive influence of consumerist values on their lives (Burbules & Berk, 1999). Such writers on spiritual education as Clive Erricker (2004) and Liam Gearon (2001, 2004) take this more radical concern for social justice to be central to the spiritual education of schoolchildren—although Ilan Gur-Zeev (2004) also draws on this same critical tradition to argue that spiritual education can only be a normalizing and therefore necessarily oppressive activity.

In addition to humanistic trends in educational thought not exclusively associated with spiritual pedagogy, increased attention has also been given over the past two decades to the question of spiritual formation in schools (e.g., Lantieri, 2001). Space does not permit a comprehensive survey of this literature, but we may here indicate some of its major themes. First, a number of authors have emphasized the "sacred" nature of childhood and children (Alexander & Ben Peretz, 2001; Brendtro & Brokenleg, 2001; Mullino-Moore, 2004). What they appear to mean by this is that children ought to be regarded as valuable in their own right, not merely as objects in the service of external social or economic goals. Thus, if the spiritual natures of children in schools are proper objects for educational influence or development, educators must respect what is valuable in the experiences that youngsters bring with them to the classroom and work to enhance or transform those experiences in appropriately positive directions.

A second point made by authors writing in this vein is that teachers also bring their spiritual lives to the classroom. For example, Parker Palmer (2001; see also 1997) writes that schools often seem to suppose that in order to operate in a more professionally responsible way teachers need to leave their most cherished beliefs and values at the classroom door. This has the effect of creating divided pedagogical selves who are unable to invest the task of teaching with whole hearts and souls. In this view, touching the spiritual lives of children requires that teachers be allowed, if not encouraged, to engage with their students as total persons: In short, to engage students as spiritual beings, teachers must be in a position to draw on and nurture their own spiritualities.

A third theme to have emerged in the recent literature of spirituality and schooling is that even where spirituality is connected to traditions or texts (and there are, as we have said, many approaches to spiritual formation that are tethered neither to traditions nor to texts), they may require interpretation in ways that take into account not only what they have meant in the past (exegesis) but also what they might mean to students seeking to find present and future meanings and purposes (eisegesis) (see McLaughlin, 2004). This approach reflects the thinking of Martin Buber (Rosenzweig, 1965, pp. 20–22), who has richly explored respects in which *Lehrnstoff,* the learning of subject matter, can be transformed into *Lehre,* teaching that transforms life.

One final theme worth mentioning in this connection is that in contrast to a picture of religion and religious and spiritual education that is obsessed with such somber topics as sin, punishment, and atonement, the cultivation of spirituality in contemporary schooling can and

perhaps ought to be a more joyous affair, celebrating our most cherished ideals of life. Indeed, if spiritual education is understood as the cultivation of moral agency, or the capacity to choose a life worth living in the context of some vision of the good, then one important consequence of spiritual formation is that what persons believe and do should matter to them. However, lives are not totally determined by external forces, and choices can be made that alter the course of lives as well as significantly affecting the lives of others. Even when one chooses a path that turns out to be less productive than one had hoped, the path might be changed or left for another. Still, in all of one's fragility, vulnerability, and fallibility, one may still make a difference. This is indeed a source of profound joy and a genuine reason for hope (Alexander, 2001, pp. 193–198; Noddings, 1984). Again, if spirituality involves emptying my self of any and all hubris concerning my worldly accomplishments, in order to experience the love of God or the inherent wonder of life—perhaps, to discover God's purpose for my life—this too can be a source of profound joy and celebration (Palmer, 1993). At all events, the potential for such joy and celebration should not be excluded from the student's spiritual journey, even when the way may be also difficult and challenging.

Spiritual Education in Families

In addition to formal schooling, families afford another key context for spiritual education, and the preparation of families to assume (or reassume) a role in spiritual education has become an important new topic of spiritual formation. In particular, the education of families to take a more active role in the spiritual formation of their children has become a major preoccupation of North American Jewish education (Wolfson & Bank, 1998). Although much earlier literature focused on successful educational programs in synagogues and schools, Vicky Kelman (1995) has developed an especially interesting theoretical framework for the education of families. Kelman draws on the social psychology of Lev Vygotsky (1980) to argue that the preparation of families to undertake spiritual education requires the creation of cognitive and affective scaffolds on which parents and children may construct an understanding of their spiritual heritage. Another approach to family education follows in the footsteps of Hope Leichter (1979), who has argued that most families have traditions of their own, marked by the names they choose for their children, the rituals they create around bedtime, the ways they commemorate birthdays and anniversaries, and, not least, their individual approaches to celebrating religious, cultural, ethnic, and national occasions. To this extent, families are already agents of this or that form of spiritual education. The task of family education is thus seen as to strengthen and empower such family traditions, and to connect them to other goals of both religiously tethered and untethered spiritual education.

Spiritual Education in Congregations and Communities

What sorts of faith congregations—churches, synagogues, mosques, and temples—may be said to educate in spirituality? Isa Aron (2000) writes of self-renewing congregations of learners and Joseph Reimer (1997) of educating synagogues. These congregations are distinguished by commitment to a common vision of the spiritual life that their members are called on to celebrate. Reimer refers to this process as "a distinctive Torah" (from the Hebrew for *scripture*: a collective narrative that connects a congregation to its past and future by situating them in a present that offers visions of lives well lived. These are examples of communities in possession of a higher good—one that embodies what Phenix (1974) and Huebner (1999) have called transcendence, or the awareness that we can always strive to be better than we are. These also seem to be the contemporary spiritual equivalents of what Cremin has called "the educational ecologies" of 19th-century America.

Still, if Aristotle is correct about the role of the polity in the education of youngsters, it is not only congregations to which we should turn for communal support in the spiritual formation of children (see Curren, 2000). Indeed, in the spiritually untethered world of much of contemporary society, many youngsters are exclusively educated in the public sphere of secular values and may be members of no congregation

whatsoever—at least not in any traditional religious sense. There needs therefore to be a role for the community of those—parents, educational professionals, and policy makers—who have care of local schools, and indeed for the democratic polity as a whole, in the spiritual education of children. Alexander (2001, pp. 92–93) has referred to this larger spiritual educational polity as a "community of communities"—a community to which adherents of competing conceptions of the good may contribute, on the condition that they do not seek to deny the basic moral freedom necessary for untethered as well as tethered spiritual growth.

It is also worth noting that such communities may fall within the realm of what Tamir, following Anderson (1983), has called "imaginary communities":

> The boundaries of such communities and the notion of recognition that flows from it, are products of its members' ability to "think the nation" by power of their imagination. Hence, rather than implying false beliefs or misrepresentations of reality, "imaginary" implies that, unlike the family, the tribe, or the people, the nation exists only when its members consciously conceive themselves as distinct from members of other groups. (Tamir, 1993, p. 8)

Although difficult to define, education in spirituality can be conceived as a normative enterprise that entails the cultivation of human agency and that is, to greater or lesser degrees, confessional or phenomenological; tethered or untethered; subjective, collective, or objective; reducible or irreducible to morality; thick or thin; and cognitive or affective. It is consistent with both affiliated liberal and liberal communitarian accounts of democratic association, and may be carried on in schools, families, congregations, and communities. Given this picture, what are some of the critical issues and opportunities for further philosophical research in this field?

FUTURE PHILOSOPHICAL RESEARCH IN SPIRITUAL EDUCATION

Conceiving spirituality in subjective, collective, or objective terms, we may classify the most pressing contemporary philosophical questions of spiritual education and development according to their concern with inner life, community, and that which transcends self and society.

A recurrent issue in the literature of spiritual education and development concerns the cultivation or nurturing of wholeness. But, what precisely is human wholeness? How is it different, if at all, from other aspects of human flourishing? A variety of different accounts have been offered of this notion, not all of which appear obviously compatible with one another. Some have suggested, for example, that wholeness might be defined as a (perhaps emotional) state of inner peace or tranquillity. Another view, however, appears to associate wholeness more with (perhaps moral) integrity. In this account, wholehearted or integrated persons are those who live the lives they believe (in good conscience) to be best without hesitation or regret. Yet a third view suggests that a whole person is at one with what he or she believes to be ultimately real or truly significant, such as nature or history or tradition or God. From a philosophical viewpoint, there would seem to be a case for further conceptual clarification, analysis, and evaluation of these views—perhaps with the goal of resolving some of the tensions between these important aspects of human wholeness.

Another theme that recurs in the literature of spiritual education and development concerns the degree to which any substantial account of spirituality or spiritual education would have to be "thick" or "tethered." Among other things, this is usually taken to mean that spirituality entails membership in and/or substantial engagement with some sort of normative community. But what kind of community would be needed to allow or enable spirituality to flourish? Ferdinand Tönnies's well-known distinction between gemeinschaft and gesellschaft communities is often quoted in this connection. The former are traditional communities defined by reference to custom, commitment, and tribal ties, whereas the latter are more modern and economically developed societies conceived more in terms of economic rationalism, bureaucratic management, and division of labor (Tönnies, 1887/1957). Durkheim (1894/1984) suggested that the ties that bind premodern communities are mechanical and arbitrary and

determined by the circumstances of birth, whereas modern forms of association tend to be more organic and created as the need for connection arises. Again, Dewey (1960b) wrote of a democratic community as defined by people who share a common life, and Bellah, Madsen, Sullivan, Swidler, and Tipton (1985) of communities of memory and purpose. It seems worth asking which, if any, of these accounts might serve to clarify the question of what sort of community best conduces to spiritual growth. More recently, indeed, feminist, radical, and postmodern educational theorists have questioned whether any such quest for community is necessarily a good thing, on the grounds that "thick" communal values are precisely erosive of individuality and personal autonomy (Noddings, 2002). On this view, it is alleged that the thickness of traditional community values serves to impede spirituality in some deep sense, so that spiritual development is best nurtured in circumstances untethered from traditional faiths and communities. But even if being thick or tethered is considered a necessary condition of developed spirituality, we may still need to ask how thick or tethered a spiritual tradition needs to be: in short, how thick is too thick, given that other values such as autonomy and tolerance are also required for democratic citizenship?

A third theme that emerges from the literature of spiritual education and development concerns the status of any "objective" reality that might be held to transcend self and society. Since Nietzsche's (1883–1892/1933) declaration that God is dead, Western and other intellectuals have grown increasingly reluctant to speak in terms of any such transcendence. Indeed, many phenomenological, subjective, or "thin" accounts of spirituality may be understood as attempts to reclaim the psychological or social benefits of faith by untethering them, as it were, from their traditional theistic trappings. Many questions have been raised about the viability of any such strategy, but it may be wondered whether or to what extent some of the difficulties might well be mitigated by attending to less traditional or tethered accounts of that which lies beyond self and society.[3] For example, Phenix has followed Tillich (1986) in conceiving transcendence as "the experience of limitless going beyond any given state or realization of being" (Phenix, 1974, p. 118). Our sense of time, place, and value is necessarily limited; there is always another time, a different place, or a better way. This is an open or dynamic account of transcendence that evolves and changes. It may to this extent be contrasted with the more closed, static, or dogmatic accounts of divinity of traditionally tethered religion (see Alexander, 2001, pp. 111–112).

In the final analysis, we might agree with spiritual "radicals" in regarding spiritual education as a significantly revolutionary enterprise. The formation of caring, morally and spiritually committed young people who reject selfishness, disregard for others, and injustice also requires the assistance of parents and politicians who are faithful to the moral and spiritual ideals by which they would want their children to live. Is this an unattainable, even utopian, educational vision? Perhaps so, but we might also do well to recall the words of the Talmudic sage: "It is not up to you to complete the work, but neither are you free to desist from it altogether" (Mishnah Avot 2:15).

NOTES

1. We are well aware that there is a large body of literature that conceives morality in cognitive developmental terms, and that many draw on this way of thinking to conceive spirituality. The question we are posing here, however, is whether this way of thinking about spirituality, as well as morality, is not a category mistake of the sort described by Ryle (1966) in his well-regarded critique of mind–body dualism in the philosophy of mind. Ryle opens his essay with the now famous story of the visitor to Oxford University, who after having been shown the colleges, libraries, laboratories, playing fields, dons, and students, responds by praising the beauty of what he has seen but asking now to be shown the university. The visitor, Ryle points out, has failed to understand the concept of what it means to be a university, which is nothing other than the colleges, libraries, laboratories, playing fields, dons, and students that he was shown. So too we are asking whether conceiving spirituality as an innate quality that develops naturally along lines similar to physiological or linguistic growth is not using categories that miss the very point of what spirituality, and morality, could possibly mean.

2. One response to this argument might be to claim that Kohlberg did not offer a particular moral vision, but rather a way of evaluating how moral thinking develops in general irrespective of particular normative content. However, this view has been severely criticized by a number of philosophers (e.g., Habermas, 1990; Phillips and Nicolayev, 1978; see also Modgil & Modgil, 1986), and repudiated by the later Kohlberg himself in embracing the idea of a seventh stage and the so-called just community (see Reed, 1998). Kohlberg's account of moral development fits clearly into the liberal tradition of moral philosophy from Kant to Rawls. It is the Kantian influence that lends meaning to the idea that moral thought can be connected to a universal cognitive structure, which simply has no analogue in Aristotelian thought. As we argue later, however, even Kant distinguished between pure and practical reason in ways that seem to have been lost on Piaget and Kohlberg.

3. This should not be interpreted in any sense as an uncritical endorsement of traditional Western religion, which has suffered historically from a variety of its own difficulties, many associated with abuse of power. These in some sense have set the stage for people to search for some of the qualities we have characterized as spiritual in untethered nonreligious contexts.

REFERENCES

Alexander, H. A. (2000). Education in the Jewish state. *Studies in Philosophy of Education, 19*(5), 489–505.

Alexander, H. A. (2001). *Reclaiming goodness: Education and the spiritual quest.* Notre Dame, IN: University of Notre Dame Press.

Alexander, H. A. (2004). Moral education and liberal democracy: Spirituality, community, and character in open society. *Educational Theory, 53*(4), 367–387.

Alexander, H. A. (in press). Education in ideology. *Journal of Moral Education, 34*(1).

Alexander, H. A., & Ben Peretz, M. (2001). Toward a pedagogy of the sacred. In J. Erricker, C. Ota, & C. Erricker (Eds.), *Spiritual education: Cultural, religious, and social difference—new perspectives for the 21st century* (pp. 34–47). Brighton, UK: Sussex Academic Press.

Alexander, H.A., & McLaughlin, T. H. (2002). Education in religion and spirituality. In

N. Blake, P. Smeyers, R. Smith, & P. Standish (Eds.), *The Blackwell guide to the philosophy of education* (pp. 356–373). Oxford, UK: Blackwell.

Anderson, B. (1983). *Imagined communities.* London: Verso.

Apple, M. W. (1990). *Ideology and curriculum.* New York: Routledge.

Aristotle. (1925). *Nicomachean ethics* (Sir David Ross, Trans.). Oxford, UK: Oxford University Press.

Aron, Isa. (2000). *Becoming a congregation of learners: Learning as a key to revitalizing congregational life.* Woodstock, VT: Jewish Lights Press.

Aronowitz, S., & Giroux, H. (1993). *Postmodern education: Politics, culture, and social criticism.* Minneapolis: University of Minnesota Press.

Bellah, R. N., Madsen, R., Sullivan, W. M., Swidler, A., & Tipton, S. M. (1985). *Habits of the heart: Individualism and commitment in American life.* Berkeley and Los Angeles: University of California Press.

Brendtro, L., & Brokenleg, M. (2001). The circle of courage: Children as sacred beings. In L. Lantieri (Ed.), *Schools with spirit* (pp. 39–52). Boston: Beacon.

Brown, G. I. (1971). *Human teaching for human learning: An introduction to confluent education.* New York: Viking.

Buber, M. (2000). *I and thou.* New York: Scribner.

Buckley, J., & Erricker, J. (2004). Citizenship education in the postmodern moment. In H. A. Alexander (Ed.), *Spirituality and ethics in education: Philosophical, theological, and radical perspectives* (pp. 172–187). Brighton, UK: Sussex Academic Press.

Burbules, N., & Berk, R. (1999). Critical thinking and critical pedagogy. In T. S. Popkewitz & L. Fendler (Eds.), *Critical theories in education* (pp. 45–66). New York: Routledge.

Cajete, G. (1994). *Look to the mountain: An ecology of indigenous education.* Asheville, NC: Kivaki Press.

Callan, E. (1997). *Creating citizens: Political education and liberal democracy.* Oxford, UK: Clarendon Press.

Carr, D. (1994). Towards a distinctive conception of spiritual education. *Oxford Review of Education, 20,* 83–98.

Carr, D. (1996). Rival conceptions of spiritual education. *Journal of Philosophy of Education, 30,* 159–178.

Carr, D. (2001). The "protean" spirit of Jeff Lewis. *Oxford Review of Education, 26,* 151–163.

Carr, D. (2002). Moral education and the perils of developmentalism. *Journal of Moral Education, 31*(1), 5–19.

Carr, D. (2003). Three concepts of spirituality for spiritual education. In D. Carr & J. Haldane (Eds.), *Spirituality, philosophy and education* (pp. 213–225). London: Routledge.

Carr, D. (2004a). Auden's great healers: Blake, Lane and Lawrence on human nature, society and education. In W. Aiken & J. Haldane (Eds.), *Philosophy and its public role* (pp. 53–68). Exeter, UK: Imprint Academic.

Carr, D. (2004b). Moral development: A reply to Richmond and Cummings. *Journal of Moral Education, 33*(2), 207–210.

Cremin, L. (1976). *Public education.* New York: Basic Books.

Curren, R. C. (2000). *Aristotle on the necessity of public education.* Lanham, MD: Rowman and Littlefield.

Dewey, J. (1960a). *A common faith.* New Haven, CT: Yale University Press. (Original work published 1934)

Dewey, J. (1960b). *Democracy and education.* New York: Free Press. (Original work published 1916)

Dewey, J. (1963). *Experience and education.* New York: Collier. (Original work published 1938)

Durkheim, E. (1984). *The division of labor in society* (W. D. Wells, Trans.). New York: Macmillan. (Original work published 1893)

Eisner, E. W. (1994). *Cognition and curriculum reconsidered.* New York: Teachers College Press.

Elkind, D. (1961). The child's conception of his religious development. *Journal of Genetic Psychology, 99,* 209–225.

Erricker, C. (2004). A manifesto for spiritual activism: Time to subvert the branding of education. In H. A. Alexander (Ed.), *Spirituality and ethics in education: Philosophical, theological, and radical perspectives* (pp. 158–171). Brighton, UK: Sussex Academic Press.

Erricker, J., Ota, C., & Erricker, C. (Eds.). (2001). *Spiritual education: Cultural, religious, and social difference—new perspectives for the 21st century.* Brighton, UK: Sussex Academic Press.

Feinberg, W. (1998). *Common schools, uncommon identities: National unity and cultural difference.* New Haven, CT: Yale University Press.

Feinberg, W., & McDonough, K. (2003). Liberalism and the dilemma of public education in multicultural societies. In K. McDonough & W. Feinberg (Eds.), *Citizenship education in liberal democratic societies: Teaching for cosmopolitan values and collective identities* (pp. 1–22). Oxford, UK: Oxford University Press.

Flier, L. (1995). Demystifying mysticism: Finding a developmental relationship between different ways of knowing. *Journal of Transpersonal Psychology, 27*(2), 131–152.

Fowler, J. (1981). *Stages of faith: The psychology of human development and the quest for meaning.* San Francisco: Harper & Row.

Freud, S. (2002). *Civilization and its discontents* (D. McLintock, Trans.). London: Penguin. (Original work published 1930)

Fromm, E. (1992). *The art of being.* New York: Continuum.

Gallie, W. B. (1955–1956). Essentially contested concepts. *Proceedings of the Aristotelian Society, 56,* 167–198.

Geach, P. T. (1977). *The virtues.* Cambridge, UK: Cambridge University Press.

Gearon, L. (2001). The corruption of innocence and the spirituality of dissent: Postcolonial perspectives on spirituality in a world of violence. In J. Erricker, C. Ota, & C. Erricker (Eds.), *Spiritual education: Cultural, religious, and social difference—new perspectives for the 21st century* (pp. 143–155). Brighton, UK: Sussex Academic Press.

Gearon, L. (2004). Hope against devastation: Children's spirituality and human rights. In H. A. Alexander (Ed.), *Spirituality and ethics in education: Philosophical, theological, and radical perspectives* (pp. 188–197). Brighton, UK: Sussex Academic Press.

Gilligan, C. (1982). *In a different voice: Psychological theory and women's development.* Cambridge, MA: Harvard University Press.

Goldman, R. (1984). *Religious thinking from childhood to adolescence.* New York: Seabury Press.

Green, T. (1999). *Voices: The educational formation of conscience.* Notre Dame, IN: University of Notre Dame Press.

Gur-Zeev, I. (2004). Contra spiritual education. In H. A. Alexander (Ed.), *Spirituality and ethics in education: Philosophical, theological, and radical perspectives* (pp. 223–232). Brighton, UK: Sussex Academic Press.

Habermas, J. (1990). *Moral consciousness and communicative action.* Cambridge, MA: MIT Press.

Heidegger, M. (1967). *Being and time* (J. Macquarrie & E. Robinson, Trans.). Oxford, UK: Blackwell.

Huebner, D. (1999). *The lure of the transcendent.* Mahwah, NJ: Erlbaum.

Hursthouse, R. (1999). *On virtue ethics.* Oxford, UK: Oxford University Press.

Jackson, R. (1997). *Religious education: An interpretive approach.* London: Hodder and Stoughton.

Jackson, R. (2004). *Rethinking religious education and plurality.* London: Routledge-Falmer.

Kant, I. (2002). *Groundwork for the metaphysics of morals* (A. Zweig, Trans.). Oxford, UK: Oxford University Press. (Original work published 1785)

Kant, I. (1967). *The critique of practical reasoning and other works on the theory of ethics* (T. K. Abbott, Trans.). London: Longmans.

Kelman, V. (1995). *Family room: Linking families into Jewish learning communities.* Los Angeles: University of Judaism, Whizin Institute for Jewish Family Life.

Kohlberg, L. (1984). *Essays on moral development: Volume 1. The philosophy of moral development.* New York: Harper & Row.

Lane, H. (1954). *Talks to parents and teachers.* London: Allen and Unwin.

Lantieri, L. (Ed.). (2001). *Schools with spirit.* Boston: Beacon.

Leichter, H. J. (1979). *Families and communities as educators.* New York: Teachers College Press.

Lickona, T. (1992). *Educating for character: How our schools can teach respect and responsibility.* New York: Bantam Doubleday Dell.

Lovat, T. (1991). *What is this thing called religious education?* Wentworth Falls, Australia: Social Science Press.

MacIntyre, A. C. (1999). How to seem virtuous without actually being so. In J. M. Halstead and T. H. McLaughlin (Eds.), *Education in morality* (pp. 118–131). London: Routledge.

MacIntyre, A. C. (1981). *After virtue.* Notre Dame, IN: University of Notre Dame Press.

MacIntyre, A. C. (1988). *Whose justice, which rationality?* Notre Dame: University of Notre Dame Press.

Marshak, D. (1997). *The common vision: Parenting and educating for wholeness.* New York: Peter Lang.

Mason, R. E. (1974). *Contemporary educational theory.* New York: McKay.

McLaren, P. (2002). *Life in schools*. Upper Saddle River, NJ: Pearson Education.

McLaughlin, T. H. (1996). The education of the whole child. In R. Best (Ed.), *Education, spirituality, and the whole child* (pp. 9–19). London: Cassell.

McLaughlin, T. H. (2003). Teaching controversial issues in citizenship education. In A. Lockyer, B. Crick, and J. Annette (Eds.), *Education for democratic citizenship: Issues of theory and practice* (pp. 149–160). London: Ashgate.

McLaughlin, T. H. (2004). Nicholas Burbules on Jesus as teacher. In H. A. Alexander (Ed.), *Spirituality and ethics in education: Philosophical, theological, and radical perspectives* (pp. 21–33). Brighton, UK: Sussex Academic Press.

Modgil, S., & Modgil, C. (Eds.). (1986). *Lawrence Kohlberg: Consensus and controversy*. Philadelphia: Falmer.

Mullino-Moore, M. E. (2004). Walking with children toward hope: The long road toward justice and reconciliation. In H. A. Alexander (Ed.), *Spirituality and ethics in education: Philosophical, theological, and radical perspectives* (pp. 83–97). Brighton, UK: Sussex Academic Press.

National Curriculum Council. (1993). *Spiritual and moral education: A discussion paper*. London: Author.

Neill, A. S. (1968). *Summerhill*. Harmondsworth, UK: Penguin Books.

Nichol Smith, D. (1921). *Wordsworth: Poetry and prose*. Oxford, UK: Clarendon Press.

Nietzsche, F. (1933). *Thus spake Zarathustra* (M. Komroff, Ed.). New York: Tudor. (Original work published 1883–1892)

Noddings, N. (1984). *Caring: A feminist approach to ethics*. Berkeley and Los Angeles: University of California Press

Noddings, N. (1993). *Educating for religious belief and unbelief*. New York: Teachers College Press.

Noddings, N. (2002). *Educating moral people: An alternative to character education*. New York: Teachers College Press.

Nozick, R. (1981). *Philosophical explanations*. Cambridge, MA: Belknap Press of Harvard University.

Office for Standards in Education (Ofsted). (1994). *Spiritual, moral, social and cultural development: An Ofsted discussion paper*. London: Author.

Palmer, P. (1993). *To know as we are known: Education as a spiritual journey*. San Francisco: HarperSanFrancisco.

Palmer, P. (1997). *The courage to teach: Exploring the inner landscape of a teacher's life*. San Francisco: Jossey-Bass.

Palmer, P. (2001). Integral life, integral teacher. In L. Lantieri (Ed.), *Schools with spirit* (pp. 1–6). Boston: Beacon.

Phenix, P. (1974). Transcendence and the curriculum. In E. W. Eisner and E. Valance (Eds.), *Conflicting conceptions of curriculum* (pp. 117–132). Berkeley: McCutchan.

Phillips, D. C., & Nicolayev, J. (1978). Kolbergian moral development: A progressing or degenerating research program? *Educational Theory, 28*(4), 286–301.

Piaget, J. (1932). *The moral judgment of the child*. New York: Free Press.

Rawls, J. (1971). *A theory of justice*. Cambridge, MA: Harvard University Press.

Rawls, J. (1993). *Political liberalism*. New York: Columbia University Press.

Reed, D. R. C. (1998). *Following Kohlberg: Liberalism and the practice of democratic community*. Notre Dame, IN: University of Notre Dame Press.

Reimer, J. (1997). *Succeeding a Jewish education: How one synagogue made it work*. Philadelphia: Jewish Publication Society.

Rogers, C. (1969). *The freedom to learn*. Columbus, OH: Merrill.

Rosenak, M. (1984). *Commandments and concerns: Jewish religious education in secular society*. Philadelphia: Jewish Publication Society of America.

Rosenak, M. (1995). *Roads to the palace: Jewish texts and teaching*. Providence, RI: Berghahn.

Rosenzweig, F. (1965). *On Jewish learning*. New York: Schocken.

Rousseau, J.-J. (1979). *Emile; or, On education* (Allan Bloom, Trans.). New York: Basic Books. (Original work published 1762)

Ryle, G. (1966). *The concept of mind*. London: Hutchinson.

Sandel, M. (1982). *Liberalism and the limits of justice*. Cambridge, UK: Cambridge University Press.

Schools Curriculum and Assessment Authority. (1995). *Spiritual and moral development* (Discussion Paper No.3). London: Author.

Schweitzer, F. (2004). Children's right to religion. In H. A. Alexander (Ed.), *Spirituality and ethics in education: Philosophical, theological, and radical perspectives* (pp. 98–104). Brighton, UK: Sussex Academic Press.

Sloan, D. (1993). *Insight-imagination: The emancipation of thought and the modern world.* Westport, CT: Greenwood.

Smith, N. (2002). *Charles Taylor: Meaning, morals, and modernity.* Cambridge, UK: Polity.

Tamir, Y. (1993). *Liberal nationalism.* Princeton, NJ: Princeton University Press.

Taylor, C. (1985). What is human agency? In C. Taylor, *Philosophical papers: Vol. 1. Human Agency and language.* Cambridge, UK: Cambridge University Press.

Taylor, C. (1989). *Sources of the self: The making of modern identity.* Cambridge, MA: Harvard University Press.

Tillich, P. (1986). *The dynamics of faith.* New York: HarperCollins.

Tönnies, F. (1957). *Community and society* (C. P. Loomis, Trans.). New York: Harper & Row. (Original work published 1887)

Vygotsky, L. S. (1980). *Mind in society.* Cambridge, MA: Harvard University Press.

Walzer, M. (1994). *Thick and thin: Moral argument at home and abroad.* Notre Dame, IN: University of Notre Dame Press.

Wilber, K., Engler, J., & Brown, D. (1986). *Transformations of consciousness.* Boston: Shambhala.

Wilf, A. (1996). *Nurturing the spirit in non-sectarian classrooms.* Hollidaysburg, PA: Parent Child Press.

Wilson, J. (1980). Philosophical difficulties and "moral development." In B. Munsey (Ed.), *Moral development, moral education, and Kohlberg* (pp. 214–231). Birmingham, AL: Religious Education Press.

Wolfson, R., & Bank, A. (Eds.). (1998). *First fruits: A Whizin anthology of Jewish family education.* Los Angeles: University of Judaism, Whizin Institute for Jewish Family Life.

7

MEASUREMENT AND RESEARCH DESIGN IN STUDYING SPIRITUAL DEVELOPMENT

RICHARD L. GORSUCH

DONALD WALKER

The purpose of this chapter is to review issues in measurement and research design of particular importance to the psychological analysis of spiritual development. The issues are those classically associated with what is known as "empirical research," which is concerned with finding data consistencies by methods others can replicate. The goal of the research is the development of theory that summarizes the data consistencies in a manner that we find easy to understand and from which we can successfully generalize. Clearly, these are human endeavors that only describe the part of religious development that fits within this paradigm, and the humanities, including theology, have other methods of approaching these topics (Gorsuch, 2002b).

"Qualitative" research is seen as a special case of general research methods. The same problems exist for anyone studying the topics addressed in this handbook, whether or not they use quantitative or qualitative methods. Avoiding quantitative methods—with their associated procedures and problems—hardly means the problems are avoided. Our perspective is that all measurement principles, research designs, and statistical procedures were invented because of the problems found with more informal methods in examining children's development. The exception is the true humanities—such as art, literature, and history—which are concerned with unique events in unique people rather than the psychological search for replicable results (Gorsuch, 2002b).

The research studies that we reference are examples to aid our discussion. Many are taken from the work of my students as we have confronted research problems. Numerous other references on the same and similar topics are not given in this chapter as the need is for examples rather than exhaustive treatment. Those wishing a general reference to the psychology of religion may consult an introductory text in the psychology of religion. Emmons and Paloutzian (2003) give a professional update on the current state of the psychology of religion, Wertlieb (2003) discusses issues of general concept to applied development, and the other chapters of this handbook examine numerous aspects of spiritual development.

The research represented in this volume has another characteristic: It is generally of North American Christianity. Therefore, most of our examples and references are to this culture. The hope is that more studies of other cultures will illuminate when results can and cannot be generalized from this one culture. While the same issues of measurement and research design can be assumed to apply to all cultures unless shown otherwise, the methods for addressing these issues and the best theory are expected to be more culturally dependent.

MEASUREMENT

Unambiguous measures are essential. Being unambiguous begins with identifying the domain of measurement and then proceeds by using high-quality measurement methods. Note that our measurement discussion will usually be in the context of questionnaires. That is primarily because that is what the literature does. But all measures—for example, drawing pictures of God—function under the same principles.

Measurement Domains

The issue of the measurement domain is that of the area of psychology within which occur the constructs being measured. Attachment, for example, is a different domain from cognitive ability. Although it may be useful to evaluate the impact of one domain on the other, that evaluation has unambiguous meaning only if some measures are clearly in the domain of attachment and others are clearly in the domain of cognitive ability.

The confusion that can occur by mixing domains is seen in the history of research on intrinsic and extrinsic religiousness. The original versions of these scales included motivation questions not only about why one might, for example, participate in a religion but also how often one attended church and participated in Bible study (Allport & Ross, 1967). It was no surprise that intrinsicness so defined correlated with religious behavior. For a meaningful correlation with religious behavior to be possible, intrinsicness needs to be measured independently of behavior, that is, as motivation

(Gorsuch, 1997). Only by having some measures that are in the motivation domain and some in the behavior domain can we explore the relationships of spiritual motivation to behavior. The major domains are as follows.

Belief. The strength of a belief is the adult's or child's judgment as to the likelihood that a statement of fact is true about conditions external to the person. The reason for considering beliefs as a separate domain is that cognitions have particular methods by which they are learned. Indeed, it appears that much of contemporary cognitive psychology and learning theory consists of explorations of how beliefs develop and so should be fertile ground for developing theories of beliefs. How beliefs interrelate to form schemas of importance to spirituality is an important and undeveloped area for the understanding of spiritual development.

The investigation of beliefs in religious and spiritual development among children and adolescents has been fairly extensive. Investigators have found, for example, that youth reporting a greater belief in God also report having higher self-esteem and more negative attitudes toward drug use (Ball, Armistead, & Austin, 2003; Mullen & Francis, 1995).

Motivation. Motivation is that which a person would do if he or she were capable of and permitted to do it. For example, the I/E-R scales measuring Intrinsic, Extrinsic-Social, and Extrinsic-Personal are motivation scales (Gorsuch, 1997); Intrinsic is being motivated to be spiritual for the sake of being spiritual, whereas Extrinsic-Social and Extrinsic-Personal find spirituality to be important because it builds interpersonal relationships or answers a personal need.

The classical manner of measuring motivation in the area of spirituality is that of attitudes. *Attitude* refers to how much a person likes it. Attitudes are based in emotions and develop through classical conditioning (and generalization through schemas). A goal has often been to identify and document the attitudes of children and youth with respect to Christianity.

Moral values are a category of motivation in which we ask what should be the case or whether we have a moral obligation, regardless of

Table 7.1 Correlations From Two Methods of Scoring the Single-Pair Measures of Religiousness

	Scoring Methods			
	Separate Scores		Combined Scores	
	Imp.	Att.	Imp. + Att.	Imp. − Att.
Religious Single Items				
Importance ratings[a]	1.00	.47	.86	.85
Attendance[b]	.47	1.00	.54	−.49
Religious Combined Scores				
Importance + Attendance	.86	.54	1.00	.04
Importance − Attendance	.85	−.49	.04	1.00
Other Measures				
Developmental assets	.37	.33	.41	.05
Thriving	.28	.24	.30	.05
Smoking	−.22	−.21	−.25	−.02
Alcohol	−.22	−.22	−.26	−.01
Drug use	−.20	−.17	−.22	−.04
Delinquency	−.20	−.15	−.20	−.05
Harm to others	−.15	−.10	−.15	−.05

SOURCE: Computed from Wagener et al. (2003).

NOTES: $N = 1,500$; r of 0.00 has standard error of .03. [a]"How important is being religious or spiritual in your life?" (rated from 1 to 5). Abbreviated as Imp. [b]"How often do you attend programs, groups, or services at a church, synagogue, mosque or other religious or spiritual place?" (rated from 1 to 5). Abbreviated as Att.

whether we like it (Gorsuch, 1986). The theories of value development and change are vague. The principal notion is that of cognitive consistency with authority and teaching as other methods of value development (Oordt, 1991).

Studies with adults have found that values add to prediction over and above attitudes (Gorsuch & Ortberg, 1983) and that values and affect are changed independently of each other (Ortberg, Gorsuch, & Kim, 2001). Studies among adolescents have typically sought to identify ways in which religious values are transmitted and internalized.

Behavior. Behavior is a function of the situation and what a person brings to the situation—including beliefs, attitudes, values, and habits. How and why individual domains relate to behavior is a question for research.

Church attendance and self-reported prayer or Bible study have been frequent measures of behavior in studies of religion and spirituality among children and adolescents. For example, research has found that higher rates of church attendance correlate with lower rates of drug

and alcohol use among adolescents (Gorsuch, 1995; Mason & Windle, 2002; see also Table 7.1). Coping behaviors are another category of behavior that Pargament (1996) has shown to be an important area of spirituality. Kneezel and Emmons (chapter 19, this volume) suggest that measures of behavior may be increasingly useful as age decreases.

Relationships Among the Domains. The importance of recognizing the domains and then interrelating them lies in the increase in theory development that is then possible. One no longer mixes apples and oranges.

With measures in several relevant domains, it is possible to use a multivariate model to bring them together to understand a particular phenomenon. We have done so on several occasions. Wong-McDonald (Wong-McDonald & Gorsuch, 2004) measured beliefs, motivations (Intrinsic and Extrinsic), and coping styles. These measures were then related to Existential Well-Being. The multiple correlation was as high as the reliabilities allow, suggesting that we now know how each domain relates to

Existential Well-Being and have covered almost all of the psychological bases of Existential Well-Being. Developmental studies on each domain could now enable us to design interventions to maximize Existential Well-Being.

Experiences. Crawford, Wright, and Masten (chapter 25, this volume) point to the sequence of religious ceremonies, experiences, and rites of passage as essential areas to be examined to understand spiritual development. Experiences have multiple impacts. They will generally affect several of the aforementioned domains. This suggests that investigations of the impact of spiritual experiences will be most profitable if they explicitly measure the more relevant of these domains.

Stages

Stages have been a useful method to understand development, particularly cognitive development. The stages may be within one area, as are Piaget's cognitive stages, or they may be broader and cover multiple domains. They may have subaspects within the cognitive system that are achieved at different times and, perhaps, by subprocesses (Feldman, 2003).

Fowler and Dell (chapter 3, this volume) clearly state that a stage includes beliefs, values, and behavioral commitments thoughtfully interrelated. For Fowler, the individuative-reflective faith has two noticeable indicators. The first, thinking critically about the previous stage, synthetic-conventional, is clearly a cognitive component. The second is self-identity and worth based on one's worldview, which anchors one's sense of being. While the second may contain some cognitive aspects, it is much broader and implies a set of beliefs integrated into a coherent schema incorporating a set of cognitively consistent values. The complexity of the stages compared to the simplicity of the measures currently existing for beliefs indicates how much remains to be done to link these paradigms.

It is possible to develop a set of scales to measure several aspects of a stage. However, one must be careful how that is done. For example, scales for Kohlberg's stages using a unidimensional technique give just one dimension, commitment to justice. While that was

mathematically the most central distinction, it reduced the complex stages to a single facet. The result leaves out other aspects of the stage, particularly the interpersonal ones. (A multivariate analysis of pilot data on Kohlberg's stages clearly shows an additional dimension of interpersonal concern.) It also fails to measure the concept of a stage being an integration of the several domains, since the integration can best be shown if the several domains are separately studied. Measuring the several domains also would allow more differentiated work on how each domain relates to and shows stage transition.

Measuring several domains in a stage would also allow for distinguishing the similarities and differences between stage theories. Each aspect could be investigated to see if one or more of them are linear and progressive (Scarlett, chapter 2, this volume). Perhaps some domains are part of soft stages and others of hard stages (Hay, Reich, & Utsch, chapter 4, this volume).

Stages as a Logical Progression. As Hay and colleagues suggest, some aspects of stages may be "hard" in the sense of being logic driven. In that case, the stages are like arithmetic and algebra. It is necessary to know arithmetic before one can learn algebra. The resulting characteristic is that anyone who can do algebra will also be able to do arithmetic; however, some of those who can do arithmetic will not be able to do algebra. Hence those at a higher stage will be able to understand the thinking of those at a lower stage, but not vice versa. This is the critical test for whether stages are logical stages.

Venable and Gorsuch (1999) hypothesized that Extrinsic and Intrinsic are stages of understanding of the Christian faith. To test whether they showed stage sequencing, adolescents read a rationale for spiritual activity. Next they wrote out what they thought the reasoning was. As predicted, those who could reproduce the intrinsic reasoning could generally reproduce the extrinsic reasoning. However, only part of those who could reproduce the extrinsic reasoning could reproduce the intrinsic reasoning. It appears that extrinsic commitment is logically prior to intrinsic commitment.

Cognitive Development as a Necessary Prerequisite to Stages. Surprisingly, the cognitive development hypothesis has centered only on Piaget-type stages, although its importance varies as a function of the purpose of the study (Ratcliff & Nye, chapter 33, this volume) and the range of abilities among the children or youth. Perhaps the reason little work has been done with the universally important general ability is because general ability is habitually defined as IQ. IQ is a normed score, adjusted so that each age has a mean of 100. Therefore it is not a measure of what a child can do but only a measure of how he or she functions relative to his or her age cohort.

To relate ability measures to religious cognitive development can be simply done by using the raw scores from the scales rather than the normed scores. This is relevant to Goldman and Fowler stages, or it may be the hypotheses of interest concerning brain functions or critical learning periods (Newberg & Newberg, chapter 13, this volume).

Given either cognitive stage or cognitive ability, the basic theory of the relationship to religious cognitive capabilities involves the same hypothesis: General cognitive development is a prerequisite for religious cognitive development; that is, a minimum level of cognitive development is required before a level of religious cognitive development can be obtained. Once that level of general development has been reached, then appropriate experience with religious materials can increase the religious cognitive development. Consider a simple example: General principles and applications of Bible knowledge require formal operations. Formal operations are then a necessary condition for this task. If the child is only at a concrete stage of cognitive development, there is no possibility of his or her showing this level of Bible application. Formal operations are not "sufficient," however, to cause this level of usage, for experience with the Bible per se is also needed. Limited cognitive capability means limited religious cognitive development, but if sufficient cognitive development is found, then we look to other variables—such as religious modeling and training—to predict more complex religious thinking. Note that special analyses—beyond correlations—are required to test these hypotheses as they require tests of interactions and standard errors conditional upon age (Gorsuch, in press).

Theoretical Measurement Issues

Aggregation. Aggregation is the degree to which a scale measures a broad area. The basic principle is that broadly aggregated independent variables correlate well with broadly aggregated dependent variables, and narrowly aggregated independent variables correlate well with narrowly aggregated dependent variables (Fishbein & Ajzen, 1974; Rushton, Brainerd, & Presley, 1983). The correlations between similarly aggregated variables range up to .7, a very strong effect, whereas the correlations between dissimilarly aggregated variables range up to .3, a much smaller effect.

Hill and Pargament (2003) note that while the global measures of spirituality are related to health, measures more specific to health issues, such as religious coping in the area of health, are more powerfully related. This is because global measures are much more aggregated than health measures. If you wish sensitive analyses and high correlations, then match on aggregation.

An example of the principle is given in Fishbein and Ajzen (1974). They had an aggregated, global scale of religiousness as the independent variable that measured global religiousness. They also had 100 questions about 100 religious behaviors. Separately, each of the behaviors is minimally aggregated, but adding them together yields a globally aggregated measure of religious behavior. The aggregated religiousness measure correlated in the .2 to .3 range with each separate behavior, but correlated .7 with the globally aggregated sum of the 100 religious behaviors.

Coping measures are good illustrations of the aggregation principle. In their classical form (Pargament, 1996), religious coping measures are broadly aggregated. They measure coping over a long time across all problems in all settings. But if the project is concerned with particular coping, such as during a child's illness, then a state coping measure needs to be given with instructions such as "while you have been ill." State coping measure examples are given in Schaefer and Gorsuch (1993).

An example of how changing the aggregation in the scoring may affect correlations can be based on Wagener, Furrow, King, Leffert, and Benson (2003) and also shows how to combine two scores to give a more aggregated score. They collected a measure of the importance of religion/spirituality and a measure of church attendance and then related both to positive and negative outcomes (columns 1 and 2, Table 7.1). Adding the scores for importance and attendance together gives a more aggregated measure (column 3), which gives higher correlations. (Also, attendance was subtracted from importance; its correlation in column 4 checks whether the two scales have different relationships to the other variables. They do not, showing that the aggregation is the best measure.)

Changes in Meaning With Age-Associated Variables. Human development has many age-conditional variables. An age-conditional variable is one for which the meaning is conditional upon age and the relationship to other variables is different from one age to another. Of course, age itself is a "stand-in" for a more specific variable—such as the changes in how adults treat a child due to how grown up he or she appears to be—but the fact is that we often first identify it as an interaction with age.

Participating in religious activities is a variable that is conditional upon age. For the new baby, a major predictor may be whether the parents believe that the baby may be exposed to a disease by being taken to church. For the child, a major predictor may be whether the family goes to church. For an older adolescent, the major factor in church attendance may be the youth's religious commitment. Church attendance has a different meaning at different ages and so interacts with or is conditional upon age. Lippman and Keith (chapter 8, this volume) note that 8th graders attend church more than do 12th graders. Perhaps partialing out parent's attendance or testing the interaction of parent's attendance and youth's attendance would be fruitful in such studies.

Technical Measurement Issues

Language. Language is an issue in two situations, both of which can be examined empirically. The first situation is when a translation is needed. In our experience, objectively oriented items, such as "How often do you go to worship services?" translate easily, but some, such as

emotions, are difficult to translate. Of course, it is best to avoid translation if possible, for if the results differ from one language group to another it is difficult to interpret the results. Miller and Kelley (chapter 29, this volume) report that Kohlberg stages replicated in some ways but not in others. When the nonreplication is at higher levels of abstraction, an alternative hypothesis is that the more abstract ideas did not translate well. Good translation is best done by two native speakers who clearly understand all the levels of the hypothesized stages or the meaning of the items on the scale, a level of expertise found in few translators.

If translation is not involved, however, linguistic differences are less viable as alternative explanations. For example, when Gorsuch and Barnes's study in Belize (1973) reported that no clear Kohlberg Stage 3 thinking was observed and that the Black Carib children rejected the individualistic approach of Western cultures, that result is less ambiguous because English is the children's primary language. It can therefore be considered a major critique of the generality of Kohlberg stages.

Unless scales are comprehended by all the children in a study, errors are introduced. Hill and Pargament (2003) state that self-report "measures may require reading and comprehension levels beyond the ability of children, poorly educated adults, and some clinical populations." The same can be said of any instructions that are given or questions asked in an interview: If they are too complex, they will be comprehended by only part of the participants. Hart (chapter 12, this volume) notes that some investigators use adult scales because they assume that true spirituality or a high stage of spiritual development requires abstract thinking, but use of adult language with nonadults is not appropriate.

Comprehensibility of the scale's items is the second situation in developmental research for which language is important. For example, Gorsuch and Venable (1983) found that the items for the I/E-R scale gave reliable results for children who scored 3 or better on the Information Inventory (items such as, "What is the opposite of south?"). The inventory can be used to drop participants from a study who are not able to understand the scales. Comprehensibility is approximated by formulas for "readability," using the number of syllables per word and the number of words per sentence to give a "grade level." It is now possible to improve on "readability" by moving to comprehensibility (Gorsuch, Walker, Lewis, & Cheung, 2005).

Scales given to children should have items that each have appropriate comprehensibility levels. To be comprehensible means that the children can understand each and every item on the scale. Some religious development scales are and some are not comprehensible (Gorsuch et al., 2005). For example, the ASC4B has items that are too difficult for elementary school children and even many in middle schools. Yet Francis, Pearson, and Stubbs (1985) investigated the relationship of personality and religion among children ages 9 to 16 with mean IQs of 78. The observed correlations were generally less than .2, and there was a small correlation of both IQ and age with the religion scale. Before deciding that these small correlations are correct, an alternative hypothesis is that the results were low because many children could not understand some items. It would have been interesting to see how much the results might have changed if those with non-normed intelligence scores too low to assure they could understand the materials had been dropped.

Developing Possible New Scales. The major question in developing a new scale is whether one should be developed at all. Two decades ago it was suggested that we needed more research with scales already in existence rather than new scales (Gorsuch, 1984). Since then more new scales have appeared and are readily accessed (Hill & Hood, 1999). While these scales have generally been developed with college students— including most in the section on "religious development"—others are age universal (Gorsuch et al., 2005). Age-universal scales are preferable because you can, at some point in your research program, compare parents and children directly on the same scale. For example, when the same items and response format are used, the religious values of children can be directly compared to those of their parents.

When a new scale is first developed, it is important to include it in research with existing scales to determine overlap. The correlations of the new scale with the old scales indicate the overlap between them; correlations with typical dependent variables show whether the new scale may be useful. The increase in prediction from adding the new scales is evaluated by a sequential (also called preplanned stepwise or hierarchical) regression analysis to determine whether the new scales add new predictive power with the old scales partialed out. For example, we hypothesized that religious coping involved not only the original dimensions of Self Directive, Deferring to God, and Collaborating with God (Pargament, 1996) but also a new dimension, Surrender to God. Wong-McDonald developed a scale and used it with the original scales, finding that Surrender did significantly increase the prediction for her dependent variables (Wong-McDonald & Gorsuch, 2000).

As there are a number of high-quality scales in existence, a new scale needs to be well done to be more useful than those already available. If you do not have the resources to carry out a research program that examines the overlap with existing scales and proves a new scale adds more than current scales, select scales from the many already available.

Design and Analysis

Cross-Sectional Designs

Age can be a variable in a cross-sectional design but only under certain conditions. First, the scales or interviews must be comprehensible for the entire age range. Second, the analysis must use age and age squared to test for curvilinear relationships. Third, the analyses need to take into account what the underlying causative agent might be in evaluating age differences. Age itself, to a psychologist, causes nothing. It is instead the change in brain functions, cognitive capabilities, or social relationships (Newberg & Newberg, chapter 13, this volume) associated with age that are the variables of interest. Age as a variable is only used as a "stand-in" until we are able to measure the independent variable directly. And we will know we have done so when we enter the causative variables first in a sequential analysis, and then enter age last and age is no longer significant. Age is only entered first when we use it as a stand-in for all age-related changes.

The analyses must also recognize the possibility of the factors being necessary but not sufficient, similar to our earlier discussion with regard to the impact of cognitive capabilities on stages. Newberg and Newberg (chapter 13, this volume) suggest that a variable such as poor infant care during a critical period may be preventive of spiritual development. In that case, interactions with age and age-conditional standard errors need to be checked (Gorsuch, in press).

Cross-sectional designs may attempt to achieve evidence on age changes by retrospective report. Retrospective report may help to identify age changes but only under one condition: The questions must be about completely objective events that others will have remarked on and so kept memories fresh. For example, studies that ask whether the person attended church during childhood (Gorsuch, 1995) have a possibility of veracity so long as detail is not expected. This is because attending church is a clearly objective event that is normally associated with a host of other childhood events. Religious rituals (e.g., Mattis, Ahluwalia, Cowie, & Kirkland-Harris, chapter 20, this volume) are also likely to be accurately recalled because they are major, communal events. Asking people how important spirituality was to them as children is more questionable.

Path analysis and structural equation modeling (SEM) are popular methods for checking for evidence that might be interpreted casually. These methods have promise but also have major problems. A major problem well known among those running such analyses is that it is the rare SEM that works the first time. If it runs at all with reasonable results (and many fail to do so for unknown reasons), it is almost always not a good fit. So most analyses depart from the initial complete set of hypothesized relationships and are adjusted to fit the data. Unfortunately, while that makes the results look significant, the changes are just as likely to be away from the population values as toward them. So a proper SEM would need to be cross-validated to be acceptable. That means one needs twice the sample size as that originally planned: One half of the sample is used to cut and fit the SEM to the data, and the other half is used to test for significance without the capitalization on chance that occurs in any sample to which SEM is cut and fit.

Path analysis and SEM have been suggested to aid in identifying casual relationships. They do, but no more so than any other statistic. All statistics need to be included in the notion that "correlation does not mean causation": No statistic can identify causation, whether it uses correlations, ANOVA, path analysis, or SEM. Causation is in the research design and the philosophy of science (Gorsuch, 2002a), not the statistics. In cross-sectional designs with developmental research, the results still only show age differences that may be due to age progression or due to cultural cohort shifts.

Longitudinal Designs

In causation analysis, time is an important variable. A cause, by definition, precedes the effect. But cross-sectional data examine differences associated with, for example, age differences and not with age changes. For this reason, it is often desirable to replace cross-sectional designs with longitudinal designs (Kneezel & Emmons, chapter 19, this volume).

Longitudinal designs have been effectively used and recommended. Some results of longitudinal studies suggest that being religious in preadolesence predicts participation in community services 2 years later (Donnelly et al., chapter 17, this volume), and that anaclitic depression in childhood predicts poorer adult spirituality (Miller & Kelley, chapter 29, this volume). Other longitudinal studies have also given interesting results for attachment (Granqvist & Dickie, chapter 14, this volume). Fowler and Dell (chapter 3, this volume) call for longitudinal data to properly study faith development stages.

Note that in the preceding paragraph the results from longitudinal studies were phrased as "predicts," and not as "causes," "reduces," "increases," or "affects." "Predicts" is all that can be concluded from the statistics of any longitudinal study. "Predicts" is the same as "is associated with" but adds the information that the design allows estimating from one time period to a later one. While this is needed for causation, it is not conclusive. Perhaps both the predictor and the outcome are influenced by another variable.

There are many problems with longitudinal designs, including:

- Very complex analyses. Velicer and Fava (2003) and McArdle and Nesselroade (2003) are good introductions to procedures available.
- Selective retention. In Tamminen (1991, 1994), the sample shrank from 1,588 on the first occasion to 277 two years later and 60 for the third testing.
- Interactions with measurement. Asking children about their families and spirituality may lead them to relate differently and so produce results in and of itself.
- Out-of-date results. A short longitudinal study might collect data for 10 years, and then take 5 more years to analyze and publish the data, with still more time needed for others to learn from it. But by that time there are cultural changes that may call into question the generalizability of the results to a new cohort.

The problems with longitudinal studies are known, and attempts have been made to counter them. Tamminen (1991, 1994) added new classmates and other children to the study to check on such effects. Dixon and Cohen (2003) consider them (from a cognitive developmental perspective). An example of a larger, more detailed approach to these problems is the Seattle Longitudinal Study of cognitive abilities (Shaie, 1996), which serves as an example both of the problems and of how, with sufficient resources, some of the problems can be addressed.

Overlapping Cohort Design: Combining Cross-Sectional and Longitudinal Designs

A simple design that combines the cross-sectional with the longitudinal, while reducing the limitations of each, and completes data collection in 1 year is the Overlapping Cohort Design. Assume that the desire is, for illustration's sake, to cover the years from 10 to 15. For a cross-sectional design, a set of 10- to 15-year-olds is measured at Occasion 1. For a longitudinal study, 10- to 15-year-olds are measured from the 1st year, Occasion 1, to the last year, Occasion 10. For the Overlapping Cohort Design, this data collection would be the first wave of measurement. Then a second wave of measures is taken at the end of a year, Occasion 2, when the 10-year-olds are now 11, the 11-year-olds are

now 12, and so on. The study is longitudinal from Occasion 1 to 2 but then uses cohorts that overlap in age. Jessor, Graves, Hanson, and Jessor (1968) provide an example of a similar design, as does Kim (2000).

Note that the analysis of the Overlapping Cohort Design tells more than a cross-sectional design and more than a longitudinal design. Its advantages are that:

- Cross-sectional analyses can be computed, such as age differences.
- Longitudinal age changes can be computed.
- Age changes can be compared with age differences, which provides useful information on how to relate longitudinal with cross-sectional studies in the literature.
- The attrition of participants is minimal because tracking is only needed for 1 year.
- The data are collected within 1 year and so are publishable while still culturally relevant.

What longitudinal, cross-sectional, and Overlapping Cohort designs cannot do is identify causation. They provide information on it, with the longitudinal and Overlapping Cohort designs adding a time perspective necessary to imply causation. (A prime reason causation cannot be proved in these designs is because of philosophical problems with the nature of causation; Gorsuch, 2002a.)

Intervention Designs

Causation is only clear in intervention studies (experimental or quasi experimental). When we can show that a program alters the religious development of children, we have shown causation.

One response to the suggestion that more experimental studies be done on spiritual development is that "it would be unethical." We would need volunteers to be in a study whose spiritual development might be advanced. That is so, but the implication that these would be hard to find is wrong. Every church—including its summer camps for children and youth—is about the business of doing exactly that: advancing spiritual development. Leaders are often delighted to have professional help in testing and improving those programs.

In addition to being concerned with needing permissions, another objection to experimental studies is that the control group would not receive the intervention. So everyone wants to be in the study's intervention group.

An experimental design is available that counters these problems, the Extended Intervention Design. The design provides for all children receiving the intervention, but just at different times. All children are tested at the start of the experiment, Occasion 1. Then children's groups are randomly assigned (or stratified randomly) to Condition A or Condition B. Those groups in Condition A receive the intervention and then are tested a second time, Occasion 2. Those in Condition B are given a control intervention and then tested at the second time, Occasion 2. So far, this is, of course, the classical randomly assigned two-occasion (pre- and post-test) design. The difference is what happens next. The study is extended by giving the intervention to those in Condition B. Then both A and B are tested a third time, Occasion 3.

The advantages of the Extended Intervention Design are several. It answers the ethical question of the control group not receiving the intervention because all receive the intervention. It also allows more powerful testing. The first two occasions are tested in the classical group by occasion ANOVA. Then the B group is tested with themselves as their own control; if the hypothesis is true, there should be greater change from Occasion 2 to Occasion 3 than from Occasion 1 to Occasion 2. Still another advantage is from analyzing changes in A from Occasion 2 to Occasion 3, which asks whether the effect maintains itself or fades with time.

Still another advantage of the Extended Intervention Design occurs when an intervention does more harm than good. The fact that we must run experiments comes from the fact that we are unsure of the possible effects. While we would not do the experiment if we thought it would be harmful, sometimes that is what happens. So in the extended design, an analysis of the first two occasions is immediately computed, and if A shows harm, two actions are taken. First, B is not exposed to the harmful intervention. Second, the time that would have been devoted to running the intervention with B is now devoted to offsetting the damage to A.

CONCLUDING COMMENTS

Spirituality is a topic on which everyone is an expert. However, each person's expertise is a function of a particular history of experience with spirituality traditions. We would not expect a fundamentalist Christian to approach spirituality in the same manner as a universalist. What methodological problems and possibilities arise from this situation? A problem arises when a scholar in one area goes beyond that area's bounds. The classical distinction of science being centered on replicable data consistencies and spirituality being centered on worldviews and values is useful here. Spiritualities cannot assume or reject the findings of science, and science cannot draw conclusions about revelation and what should be (Gorsuch, 2002a, 2002b). While such a brief statement regarding such a complex topic is quite limited, it does point to the need for clarity about what psychology can and cannot do.

An illustration of the need for clear boundaries is seen in the use of terms with clear value connotations. Consider the use of the term *mature* for spirituality. The term itself implies that it is the highest and best possible state of spirituality. But how can psychology define the "highest and best" spirituality? Different spiritual traditions will have different answers to this question.

From a science perspective, psychology itself can only define *mature* in terms of growth curves across age. Of course, mature is not identified as the oldest age, for decline occurs as a person grows older. For example, the intellectually mature person is the person who has reached the height of his or her cognitive development, and height can be defined as the highest point on a graph plotting ability across age. But there is no such graph for spirituality.

From a spirituality perspective, the elements a psychologist considers part of maturity may be irrelevant or misleading. For example, psychologists commonly view the ability to process complex materials to be a function of maturity, and so the spiritually mature person is the one who is able to deal with spirituality in a cognitively complex manner. But spiritualities can reject cognitive capabilities as a criterion, preferring others such as belief or compassionate service as being the highest level of spirituality (a level attainable by those developmentally challenged children and youth who will continue to have difficulties with cognitive complexity).

The problem of defining spiritual maturity is a reminder that a dialogue is needed between psychology and spirituality to enable each to do its best work. Methodologically, issues such as spiritual maturity and how it is reached need to be enriched by that dialogue.

REFERENCES

Allport, G. W., & Ross, J. M. (1967). Personal religious orientation and prejudice. *Journal of Personality and Social Psychology, 5,* 432–443.

Ball, J., Armistead, L., & Austin, B. (2003). The relationship between religiosity and adjustment among African-American, female, urban adolescents. *Journal of Adolescence, 26*(4), 431–446.

Dixon, R. A., & Cohen, A. (2003). Cognitive development in adulthood. In R. M. Lerner, M. A. Easterbrooks, & J. Mistry (Eds.), *Handbook of psychology: Vol. 6. Developmental psychology* (pp. 443–461). Hoboken, NJ: Wiley.

Emmons, R. A., & Paloutzian, R. F. (2003). Psychology of religion. In S. T. Fiske, D. Schacter, & C. Zahn-Waxler (Eds.), *Annual Review of Psychology, 55,* 377–402.

Feldman, D. H. (2003). Cognitive development in childhood. In R. M. Lerner, M. A. Easterbrooks, & J. Mistry (Eds.), *Handbook of psychology: Vol. 6. Developmental psychology* (pp. 195–210). Hoboken, NJ: Wiley.

Fishbein, M., & Ajzen, I. (1974). Attitudes toward objects as predictors of single and multiple behavioral criteria. *Psychological Review, 81,* 59–74.

Francis, L., Pearson, P., & Stubbs, M. (1985). Personality and religion among low ability children in residential special schools. *British Journal of Mental Subnormality, 31,* 41–45.

Gorsuch, R. (1984). Measurement: The boon and bane of investigating religion. *American Psychologist, 39*(3), 228–236.

Gorsuch, R. (1986). Measuring attitudes, interests, sentiments, and values. In R. Johnson & R. B. Cattell (Eds.), *Functional psychological testing* (pp. 316–333). New York: Brunner/Mazel.

Gorsuch, R. (1995). Religious aspects of substance abuse and recovery. *Journal of Social Issues, 51*(2), 65–83.

Gorsuch, R. (1997). Toward motivational theories of intrinsic religious commitment. In B. Spilka & D. N. McIntosh (Eds.), *The psychology of religion: Theoretical approaches.* Boulder, CO: Westview.

Gorsuch, R. (2002a). *Integrating psychology and spirituality?* Westport, CT: Praeger.

Gorsuch, R. L. (2002b). The pyramids of sciences and of humanities. *American Behavioral Scientist, 45,* 1822–1838.

Gorsuch, R. (in press). Continuous parameter estimation model: Expanding the standard statistical paradigm. *Thailand Journal of Statistics.*

Gorsuch, R. L., & Barnes, M. L. (1973). Stages of ethical reasoning and moral norms of Carib youths. *Journal of Cross-Cultural Psychology, 4,* 283–301.

Gorsuch, R. L., & Ortberg, J., Jr. (1983). Moral obligations and attitudes: Their relationship to behavioral intentions. *Journal of Personality and Social Psychology, 44*(5), 1025–1028.

Gorsuch, R. L., & Venable, G. D. (1983). Development of an "age universal" I-E scale. *Journal for the Scientific Study of Religion, 22*(2), 181–187.

Gorsuch, R., Walker, D., Lewis, H., & Cheung, T. (2005). *Measurement of religion and spirituality among youth: A review.* Presented at the American Psychological Association Annual Meeting, Washington, DC.

Hill, P. C., & Hood, R. W. (1999). *Measures of religiosity.* Birmingham, AL: Religious Education Press.

Hill, P. C., & Pargament, K. I. (2003). Advances in the conceptualization and measurement of religion and spirituality: Implications for physical and mental health research. *American Psychologist, 58,* 64–74.

Jessor, R., Graves, T. D., Hanson, R. C., & Jessor, S. L. (1968). *Society, personality and deviant behavior: A study of a tri-ethnic community.* New York: Holt, Rinehart and Winston.

Kim, G. (2000). *A comparative analysis of value socialization within the school setting.* Unpublished doctoral dissertation, Fuller Theological Seminary, Pasadena, California.

Mason, W. A., & Windle, M. (2002). A longitudinal study of the effects of religiosity on adolescent alcohol use and alcohol-related problems. *Journal of Adolescent Research, 17*(4), 346–363.

McArdle, J. J., & Nesselroade, J. R. (2003). Growth curve analysis in contemporary psychological research. In J. A. Schinka & W. E. Velicer (Eds.), *Handbook of psychology: Vol. 2. Research methods in psychology* (pp. 447–480). Hoboken, NJ: Wiley.

Mullen, K., & Francis, L. J. (1995). Religiosity and attitudes towards drug use among Dutch school children. *Journal of Alcohol & Drug Education 41*(1), 16–25.

Oordt, M. (1991). *Value change, authority, and religious tolerance: A re-examination of the cognitive consistency model.* Unpublished doctoral dissertation, Fuller Theological Seminary, Pasadena, California.

Ortberg, J. C., Jr., Gorsuch, R. L., & Kim, G. J. (2001). Changing attitude and moral obligation: Their independent effects on behavior. *Journal for the Scientific Study of Religion, 40*(3), 489–496.

Pargament, K. (1996). *The psychology of religion and coping: Theory, research, and practice.* New York: Guilford.

Rushton, J. P., Brainerd, C. J., & Presley, M. (1983). Behavioral development and construct validity: The principle of aggregation. *Psychological Bulletin, 94,* 18–38.

Schaefer, C. A., & Gorsuch, R. L. (1993). Situational and personal variations in religious coping. *Journal for the Scientific Study of Religion, 32*(2), 136–147.

Schaie, K. W. (1996). *Intellectual development in adulthood: The Seattle Longitudinal Study.* Cambridge, UK: Cambridge University Press.

Tamminen, K. (1991). *Religious development in childhood and youth: An empirical study.* Helsinki, Finland: Suomalainen Tiedeakatemia.

Tamminen, K. (1994). Religious experiences in childhood and adolescence: A viewpoint of religious development between the ages of 7 and 20. *International Journal for the Psychology of Religion, 4,* 61–85.

Velicer, W., & Fava, J. (2003). Time series analysis. In J. A. Schinka & W. E. Velicer (Eds.), *Handbook of psychology: Vol. 2. Research methods in psychology* (pp. 581–606). Hoboken, NJ: Wiley.

Venable, G., & Gorsuch, R. (1999). I and E in developmental perspective. In L. Rector & W. Santaniello (Eds.), *Psychological perspectives and the religious quest* (pp. 81–101). Lanham, MD: University Press of America.

Wagener, L. M., Furrow, J. L., King, P. E., Leffert, N., & Benson, P. L. (2003). Religious involvement and developmental resources in youth. *Review of Religious Research, 44,* 271–284.

Wertlieb, D. (2003). Applied developmental science. In R. M. Lerner, M. A. Easterbrooks, & J. Mistry (Eds.), *Handbook of psychology: Vol. 6. Developmental psychology* (pp. 43–61). Hoboken, NJ: Wiley.

Wong-McDonald, A., & Gorsuch, R. (2000). Surrender to God: An additional coping style? *Journal of Psychology and Theology, 28,* 149–161.

Wong-McDonald, A., & Gorsuch, R. (2004). A multivariate theory of God concept, religious motivation, locus of control, coping, and spiritual well-being. *Journal of Psychology and Theology, 32,* 318–334.

PART II

Descriptive Approaches to Spiritual Development

Introduction to Part II

The processes of spiritual development transcend cultures, traditions, and contexts. Yet they are manifested in widely different ways, from the pervasive sense of the spiritual in all of daily life to the ritualized practices of formal religious traditions of Buddhism, Christianity, Hinduism, Islam, and Judaism, to the individual quests of those young people who seek meaning, purpose, and contribution outside of organized faith traditions. Furthermore, broad social, political, and economic realities influence the diverse paths of spiritual development for the world's children and adolescents.

It is therefore not enough to argue that spiritual development is a universal process; it is important also to see how the spiritual dimension is manifested in the lives of children and adolescents globally. The chapters in this section offer important insights into what spirituality looks like among children and adolescents at both the macro and micro levels.

The first three chapters of this section take broad views. First, Laura H. Lippman and Julie Dombrowski Keith profile young people's spiritual and religious commitments, highlighting major differences among continents and countries that are evident in international studies of adolescents. They find wide variation among population groups in measures of religiosity and in the prevalence of spiritual beliefs and practices—patterns that are suggestive of individual differences as well as social forces that may influence spiritual development.

Then, using findings from the Study Group on Adolescence in the 21st Century, Suman Verma and Madelene Sta. Maria highlight macro societal trends and trends in young people's family, education, and peer relationships that have implications for spiritual development. They emphasize that social forces shape not only adolescents' spiritual development but also the ways in which young people's spiritual commitments can be powerful forces for social change.

Next, Linda M. Wagener and H. Newton Malony offer an important corrective to the mistake of assuming that all spiritual development is positive by examining spiritual and religious pathology in childhood and adolescence. After reviewing the history of the study of spiritual and religious pathology and definitional approaches to the phenomenon, they discuss four areas of religious and spiritual pathology: delusions, terrorism, cults, and young people who have experienced trauma.

The final two chapters in part II shift from these broader perspectives to more focused explorations of spirituality in particular contexts and, in these cases, with preadolescent children. First, Alma Gottlieb presents a case study of West African society—the Beng of Ivory Coast—that illustrates how the belief in reincarnation and children's spiritual nature shapes child-rearing practices. Gottlieb challenges scholars to consider the possibility of infant spirituality as it is developed beyond the West, which has dominated the study of religion and spirituality.

The section concludes with Tobin Hart's phenomenological, narrative approach to children's spirituality and spiritual experiences. He focuses on four capacities—wonder, wondering, relational spirituality, and wisdom—and describes the diverse ways in which children pursue their spiritual drives, noting that these developmental capacities and formative moments may unfold through the course of a lifetime.

These chapters only begin to mine the rich terrain of young people's spiritual experiences and practices. The international survey research reported by Lippman and Keith is an essential step in detailing broad sociological patterns that merit more comprehensive analysis. Wagener and Malony point to the need for more sophisticated ways of grasping the complex dynamics of spiritual development that sometimes goes awry. Gottlieb's nuanced description of spirituality in Beng society is suggestive of the rich possibility of anthropological exploration of children's spirituality in many other cultural contexts around the world. Hart's phenomenological methodology points to the ongoing need to listen to children's own words and perspectives to ground theory in their experiences.

When drawn together, these chapters underscore the value of multidisciplinary approaches to the study of child and adolescent spirituality, ranging from sociology and demography to psychology and anthropology. When these disciplines, perspectives, and levels of analysis actually inform and shape each other, the available knowledge on child and adolescent spiritual development is expanded and strengthened for all.

8

THE DEMOGRAPHICS OF SPIRITUALITY AMONG YOUTH: INTERNATIONAL PERSPECTIVES

LAURA H. LIPPMAN

JULIE DOMBROWSKI KEITH

A high proportion of American young adults report that religion and spirituality are important in their lives. According to a recent Gallup poll (2004), 48% of young adults ages 18 to 29 report that religion is "very important" in their own lives. Among youth at the lower end of that age range, integrating spirituality into life was considered to be an "essential" or "very important" objective for 43% of first-year college students in 1999 (Sax, Astin, Korn, & Mahoney, 1999). Levels of religious engagement have been found to be high in the United States in comparison to those of Western Europe (Eck, 2001). However, these levels of self-reported religiosity and spirituality are not uniform across demographic groups in the United States, nor are they universal among countries of the world. This chapter documents the prevalence of adolescent and young adult religiosity and spirituality around the world and how it compares to that among adolescents and young adults in the United States. We also present international evidence on the phenomenon among young people who consider themselves to be "spiritual, but not religious" (Fuller, 2001).

Finally, we examine the variation in reported spirituality and religiosity among demographic groups within the United States.

Undertaking an exploration of the demographics of spirituality may appear to be a questionable task, since demography is about measurement and spirituality is not easy to measure (and some would say it is not measurable at all). In particular, the survey measures that are available, and on which this chapter draws, are often quite limited, which we later comment on more specifically. In addition, one would expect that the basic human need or inclination to connect to a supreme being or to have transcendent experiences would be equally distributed in the population. However, surveys consistently find wide variation among population groups in measures of religiosity, such as frequency of religious attendance or religious identity, and in the prevalence of spiritual beliefs and practices, such as belief in God and frequency of prayer. We document this variation in spirituality among adolescents and young adults in population groups within the United States and across countries, and demographers may be intrigued with that variation alone. But this variation is of interest to scholars of spirituality as well, since the patterns that emerge are suggestive of conditions that may be related to the development of spirituality, such as the history, culture, and economic level of development of a country, as well as characteristics of adolescents (e.g., gender and race).

This chapter focuses on measures of spirituality, but since there are few available, we also address related measures of the importance of religion. A note is in order to clarify the difference between the two. Spirituality is generally considered to be beliefs, experiences, or practices, such as prayer or meditation, that foster a connection to a higher power that transcends daily physical existence, and which may be unrelated to the practices of any religion per se. Religiosity is generally considered to involve following the specific practices, attending services of, or identifying with the beliefs of a specific religion or religious community.

The measures of spirituality and religiosity that are discussed are limited by the survey questions that were administered, and by the imaginations of their creators. They generally reflect a Western monotheistic frame of reference vis-à-vis spirituality and religion, and use terminology and concepts that are found in Judaism, Christianity, and Islam, such as the concept of one God who influences one's life. When these questions are applied to cultures in which other religions predominate, such as Buddhism and Hinduism, some may suggest that they lose validity, and the responses to the surveys may be affected. However, an analysis of construct validity constructed by the designers of the World Values Survey, which asks questions about God and religiosity that are examined later here, found that being religious was related to attaching importance to God, across countries with a wide variety of religious cultures, and that these questions worked well regardless of potentially different understandings of the concepts. In a test of criterion-related validity, the authors used the Human Development Index (HDI), which measures income, education, and life expectancy as an outcome variable that is related to the construct of religiosity and faith, since research has shown that these are negatively related to higher levels of income, education, and standards of living. The authors found that the HDI for each country explained 40% of the variance across countries in the importance-of-God question (Inglehart, Basañez, Díez-Medrano, Halman, & Luijkx, 2004), demonstrating the criterion-related validity of these questions as well. The authors conclude that the data show a high degree of cross-cultural validity. Within-country surveys also struggle with the same problems with validity across many constructs across cultures, yet they do not always perform as well as these questions do. All of the data cited in this chapter derive from surveys in which scientific sampling methods have been used and that have demonstrable reliability.

We begin the chapter with a global survey, extracting data from international surveys on values among young adults and participation in religious youth groups, which elucidate global patterns of spirituality and religiosity in relation to economic development. Then we focus on Europe, where we find among the most economically developed nations, a dichotomy between spiritual beliefs and religious practices. Then, we return to the United States, an outlier in spirituality and religiosity among developed countries, for a closer look at demographic patterns among youth in the United States in spiritual beliefs and religious practices.

INTERNATIONAL COMPARISONS

International comparisons of the prevalence of spirituality and religiosity among youth can be extracted from several international surveys that tap into general values and attitudes. The measures available vary across the surveys, and the populations sampled also vary, making comparability across surveys impossible. We find, however, that the overall patterns are consistent across the surveys. The World Values Survey provides information on the importance of religion, belief in God, and the importance of God among 18- to 24-year-olds in all regions of the world. The International Association for the Evaluation of Educational Achievement's Civic Education study provides data on the proportion of 14-year-olds who are involved in religious groups for selected countries around the world.

The "Young Europeans" Survey details the relationship between religious beliefs and practice among 15- to 24-year-olds in Europe.

The World Values Survey, 1999–2001

The World Values Survey has been conducted four times since 1981, interviewing adults age 18 and older in nationally representative samples in 81 countries around the world about their views on civic values and beliefs. These countries represent the full range of regions of the world, levels of economic development, types of government, and religious and cultural histories. We have selected 41 countries representing the regions of the world: the United States, Canada, and Mexico for North America; the South American countries of Argentina, Brazil, the Dominican Republic, and Uruguay; the Western European countries of Great Britain, France, Italy, Finland, Norway, Spain, Sweden, Switzerland, and Germany; and the Eastern European countries of Bulgaria, Croatia, Estonia, Georgia, Lithuania, Poland, Russia, Serbia, and Ukraine. Egypt, Nigeria, and South Africa represent Africa, and representing the Asian and Pacific region are Australia, China, Indonesia, Japan, Philippines, South Korea, and Taiwan. Representing the Middle East region are Azerbaijan, Iran, and Turkey, and in South Asia are Bangladesh, India, and Pakistan.

From the most recent data available for analysis, the 1999–2001 World Values Survey, we have analyzed the responses to three questions on the importance of religion, belief in God, and the importance of God in one's life, using a sample of 20,000 18- to 24-year-olds from the 41 countries. The first question asked, "How important is religion in your life?" and the response categories were "Very," "Rather," "Not very," and "Not at all." The second question simply asked respondents whether they believed in God, with a "yes" and "no" response choice. The third question asked respondents to indicate on a scale of 1 to 10 how important God was in their lives, with 1 being "Not at all important" and 10 being "Very important." Because of space limitations, Table 8.1 displays data only for the response categories of "very important" on the importance of religion and

God in the respondent's life, and the percentage responding "yes" to the question on belief in God.

As seen in Table 8.1, there is a wide range in the presence of a belief in God and in the rating of the importance of religion and God to the respondent's life. Belief in God ranges from a low of 40% in Sweden to a high of 100% in Pakistan, and a rating of the importance of God in one's life as "very" ranges from a low of 2%, also in Sweden, to 100% in Pakistan. The percentage who reported that religion was very important to their life ranges from a low of 0 in Japan to 93% in Nigeria.

In general, young adults in less economically developed countries are more likely to be spiritual, as well as religious, than those in more economically developed countries. Also, there are often similar patterns among the countries within a region. In the less developed regions of South America, Africa, the Middle East, and South Asia, higher proportions of young adults reported a belief in God, and reported that religion and God were very important in their lives, than those living in more developed countries. For example, in Brazil, 99% of young adults reported a belief in God, 87% felt that God was very important in their lives, and 59% reported that religion was very important in their lives. In the African country of Nigeria, belief in God was universal among 18- to 24-year-olds, and 84% said that God was very important in their lives, while 93% said that religion was very important. In Turkey, 97% reported a belief in God, 75% said God was very important in their lives, and 76% said that religion was very important in their lives. In South Asia, 100% of Pakistani young adults reported a belief in God and also reported that God was important in their lives, while 74% reported that religion was very important in their lives. A characteristic of many of the countries where youth reported the highest levels of belief and importance of God and religion is that they tend to be societies with large Muslim populations, such as Pakistan, Nigeria, Egypt, Indonesia, Iran, Turkey, and Bangladesh. The Philippines is the only non-Islamic country in which such high proportions of young adults reported a belief in God and similarly high ratings of the importance of God and religion in their lives. Historically, the

Table 8.1   Spirituality of 18- to 24-Year-Olds, 2000 World Values Survey

	Importance of Religion in Respondent's Life	Does Respondent Believe in God?	Importance of God in Respondent's Life
	Very	Yes	Very
North America			
Canada	21.0	84.3	26.6
United States	47.2	92.9	50.3
Mexico	55.6	97.2	72.6
South America			
Argentina	35.2	95.1	46.9
Brazil	58.9	98.5	87.2
Dominican Republic	51.5	94.7	77.2
Uruguay	10.9	76.3	29.1
Western Europe			
Great Britain	10.2	64.0	8.6
France	5.1	52.4	2.8
Italy	18.0	94.4	17.7
Finland	7.8	70.1	6.4
Norway	9.2	53.3	8.5
Spain	7.1	69.0	6.5
Sweden	7.8	40.4	1.6
Switzerland	11.3	68.1	12.6
Germany	5.6	54.4	4.1
Eastern Europe			
Bulgaria	15.6	62.7	9.2
Croatia	14.9	87.9	22.5
Estonia	2.4	40.9	3.9
Georgia	58.6	96.4	43.9
Lithuania	7.9	78.0	17.7
Poland	37.8	98.7	45.2
Russia	7.1	71.1	8.2
Serbia	27.6	82.9	18.2
Ukraine	15.8	84.7	19.6
Africa			
Egypt	96.1	100.0	76.9
South Africa	62.1	98.7	69.3
Nigeria	93.4	99.7	84.4
Asia/Pacific			
Australia	14.8	74.3	11.2
China	1.3	–	–
Indonesia	100.0	100.0	97.1
Japan	0.0	50.0	1.8
Philippines	86.9	99.5	86.8
South Korea	22.0	–	14.1
Taiwan	4.3	73.2	6.1
Middle East			
Azerbaijan	38.2	98.6	63.4
Iran	76.3	99.3	82.2
Turkey	76.1	97.4	75.2
South Asia			
Bangladesh	87.1	98.8	91.7
India	52.9	94.3	0.0*
Pakistan	74.0	100.0	100.0

NOTE: Dashes indicate there was no response to that question. * = 91% responded affirmatively to the next highest category.

SOURCE: Original analysis by Child Trends of World Values Survey data, 1999–2001.

Philippines has a strong traditional Catholic culture and has low levels of education and income among the population.

North American young adults fall between those in the developing and developed world in their spirituality and religiosity, with very high levels of belief in God, but lower levels of the population who regard religion and God as important to their lives. More than 90% of 18- to 24-year-olds in the United States and Mexico reported that they believed in God, whereas about half of that population in the United States and more than half in Mexico reported that they felt religion and God were very important to their lives. In Canada, 84% of young adults believed in God, but only 21% regarded religion as very important in their lives and only 27% reported that God was very important in their lives.

Young adults in the Asia/Pacific area were generally less likely than those in the less developed regions or those in North America to believe in God, or to feel that religion and God were important, but they were more likely to believe in God and place a high value on religion than those in Western Europe. Young adults who believed in God ranged from a low of 50% in Japan to 100% in Indonesia. No young adults in Japan reported that religion was very important in their lives, and only 2% reported that God was very important. Likewise in China, where only 1% reported that religion was very important, but there are no data on belief in and importance of God. Other countries in the region, with exceptions, have similar patterns of extremely low percentages of youth rating religion and God as very important, but have relatively high proportions believing in God. Indonesia and the Philippines have very different patterns than the other countries in this region, both of which, as noted, have strong traditional religious cultures and are less developed than other countries in the region. Belief in God is almost universal in both countries, and while Indonesians universally reported that God and religion were very important, 87% of Filipinos did so.

Western European countries in the World Values Survey had relatively low proportions of young adults reporting that religion was very important to them, ranging from 5% in France to 18% in Italy. However, they were more likely to believe in God, ranging from 40% in Sweden to 94% in Italy, but the importance of God was not considered to be as strong (ranging from 2% in Sweden to 18% in Italy). These findings from the World Values Survey correspond to those of the Eurobarometer's "Young Europeans" study, which will be discussed later, in which many European countries had low proportions of young adults who practiced religion, but high proportions who identified as nonpracticing believers.

Eastern Europe had a wide range of responses on these questions. Young adults in Russia and several other members of the former Soviet Union were highly unlikely to report that God or religion was very important in their lives, with percentages in the single digits, yet strong majorities reported believing in God. In Eastern European countries with strong religious traditions, such as Poland and Georgia, moderate levels of young adults responded "very" on the importance questions and almost all reported a belief in God.

While we did not conduct subgroup analyses on the young adult sample, in the overall population surveyed in each country, there were patterns noted across demographic groups of age, gender, and socioeconomic status. Young adult respondents tended to be less likely to say that religion was very important in their lives than were older adults in advanced industrial societies, suggesting that younger generations have a more secular outlook. In Islamic societies, however, the importance of religion was deemed universally high by all age groups. Women are more likely to attach greater importance to religion in their lives across most countries. The more highly educated and higher income groups are less likely to attach high importance to religion in advanced industrial societies, whereas in many less developed and Islamic societies, there are no differences by SES (Inglehart et al., 2004).

The World Values survey has also documented changes in the importance of religion since 1990. In most advanced industrialized countries, the importance of religion dropped over the decade, again reflecting increased secularization, while in less developed countries, the importance of religion grew. In the United States, an outlier among more developed countries, there was a slight increase in importance as well (Inglehart et al., 2004). There has been widespread recent growth in participation in Christianity, particularly in evangelical groups, in developing countries. This growth, coupled with higher population growth rates, could help explain the growing importance of religion in those countries (Jenkins, 2002; Johnson, 2004).

The IEA Civic Education Study

While the World Values Survey can report on young adults, international data on adolescent spirituality are scarce. One way adolescents express their attachment to religion and spirituality is through participation in religiously sponsored organizations. We draw from one survey for data on this participation: the IEA Civic Education Study, which was administered in 28 countries in 1999 to nationally representative samples totaling 90,000 students at age 14. These countries do not represent the complete range of regions of the world, however, as in the World Values Surveys. The participating countries are heavily European, with a few in South America and the Asia/Pacific regions, as well as the United States. Participating students were asked about their knowledge of fundamental democratic principles, their attitudes toward government, and their participation in civic activities (Torney-Purta, Lehmann, Oswald, & Schultz, 2001). One of the civic activities listed was "An organization sponsored by a religious group," and we present the responses to this item across the 28 countries in Table 8.2.

Participation in religious organizations by 14-year-olds is quite low across the world. However, there are similarities among countries in certain geographical areas. Students in Eastern European countries were again least likely to participate in a religious organization, with an average of only 10% of 14-year-olds participating. Northern European countries (13%) and Western European countries (14%) also had low average religious organization rates among 14-year-olds, with the exceptions of Germany and Slovenia, which had rates of more than 20%. The Asian/Pacific countries had slightly higher average participation rates, with about one out of five 14-year-olds in Australia and Hong Kong participating in a religious organization, as did all of the Southern European countries except Cyprus, where 47%

participated. In the two South American countries surveyed, Chile and Colombia, participation rates ranged from 26% to 30%. The United States was the lone representative for North America and had much higher rates of participation than all countries except Cyprus, with 42% of its 14-year-olds participating in a religious group or organization.

So although more limited in age, geographic reach, and in the construct measured, the IEA Civic Education Study corroborates some of the general patterns of the World Values Survey, at about the same time period (1999 and 1999–2001, respectively), for the regions for which we have data. European youth, particularly those in Eastern Europe, are least likely to be involved with religious organizations, just as their young adult counterparts are the least likely in the world to attach a lot of importance to religion and God. American youth are the most likely (except for Cyprus) to be involved, and such high levels of involvement in religious organizations at age 14 are, no doubt, reflected in the high levels of importance attached to religion and God by American young adults in the World Values Survey. South American youth are involved at slightly lower rates, while Asian/Pacific and Southern European youth fall intermediate between the Americas and the rest of Europe in their rates of participation in religious organizations.

"The Young Europeans" Survey

The European situation bears closer examination. Why is it that the vast majority of young adults in Europe report a belief in God, but do not regard God or religion as very important and are unlikely to participate in religious groups in adolescence? An interesting survey explores this phenomenon in detail. "The Young Europeans" is an opinion survey administered by the Eurobarometer in 1997 at the request of the European Commission's Directorate General XXII–Education, Training, and Youth. It has a wealth of information about spiritual beliefs and religious practices among 15- to 24-year-olds in 15 countries: Austria, Belgium, Denmark, Finland, France, Germany, Greece, Ireland, Italy, Luxembourg, the Netherlands, Portugal, Spain, Sweden, and the United Kingdom.

Table 8.2   Religious Group Participation, IEA Civic Education

	Participated in Religious Group	*Did Not Participate in Religious Group*
North America		
United States	41.9	51.7
South America	27.9 avg.	52.6 avg.
Chile *	30.3	53.9
Colombia *	25.5	51.2
Western Europe	14.4 avg.	74.3 avg.
Belgium *	9.0	72.7
England	13.2	86.0
Germany	20.1	65.4
Switzerland	15.2	73.1
Eastern Europe	10.3 avg.	82.7 avg.
Bulgaria	5.5	90.2
Czech Republic	8.1	89.8
Estonia	9.3	82.7
Hungary	15.2	83.3
Lithuania	4.4	80.6
Latvia	4.9	85.8
Poland	10.0	84.7
Romania	12.0	80.8
Russian Federation	2.0	84.3
Slovak Republic	12.6	83.4
Slovenia	29.7	64.5
Northern Europe	13.1 avg.	73.3 avg.
Denmark	6.3	81.4
Finland	11.0	82.3
Norway *	16.9	67.2
Sweden *	18.1	62.3
Southern Europe	27.6 avg.	64.1 avg.
Cyprus	47.1	43.8
Greece	21.4	76.6
Italy	20.3	75.7
Portugal *	21.6	60.2
Asia/Pacific	19.9 avg.	71.5 avg.
Australia	20.8	69.6
Hong Kong	19.1	73.4

NOTE: * These countries had a nonresponse rate of more than 15% for the religious organization variable.

SOURCE: IEA Civic Education Dataset, final version.

A total sample of 9,400 respondents between the ages of 15 and 24 was obtained, with an average of 600 respondents per country, with the exception of Germany (1,200), the United Kingdom (800), and Luxembourg (200). Respondents were asked to choose a category that best corresponded to their personal spiritual and religious beliefs. Category choices were "I believe and I practice"; "I believe, but I don't practice"; "I practice religion, but I don't really believe"; "I belong to a spiritual group which is not a recognized religion"; "I would like to join a religious group, but I haven't found a suitable one yet"; "I am agnostic, I don't know whether there is a God and I do not belong to a religious group"; and "I am an atheist, I do not believe in any God" (European Commission, 1997).

Table 8.3 shows the distribution of responses for respondents in all 15 countries. Across all 15 countries combined, 19% of the respondents

Table 8.3 Religious Involvement, Eurobarometer

	Practicing Believer	Non-practicing Believer	Practicing non-Believer	Belongs to Spiritual Group	Wants to Belong to Religious Group	Agnostic	Atheist	Don't know
Western Europe								
Austria	26.1	38.0	18.0	1.0	0.6	2.7	4.9	8.8
Belgium	8.9	33.8	23.4	0.5	0.8	11.7	14.3	6.1
France	8.6	44.2	3.8	1.1	2.1	13.9	23.4	3.0
Germany	17.2	32.9	12.2	0.5	0.9	7.5	22.2	6.4
Fmr. W. Ger.	19.6	38.4	13.8	0.5	0.8	6.3	14.2	6.3
Fmr. E. Ger.	7.3	9.8	5.4	0.5	1.3	12.4	55.6	7.2
Ireland	48.9	32.5	7.2	0.4	0.0	3.4	4.8	2.5
Luxembourg	13.9	35.1	15.8	0.0	0.9	9.5	21.1	3.0
Netherlands	15.1	25.5	5.2	2.3	0.8	24.7	22.7	3.7
United Kingdom	8.2	42.6	1.8	0.6	0.2	20.2	18.5	7.1
Northern Europe								
Denmark	5.1	43.4	8.7	1.6	1.0	15.3	19.3	5.7
Finland	14.1	47.6	5.2	0.6	1.5	16.1	10.4	4.5
Sweden	7.5	35.3	12.2	0.5	0.7	22.8	16.4	4.5
Southern Europe								
Greece	41.9	52.8	1.5	0.0	0.7	0.7	1.9	0.5
Italy	41.0	46.3	2.3	0.4	1.7	4.7	2.9	0.7
Portugal	32.6	48.9	2.0	0.6	1.7	7.9	6.2	0.1
Spain	16.5	56.2	2.6	0.0	0.1	11.5	11.1	2.0
EU Total	19.4	42.6	5.6	0.6	1.0	11.6	15.1	3.9

SOURCE: Table reproduction from *The Young Europeans, Eurobarometer 47.2, 1997.*

indicated that they believed and practiced a religion, while 43% of respondents said that they had religious beliefs but they did not practice a religion, and 6% practiced a religion but did not believe. This pattern of low religious involvement yet moderate adherence to beliefs is similar to that reported in the World Values Survey as well. Also, as in other data sets, the variation across countries reflects religious heritage. Ireland, Greece, and Italy, with strong Catholic traditions, had rates of practicing youth believers that were double the European average (49%, 42%, and 41%, respectively, compared with 19%). In most other countries, less than 19% of youth believed and practiced a religion. The least likely to practice and believe a religion were in Denmark, Sweden, the United Kingdom, France, and Belgium, all with less than 10%.

Nonpracticing believers are the largest group in most countries, and they are more common than practicing believers in all countries participating except Ireland, ranging from 26% in the Netherlands to 56% in Spain. Where are these believers taking their beliefs if not within organized religion? Is there a demand for alternative spiritual groups? Less than 1% overall belong to a spiritual group, and the Netherlands, with 2%, is the only country where more than 1% belong to such a group. An average of 12% of youth overall identify as agnostic, but in the Netherlands, UK, and Sweden, that percentage exceeds 20. Fifteen percent overall are atheist, but in France, Germany, Luxembourg, and the Netherlands, that percentage again exceeds 20.

Small differences by age groups are evident between youth ages 15 to 19 and 20 to 24. Youth in the age group of 15–19 are "more likely to practice religion without really believing in it, while the older group (20–24) is more likely to believe but not practice" (European Commission, 1997). Youth younger than 19 are more likely to live at home, and to conform to family tradition by practicing religion with the family while still in the family home. When young adults ages 20–24 move out of the family home and away from the family's religious practices, the turbulence in residence may reduce their involvement in a religious community, and they may assert individual choices about religion for the first time.

"The Young Europeans" included demographic data for all Europeans combined. There are some differences in religious involvement by gender, education, and religious affiliation. Women are more likely than men to be practicing believers, and men are nearly 50% more likely than women to be agnostic or atheist. Education level also plays a role in religious belief and practice. The more education a person has, the less likely he or she is to be a practicing believer and the more likely he or she is to be a nonpracticing believer. Approximately 21% of young Europeans with less than 15 years of education identify as practicing believers, while 43% of this group identify as nonpracticing believers. For young Europeans who have had 20 or more years of education, 16% identify as practicing believers, while 47% identify as nonpracticing believers. Catholic respondents are more likely than others to be nonpracticing believers (56%) (European Commission, 2001).

Discussion of International Data

This quick tour of data from around the world has identified several patterns. One is the aforementioned relationship between a country's level of economic development and the spirituality and religiosity of its population. As countries develop economically, there is less emphasis on traditional religious values and more emphasis placed on secular institutions, as well as educational and economic accomplishment, powered by the need for trained workforces in industrialized societies (Inglehart et al., 2004). In addition, with development there is a growth in individual choice and freedom of expression, which can help explain the lack of attachment to religious practice among the Young Europeans, despite moderately high levels of the population who believe but do not practice, and majorities who believe in God. The fact that the more highly educated are the most likely to believe and not practice provides support for the inverse relationship between education and religious practice. When countries are arrayed on a continuum between survival values and self-expression values on the one hand, and traditional values versus secular-rational values on the other, high income countries cluster in the upper right corner, scoring high on self-expression and secularism, while low income countries cluster in the lower left quadrant, having traditional/survival values (Inglehart et al., 2004). The U.S. population, as reflected in the responses of young adults to the questions on religiosity and spirituality in these global surveys, has a more traditional value system than other advanced industrial societies, and thus is an outlier among wealthy nations. In addition, it has been argued that the higher levels of competition among churches in the United States compared to Europe, where the church is often state supported, account for differences in religious participation between the two regions (Stark & Finke, 2000).

Another pattern is the clear and continuing imprint of religion on beliefs in countries with a history of an influential traditional religion, such as Islam or Catholicism, so that young adults from countries who share a traditional religious heritage score similarly high on these questions. In addition, there is evidence that the recent revitalization of Islam is a nationalist movement as well, particularly appealing to young adults who wish to reject domination by Western culture (Stark & Finke, 2000).

Likewise, there is an imprint of the secular traditions of communist, socialist, and welfare states, reflected in the low importance given to religion and God in countries of the former Soviet Union, where religion was suppressed for so long and atheism was espoused by the state and widely adopted by citizens, and in the Nordic welfare states. In addition, Confucian societies (Japan, China) have a tradition of secular bureaucratic authority that is reflected in the low importance attached to God and religion in those countries (Inglehart et al., 2004). These international patterns are apparent in all of the data sets presented.

THE DEMOGRAPHICS OF ADOLESCENT SPIRITUALITY IN THE UNITED STATES

To date, the most commonly available measures of adolescent spirituality and religiosity in the United States were measures of the frequency of religious service attendance and the degree of importance that respondents attach to religion (Benson, Scales, Sesma, & Roehlkepartain, 2005). In addition, there have been measures of religious affiliation, religious identification, and participation in religious youth groups in various surveys. Of those data available, we have chosen to present only data on the importance of religion to parallel the international data presented earlier. With the upcoming release of data from the National Study of Youth and Religion (NSYR), the data landscape completely changes, and for the first time we have a rich data source on the spiritual lives of adolescents. We summarize some data from that study here, with permission of Christian Smith, whose recent book, *Soul Searching: The Religious and Spiritual Lives of American Teenagers*, presents the findings of the survey (Smith & Denton, 2005).

The NSYR was conducted in two phases. A nationally representative telephone survey of households containing at least one teenager age 13–17 was conducted from July 2002 to January 2003, followed up with in-person interviews in 2003 of a subsample of 267 respondents. Although the survey contains a vast array of fascinating items on spirituality, we have chosen to describe the results that are similar to those questions we were able to uncover in the international surveys.

In the United States, adolescents ages 13 through 17 reported that religion played a very strong role in their lives. Their faith was important in shaping their daily lives as well as the major life decisions they face. These teenagers also reported feeling close to God and had very few doubts about their religious beliefs. When asked about the importance of their religious faith in shaping daily life, 51% said that their faith was extremely important or very important, 31% stated that religious faith was somewhat important, and only 18% said that religious faith was not very important or not at all important in shaping their daily life.

Similar percentages were reported for the importance of religious faith in shaping major life decisions: 49% said that their faith was extremely important or very important in shaping decisions, 31% stated that their faith was somewhat important, and 19% said that their faith was not very important or not at all important when it came to shaping major life decisions.

U.S. adolescents also show strong belief in God and the influence of God over people's lives. Most adolescents have a core belief in the existence of God. They also believe that God is personally involved in the individual lives of people. More than four out of five adolescents (84%) believe in the existence of God; 12% are unsure in their belief of God, and only 3% do not believe in God. Two-thirds of adolescents (65%) believe that God is a personal being involved in the lives of people today, while 13% believe that God created the world but is not involved in the world today; 14% believe that God is not personal and is more like a cosmic life force. The extent of belief in a personal God is reflected in feelings of closeness to God: 36% of adolescents feel extremely close or very close to God, while 35% feel somewhat close to God. Seventeen percent feel somewhat distant to God, while only 8% feel very or extremely distant to God.

The NSYR data, then, corroborate and extend the findings of the international surveys on American spirituality. Very high levels of belief in God were reported in both surveys, and about half the population reported that faith or religion was at least very important in shaping one's life. That two-thirds believe in a personal God involved in their life helps characterize American adolescent spirituality in a way that other surveys have not been able to before.

Another new survey, Spirituality in Higher Education: A National Study of College Students' Search for Meaning and Purpose, sheds light on the spirituality of American college students. Data from a pilot study conducted in 2000 are suggestive. With a sample of 3,680 undergraduates attending 46 diverse colleges and universities across the country, it found that college students reported high levels of spiritual engagement and commitment, with 58% placing a high value on "integrating spirituality" in their lives, 77% believing that "we are all spiritual beings" and engaging in prayer, 71% stating that they "gain spiritual strength by trusting in a higher power," and 67% reporting that religious/spiritual beliefs had given meaning and/or purpose to their lives. As shown in other studies, women appear to be more spiritual and have a greater commitment to religion than do men. Approximately 37% of women scored high on the religious commitment scale, while only 25% of men had high scores of religious commitment; 26% of women scored high on the spirituality

scale, and only 16% of men had high scores of spirituality. A pretest was administered in fall 2004 to first-year college students, and a longitudinal follow-up is planned for spring 2007, when the students will be juniors (University of California, Los Angeles, Higher Education Research Institute, 2004).

Data on the importance of religion among U.S. adolescents can also be obtained from the Monitoring the Future Study (MTF). The big advantage of MTF is that it provides information on changes over time. Monitoring the Future is an annual study funded by the National Institutes of Health and administered in the United States. Nearly 50,000 students per year in grades 8, 10, and 12 have been questioned about their behavior, attitudes, and values. Approximately 420 middle and high schools, both public and private, are selected each year to provide an accurate representative sample of students in each grade targeted in the survey. Many of the items in the survey are geared toward understanding teenage drug and alcohol use and risk-taking behaviors; there is, however, a question asking students to indicate how important religion is in their lives, with response categories of "Not important," "Little importance," "Pretty important," and "Very important."

The Monitoring the Future study is unique in assessing long-term trends on the importance of religion in the lives of 12th graders since 1975, and for 8th and 10th graders since 1991. There appears to have been a slight increase in the importance of religion to 12th-grade students since data collection began (see Figure 8.1). In 1976, 29% of students in grade 12 reported that religion played a "very" important role in their lives. There was very little difference by grade in student reports of the importance of religion when 8th and 10th graders were added in to the sample, a finding corroborated by other analyses (Smith, Faris, & Denton, 2003). In 1991, 29% of 8th graders, and 28% of 10th and 12th graders reported that religion played a "very" important role in their lives. Religious importance increased only slightly for all grade levels throughout the decade of the 1990s, such that 34%, 33%, and 31% of students in 8th, 10th, and 12th grade, respectively, reported that religion was very important in their lives in 2003.

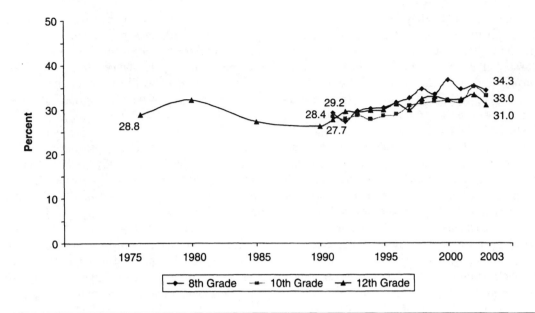

Figure 8.1   Religiosity: Percentage of Students in Grades 8, 10, and 12 Who Report That Religion Plays a Very Important Role in Their Lives, Selected Years 1976-2003 (Source: Original analysis by Child Trends of Monitoring the Future data, selected years 1976-2003)

NOTE: Data from 1997–2001 exclude students living in California

Gender

Gender differences in the value placed on religion are much larger than differences by grade: 68% of 12th-grade girls surveyed in MTF reported that religion is "pretty" important or "very" important in their lives compared with 57% of 12th-grade boys. Nearly 43% of boys in the 12th grade said that religion was "not" important or only "a little" important to them, whereas only 33% of girls in the 12th grade believed the same about religion in their own lives. Smith and colleagues (2003) noted this gender difference as well in the frequency of prayer, as reported in the National Longitudinal Survey of Adolescent Health. It was also noted in the findings from the World Values Survey discussed earlier that women across the globe were more likely to place high importance on religion, and the United States is no exception.

Several explanations have been offered for the religious differences between men and women. In two separate studies, Miller and Hoffman (1995) and Miller and Stark (2002) use data from Monitoring the Future, the American General Social Survey, the World Values Survey, and the National Jewish Population Survey to explore the relationship between risk preferences and religiosity among males and females. They tested two common explanations for religious differences among men and women. The first is the commonly held notion that differences in socialization between girls and boy are responsible, so that girls are "taught to be more submissive, passive, obedient, and nurturing than are males, and these traits are associated with higher levels of religiosity" (Miller & Hoffman, 1995, p. 63). The second explanation commonly offered is that since women traditionally participate less in the labor force and have the majority of the responsibility for raising children, women have less social power, more time for religious activities, and a "greater need for a source of personal identity and commitment" (Miller & Hoffman, 1995, p. 64). They suggest, however, that religious behavior is risk-averse and nonreligious behavior is risk-taking, and find that higher levels of risk-taking behavior among boys, and more risk-averse behavior among girls, explain religious differences rather than socialization or social power. They found that their risk preference hypotheses were consistently supported over time, across cohorts, religions, and cultures. All of these explanations promote a negative frame of reference (i.e., that attributes such as passivity, a greater need for a source of personal identity, and risk aversion drive women toward religiosity to fill their needs). An alternative explanation is that women are often considered to be the connective tissue in families and society, and so have more evolved moral compasses about human relationships. Likewise, they are more likely to experience and honor a relationship with God, and to identify with and practice the moral codes offered by religion.

Race

The importance of religion to adolescents in the United States differs according to race, and these differences have persisted over the time in which trends have been monitored by Monitoring the Future. In 2003, Black 12th graders were more than twice as likely as Whites (56% compared with 26%) to report that religion played a very important role in their lives (Child Trends Databank, 2003). Other analyses of MTF and the National Longitudinal Study of Adolescent Health survey have found the same pattern (Smith et al., 2003). Some have suggested that this difference is related to the central position of the church in Black society, and that involvement in religion, particularly in rural communities, is a means to achieve "respectability" and social opportunity (Ellison & Sherkat, 1995). Churches house social networks, including relatives, coworkers, neighbors, and friends, as well as members of the same race. Therefore, it is suggested that the importance of religion for Blacks living in the rural South goes beyond personal spirituality and is nested with social desirability and solidarity with a broader community (Ellison & Sherkat, 1995, 1999).

Summary of Demographic Patterns in the United States

While large proportions of high school and college students in the United States report high levels of spirituality and say that religion is very important in their lives, differences by demographic group have been noted. Adolescent girls are more likely than boys to attach high importance to religion. Black students are more likely than White students to rate religion as very important in their lives. Only very small differences have been noted across grade or over time, demonstrating more stability than not in adolescent spirituality, despite numerous claims to the contrary (Smith et al., 2003).

DISCUSSION

The survey data presented in this chapter document patterns of spirituality and religiosity among youth and young adults in the United States in relation to other countries. We have presented data on belief in God and the importance of religion and God for young adults in every region of the world; cross-national rates of involvement in religious organizations among 14-year-olds; European young adults' beliefs compared with their religious practices; and the religious importance and beliefs among American high school and college students. Less than 20% of young adults in Western Europe think that religion is "very important," and only 19% of "Young Europeans" believe and practice a formal religion. However, 43% of Young Europeans consider themselves to be "nonpracticing believers," providing evidence for the "spiritual but not religious" phenomenon. This phenomenon is also suggested by the results of the World Values Survey, which finds widespread belief in God, even among slim majorities of young adults in Western Europe, but low levels of support for the importance of religion in their lives. The United States looks more like developing countries in the Southern Hemisphere in the prevalence of belief in God (above 90%), but here also there is less importance given to religion and God than in developing countries, with 40% of young adults reporting that religion and God are very important to their lives, as opposed to more than 75% of the population in most developing countries. The United States appears to be unique among wealthy countries in the strength of young people's belief in God, in their participation in religious organizations, and in the importance they give to religion and spirituality in their lives. Black and female high school students were found to place higher importance on religion in their lives, confirming other studies. There are also high rates of religious involvement prior to high school. Over 40% of 14-year-old students in the United States are involved with a religious organization, whereas it is less than 25% in most other countries.

While these data come from disparate surveys, the patterns noted are consistent across surveys, which supports their credibility. The variation observed across countries, and within the United States, fits with prior research explaining how levels of religiosity and spirituality relate to country levels of economic development, as well as cultural, religious, and political histories of countries and subpopulations within the United States.

Data Gaps

Before identifying gaps in existing data, we wish to pause to appreciate the fact that internationally comparable data on young adult spirituality and the importance of religion *do* exist from the World Values Survey, and have been collected using scientific sampling methods. These data present a coherent and valid picture of cross-national variations in basic concepts of interest such as belief in God and the importance of religion and God in one's life for 18- to 24-year-olds. Furthermore, the IEA Civic Education Study, also conducted under scientific sampling conditions, provides data for a more limited set of countries on the involvement of 14-year-olds with religious organizations. The Young European study allowed us to focus in more detail on the phenomenon of nonpracticing believers in Europe. These data sets are a good start. Missing are internationally comparable data on adolescent spirituality for youth ages 12–17, similar to that in the National Study of Youth and Religion, which could provide a detailed profile of spiritual beliefs and practices across countries. While we can hypothesize that the beliefs and practices of youth may parallel those of young adults, or even lay the groundwork for those beliefs later on, we do not have a source of data with which to explore the

relationships between youth and young adult or later adult spirituality across cultures. The patterns in the IEA religious group data are suggestive, but religious group involvement at age 14 may be a result of circumstances that are totally unrelated to spirituality or religion. Also missing are consistent data for subgroups within countries, such as data on racial, cultural, and religious groups within countries. Gender and age seem to be the only characteristics widely available. We look hopefully to the future for the development of sources of international data on adolescent spirituality that can further illuminate spiritual development in adolescents across the globe.

REFERENCES

Benson, P. L., Scales, P. C., Sesma, A., Jr., & Roehlkepartain, E. C. (2005). Adolescent spirituality. In K. A. Moore & L. H. Lippman (Eds.), *What do children need to flourish? Conceptualizing and measuring indicators of positive development* (pp. 25–40). New York: Springer Science + Business Media.

Child Trends Databank. (2003). *Religiosity indicator: Original analysis by Child Trends of Monitoring the Future Data*. Retrieved January 18, 2005, from http://www.childtrendsdatabank.org/figures/35-Figure-2.gif

Eck, D. L. (2001). *A new religious America: How a "Christian country" has become the world's most religiously diverse nation*. San Francisco: Harper.

Ellison, C. G., & Sherkat, D. E. (1995). The "semi-involuntary institution" revisited: Regional variations in church participation among Black Americans. *Social Forces, 73*(4), 1415–1437.

Ellison, C. G., & Sherkat, D. E. (1999). Identifying the semi-involuntary institution: A clarification. *Social Forces, 78*(2), 793–800.

European Commission. (1997). *The Young Europeans: Eurobarometer 47.2*. Retrieved February 11, 2004, from http://europa.eu.int/comm/public_opinion/archives/eb_special_en.htm

European Commission. (2001). *The Young Europeans in 2001: Eurobarometer 55.1*. Retrieved February 9, 2004, from http://europa.eu.int/comm/public_opinion/archives/eb_special_en.htm

Fuller, R. C. (2001). *Spiritual but not religious: Understanding unchurched America.* New York: Oxford University Press.

Gallup Organization. (2004*). American public opinion about religion.* Retrieved May 21, 2004, from http://www.gallup.com/poll/focus/sr040302.asp

Inglehart, R., Basañez, M., Díez-Medrano, J., Halman, L., & Luijkx, R. (2004). *Human beliefs and values: A cross-cultural sourcesbook based upon the 1999–2002 values surveys.* Mexico City: Siglo Veintiuno Editores.

Jenkins, P. (2002). *The new Christendom.* New York: Oxford University Press.

Johnson, T. (2004). Demographic futures for Christianity and the world religions. *Dialog: A Journal of Theology, 43*(1), 10–19.

Miller, A. S., & Hoffman, J. P. (1995). Risk and religion: An explanation of gender differences in religiosity. *Journal for the Scientific Study of Religion, 34*(1), 63–75.

Miller, A. S., & Stark, R. (2002). Gender and religiousness: Can socialization explanations be saved? *American Journal of Sociology, 107*(6), 1399–1423.

Sax, L. J., Astin, A. W., Korn, W. S., & Mahoney, K. M. (1999). *The American freshman: National norms for fall 1999.* Los Angeles: University of California at Los Angeles, Higher Education Research Institute.

Smith, C., & Denton, M. L. (2005). *Soul searching: The religious and spiritual lives of American teenagers.* New York: Oxford University Press.

Smith, C., Faris, R., & Denton, M. L. (2003). Mapping American adolescent subjective religiosity and attitudes of alienation toward religion: A research report. *Sociology of Religion, 64*(1), 111–133.

Stark, R., & Finke, R. (2000). *Acts of faith: Explaining the human side of religion.* Berkeley and Los Angeles: University of California Press.

Torney-Purta, J., Lehmann, R., Oswald, H., & Schulz, W. (2001). *Citizenship and education in twenty-eight countries: Civic knowledge and engagement at age fourteen.* Amsterdam: International Association for the Evaluation of Educational Achievement.

University of California, Los Angeles, Higher Education Research Institute. (2004, October). *Spirituality in higher education: A national study of college students' search for meaning and purpose. Summary of selected findings (2000–2003).* Retrieved January 19, 2005, from University of California, Los Angeles, Higher Education Research Institute Web site: http://www.spirituality.ucla.edu/results/Findings_Summary_00–03.pdf

9

THE CHANGING GLOBAL CONTEXT OF ADOLESCENT SPIRITUALITY

SUMAN VERMA

MADELENE STA. MARIA

Understanding the role of spirituality as a developmental force during adolescence is important in the context of the widespread societal changes confronting youth today that affect their relationships, notions of identity, and attitudes toward religion and spirituality.

Adolescents around the world are exposed to varied sets of experiences, leading to unstable environments such as increases in adolescent pregnancy rates, divorce rates, and increased mobility of families (Allen & Coy, 2004; Santrock, 2001). The increasing rates of youth crime, substance abuse, suicides, and violence all are pointers to the adolescent population struggling to draw meaning from their lives (Miller, 2002). In such a milieu, spirituality serves as an important force that guides adolescents' interests and participation during a developmental period when institutional religion loses its hold on many young people (Bruce & Cockreham, 2004).

Many of today's youth also experience a sense of meaninglessness resulting from outdated social and religious traditions that fail to provide a sense of purpose, continuity, or belongingness in a larger social world (Kessler, 2002). Their lack of spiritual guidance and opportunity manifest in and contribute to high-risk behaviors, which can be both a search for connection, transcendence, meaning, and initiation as well as an escape from the reality of not having a genuine source of spiritual fulfillment and direction (Bruce & Cockreham, 2004). We need to address spiritual dimensions and connections to enhance adolescents' optimal development (Miller, 2002).

As adolescents search for their identity and learn about themselves through their relations with others (Gilligan, 1982), psychosocial support is crucial in helping them examine this aspect of their spirituality. They draw meaning from their lives; they need to explore their place in the world and in their relationships to discover their individual selves and talents (Bruce & Cockreham, 2004). Adolescence is also an age when young minds are involved in questioning and deliberating important existential issues; are conflicted about their values, beliefs, and morals; and explore religious and spiritual topics that affect their daily lives (Coles, 1990). Thus, spirituality is a central part of human development and wellness (Coles, 1990; Myers & Williard, 2003).

There is ample support for understanding spirituality as a normal human line of development like cognition, emotion, or sexual identity

(Ingersoll, 1998; Sink, 2004). In this chapter we discuss the importance of spirituality in the daily contexts of adolescents' life space, recognizing that spirituality develops across behavioral, psychological, cultural, and social contexts. We begin by highlighting some macrosocietal trends shaping adolescence across the globe wherein we draw on the work of the Study Group on Adolescence in the 21st Century. We then examine trends within the contexts of adolescents' relationships: Family, peers, school, and community all can serve as necessary spiritual resources for preparation for adulthood. Against this backdrop, we portray the place of religion and spirituality in the daily ecology of adolescent life experiences from a global perspective. Stressing a view of adolescents as resources, as active agents of change, and as a group that should be viewed in terms of their enormous potential for having a positive influence on society (Larson & Verma, 2002), we elaborate on the relation between spirituality and civic involvement among youth to demonstrate how they create their own contexts for positive youth development. The final section considers several critical issues that must be addressed in future research and theory development to more fully understand the relationships among religion, spirituality, and culture.

TRENDS SHAPING ADOLESCENCE

At the core of this chapter is a summary of the work of the Study Group on Adolescence in the 21st Century, which examined across cultures the societal trends that young people are likely to experience in the next several decades and considered the implications of these trends for the acquisition of various interpersonal competencies and resources in preparation for adulthood. This study group, made up of 25 scholars from different countries, was chaired by Reed Larson, with Jeylan T. Mortimer and B. Bradford Brown. It was sponsored jointly by the Society for Research on Adolescence and the International Society for the Study of Behavioral Development, with primary support from the William T. Grant Foundation.

The group deliberated on the possible life scenarios for adolescents across nations, and over the next 3 to 5 decades. Regional authors provided empirically based analyses of the transformation from childhood to adulthood with regard to various issues and social contexts that affect adolescents' lives and their roles as adults (Brown, Larson, & Saraswathi, 2002). Other experts were asked to forecast major trends in their domains of study and ways in which these trends might shape adolescent development and their transition to adulthood (Mortimer & Larson, 2002). The third volume deals with the influence of societal changes on adolescents' competence and well-being in four domains (Larson, Brown, & Mortimer, 2002).

We present a few key highlights of the issues the group deliberated on, details of which are available in Larson, Wilson, Brown, Furstenberg, and Verma (2002). These trends focus on some of the most significant settings and contexts that youth live in and highlight how changes in these settings require adolescents to develop a wider range of interpersonal skills and competencies. For each set of trends, this chapter articulates potential implications for spiritual development in adolescence.

Macrosocietal Trends

An important development influencing adolescent life is rapid population growth, especially in the urban areas of developing countries, which has led to crowding, competition for resources, and challenges to the quality of daily life. The young person is now exposed to issues of intergroup relations, which have become paramount with the steady flow of immigrants into Western countries. Urbanization has also facilitated this increased contact between diverse cultural and religious groups. Cultural globalization has brought with it a host of consequences for adolescent life in many societies. There is emerging a worldwide materialistic youth culture for the middle class. Moreover, cultural disenfranchisement is happening with some of the youth, who, as a result of embracing new values, lose traditional systems of support and meaning that are not being replaced. Globalization has likewise produced reactions that result in stronger ethnic group identification. Youth are now required to operate in multicultural settings and to be culturally pluralistic.

The globalized world is to a large extent a consequence of the progress in information and communication technology. Youth have lived through tremendously rapid change in this technology. We see new paths and patterns to communication recently emerging as a result of this worldwide phenomenon. However, access to technology will be limited to those with sufficient wealth and resources.

Required longer education for careers and the decision among youth to delay marriage have considerably lengthened adolescent transition in many societies. There is also a worldwide trend toward greater female empowerment. More girls and women are recognizing and claiming their rights. This trend is changing the nature of social relationships among youth. The convergence of gender roles, which has become more salient in the middle class, and the ability to switch gender codes have a pronounced impact on the identity formation of the young. Because the social and psychological features of adulthood have become less coordinated, a sense of an integrated identity becomes more difficult to achieve.

What characterize the macrosocietal trends that influence adolescents' life in the present time are changes in contexts that nurture their development in an increasingly globalized world. The effects of these general trends on the spiritual development of the young person may be assessed through an examination of how these trends have affected the values of the society to which the young person belongs and the institutions that shape those values. Inglehart and Baker (2000) emphasize that it is inaccurate to view the effects of globalization as producing an increasingly uniform world. Therefore, youths' exposure to a vast range of spiritual beliefs and practices may take away from them the secure grounding of traditional values, but the exposure may also produce a wide array of meaning systems that youth can explore as they begin to deal with the changes in their world. Still, the spiritual trajectory youth may take will depend on their cultural heritage, as well as the level and nature of economic development in society.

Using the data from three waves of the World Values Surveys, which included 75% of the world's population, Inglehart and Baker (2000) found that broad cultural heritage (Roman Catholicism, Confucianism, Protestantism) has an enduring influence on the lives of members of a society despite modernization. Great religious traditions shape the national cultures of some societies, and the impact of these traditions is transmitted through nationwide institutions. Consistent with this conclusion is Kelley and De Graaf's (1997) findings that show family religious background to be more important in socialization of youth in more secular nations, while national context was found to be more important in religious nations. The religious context of the nation may thus remain the primary source of beliefs for the young person. Therefore, despite globalization, the nation remains as the center of shared experience, and its institutions continue to play a vital role in the transmission of beliefs and values (Inglehart & Baker, 2000).

Inglehart and Baker were also able to determine that although growing materialism may be linked to economic development, the existential security and changes in the nature of work in advanced industrialized societies are producing a shift to postmaterialist and postmodern values, for example, an emphasis on the quality of life, environmental protection, and self-expression. Therefore, the spiritual life of most youth in postindustrial societies may be influenced by a prevailing emphasis on communication and relationships, as well as a decrease in allegiance to religious institutions. In advanced industrial societies, what takes place is a growing interest in spiritual concerns at the individual level. Inglehart and Baker add that unlike materialists, the postmaterialists are less attached to traditional forms of religion, and tend to reflect more on the meaning and purpose of life. Technology is aiding youth in this quest. According to Lopiano-Miscom and De Luca (1998), young people are using technology to create traditions, customs, and communities. They work with the computer and imbue it with their sense of spirituality. As Lopiano-Miscom and De Luca claim, "By day, they may look like pacifists, and work within the mainstream; but by night, they are existentialists, hacking into the latest programs and creating their own communities" (p. 22).

Family

In addition to the broad, macrosocietal trends, significant trends are evident when examining the interpersonal contexts of adolescents, particularly their families, which are the primary context in which spiritual development is nurtured (Boyatzis, Dollahite, & Marks, chapter 21, this volume). The following trends are among those identified by the Study Group on Adolescence in the 21st Century:

- In all parts of the world, links between the family and community are threatened by urbanization and family mobility.
- In addition to a global trend toward smaller families (with fewer siblings, aunts, uncles, and cousins), there are a growing number of childless couples. There are also increasing diversity of family forms, and more improvisation of family roles and relationships. At the same time, there is also evidence of the persistence and renewal of the extended family in most nations.
- In all parts of the world, there are increasing income disparities between families, leaving adolescents and emerging adults in poor families handicapped by lack of family resources. In addition, they point to increasing numbers of homeless adolescents in all nations.
- With these changes in families, some of the instrumental functions of families have been given over to other institutions in all nations.
- At the same time, there is greater investment of financial resources, time, and emotional energy in children by many parents, particularly the middle class in most nations, with more monitoring and "oversupervision" of children.
- The way in which parents rear their children is also changing in most nations, particularly within the middle classes. Parents are less authoritarian, with more emphasis on the interpersonal quality of parent–adolescent relationships. There tends to be more equitable treatment and expectations for boys and girls in families. At the same time, parents are putting increased pressure on adolescents' school performance.
- In all nations—but especially those experiencing the most rapid change—there is evidence of an increasing generation gap between parents and adolescents in, for example, knowledge about information technology and popular culture.

These changes in families around the globe have significant implications for young people's spiritual development. For example, fewer siblings and cousins mean fewer opportunities to acquire spiritual concepts and skills through these relationships, including empathy and spiritual nurturance. In addition, family mobility, dissolution, and reconstitution may impair spiritual socialization and force adolescents to learn skills for creating and negotiating relationships within the family (e.g., renegotiating autonomy and connection, repair and maintenance skills, communication skills). And the growing numbers of homeless and parentless young people are deprived of parental support and spiritual nurture, resulting in deficits in transmission of spiritual beliefs and values, religious affiliations, and a less secure sense of self.

Changes in the family heighten the need for resources to create and renegotiate ad hoc family relationships in adulthood. Codified, traditional hierarchal norms of relating may be of less value. This factor will require a redefining of oneself outside the family and the development of an individual set of moral, ethical, religious, and spiritual principles.

Peer Relationships and Schools

In addition to families, peer relationships (see Schwartz, Bukowski, & Aoki, chapter 22, this volume) and school (see Alexander & Carr, chapter 6, this volume) play significant roles in young people's spiritual development. These dynamics are markedly different between the developing world and the developed world, according to the working group's conclusions.

In the developing world:

- For youth in many traditional societies, peers are becoming more important than was true in the past. Peer relationships in many societies in the developing world have been much less important than family relationships (and thus less studied). This is particularly true of girls, who are more closely monitored by parents and have more household responsibilities. This pattern is being altered by smaller families and by schooling, which removes children from their families for 5 to 8 hours a day and puts them in contact with large numbers of same-aged peers.
- Family mobility, urbanization, longer schooling, and exposure to mass media also contribute to

peer relations becoming more salient in cultures where peers were historically of less importance (e.g., Arabic and South Asian countries). The increased importance of peers leads to (a) age-segregated peer groups and (b) cliques and crowds. Exposure to worldwide youth cultures has recast peer relationships within a larger materialistic or ideological frame.

- Community supports and structures for peer groups are diminishing. Some traditional societies—notably those in sub-Saharan Africa—have formalized peer groups, especially for boys. These provide institutions for socialization, learning self-regulation, and learning to take care of each other. In rural life, including in rural America, adolescent peer groups often play important roles in organizing community festivals, projects, or rituals (Schlegel & Barry, 1991; Verma & Saraswathi, 2002). Urbanization reduces or takes away this form of peer group embeddedness in the community.

- Urbanization and crowding throughout the world, but especially in developing countries, are creating the conditions for gang formation, as adolescents struggle for identity in a condition of scarce material and symbolic resources.

In the developed world:

- Among the middle class and in Western nations, much about the nature of adolescent peer relationships will remain the same, even as they appear to change.

- In some developed nations, communities are playing a renewed and increasing role in providing structures for adolescent friendship. Governments and families are investing more in after-school programs, sports and music programs, clubs, and camps that are a major source of peer affiliation, particularly for middle-class kids.

- Increased contact between different ethnic groups brings issues of intergroup relationships to the fore, increasing the need for young people to learn not just tolerance but a capacity to be multicultural.

- Information and communication technologies (ICT) are bringing about changes in adolescents' social networks. Adolescents are frequent users of the Internet for social functions, opening the potential for new paths of adolescent communication with people outside their immediate community.

- In addition, ICT may also lead to changes in the *nature* of adolescents' communications and relationships. The Internet provides a unique opportunity for exploration of new selves, and young people can obtain affirmation for identities that are outside the mainstream (e.g., gay/lesbian/bisexual). However, there may be shortcomings in these relationships and they become more anonymous, less intimate, and may, in some cases, substitute for face-to-face interactions.

- Despite increased pluralism within most societies, the possibility that schools will become more tiered economically may mean that adolescents have less contact with young persons from other socioeconomic groups, thus reducing opportunities to learn about others. Furthermore, the increased incidence of home schooling and use of communication technology for schooling may lead to less peer group contact. At the same time, the increased use of communication technology in schools may lead to more communication across cultural groups.

These changes in peer and school relationships have the potential to profoundly affect the patterns of spiritual development. For example, the ability to manage and maintain relationships by means of ICT can provide a sense of spiritual connectivity and sharing across national boundaries. At the same time, different youth cultures may encourage learning about (or scorning) different types of religious and spiritual values and beliefs. Youth culture plays a particularly important role in religious tolerance and in defining relationships between ethnic groups and between genders.

Yet urbanization and diminishing of primary community may mean that peer groups are less under social control than in the past. There may be more peer groups and gangs that function outside the norms of society, and do not provide training in normative moral and social skills, thus becoming potential sources of negative expressions of spiritual commitment and connections.

New patterns of adolescent peer relationships on the World Wide Web (for those with access to the Internet) may mean more links across distance, culture, nation, language, age, and so forth, leading to richer opportunities for learning and sharing a broad variety of social skills, including skills for relationships with people different from oneself, negotiating hierarchical and horizontal relationships, and managing impersonal relationships. These opportunities will enhance young persons' abilities to navigate multiple worlds and develop a sense of purpose and self-worth.

RELIGION AND SPIRITUALITY IN THE LIVES OF YOUTH IN DIFFERENT PARTS OF THE WORLD

As is evident from this sampling of trends, adolescent experiences are being altered by globalization, and by socioeconomic and technological changes occurring worldwide. These changes will inevitably have an impact on their spiritual development. To understand patterns of spirituality in adolescence, we need to look more closely at youth spirituality as it is experienced in various regions of the world, complementing the demographic information provided by Lippman and Keith (chapter 8, this volume). We are afforded this view in the accounts of young persons' religious and spiritual life from a global perspective in Brown, Larson, and Sarawathi (2002), one of the volumes that also emerged from the Study Group on Adolescence in the 21st Century. This group's work focused primarily on religion, not spirituality per se.

Religion and spirituality provide contour to the experience of the youth, particularly in their adolescent life stage, in different parts of our globe. Adolescents find in religion the boundaries and pathways for expression as they participate more actively in their expanding contexts of interaction and experience. Spirituality takes on for them meanings emerging from the sociopolitical conditions and the historical-cultural contexts within which they live, influencing both their social role as well as their individual behaviors.

Verma and Saraswathi (2002) describe how religion plays a direct or indirect role in the daily lives of the youth in India. One may find a shrine in most homes, which allows youth to engage in brief periods of daily worship. Places of worship are also a ubiquitous feature in the local scene, and adolescents, together with their families, pay visits to these sites to offer prayers to several deities. Verma and Saraswathi point out that religion plays more of a social role than a religious one in most instances in young persons' lives. An important example of this role is seen in the practice of the caste system in marriage, whereby the choices for marriage partners are made from within the caste or a sect that is very close to it. One's family risks social ostracism when the choice of a partner transgresses religious and caste barriers.

Among Latin American youth, religion likewise plays a social role, specifically in peer socialization (Welti, 2002). Adolescents in Latin America are said to identify more with peers with whom they attend private, religious sectarian schools. These youth have more opportunities to interact with their peers whenever they participate in religious services.

Another important phenomenon, the rise of religious conservatism in the Arab world, has brought about certain kinds of peer influence. Booth (2002) reports that, in Egypt, adolescents use fundamentalist peer groups as a reference point to alienate themselves from their more conservative parents. Indeed, expressions of religious fundamentalism may be observed among youth in other parts of the world. In India, these expressions lead to communal clashes among adults and young people (Verma & Saraswathi, 2002). Youth have found in religion a pathway through which they can participate in challenging an existing social order and introduce change in society, a theme that will be addressed more fully later.

Religion and spirituality also affect individual behaviors in different ways around the world. One area that has received attention in this regard is adolescent sexuality. Sta. Maria (2002) reports that a survey on Filipino youths' sexual behaviors showed the use of contraceptives to be higher among male and female youths with greater religiosity, greater urban exposure, and more education. From this general finding, one may deduce that youth with greater religiosity are more responsible about the consequences of their sexual behaviors, especially since religion makes them aware of the sanctions of the community regarding premarital sex and pregnancy. Similarly, Muslims and Christians in the Arab world view adolescence as a stage particularly filled with sexual temptations, and perhaps as in the example from the Philippines, they use religious authority to regulate youths' sexual activities at this stage (Booth, 2002).

In contrast, Africa's pronationalist values and religious beliefs about fertility hinder HIV/AIDS prevention messages for adolescents in sub-Saharan Africa, resulting in an increase of its incidence among youth (Nsamenang, 2002).

In Latin America, however, religion is seen to have a diminishing influence on youths' sexual behavior (Welti, 2002). Young individuals increasingly perceive religious institutions as distant from the realities of everyday life. The religious hierarchy is thought to represent old regimes, legitimizing a social order that perpetuates exploitation. The church is viewed as taking a position against practices that youth find as natural (e.g., premarital sex and cohabitation, the use of modern methods of contraception, and divorce or separation).

Each of these instances points to the ways in which broader societal forces and trends interact with young people's spiritual development in complex ways. Adolescents in some cultures seem to turn away from religious practices in the face of the confusion resulting from the rapid social and technological changes characterizing life in the modern world. Other young people have embraced religion and spirituality as tools for dealing with the change. In Southeast Asia, for example, traditional religious practices serve as a soothing relief from stresses and strains of living in the modern world for participating adolescents (Sta. Maria, 2002).

In the Arab world, Islamist calls for reassertions of indigenous cultural identity are reassuring to the young people who are caught in contradictory circumstances (Booth, 2002). Many of those who have committed themselves to an Islamic outlook find a pathway to serve their society and religion. They believe that by doing so, they become worthy of an eternal reward—a thought that, according to Booth, holds great appeal given the conditions in which most of them live. They have found in Islam-oriented activism the hope and services they find lacking in other sectors of their society. This dissatisfaction is exemplified most poignantly in the following words of a young person from Algeria:

You have only four choices: you can remain unemployed and celibate because there are no

jobs and no apartments to live in; you can work in the black market and risk being arrested; you can try to emigrate to France to sweep the streets of Paris or Marseilles; or you can join the FIS [Front Islamic du Salut, the Islamist opposition party in Algeria] and vote for Islam. (cited by Booth, 2002, p. 235)

Aside from the fact that they provide a channel for oppositional activity within a political system, Booth notes that organized religious activities may likewise allow youth opportunities to participate in peaceful activities (e.g., charity work) that also give order and direction to Arab adolescents' lives.

It is apparent that the rise in youth participation in religious activities may be seen as an indication of a growing dissatisfaction felt in existing societal conditions. In Russia, where religious faith was formerly uncommon among youth, more young people are beginning to describe themselves as believers, with nontraditional forms of religion becoming more popular among educated youth (Stetsenko, 2002). In Latin America, the political function of religious institutions is observable in the attraction among the young to liberation theology, which, with its central thesis regarding the church standing with the poor, provides youth with an alternative to social change in the region (Welti, 2002). In the West, participation in religious organizations among youth varies with age and many perform community service through affiliations with religious organizations (Arnett, 2002).

In summary, the significance of religion in adolescent life may be found in their participation in organized religious activities, which provide them with opportunities to interact meaningfully with others within and outside the family. Religion and spiritual activities such as yoga and meditation also give youth a way to cope with the confusion, chaos, and lifestyle-related stress that come with the accelerated changes occurring in contemporary society. Finally, religion and spirituality seem to be the resources youth use to contribute meaningfully to the world they are now slowly coming to terms with as they enter the world of adulthood. The accounts of youth in the different regions of our globe indicate the significant role religion is playing in civic engagement among them—a theme to elaborate on in the next section.

ADOLESCENT SPIRITUALITY
AS A FORCE FOR SOCIAL CHANGE

The role of religion in young persons' lives in different parts of the world highlights the participation of youth in contexts beyond the family, where youth are exposed to opportunities to contribute to society. Although the nature of the relationship between civic involvement and spiritual commitment needs further investigation (Donnelly et al., chapter 17, this volume), involvement in religious organizations can be seen as a form of youth civic engagement. In the United States, for example, many youth engage in community service through their participation in church-sponsored programs for the homeless (Arnett, 2002). This emphasis further highlights that young people's spiritual development and commitments are not only shaped by societal changes, they also can become potent forces for social change, both positive and negative.

Spiritual and religious commitments are important factors in young people's contributing to—and sometimes leading—social change, at the level of humanitarian concern as well as systemic political and social change. An example of the former was seen in the aftermath of the tsunami that hit southern Asia coastlines on December 26, 2004. With a death toll exceeding 150,000, the disaster prompted unprecedented humanitarian efforts and aid from across the globe to help families of the victims who died in the tragedy and to rehabilitate those whose homes and possessions (including their means of livelihood) were destroyed. While innumerable organizations and governments have reached out to the needy following this disaster, a focused group discussion with one such organization highlighted the linkages between youth, spirituality, and civic engagement.

In discussions with members of a Buddhist organization in the city of Chandigarh, India (the Soka Gakkai International, a nongovernmental organization registered with the United Nations), the first author learned that members of the organization, a substantial percentage of them being adolescents and young adults, had contributed selflessly and with a great deal of empathy toward the cause, even at the cost of their own financial resources. When asked what led them to make such generous contributions, the immediate response was that providing this humanitarian

relief was in keeping with the traditions of humanism that were taught to them in their religious tenets and practice. The youth of this organization also felt that they needed to practice wholeheartedly what they had been learning through their practice: that "none of us can be truly happy if others around us are struggling," and "the true world citizen can share, as a fellow human being, the sufferings and sadness as well as the happiness and joy of others regardless of their nationality or ethnic background" (Ikeda, 2000, pp. 144, 164). Through a common spiritual link the members were able to get together and contribute toward a larger civic cause. This is just one of numerous examples that have been observed of youth coming forward and contributing during the trying days following the tidal waves.

There are instances, however, where this kind of civic participation appears to be in decline owing to some of the social forces mentioned earlier. For example, in the Hindu model of human development, emphasis is laid on the acquisition of specific tasks at each stage of life that also represent the developmental milestones. During *brahmacharya* (adolescence), the specific task and virtue that is expected is knowledge of *dharma* (apprenticeship, competence, and fidelity). In today's competitive times, the main expectation that educated families have of their children is that of completing their education and attaining a professional qualification. With increasing academic stress and competition for resources at all entry levels to higher education, the role of youth in the community has gradually diminished. Voiced concerns regarding this alienation have resulted in programs by religious organizations that engage youth in humanitarian causes by involving them in social welfare programs (Verma & Saraswathi, 2002). Serious involvement in matters related to religion, spirituality, and civic engagement is often thought of in the later years, when adults are free from their commitment toward their jobs and families.

Community involvement for youth also varies from being informal (as in collectivist cultures of Asia and Africa) to organized, as in individualist societies such as Israel and Germany, which require youth to perform national service in the military (Youniss et al., 2002).

Youth have played a key role in transforming the sociopolitical economic reality in various parts of the world. For example, in India, youth power has been available for revolutionary activities (the Quit India Movement), social movements, or for rebellious and retrogressive activities. In the latter part of the 1960s and the early 1970s, politically and socially oriented middle-class youth movements led to unrest: Propelled by the anxiety caused by unemployment, a defective educational system, and the lack of effective governance and university–state relations (Upreti, 1987), youth demanded a greater student role in the decision-making process. Students started becoming active agents of opposition and change, staging protests, demonstrations, strikes, boycotts, and other methods of exerting pressure. They eventually succeeded in forming the first-ever student government in the country—All Assam Students Union (Kumari & Sree, 1992).

In post-Independence India, there has been a gradual qualitative shift in politics and politicians. As politics degenerated, the role models for youth diminished. The nature of youth involvement came to be questioned, as did their contributions to social change. With the socioeconomic gap widening and employment opportunities dwindling, frustration became part of life for a segment of youth (H. Jaisingh, personal communication, July 6, 1999). Regional aspirations and religious conflicts combined with declining opportunities altered the course and quality of youth movements. Instances of substantial youth involvement are evident in subversive activities in the sensitive regions of Kashmir and Punjab. In this scenario, youth also became the victims of change. Religion played a key role. The involvement of youth in various terrorist activities raised issues related to territorial unity and secular notions. Youth power in India was used both for revolutionary social movements and for militant activities, and in the process religion became enmeshed with political activities.

Elaborating on the issue of spiritual connection in the use of children as combatants, Machel (2001) explains that adolescents, attracted by ideologies, may arm themselves to fight for religious expression, self-determination, or national liberation. In the Philippines, for example, some of the young people who have joined rebel movements have been known to admit that they joined to fulfill a religious duty or obligation, for example, to wage jihad (Cagoco-Guiam, 2002).

These contrasting images of youth as agents of both constructive and destructive social change—driven, at least in part, by their religious or spiritual commitments—raise important questions about how societies and their leaders are being intentional in addressing these issues in a contradictory world whose people are differentiated on the basis of religious affiliation, on the one hand, and that is continuously seeking to close the gap between Eastern and Western philosophies of spirituality like never before. What is the spiritual legacy that we are passing on to our adolescents as global citizens who will shape the future for tomorrow? Are we leading our youth to constructive civic participation as adults (see Youniss et al., 2002)? Linking these two questions is a third issue: If we are to visualize a scenario that has an ideal combination of spirituality and civic engagement in a continually violent global scenario, what are some of the precursors that act as catalysts? Some of the crucial influences during the adolescent years for civic engagement, as reviewed by Youniss et al. (2002), remain the family, educational institutions, and conventional and new media. It is here that adolescents gain the maximum knowledge about religious affiliations, spiritual linkages, and the process of suitably directing this knowledge (or not) toward civic engagement and participation. And, as we have noted, these same influences are undergoing significant change around the globe.

The significance, therefore, lies in the capacity of researchers to examine the processes of transformation and translation that characterize spiritual development as these occur in social contexts where young persons participate more actively as they move from childhood to adulthood. An examination of contexts of interaction and activity would entail an inclusion of culture to the study of spiritual development. This approach will allow researchers to view spiritual experience as part of a process of socialization into meaning systems that make participation in group life possible. Some of the factors that can promote spiritual development among youth through civic engagement are as follows:

1. Youth with a religious and spiritual identity have an enhanced chance of being aware of their civic obligations.

2. In an increasingly violent world it is important that we foster spiritual development as an integral part of the school curriculum, since that is one of the important learning contexts for children.

3. Organized civic participation opportunities, clear-cut guidelines, and religious organizations that can create a balance between the old and the new will go a long way in encouraging greater involvement of the youth in civic activities.

DEEPENING UNDERSTANDING OF RELIGION, SPIRITUALITY, AND CULTURE

A consideration of the cultural context has been raised repeatedly by contributors to this volume, as well as by others involved in the study of spiritual development. Newberg and Newberg (chapter 13, this volume) cite Katz, who, in 1978, argued that spiritual experiences will differ in terms of the language of the culture in which they are embedded, and that spiritual experiences may be altered by the cultural experiences a person brings to them. Benson, Roehlkepartain, and Rude (2003) underscore the importance of studying the salience of spirituality among young people in different cultures and traditions. Hill and Pargament (2003) point to the need to develop measures of religion and spirituality that reflect greater sensitivity to cultural characteristics and issues. They further point out that differences in spiritual and religious beliefs and practices are interwoven into other features of cultural life.

An examination of spirituality and religion from a cultural perspective may inevitably lead us to suspend assumptions regarding the divergence between religion and spirituality. Hill and Pargament (2003) provide substance to this caution by stating that religion and spirituality may not be separate in many cultures. They further argue that a polarization of religion and spirituality into their institutionalized and individual domains leads one to disregard the fact that expressions of spirituality occur in social contexts. This polarization also ignores the fact that organized faith traditions are interested in providing order to personal spiritual experiences. Most people would thus experience spirituality

in an organized religious context, and, according to Hill and Pargament, in empirical reality people fail to see the distinction between spirituality and religion. A polarization would therefore only lead to a duplication of concepts and measures.

Not only do we have to anticipate the convergence of spirituality and religion in a cultural perspective; we may also have to view all aspects of social and symbolic life as contributing to spiritual and religious experience. Mattis, Ahluwalia, Cowie, and Kirkland-Harris (chapter 20, this volume) emphasize that research in spiritual development will need to unravel the ways in which a group shapes the form, content, and trajectory of a people's religious and spiritual development. Because religion and spirituality are interwoven into all aspects of life, the authors maintain that relevant to the discourse on spiritual development are the cultural definitions of adolescence, childhood, selfhood, and personhood. What are significant would be the processes of integration into religious and spiritual communities (e.g., religious rituals), and how others in these communities contribute to the construction of one's spiritual and religious identity (e.g., experience of spirituality).

These issues are illustrated through Whiting's (1990) recounting of how pubescent boys undergo spiritual transformation among the Ojibwa of North America:

> The quest for a guardian spirit is widespread among the Indians of North America. Guardian spirits appear to an individual in a dream or vision. Such dreams are believed to be induced by fasting and isolation. Landes (1938) reports for the Southern Ojibwa that the pubescent boy is encouraged to seek a supernatural power who will "adopt him and care for him as a parent or grandparent cares for a child." By isolating himself and fasting, the pubescent boy will arouse pity in the supernatural, which will take him as a protégé, bound to him "by the firmest loyalties what exists in Ojibwa." In the Ojibwa idiom, to "pity" another is to adopt and care for them. (p. 363)

Spiritual experiences during adolescence are, therefore, not only closely tied to cultural notions of adolescence, childhood, selfhood, and personhood. They are also linked closely to notions about the nature of relations one has with others in one's social world, as well as the emotions that one invests in these relationships.

Moreover, transformation in spirituality as it occurs within the adolescent stage hinges on the changes in relationships and the emotional experiences that occur with these changes. This would be particularly true in most Asian cultures. Among the Japanese, for example, a personally related deity is unavailable, and there is little recourse for religious beliefs that can compensate for the needed benevolence and concern that comes during different stages in one's life (DeVos, 1985). Youth in Japan are thus likely to be taught to participate in the expression of religion through the idealization of the family as part of a quasi-religious security system and particularly through the idealization of the maternal relationship as it has been experienced within the family (DeVos, 1985). This arises from the Confucian ideology regarding the family and social relationships, which emphasizes an ideal of ordered human feelings based on harmony and on one's proper maintenance of expected roles within one's social group (DeVos, 1985). Among the Chinese, spiritual development entails the Confucian quest for self-transformation as a communal act (Tu, 1985):

> It is through the disciplining of the body and mind that the Confucian acquires a taste for life, not as an isolated individual, but as an active participant in the living community—the family, the province, the state, and the world. The idea of "ritualization," which implies a dynamic process of self-cultivation in the spirit of filiality, brotherhood, friendship, and loyalty, seems to capture well this basic Confucian intention. (p. 232)

In summary, giving serious consideration to culture as an important facet of spiritual development will involve a view to this process of development within contexts of activities organized through religious symbolism and social relationships that are imbued with meanings collectively shared by the young person's group. The paths to spiritual development seem therefore to be determined by notions of an idealized personhood, as well as of an idealized social order, that are nurtured within the complexity of one's culture.

A final point has to be made regarding the analytical agenda that needs to be worked out in examining spiritual development from a cultural perspective. It would be useful to heed Clifford Geertz's (1973) caution regarding confusing the intrinsic double aspect of culture patterns. According to Geertz, culture patterns "give meaning, that is, objective conceptual form, to social and psychological reality both by shaping themselves to it [being models of] and by shaping it themselves [being models for]" (p. 93). He further clarifies that concrete symbols involved in religion "point in either direction, they both express the world's climate and shape it. They shape it by inducing in the worshipper a certain distinctive set of dispositions . . . which lend a chronic character to the flow of his activity and the quality of his experience" (p. 95). Geertz explains how confusion can result when the two aspects of cultural patterns and symbolism are not disentangled in analysis:

> Religious belief has usually been presented as a homogeneous characteristic of an individual, like his place of residence, his occupational role, his kinship position, and so on. But religious belief in the midst of ritual, where it engulfs the total person, transporting him, so far as he is concerned, into another mode of existence, and religious belief as the pale remembered reflection of that experience in the midst of everyday life are not precisely the same thing, and the failure to realize this has led to some confusion. (pp. 119–120)

Religion as "pure" and religion as "applied" need to be distinguished analytically. The terms, according to Geertz, represent two forms of thought. Therefore, in the study of spirituality and religion from a cultural perspective, one needs to determine how these two modes of symbolic formulations interact with each other. Determining the interaction between how religion and spirituality provide a source of the general conceptions of the world, the self, and the relations between them (the models of), on the one hand, and how religion and spirituality represent mental dispositions (i.e., motives and moods), on the other, will allow us a way to examine process. As Geertz asserts, "Only when we have a theoretical analysis of symbolic action . . . will we be able to cope effectively with those aspects of social and psychological life in which religion . . . plays a determinant role" (p. 125).

CONCLUSIONS

Adolescent experiences across the globe are being altered by macrosocietal changes that are affecting their preparation for adulthood (Larson & Verma, 2002). Amidst all these unstable and stressful life situations, adolescents are emerging as active agents of change, creating their own contexts for development, including search for self, a sense of purpose and deriving meaning in the varying contexts that they live in. Creating the research agenda for spiritual development in the adolescent stage brings us to the issues of transformation and translation. Transformation issues will lead us to examine the changes in faith and notions of the sacred, as the young person moves away from childhood spirituality and religion. Translation issues take us to the investigation of the outcome of this movement in the social and emotional life of adolescents, specifically in the processes involved in the formation of identity, relationships, aspirations, and life projects.

The conditions that prepare youth for transformation may be said to spring from three sources. The first involves their entry into more expanding contexts of interaction as they journey toward adulthood. Another source consists of their confrontations with situations that require from them comprehensive ideas of order that are consistent with what they perceive their world to have become. Yet another source is the organized and collective system of meanings from which youth draw and actualize their notions of idealized personhood within an idealized system of relating in one's social world. An intensive study of process is needed—a study that may be well informed by the analysis of symbolic action within a cultural perspective.

REFERENCES

Allen, J. M., & Coy, D. R. (2004). Linking spirituality and violence prevention in school counseling. *Professional School Counseling, 7*(5), 351.

Arnett, J. (2002). Adolescents in western countries in the 21st century: Vast opportunities for all? In B. B. Brown, R. W. Larson, & T. S. Saraswathi (Eds.), *The world's youth: Adolescence in eight regions of the world* (pp. 307–343). Cambridge, UK: Cambridge University Press.

Benson, P. L., Roehlkepartain, E. C., & Rude, S. P. (2003). Spiritual development in childhood and adolescence: Toward a field of inquiry. *Applied Developmental Science, 7* (3), 204–212.

Booth, M. (2002). Arab adolescents facing the future: Enduring ideals and pressures to change. In B. B. Brown, R. W. Larson, & T. S. Saraswathi (Eds.), *The world's youth: Adolescence in eight regions of the globe* (pp. 207–242). Cambridge, UK: Cambridge University Press.

Brown, B. B., Larson, R. W., & Saraswathi, T. S. (2002). *The world's youth: Adolescence in eight regions of the globe.* Cambridge, UK: Cambridge University Press.

Bruce, M. A., & Cockreham, D. (2004). Enhancing the spiritual development of adolescent girls. *Professional School Counseling, 7*(5), 334.

Cagoco-Guiam, R. (2002). *Child soldiers in Central and Western Mindanao: A rapid assessment.* Manila: International Labour Office–International Programme on the Elimination of Child Labour.

Coles, R. (1990). *The spiritual life of children.* Boston: Houghton Mifflin.

DeVos, G. (1985). Dimensions of self in Japanese culture. In A. J. Marsella, G. DeVos, & F. L. K. Hsu (Eds.), *Culture and self: Asian and western perspectives* (pp. 141–184). New York: Tavistock.

Geertz, C. (1973). *The interpretation of cultures.* New York: Basic Books.

Gilligan, C. (1982). *In a different voice.* Cambridge, MA: Harvard University Press.

Hill, P. C., & Pargament, K. I. (2003). Advances in conceptualization and measurement of religion and spirituality: Implications for physical and mental health research. *American Psychologist, 58*(1), 64–74.

Ikeda, D. (2000). *The way of youth.* Santa Monica, CA: Middleway Press.

Ingersoll, R. (1998). Redefining dimensions of spiritual wellness: Across-traditional approach. *Counseling and Values, 42,* 156–165.

Inglehart, R., & Baker, W. E. (2000). Modernization, cultural change, and the persistence of traditional values. *American Sociological Review, 65*(1), 19–51.

Kelley, J., & De Graaf, N. D. (1997). National context, parental socialization, and religious belief: Results from 15 nations. *American Sociological Review, 62*(4), 639–659.

Kessler, R. (2002). *Passages: Fostering community, heart, and spirit in adolescent education.* Retrieved January 2004, from http://www.newhorizons.org/lifelong/adolescence/kessler1.htm

Kumari, M. K., & Sree, K. J. (1992). Role of youth in religion and politics of India. In Y. C. Simhadri (Ed.), *Global youth, peace and development* (Vol. 2). Delhi: Ajanta.

Larson, R., Brown, B. B., & Mortimer, J. (2002). *Adolescents' preparation for the future: Perils and promise.* Oxford, UK: Blackwell.

Larson, R., & Verma, S. (2002). Globalization and the emergence of new adolescences: Findings from the work of an interdisciplinary Study Group on Adolescence in the 21st Century. *ISSBD Newsletter, 1*(4), 23.

Larson, R. W., Wilson, S., Brown, B. B., Furstenberg, F. F., & Verma, S. (2002). Changes in adolescents' interpersonal experiences: Are they being prepared for adult relationships in the twenty-first century? *Journal of Research on Adolescence, 12*(1), 31.

Lopiano-Miscom, J., & De Luca, J. (1998). Tune in, turn on, link up. *Brandweek, 39*(2), 22.

Machel, G. (2001). *The impact of war on children.* London: Hurst.

Miller, R. (2002). An outpouring of new books on spirituality in education. *Paths of Learning, 12,* 37–44.

Mortimer, J. T., & Larson, R. W. (2002). *The changing adolescent experience: Societal trends and the transition to adulthood.* Cambridge, UK: Cambridge University Press.

Myers, J. E., & Williard, K. (2003). Integrating spirituality into counselor preparation: A developmental and wellness approach. *Counseling and Values, 47,* 142–155.

Nsamenang, A.B. (2002). Adolescence in Sub-Saharan Africa: An image constructed from Africa's triple inheritance. In B. B. Brown, R. W. Larson, & T. S. Saraswathi (Eds.), *The world's youth: Adolescence in eight regions of the globe* (pp. 61–104). Cambridge, UK: Cambridge University Press.

Santrock, J. W. (2001). *Adolescence* (8th ed.). Boston: McGraw-Hill.

Schlegel, A., & Barry, H. (1991). *Adolescence: An anthropological inquiry.* New York: Free Press.

Sink, C. A. (2004). Spirituality and comprehensive school counseling programs. *Professional School Counseling, 7*(5), 309.

Sta. Maria, M. (2002). Youth in Southeast Asia: Living within the continuity of tradition and the turbulence of change. In B. B. Brown, R. Larson, & T. S. Saraswathi (Eds.), *The world's youth: Adolescence in eight regions of the globe* (pp. 171–206). Cambridge, UK: Cambridge University Press.

Stetsenko, A. (2002). Adolescents in Russia: Surviving the turmoil and creating a brighter future. In B. B. Brown, R. W. Larson, & T. S. Saraswathi (Eds.), *The world's youth: Adolescence in eight regions of the globe* (pp. 243–275). Cambridge, UK: Cambridge University Press.

Tu Wei-ming. (1985). Selfhood and otherness in Confucian thought. In A. J. Marsella, G. DeVos, & F. L. K. Hsu (Eds.), *Culture and self: Asian and western perspectives* (pp. 231–251). New York: Tavistock.

Upreti, H. C. (1987). *Youth politics in India.* Jaipur, India: Printwell.

Verma, S., & Saraswathi, T. S. (2002). Adolescence in India: Street urchins or Silicon Valley millionaires? In B. B. Brown, R. W. Larson, & T. S. Saraswathi (Eds.), *The world's youth: Adolescence in eight regions of the globe* (pp. 105–140). Cambridge, UK: Cambridge University Press.

Welti, C. (2002). Adolescents in Latin America: Facing the future with skepticism. In B. B. Brown, R. W. Larson, & T. S. Saraswathi (Eds.), *The world's youth: Adolescence in eight regions of the globe* (pp. 276–306). Cambridge, UK: Cambridge University Press.

Whiting, J. W. M. (1990). Adolescent rituals and identity conflicts. In J. W. Stigler, R. A. Shweder, & G. Herdt (Eds.), *Cultural psychology: Essays on comparative human development* (pp. 357–365). Cambridge, UK: Cambridge University Press.

Youniss, J., Bales, S., Christmas-Best, V., Diversi, M., McLaughlin, M., & Silbereisen, R. (2002). Youth civic engagement in the twenty-first century. *Journal of Research on Adolescence, 12*(1), 31.

10

Spiritual and Religious Pathology in Childhood and Adolescence

Linda M. Wagener

H. Newton Malony

Any discussion of spiritual pathology necessarily wades into a realm of value-laden contructs and becomes particularly difficult in the absence of a universally accepted notion of "normal" spiritual development. Yet, insofar as spiritual development implies a trajectory toward an ideal end state (see Scarlett, chapter 2, this volume), it ought to be possible to articulate and to identify whether a particular individual is "on the right track." In fact, we might argue that this is a commonplace practice. We are generally inclined to recognize that there is something "wrong" with the spirituality of someone who kills innocents in the name of God or believes that he or she has been taken over by an evil spirit.

A foundational assumption of this chapter is that it is possible to draw a distinction between pathological and normal spiritual development. An alternative approach is, however, possible. Some might argue that spiritual development is socially constructed such that the designation of a particular form of spirituality as pathological is a matter of interpretation, based entirely on social convention, rooted as it may be in historicopolitical structures. Thus, the religious terrorist who views globalization and the spread of Western values as leading to the corruption of the fundamental tenents of a pure faith will view Western capitalists as an appropriate target for holy war. A young woman who has been raised to believe that multitudes of spirits, both benign and malevolent, can inhabit persons may be using constructs and language familiar to her culture to explain a moral lapse. In the end, the radical relativism of such a position is philosophically and even functionally unsatisfying. However, this perspective is valuable in elucidating the cultural influences on the understanding of spiritual development and its location in a particular context.

We will begin by briefly discussing the history of attention paid to spiritual and religious pathology in the social sciences, followed by definitional issues and four "methods" for identifying pathological development. We will then turn to specific examples of spiritual pathology. In this chapter we will address four areas of religious and spiritual pathology that make their appearance in youth and have been given attention within the social sciences: delusions, terrorism, cults or new religious movements, and the special case of young people who have been subjected to trauma.

THE STUDY OF RELIGIOUS AND SPIRITUAL PATHOLOGY

The social sciences have historically treated the issue of spiritual and religious development with either neglect or attention to eclectic issues, primarily dealing with odd or pathological expressions of religious or spiritual beliefs and practices. A review of a typical index from a basic developmental psychology text of the modern era (Sroufe & Cooper, 1988) cites no entries for spiritual development and one entry pertaining to religion: "religious cults." Other common entries in introductory psychology texts include "religion and psychoactive drug use," "religious delusions," and "spirit possession." Only recently have texts begun to describe, though still minimally, nonpathological processes of spiritual development (see, e.g., Myers, 2001).

This overemphasis on the pathological, particularly in regard to religious functioning, has its roots in the foundational theories of psychology. Enlightenment constructs including positivism, materialism, rationalism, and humanism in part derived from a repudiation of any kind of transcendence of the external world, of personal immortality, or of the existence of a spiritual dimension of human functioning. From Freud and Watson onward, social scientists have been shaped by psychological theories that have considered religious and spiritual beliefs and practices to be examples of illusional functioning.

In multiple writings (*Civilization and Its Discontents*, 1930/1961; The *Future of an Illusion*, 1927/1928; *Totem and Taboo*, 1913/1927), Sigmund Freud articulated the theory that religious ideation and beliefs were the result of a projection of immature psychic needs for dependency. Freud theorized that in monotheistic forms of religion the fallible father of reality is replaced by an omnipotent and infallible father-God. According to Freud, people created God in the image of an all-powerful parent in order to deny their vulnerability and maintain their child status. Freud believed that religious beliefs are a particularly dangerous form of illusion because they interfere with our scientific efforts to distinguish reality from our wishes:

> The whole thing [religion] is so patently infantile, so incongruous with reality, that to one whose attitude to humanity is friendly it is painful to think that the great majority of mortals will never be able to rise above this view of life. It is even more humiliating to discover what a large number of those alive today, who must see that this religion is not tenable, yet try to defend it inch by inch, as if with a series of pitiable rearguard actions. (1930/1961, p. 22)

The American behaviorist movement, founded as a protest against the mind–body split, the concept of consciousness, and any use of introspective methods, furthered the inhospitable climate for the examination of religious and spiritual phenomena.

The only notable exceptions to this trend in the early 20th century were William James's "descriptive" treatment of religion in *The Varieties of Religious Experience* (1902) and G. Stanley Hall's "world soul" approach in *Jesus the Christ in the Light of Psychology* (1917). The Clark School of Religious Psychology, which Hall directed, spawned many analyses of religious development—most of which either "bracketed" the validity question of religion or recommended an approach to childrearing that led to benign acceptance but not religious conviction. Hall's theory of Christian conversion described it as a normal developmental process. He suggested that youth would be swayed more by the idea of someone loving them enough to die for them than they would by the idea of a martyr dying for what he believed (Malony, 1984). It is interesting that Hall, who is considered the first developmental psychologist, would incorporate into his philosophical ideas a model that included religious experience. Beit-Hallahmi (1977) noted how the appropriation of this early 20th-century interest in religion by religious educators led to a rejection of interest by mainline psychology. Religion became one of psychology's taboo subjects until the mid-1950s.

More recently there has been a tendency to align positive aspects of functioning with "spirituality" and negative aspects with "religion." The story of Bill W., founder of Alcoholics Anonymous, illustrates the modern trend toward this split:

On a chill, rainy afternoon in November, 1934, two men sat catercorner at the kitchen table of a brownstone house in Brooklyn, New York. On the white oilcloth-covered table stood a pitcher of pineapple juice, two glasses, and a bottle of gin, recently retrieved from its hiding place in the overhead tank of the toilet in the adjacent bathroom.

The visitor, neatly groomed and bright-eyed, smiled gently as his tall, craggy faced host reached for the bottle and offered him a drink.

"No thanks," Ebby said. "I'm not drinking."

"Not drinking! Why not?" Bill was so surprised that he stopped pouring to look with concern at his old friend. "What's the matter?"

"I don't need it anymore," Ebby replied simply. "I've got religion."

Religion? Damn! For a fleeting moment, Bill wondered about his friend's sanity. Ebby, after all, was a drinking buddy from way back. Now, apparently he had gone off the deep end—his alcoholic insanity had become religious insanity!

Bill gulped a slug of gin. Well, dammit, not him. Religion was for the weak, the old, the hopeless; he'd never "get religion."

Bill Wilson never did "get religion" but he did get sober, and unlike Ebby, who would die destitute after 30 years of sporadic drinking, Bill stayed sober. How? Through a spiritual program that grew precisely from his realization that religion with its canons and commandments, wouldn't work for him and seemingly contradictory understanding that without help from a power greater than himself, he was lost. "*We must find a spiritual basis for living,*" Bill later said about himself and other alcoholics, "*else we die.*" (Kurtz & Ketchum, 1992, p. 4)

Alcoholics Anonymous, a significant 20th-century grassroots psychological movement, has always presented its program as "spiritual" rather than "religious" and has been consistently wary and critical of the dogma and directives of conventional religions.

These examples are but a few illustrations of the social sciences' penchant for considering religion pathological. Any treatment of spiritual and religious pathology must therefore be situated within a foundational theoretical approach that respectfully addresses the full range of religious and spiritual functioning and particularly works to identify positive aspects. Empirical research has demonstrated no relationship between religion and dysfunction (Bergin, 1983). In fact, religion has often been linked with lowered psychological distress (Ross, 1990) and positive developmental outcomes (King and Benson, chapter 27, this volume).

DEFINITIONAL ISSUES

Spirituality, as we use the term in this chapter, is the essential potentiality for addressing the ultimate questions that are intrinsic to the experience of being human. It includes experiences of transcendence, good and evil, belonging and connectedness, meaning and purpose. Spirituality is an integrative function that leads to an experience of personal wholeness and defines the links between the self and the rest of creation, locating the individual within a transcendent system of meaning. As Alexander and Carr (chapter 6, this volume) have summarized, rival conceptions of spirituality function to locate the focal point of a meaningful and purposeful life. Although they may differ in their emphasis on the subjective, collective, or objective, any coherent conception of spirituality will integrate these various dimensions of meaning. As we use the terms, *spirituality* refers to the personal and experiential dimensions; *religion* is the shared belief and social structure within which, for most but not all, spirituality is primarily shaped. We recognize that secular spiritualities also have legitimacy related to this domain.

Pathology will be understood as that which reflects a distortion of reality or leads to potential harm to self or others. Distinctions will be drawn between those beliefs and practices that are pathological and those that are culturally idiosyncratic. Absent from this discussion is attention to the concept of *heresy,* defined as an opinion or a doctrine at variance with established religious beliefs. While this may constitute spiritual pathology from the perspective of a religious tradition, it has not been addressed from a social science perspective. In fact, we "bracket" all questions as to which interpretation or religious tradition has more validity than another as the domain of theology.

PATHOLOGICAL SPIRITUAL DEVELOPMENT

An underlying assumption of this chapter is that spiritual and religious pathology in children and adolescents should be regarded as deviation from a normal developmental pathway. Normal development is defined by emerging competencies in a series of interconnected social, emotional, and cognitive skills. Pathological development is a lack of integration of competencies that are important to achieving particular developmental tasks. In the area of spirituality, normal development involves the integration of experiences into a system of meaning that addresses questions of ultimate purpose, connectedness, good and evil, and transcendent reality. We assume that such questions are imbedded in what it means to be human. Organic, intrapersonal, interpersonal, contextual, and even supervenient factors can influence the course of spiritual development. Challenges arise in identifying the influences that divert development from its typical course. As examples, the onset of a psychosis may lead to religious delusions; intrapersonal experiences of guilt and shame may be interwoven with compulsions and obsessions about salvation; experiences of abuse by a religious leader may affect one's concept of God; and contextual influences such as membership in a religious organization that promotes violence or self-sacrifice may lead to acts of terrorism or suicide. Spiritual development, in some cases, might involve experiences of the supernatural or miracles. In each of these cases the task of the social scientist is to evaluate the adaptiveness of these potential realities.

To add to the complexity of the issue, spirituality can be connected to the entire range of children's mental and emotional life. Their experiences and understanding of death, illness, trauma, despair, joy, hope, guilt, shame, sexuality, and identity may be relevant to their spiritual development. Particular experiences of trauma, suffering, and loss may, in fact, provoke spiritual development as children draw on the religious and spiritual resources available to them to understand and give meaning to the challenges they face (see Mahoney, Pendleton, & Ihrke, chapter 24, this volume)

Adolescence can be a time of particular vulnerability to spiritual pathology. As Erikson (1963) noted, during adolescence, youth begin to appreciate their own history at the same time that they consider what role they will play in culture. The process of the development of a coherent identity requires that adolescents draw from models found within their social context yet, paradoxically, define themselves uniquely. Traditionally, adolescents have been critical of traditional values and established patterns of society. In some cases, their idealism may lead them to believe in new social movements and leaders. As higher order cognitive skills become engaged, adolescents are likely to become intellectually curious and drawn to seeking truth in novel ways. Without the wisdom and experience of maturity, adolescents have more difficulty critiquing complex philosophical systems or delineating long-term consequences of choices.

Adolescents, by virtue of their developmental status, are prone to forms of spiritual pathology that infrequently occur in childhood. Their developmental focus on formation of identity includes, to a greater or lesser extent, their sense of self as a spiritual and/or religious person. For the majority of adolescents, these developmental strivings will be housed in the context of traditional approaches, most often within the faith tradition or secular "soul-searching" of their family. For a minority, particularly those who are vulnerable owing to psychopathology, family or cultural disintegration, or trauma, their religious and spiritual development may become pathological, leading to harm to self or others.

IDENTIFYING SPIRITUAL PATHOLOGY

We propose that there are four common "methods" for determining whether a particular form of spirituality is pathological. These include functional, culturally consensual, rational, and authoritarian approaches, each with its own strengths and limitations. We begin by distinguishing between questions of pathology that refer to whether a particular form of development has deleterious effects on the health, well-being, or life adjustment of the young person and questions of truth that refer to whether a particular belief system reflects some objective reality. These questions are not synonymous (Meissner, 2002). Identification of a form of spiritual development as pathological depends on assessing the degree to which spiritual development contributes to a pattern of meaningful life experience and adaptive functioning or, conversely, leads to disorganization and disturbances in functioning.

The Functional Approach

The functional approach to defining pathology primarily relies on empirical investigation to demonstrate the association between particular forms of spirituality and other either positive or negative outcomes. As an example, in a study of college students Mahoney et al. (2002) demonstrated that students who made demonic interpretations of the events of September 11 were more likely to feel threatened and experience post-traumatic stress symptoms. A second case in point is that participation by Palestinian youth in political violence through the intifada is positively associated with religiosity (Barber, 2001).

A functional approach has the capacity to generate significant research opportunities that are as yet unstudied. Complicating the picture, however, is that because religious and spiritual strivings are complex and multidimensional, they may have both negative and positive effects. For example, some spiritual practices that might be considered exemplary, such as dedicating one's life to serving the poor, may also lead to psychological distress. As another example, while fundamentalist religious orientations are linked to greater prejudice and intolerance (Altemeyer, 2003), they are also linked to greater optimism and felt well-being (Sethi & Seligman, 1993).

The Culturally Consensual Approach

A second approach to identifying pathology relies on consensus within particular communities or traditions. Many spiritual practices that are considered normal within one tradition might be seen as pathological in another. Examples include the experience of visions, receiving direct communication from God, speaking in tongues, encountering a variety of spirits, and receiving healing from the laying on of hands.

Zar is a term applied in some North African and Middle Eastern societies to refer to spirit possession. Within these cultures, spirit possession is not considered pathological, although the individual may experience dissociative episodes that include intense emotional lability or extreme apathy and withdrawal or perhaps even the development of a long-term relationship with a spirit.

A culturally sensitive approach to defining pathology will take into account the norms of the individual's ethnic or cultural reference groups regarding their behavior, its causes and meaning. Culturally relevant interpretations include attention to social stressors, available social supports, and local illness categories.

A challenge to this approach is that often the values of a particular subculture may clash with those of the majority culture or may change across time. In particular, issues of childrearing and protection of minors can become a focal point of contention. Allegations of child endangerment and abuse, for example, sparked government intervention in the case of the Branch Davidians, leading unfortunately to the deaths of 81 adults and children living in the group's Waco, Texas, compound (Ellison & Bartkowski, 1995).

In an increasingly global culture, important questions are raised when the spiritual norms of cultures clash. Rapid cultural change can also lead to generational divides that leave grandparents, parents, and children with little common ground to reflect on questions of ultimate concern. Intersecting traditions need to create agreement that unites rather than divides, with a spirituality that is meaningful to self and the collective.

The Rational Approach

In contrast to the approaches elucidated so far, we can identify pathology by appealing to reason and theory. According to this classical view, rooted in moral philosophy, human beings have the capacity to recognize virtuous goals and act in accordance with them. A modern version of this approach is to identify spiritual exemplars in order to learn what is distinctive about them or, conversely, to examine the lives of those whose spirituality is universally understood to be pathological (e.g., murderers). This approach has a rich history and tradition and has generated significant dialogue about human nature.

The Authoritarian Approach

Finally, one can appeal to a higher source of authority in order to discriminate both appropriate and pathological spiritual development. This is the realm of theology, and traditional religions have relied on sacred texts and scriptures both to define the ideal state of spirituality and to give definition to spiritual pathology. Political and philosophical movements give shape to secular spiritualites as well.

The limits of this approach are illustrated in the multitude of historical examples of destructive movements, both religiously and politically motivated, including the Crusades, the Inquisition, the Holocaust, and other ethnic cleansing movements.

EXAMPLES OF SPIRITUAL PATHOLOGY

Our examples of spiritual pathology include deviations from the normal developmental progression due to aberrant developmental process in the organic, intrapersonal, interpersonal and cultural spheres. We will discuss the special cases of delusions, new religious movements, and terrorism as illustrative of pathological spiritual development.

Religious Delusions

Religious delusions and hallucinations are thought to derive primarily from disturbances in the basic perceptual and organizational sphere of development that lead to disorganization and lack of coherence in the spiritual functioning of the young person. A belief is considered to be delusional only to the extent that it violates what is known to be true about objective reality. The identification of delusions does not apply in

those cases where it is not possible to test the validity of a belief. A belief that Jesus walked on water is empirically untestable; a belief that I can walk on water is testable and hence delusional since it is not true.

In some cases a belief may be illusional as opposed to delusional, in that it is based on a wish or need of the individual, rather than an assessment of some empirically testable set of evidence. Such a belief would be pathological only to the degree that the wish or need is pathological (Meissner, 2002) or leads to maladaptive functioning. A nonpathological illusion would be the belief that one's prayers to God will help one survive cancer despite negative odds. Such "positive illusions" have been demonstrated to lead to better health outcomes (Taylor, Kemeny, Reed, Bower, & Gruenewald, 2000) and thus function as resources rather than as risks.

The grandiose and persecutory ideology that is reflected in delusions and hallucinations can be understood as a distortion of the spiritual impulse to connect with the transcendent and the sacred. The content of religious delusions is often concerned with supernatural power or good and evil. Religious delusions, associated with schizophrenia and other psychoses, often make their first appearance in adolescence, and rarely in childhood. While they result from neurological, neurochemical, or other forms of biological dysfunction, they are shaped by personal history and culture, and so often incorporate personally and culturally relevant meaning.

An example of how personal context affects the content of delusions is the disorder that has been labeled the Jerusalem syndrome. In this syndrome, visitors to the holy city gradually become withdrawn and assume a sudden identity shift, donning makeshift robes and preaching in the streets. Jerusalem psychiatrist Yair Bar-El (1994) notes that the religious tradition of the patient affects the form of the delusion. Christians tend to believe that they are Jesus Christ, John the Baptist, or the Virgin Mary. Jews will more often believe that they are Moses, Samson, or King David, whereas Muslims tend to identify with the Mahdi, the Savior who will be sent before the end of time to establish the global dominion of Islam.

Religious hallucinations are often tied to the patient's delusional system of beliefs. The most common is auditory hallucinations, which take the form of voices. The content can reinforce a sense either of grandeur, as in communicating instructions from God or angels, or persecution, as in hearing threatening or accusing voices. A young person in the midst of a severe psychotic episode often cannot distinguish hallucinations from reality. With improvement, however, the voices are recognized as hallucinations or may even stop completely.

Delusional beliefs can be distinguished from other religious experiences such as mountaintop experiences at camp or decisions made in revivals or other religious meetings, since the former most frequently occur as part of a complex pattern of symptoms indicating psychosis, including apathy, anhedonia, withdrawal, and peculiar disorganized thinking. This quality of organizational instability is noteworthy and helps to distinguish delusional beliefs from those that are part of a coherent system of belief. Additionally, youth who are in the midst of a process of psychological deterioration associated with psychosis will most likely demonstrate significant difficulties in functioning competently in their daily living. Social activities, schoolwork, and self-care are noticeably affected. This typically results in the young person's becoming excessively dependent on others.

Yet another rare form of adolescent spiritual pathology is grandiosity or claiming of special status or personhood. John Edward (1999), the psychic host of the television program *Crossing Over,* tells of his concern during adolescence that his budding ability to receive messages from the dead would label him as a "freak." That he was able then to fit into other behavioral norms for teenagers and has been able to turn his skill into a lifework have prevented him from being thought of as suffering from a mental illness. Others are not so fortunate. They hear voices and claim special status, such as was the case of Joan of Arc. Church youth who have mystical experiences while attending summer camp would also border on being considered psychopathological were it not for the fact that many others share the events and they are protected by church bodies who, in fact, nurture their development, providing them resources with which to process and give meaning to their experience.

A third pathway to religious hallucinations and distortions of consciousness is through the use of psychoactive substances. The appeal of extraordinary experience is high among adolescence. The introduction of psychedelic drugs into the youth culture during the 1960s was accompanied by the promise of revelation of spiritual truths. Harvard professor Timothy Leary conducted a series of psychological studies of "insight" experiences produced by consciousness-altering drugs, notably psilocybin (Leary, 1965). Among the effects on behavior and consciousness Leary discussed was an openness to religious influence and spiritual experience (Leary & Clark, 1963). In fact, Clark recommended the regular ingesting of these drugs for the induction of spiritual experiences in a culture that he felt militated against such events. It is unclear whether he would have approved of such drug use among adolescents (see Clark, Malony, Daane, & Tippett, 1973).

While this movement has been generally discredited within the social sciences, it still reappears among youth who draw on various influences, including an attraction to the religious ceremonies of native peoples. Mescaline derived from the peyote cactus and psilocybin derived from the psilocybe mushroom have been used in religious rites in Mexico and Central America since 500 BCE. In these traditional societies the use of psychoactive drugs is tightly controlled and integrated, so abuse is rare. However, when traditional structures begin to break down, ritual use may deteriorate into drug abuse. As an example, kava is a substance that has been used in the South Pacific islands as part of traditional religious rituals. In recent years, kava abuse has been a significant social problem as young people have dissociated its use from the context of the religious training and ceremonies (Trimble, 1994).

New Religious Movements

New religious movements or charismatic groups are typically defined by the presence of four characteristics: strict adherence to a consensual belief system, a high level of social cohesiveness, strict behavioral norms, and the imputation of charismatic or divine power to the group or its leadership (Galanter, 1996). It is particularly important in the area of new religions to distinguish between movements that are not yet accepted by the mainstream culture and those that are pathological in that they influence members toward self-harm or harming others. Many new religious movements (NRMs) have been subjected to radical forms of social control by a culture swayed by stories of brainwashing and other coercive techniques (Richardson, 1993). Public opinion research reveals widespread popular belief that NRMs are exploitative (Bromley & Breschel, 1992). Despite First Amendment protection in the United States, the sustained punitive nature of social control has a deleterious effect on the long-term survival of NRMs. Without significant social and financial resources, NRMs frequently cannot mount a successful legal defense without diverting from their religious missions, which are often socially constructive.

The well-known case of Robin George, an adolescent who became enamored with the Hare Krishnas, illustrates how easy it is for nontraditional, minority religious movements to be labeled as using coercive persuasion. Like many adolescents who are not into the more popular religious movements and who may be experiencing social disfavor, Robin George attended Hare Krishna meetings and set up an altar in her home. Against her parents' wishes, she moved into the Krishna center. Although she later left the group and claimed she was influenced against her will, the Krishnas have demonstrated in court that they had not used any brainwashing techniques ("$9.7 Million Hare Krishna Award Reviewed," 1988).

This tendency to try alternative spiritual movements continues. Among more recent NRMs, now extending into their second generation, are Wicca, paganism, Scientology, Osho Ko Hsuan, Shaja Yoga, In Search of Truth, and The Family. It is often difficult to assess whether the natural tendency for adolescents to try new behaviors explains choices that are perceived as pathological or whether these smaller NRMs actually engage in coercive persuasion and thereby create pathology. While the study of children in new religious movements is relatively rare, there are some interesting examples. Those children who have grown up in NRMs are likely to be in a very different situation from their parents, who

often made the choice to join an alternative and radical religious organization (Palmer & Hardman, 1999).

In particular, recent decades have seen a rise in accusations of child abuse against members of new religious movements as a means of social control. Charges have been brought against individual members, usually parents, accused of mistreating their own children and also collectively against entire communities. Often these incidents arise in the context of custody disputes between parents who have split over the family commitment to the NRM. Examples of accusations of collective abuse include the well-known suit in 1984 brought against the Northeast Community Kingdom Church in Island Pond, Vermont (Malcarne & Burchard, 1992), and the Branch Davidians of Waco (Ellison & Bartkowski, 1995). In each of these examples, it was assumed that children were being mistreated simply as a result of their membership in a particular religious collective whose beliefs and practices were considered to be harmful. These practices typically include religious home schooling, corporal punishment, or allegations of aberrant sexual practices. In the most extreme cases, children were separated from their families in "raids" and placed for extended periods in state care. Extensive psychological assessment revealed that the children were generally healthy, well educated, and relationally skilled. Any anxiety or trauma resulted from the forced separation from their families, rather than from the religious practices of their community (see Goddard, 1994a, 1994b).

As a further example, accusations against the communal group called The Family have been legally proved to be unfounded in Australia, Argentina, England, France, and the United States. One unpublished doctoral dissertation (Vogt, 1999) found that second-generation youth growing up in The Family identified more strongly with proscriptions against sexual promiscuity and in favor of fidelity than did a western U.S. sample of youth raised in nuclear families.

Many youth movements draw on the spiritual longings of young people to find truth, experience the transcendent, and connect with others in a way that moves them beyond narrow self-interest. Powerful spiritual experiences of belonging and connectedness are often influential in attracting young people to religious subgroups that may function at odds with the dominant culture. Those adolescents particularly susceptible to recruitment may be experiencing identity confusion, alienation from family, weak cultural and community ties, and feelings of powerlessness (Hunter, 1998). A study of 15 subjects previously belonging to "cults" demonstrated that the process of so-called mind control originated with adolescent needs following a period of loneliness and personal search, loosening of church ties, feelings of guilt, and a background of rigid family beliefs (Venter, 1998). It would be a mistake, however, to think that adolescent members of NRMs are easily identifiable by atypical demographics given that a surprising number come from democratic and egalitarian homes and upper socioeconomic levels (Andron, 1983).

Religious Terrorism

It is chilling to note that a disturbing number of young people become involved in violent religiously motivated activities. Adolescents and even children in countries such as Colombia, Rwanda, Sierra Leone, Palestine, and Ireland have become soldiers and rebels engaged in brutal acts of violence. Young people who become involved in religious terrorism are struggling with the spiritual questions that define good and evil and their connection to structures of power. Terrorism, whether secularly or religiously motivated, is seen in violent acts against perceived evil and thus can be understood to be related to one's spiritual worldview and development. In these cases, it is often difficult to assess pathological functioning at the individual level, unless one uses the criterion of whether the young person has engaged in activities that led to harm. Examples in adolescence include joining terrorist organizations (e.g., the IRA or Hamas), school shootings, and suicide bombings. The process of becoming a terrorist results from a combination of factors, including individual characteristics, coercion, social identification and marginalization, a desire for vengeance status and personal rewards, and opportunity (Silke, 2003).

The most common biological factors that are associated with terrorism are age and gender.

Young men are the most common terrorist recruits. This may be related to the well-documented gender effect on aggressive and deviant risk-taking behavior. It is often the younger members of terrorist groups who carry out the most violent attacks (Silke, 1999). Research has not supported the idea that terrorists have a particular pathological personality structure or mental illness (Silke, 2003).

Many recruits to terrorist groups are brought up in families and subcultures that strongly support the aims and methods of the terrorist groups such that the views and values are part of their socialization. Membership in a marginalized and disadvantaged group, either by birth or life experience, increases the receptivity of the teenager to radical ideologies. In some communities during especially disruptive periods it may become normative to join a terrorist group.

One young recruit explained: "My motivation in joining Fatah was both ideological and personal. It was a question of self-fulfillment, of honour, and a feeling of independence . . . the goal of every young Palestinian was to be a fighter" (Post & Denny, 2002).

Examples can be found within other cultures and regions. Gerry Adams, the leader of the Irish independence party, Sinn Féin, is a case in point. Adams joined the Irish Republican Army as a teenager, motivated by his strong family background in the organization. His father and uncle had both participated in violent republican activities, so for Adams joining was a family tradition (Sharrock & Davenport, 1977).

A primary motivation for terrorism often revolves around a desire for revenge (Schmid & Jongman, 1988; Silke, 2003). This factor links group-related terrorism, such as is found in Palestinian suicide bombings in Israel and individual acts of terror such as school shootings. In these cases, the terrorist acts were perceived as acts of justice aimed at restoring the self-worth of the individuals who perceived themselves as victims. Engaging in an act of terror or joining a terrorist group in the aftermath of perceived violence against oneself, one's loved ones, or one's community appears to be a common theme in the historical narratives of terrorists. The shooters at Columbine High School in Colorado in 1999 were apparently upset by perceived harassment and ridicule that they received at the hands of classmates who called them "fags" or "outcasts," and threw bottles at them. Eamon Collins, who joined the IRA during his university years, did so only after a pivotal experience in which he and his family suffered unjustly at the hands of the British Army (Collins, 1997). The sparse research that exists on this subject indicates that while a desire for vengeance appears to be a generally held human characteristic, males, young people, and certain religious groups appear to be more vengeance prone (Cota-McKinley, Woody, & Bell, 2001).

A surprising factor accompanying the desire to retaliate is the willingness of individuals to engage in even extreme acts of self-sacrifice in order to carry out an act of revenge. This facet of personality may help explain the existence of forms of terrorism that include suicide. Cota-McKinley and colleagues (2001) state: "vengeance can have many irrational and destructive consequences for the person seeking vengeance as well as for the target. The person seeking vengeance will often compromise his or her own integrity, social standing, and personal safety for the sake of revenge" (p. 343).

In some cases, joining a terrorist group can also lead to increased status and secondary rewards. From within the group, the members are perceived as "freedom fighters" and often garner considerable respect. As one Palestinian youth described it: "After recruitment, my social status was greatly enhanced. I got a lot of respect from my acquaintances, and from the young people in my village" (Post & Denny, 2002, p. 4). As well as enhancing the social status of the individual recruit, terrorist organizations can provide increased protection for its members.

Although it may appear that the decision to engage in acts of terrorism is a form of highly deviant behavior, in many communities the process is more akin to a decision to join the military or the police force. It is closely aligned with the young person's perception of justice and morality, sense of meaning and purpose, and worldview. Crucial socialization processes play a role in determining whether a young person will become attracted to terrorism. Belonging to a disenfranchised cultural group, being subjected to injustice, and internalizing the values of a culture of violence are three critical dimensions in the formation of the psychology of terrorism.

Trauma

We now switch perspectives to address the effect that traumatic events such as abuse, war, natural disasters, and death may have on spiritual development. Such events almost invariably lead to spiritual and religious questioning about the nature of the transcendent, good and evil, and the meaning and purpose of life, even in very young children.

Spiritual abuse is the misuse of social or political power in a spiritual context. Because of the context, the power is often interpreted as spiritual in nature and thus given unwarranted authority (Wehr, 2000). In cases of spiritual abuse, spirituality becomes contaminated with the abuse experience and linked to that which the young person considers to be sacred.

A recent example that received much media coverage was the case of 15-year-old Elizabeth Smart, who was kidnapped from her Salt Lake City, Utah, home in 2002 and held for months by a psychotically grandiose couple. The abductors apparently believed it was their sacred destiny to marry a number of adolescent girls and have them deliver babies who would be part of a messianic family. Although Elizabeth was living near enough to hear people searching for her, she did not escape and seemingly adopted the couple's delusion. Interestingly, when rescued by her family, she apparently quickly gave up the delusion and returned to normal teenage interests and life.

Stockholm syndrome was a term coined by Professor Nils Bejerot to describe the phenomenon of hostages bonding with their captors. The Norrmalmstorg bank robbery in Stockholm, Sweden, in 1973 received much attention because four hostages, held for 6 days by two bank robbers, came to care about their captors and believe that they were protecting them from the police. Stockholm syndrome was used to explain the behavior of Patricia Hearst following her abduction in 1974 by the Symbionese Liberation Army.

Stockholm syndrome is a cluster of symptoms thought to be a survival strategy under conditions of extreme threat. It is often observed in hostages, cult members, and victims of battering and abuse. The symptoms include identification and bonding with the perpetrator, including adoption of his or her point of view, extreme dependence on the captor and valuing every act of kindness, and seeking approval from the captor. The most extreme symptoms include viewing potential rescuers as dangerous and resenting them for their rescue attempts.

The psychological motivations that underlie Stockholm syndrome include that of physical and mental survival and an avoidance of fear and pain. Positive motivations for relationship and acceptance, security, hope, and meaning are also present. It is most likely to occur under conditions of extreme trauma that have shattered previous systems of meaning and when the individual is isolated from sources of support.

Those who are most vulnerable to Stockholm syndrome lack a clear identity, sense of meaning and purpose, or have little experience overcoming adversity. Those who have a history of having powerful authorities in control over their life, or a strong need for approval, may also be particularly susceptible. It is clear that immature developmental status in itself includes all of these factors.

FUTURE DIRECTIONS

The study of spiritual and religious pathology has been largely conducted with case study and illustrative examples, as is apparent in this review. Significant obstacles remain in the path of those who would attempt a serious approach to this area of inquiry. Notably, lacking a coherent theory and definition of spiritual development inhibits the attempt to discuss pathological development. Furthermore, except in the more extreme cases discussed herein, the researcher labeling forms of spirituality as pathological risks treading on cultural values of those whose ideologies differ from the secular humanist tradition that provides the foundation for the social sciences.

Yet the problems created by spiritual pathology and religious ideological difference are critical to the gravest issues that we face. Should developmentalists remain silent? Pargament (2002) has called for psychological researchers to get closer to religious experience, "asking how helpful and harmful are particular kinds of religious expressions for particular people dealing with particular situations in particular social contexts according to particular criteria" (p. 178).

To do so requires not only theoretical development but also advances in our measurement of both religious and spiritual variables, using a range of approaches, both qualitative and quantitative, cross-sectional and longitudinal. The rich diversity of spiritual and religious traditions and cultures has largely escaped the lens of developmental researchers. The literature that exists today is almost exclusively drawn from Judeo-Christian perspectives, and conducted with North American samples. Clearly the phenomena are too complex to be captured by simplistic theories and methods of study.

CONCLUSIONS

Although it is not appropriate for social scientists to sit in judgment regarding the truth of any system of spiritual or religious beliefs, it is necessary and helpful to offer criteria that can help distinguish pathological from adaptive forms of functioning. As with other aspects of development, it is possible to discriminate aspects of functioning that are supportive, mature, organized, purposeful, and meaningful from those that are destructive and needlessly promote excessive levels of anxiety, despair, guilt, or violence. An initial attitude of respect for religious and spiritual worldviews, with attention to the way they promote an effective adaptation, will enable social scientists to avoid what is essentially the theological task of determining the truth of any particular set of transcendent beliefs. The value of a set of beliefs for a developmentalist depends on the extent to which they enable the young person to pursue a life of meaning and purpose, commitment and service, sustain their relationships to creation, the sacred, their fellow human beings, and respond adaptively to challenges.

REFERENCES

Altemeyer, B. (2003). Authoritarianism, religious fundamentalism, quest, and prejudice. *International Journal for the Psychology of Religion, 13,* 17–28.

Andron, S. (1983). Our gifted teens and the cults. *Gifted, Creative, Talented Children, 26,* 32–33.

Barber, B. K. (2001). Political violence, social integration, and youth functioning: Palestinian youth from the intifada. *Journal of Community Psychology, 29*(3), 259–280.

Bar-El, Y. (1994, October 2). Syndrome strikes spiritual senseless. *Tulsa World,* p. 10.

Beit-Hallahmi, B. (1977). Psychology of religion 1880–1930: The rise and fall of a psychological movement. In H. N. Malony (Ed.), *Current perspectives in the psychology of religion* (pp.17–26). Grand Rapids, MI: Eerdmans.

Bergin, A. (1983). Religiosity and mental health: A critical re-evaluation and meta-analysis. *Professional Psychology: Research and Practice, 14,* 170–184.

Bromley, D., & Breschel, E. (1992). General population and institutional support for social control of new religious movements: Evidence from national survey data. *Behavioral Sciences and the Law, 10,* 39–52.

Clark, W. H., Malony, H. N., Daane, J., & Tippett, A. R. (1973). *Religious experience: Its nature and function in the human psyche.* Springfield, IL: Thomas.

Collins, E. (with McGovern, M.). (1997). *Killing rage.* London: Granta Books.

Cota-McKinley, A., Woody, W., & Bell, P. (2001). Vengeance: Effects of gender, age, and religious background. *Aggressive Behavior, 27,* 343–350.

Edward, J. J. (1999). *One last time: A psychic medium speaks to those we have loved and lost.* New York: Berkely.

Ellison, C., & Bartkowski, J. (1995). "Babies were being beaten": Exploring child abuse allegations at Ranch Apocalypse. In S. Wright (Ed.), *Armageddon in Waco: Critical perspectives on the Branch Davidian conflict* (pp. 111–149). Chicago: University of Chicago Press.

Erikson, E. H. (1963). *Childhood and society* (2nd ed.). New York: Norton.

Freud, S. (1927). *Totem and taboo* (A. A. Brill, Trans.). Oxford, UK: New Republic. (Original work published 1913)

Freud, S. (1928). *The future of an illusion* (W. D. Robson-Scott, Trans.). London: Hogarth. (Original work published 1927)

Freud, S. (1961). *Civilization and its discontents.*In *The standard edition of the complete psychological works of Sigmund Freud* (James Strachey, Ed. and Trans., in collaboration with Anna Freud). London and New York: Norton. (Original work published 1930)

Galanter, M. (1996). Cults and charismatic group psychology. In E. P. Shanfranske (ed.), *Religion and the clinical practice of psychology* (pp. 269–296). Washington, DC: American Psychological Association.

Goddard, C. (1994a). Governing the "Family": Child protection policy and practice and the "Children of God." *Just Policy, 1,* 9–11.

Goddard, C. (1994b, May 6). Still in the dark over "The Family" raids. *The Age* (Melbourne), p. 17.

Hall, G. S. (1917). *Jesus the Christ in the light of psychology.* New York: Appleton.

Hunter, E. (1998). Adolescent attraction to cults. *Adolescence, 33,* 709–714.

James, W. (1902). *The varieties of religious experience.* New York: Longmans.

Kurtz, E., & Ketchum, K. (1992). *The spirituality of imperfection: Storytelling and the journey to wholeness.* New York: Bantam Books.

Leary, T. (1965). A new behavior change program using psilocybin. *Psychotherapy: Theory, Research, & Practice, 2*(2), 61–72.

Leary, T., & Clark, W. H. (1963). Religious implications of consciousness expanding drugs. *Religious Education, 58*(2), 251–256.

Mahoney, A. M., Pargament, K. I., Ano, G., Lynn, Q., Magyar, G., McCarthy, S., et al. (2002, August). *The devil made them do it? Demonization and the 9/11 attacks.* Paper presented at the meeting of the American Psychological Association, Chicago.

Malcarne, V., & Burchard, J. (1992). Investigations of child abuse/neglect allegations in religious cults: A case study in Vermont. *Behavioral Science and the Law, 10,* 75–88.

Malony, H. N. (1984). G. S. Hall's theory of conversion. *Journal of Psychology and Christianity, 3*(3), 2–8.

Meissner, W. W. (2002). The pathology of beliefs and the beliefs of pathology. In E. P. Shanfranske (ed.), *Religion and the clinical practice of psychology* (pp. 241–268). Washington, DC: American Psychological Association.

Myers, D. G. (2001). *Exploring psychology* (5th ed.). New York: Worth.

Palmer, S. J., & Hardman, C. E. (1999). *Children in new religions.* New Brunswick, NJ: Rutgers University Press.

Pargament, K. I. (2002). The bitter and the sweet: An evaluation of the costs and benefits of religiousness. *Psychological Inquiry,13*(3), 168–181.

Post, J., & Denny, L. (2002, July). *The terrorists in their own words.* Paper presented at the meeting of the International Society of Political Psychology, Berlin, Germany.

Richardson, J. T. (1993). A social psychology critique of "brainwashing" claims about recruitment to new religions. In D. Bromley & J. Hadden (Eds.), *Sects and cults in America* (pp. 75–97). Geenwich, CT: JAI Press.

Ross, C. E. (1990). Religion and psychological distress. *Journal for the Scientific Study of Religion, 29*(2), 236–245.

Schmid, A. P., & Jongman, A. J. (1988). *Political terrorism* (2nd ed.). Oxford, UK: North Holland.

Sethi, S., & Seligman, M. E. (1993). Optimism and fundamentalism. *Psychological Science, 4,* 256–259.

Sharrock, D., & Devenport, M. (1997). *Man of war, man of peace? The unauthorised biography of Gerry Adams.* London: Macmillan.

Silke, A. (1999). Ragged justice: Loyalist vigilantism in Northern Ireland. *Terrorism and Political Violence, 11*(3), 1–31.

Silke, A. (2003). Becoming a terrorist. In A. Silke (ed.), *Terrorists, victims, and society* (pp. 29–54). New York: Wiley.

Sroufe, L. A., & Cooper, R. G. (1988). *Child development: Its nature and course.* New York: Knopf.

Taylor, S. E., Kemeny, M. E., Reed, G. M., Bower, J. E., & Gruenewald, T. L. (2000). Psychological resources, positive illusions, and health. *American Psychologist, 55*(1), 99–109.

Trimble, J. E. (1994). Cultural variation in the use of alcohol and drugs. In W. J. Lonner & R. Malpass (Eds.), *Psychology and culture* (79–84). Boston: Allyn & Bacon.

Venter, M. A. (1998). Susceptibility of adolescents to cults. *Southern African Journal of Child and Adolescent Mental Health, 10* (2), 93–106.

Vogt, N. (1999). *Sexual mores in The Family: A comparison of second-generation members with a national sample.* Unpublished doctoral dissertation, Fuller Theological Seminary, Graduate School of Psychology, Pasadena, California.

Wehr, D. (2000). Spiritual abuse: When good people do bad things. In P. Young-Eisendrath and M. E. Miller (Eds.), *The psychology of mature spirituality: Integrity, wisdom, transcendence* (47–61). London: Brunner-Routledge.

Zimbardo, P. G., & Hartley, C. (1985). Cults go to high school: A theoretical and empirical analysis of the initial steps in the recruitment process. *Cultic Studies Journal, 2,* 91–147.

11

Non-Western Approaches to Spiritual Development Among Infants and Young Children: A Case Study from West Africa

Alma Gottlieb

Discussions of religion have tended to focus on the lives, experiences, and viewpoints of adults. The great canonical works on religion say scarcely a word about how religion might affect children and shape their lives. For example, in chronicling the early history of Judaism, the renowned 19th-century scholar Robertson Smith (1889/1927) wrote nothing about the religion of *young* Semites. In his legendary work on divine kingship, Sir James Frazer (1906–1915) never considered how that institution might influence children's play styles. The great French sociologist Emile Durkheim (1912/1925), who famously explored collective rituals of several Aboriginal Australian groups, did not investigate how Aboriginal boys and girls might influence their elders in creating an effervescence of spirit. And the esteemed theorist of world religions Max Weber (1904/1958) neglected to speculate on the effect that Protestant faith might have on child-rearing practices. More recently, and beyond this volume, most current social scientists have continued to assume the irrelevance of early childhood to spirituality.

AUTHOR'S NOTE: This chapter is adapted, in part, from the following two sources: Gottlieb, A. (1998). Do infants have religion? The spiritual life of Beng babies. *American Anthropologists, 100* (1). 122–135. Copyright © 1998 by the American Anthropological Assoication. Used with permission. Gottlieb, A. (2004). *The afterlife is where we come from: The culture of infancy in West Africa.* Chicago: University of Chicago press. Copyright © 2004 University of Chicago Press. Used with permission. For support of my field research and writing, I am grateful to the John Simon Guggenheim Memorial Foundation, National Endowment for the Humanities, Wenner-Gren Foundation for Anthropological Research, Social Science Research Council, United States Information Agency, and several units at the University of Illinois (Center for Advanced Study, Research Board, and Center for African Studies). For intellectual support during my field research, I owe a continuing debt, which I always strive in vain to repay, to the Beng community. This chapter pertains to life in Beng villages before the major disruptions of the current civil war in Ivory Coast, which has caused enormous hardship and upheavals in villagers' lives.

One exception to this tendency is a small body of literature addressing children in the context of organized initiation rituals in some non-Western societies. Africanist discussions of this topic are particularly well known. Audrey Richards's (1956) and Victor Turner's (1967) explorations of Chisungu girls' and Ndembu boys' initiations in Zambia set the tone for many subsequent scholars' writings on such rituals (e.g., LaFontaine, 1985; Ottenberg, 1989; Schloss, 1988). Yet apart from these and a few other exceptions, including the current collection, silence generally reigns concerning the religious and ritual experiences of minors. If this is true of children in general, it is especially so of infants, who are perhaps the most systematically ignored of all human groups by scholars of religion (as well as by anthropologists and other social scientists in general, other than psychologists).[1] Even when discussions of spirituality include adolescents and older children, infants and toddlers are rarely considered relevant to the topic.

This neglect is especially inappropriate in certain world regions. One such area is West Africa. In this part of the world, infants are often considered the most spiritual of all humans, and in many local societies, much of the goal of adequate childcare focuses on accommodating the imputed spiritual nature of infants and young children. In West Africa, an ideology of reincarnation generally lies behind this model of infants and an array of child-rearing practices that are meant to serve it.

This chapter discusses one West African society—the Beng of Ivory Coast—as a striking exemplar of the view that young children embody the purest spiritual orientation. Among the Beng, babies are raised with the goal of gradually and lovingly luring them back from the culturally imagined space that I translate as "the afterlife," and into this life, by accommodating spiritually based desires that are routinely attributed to infants. In keeping with this volume, the Beng case challenges us to rethink the common Western tendency to focus on adults (and, to a lesser extent, adolescents) when it comes to discussing religious practice, and encourages us to consider the possibility of infant spirituality (as postulated by adults), and child rearing as a site of religious practice, as these may be developed in a variety of local settings in West Africa and elsewhere beyond the mainstream West.[2]

The Spiritual Lives of Beng Infants: The Afterlife Is Where We Come From

Most secular, Western folk models of child development imply a mute and uncomprehending newborn arriving for the first time in the world of humans from a restricted uterine life of minimal stimulation, and no social interaction as such. Before that, the underlying biological model further implies, the fetus was a mere zygote of a few cells, and before those cells were joined, it had no existence whatsoever. Hence the Western caretaker of an infant, whether the mother or anyone else, usually attends to the bodily needs of the young tot with great care but typically pays less attention to social concerns, and virtually none to spiritual ones.[3]

In West Africa, the Beng view of fetal development is quite different. Beng adults maintain that infants lead profoundly spiritual lives. In fact, the younger they are, the more thoroughly spiritual their existence is said to be. It follows that newborns are considered the most spiritual of all living humans. This doctrine derives from a widespread conviction that all current human lives follow from reincarnation from a previous life. Associated with the imputed spirituality of infants is a set of infant care practices demanded of a caretaker.

In Beng villages, then, each baby is said to be a reincarnation of someone who died. By itself this ideology is by no means rare in Africa (e.g., Creider, 1986; MacGaffey, 1986; Okri, 1991; Oluwole, 1992; Uchendu, 1965); it is also well known for South Asia and Native North Americans (Mills & Slobodin, 1994). But scholars have rarely asked what the implications of this common ideology may be for the treatment of infants and their experiences. Focusing on rural Beng, let us trace their life course; to understand the Beng conception of infants' spirituality, we begin by investigating life before the womb.

In the Beng world, infants are believed to emerge not from a void before gaining life inside a woman's womb, but from a rich, social existence in a place invisible to the living that adults call *wrugbe*. Beng adults understand *wrugbe* as a place that is dispersed among invisible neighborhoods in major cities throughout Africa and Europe.[4]

The literal meaning of *wrugbe* is "spirit village" or "spirit town." In English, a likely translation of *wrugbe* would be "afterlife": the place to which the *wru*, or spirit, of a person travels once that person's body dies and the *neneŋ* or soul, transforms to a *wru*. In the Beng model, the souls of the recently deceased journey to *wrugbe* as a waystation; after some time (whose duration is variable), they are reborn as newborn humans. The doctrine of reincarnation is thus based on a cyclical trajectory, with no beginning and no end, and death itself is another kind of life. "This life" is seen by at least some Beng—certainly by religious specialists (diviners and Masters of the Earth) and others who think deeply about such matters—as the ephemeral site of transit whose ultimate goal is to reach the land of the ancestors (cf. MacGaffey, 1986). As articulated by Beng adults, then, infants have just recently been living in a previous and invisible existence.

An understanding of the contours of *wrugbe* is best gained from conversations with religious specialists, both Masters of the Earth and diviners. These two authorities play an important role in Beng religious practice. People consult diviners to discover the cause of a wide range of misfortunes, from illness to poverty. In turn, depending on what they see as the cause of the misfortune, diviners prescribe a broad spectrum of remedies, from herbal medicines (which are often quite effective) to sacrifices. If the sacrifice is meant to be offered to a spirit inhabiting the Earth, the diviner then instructs the client to consult a Master of the Earth to carry out the sacrifice. Both these religious specialists, then, are intimately involved in a range of spiritual activities and have much to say about the cycle of reincarnation. Here is how one Beng diviner, Kouakou Ba, explained his understanding of the temporal and, we might say, demographic dimensions of *wrugbe:*

Every day, there are deaths and births. The number of people living here and in *wrugbe* keeps going up and down. You know who you're replacing from *wrugbe* if someone dies on the same day that you're born. Otherwise, if no one dies on the day you're born, you don't know who you're replacing.

Two issues emerging from Kouakou Ba's statement bear discussion. The first is that of personal identity. In the Beng model, everyone is considered to be a reincarnation of an ancestor, although not all people know which ancestor has been reborn in them. If an individual knows his or her prior identity, others may treat this person in particular ways according to the ancestor's remembered personality and life circumstances.

Kouakou Ba's statement also carries demographic implications that we might be tempted to put in economic terms. That is, the indigenous conception of demography in which each human life given from *wrugbe* must be counterbalanced by one taken back to *wrugbe* might be recast as a zero-sum conception of human life. Does this necessarily imply an empirically stable population, with births and deaths delicately balanced? This would hardly be possible at any given moment, as the number of births and deaths may vary according to a complex array of factors that are surely impossible to balance. For our purposes, what is significant is that the idea of reincarnation as demographic balance operates at the ideological level regardless of actual demographic fluctuations (cf. Ardener, 1989, pp. 117, 123, et passim).

This possible lack of fit between ideology and practice is mirrored at another level. Once someone dies, the *neneŋ* or soul, is transformed into a *wru*, or spirit. Yet when that person is reincarnated into someone else, the *wru* nevertheless continues to exist as an ancestor. This model posits a dual, rather than an either-or, existence. Unlike the classical Aristotelian framework, which demands that an identity be either one thing or another but not both simultaneously, the Beng view allows that a being may exist simultaneously at two levels of reality— one visible and earthly, the other invisible and ghostly. This dualistic perspective occurs elsewhere in West Africa. For example, a somewhat similar "contradiction" (by Western standards) exists in Nigeria: Among the Yoruba, ancestors are said to exist at two levels simultaneously, both individual and collective, with no problem perceived concerning what appears to Western logic as internal inconsistency (John Peel, personal communication).

Among the Beng, the boundary between *wrugbe* and this life is held to be permeable in another way. Although *wrugbe* is said to be located in distant countries or metropolises, where the lifestyle of the living is quite different from that of rural Beng villagers, Beng adults do not perceive *wrugbe* as unreachable. Indeed, I was told of several living adults who had managed to travel to *wrugbe* in their dreams in order to converse with ancestors, and had then returned easily to tell the tale. When I expressed amazement—perhaps influenced unconsciously by the classical Greek conception of the afterlife, with its formidable Cerberus guarding the gate to Hades—my interlocutor assured me that anyone could converse with an ancestor and that the (dreamtime) journey to *wrugbe* is not dangerous.

Reciprocally, the *wrus* of Beng ancestors are said to traverse back and forth between *wrugbe* and this life on a daily basis. Before local officials of the Ivoirian government ordered all thatch-roofed houses destroyed in the late 1960s, the Beng lived in large, round dwellings that accommodated an extended family (Gottlieb, 1992, pp. 135–136). These houses were meant to shelter not only the living but also the dead. Every night, someone in the household put out a small bowl of food for the family's ancestors, and the last person to retire would close the door, locking in the living and the dead to sleep together. In the morning, the first person to open the door released the *wrus*, who traveled back to *wrugbe* for the day—to return at night for their dinner and sleeping spot once again.

Considering this model of a regular traffic between *wrugbe* and this life, and considering Beng adults' assertion that infants have just emerged from *wrugbe*, what ramifications does the Beng ideology of reincarnation have for the daily experiences of actual babies and those who take care of them? In the sections below, we will explore a variety of caretaking strategies much of whose meaning derives from the Beng model of infants as profoundly spiritual people.

The Umbilical Cord: Lifeline to *Wrugbe*

According to Beng adults, until the umbilical cord stump falls off, a newborn is not considered to have emerged from *wrugbe* at all, so the tiny creature is not yet classified as a person (*sòŋ*). If the newborn dies during those first few days, no funeral is held. The event is not announced publicly, for the infant's passing is conceived not as a death but as a return in bodily form to the space the infant was still fully inhabiting.

Beng women told me that the umbilical stump usually drops off on the third or fourth day; this was indeed the case for all of the Beng newborns I have observed during my fieldwork. This schedule is rather on the fast end of the scale when viewed cross-culturally (cf. Bhalla, Nafis, Rohtagi, & Singh, 1975; Novack, Mueller, & Ochs 1988, pp. 221–222). How can we account for this relatively rapid development on the part of Beng infants? Beng women apply an herbal mixture to a newborn's umbilical stump that may shorten the number of days the cord remains attached to the navel (cf. Novack et al., 1988, p. 220, citing Arad, Eyal, & Fainmesser, 1981). The intention is to dry out the moist cord fragment quickly, enabling it to wither and drop off—and thus allowing the infant to begin its spiritual journey from *wrugbe* to this life. Beng women take this responsibility seriously. Next to every newborn sits an older woman, usually the baby's maternal grandmother, who dabs a tiny bit of the herbal mixture on the dangling cord every few minutes.

Extended symbolic elaboration or ritual treatment of the umbilical stump in one way or another is by no means uncommon in West Africa (for a notable example from the Igbo of Nigeria, see Uchendu, 1965, pp. 58–59). Among the Beng, the day that a baby's umbilical cord stump falls off is a momentous one, for the newborn is considered to have just begun to emerge from *wrugbe*. However, this emergence is said to be a gradual process that will take several years to complete. Both to mark the beginning of this passage, and to inaugurate it more actively, the infant's mother and some of her female relatives conduct two or three bodily rituals of transformation on the tiny new person.

First, they administer an enema to the baby, with a new mother taught the technique by a female elder who has been bathing the baby four times a day since the birth. The mother learns to use the leaves of the *kprɔkprɔ* plant crushed together with a single chili pepper and some warm water. After the initial treatment the mother will give such an enema to her baby twice a day, in the morning and at night. Older children often take regular enemas as well, and many adults give themselves enemas on a regular basis as a means of controlling their intestinal production and, they say, maintaining general health. Thus the baby starts to be "toilet trained" from the first week of life, as part of a series of "civilizing" processes that marks the baby's entry into "this life" (for a discussion of a pragmatic rationale for enemas from the perspective of a mother's labor demands, see Gottlieb, 2004, pp. 130–134).

Typically a few hours after the first enema, the newborn is the subject of a second major ritual. The maternal grandmother or another older woman makes a necklace (*dɛ̃*) from a savanna grass of the same name. This necklace will be worn night and day by the infant to encourage general health and growth until it eventually tears and falls off. At that point, depending on the baby's age and the mother's industry, it may or may not be replaced. The ritual to attach the first necklace is held with a somewhat solemn tone in a rather secluded and dimly lit space inside the bedroom of the infant's mother. After this first necklace is applied, the mother or grandmother is permitted to add other items of jewelry. For an infant girl, a third ritual manipulation of the body occurs on the day the umbilical stump falls off: Her ears are pierced. Now she is authorized to enter into the gendered space of feminine beautification. This set of rituals collectively inaugurates a series of aftereffects relative to the doctrine of reincarnation.

The Call of *Wrugbe*

As soon as the umbilical stump drops off, the baby is said to start the spiritual journey of emerging from *wrugbe;* however, as some other societies in Africa and elsewhere have posited (e.g., Diener, 2000; Leis, 1982, p. 154), the process of moving from one sociospiritual space to another is believed to be long and difficult, and it takes several years to complete. Here is what the Beng diviner Kouakou Ba said on the subject:

KB: At some point, children leave *wrugbe* for good and decide to stay in this life.

AG: How do you know when this has happened?

KB: When children can speak their dreams, or understand [a drastic situation, such as] that their mother or father has died, then you know that they've totally come out of *wrugbe.*

AG: When does that happen?

KB: By seven years old, for sure! At three years old, they're still in between: partly in *wrugbe,* and partly in this life. They *see* what happens in this life, but they don't understand it.

During the time that young children are still partly inhabiting *wrugbe,* they remain vulnerable to returning to that other life. They might do so by means of another spiritual intermediary. For in the Beng pantheon, the souls of ancestors are complemented by bush spirits (*bɔŋzɔ*) that may be in contact with the ancestors living in the afterlife. Some spirits of the bush may find young children attractive, as babies and toddlers are said to retain a spiritual identity to which the spirits can relate. Certain signs may make some children in particular especially attractive to the spirits. For example, bush spirits are said to prefer the color red. If they see children wearing red, they are tempted to kidnap the children and bring them back to the land of spirits. To protect infants and young children from being snatched away by spirits, caretakers often avoid dressing their babies and toddlers in red clothes.

Another reason that adults invoke to explain why some children return to the land of spirits concerns the babies' own consciousness. During the liminal time of early childhood, as we might term it, the consciousness of the infant or toddler is sometimes in *wrugbe* and sometimes in this life. In the Beng view, parents ought to do all they can to make this life comfortable and attractive for their infant, to ensure that their child is not tempted to return to *wrugbe.* For help with the child's bodily needs, a mother regularly consults her mother, her grandmother, and other experienced mothers around her (see

Gottlieb, 2000). But sometimes infants appear miserable for no obvious reason. In this case, the Beng say the baby is endeavoring to communicate a spiritual need, based in their memories from *wrugbe,* that the parents are unable to understand. This need signals that the infant is probably homesick for *wrugbe.*

This is where diviners enter the picture, for these specialists are seen as intermediaries between the living and the ancestors, as well as between the living and the bush spirits (Gottlieb, 1992, chapter 2; Gottlieb & Graham, 1993). Given the culturally valued space occupied by diviners, Beng mothers are expected to consult them regularly during the early years of their children's existence, even if their children are not sick. A Beng college student, Bertin Kouadio, explained that in the "old days," mothers automatically consulted a diviner almost immediately after the birth of each of their babies. This statement may well index a goal that was not always realized. For one thing, diviners cost money, even if the fee is modest by local standards (typically 50 CFA; currently $1 U.S. = approximately 500 CFA). As elsewhere, some mothers are more devoted to their children than others; some are more willing to spend scarce resources to gather items that are judged culturally necessary for their children's well-being; and some simply have more available cash. Still, the practice outlined by Bertin represents an operative ideal that is consistent with the Beng ideology of the life course.

Almost invariably, when Beng diviners are consulted by parents—usually mothers—the specialists recommend that the new mother give their baby a cowry shell. Bertin put it this way:

All babies must be given a cowry shell [a small white shell, originally from the Indian Ocean] as a first gift, when the baby is born, because the cowry was important as currency for the ancestors—it was the second most important thing, after gold. The newborn had contact with the ancestors before birth, and the cowry shell reminds the baby of the previous life in *wrugbe.*

Nowadays not all women contact a diviner immediately after the birth; they may wait for a day when the baby is in distress. Other mothers may give a cowry shell to the baby as a personal gift, though they weren't told to do so by a diviner.

Another Beng friend added this commentary:

Infants like money because they had money when they were living in *wrugbe.* In coming to this world, they all choose what they want. This could be *wali pu* [French coins from the colonial era], or jewelry [usually cowry shells]—whatever is like what they had in *wrugbe.*

The ancient French coins are sometimes sold in local markets, although they are increasingly rare; by contrast, cowry shells are still fairly easy to come by, though they no longer line the ground as elders say they used to in precolonial days (for more about cowry shells, see Gottlieb, 2004). As with the *dē,* an infant may wear a cowry shell or coin as an item of jewelry, usually a bracelet. Diviners may recommend a single shell or coin, or they might suggest a number of cowries strung close together on a bracelet, or two or three coins strung on a cotton thread. The mother may leave the jewelry on the baby continually, washing it carefully during the baths she gives her child (see Gottlieb, 2004, pp. 105–135); or she may put the bracelet or necklace on the infant on particular days according to the spiritual calendar.

At the psychological level, the diviner is communicating to the parents the message that the infant needs to be valued more, and needs to wear a visible sign of this valuing. Western-trained child psychologists would probably applaud this practice, as it encourages parents of a small creature who cries regularly to devote themselves to the needs of the often stressed, and stress-inducing, newborn (cf. Lewis & Rosenblum, 1974). At the level of local belief, a diviner's instructions to parents to buy jewelry for their crying child may serve to remind them that although the infant seems helpless and unable to communicate, the little one was recently living a full life elsewhere and thus needs to be respected as a fellow person rather than being viewed as a suffering, wordless creature.

Another *wrugbe*–currency connection concerns a bodily position that psychologists would classify as a reflex devoid of significance but that Beng adults interpret otherwise. Newborns everywhere may clench their hands into a surprisingly tight fist for no apparent reasons. Beng elders interpret this position as culturally meaningful: They claim that the babies are concealing gold in their fists—invisible, since it is from the spirit world—and that this is yet another sign of the deep memories that infants retain of their life in *wrugbe,* where gold is said to be abundant.

The fact of reincarnation may prove critical in the life of a given newborn in another way. It may be apparent as early as the childbirth whose *wrugbe* ancestor the newborn embodies. If a relative dies on the day a baby is born, this is taken as a sign of instant reincarnation ("s/he came, s/he returned"). Alternatively, a name that is shared, seemingly by coincidence, between infant and ancestor may indicate a reincarnation. For example, a 9-month-old girl had a series of names, but most villagers called her *mama,* or "grandma." This is because the baby was said to be the reincarnation of her father's mother, Bande Kla Ajua, with whom she had two names in common ("Kla," an ancient family name, and "Ajua," a day name for girls born on a Tuesday); the infant was spoken to (and about) as if she were that ancestor.

A baby's identity may make itself known through misery. The diviner may pronounce that the infant is unhappy with his or her name and prefers another one. The new name usually commemorates the baby's *wrugbe* identity, which the baby is said to remember and to miss. Alternatively, a baby can be renamed for a spirit rather than an ancestor. For example, a baby named Kouassi cried day and night when he was a month old. In despair, his mother consulted Kouakou Ba, who said that Kouassi was crying for two reasons. First, Kouassi wanted two bracelets on his left hand, one with cowry shells, the other of *ŋà ti* (silver). Second, he had been misnamed; his real name—which he apparently remembered from *wrugbe* and now missed— was Anie, after a local sacred pool of water that is said to hold resident spirits. After hearing Kouakou Ba's pronouncement, the baby's mother found the required bracelets, and the baby's family began calling the infant "Anie." According to reports, after these two changes, Anie stopped crying.

Bearing an ancestral identity can have ramifications for the baby's life far beyond naming. The imputed identity can organize the manner in which the infant is treated in many other

contexts. For example, a baby who is born following the deaths of two siblings in the family is inevitably called "Sunu" (for a girl) or "Wamyã" (for a boy). The infant is seen as the reincarnation of one of the two deceased siblings. Like all Beng children who die, the dead siblings will have been buried in a muddy patch behind the home. As babies and toddlers, Sunus and Wamyãs are said to remember the spot that is considered their recent resting place; thus they are said to like mud, so their mothers may pat mud over their small bodies.

The reincarnated identities of Wamyãs and Sunus may continue to have consequences for their personality development well beyond infancy. As older children and adults, it is said, they are prone to depression and they can predict someone else's demise. When a Wamyã or Sunu appears depressed or acts aggressively without obvious cause, people worry that someone is about to die. For instance, one day a 9-year-old Sunu spent an entire afternoon hitting her older sister for no apparent reason. Family members and neighbors worried aloud that it was a bad omen. The next morning, two deaths were announced in the village. On hearing the news, the girl's mother and aunts proclaimed, "So that's why she was hitting her older sister yesterday!" The deaths confirmed for them the ability of this Sunu—and that of all Sunus—to foretell death.

A funeral is said to remind all Sunus and Wamyãs of the deaths of their infant siblings; hence they are always among the saddest mourners. To commemorate this, all Sunus and Wamyãs—both female and male, from infants to elders—wear a special necklace or bracelet of scorpion tails during any funeral they attend. Considering their propensity for depression, some Beng claim that a Sunu and a Wamyã should never marry. On days they were both sad, they would be unable to take care of their children: A mourning or depressed Sunu may fail to nurse her infant, and both parents might refuse to work in the fields.

People named Sunu or Wamyã are generally said to have a "difficult personality" (*sie grégré*). Their parents may find validation of this psychological diagnosis through divination. Sometimes the divination reveals an unexpected Sunu or Wamyã identity brought to this world from the afterlife. For instance, when a Beng woman named Au was pregnant with her son, her uncle consulted a diviner, who predicted that his niece would have a child who would be very difficult, prone to crying. However, Au was told that she shouldn't become too upset or angry about this child's behavior, or the baby would leave the family and return to *wrugbe*—in other words, die.

Au assumed that this prediction applied to the baby she was carrying, but in fact he turned out to be easygoing. During her next pregnancy, she thought back to the diviner's prediction, but this child too turned out to be relatively unflappable, as was her next. It was only with her last child that the prediction was finally validated: Her daughter Jeanne turned out to be a "*wrugbe* Sunu" who indeed exhibited a difficult personality. During a village funeral, one of Au's older female relatives dreamed that Jeanne had been a Sunu while in *wrugbe*. Word circulated, and soon relatives and neighbors classified Jeanne as a Sunu. Because she was a "*wrugbe* Sunu," they thought, Jeanne would have an even more difficult personality than an ordinary Sunu would.

Not surprisingly, this foretelling proved accurate. When she was just starting to walk, Jeanne wanted to stay on her mother's back all day while Au worked in the fields. If Au put her down, Jeanne stamped right in front of her mother wherever she was walking, or she dared Au to cut her with a machete, then had a temper tantrum when her mother failed to comply. Jeanne's older sister Afwe had been designated as Jeanne's babysitter (*lɛŋ kũli*), and Afwe's primary job was to carry her younger sister; but Jeanne frequently hit Afwe while being carried on her back, and Afwe wasn't always able—or willing—to carry the rambunctious Jeanne.

As she grew older, Jeanne's difficult personality remained. She frightened other children in the neighborhood and provoked disputes and physical fights. One day I videotaped about half an hour of a temper tantrum Jeanne threw in two adjoining courtyards. Enraged at a perceived slight, she toppled furniture and hurled pails around her—behavior that would be quite unheard of for someone without the spiritual profile that Jeanne possesses.

In short, Jeanne internalized her identity as a "*wrugbe* Sunu." This should not be surprising. Because she often heard others discuss the difficult personality that is assumed to accompany a *wrugbe* Sunu identity, Jeanne was aware of the expectation that she act "difficult." As psychologists might say, the labeling proved successful (Rosenthal & Jacobson, 1968).

Not only do the Beng believe that children continue after birth to retain a memory of the previous life in *wrugbe,* but it is said that they retain their parents from *wrugbe,* who continue to look out for their baby even after the infant has begun to leave the afterlife. In some instances, this can cause conflict with the parents of this life. The child's *wrugbe* parents will be displeased if they judge that the child's parents of this life are mistreating the baby, either through abuse or neglect. The mother may not be breastfeeding her infant often enough, or may not be offering enough solid foods to an older infant. She may leave her baby to cry, may wait before taking her sick baby to a diviner or a healer, or may use poverty as an excuse to avoid buying the items or conducting the sacrifices that a diviner declares necessary to the baby's spiritual well-being. Any of these can have dire consequences: The *wrugbe* parents may decide to snatch the infant away back to the other life, where they will raise the child temporarily, as they await a more suitable couple to emerge as responsible parents for their *wrugbe* baby. This is, then, one explanation that is offered by Beng adults to account for the high infant and young child mortality rate in the region (for further discussion of infant illness and mortality, see Gottlieb, 2004).

Bearing this in mind, the diviner Kouakou Ba described how a good living parent should behave:

> You should go to a diviner to find out what the baby wants, then go and buy that thing for the child. It's the child's *wrugbe* relatives—usually one of the baby's *wrugbe* parents—who has told the baby to cry, to say what the baby wants. Or sometimes it may be a spirit who's told this to the baby. Infants choose these desires to copy the objects they liked back in *wrugbe*—usually jewelry, money, or cowries. In any case, once the parents of this life discover the baby's desires, they should do all they can to indulge them.

From Kouakou Ba's statement we learn that the baby has desires but is unsure how to communicate them directly. We also learn that *wrugbe* parents continue to take an active role in their infant's life even after the child has begun to enter this life, to the point of instructing the baby to cry to make a particular desire known. Through the infant, the *wrugbe* parents indirectly communicate to and instruct their counterparts in this life. But how can babies and *wrugbe* parents make their desires understood to this-life parents?

THE LANGUAGE OF *WRUGBE*

In the Beng model of the afterlife—unlike life in this world—different ethnic groups do not live apart from one another. Rather, members of all the world's ethnic groups are said to live together in *wrugbe* harmoniously. Associated with this ethnic mixture is a striking degree of linguistic ecumenicism: When the residents of *wrugbe* speak to each other in their own languages, everyone understands, with full mutual comprehension. This model of the afterlife has implications for how Beng adults view infants' linguistic development.

In the minds of many middle-class Western parents, young infants are seen as lacking linguistic abilities. As the popular British childcare author Penelope Leach has written, "At the beginning a new infant has no language other than crying" (1983, p. 62). The Beng model poses a stark contrast, for it posits a baby who is anything but "prelinguistic"—in fact, among the Beng, infants are said to be multilingual. Having only recently emerged from *wrugbe,* where everyone understood every language, Beng newborns are said to have full comprehension not only of Beng but of every language spoken on this earth.

Furthermore, as Beng infants are said to begin gradually to leave their previous existence behind, this includes gradually giving up their knowledge of languages other than the one(s) spoken around and to them daily. But as we have seen, this emergence from *wrugbe* is a very slow process that takes several years. Until it is complete, the child is said to continue to understand the many languages spoken in *wrugbe*—though with only sporadic and diminishing comprehension. In sum, Beng infants are doing the opposite of learning new languages

subsequent to a "prelinguistic" phase, as a popular Western folk model posits. Instead, they are said to shed their understanding of numerous languages in order to strip away excess linguistic baggage, as we might put it, and leave room for the language(s) that will be most appropriate for this life (cf. Werker, 1989).

Because Beng babies are said to have a passive understanding of all languages spoken to them, adults consider it appropriate to make use of that passive understanding. Older people address speech directly even to newborns, often continually. In hundreds of hours observing babies with their caretakers, rarely did 5 minutes go by when someone was not speaking directly to an awake infant.

For instance, a new mother I was visiting was holding her 4-day-old daughter on her lap. The woman sat with her legs outstretched, leaning over the baby a bit while chatting with me and two other friends. In between talking to us, she spoke to her baby regularly. At one point, her tiny daughter's eyes were open wide, and the new mother asked her tenderly, "*myé blicalò?*" ("Are you looking around?") I saw linguistic encounters such as this replicated by virtually every mother and caretaker whom I visited during my research. On offering her baby her breast, for example, a mother often instructs her infant, "*nyo mi!*" ("Nurse!") After the breastfeeding session, many mothers of infants, including newborns, typically question the little one, "*mí kanà?*" ("Are you full?") This linguistic attention extends to nonsomatic contexts. For instance, a newborn is introduced to each visitor by being asked, "*dɛ kána? mí dɔ̃?*" ("Who's this? Do you know?") In my observations, people talking to infants tend to simplify and slow their speech, presumably making it more "user-friendly" for the babies themselves (see Ferguson, 1977; Snow, 1977).

This very active level of verbal interaction that Beng adults have with babies is consistent with the local ideology of the afterlife. For as recent exiles from *wrugbe,* Beng infants are said to be capable of understanding speech in any language that is addressed to them. Behavior replicates the conceptual model in a directly observable way.

If Beng adults believe that infants can understand language due to their previous life in *wrugbe,* what of the babies' own verbalizing abilities? Beng infants' babble is routinely remarked upon, delighted in, and encouraged as protolinguistic—not only by Beng mothers, but by siblings, grandparents, other relatives, neighbors, indeed anyone who observes it. As an example, let us consider the case of Tahan, a mother who once observed her 7-month-old son as he looked with interest at two nearby pigs who were grunting. When the pigs quieted, her baby made noises that Tahan interpreted as an imitation of the animals. She clapped her hands with pleasure and exclaimed, "*ja, e za dǒ!*" Literally, this meant, "So, he understands things!"; figuratively, it meant, "So, he's smart!" attesting to a perceived connection between speech and intelligence even in a young infant.

Moreover, adults take an active role in teaching their infants to speak the Beng language by engaging in a formal routine of speaking for their infants. In this discursive routine, an adult asks a question directly of an infant, and another adult—the mother or whoever is currently minding the baby—answers for the child in the first person as if she were the baby, in effect prompting the child with lines the infant will presumably repeat months later when capable of such speech. For example, a visitor may directly ask the baby her name. In response, whoever is tending the baby holds up the infant and, much as a puppeteer might speak through a puppet, she answers in the first person as if she were the child: "My name is So-and-So." This practice is so deeply entrenched that adults sometimes apologize if they fail to engage in it.

Despite Beng adults' positive and encouraging attitude toward the speech of their babies, the verbalizing abilities of infants are said by adults to be in some respects problematic. Beng adults assert that, sadly, although infants are able to express their desires and thoughts, most adults are not capable of understanding the youngest children's utterances. The diviner Kouakou Ba explained that when babies cry, they are speaking the language of *wrugbe.* Babies may also communicate their wishes by failing to defecate or to nurse. However, none of these means of communication is readily understandable to the baby's parents, who emerged from that other life too long ago to remember its language. Thus parents of an obviously unhappy

baby typically take their child to a specialist to have their infant's cries or digestive irregularities translated.

In Beng villages, diviners serve as intermediaries between the land of the currently living and the land of the previously living. They do this by themselves using the services of intermediaries: the spirits (*bɔŋzɔ*), who speak both the language of the other world and that of this world. It is therefore a multitiered system of translation: The spirits speak first with the infant, who then announces—albeit ineffectively—his or her desires to the parents of this life, through crying or digestive upsets. Eager to soothe their child, the parents consult a diviner, who summons the spirits or the baby's *wrugbe* parents, who then speak for the baby after speaking with the infant. Finally, the diviner conveys the baby's desires to the bewildered parents of this life. In this way, the *wrugbe* identity of the infant is maintained in this world and through a series of intermediaries, the infant manages to communicate complex desires rooted in memory, to the parents of this life.

CONCLUSIONS

In this chapter we have seen that Beng infants occupy a culturally liminal space. Because babies are said to have barely emerged from *wrugbe* and at the same time are said to have barely entered into this life, their consciousness is believed to be oriented sometimes toward this life, sometimes toward the other life. This model of infancy produces a range of behaviors in Beng mothers and other caretakers that goes a long way toward accounting for how babies are cared for in daily life. Infants themselves are accorded a high level of agency in this indigenous model, as Beng babies are attributed consciousness requiring decoding by an elite group of adults with special translation skills. In these ways, Beng ideas about infant care challenge dominant Western models of child rearing at the same time that they challenge the scholar both to take spirituality seriously in understanding infancy and to take infancy seriously in understanding spirituality.

Anthropologists have long promoted the notion that customs that are assumed by the members of one society to be "natural" may be surprisingly absent elsewhere, and that such customs, seemingly "unnatural" in the views of outsiders, make sense when viewed in the context of a variety of cultural factors whose meanings can be discerned after systematic analysis of the local system. Some time ago, Clifford Geertz (1983) articulated this argument with relation to the notion of common sense, arguing that what passes as common sense is anything but common. Instead, it is a deeply culturally constructed artifice that is so convincingly structured as to appear transparent, self-evident. At one level, this chapter has taken up this line of thinking, seeking to apply Geertz's insight to the seemingly commonsensical realm of infant care by showing how it is surprisingly but deeply embedded in the realm of the spiritual in the West African context of the Beng. As we have seen, the everyday decisions that Beng mothers and other caretakers make concerning infants are anything but "common" when viewed from an outsider's perspective. At the same time, religion, that topic of adult contemplation occupying the thoughts of all the great philosophers and social theorists, turns out to be critical to, and critically defining of, the lives of the tiniest humans in the Beng world.

Perhaps religion and infant care have typically inhabited different realms of scholarly inquiry as a result of prefeminist assumptions about the nature of society and its assumed structure of gender roles. Most social scientists writing before the current feminist era saw the domestic world of the household as the bastion of women's lives. In turn, the lives of women themselves—especially their typically intense involvement with child rearing, most particularly with infants—were long seen as more natural than cultural, and more private than public (for explanations of this double tendency, see Ortner, 1974, 1989–1990; Rosaldo, 1974, 1980). Happily, feminism has challenged this easy set of associations, inspiring a generation of scholars to investigate women's lives, including the world that is commonly defined as domestic, as entirely cultural (e.g., Behar & Gordon, 1995; Ginsburg & Rapp, 1995; Glenn, Chang, & Forcey, 1994; Rich, 1976). Now that women are accepted as proper scholarly subjects, their inevitable involvements with children—including infants, those seemingly humblest and least spiritual of all humans—are beginning to be rich sources of scholarly investigation.

In West Africa, the imputed religious lives of infants and toddlers constitute an especially promising site for analytic inquiry, as the doctrine of reincarnation that is common throughout the region attributes deep spiritual activity to young children as revered, reincarnated ancestors with active memories of an afterlife. In other regions outside the Euro-American world, local doctrines of the afterlife and other models of a spiritually organized life cycle may provide alternative visions for young children's spirituality. Opening up the realm of religion to children allows the possibility of unexpected models, as old sites are revisited with new analytic lenses and the possibility of spiritual reflection is acknowledged for even the youngest of humans.

NOTES

1. For a brief review of the scanty anthropological and related literature on children, and an extended analysis of why anthropologists in particular have tended to neglect the study of infants overall, see Gottlieb (2004, pp. 38–61).

2. For a discussion of appropriate field methods and their challenges in studying infants' lives, see Gottlieb (2004, pp. 3–37).

3. Of course, Westerners with active religious affiliations may involve their infants to some extent (and their older children far more so) in religious activities geared to the life cycle, including baptisms, circumcision rituals, and adolescent initiations (e.g., Kirshenblatt-Gimblett, 1982). Members of certain contemporary Western religious communities, including the Amish, some Mennonites, and Chasidic Jews, also promote systematic child-rearing agendas based explicitly on religious doctrines. My remarks here pertain particularly to middle-class, Euro-Americans whose lifestyles are discursively taken in popular media to signal the mainstream of Western daily practice.

4. Such cities are indeed envisioned as "other," since as of this writing, only a handful of Beng have themselves ever traveled to major cities beyond Abidjan.

REFERENCES

Arad, I., Eyal, F., & Fainmesser, P. (1981). Umbilical care and cord separation. *Archives of Disease in Childhood, 56,* 887–888.

Ardener, E. (1989). Social anthropology and population. In E. Ardener, *The voice of prophecy and other essays* (M. Chapman, Ed.) (pp. 109–126). Oxford, UK: Basil Blackwell. (Original work published 1974)

Behar, R., & Gordon, D. A. (Eds.). (1995). *Women writing culture.* Berkeley and Los Angeles: University of California Press.

Bhalla, J. N., Nafis, N., Rohtagi, P., & Singh, J. (1975). Some observations on separation of the umbilical stump in the newborn. *Indian Journal of Pediatrics, 42,* 329–334.

Creider, J. T. (1986). *Two lives: My spirit and I.* London: Women's Press.

Diener, M. (2000). Balinese child care. In J. DeLoache & A. Gottlieb (Eds.), *A world of babies: Imagined childcare guides for seven societies* (pp. 91–116). Cambridge, UK: Cambridge University Press.

Durkheim, E. (1995). *The elementary forms of the religious life* (K. E. Fields, Trans.). New York: Free Press. (Original work published 1912)

Ferguson, C. (1977). Baby talk as a simplified register. In C. Snow & C. Ferguson (Eds.), *Talking to children: Language input and acquisition* (pp. 209–235). Cambridge, UK: Cambridge University Press.

Frazer, J. (1906–1915). *The golden bough: A study in magic and religion* (Vols. 1–12, 3rd ed.). London: Macmillan. (Original work published 1890)

Geertz, C. (1983). Common sense as a cultural system. In C. Geertz, *Local knowledge: Further essays in interpretive anthropology* (pp. 73–93). New York: Basic Books.

Ginsburg, F. D., & Rapp, R. (Eds.). (1995). *Conceiving the new world order: The global politics of reproduction.* Berkeley and Los Angeles: University of California Press.

Glenn, E. N., Chang, G., & Forcey, L. R. (Eds.). (1994). *Mothering: Ideology, experience, and agency.* New York: Routledge.

Gottlieb, A. (1992). *Under the kapok tree: Identity and difference in Beng thought.* Bloomington: Indiana University Press.

Gottlieb, A. (2000). Luring your child into this life: A Beng path for infant care. In J. DeLoache & A. Gottlieb (Eds.), *A world of babies: Imagined childcare guides for seven societies* (pp. 55–89). Cambridge, UK: Cambridge University Press.

Gottlieb, A. (2004). *The afterlife is where we come from: The culture of infancy in West Africa.* Chicago: University of Chicago Press.

Gottlieb, A., & Graham, P. (1993). *Parallel worlds: An anthropologist and a writer encounter Africa.* New York: Crown/Random House.

Kirshenblatt-Gimblett, B. (1982). The cut that binds: The Western Ashkenazic Torah binder as nexus between circumcision and Torah. In V. Turner (Ed.), *Celebration: Studies in festivity and ritual* (pp. 136–146). Washington, DC: Smithsonian Institution Press.

LaFontaine, J. (1985). *Initiation.* Harmondsworth, UK: Penguin.

Leach, P. (1983). *Babyhood* (2nd ed.). New York: Knopf.

Leis, N. (1982). The not-so-supernatural power of Ijaw children. In S. Ottenberg (Ed.), *African religious groups and beliefs: Papers in honor of William R. Bascom* (pp. 151–169). Meerut, India: Folklore Institute/Archana.

Lewis, M., & Rosenblum, L. A. (Eds.). (1974). *The effect of the infant on its caregiver.* New York: Wiley.

MacGaffey, W. (1986). *Religion and society in Central Africa: The BaKongo of Lower Zaire.* Chicago: University of Chicago Press.

Mills, A., & Slobodin, R. (Eds.). (1994). *Amerindian rebirth: Reincarnation belief among North American Indians and Inuit.* Toronto: University of Toronto Press.

Novack, A. H., Mueller, B., & Ochs, H. (1988). Umbilical cord separation in the normal newborn. *American Journal of Diseases of Children, 142,* 220–223.

Okri, B. (1991). *The famished road.* London: Jonathan Cape.

Oluwole, S. B. (1992). Reincarnation: An issue in African philosophy? In S. B. Oluwole, *Witchcraft, reincarnation and the God-head* (pp. 39–54). Lagos: Excel Publishers.

Ortner, S. (1974). Is female to male as nature is to culture? In M. Z. Rosaldo & L. Lamphere (Eds.), *Woman, culture, and society* (pp. 67–87). Stanford, CA: Stanford University Press.

Ortner, S. (1989–1990). Gender hegemonies. *Cultural Critique, 14* (Winter), 35–80.

Ottenberg, S. (1989). *Boyhood rituals in an African society: An interpretation.* Seattle: University of Washington Press.

Rich, A. (1976). *Of woman born: Motherhood as experience and institution.* New York: Norton.

Richards, A. (1956). *Chisungu: A girls' initiation ceremony among the Bemba of Northern Rhodesia.* London: Faber and Faber.

Rosaldo, M. Z. (1974). Woman, culture, and society: A theoretical overview. In M. Z. Rosaldo & L. Lamphere (Eds.), *Woman, culture, and society* (pp. 17–42). Stanford, CA: Stanford University Press.

Rosaldo, M. Z. (1980). The use and abuse of anthropology: Reflections on feminism and cross-cultural understanding. *Signs, 5*(3), 389–417.

Rosenthal, R., & Jacobson, L. (1968). *Pygmalion in the classroom: Teacher expectations and pupils' intellectual development.* New York: Holt, Rinehart and Winston.

Schloss, M. R. (1988). *The hatchet's blood: Separation, power, and gender in Ehing social life.* Tucson: University of Arizona Press.

Smith, R. (1927). *The religion of the Semites* (3rd ed.). London: A & C Black. (Original work published 1889)

Snow, C. (1977). Mothers' speech research: From input to interaction. In C. Snow & C. A. Ferguson (Eds.), *Talking to children: Language input and acquisition* (pp. 31–49). Cambridge, UK: Cambridge University Press.

Turner, V. (1967). *The forest of symbols.* Ithaca, NY: Cornell University Press.

Uchendu, V. C. (1965). *The Igbo of southeast Nigeria.* New York: Holt, Rinehart and Winston.

Weber, M. (1958). *The Protestant ethic and the spirit of capitalism.* New York: Scribner's. (Original work published 1904)

Werker, J. F. (1989). Becoming a native listener. *American Scientist, 77,* 54–59.

12

SPIRITUAL EXPERIENCES AND CAPACITIES OF CHILDREN AND YOUTH

TOBIN HART

There is a growing body of evidence that children have spiritual capacities and experiences—moments, both little and large, that shape their lives in enduring ways. These varied experiences reveal a rich and significant spiritual life that has gone largely unrecognized in the annals of child development and yet may provide one of the most fundamental sources of human motivation. The evidence of these experiences and innate capacities challenges conventional views of childhood spiritual life and therefore has significant implications for the care and nurture of young people both within and outside of religious contexts.

Yet it has often been difficult for adults to recognize this spiritual life. Traditionally, developmental theory has been largely dismissive of the idea that children have genuine spiritual experiences and capacities (e.g., Goldman, 1964; Wilber, 1996). Children have generally been seen as developmentally immature, without sufficient intellectual growth to manifest anything that might be understood as meaningfully reflective and/or spiritual. For example, even contemporary transpersonal theorists like Wilber (1996) describe children's modes of thinking and being as merely "instinctual,

impulsive, libidinous, id-ish, animal, apelike" (p. 2). Assumptions about children's capacities have frequently remained guided by Piaget's (1968) stage model of cognitive development, in which young children are viewed as largely incapable of meaningful reflection. Tied to this understanding of cognition, there is a prevalent presupposition that genuine spirituality requires adult abstract thinking and language ability as exhibited in the higher stages of adolescence and adulthood (for a discussion see, e.g., Dillon, 2000). Many researchers have therefore concluded that children, especially preadolescents, do not, and cannot, have a genuine spiritual life.

In addition, until recently research on childhood spirituality has typically equated spirituality with "God talk"—how children think and talk about God or other religious concepts (e.g., Coles, 1992; Heller, 1986; Tamminen, 1991). Through the imposition of such cognitive and religious standards, children's spiritual expressions often go unrecognized or are interpreted as merely immature religiosity. However, children's spirituality may exist apart from adult rational and linguistic conceptions and from knowledge about a religion. Although children may not be able to articulate a moment of wonder or conceptualize a religious concept, their *presence*—their mode of being and knowing in the world—may be distinctly spiritual. As Gordon Allport (1955) suggested, "The religion of childhood may be of a very special order" (p. 101).

Some theorists have recognized children's more immediate, intuitive knowing as an innate source for character and spiritual growth (Froebel cited in Lilley, 1967; Richter, 1887; Steiner, 1909/1965). Rather than focusing on religious knowledge, adherence, or thinking and language capacity, William James (1936) emphasized the significance of *personal religion* as opposed to *institutional religion*. For James, institutional religion implies approaches to spiritual growth formed around doctrines, various practices or rituals, and standards of behavior.

Spirituality—what James called personal religion—is the very direct and intimate experience of divinity. That divinity is the incomprehensible life force that remains so difficult to pin down, but to which we try to point with words like *God* or *spirit*. These experiences may emerge as a sense of interconnection or compassion, a revelatory insight, a quest for meaning, a sacred other, and so forth. These phenomena emerge as ways of being-in-the-world, intuitive epistemic styles and types of immediate awareness or perception that may take place within or outside the context of religion (see, e.g., Hart, Nelson, & Puhakka, 2000). The original seed of religion— the "word in the heart from which all scriptures come," as the Quaker William Penn (cited in Huxley, 1945) wrote—is the spiritual. Spiritual moments are direct, personal, and often have the effect, if only for a moment, of waking us up and expanding our understanding of who we are and what our place is in the universe. They can serve as benchmarks and catalysts for spiritual growth.

In addition to the evidence of particular types of experiences in adults (e.g., Bucke, 1969; James, 1936; Maslow, 1971; Underhill, 1911/ 1961), there is a growing body of evidence documenting spiritual experiences and capacities in childhood (Armstrong, 1985; Hart, 2003; Hay & Nye, 1998; Hoffman, 1992; Piechowski, 2001; Robinson, 1978, 1983). For this chapter I have drawn from these existing case studies with children and recollected childhood accounts, as well as autobiographical documents of historic figures, along with my own long-term qualitative

study (see Hart, 2003), and have interwoven these with insights from various faith traditions. Beyond documented cases and autobiographical accounts, in my direct qualitative study more than 150 cases were collected through contacts with individuals and families over a span of 5 years. Participants were purposefully sampled and included adults who recalled childhood experiences, young people who described spiritual encounters, and families. The notion of spiritual experience or awareness was left generally open-ended and was informed by extensive previous literature on religious, mystical, psychospiritual and transpersonal experience for adults, recent research on children, and autobiographical accounts. Participants were mainly, but not exclusively, North American and encompassed a wide range of cultural diversity and faith traditions as well as those with no religious affiliation. Several different means were employed to open intentional conversation, including focus groups, participant observation (e.g., during summer camp), and formal interviews with families, adults, or youth. Frequently, an initial contact would be serendipitous (a conversation on an airplane or a call from a parent) or a referral ("You should talk to so-and-so . . ."), and this would be followed up with an in-depth semistructured interview or a less structured visit to a family. The organizing principle of this varied approach was to gather credible narrative accounts of the spiritual life and capacities of childhood and to understand those in the context of daily life and development.

Supplementing narrative approaches, evidence is drawn from a survey of recalled childhood spiritual experiences in order to assess the frequency and variety of the phenomena (Nelson & Hart, 2003). In this study a series of questions was derived from the phenomenological descriptions of case accounts gathered in previous qualitative inquiry and then posed to approximately 450 undergraduate students at the State University of West Georgia in an anonymous survey. Students were enrolled in one of several different sections of an introductory psychology class, a core requirement of the university, taught by different instructors. All university majors were represented in the sample; students had had no previous organized exposure to the material. Excerpts of the results are reported here to provide some preliminary idea of just how common these experiences might be. If a rare few prodigious children have spiritual capacities or experiences, then this might imply significance along the lines of research on gifted education or child prodigies. However, if a larger percentage of children have spiritual experiences and capacities, a fundamental revision in how we view children may be required. These results, though very preliminary, suggest both a surprisingly widespread occurrence and the need for further, more wide scale research.

The data are organized around four general types of experiences and capacities: wonder, wondering, relational spirituality, and wisdom. These categories were induced from the extensive case material examined, and clarified, in part through various spiritual traditions and writers. The experiences of awe and wonder, wisdom, love or compassion, and metaphysical pondering are frequently described as outcomes or processes inherent in a spiritual life. For example, love or compassion—what I have included as relational spirituality—is commonly described across the faith traditions. Likewise, the pursuit of wisdom is a common principle in spiritual texts and among spiritual leaders. These general themes appeared repeatedly in the case material.

These ways of being-in-the world may help provide a multifaceted definition of spiritual life, demonstrating the diverse ways in which spirituality manifests. They also appear to represent general nonexclusive spiritual styles or temperaments. For example, one child's way of being may be especially empathic or compassionate, whereas another may be more philosophical—asking big questions of life and meaning. It is important to note that these are broad and general categories and that children express their spirituality in very individualized ways—a kind of personal "signature" tied to one's personality, as Nye has suggested (Hay & Nye, 1998).

This evidence may shed light on the diverse ways in which children pursue their spiritual drives and may help us recognize the innate spiritual capacities in our own life. It is also significant that the innate spiritual tendencies of

children coexist with immaturity, selfishness, and naïveté. These are developmental capacities and formative moments whose full potential and meaning may unfold through the course of a life.

In what follows, I will very briefly outline four domains and will do so especially by including a few examples that are intended to provide some concrete sense of the spirituality of children and youth.

WONDER

Childhood is a time of wonder and awe as the world grabs attention through fresh eyes and ears. Wonder includes a constellation of experiences that can involve feelings of awe, connection, joy, insight, and a deep sense of reverence and love. Surprisingly, the reports of wonder from contemporary children are often indistinguishable from those of the great mystics of the world for whom wondrous moments provided a touchstone and a beacon for the spiritual life that was to come.

Mechanism, materialism, and modernism tend to "desacralize" the world, leaving it as inert matter for our manipulation. Wonder keeps the sacred in view and recognizes it alive in our midst. Karen (I will use pseudonyms for case material throughout this chapter) remembers a powerful moment in her own secret place: "I was 15, sitting in silence in my 'special spot' outside, a short walk from my family's house. I was just sort of tuning in to nature, the little birds and insects here and there. Then suddenly I had this experience of everything being connected. Both in the sense of just part of the same, but then, what was most amazing to me was there was also a sense of everything being equal—the majestic mountain, the blade of grass, and me."

As it was for Karen, it appears that time in nature is the most common catalyst for moments of wonder (Laski, 1968). Children sometimes have a "special spot" that seems to provide a kind of spiritual nourishment.

Wonder comes in all shapes and sizes, ranging from awesome spiritual epiphanies to a small moment of being overwhelmed by the color or fragrance of a flower, for example. But these special moments, especially the "larger" ones, share particular qualities that help define them. As William James (1902/1936) recognized more than 100 years ago, they are *ineffable*—words fail to convey their depth and meaning. Like so many others, Black Elk said he was just speechless in trying to convey his own childhood spiritual visions: "As I lay there thinking of my vision, I could see it all and feel the meaning with a part of me like a strange power glowing in my body; but when the part of me that talks would try to make words for the meaning, it would be like a fog and get away from me" (Neihardt, 1972, pp. 40–41).

These moments are also *timeless.* A few hours in the surf may feel like a few seconds when we are absorbed in the "eternal now," as theologian Paul Tillich (1957) called it. The ability to be lost in the moment—absorption—is a capacity that is natural for children and seems to provide a gateway for opening perception toward a mystical encounter. Indeed, absorption appears significantly correlated with ecstasy and states of flow (Irwin, 1985; Nelson, 1989; Nelson & Hart, 2003). Yet in a fast-paced, modernist culture we are often discouraging of contemplative absorption that may appear as daydreaming or idleness (see Hart, 2004).

However novel these moments seem, there is often a sense of their being both *absolutely true* and *strangely familiar.* Plato called this depth of knowing "anamnesis," the soul's remembrance of truth. A moment of such communion can announce our spiritual homecoming and serves as a reminder of our spiritual address. Fifteen-year-old Jane said, "I'm having the hardest time finding the right words. Sometimes I feel like what I experience isn't really another reality at all, it's just a bigger view of this one. A few months back I had this experience while taking a walk where I felt so connected to everyone and everything—I could see, feel, and hear the web between us. It dissolves all fear. It felt so totally fresh and like coming home at the same time."

Wonder is also nonrational or transrational; it involves a *direct knowing.* Debbie's account at 11 years old described this shift: "I was outside lying back on my swing set by myself; I was looking at the sky, just watching. I don't know how it happened, but all of a sudden it all opened up to me. I don't know how to say it, but I was frozen right there and felt like everything

was perfect and connected. I can't say I was thinking anything; it's like there was no room even to think. The feelings were so much bigger than thinking. My thinking stopped and was blank. At the same time, it literally felt like my chest could just burst open and fly into a million pieces. I felt like I could explode and be the sun and the clouds." Saint John of the Cross described this mystical knowing that is beyond our intellect's ability to pin it down as "infinite incomprehension" (Underhill, 1911/1961).

Wonder may sometimes involve an awareness of a *sacred other.* For example, Catherine of Siena had her most formative revelation of Jesus when she was 6 years old (Vineis, 1934/1960). Hildegard von Bingen "saw so great a brightness that my soul trembled" at age 3 (Bowie & Davies, 1990, p. 20). Ramakrishna had a profound spiritual opening at 6 years old. Sometime following this he was taking food as an offering to the Divine Mother. The custom was to place it on an altar as he said prayers. This day he stopped as he was approaching the altar and noticed a cat nearby. Much to his surprise he reported that he clearly perceived that the Divine Mother Herself had become everything, even the cat. Instead of leaving the food on the altar, he gave it to the cat. The heart of his vision was that divinity is immanent—it is here and now in all things, even the cat (Nikhilananda, 1970).

During such moments, perception of the distinction between subject and object or self and other blurs. While the spiritual has sometimes been portrayed as separate and transcendent—beyond our reach or not of this world—what children tell us is that the other world is often perceived as right here and right now. This profound sense of immanence often comes with a sense of perfection, understanding, appreciation, and love. For many, a "reverence" and "appreciation" toward life arise naturally out of wonder and form a moral backdrop, as has been documented among adults (e.g., James, 1902/1936; Bucke, 1969; Maslow, 1971). Albert Schweitzer called this reverence the most profound attitude that we can have as human beings (Pierhal, 1957). A sense of gratitude, which has been described as a fundamental virtue (Emmons & McCullough, 2004), and even a spontaneous desire toward devotion may emerge, as it did for Saint Catherine and

Ramakrishna. Childhood moments of wonder are not merely passing reveries but may be translated into a moral benchmark.

Wonder and awe describe not only a spiritual *experience* but also a spiritual *attitude*. In Zen Buddhism, this attitude or way of seeing is called *Beginner's Mind*. It means being open to the world, appreciating and meeting it with fresh eyes—just watching it (and ourselves) with lessened preset expectations or categories. In what may be a similar vein, the Bible tells us that one enters the Kingdom of Heaven by becoming like a child: "unless you turn and become like children, you will never enter the kingdom of heaven" (Matthew 18:3). The same hint is offered in Taoism, whose founder's name, Lao-Tze, means "old child." I think it is safe to conclude that this does not mean childish, but instead childlike—full of wonder and openness, seeing in a more immediate, open, and less categorical fashion.

Beyond the reverence and joy, at times the divine can create a demand. A moment of ecstasy, unity, or a sacred other can be overwhelming and difficult to integrate. For example, in Atwater's (1999) research on children's near-death experiences, more than half dealt with serious bouts of depression. A staggering 21% attempted suicide (this number compares with 4% in adult near-death experiencers in her research). Such overwhelming experiences can be difficult to reconcile with one's daily life. But confusion, guilt, shame, lack of understanding, and family and religious members who felt threatened were the greatest source of difficulty. As one person learned, "I found it was O.K. to listen to talks about Jesus [in church] but not to be talked to by Jesus" (Hollander, 1980, p. 27).

There has been a long tradition of suspicion of ecstasy and mystical encounters. Documents like the *Malleus Maleficarum,* better known as *The Witches' Hammer,* written in 1486 by two Catholic monks from Germany, insist that mystical experiences, moments of ecstasy, visions, and the like are the mark of satanic influence (Liester, 1996). Such attitudes have helped institutionalize misunderstanding, repression, and persecution of those having spiritual experiences. Contemporary psychiatry also tends to dismiss such moments as mere fantasy or, worse, as a sign not of divinity but of pathology.

Recently, the primary diagnostic manual for psychiatric disorders has added a category, "Spiritual Emergency," to describe crises of meaning and experiences that have a spiritual flavor (American Psychological Association, 2000). Children's experiences reflect natural emergence and not necessarily an emergency, but we are beginning to recognize that the spiritual is central to our well-being, not a marker of our pathology.

In our study of recalled childhood experiences, nearly 80% of young adults said they sometimes feel a sense of awe and wonderment inspired by the immediate world around them and of those, 85% reported that their first occurrence was before the age of 18, with 12% indicating their first occurrence prior to 6 years old, 27% between 6 and 12, and 46% between 12 and less than 18 years old. In addition, 39% indicated that they had had a moment of unitive connection ("Have you ever had an experience in which you perceived that all was really connected together as one?"), and of those, 70% said it occurred at least once in childhood or youth (Nelson & Hart, 2003). As indicated previously, this study is preliminary.

Although moments of wonder appear to reflect powerful ways of knowing that in turn may shape a worldview and orientation toward life, there remains a lack of psychological theory appreciating the significance and nature of wonder in children. For example, Piaget (1968) recognized that children have an intuitive capacity, but he did not see much value in it. Fowler's (1981) "intuitive-projective" stage of faith recognizes that the child is continually encountering novelty and has a rich fantasy life, but this does not really address the transformative nature of wonder that children are describing. Washburn (1995) recognizes children's openness to the "dynamic ground" but presumes this openness must close off as the ego develops, and his map does not account for its developmental significance. Increasing evidence suggests, however, that wonder is of developmental significance for children and that children's capacity for wonder may be engendered owing to several factors, including their lack of rigid egoic structure, which permits an intimacy of contact—a crossing or blurring of subject and object—the natural capacity for absorption, their intuitive style of knowing, the perception of novelty all mixed with the mystery of life.

Literature on peak experiences (e.g., Bucke, 1901/1969; James, 1902/1936; Maslow, 1971), ecstasy (e.g., Laski, 1968; Underhill, 1911/1961), and absorption (e.g., Csikszentmihalyi, 1990; Nelson, 1989) articulates the significance of "wonder" in adults and its important impact on spiritual growth. The present research suggests that childhood wonder can also shape a worldview and even the course of one's life. While I have offered somewhat dramatic examples of discrete moments, it may be the everyday way of being and knowing that describes childhood wonder best. And the greatest significance is not in how small or large an experience is, but in how those moments are integrated and expressed in one's life. For example, how does a flash of interconnection translate into character and compassion? In addition, how might the presence of children help remind us, as adults, to find wonder in the midst of our lives (see Hart, 2003)?

WONDERING

Children can be natural philosophers. Much to our amazement, they often ponder *big questions*. They ask about life and meaning, knowing and knowledge, truth and justice, reality and death. These questions are what philosophy and religion have attempted to address.

"Why am I here?" 7-year-old John asked his father at the grocery store. "We're getting food for dinner. You said you wanted to come," his father reminded him. "No! No! Why are we *here;* you know, alive?" John said. "Huh? You mean why are we on Earth?" his father asked, a little stunned. "Yeah!" John said with some exasperation in his voice, as if it was the most obvious question he could ask. His father quickly gathered himself together and began to wind up an answer in his mind. But before he offered it, he had the good sense to ask John instead, "Why do *you* think we're here?" "I don't know yet; I'm working on it," John replied. Fair enough.

For many, the spiritual quest is focused and explored through pondering, puzzling over, and playing with such questions. For individuals like Gandhi, who was described as hungering for

truth even as a child, entertaining the big questions is a way to enter a dialogue with mystery, with the spiritual (Erikson, 1969). Emmons (1999) and Fowler (1981) recognize that "striving for the sacred" is integral to human personality and motivation. However, children's striving through questioning and pondering has been underappreciated.

Piaget's (1968) model of development maps cognition through progressive developmental stages—from the very body-based knowing of an infant to increasing abstraction. He believed that a child lacks the ability to reason and reflect with any degree of sophistication. There is increasing evidence, though, that he was both right and also quite wrong or, at least, incomplete. It does appear that children do go through cognitive development in stages. But these stages are general and broad, and represent merely a rough sketch. When we look a little closer, we can find grand exceptions to Piaget's model. Even young children have shown a capacity for thoughtful consideration of the "big questions" (metaphysics), inquiring about proof and the source of knowledge (epistemology), reasoning through problems (logic), questioning values (ethics), and reflecting on their own identity in the world. As previously indicated, the style of children's thinking may be more intuitive than sequentially analytic and therefore may have been missed by conventional standards of adult rational thought. Young people (as well as adults) may grasp a key insight or a broad understanding that captures the heart of an issue, but they may not be able to explain it in adult logic and language. Of course, this is true of other styles of thinking as well, such as a predominantly visual-spatial learner (Silverman, 2002) whose descriptions may be unfathomable to a less visual thinker.

Children's openness, vulnerability, and tolerance for mystery enable them to entertain perplexing and paradoxical questions. Matthews (1980) has said that children may be especially good at philosophy because they have "fresh eyes and ears for perplexity and incongruity . . . and a [high] degree of candor and spontaneity" (p. 85). Especially important to the consideration of spirituality, they often naturally ponder what Tillich (1957) called *ultimate concerns:* "Why are we here?" "What is life about?" Or, as my youngest daughter asked the other day, "Where did the first people come from?" Unfortunately, children may find prohibitions against their natural questioning in favor of pre-determined answers and ideologies, and this can be a source of great frustration and suffering. Jim, 14, looked back on his earlier school career:

I couldn't get my teachers to take my questions and ideas seriously. I thought this was what school was going to be about. There was such a big deal about going off to first grade, but I kept waiting for us to talk about life—you know, why we're all here? What's this world's about? The nature of the universe. Things like that. When I'd ask or say my ideas just to sort of get things going, there would be dead silence, and then the teacher would move on to spelling or something. I thought, "OK, I guess we're getting the basic stuff this year, and then we'll get into the good stuff in second grade. I can wait that long if I have to." Well, second grade came and went and it wasn't any better—maybe worse—since we didn't even get to play as much. By fourth grade I remember thinking, "I must be an alien. These people don't under-stand. I'm not a social zero; I have friends. But no one, especially not the teachers, are talking about this." School seems not to be very interested in my questions or any questions really; it is all about the answers. We're only supposed to give them the right answer.

The depth of children's concerns and ques-tions can surprise us. Jesse was about to turn 9 years old. It was the night before his birthday, and his dad was saying good night and giving him a kiss on the head. Jesse started to cry. "What's wrong?" his father asked. Jesse couldn't control himself; he was sobbing heavily as his father looked on helplessly with no idea what was happening. Was it about a present that he was afraid he might not get? Did he get in trou-ble at school? His father had no idea. Finally, Jesse was able to calm down enough to explain: "My birthday means I'm another year closer to death, and it means you are, too. I know that there's such a thing as reincarnation, but I don't want things to change." His dad didn't have an answer. They held each other while they both cried. Children certainly do think about toys and getting in trouble at school, but they also ponder

deeply the mysteries of being human—like death and love—and therefore their questions and concerns deserve our deepest respect and reverence.

Children's questions and comments reveal that they do not take for granted the same things that adults do. One mother described a moment when she and her daughter were sitting on their couch in front of the television: "I was laughing at something on TV, and my 8-year-old was scared by it and she said, 'You know, Mommy, I don't know yet what's real and what's not real.'" This reflects a powerful self-awareness and poses a bedrock philosophical question about proof and evidence: How does one know what is real? What are the requirements to determine validity?

This question of evidence extends to all sorts of questions. Ten-year-old Tim reports: "I some-times think about if there is one God.... Different people believe in different gods. Which God is real?... I just can't figure that out" (Hay & Nye, 1998, p. 97). After pondering the idea that Jesus was the only perfect person, as had been explained to her in church, 9-year-old Kathy offered a flurry of questions. "This is so weird," she said. "I can't understand how he could be the only one. What about all the other people around the world who don't believe in Jesus? What do they think about him being the only perfect one? What do they believe in? And why shouldn't they be able to go to heaven too?" She then dug deeper still: "How do you even know there is a God?"

Conceptual play and "philosophical whimsy," as Matthews (1980) names it, free us to imagine a world of endless possibilities. For example, Jung (1965), describing his own childhood, wrote: "Often, when I was alone, I sat down on this stone, and began an imaginary game that went something like this: I am sitting on the top of this stone and it is underneath. But the stone could also say 'I' and think: 'I am lying here on this slope and he is sitting on top of me.' The question then arose: 'Am I the one who is sitting on top of the stone, or am I the stone on which *he* is sitting?'" (p. 20).

Children's natural radical questioning is very much akin to a long history of spiritual practice designed to help free the mind to see more clearly and immediately. For example, Merton

(1948/1978) referred to unraveling questions as a "dark knowing," by which he meant that the result of the questioning process was mainly an "unknowing"—taking down rather than adding to. The Buddhist Madhyamika method intentionally deconstructs core concepts, even of Buddhism (Fenner, 1991). The approach called negative theology in Christianity systematically suspends core beliefs, even the basic tenets of Christianity, as a way of arriving at the profoundest knowing. Postmodern deconstruction is designed to render transparent the underpinnings of our beliefs and the structures of power and knowledge by questioning the origins of our assumptions. The 20th-century Indian sage Ramana Maharshi (1982) had momentous epiphanies as a teenager that opened him to his own spiritual identity. The center of his own quest and the heart of his spiritual teaching was a very direct question: "Who am I?" He understood that if this question is asked honestly and fully, it leads deeper and deeper, through layers of identity, roles, and attachments. Remarkably, because of their curiosity, candor, and freshness, children often find and ask these deep questions quite naturally.

As physicist David Bohm (1981) explains, "Questioning is . . . not an end in itself, nor is its main purpose to give rise to answers. Rather, what is essential here is the whole flowing movement of life, which can be harmonious only when there is ceaseless questioning" (p. 25). If you are around young children, you may be familiar with ceaseless questioning— Why? Why? Why?—or perhaps with children who pose difficult questions that defy easy answers. At 6, Julian asked, "What are heaven and hell? And what about the devil? Is it real?" He not only ponders how to get his little brother to leave him alone, but also earnestly puzzles over infinity, zero, God, and death. Such wondering may focus priorities in one's life and serve as a kind of trailhead in the search for meaning.

WISDOM

The spiritual traditions from around the world are also referred to as the wisdom traditions. In a spiritual life, wisdom seems to be something both to strive for and to use to reach toward the goal. We might reasonably assume that wisdom comes only with a great deal of experience, reserved for elders or for a rare few. However, in spite of their naïveté in the ways of the world, children often show a remarkable capacity for cutting to the heart of a matter, for accessing profound insight and wise guidance.

While the meaning of wisdom is difficult to pin down, we can take a moment to circle it for this discussion. Aquinas suggested that wisdom involves looking at things from a greater height. It involves *gnome,* or the ability to see through things (Gilby, 1967). Ralph Waldo Emerson captures a further dimension of wisdom in describing it as a blend of the perception of what is true with the moral sentiment of what is right (Sealts, 1992, p. 257). The courageous and very risky acts of persons like Gandhi, Jesus of Nazareth, and Martin Luther King imply that wise action moves beyond self-interest. We would not say that their actions were "smart," but they were deeply wise. And finally, wisdom is distinguished from bare intellect especially by its integration of the heart.

Donna described an opening to insight that took place when she was 8 years old:

> I was in church thinking about praying. Suddenly, in a flash, I understood that I should be praying for love and wisdom. I suddenly "got" that this was the way to use prayer. This was never suggested to me or even really talked about; but this insight came to be my regular way of praying. Whenever I prayed, I prayed for love and wisdom. This sounds simple, but it provided an incredible focus for me. This was my special secret. Even up until this moment, I have never told anyone about it. Up until my late 20s, I continued this style of prayer. Around the time of my marriage, it changed somewhat. I started to pray to have my heart opened . . . this seems like a different version of the same theme. I think that at some point I was expecting transcendence or something from my prayers, and it wasn't until later that I realized that what I was getting were small glimpses, a direction, an insight or attitude about handling situations. I didn't have the maturity to realize until later that wisdom involves acting on what we know—walking it out in the world. I had to take those glimpses and live them in order to learn from them.

Wisdom is not just about what we know, but especially about how we live, how we embody knowledge and compassion in our life and, as Emerson said, blend a sense of what is true with what is right. While this is often the daily challenge played out over the course of our life, some children seem to have mastered it surprisingly well.

As an 11-year-old, Mattie Stepanek seemed to have a remarkable embodied wisdom. His clarity and single-minded mission to "spread peace in the world" were impressive to those who met him. Mattie died in 2004 from multiple sclerosis and, for many years, had been precariously poised between life and death. Mattie had three wishes for his life, all of which were accomplished before his death: (1) to get his book of poetry published, (2) to meet his hero, Jimmy Carter, and (3) to be on Oprah Winfrey's show so that he could "spread peace." Television interviewer Larry King asked Mattie about his meeting with Carter, and Mattie described it in a lively and funny way and said they had a wonderful one-on-one conversation. Jimmy was his hero because he is a "humble peacemaker." Mattie said he liked to stay in touch with Carter to "make sure that Jimmy stays on track" with his peace work. Carter once remarked that Mattie was the wisest person he had ever met.

In response to the 9/11 tragedy, Mattie wrote three poems. The first he wrote when the World Trade Center Towers were falling, and he was "very, very sad and scared." The poem expresses this sadness, almost despair, about what is happening to people and their suffering, without in any way getting stuck in the "good" here and the "evil" there. In the third poem, he called on all people to "STOP" and stay still. Just "BE" before making any move in reaction to what just happened.

While intelligence is usually associated with an ability to identify or articulate complex patterns of thought, wisdom often emerges as an elegantly simple proposition. This is not simplicity born of ignorance, but a simplicity that is tuned into what is essential in life. It cuts through the cloud of complexity. Children can go right to the heart of an issue. They often recognize pain, injustice, and phoniness very quickly.

Meacham (1990) proposes that wisdom, normally associated with experience and maturity, is in reach of the child and may actually decrease with age. He views wisdom in terms of one's knowledge that one doesn't know and suggests that balancing knowing and doubting or, said differently, knowing without excessive confidence or cautiousness, may capture the simple essence of wisdom.

Wisdom does not come from amassing bits of information; it is not a thing that's accumulated, not an *entity*. Instead, it is an *activity* of knowing, perhaps most simply named as a shift in a state of consciousness or awareness. In some moments children find remarkable insight as they access this contemplative knowing that complements the rational and sensory (see Hart, 2000, 2004).

Although such knowing often arrives spontaneously, children sometimes find their own unique ways to open the contemplative mind. (See Hart, 2003, 2004, for an exploration of ways in which children spontaneously open this contemplative mind and also the means to cultivate this in secular and religious contexts.)

In our survey of young adults who were asked "Have you ever had the experience of receiving guidance from some source that is not part of our usual physical world?" 61% answered affirmatively and 85% of those indicated that this occurred before the age of 18. Asked the question "Have you ever found yourself knowing and/or saying something that seemed to come through you, rather than from you, expressing a wisdom you don't feel you usually have?" 54% said they had and of those, 80% indicated that this occurred in childhood and or youth (Nelson & Hart, 2003).

As a teenager, George left home to try to find a person who would inspire and serve as his spiritual guide. He came away from each visit with a different preacher more disappointed and discouraged. Finally, sitting in silence one day, he began to hear a deep inner source, what he called the "Inner Light." This was George Fox, who founded the Society of Friends, better known as the Quakers, in the 17th century (Liester, 1996). In recognition of the inner light, Quaker worship services are dominated by silence, so that worshippers may listen for their own inner voice or inner wisdom that is beyond shrewdness and calculation.

The great Native American Black Elk had visions that would shape his life at 5 and 9 years old. In his most formative vision, he was led by a horse and an eagle through a rainbow doorway into a teepee where there were six old men sitting in a row. The old men said, "Your grandfathers from all over the world have called you here to teach you." Each offered a medicine—a power—that would shape his life (Neihardt, 1972, p. 21).

When unacknowledged, childhood wisdom can lead to a sense of alienation. One participant in Edward Hoffman's (1992) study found little support or appreciation for this way of knowing:

> In simple terms, these meditative experiences led me to feel as a child that the grown-ups around me were out of touch with something and were deceiving themselves—and me—with unfounded opinions. As a result I often felt the need to retreat to a private reality among the woods and in nature. (pp. 96–97)

BETWEEN YOU AND ME

"Spirit is not in the I but between the I and you. It is not like the blood that circulates in you, but like the air in which you breathe," wrote Buber (1923/1970, p. 89). Spirituality is often lived out at the intersection of our lives—at the meeting *between you and me*. It is the quality of these human encounters that is the basis of a *relational* spirituality. This is typically recognized as love or compassion in the wisdom traditions and begins as an experience of empathy. Young people have the capacity to know the other quite directly, and in so doing they often sense pain, anger, or joy, for example, very quickly. Sometimes they may be overwhelmed or confused by the feelings of another person; in other moments that deep connection leads to surprising understanding.

Jeff remembers a moment of deep recognition as he was turning 10:

> More than anything I wanted a wristwatch for my birthday, and I kept letting my mother know. I had never had one before, and I thought this would be the greatest thing I could get. But we were very poor. My birthday came and my mother gave me an unwrapped box. I opened it and saw my new watch. But in the next moment, I looked into my mother's eyes and I saw this incredibly deep pain.

In that instant I saw that she was someone's child, she was someone's mother, and she would become an old woman. I knew that my mother was feeling pain and a sense of desperation. I had no way to talk about it then, but I knew who she was and what she felt, although I'm sure she had no idea of what I saw. I knew that somehow I was different after that moment. I went out to play and lost the watch before I returned for dinner.

At the age of 22, a dozen years later, I had been reading Martin Buber on the "I-thou" experience. It was then that I had an image for understanding what I had felt with my mother on my 10th birthday. I decided that I should telephone her. I asked her if she remembered that day and that gift. She did. I told her about the pain that I knew she was in. She was amazed because it seemed exactly right to her. She wondered how I could have known and understood it so clearly.

The word *understanding* means literally "standing among or under." Children appear to have an epistemic capacity that is naturally interconnective, less self-separate, related perhaps to the lack of refined ego identity. This rather direct and, we could say, "open-hearted" way of knowing is not limited to human relationships. Young people can feel that concern and care for a dead squirrel along the roadway, a dying tree, or nature as a whole. On the way to school just yesterday my daughter asked, "Dad, will you go back and make sure that turtle [that was in the middle of the road] gets across OK." And my 13-year-old friend wrote that her biggest fear is that we will continue to harm the earth and even destroy it. With similar care and intimacy, Nobel laureate Barbara McClintock (who explored genetics through working with corn plants) described a less detached empiricism, one in which she gained "a feeling for the organism" that required "the openness to let it come to you" (quoted in Keller, 1983, p. 198). In this epistemic style, the other is no longer separate but becomes part of our world and ourselves in a profoundly intimate way.

This empathy and "openness to let it come to you" can be a spiritual knowing especially because it awakens our interconnection, compassion, and love. Because of the profound importance of this kind of meeting, empathy has been described as the basis of moral development

(Hoffman, 1990) and even the trait that makes us most human (Azar, 1997). We realize our humanity and our divinity through the quality of our meetings. And when we really meet others, feel into their world and understand them, it becomes much more difficult to perpetrate violence against them. This is the root of a living relational morality:

> What I wanted I took—until about age 11, as I was about to take some nice marbles, I had a flash of insight into what the girl would feel like when she found them missing. The thought of her distress cured me of stealing, not the knowledge that what I was doing was wrong. (Robinson, 1983, p. 138)

While modern conceptions generally locate "knowing" in the head, sacred traditions identify the most essential knowing with the heart. For example, the Chinese word *hsin* is often translated as "mind" but includes both mind and heart. Heart knowing is recognized as the eye of the Tao in Chinese philosophy. Plato called it the eye of the soul (Smith, 1993). And the power of the heart is identified as "south" on the Native American medicine wheel (Storm, 1972). Seeing through the eye of the heart is a capacity present even at very tender ages.

Early in their new preschool program a 3-year-old boy, who was having trouble fitting in, bit Chessie, also 3, on the arm. She was naturally upset and was then very vigilant about the boy's whereabouts for the rest of the day. The next day, when he was sneaking up behind her and was just about to pounce, she spun around, pointed her finger at him, and shouted, "No!" like a parent. He stopped dead in his tracks and then moved away, leaving her alone for the remainder of the day.

The next day, he again tried to sneak up on her. Once again, Chessie spun around just as he was about to strike. He stood up straight and froze. She then stepped up and gave him a big hug. From that day on he never sneaked up on her. She made sure he wasn't left out during games or other activities and made certain that he had someone to sit next to during a video or story. As her teacher said, "She seemed to know exactly what this boy needed and took care of him while still setting limits."

Traditionally, developmental theorists have told us that children are self-centered and incapable of real empathy or compassion; they have not developed cognitively sufficiently to really put themselves in someone else's shoes. Indeed, children can be enormously selfish and self-centered. However, there has been some important recognition of the moral concerns and natural compassion of children (e.g., Coles, 1986; Damon, 1990). Children's openness and intuitive capacity allow them to experience a kind of direct empathic interconnection with the world—*deep empathy*—and their compassion can arise very naturally (Hart, 2000). The capacities for separateness and connection, selfishness and compassion exist simultaneously.

As with any faculty, young people may have varying proficiency—some are remarkably empathic, others seem only slightly so. However, from our initial survey results it appears that there is the possibility that the general phenomenon may be quite common. In answer to the question "Do you ever feel that at times you know people's thoughts/feelings unusually accurately without being told or shown in any direct, physical way?" 70% in our survey indicated they had; 31% indicated that the first occurrence was before 12 years old, and 48% said their first recalled occurrence was between 12 and 17 years old (Nelson & Hart, 2003).

Such direct knowing and intensity of feeling can be overwhelming. Self–other boundaries vary a great deal from one individual to the next. Individuals who are highly empathic often have a flexible or highly permeable boundary—a fundamental and primary way of knowing the world—that can be a great gift as well as a source of confusion and suffering. Seventeen-year-old Sarah tells about a surprisingly typical circumstance of being a kind of psychic sponge, seemingly absorbing others' emotions: "I'm an empath, and I hate school. I walk around and people walk in and out of classes, and I get everything from them—their anger, frustration, even happiness or joy. But it's no fun. I'm not a big fan of crowds . . . but I'm working on turning the empathy on and off."

Many teenagers and adults use compensatory measures such as drugs and alcohol to numb their sensitivity or, alternatively, develop a hostile or withdrawn personality in order to create a pseudoboundary. At times their empathic sensitivity has been a source of confusion because they have not learned to shut out empathic perceptions or to distinguish between what feelings are theirs and which belong to someone else, or they fail to interpret information in a helpful way (Hart, 2003).

Relational spirituality is about communion—a profound sense of interconnection with the cosmos; connection—a sense of intimacy with someone or something; community—a sense of belonging to a group; and compassion—the drive to help others. It is about the way one knows and meets the world. The spirit is brought to life in a genuine and open meeting, just as children can remind us to do, and Buber (1923/1970) tells us that ultimately, "all real living *is* meeting" (p. 11).

CONCLUSIONS

The pleasure principle, instinctual drives toward survival and procreation, and early object relations certainly shape motivation and behavior; however, another coexistent source of motivation may be of a very different order. Childhood spiritual awareness and experience may serve as touchstones and catalysts for psychospiritual development. Recognition of empathic interconnection or *interbeing* (Hanh, 1995) may help shape a morality emphasizing interdependence or care. Entertaining big questions about meaning, suffering, and so forth may help shape character by validating such ultimate concerns amid a media deluge that seems to emphasize sexuality, materiality, consumerism, and celebrity. Experiences of accessing wisdom may activate a lifelong capacity for listening for that still small voice, reflection and contemplation. Moments of wonder, peace, perfection, joy, or of seeing the Golden World, as Eliade (1964) called it, may provide a sense of perspective, hope, or optimism.

The evidence of the innate spiritual capacities of children and youth and its significance for development raises questions for the care and nurture of the spiritual life of young people. How do we draw out and work with the organic spiritual character, capacities, and compassion within the child, and when do we offer our view of the "good life" from the outside in? What is

the right balance in this dialectic? In light of the diet of materialism, violence, and so forth offered by the mass media, the value in reinforcing and offering "spiritual" perspectives seems clear. But how do we avoid squelching and overwhelming children's world presence—their way of being and knowing in the world—with an adultcentric worldview? When are our messages and expectations imperialistic toward children and when are they liberating? What is the relationship between religion and childhood spirituality? What kinds of religious participation enhance and help actualize psychospiritual development and what activities actually thwart development? These questions and this relationship are not simple ones. Childhood spirituality tends toward the immanent and existential, and is diverse and direct. It may or may not match our adult worldview or religious concepts (e.g., original sin) and may not be articulated but is deeply felt nonetheless. If there is a single general idea that could be said about how to enhance or inhibit childhood spiritual life, perhaps it is that the foremost concern is respect for the child's innate spiritual capacities. As Black Elk said, "Grown men may learn from very little children, for the hearts of little children are pure, and, therefore, the Great Spirit may show to them many things which older people miss" (Brown, 1953, pp. 74–75). It is the assumptions and the agenda we hold that may be the most significant factor in determining whether religious, educational, parenting, and psychiatric efforts harm or heal. Our assumptions shape our perceptions. Do we assume, for example, that the child is immoral or amoral and incapable of meaning and spiritual experience, or is the child a spiritual being with spiritual capacities? First and foremost, and before we try to mold who they are from the outside in, can we try to understand and appreciate who the child is from the inside out? This kind of inquiry of the inner life continues to be best served with subtle human sciences research approaches—such as narrative accounts, phenomenological description, the use of art or other expressive means, and participant observation where appropriate. Data derived from such approaches could be followed with survey or similar means of inquiry. In addition, as the vast majority of research on children's spirituality is from North America and Europe, cross-cultural studies that might help us reveal unexpected presuppositions and see alternative approaches to development and education would be very welcome.

What we can begin to understand is that children already have a spiritual life; they have access to wisdom and wonder, struggle with questions of meaning and morality, and have a deep sense of compassion. Elsewhere I have attempted to highlight in more detail those qualities and conditions that tend to thwart and those that may enhance childhood spirituality (Hart, 2003).

Perhaps most important at this stage in our understanding of the spiritual life of young people, can we be as willing to let what we learn from children change *our* theology and theory as we are willing to change children by the imposition of our theology and theory on them?

REFERENCES

Allport, G. (1955). *The individual and his religion.* New York: Macmillan.

American Psychological Association. (2000). *Diagnostic and statistical manual of mental disorders* (4th ed.). Washington, DC: Author.

Armstrong, T. (1985). *The radiant child.* Wheaton, IL: Theosophical Publishing House.

Atwater, P. M. H. (1999). *Children of the new millennium: Children's near-death experiences and the evolution of humankind.* New York: Three Rivers Press.

Azar, B. (1997). Defining the trait that makes us most human. *APA Monitor, 28*(11), 1–15.

Bohm, D. (1981). Insight, knowledge, science, and human values. In D. Sloan (Ed.), *Toward the recovery of wholeness* (pp. 8–30). New York: Teachers College Press.

Bowie, F., & Davies, O. (Eds.). (1990). *Hildegard of Bingen* (R. Carver, Trans.). New York: Crossroad.

Brown, J. E. (Ed.). (1953). *The sacred pipe: Black Elk's account of the seven rites of the Oglala Sioux.* Norman: University of Oklahoma Press.

Buber, M. (1970). *I and thou* (W. Kaufmann, Trans.). New York: Charles Scribner & Sons. (Original work published 1923)

Bucke, R. M. (1969). *Cosmic consciousness: A study in the evolution of the human mind.* New York: Dutton. (Original work published 1901)

Coles, R. (1986). *The moral life of children.* New York: Atlantic Monthly Press.

Coles, R. (1992). *The spiritual life of children.* New York: HarperCollins.

Csikszentmihalyi, M. C. (1990). *Flow: The psychology of optimal experience.* New York: Harper & Row.

Damon, W. (1990). *The moral child: Nurturing children's natural moral growth.* New York: Free Press.

Dillon, J. J. (2000). The spiritual child: Appreciating children's transformative effects on adults. *Encounter: Education for Meaning and Social Justice, 13*(4), 4–18.

Eliade, M. (1964). *Shamanism: Archaic techniques of ecstasy.* Princeton, NJ: Princeton University Press.

Emmons, R. A. (1999). *The psychology of ultimate concerns: Motivation and spirituality in personality.* New York: Guilford.

Emmons, R. A., & McCullough, M. E. (Eds.). (2004). *The psychology of gratitude.* New York: Oxford University Press.

Erikson, E. H. (1969). *Gandhi's truth: On the origins of militant nonviolence.* New York: Norton.

Fenner, P. (1991). *The ontology of the middle way.* Dordrecht, Holland: Kluwer.

Fowler, J. W. (1981). *Stages of faith: The psychology of human development and the quest for meaning.* San Francisco: Harper & Row.

Gilby, T. (Trans.). (1967). *St. Thomas Aquinas: Philosophical texts.* New York: Oxford University Press.

Goldman, R. (1964). *Religious thinking from childhood to adolescence.* London: Routledge Kegan & Paul.

Hanh, T. N. (1995). *The heart of understanding: Commentaries on the Prajnaparamita Heart Sutra.* Berkeley, CA: Parallax Press.

Hart, T. (2000). Deep empathy. In T. Hart, P. L. Nelson, & K. Puhakka (Eds.), *Transpersonal knowing: Exploring the horizon of consciousness* (pp. 253–270). Albany: State University of New York Press.

Hart, T. (2003). *The secret spiritual world of children.* Makawao, HI: Inner Ocean.

Hart, T. (2004). Opening the contemplative mind in the classroom. *Journal of Transformative Education, 2*, 28–46.

Hart, T., Nelson, P., & Puhakka, K. (Eds.). (2000). *Transpersonal knowing: Exploring the horizon of consciousness.* Albany: State University of New York Press.

Hay, D., & Nye, R. (1998). *The spirit of the child.* London: Fount/HarperCollins.

Heller, D. (1986). *The children's God.* Chicago: University of Chicago Press.

Hoffman, E. (1992). *Visions of innocence: Spiritual and inspirational experiences of childhood.* Boston: Shambhala.

Hoffman, M. L. (1990). Empathy and justice motivation. *Motivation and Emotion, 14*(2), 151–172.

Hollander, A. (1980). *How to help your child have a spiritual life: A parent's guide to inner development.* New York: A & W.

Huxley, A. (1945). *The perennial philosophy.* New York: Harper & Row.

Irwin, H. J. (1985). Parapsychological phenomena and the absorption domain. *Journal of the American Society for Psychical Research, 79,* 1–11.

James, W. (1936). *The varieties of religious experience.* New York: Modern Library. (Original work published 1902)

Jung, C. G. (1965). *Memories, dreams, reflections.* New York: Vintage Books.

Keller, E. F. (1983). *A feeling for the organism: The life and work of Barbara McClintock.* New York: Freeman.

Laski, M. (1968). *Ecstasy: A study of some secular and religious experiences.* London: Cressent Press.

Liester, M. B. (1996). Inner voices: Distinguishing transcendent and pathological characteristics. *Journal of Transpersonal Psychology, 28*(1), 1.

Lilley, I. M. (1967). *Friedrich Froebel: A selection from his writings.* Cambridge, UK: Cambridge University Press.

Maharshi, R. (1982). *Who am I?* Tiruvannamalai, India: Sri Ramanasramam.

Maslow, A. (1971). *The farther reaches of human nature.* New York: Penguin.

Matthews, G. B. (1980). *Philosophy and the young child.* Cambridge, MA: Harvard University Press.

Meacham, J. A. (1990). The loss of wisdom. In R. J. Sternberg (Ed.), *Wisdom: Its nature, origins, and development* (pp. 181–211). Cambridge, UK: Cambridge University Press.

Merton, T. (1978). *What is contemplation?* Springfield, IL: Templegate. (Original work published 1948)

Neihardt, J. G. (1972). *Black Elk speaks: Being the life story of a holy man of the Oglala Sioux.* New York: Pocket Books.

Nelson, P. L. (1989). Personality factors in the frequency of reported spontaneous præternatural experiences. *Journal of Transpersonal Psychology, 21*(2), 193–209.

Nelson, P. L., & Hart, T. (2003). *A survey of recalled childhood spiritual and non-ordinary experiences: Age, rate and psychological factors associated with their occurrence.* Retrieved January 13, 2004, from http://www.childspirit.net/survey%200f%20childhood%20experiences.pdf

Nikhilananda, S. (Trans.). (1970). *The gospel of Sri Ramakrishna* (Abridged ed.). New York: Ramakrishna-Vivekananda Center.

Piaget, J. (1968). *Six psychological studies.* New York: Random House.

Piechowski, M. (2001). Childhood spirituality. *Journal of Transpersonal Psychology, 33*(1), 1–15.

Pierhal, J. (1957). *Albert Schweitzer: The story of his life.* New York: Philosophical Library.

Richter, J. P. (1887). *The doctrine of education for English readers* (B. Wood, Trans.). London: Swan Sonnenschein.

Robinson, E. (1978). *Living the questions: Studies in the childhood of religious experience.* Oxford, UK: Manchester College, Religious Experience Research Unit.

Robinson, E. (1983). *The original vision: A study of the religious experience of childhood.* New York: Seabury. (Original work published 1977)

Sealts, M. M. (1992). *Emerson on the scholar.* Columbia: University of Missouri Press.

Silverman, L. (2002). *Upside-down brilliance: The visual-spatial learner.* Glendale, CO: DeLeon.

Smith, H. (1993). Educating the intellect: On opening the eye of the heart. In B. Darling-Smith (Ed.), *Can virtue be taught?* (pp. 17–31). Notre Dame, IN: University of Notre Dame Press.

Steiner, R. (1965). *Education of the children in light of anthroposophy.* London: Rudolf Steiner Press. (Original work published 1909)

Storm, H. (1972). *Seven arrows.* New York: Ballantine.

Tamminen, K. (1991). *Religious development in childhood and youth: An empirical study.* Helsinki, Finland: Suomalainen Tiedeakatemia.

Tillich, P. (1957). *Dynamics of faith.* New York: Harper & Row.

Underhill, E. (1961). *Mysticism.* New York: Dutton. (Original work published 1911)

Vineis, R. (1960). *The life of St. Catherine of Siena* (G. Lamb, Trans.). New York: P. J. Kennedy & Sons. (Original work published 1934)

Washburn, M. (1995). *The ego and the dynamic ground: A transpersonal theory of human development* (2nd ed.). Albany: State University of New York Press.

Wilber, K. (1996). *The atman project: A transpersonal view of human development*. Wheaton, IL: Quest.

Part III

SPIRITUALITY AND HUMAN DEVELOPMENT:
EXPLORING CONNECTIONS

Introduction to Part III

Definitions of spirituality have largely failed in the attempt to articulate a separate domain for the spiritual. It becomes inescapable that spirituality is not separate from the biological, social, cognitive, emotional, moral, civic, and religious domains. Spirituality by its very nature begs us to take a holistic view of persons. Human development cannot ultimately be understood or represented in terms of cognition, emotion, attachment, neurology, or any single set of human functions. Inevitably the need to account for the connection between these separated domains arises. Might spirituality be considered as the process of connection and organization, in other words, the integrative function of development?

The authors in part III take on the task of exploring the connection of spirituality to traditional subdisciplines within the field of human development. In doing so they are able to reflect on and contribute to the models and methods of integrative research, generating coherent ways of thinking about spirituality.

Andrew B. Newberg and Stephanie K. Newberg begin by asking the question of how religion and spirituality are intimately linked with human biology throughout the life cycle. They argue that the basic mechanisms associated with spiritual experiences are correlated with essential brain functions and that the two processes mirror each other in development.

Pehr Granqvist and Jane R. Dickie use attachment theory to elucidate the structural and functional similarity between child–parent and believer–God relationships. Granqvist and Dickie propose correspondence and compensation hypotheses as models for investigating the links between attachment and religiosity/spirituality in adulthood.

The links between cognitive and spiritual development are examined by Carl N. Johnson and Chris J. Boyatzis. The theoretical models traditionally applied to cognitive development are critiqued for their usefulness for understanding spiritual development. The authors provide a cognitive framework for understanding spiritual development and present the empirical research on domains related to conceptual–spiritual development. Religious concepts such as God, prayer, and soul are reviewed, and the relationships among culture, family transmission, and cognition are explored.

Lawrence J. Walker and Kevin S. Reimer have provided a careful treatment of the connections between moral and spiritual development grounded in historical-classical sources and augmented with recent empirical work on naturalistic conceptualizations. Walker and Reimer use a case study approach to delve into the morality and spirituality of a community of care exemplars.

Thomas M. Donnelly, M. Kyle Matsuba, Daniel Hart, and Robert Atkins explore the intertwining of spirituality and civic involvement. The model they put forth demonstrates the path from spirituality through either organized religion or virtue to outcomes that focus on self-perfection/salvation or, alternatively, to a concern for others. These authors also review the extant research supporting the bidirectional and largely positive association between the two streams of spirituality and civic engagement in adolescence.

Identity and spiritual development are ultimately linked through the question, "Who am I?" Janice L. Templeton and Jacquelynne S. Eccles discuss the theories that inform our thinking about spiritual identity development. Erik Erikson's psychosocial stages are provided as a foundational model for understanding both identity and spiritual development. The numerous social identities revealed in a person by context developmental perspective alert us to the importance of understanding the social, cultural, ethnic, and historical influences on spiritual identity formation.

In this section's final chapter, Teresa T. Kneezel and Robert A. Emmons present self-determination theory as a useful heuristic for looking at spiritual development as well as personality and motivation. The key organismic proposal that people intrinsically strive toward differentiation and integration of self is expanded to include a transcendent function that integrates self with others and the sacred.

As is true in any vital field of research, the questions these chapters raise outnumber the answers they provide. Is there a unique domain of spiritual development? Or, as has been suggested, is spirituality an integrative function? As the field of human development progresses, the methods and models generated by the study of spiritual development may provide critical foundations for integrative research.

13

A Neuropsychological Perspective on Spiritual Development

Andrew B. Newberg

Stephanie K. Newberg

The study of religious and spiritual phenomena from a neuropsychological and developmental perspective presents a number of complex issues, the most important of which is to determine whether such an approach may open a window to understanding how religion and spirituality are intimately linked with human biology and psychology throughout the life cycle. We will argue that the basic mechanisms associated with religious and spiritual experiences are correlated with essential brain functions and that the development of each mirrors that of the other. The notion that as the brain develops physiologically, the human concept of religion and spirituality evolves accordingly, supports the intimate link between human biology and spirituality. By exploring this link, we hope to elucidate how religion and spirituality become hard associated with various brain functions.

EPIDEMIOLOGY AND DESCRIPTION

Spirituality, religion, and faith are complex concepts that have been defined in many different ways. For the purposes of this chapter, we will define spirituality as distinct from religion or religiousness. Spirituality is usually regarded as less institutionally based and as more encompassing and inclusive of all groups and cultures than religiousness. Spirituality is also used to describe individual experiences such as those of transcendence and meaningfulness (Larson, Swyers, & McCullough, 1998; Spilka & McIntosh, 1996). According to a recent consensus conference report sponsored by the National Institute for Healthcare Research, the criteria for spirituality were described as "the feelings, thoughts, experiences, and behaviors that arise from a search for the sacred. The term 'search' refers to attempts to identify, articulate, maintain, or transform. The term 'sacred' refers to a divine being or Ultimate Reality or Ultimate Truth, as perceived by the individual" (Larson et al., 1998). This definition of spirituality was distinguished from that for religiousness. Religion and religiousness not only contained the preceding criteria, they also included a "search for non sacred goals (such as identity, belongingness, meaning, health, or wellness)." Religiousness also implies that the means and methods of the search "receive validation and support from within an identifiable group"

(Larson et al., 1998). It should be emphasized that these definitions were specifically intended to be operationalized approaches that would facilitate future scientific research and were not necessarily meant to be the most accurate from a religious or theological perspective.

The concept of faith is also extremely difficult to characterize clearly. Although the term *faith* has religious implications in terms of being a belief in a specific religious conceptualization of God and humankind's relation to God, faith also can be considered from a neuropsychological perspective. A neuropsychological perspective posits that all human experience is ultimately processed by the brain. The brain therefore can only provide a "secondhand rendition" of external reality. If this is the case, then human beings always have to have faith in their interpretation of that external reality as it is processed by the brain. Faith, in some sense, becomes absolutely essential for the human brain to function properly so that it assumes that the world as it is perceived and interpreted represents a reasonable one-to-one correlation with what is actually "out there." With this perspective in mind, faith clearly underlies the experiences and ideas associated with religion and spirituality. Fowler (1981) has observed that faith is universal and recognizably similar regardless of one's specific beliefs or religion. In this regard, faith might be considered to refer to the quest for meaning and its relation to transcendence and how one uses the concept to derive purpose and set priorities within life. Thus, faith can evolve over the course of an individual's life span, and will have mutual interactions with the person's sense of spirituality and religion.

In order to better understand spirituality and religion, scholars have attempted to identify the specific characteristics of experiences associated with these two concepts. A spiritual experience has been defined as a melting of boundaries and a merging with the surrounding environment (Rolbin, 1985) and as a unitary or "cosmic consciousness" (Bucke, 1961; Rowan, 1983). Spirituality has been discussed as a transcendence that occurs along a specified spiritual path that can be attained through practices such as meditation. "Through therapy or personal growth, we learn to open up to our own inner process, through mysticism we learn how to

carry on with that same process into the deepest depths of all" (Rowan, 1983, p. 9). Spirituality has been described by Maslow (1970) as a unity with all and the attainment of self-actualization. According to Rowan (1983), in order to attain a spiritual experience one must have discovered one's self through mindful awareness, therapy, personal growth, and/or meditation. However, there are clearly many examples of spontaneous spiritual experiences that include near-death experiences and religious conversions. It is also important to acknowledge that spiritual experiences likely reside along a continuum from relatively brief feelings of "awe" to profound unitary states; we will consider this issue later in this chapter (d'Aquili & Newberg, 1999).

In order to explore fully the biology of spiritual development, it seems necessary to consider briefly spiritual experiences from a neuropsychological as well as a clinical perspective to provide some insight into the significance of such experiences and to begin to consider how to incorporate the exploration of these experiences into therapy.

THE NEUROPSYCHOLOGY OF SPIRITUAL EXPERIENCES

The study of spiritual experiences has important implications for a developmental spirituality since it is frequently such experiences that can propel an individual along the developmental path. Furthermore, it may be that certain stages of spiritual development are associated with different types of spiritual experiences. There is clearly a wide variety of spiritual experiences that exist along a continuum ranging from mild feelings of "awe" to the sense of the "wholly other" of the divine being, to what has been called "absolute unitary being" (AUB) in many of the Eastern traditions such as Buddhism and Hinduism (Otto, 1970; Streng, 1978). Smart (1967, 1969, 1978) has argued that certain strains of Hinduism, Buddhism, and Taoism differ markedly from prophetic religions such as Judaism and Islam and from religions related to the prophetic-like Christianity, in that the religious experience most characteristic of the former is "mystical," whereas that most characteristic of the latter is "numinous." Of these two terms, it is the numinous that Smart seems to have an easier time explaining, since it obviously arises more spontaneously out of Western religious traditions. Stace (1961) goes further by distinguishing between what he calls extrovertive mystical experiences and introvertive mystical experiences. Extrovertive mystical experiences are differentiated by including a unifying vision in which all things are perceived as one and the more concrete apprehension of the One as an inner subjectivity, or life, in all things. Introvertive mystical experiences are distinguished by including a Unitary Consciousness that is nonspatial and nontemporal.

A neurobiological analysis of spiritual experiences might clarify some of the issues regarding these experiences by allowing for a typology based on the underlying brain functions. With regard to the continuum of spiritual experiences, unitary states appear to play a crucial role. While it is difficult to define what makes a given experience spiritual, the sense of having a union with some higher power or fundamental state of being seems a crucial part of spiritual experiences. To that end, this union helps reduce existential anxiety as well as provide a sense of control over the environment (d'Aquili, 1978; d'Aquili & Newberg, 1998; Smart, 1967, 1969). The bottom line in understanding the phenomenology of subjective spiritual experience is to understand that every experience involves a sense of the unity of reality at least somewhat greater than the baseline perception of unity in day-to-day life (d'Aquili, 1986). This may be related to altered functioning of the brain structures typically involved in helping to construct the self/other dichotomy. Usually the self/other dichotomy functions to help us distinguish our self from the rest of the external world. It has been suggested that the left posterior superior parietal lobe may be responsible for this function because it is involved in differentiating graspable from nongraspable objects (Van Heertum & Tikofsky, 1995). In human beings, it has been suggested that the functions of this structure have been elaborated to allow for the self/other dichotomy (Joseph, 1996). This dichotomy is normally based on input from all of the sensory systems. In cases of meditation, it has been suggested that there is a differential blocking, or "deafferentation," of input into the

posterior superior parietal lobe that progressively diminishes the strength of the self/other dichotomy (d'Aquili & Newberg, 1993; Newberg & Iversen, 2003). Thus, the continuum of spiritual experience relies heavily on the progressive sense of unity that is associated with a progressive blocking of input into the posterior superior parietal lobe. We have hypothesized that this progressive blocking of input into the posterior superior parietal lobe creates a sense of increased unity over multiplicity. It should also be mentioned that the right posterior superior parietal lobe is involved in orienting us within three-dimensional space (Joseph, 1996). We have proposed that the blocking of input into this structure may result in the alterations in the sense of space and time that are often described during spiritual experiences. Thus, both the left and right posterior superior parietal lobe are likely involved in spiritual experiences.

At the extreme end of the continuum of spiritual experiences is the state of absolute unitary being, which is described in the mystical literature of all the world's great religions. When a person is in that state he or she loses all sense of discrete being, and even the difference between self and other is obliterated. There is no sense of the passing of time, and all that remains is a perfect timeless undifferentiated consciousness. When such a state is suffused with positive affect there is a tendency to describe the experience, after the fact, as personal. Such experiences are often described as a perfect union with God (the *unio mystica* of the Christian tradition) or else the perfect manifestation of God in the Hindu tradition. When such experiences are accompanied by neutral affect they tend to be described, after the fact, as impersonal. These states are described in concepts such as the abyss of the German mystic Jakob Böhme, the Void or Nirvana of Buddhism, or the Absolute of a number of philosophical/mystical traditions. There is no question that whether the experience is interpreted personally as God or impersonally as the Absolute, it nevertheless possesses a quality of transcendent wholeness without any temporal or spatial division whatsoever. We have postulated that these rare states of AUB are associated with the total blocking of input into the posterior superior parietal lobe (d'Aquili, 1982; d'Aquili & Newberg, 1993).

We propose that even in more ordinary perceptions, whenever the sense of wholeness exceeds the sense of multiplicity of parts or of discrete elements in the sensorium, there is an affective discharge via the right brain–limbic connections that Schwartz, Davidson, and Maer (1975) have shown to be of such importance. This tilting of the balance toward an increased perception of wholeness, depending on its intensity, can be experienced as beauty, romantic love, numinosity or the religious awe described by Smart, religious exaltation in the perception of unity in multiplicity (described by Stace as extrovertive mystical experience), and eventually various trance states culminating in AUB.

As there is an increasing sense of unity, there is the perception of ever greater approximations of some more fundamental reality (d'Aquili, 1986). Furthermore, the more the blocking of input into the right posterior superior parietal lobe is in excess of a state of balance with the analytic functions of the left hemisphere, the stronger will be the associated emotional charge. Thus, in any perception such as a piece of music, a painting, a sculpture, or a sunset, there is a sense of meaning and wholeness that transcends the constituent parts. In aesthetic experiences such as those just described, this transcendence is mild to moderate. We would locate the overarching sense of unity between two persons in romantic love as the next stage in this continuum. Feelings of numinosity or religious awe occur when there is a marked sense of meaning and wholeness extending well beyond the parts perceived or well beyond the image generated, but in a "wholly other" context. Both Otto (1970) and Smart (1969) have described this experience in detail. It is often considered (rather incorrectly we feel) to be the dominant Western mystical experience. It is experienced when an archetypal symbol is perceived or when certain archetypal elements are externally constellated in a myth. As we move from numinosity along the continuum, we reach the state of religious exaltation that Bucke (1961) has called "Cosmic Consciousness." This state is characterized by a sense of meaning and wholeness extending to all discrete being whether subjective or objective. The essential unity and purposefulness of the universe are perceived as a primary datum despite the perception and

knowledge of evil in the world. During this state, there is nothing whatsoever that escapes the mantle of wholeness and purposefulness. But this state does not obliterate discrete being, and it certainly exists within a temporal context. This roughly corresponds to Stace's extrovertive mystical experience.

There are several other brain structures that are likely to be important with regard to spiritual experiences. It is likely that there is increased activity in two structures of the limbic system, called the amygdala and hippocampus, resulting in the strong affective component described as part of spiritual experiences (Saver & Rabin, 1997). Electrical stimulation of these two structures has also resulted in various sensory experiences, visions, and emotional discharges similar to some of those that occur during spiritual experiences (Penfield & Perot, 1963; Valenstein, 1973). Limbic stimulation during spiritual experiences may be modulated by activity in the posterior superior parietal lobes as well as the frontal lobes since these structures are all intimately interconnected (Joseph, 1996). During practices such as meditation, stimulation of the limbic system may result from activity in the frontal cortex, which is known to modulate emotional responses via its connections with two limbic structures, the amygdala and hippocampus. Increased frontal lobe activity has been shown to occur during meditation and likely occurs during other types of spiritual practices (Herzog et al., 1990–1991; Lazar et al., 2000; Newberg, Alivi, Baime, Mozley, & d'Aquili, 2001). This frontal lobe activity is also likely associated with the concomitant experience of intense awareness and alertness reported during such experiences. Mention should also be made of the connections between the limbic system and autonomic nervous system with regard to spiritual experiences. Alterations in autonomic activity during various spiritual practices have been demonstrated in a number of studies (Corby, Roth, Zarcone, & Kopell, 1978; Jevning, Wallace, & Beidebach, 1992; Kesterson, 1989; Sudsuang, Chantanez, & Veluvan, 1991). It seems likely that the feelings of the heart racing or of extreme calmness that may occur during different spiritual practices may be associated with alterations in the functioning of the autonomic nervous system. Such alterations may also help explain other physiological changes, including those in heart rate, blood pressure, and respiratory rate.

Although spiritual experiences and the unitary continuum are crucial, it is also important to realize how they are elaborated into myth formation. A myth presents a problem of ultimate concern to a society. We have typically considered myth formation based on several prominent cognitive functions. These cognitive functions include those of causality, binary operations, affect value response, and holistic perceptions. These basic brain functions are also subserved by specific brain structures and their interactions within the brain's neural network. The ability to observe causality and to relate one event to another in a sequential ordering appears to be located in the superior temporal lobe in conjunction with the inferior parietal region (Mills & Rollman, 1980; Pribram & Luria, 1973; Swisher & Hirsch, 1971). The ability to generate a sense of binary opposites, so that we can compare concepts such as good to evil or right to wrong, is also likely associated with the inferior parietal regions (Gardner, Silverman, Wapner, & Surif, 1978; Gazzaniga & Miller, 1989). This binary function has particular relevance to religious experiences and, particularly, myth formation. Religious myths tend to involve opposites that are in some form of conflict and are then resolved through the myth process (d'Aquili, 1978). When we initially observe a pair of opposites, we encounter a sense of arousal because of the incongruity between the opposites. We desire a resolution and revised understanding because of the holistic abilities of the brain, most likely associated with the superior parietal region (Nebes & Sperry, 1971; Schiavetto, Cortese, & Alain, 1999; Sperry, Gazzaniga, & Bogen, 1969). The initial binary tension enhances activity in the autonomic nervous system, particularly in the sympathetic system, which subserves the sense of arousal and the "fight or flight" response. The parasympathetic system, which underlies quiescent functions, may be stimulated upon resolution of the opposites within a myth. Thus, the existential problem presented in the myth is solved by some resolution or unification of the seemingly irreconcilable opposites that constitute the problem, and such a resolution is associated with strong emotional and visceral experiences. The ability to assign emotional valence to various thoughts and stimuli involved in the myth is associated with the connections between the limbic system and the other cognitive processes. Clearly, this emotional response is crucial for religious myth as well as spiritual experiences.

DEVELOPMENTAL SPIRITUALITY

Given the preceding description of the neuropsychological correlates of religious and spiritual experiences, as well as their elaboration in myth, it is now possible to consider a developmental spirituality. This developmental spirituality considers how spiritual experiences, perspectives, and concepts evolve over the course of the human life span and how they parallel human brain development. It is well known that the human brain is not static in its structures or functions throughout life. It is this ability to change and adapt that gives the brain its power to enable human beings to survive, grow, and learn new things to ever enhance and modify thoughts and behaviors and experiences. Enough studies of brain function and structure have been performed to yield an overall model of human brain development from infancy, through adolescence, and into adulthood and old age. The brain changes that occur should have a direct impact on human thoughts and behaviors and consequently on religious and spiritual experiences. In this section, we will outline a neuropsychologically based developmental spirituality in which we consider the developmental stages of brain function and compare them to the stages of spiritual development. We will primarily use Fowler's (1981) conception of faith development in his book *Stages of Faith* as a framework for this analysis. It should be stated clearly, however, that spiritual development is likely to be more complex (Oser, 1991; Tamminen, 1994) and involve subtler changes than will be elaborated here. Other cultures and traditions may have a different development of spirituality as well. Furthermore, this chapter represents an initial attempt to intimately link brain development with spiritual development. Some of the speculative concepts considered will hopefully lay the foundation for future analyses and studies in order to more clearly establish and substantiate this link.

Infancy

Fowler described the stage that precedes the first structural, developmental faith stage as "undifferentiated faith." Since there is little in the way of higher cognitive functions, especially with regard to integrating sensory phenomena, there can be no identifiable or differentiated faith or belief system. The infant operates almost exclusively in a stimulus/response mode. This notion implies that at this level, there can be no conception of a well-defined religion or spiritual viewpoint. Even if the person is raised in a highly devoted religious family, the infant cannot cognitively absorb this information in order to derive an understanding of any particular religious perspective. In spite of the lack of higher cognitive processing, this is the stage in which the seeds of trust, hope, and love are developed through the actions of the infant's caregivers. It is imperative at this stage that the environment in which an infant is raised provide enough consistency and nurturance and is not one in which there is deprivation. Such deprivation, at least in animal models, results in a significant lack of neuronal complexity and interconnectedness (Black, 1998; Kuhn & Schanberg, 1998). This prestage is therefore critical for the overall development, both psychologically and spiritually, of the individual.

Even though there are no higher processing steps, this prestage helps to lay the foundation for future development and benefits from an environment that provides the basis for courage, autonomy, hope, trust, and strength to prepare for faith and spiritual development and subsequent stages. If there is neglect or inconsistencies in care, the infant may lock into patterns of isolation and despair and not integrate the concept of mutuality. Such isolation is arguably associated with an overall lack of connection, not only between the neurons in the individual's brain, but between the individual and the rest of his or her environment. If such a lack of connection persists beyond this stage, then the individual's association areas may not form adequately, thus preventing the person from being able to explore spirituality and meaning in the first place. Such a phenomenon is known to occur with specific sensory systems in which an inability to make the appropriate neuronal connections early in life causes a reorganization of the brain's structure and function. This reorganization typically prevents these brain structures from functioning in their "normal" capacity even though they might be able to acquire new functions (Gazzaniga, 2000).

From the physiological developmental perspective, the undifferentiated stage is associated with the state of brain function during this infancy period. It has been shown that the brain function pattern changes throughout the first year of life with initial increases in the sensorimotor cortex, thalami, brain stem, and cerebellar vermis (Chugani & Phelps, 1986; Chugani, Phelps, & Mazziotta, 1987). These are central systems that subserve brain stem reflexes and visuomotor integrative performance that are typically displayed in infant behavior (Chugani, 1992). There are no significant higher cortical functions, however, and subsequently no strong evidence of well-integrated cognitive functioning. As visuospatial and visuo-sensorimotor integrative functions are acquired and primitive reflexes are reorganized, there is increasing activity in the primary visual cortex, parietal and temporal regions, basal ganglia, and cerebellar hemispheres (André-Thomas & Saint-Anne Dargassies, 1960; Parmelee & Sigman, 1983).

This increased activity also coincides with maturation of the EEG at around 2–3 months of age (Kellaway, 1979). At this time, there is still relatively decreased activity in the association areas that are necessary for higher cognitive processing. At 8–9 months there is increasing activity in the frontal lobes and association areas coinciding with the advent of cognitive thinking and hypothesis forming, social interaction, and higher order thinking. This also correlates with the time that a child begins to develop the concept of object permanence such that he or she understands that things that are removed from immediate sensory perception can still exist. This is likely associated with the ability for neurons representing sensory information to connect with memory functions as the association areas become more activated.

We would argue that the initial prestage lasts up to approximately 1 year, at which time the metabolic pattern observed on brain scans *qualitatively* resembles that of the adult brain (Chugani, 1992). However, this stage may extend up to 2 years until verbal skills are more highly developed (as suggested by Fowler). From the spiritual development perspective, an undifferentiated state is likely associated with the structures that are functioning during the first year with no clear evidence of higher cognitive processing, no clearly defined sense of self, and a strong reliance on visual and motor responses. Since the association areas are not mature, any information coming into the infant is essentially unprocessed and in that respect is viewed by the infant in an undifferentiated manner. The inability to process sensory information is somewhat similar to the notion of "deafferentation," which refers to the ability to block or prevent incoming sensory or neuronal input from reaching a structure (d'Aquili & Newberg, 1993). Since sensory input arriving at the association areas cannot be further processed, the result would be a state similar to a deafferented association area observed during spiritual experiences. However, because there is no higher cognitive processing, even the association areas cannot respond normally due to an immature functional status. Thus, this state is not exactly the same as absolute unitary states that are attributed to high spiritual experiences. Specifically, there is an absence of any notion of self either in an ego context or a universal context. On the other hand, there should theoretically be some remarkable similarities, and it has been remarked by a number of mystical traditions that the ultimate goal of spiritual pursuits is to return to a time in which the mind was at its beginning. For example, the ancient Taoist text, *Tao Te Ching,* contains the following passages (Chan, 1963):

Chapter 10:

Can you keep the spirit and embrace the One without departing from them?

Can you concentrate your vital force (*ch'i*) and achieve the highest degree of weakness like an infant?

Chapter 55:
He who possesses virtue in abundance May be compared to an infant.

Childhood

Fowler (1981) refers to the first stage of faith as the "intuitive-projective" stage and he describes this as occurring between the ages of 2 and 6 years. A child in this stage is beginning to develop the ability to use speech to organize his sensory experience into meaning. A child is able to sort out and gain some control over the world through her use of language and symbolic representations. At this point, children's thought processes are not reversible, and the concept of causality is poorly understood. Children at this stage assume that their perspective is the only perspective, and their thinking is magical, episodic, and not constrained by stable logical operations. Their conversations can be described as dual monologues in which they have their own train of thought and cannot respond to another in a reciprocal manner. In general, during this stage a child has integrated and conceptualized God in the way in which society has ingrained it into her through fantasy, stories, and dramatic representations. This stage is largely characterized by fantasy-filled, imaginative processes that are unconstrained by logical thought processes.

It is interesting that during this stage, neurophysiological development is associated with a progressive increase in overall brain metabolism. The neonate's brain typically has an absolute brain metabolism 30% lower than adults, but this continually increases until it reaches the adult level at about age 2 (Chugani, 1992; Kennedy & Sokoloff, 1957). It continues to increase until about age 4, at which point a plateau is reached. We would suggest that because of this aspect of neurophysiological development, the intuitive-projective stage of spiritual development may actually last up to the age of 4 with an overlap with the next stage up to approximately age 6. The initial increase in metabolism is primarily in the neocortex, which has almost twice the metabolic activity as in adults (Kennedy & Sokoloff, 1957). Central structures such as the brain stem and cerebellum do not demonstrate an increase during this time. Intermediate increases occur in the basal ganglia and thalamus. The initial increased metabolism is likely associated with the overproduction of neurons and their connections (Huttenlocher, 1979; Huttenlocher & deCourten, 1987). We would suggest that this may explain the increase in fantasy and imaginative powers of children at this age. Their brain is establishing so many different connections all of the time that there is tremendous expansion and overconnectedness between neurons that are not typically related in the adult brain. The result psychologically and cognitively is that there are few clearly defined rules, and there is a sense of blending many different experiences and ideas. The child would therefore perceive the world as being composed of many overlapping ideas, experiences, and feelings and would likely see things in ways that appear to be a fantasy to older individuals. These latter individuals have already reduced their neural interconnections and developed more concrete rules associated with their better defined neural connections.

Children in the Intuitive-Projective stage will likely not see any problem blending ideas about God with very mundane issues. They may not form clear senses of opposites such as right and wrong or justice and injustice, which will come when the overconnectedness is cut back during the developmental process. Children in this stage begin to form their first sense of self-awareness, which is most likely attributable to a greater maturity of the association areas, particularly the superior parietal region in which the sense of self, in conjunction with the other association areas, is ultimately formed. However, due to the overconnectedness of sensory neurons with the association areas, the developing self is seen as highly interwoven with the external world. This may result in the self participating in various fantasies and dream states. On the other hand, with this developing sense of self comes the beginning of experiencing concepts of death, sex, strong taboos within society, and the ultimate conditions of existence. They will not likely be able to make sense of these complex issues in the same way a mature adult would, however, since they might not be able to clearly distinguish death from life and wrong from right until their association areas are able to fully process such ideas.

This stage of development can be significantly influenced by the external environment. Problems can arise during this time if a child develops images of terror and destructiveness in the reinforcement of societal taboos. For example, primary caretakers who are very critical, rigid, and use violent and destructive images can result in a child internalizing these negative concepts. Similar negative ideas may become associated with religion and spirituality rather than more positive conceptions of something greater than themselves. Children may also develop mood disorders that can delay their ability to incorporate religious and spiritual ideals, symbols, and rituals into their life. Consequently, the child may not be able to develop a strong sense of self, independence, or autonomy that is crucial to progress to future stages. From a neurophysiological perspective, the neuronal connections associated with negative fantasies may become stronger, making such a negative perspective more pervasive during subsequent stages of development.

The initiating factor that propels a child to the next stage is the capacity for concrete operational thinking (Piaget, 1932), at which point the child begins to discern and become curious about what is and is not "real." The second stage is referred to by Fowler as the "Mythic-Literal" stage, which he describes as occurring at approximately 6–10 years of age. During this stage, a child begins to internalize stories, beliefs, and observances that symbolize belonging to a community or group enabling the composition of a worldview and ideology. Beliefs are related to literal interpretations of religions or doctrines and are usually composed of moral rules and attitudes. From the neurological perspective, this stage appears to coincide with a plateau phase in brain metabolism such that the overall activity throughout the brain remains higher than in the adult, but there is no longer an increase in activity (Chugani et al., 1987). It is believed that during this time, from the age of 4 to 9, there continues to be a slower overproduction of neuronal connections, and there is a very active cutting back of connections (Chugani, Phelps, & Mazziotta, 1989). The removal of inappropriate connections is likely associated with the establishment of specific rules by which neural connections are allowed to continue. If the connection that $1 + 2 = 3$ is correct, then other connections that might lead to $1 + 2 = 2$ and $1 + 2 = 4$ will be pruned away. In this manner, specific and possibly literal rules of behavior, language, emotion, and thought are established. Although there is still some over-production of neuronal connections during this stage, the emphasis on the cutting back of these connections may account for the transition from an imagination- and fantasy-oriented stage to a literal and rule-based stage.

As we have described in previous work, these rules are likely associated with the elaboration of myth in order to provide information and understanding of the world (d'Aquili & Newberg, 1999). These myths are also based on a number of specific cognitive functions, including those that subserve the ability to view things in a binary, quantitative, linguistic, holistic, and abstract manner. Thus, in this stage of development, stories, drama, and myth are the primary venues in which ideas are experienced. This is particularly relevant to the development of the sense of self and the connection of this self to the world. In terms of establishing the sense of self, this stage also begins to provide concrete rules for determining what is and what is not the self and what is and is not "real" (Fowler, 1981). These rules guide the orientation function of the brain to provide a definitive sense of self that is now more clearly separated from the fantasies and holistic world experience. However, this sense of self is still not fully matured. All of these developments, if they become too rigidly determined, can lead the person's cognitive and emotional perspectives, as well as faith-based concepts, to become trapped in the "narrative." Thus, if a child's environment is constantly controlling and judging, she ultimately will have difficulty formulating her own spiritual concepts and reflecting on the value of those concepts. Although there is increased accuracy in taking the perspective of other people, there is also an excessive sense of reliance on reciprocity with the sacred (Fowler, 1981). This can even lead to the distortion of the individual's sense of self or possibly becoming self-destructive if he feels he deserves punishment on the basis of his relationship with the sacred.

Adolescence to Early Adulthood

The factor initiating transition to the third stage is the implicit contradiction within authoritative stories that leads to reflection on meanings and conflicts. In this regard, the concrete thinking that establishes myths is confronted by new information, exposure to other perspectives, and higher cognitive processes that result in a reconsideration of the literal aspect of Stage 2. The third stage, which usually takes place during adolescence and into early adulthood, is referred to by Fowler as the "synthetic-conventional" stage. Formal operational thinking and mutual perspective taking characterize it. Neurophysiologically, this corresponds to a time in which the overall metabolism in the brain begins to decrease (probably from the age of 11 to 20). This is associated with the pruning of neuronal connections in order to establish the primary connections that will take the person into adulthood. Plasticity of the brain decreases notably during the decreasing metabolism phase of brain development (Chugani et al., 1989). There is still significant room for developing and learning new ideas and concepts, however. It is simply that these new ideas are not as likely to be foundational concepts so much as they are building upon the connections made during the previous stages of development. Thus, new concepts of mathematics might continue to be learned, but they are built upon the fundamental laws of quantitation that have become engrained in the person's brain structures. Likewise, a person's sense of spirituality is more likely to be built upon previously established notions of religion and spirituality. It is during this time that there is significant elaboration of basic ideas and deeper incorporation into the person's overall world perspective. Since the connections that are established and lost during this time will likely become the individual's neurophysiological "setup" throughout the rest of her life, this is a crucial period of development. This is the period in which the person's basic approach to life, relationships, his self, and spirituality are galvanized and fully elaborated.

This is also a complex stage due to a variety of factors, including biological ones associated with various hormonal states associated with puberty and sexual maturation as well as this being the time in which the individual's world begins to extend beyond the family into peer and other cohort groups. The individual begins to develop a more coherent orientation within the world in the midst of more complex and diverse involvements and understandings. In this stage, values and information become synthesized, which provides for a sense of identity and outlook. Conversely, this stage can also be characterized as conformist because one is tuned in to the expectations and judgments of significant others that can actually prevent the development of independent perspectives and provide less opportunity to examine individual beliefs and doctrines systematically. All of these factors impact the pruning process of the neuronal connections, establishing which will survive and which will fall away. As a result, the person's individual approach to life and various ideologies is beginning to solidify. Such a process also can result in defining differences among ideologies and the individuals who adhere to discrepant ideologies. This can lead to alienation and possible violence toward others if the environment is depriving and prone to scapegoating. This is where hatred and intergroup rivalries can emerge and where cults and powerful leaders can provide a safe and important context to nurture vulnerabilities relating to the need to conform. In particular, rituals that can activate the same biological mechanisms described above for spiritual experiences also can enhance a sense of unity among individuals adhering to the same ideology or myth (d'Aquili & Newberg, 1999). Thus, if the myth is embodied within a ritual, then the participants experience a sense of unity and a decrease in intragroup aggression. However, there is a subsequent increase in intergroup aggression toward those individuals and groups that are not participating in the same myth or ritual.

The initiating factor to the next stage is frequently the experience of leaving home or receiving more education, which precipitates the examination of self, values, and background that gives rise to the transition to the next stage. In addition to the establishment of the basic functionality of the brain as determined by the neuronal connections, this is also the stage in which the cognitive functions described in the previous section become fully established. The binary and causal functions, for example, are now fully operational and base that function, in part, upon the connections established between and within the brain structures subserving these functions. However, these functions have not yet been used to their fullest extent to help the person examine beliefs and doctrines systematically. This appears to occur in the fourth stage.

Adulthood

While the focus of this book is on child and adolescent development, several issues pertaining to spiritual development into adulthood may help to demonstrate the full range of spiritual experience. The fourth stage that begins in adulthood is referred to by Fowler as the "individuative-reflective" stage. This stage occurs when there is an interruption of reliance on external sources of authority, usually during young adulthood but sometimes as late as age 30–40; it is a time when one begins to take responsibility for one's own choices, irrespective of what others feel. Neurophysiologically, this stage is associated with the full development of the cognitive and emotional processes that are now significantly more stable than in all of the previous stages. There are limited new connections and limited pruning (at least connections are in balance). Thus, the cognitive functions of the individual are operating for their first time in their full manner and can be brought to bear on all types of experiences and ideas (both internally and externally generated). The more mature functioning of the brain is likely associated with the ability to establish a well-defined identity and to imbue that self with a set of cognitive, affective, and behavioral processes that together help to define the self. The overall brain metabolism is highly stable as well, reflecting this overall mature stage of the human brain. In fact, the metabolism remains at this level until the end of the fourth decade of life. There is an ability at this stage to critically and objectively reflect on identity and outlook and translate symbols into concepts with deeper meanings. There is also the struggle for self-fulfillment as a primary concern versus service to and being for others and the question of being committed to the relative versus struggle with the possibility of an absolute.

Fowler refers to the fifth stage as "conjunctive faith" and it generally occurs at midlife.

At this stage the individual is ready for significant encounters with other traditions in a quest for meaning and value in life. As the individual gains access to various perspectives, each one will augment and correct aspects to eventually sort out the realest and truest ones. The end result is a reclaiming and reworking of one's identity and faith through understanding their own life and how it relates to humanity. Neurophysiologically, this stage is associated with a decrease in overall brain metabolic and neurotransmitter activity (Newberg & Alavi, 1997). This decrease begins around the age of 40 and slowly progresses throughout the remainder of the individual's life. This decrease, while unknown to the person, may reflect or at least contribute to the notion of disillusionment since the brain no longer appears to be able to find the answers it was striving so hard to find with its full complement of functions. As connections are lost, there may be a sense that the answers are slipping away, and that it is unlikely that they will be obtained on the present path. The self may also be perceived to be somewhat slipping away since the connections between the neurons subserving the self and the sensory and cognitive input become diminished. The result may be a concern that the self can no longer face the struggle to know and understand.

The last stage Fowler refers to is that of a "universalizing faith." In universalizing faith, there is a sense of unity between the self and the tenets of the individual's religious tradition. This may represent a sense of union of the self with God or ultimate reality. This union may result from various spiritual practices or experiences such as those described earlier in this chapter. In fact, this type of experience likely arises from the deafferentation of sensory and cognitive inputs into the association areas that subserve the orientation abilities of the brain. That there is already a concomitant decrease in overall neuronal function and interconnectedness may actually contribute to this type of experience typically occurring in older individuals. There may also be a notion of universalization across traditions, namely, that all faiths have similar perspectives and derive from a similar root. It is interesting to note that physiologically, the brain of an older individual begins to decrease activity in the association areas similar to what is found in the infant brain. It is not a coincidence that individuals suffering from disorders such as Alzheimer's disease can actually have brain metabolic patterns that appear almost identical to that of an infant (Newberg & Alavi, 1996). The difference here is that such an experience is built upon the entire developmental basis of the individual as he or she progresses through the various stages.

CONCLUSIONS

Our purpose here has been to outline a neuropsychological developmental spirituality. This initial attempt at combining the phenomenological aspects of spiritual development with observed changes in brain function over the life span of the human being provides a hypothetical framework upon which to base future studies of normal and abnormal development. In particular, an updated phenomenological model of faith development is required. Although few models developed in recent years have had the same depth as those of Fowler's, with the advances in child development and pediatric neuropsychology, it is likely that future work can also address issues pertaining to the development of the sense of self, moral development, and concepts such as theory of mind. However, the purpose of this chapter was to provide a potential starting point with a relatively well-known and comprehensive account of spiritual development. Future work might also explore how tight the correlation is between neurophysiological changes in the brain and various elements of spiritual development. The ability to observe potential physiological and clinical sources of "abnormal" spiritual development may prove to be a valuable interface to begin to design interventions that may help prevent such problems from arising. Finally, it appears that there is a strong correlation between a number of the characteristics of spiritual development and the changing function of specific brain structures over time from infancy through adulthood. Thus, this developmental approach suggests a deep interconnection between neurophysiology and spirituality.

REFERENCES

André-Thomas, C. Y., & Saint-Anne Dargassies, S. (1960). *The neurological examination of the infant.* London: Medical Advisory Committee of the National Spastics Society.

Black, J. E. (1998). How a child builds its brain: Some lessons from animal studies of neural plasticity. *Preventive Medicine, 27,* 168–171.

Bucke, R. M. (1961). *Cosmic consciousness.* Secaucus, NJ: Citadel Press.

Chan, W. T. (1963). *The source book in Chinese philosophy.* Princeton, NJ: Princeton University Press.

Chugani, H. T. (1992). Functional brain imaging in pediatrics. *Pediatric Clinics of North America, 39,* 777–799.

Chugani, H. T., & Phelps, M. E. (1986). Maturational changes in cerebral function in infants determined by [18]FDG positron emission tomography. *Science, 231,* 840–843.

Chugani, H. T., Phelps, M. E., & Mazziotta, J. C. (1987). Positron emission tomography study of human brain functional development. *Annals of Neurology, 22,* 487–497.

Chugani, H. T., Phelps, M. E., & Mazziotta, J. C. (1989). Metabolic assessment of functional maturation and neuronal plasticity in the human brain. In C. von Euler, H. Forssberg, & H. Lagercrantz (Eds.), *Neurobiology of early infant behavior* (pp. 323–330). New York: Stockton Press.

Corby, J. C., Roth, W. T., Zarcone, V. P., & Kopell, B. S. (1978). Psychophysiological correlates of the practice of tantric yoga meditation. *Archives of General Psychiatry, 35,* 571–577.

d'Aquili, E. G. (1978). The neurobiological bases of myth and concepts of deity. *Zygon, 13,* 257–275.

d'Aquili, E. G. (1982). Senses of reality in science and religion. *Zygon, 17,* 361–384.

d'Aquili, E. G. (1986). Myth, ritual, and the archetypal hypothesis: Does the dance generate the word? *Zygon, 21,* 141–160.

d'Aquili, E. G., & Newberg, A. B. (1993). Religious and mystical states: A neuropsychological substrate. *Zygon, 28,* 177–200.

d'Aquili, E. G., & Newberg, A. B. (1998). The neuropsychological basis of religion: Or why God won't go away. *Zygon, 33,* 187–201.

d'Aquili, E. G., & Newberg, A. B. (1999). *The mystical mind: Probing the biology of religious experience.* Minneapolis, MN: Fortress Press.

Fowler, J. W. (1981). *Stages of faith.* San Francisco: HarperCollins.

Gardner, H., Silverman, J., Wapner, W., & Surif, E. (1978). The appreciation of antonymic contrasts in aphasia. *Brain and Language, 6,* 301–317.

Gazzaniga, M. S. (2000). *The new cognitive neurosciences.* Cambridge, MA: MIT Press.

Gazzaniga, M. S., & Miller, G. A. (1989). The recognition of antonymy by a language-enriched right hemisphere. *Journal of Cognitive Neuroscience, 1,* 187–193.

Herzog, H., Lele, V. R., Kuwert, T., Langen, K.-J., Kops, E. R., & Feinendegen, L. E. (1990–91). Changed pattern of regional glucose metabolism during yoga meditative relaxation. *Neuropsychobiology, 23,* 182–187.

Huttenlocher, P. R. (1979). Synaptic density in human frontal cortex: Developmental changes and effects of aging. *Brain Research, 163,* 195–205.

Huttenlocher, P. R., & deCourten, C. (1987). The development of synapses in striate cortex of man. *Human Neurobiology, 6,* 1–9.

Jevning, R., Wallace, R. K., & Beidebach, M. (1992). The physiology of meditation: A review. A wakeful hypometabolic integrated response. *Neuroscience and Biobehavioral Reviews, 16,* 415–424.

Joseph, R. (1996) *Neuropsychology, neuropsychiatry, and behavioral neurology.* Baltimore: Williams & Wilkins.

Kellaway, P. (1979). An orderly approach to visual analysis: Parameters of the normal EEG in adults and children. In D. W. Klass & D. D. Daly (Eds.), *Current practice of clinical electroencephalography* (pp. 69–147). New York: Raven Press.

Kennedy, C., & Sokoloff, L. (1957). An adaptation of the nitrous oxide method to the study of the cerebral circulation in children: Normal values for cerebral blood flow and cerebral metabolic rate in childhood. *Journal of Clinical Investigation, 36,* 1130.

Kesterson, J. (1989). Metabolic rate, respiratory exchange ratio and apnea during meditation. *American Journal of Physiology, R256,* 632–638.

Kuhn, C. M., & Schanberg, S. M. (1998). Responses to maternal separation: Mechanisms and mediators. *International Journal of Developmental Neuroscience, 16,* 261–270.

Larson, D. B., Swyers, J. P., & McCullough, M. E. (1998). *Scientific research on spirituality and health: A consensus report.* Rockville, MD: National Institute of Healthcare Research.

Lazar, S. W., Bush, G., Gollub, R. L., Fricchione, G. L., Khalsa, G., & Benson, H. (2000). Functional brain mapping of the relaxation response and meditation. *NeuroReport, 11,* 1581–1585.

Maslow, A. H. (1970). *Religions, values, and peak experiences.* New York: Viking.

Mills, L., & Rollman, G. B. (1980). Hemispheric asymmetry for auditory perception of temporal order. *Neuropsychologia, 18,* 41–47.

Nebes, R. D., & Sperry, R. W. (1971). Hemispheric disconnection syndrome with cerebral birth injury in the dominant arm area. *Neuropsychologia, 9,* 249–259.

Newberg, A. B., & Alavi, A. (1996). The study of the neurological disorders using positron emission tomography and single photon emission computed tomography. *Journal of the Neurological Sciences, 135,* 91–108.

Newberg, A. B., & Alavi, A. (1997). Neuroimaging in the in vivo measurement of regional function in the aging brain. In S. U. Dani, A. Hori, & G. F. Walter (Eds.), *Principles of neural aging* (pp. 397–408). Amsterdam: Elsevier Science.

Newberg, A. B., Alavi, A., Baime, M., Mozley, P. D., & d'Aquili, E. (2001). The measurement of regional cerebral blood flow during the complex cognitive task of meditation: A preliminary SPECT study. *Psychiatry Research: Neuroimaging, 106,* 113–122.

Newberg, A. B., & Iversen, J. (2003). The neural basis of the complex mental task of meditation: Neurotransmitter and neurochemical considerations. *Medical Hypothesis, 61,* 282–291.

Oser, F. K. (1991). The development of religious judgment. *New Directions for Child Development, 52,* 5–25.

Otto, R. (1970). *The idea of the holy.* New York: Oxford University Press.

Parmelee, A. H., & Sigman, M. D. (1983). Perinatal brain development and behavior. In M. Haith & J. Campos (Eds.), *Biology and infancy* (Vol. 2, pp. 95–155). New York: Wiley.

Penfield, W., & Perot, P. (1963). The brain's record of auditory and visual experience. *Brain, 86,* 595–695.

Piaget, J. (1932). *The moral judgment of the child.* London: Routledge & Kegan Paul.

Pribram, K. H., & Luria, A. R. (1973). *Psychophysiology of the frontal lobes.* New York: Academic Press.

Rolbin, S. B. (1985). The mystical quest: Experiences, goals, changes, and problems. *Dissertation Abstracts International, 47,* 940A–941A.

Rowan, J. (1983). The real self and mystical experiences. *Journal of Humanistic Psychology, 23,* 9–27.

Saver, J. L., & Rabin, J. (1997). The neural substrates of religious experience. *Journal of Neuropsychiatry and Clinical Neurosciences, 9,* 498–510.

Schiavetto, A., Cortese, F., & Alain, C. (1999). Global and local processing of musical sequences: An event related brain potential study. *NeuroReport, 10,* 2467–2472.

Schwartz, G. E., Davidson, R. J., & Maer, F. (1975). Right hemisphere lateralization for emotion in the human brain: Interactions with cognitions. *Science, 190,* 286–288.

Smart, N. (1967). History of mysticism. In P. Edwards (Ed.), *Encyclopedia of philosophy* (pp. 419–428). London: Macmillan.

Smart, N. (1969). *The religious experience of mankind.* London: Macmillan.

Smart, N. (1978). Understanding religious experience. In S. Katz (Ed.), *Mysticism and philosophical analysis* (pp. 10–21). New York: Oxford University Press.

Sperry, R. W., Gazzaniga, M. S., & Bogen, J. E. (1969). Interhemispheric relationships: The neocortical commissures; syndromes of hemisphere disconnection. In P. J. Vinken & C. W. Bruyn (Eds.), *Handbook of clinical neurology* (Vol. 4, pp. 273–290). Amsterdam: North Holland.

Spilka, B., & McIntosh, D. N. (1996, August). *Religion and spirituality: The known and the unknown.* Paper presented at the annual meeting of the American Psychological Association, Toronto, Canada.

Stace, W. T. (1961). *Mysticism and philosophy.* London: Macmillan.

Streng, F. (1978). Language and mystical awareness. In S. Katz (Ed.), *Mysticism and philosophical analysis* (pp. 141–169). New York: Oxford University Press.

Sudsuang, R., Chentanez, V., & Veluvan, K. (1991). Effects of Buddhist meditation on serum cortisol and total protein levels, blood pressure, pulse rate, lung volume and reaction time. *Physiology and Behavior, 50,* 543–548.

Swisher, L., & Hirsch, I. (1971). Brain damage and the ordering of two temporally successive stimuli. *Neuropsychologia, 10,* 137–152.

Tamminen, K. (1994). Religious experiences in childhood and adolescence: A viewpoint of religious development between the ages of 7 and 20. *International Journal for the Psychology of Religion, 4,* 61–85.

Valenstein, E. S. (1973). *Brain control: A critical examination of brain stimulation and psychosurgery.* New York: Wiley.

Van Heertum, R. L., & Tikofsky, R. S. (Eds.). (1995). *Cerebral SPECT imaging.* New York: Raven Press.

Worthington, E. L., McCullough, M. E., & Sandage, S. J. (1995). Empirical research on religion and psychotherapeutic processes and outcomes: A 10 year review and research prospectus. *Psychological Bulletin, 119,* 448–487.

14

ATTACHMENT AND SPIRITUAL DEVELOPMENT IN CHILDHOOD AND ADOLESCENCE

PEHR GRANQVIST

JANE R. DICKIE

Affective aspects of religious development in childhood have largely been neglected in research. The main focus has instead been on the cognitive underpinnings of religious development, using a variety of cognitive stage theory applications, particularly Piagetian theory (e.g., Elkind, 1970; Oser, 1991). In a review of the religious development literature, Spilka, Hood, Hunsberger, and Gorsuch (2003) argue that "fresh conceptual approaches are needed to revitalize the study of children's religious development" (p. 103). They specifically mention the possibility that attachment research may provide a strong socioemotional supplement to the near exclusive cognitive focus of the developmental psychology of religion.

The scarce literature on more affective aspects of religious and spiritual development that does exist has been highly theoretically oriented, mostly consisting of post hoc reconstructions in the service of different psychoanalytic theories (e.g., Jones, 1991; Rizzuto, 1979). Unfortunately, these endeavors have all suffered from serious theoretical and/or methodological shortcomings (see Granqvist, in press a, for a critique). In other words, there has been little psychoanalytic research on the observed, as opposed to the inferred, child (for an exception using a case study design, see Coles, 1990). Luckily, through research inspired by attachment theory, this situation is changing in a favorable direction, as will be outlined in the present chapter.

This chapter details the contribution of attachment theory and research to understanding the development of spirituality and religiosity in childhood and adolescence. The application of attachment theory to spirituality and religion is motivated by a high degree of

AUTHORS' NOTE: During the writing of this chapter, Pehr Granqvist was supported by Grant No. Dnr 1999–0507:01,02 from the Bank of Sweden Tercentenary Foundation and by a Sasakawa Young Leaders postdoctoral fellowship.

structural and functional similarity between child–parent and believer–God relationships. After providing a brief conceptual and empirical overview of attachment theory, the chapter reviews the relevant literatures on attachment in relation to spiritual and religious development in childhood and adolescence. Relevant findings will be discussed in relation to the correspondence and compensation hypotheses, both of which highlight the presumed influence of early child–parent attachment on subsequent spiritual and religious development. In the concluding section we point to shortcomings in the research conducted to date and suggest several avenues for future research in this area.

Before proceeding, it should be noted that most of the research based on attachment theory has concerned institutionalized forms of religion. From an attachment perspective, however, it does not matter whether "the search for connectedness" (from this handbook's definition of spirituality) has occurred within institutionalized religion so long as the search is for something greater than the self. We will see this later when we consider individual differences in attachment in relation to institutionalized religion, on the one hand, and in relation to such noninstitutionalized forms of spirituality as the adoption of a new age orientation, on the other. What matters is the particular pathway taken to the spiritual destination and the affective tone of the self-transcendence.

INTRODUCTION TO ATTACHMENT AND SPIRITUAL DEVELOPMENT

An Outline of Attachment Theory and Research

To explain the affectional bond developing between mammalian offspring and caregivers, Bowlby (1969, 1973, 1980) proposed that the offspring possesses an attachment behavioral system, which is designed by natural selection and manifested in infants' signal behaviors (e.g., crying, smiling, following). These attachment behaviors are activated particularly during situations that are threatening to the offspring. In conjunction with the caregiver's complementary caregiving system, the predictable outcome of these signaling behaviors is physical proximity between offspring and caregiver, which in turn leads to an increased likelihood of offspring protection and survival to reproductive age. Attachment system functioning is evident in infants turning to their attachment figures when distressed (i.e., safe haven behaviors) and occasionally monitoring their attachment figures' responses when exploring the environment (i.e., secure base behaviors), thereby achieving increased confidence for continued exploration. Bowlby also argued that the caregiver's responses to the child in attachment-activating situations determine the nature of the child's internal working models (IWMs; i.e., cognitive-affective representations of self and others). Presuming contextual stability, IWMs are held responsible for the continuity observed in attachment functioning.

Particularly by considering individual differences (Ainsworth, Blehar, Waters, & Wall, 1978) in infant–caregiver attachment security, attachment theory has been useful for understanding the socioemotional development of children (see Cassidy & Shaver, 1999). For instance, attachment security in infancy predicts empathy, social competence, and ego resiliency, and attachment insecurity predicts externalizing (e.g., aggression, conduct problems) as well as internalizing (e.g., social anxiety, psychosomatic complaints) behavior problems throughout childhood and adolescence (e.g., Weinfield., Sroufe, Egeland, & Carlson, 1999).

A key to understanding these predictions is provided by considering the balance that securely attached children strike between attachment and exploration. When distressed, they typically turn to their caregivers, who help them in a sensitive way to handle the distressing situations and affects, thereby giving them increased confidence for exploration while at the same time demonstrating that other humans are available in times of need and that distress can be dealt with, without being overwhelming (Cassidy, 1994). Insecurity, on the other hand, is characterized either by defensive exploration at the expense of attachment in response to rejecting caregiving (avoidant attachment) or passive clinginess to an inconsistent caregiver at the expense of exploration (ambivalent attachment). Insecure/disorganized attachment is characterized by a stress-provoked breakdown in behavioral organization in relation to a frightened or frightening caregiver (Main & Hesse, 1990).

During the past 15 years, attachment research has also been directed at understanding attachment processes in adolescence and adulthood. Although there are multiple transition points in development, adolescence has been of interest to attachment researchers because it signifies an important transitional period during which attachment functions are gradually transferred from parents to peers, most often long-term love partners. Attachment transfer occurs sequentially, beginning with the proximity maintenance function in early childhood, followed by the safe haven function in midadolescence, and finally the secure base function in early adulthood being primarily directed toward reciprocal relationship partners rather than parents. Hence, even though attachment transition is by no means typically concluded in adolescence, the transfer process is well in the making (Fraley & Davis, 1997; Friedlmeier & Granqvist, submitted; Hazan & Zeifman, 1999).

Religion and Spirituality in Relation to Attachment: Conceptual Considerations

Normative Aspects: Proximity, Safe Haven, and Secure Base. The most obvious point of departure for an attachment theoretical application to "the search for connectedness" is the centrality of the believer's personal relationship with God (see Kirkpatrick, 1999). However, the term *attachment relationship* does not refer to all types of close relationships, but exclusively to relationships that meet three criteria: proximity maintenance, safe haven, and secure base (see Hazan & Zeifman, 1999). Bowlby (1973) included a fourth criterion: that the attachment figure should be perceived as stronger and wiser during stress. These criteria have been shown to be reasonably met in believers' relationships with God.

For instance, regarding proximity maintenance, adult attachment experiments have documented an increase in believers' wish to be close to God following primes with separation stimuli targeting their relationship with God (Birgegard & Granqvist, 2004). Regarding safe haven, a well-documented finding in the behavioral sciences of religion is that individuals turn to God in situations of distress, and the more distressing the situation is, the more likely people are to do so (Pargament, 1997). God also possesses sensitivity-related attributes that are supposedly ideal for a secure base (Kirkpatrick, 1999). Moreover, correlates of religiosity suggest that possessing an image of and relating to God as a sensitive secure base are associated with positive outcomes, over and above the effects of virtually every conceivable covariate (George, Ellison, & Larson, 2002). Finally, by being described as omnipotent and omniscient, God is perceived as both stronger and wiser than the believers themselves.

The preceding analysis focused almost exclusively on monotheistic, and particularly Christian, religions. In portraying a personal God who is involved in the individual's private life and affairs, religiosity and spirituality within these traditions suit an attachment theoretical conceptualization intuitively better than, for instance, in the case of pantheistic religions. As discussed by Kirkpatrick (1995), however, there are notable attachment aspects occurring also in the context of nontheistic religions, such as Mahayana Buddhists' devotion to ancestral spirits.

Individual Differences: Compensation and Two Levels of Correspondence. Two general hypotheses concerning the relationship between individual differences in attachment security and religiosity have been derived from attachment theory and supported in empirical research on adults (see Granqvist, in preparation a; Kirkpatrick, 1999). The compensation hypothesis assumes that individuals who have experienced insecure, as opposed to secure, childhood attachment relationships with their primary attachment figures are in greater need to establish compensatory attachment relationships to regulate distress and obtain felt security. In the context of religion, God was suggested to function as such a surrogate attachment figure (Ainsworth, 1985). This hypothesis has received support, for example, in findings showing that distress-driven religious changes and conversions are linked to attachment insecurity.

The correspondence hypothesis, as revised by Granqvist (2002; Granqvist & Hagekull, 1999), suggests that individuals who have experienced secure, as opposed to insecure, childhood attachments (1) have established the foundations on which a corresponding relationship with God could be built (IWM correspondence; see also Kirkpatrick, 1992) and (2) are successfully socialized to adopt the attachment figure's religious or nonreligious standards (socialized correspondence; Granqvist & Hagekull, 1999). The former part of this hypothesis was based on Bowlby's (e.g., 1969) discussion of IWMs of attachment as being responsible for continuity in attachment functioning. IWM correspondence has been supported, for example, in associations between attachment security and loving and caring God images. The socialized correspondence part of the hypothesis was based on findings showing that securely, as compared to insecurely, attached offspring are better socialized with respect to parental standards in general (e.g., Londerville & Main, 1981; Richters & Waters, 1991). In the context of religion, the notion of socialized correspondence has been supported in significantly higher associations between parent and offspring religiosity in secure compared to insecure dyads.

The attachment theoretical studies have mostly concerned spirituality in the context of organized, theistic religion. However, two studies on adults have now been conducted showing expected support for the compensation hypothesis in relation to such a nonorganized form of spirituality as the adoption of a new age orientation in adults (Granqvist, in preparation b; Granqvist & Hagekull, 2001).

ATTACHMENT AND RELIGIOUS AND SPIRITUAL DEVELOPMENT IN CHILDHOOD

The Need for Connection: Universal in Children?

After interviewing hundreds of 6- to 13-year-old children of Jewish, Christian, Muslim, and Native American (Hopi) faith communities and children from secular homes, Coles (1990) concluded that all children hunger for an answer to the spiritual questions: "Where do we come from? What are we? What is the meaning of life?" Of course, children approach these questions using their own cultural discourse and level of developmental sophistication. Coles asserted: "Even agnostics and atheists have ideas about God, giving Him some private form—a mental picture, some words, a sound. In the lives of children God joins company with kings, superheroes, witches, monsters, friends, brothers and sisters, parents, teachers, police, firefighters and on and on" (p. 5).

Using more empirical approaches, others found that whether children were part of a faith community or not, they had concepts of God, and these concepts strongly related to images of and relationships with parents (Dickie et al., 1997; Tamminen, 1994). The parent–child relationship, it seems, is key to understanding children's experiences of God as loving, powerful, caring, nurturing, punishing, close, or distant.

Children's spiritual needs seem to be closely linked with their social-emotional needs. Fowler (1994) succinctly described these needs, including experiencing well-being through belonging, interrelationships of mutual love and trust, and being cherished and loved as unique and irreplaceable. These qualities constitute the essence of the sensitive, responsive relationship that is known to foster secure attachment (DeWolff & van IJzendoorn, 1997), and its importance for health and competent functioning in children is well established (Bowlby, 1969; Cassidy & Shaver, 1999).

Normative Developmental Shifts in Children's Search for Connection

This section will examine research on children's concepts and experience of God from a developmental attachment framework, first looking at normative aspects of attachment, then at the empirical studies of children's spiritual and religious development from early to middle childhood. We will make the case for parallel development between the parent–child attachment and the God–child relationship and for children's increasing reliance on God as they become increasingly independent of parents from early to middle childhood.

Functionally and structurally, the need for connection to human attachment figures parallels that of connection to the sacred or divine. How then does this normative developmental need for attachments to nurturing adults relate to spiritual development in children? In spite of the assumptions by religious educators that children's attachments with adults, particularly parents, are critical for spiritual development, most of the research on parental influences on God concepts has been carried out with adults (see Kirkpatrick, 1999). It is important to look at actual children to test whether attachment theory helps account for the form and function of children's connection with the divine.

Most of the studies of children's faith have not used attachment theory as their central framework. It is possible, however, to use attachment theory to understand their results.

Attachment and Faith in Early Childhood. As children move from infancy into early childhood, physical development allows movement away from attachment figures while emotional and cognitive development allows carrying attachment figures symbolically in language and emotional constancy and the use of the attachment figures as a safe haven in times of distress even when physically distant. Most children develop multiple attachment figures although they are not equally sought (Myers, Jarvis, & Creasey, 1987), opening the way for attachment to God. Still, in early childhood, ages 3 to 6, children's emotional connections are with primary caregivers, usually parents.

At these ages children are developing a concept of God that they describe or draw as a person (Heller, 1986) who is more loving than powerful or wrathful (Dickie et al., 1997; Johnson & Eastburg, 1992; Nelson & Kroliczak, 1984). As with attachment figures that are not primary, God is not yet the "perfect substitute" for parents. At this time, the children's God images are less like parents, less nurturing and less powerful than will be the case in middle childhood. Presumably through their IWMs of parents (such as nurturing, caring, loving, powerful, protecting, punishing), their perceptions of God are formed (Dickie et al., 1997).

In a study designed specifically to look at 5-year-olds' attachment representations in

relation to their mothers through a story completion task, children from the Netherlands described a more loving God if they also had close and harmonious relationships with their teachers and were rated by the teachers to have positive self-esteem. However, the children's story completion tasks with regard to their mothers were unrelated to the children's concepts of God (De Roos, Meidema, & Iedema, 2001), possibly due to limitations in the validity of the attachment measurement. Another possibility is that the variability in mother–child relationships (not reported) was less than in the teacher–child relationships, masking the effect of mother–child relationships. Of course, it is also possible that young children relate God image to figures other than the likely primary figure, mother. In the study performed by Dickie et al. (1997), God was perceived as more like father than like mother in early childhood. Interestingly, it was the father's nurturance that best predicted seeing God as nurturing, and the mother's power that best predicted seeing God as powerful.[1] Because De Roos et al. only looked at loving (not powerful) images of God, and only at attachment to mother (not father), they may have missed the essential point that in early childhood, God is still a relatively distant figure and more like, though not as nurturing or powerful as, the father (Eshleman et al., 1999). In other words, God is not yet the perfect parent substitute.

Attachment and Faith in Middle Childhood. During the transition from early to middle childhood, from ages 7 to 11, children are making another shift. As parents are less available and more distant, reliance on other authority figures, such as teachers, may increase. Although the gradual shift to peer attachments has begun, during middle childhood, parents are still the main attachment figures. Attachment figures in secure dyads serve as a secure base that allow greater physical, though not emotional, distance. It is important that children have internal mechanisms to bridge the physical gap from primary attachment figures, for it is being alone versus being with a friendly other or alternative attachment figure that is the most likely event to elicit distress (Bowlby, 1969; Marvin, 1977). Children at this age are more able to discuss shared goals, feelings, plans, and reunion as they refine their goal-corrected partnership with the attachment figures (Main & Cassidy, 1988; Marvin & Greenberg, 1982). Now the child is more in control of proximity and is able to maintain separation. However, children still need to believe that communication, physical accessibility, and responsiveness are possible with the attachment figure (Ainsworth, 1990). It is not until adolescence that attachment to parents shifts more fully to peer attachments and particularly love partners.

In middle childhood, children can comprehend the existence of loved ones who are not immediately accessible. So it is now that the God image and children's felt closeness to God are capable of serving as "parent substitutes." Children now describe God in anthropomorphic terms, often in heaven (Tamm, 1996). There is a stronger correspondence between the ways in which children view their parents and the way in which they view God than there was in early childhood. God is the "more perfect" parent, however: God is more powerful, more loving, and more nurturing than their parents (Dickie et al., 1997; Johnson & Eastburg, 1992). God is also viewed as more loving than punishing and more like mother than father (Dickie et al., 1997; Heller, 1986; Hertel & Donahue, 1995). God is viewed as closer now than in early childhood or adolescence (Eshleman et al., 1999; Tamminen, 1994).

So, just as children are entering school and moving farther from parents' immediate care, God becomes the more perfect attachment substitute, available at all times; the child need not feel alone. God also serves as a safe haven in times of stress. Eshleman et al. (1999) found that when 7- to 10-year-old American children were told stories about children who were sick, hurt, or crying, they placed a figure that they selected to represent God closer to the child; they did not do this in response to stories in which children were not distressed. Tamminen (1994) found that Finnish 7- to 12-year-old children reported feeling close to God particularly when they felt threatened. They were more likely to call on God than were adolescents in the same sample.

Perceptions of parents, more than perceptions of self, are still more powerful predictors of perceptions of God (Dickie et al., 1997). It seems likely that the IWM of self is less important at this age than the IWM of others, particularly the parents. Only later, in adolescence, does the model of self, more than the model of the other (parents), better predict the concept of God (Dickie, Woodall, Hankamp, & Nixon, submitted; Kirkpatrick, 1998).

Individual Differences and Contextual Influences on Children's Search for Connection

Support for Two Levels of Correspondence: Secure Attachment. When the attachment between adult and child is secure, the IWM correspondence model predicts loving relationships with others, including God. In the previously reported normative studies, children's God concepts most followed the correspondence model in that children's images of loving and powerful parents predicted images of a loving and powerful God (Dickie et al., 1997; Hertel & Donahue, 1995). However, security of attachment can only be inferred from these studies.

The one study (DeRoos et al., 2001) that looked explicitly at 5-year-old children's security of attachment, and their God concepts, did not find a relation. Potential reasons for this were given earlier. Clearly, more research that explicitly assesses children's attachment with well-validated methods is needed.

Regarding socialized correspondence, parents socialize their children directly in their own religious beliefs (Spilka et al., 2003), and mothers seem particularly important in this role (Acock & Bengtson, 1978). In line with the notion of socialized correspondence, Tamminen's (e.g., 1994) longitudinal study of religious development in Finnish children and adolescents showed the main effects of parental importance of religion on their offspring's experiences of God's nearness, but the crucial test of an interaction between relationship quality and parental religiousness was not performed.

Research on parental discipline style may provide an indirect estimate of parent–child attachment (Rutter & O'Connor, 1999) and, as such, may allow an estimation of support for the two levels of correspondence. As child-rearing methods have shifted more toward love-oriented techniques and away from more punitive methods, children's concepts of God have become more loving and less punitive as well (Nelson & Kroliczak, 1984). Hertel and Donahue (1995), in their sample of nearly 3,000 child–parent dyads, reported that parenting styles that were loving or authoritarian predicted children's and the parents' own views of God as correspondingly loving or authoritarian. Dickie et al. (1997), in a diverse group of 4- to 11-year-old children, found that discipline style had a significant effect on girls', though not boys', concepts of God. When parents used more love oriented techniques (reasoning, praising, explaining) and less power oriented techniques (yelling, threatening, hitting), girls viewed God as more loving and more powerful. This finding supports the correspondence model as well. However, in cases where discipline becomes abuse, the compensation model may account for children's views of God.

Support for Compensation: Abuse, Uninvolvement, and Father Absence. While circumstances that produce secure attachments likely lead to corresponding models of parents and God as loving and available, in the case of insecure attachments, compensation for states of insecurity may be at work. If prior experience precludes access to a secure attachment figure, the compensatory model would predict turning to God as a more "perfect attachment substitute" in times of stress (Granqvist, in press b; Kirkpatrick, 1999).

In a study comparing 30 abused children living in residential treatment with 30 nonabused children living at home, the children's images of their parents differed significantly. Abused children saw parents as less kind and more wrathful, and themselves in a less favorable way, than did nonabused children. However, the two groups did not differ in their views of God as kind and close (Johnson & Eastburg, 1992). Attachment theory may help explain this discrepancy. Children who are more likely to have a secure attachment (the nonabused children) would be expected to follow the IWM correspondence model, whereas children who are more likely to be insecurely attached, and face difficult and frightening life experiences (the abused children), are more likely to follow the

compensation model, seeking a more "perfect attachment substitute."

Further support for the compensation model comes from children whose parents are divorced. Dickie et al. (1997) found that children whose fathers were absent from home imagined a more loving and powerful God than did children from intact homes. Eshleman et al. (1999) found that when parents spent less quality time with their children and had less identity in the parenting role, children viewed God as closer even when controlling for the age of children. It appears that these children find God to fulfill the role of an attachment figure, to be close and available, particularly in times of stress, or when feeling alone.

ATTACHMENT AND RELIGIOUS AND SPIRITUAL DEVELOPMENT IN ADOLESCENCE

Adolescence signifies a major period of attachment transition for most individuals, during which attachment components are gradually transferred from parents to peers. This is not always easily accomplished, as adolescents may be struggling for more autonomy than their parents are willing to give them, presumably because of lingering perceptions of immaturity in the offspring on the part of the parents (e.g., Allen & Land, 1999). In other words, adolescence is sometimes a period of attachment-related turbulence.

However, there are important individual differences to consider here. Security, unlike insecurity, of attachment is associated with generally favorable outcomes (Allen & Land, 1999; Kobak, Cole, Ferenz-Gillies, & Fleming, 1993; Kobak & Ferenz-Gillies, 1995; Kobak, Ferenz-Gillies, Everhart, & Seabrook, 1994) and, hence, seems to foster continuity of adaptation throughout adolescence (e.g., Armsden & Greenberg, 1987; Lapsley, Rice, & Fitzgerald, 1990; Rice, 1990). In addition, although often making a premature transfer of attachment (Friedlmeier & Granqvist, 2004), adolescents with an insecure attachment history are less likely to build close, trusting, and satisfactory peer relations (Allen & Land, 1999). Thus, insecurely attached adolescents may be left in a state wherein experienced security cannot be derived by turning either to parents or to peers for support. In other words, attachment turbulence is likely to be especially pronounced for adolescents with insecure attachment characteristics.

This period of attachment transition coincides with one of the major periods of religious and spiritual transformations in many people's lives. Adolescence and young adulthood have been noted as major religious transitional periods since the infancy days of the psychology of religion (e.g., James, 1902). Why this is so, however, has remained unclear. Besides being linked to increased religiousness, as in the experience of religious conversion, adolescence and early adulthood are associated with apostasy, that is, the decline of religiosity among those raised in a religious home (e.g., Roof & McKinney, 1987; Tamminen, 1994). One important reason why adolescence is a religious transitional period may be because attachment transfer is co-occurring. That is to say, attachment components may not only be transferred to peers, but also, in some cases, to God, and away from God.

Several studies have now been conducted on individual differences in attachment in relation to religious and spiritual changes in adolescence. These studies have consistently supported the compensation and correspondence hypotheses described above, regardless of attachment target (attachment history with parents or current romantic attachment), nation (United States or Sweden), and denominational characteristics (Swedish Lutherans or new agers, or diverse U.S. denomination members).

Insecure Attachment and the Compensatory Search for Connectedness

Taken together with the findings showing adolescence to be a religious transitional period, the fact that it is particularly in the case of insecure attachment that the transition from parents to peers unfolds unfavorably might suggest that the search for God would be particularly tempting for insecurely attached adolescents. In support of this line of reasoning, Kirkpatrick and Shaver (1990) found a significant overrepresentation of an insecure/avoidant attachment history among adults who retrospectively reported to have experienced sudden religious conversions in adolescence. Furthermore, the life situations during which these conversions were experienced (e.g., emotional turmoil, relationship problems with parents and relationship partners) suggested that the conversions served an emotionally supportive function for the converts (henceforward labeled *themes of compensation*).

In a subsequent prospective longitudinal study of late adolescents/young adults, Kirkpatrick (1998) found that participants with an insecure romantic attachment orientation, and particularly those with a negative self-model (ambivalent and fearful avoidant attachment; Bartholomew & Horowitz, 1991), increased in religiousness (e.g., relationships with God, loving God image) compared to securely attached/positive self-model participants over a 4-month period, controlling for Time 1 religion assessments. These latter findings suggest that it is particularly a negative model of self, rather than of others, that is conducive to the compensatory use of God in adolescence. Adolescents with a negative other model are likely to view God in a similarly negative fashion and hence cannot efficiently use God as a surrogate.

In a prospective longitudinal study of Swedish midadolescents (Granqvist, 2002), participants with an insecure attachment history with mother were found to have experienced religious changes in both directions (i.e., increases and decreases) to a larger extent than adolescents reporting a secure attachment history. Moreover, among participants who had experienced a 15-month prospective increase in religiousness, an insecure history with mother was positively related both to the suddenness/intenseness of change and themes of compensation, again attesting to the emotionally supportive function that increased religiousness fills for these individuals. Romantic attachment failed to systematically predict religious changes in these analyses. However, when considering a theoretically relevant contextual factor that pointed to the need for a surrogate use of God (i.e., a prospective breakup from a romantic relationship), further analyses of this material showed that insecure attachment (both attachment history and current romantic orientation) was linked to increased religiousness over the

15-month time span (Granqvist & Hagekull, 2003). Further, when insecurely attached adolescents instead had formed a new romantic relationship between assessments, their religiousness actually decreased over time. Again, these findings suggest that it is specifically in distress that the insecurely attached are likely to search for connectedness.

Besides the search for connectedness in institutionalized settings, the Swedish adolescents constituted one subsample in the new age studies mentioned earlier (Granqvist & Hagekull, 2001). The conclusions reached about the new age as a compensatory arena of spirituality holds true also when specifically considering the adolescent subsample. High adolescent new age scorers reported a comparatively insecure attachment history with mother, as well as a current avoidant-fearful romantic attachment orientation. Avoidant-fearful attachment is the worst-case romantic attachment scenario because it is characterized by negative models of both self and others (Bartholomew & Horowitz, 1991) or, according to a more recent conceptualization (Brennan, Clark, & Shaver, 1998), by both high anxiety (about being abandoned, insufficiently loved) and high avoidance (of closeness and dependency). Avoidance and anxiety are typically thought of as antithetical strategies that, when combined, lead to a type of romantic attachment disorganization (e.g., seeking closeness but at the same time avoiding it) similar to the subset of children in the Strange Situation Procedure (Ainsworth et al., 1978) that are classified as insecure/disorganized (Brennan et al., 1998; Main & Hesse, 1990). These findings also correspond well conceptually to the Adult Attachment Interview (George, Kaplan, & Main, 1996) study, which showed an overrepresentation of disorganized states in high adult new age scorers (Granqvist, Hagekull, Broberg, & Iverson, 2004). They are also in line with George and Solomon's (1999) study, in which disorganized mothers, according to their caregiving interview, tended to attribute psychic powers to their offspring. Given the absence of internal organization, it may not be so surprising that the search for connectedness is similarly a project without an overarching organization that could help the individual achieve mental integration.

Secure Attachment and Correspondence in the Search for Connectedness

As in the case for adults, adolescents with secure attachment characteristics tend to be comparatively likely to identify themselves with their parents' religious standards, even though they may be in the midst of attachment transfer. For instance, Granqvist (2002) reported significant correlations between secure attachment characteristics and scores on the socialization-based religiosity scale (Granqvist & Hagekull, 1999). An implication of these findings is that apostasy is not necessarily a normative adolescent phenomenon, but rather is associated with insecure attachment characteristics and the forming and breaking of other affectional bonds.

The IWM part of the correspondence hypothesis has been supported in contemporaneous associations between late adolescents' images of God as nurturing, caring, and loving, on the one hand, and nurturing images of parents (Dickie et al., submitted) and secure romantic attachment (Kirkpatrick, 1998), on the other. In Kirkpatrick's study, contemporaneous support for the correspondence hypothesis was obtained in spite of the fact that insecure attachment/negative model of self predicted increased religiousness over time in the same sample. Although causal direction cannot be inferred on the basis of correlational research, the dynamics of these findings may suggest that insecurity leads to a search for spiritual solutions, and that, at least in institutionalized settings, this in fact works in the sense of helping the individual achieve increased security of attachment (see also Granqvist, 2003).

The research reviewed here points to the conclusion that the religiosity of adolescents with secure, compared to insecure, attachment characteristics is less dramatic. However, there are conditions under which fluctuations in religiousness are to be expected also for securely attached adolescents. Two such conditions are the formation of and breakup from romantic relationships. As predicted by the correspondence hypothesis, in the case of secure attachment, the formation of a new attachment relationship is associated with increased religiousness and the breakup from an attachment relationship with decreased religiousness over time (Granqvist & Hagekull, 2003).

CONCLUSIONS, METHODOLOGICAL RESERVATIONS, AND FUTURE DIRECTIONS

After a period of interest in adulthood, researchers have finally initiated the empirical study of how attachment and spirituality/religiosity in childhood and adolescence are related. More specifically, in the case of secure attachment characteristics, spirituality and religiosity have been found to parallel the affective tone of the individual's attachment relationships and representations (internal working model correspondence), and her or his attachment figures' religious and spiritual standards (socialized correspondence). In adolescence, spirituality and religiosity of securely attached individuals are relatively stable over time. To the extent that securely attached adolescents display spiritual transformations, they tend to do so in the context of forming other close relationships.

We have also seen that in the case of insecure attachment characteristics, the individual's spirituality and religiosity may reflect stress-provoked distress regulation strategies, in which God is used as a substitute attachment-like figure. For children thus at risk, God is more loving and more powerful, hence providing the security needed to function. The religious changes of insecurely attached adolescents tend to be driven in particular by a negative self-model. When undertaken in institutionalized settings, there are some suggestions that the religious quest may have served self-integrating functions in that security is linked to higher religiousness at a given time (i.e., the formerly insecure individuals may have "earned security"). When undertaken in a noninstitutionalized context such as the new age, however, current insecurity of the most serious kind seems to linger.

Finally, a number of normative developmental attachment issues have been considered in relation to the development of spirituality and religiosity in childhood and adolescence. Children's God images gradually become more like their parents, at first most like fathers'

qualities, and later most like mothers' qualities. Through middle childhood God becomes the "more perfect" attachment figure who is sought particularly in times of separation from parents and in times of distress.

Even though findings support the utility of an attachment framework, much remains to be done before precise conclusions can be drawn with any satisfactory degree of confidence. In particular, there is an absence of long-term prospective studies on children that utilize well-validated assessments of attachment, such as the Strange Situation Procedure for infants and toddlers (Ainsworth et al., 1978) and the 6-year reunion procedure or Separation Anxiety Test for somewhat older children (Main, Kaplan, & Cassidy, 1985). It is a practical challenge to implement such projects, but there is no satisfactory shortcut.

Unlike the case of children, research using standard attachment methods has been conducted on adolescents. However, relevant research has used questionnaire measures of attachment, which are susceptible to a variety of self-presentation and defensive biases. Therefore, we suggest the use of the Adult Attachment Interview (AAI; Main et al., 1985) in future adolescent studies. In adulthood, the patterns of findings using the AAI and questionnaires are congruent (Granqvist, in press b), so we may expect likewise in adolescence.

A problem with the attachment account of religion is that when the compensation and correspondence hypotheses are couched as opposing, they predict the same outcome (e.g., secure attachment characteristics are associated with loving God images, but so are experiences of abuse). One way of eliminating this problem is to look at difference scores between parent and God images for offspring differing in attachment security. Hence, even if no attachment main effects were to be observed on God image, it could be predicted that the God image would differ more (in the positive direction) from the image of parents in the case of insecure attachment.

There is a need for more studies concerning other nontraditional forms of spirituality in the West besides the new age. The new age may in fact be considered "semi-institutionalized" (cf. Kwilecki, in press), and hence involvement therein may not be representative of even more private forms of spirituality. In addition, attachment studies should be conducted outside of the Western world to examine the cross-cultural validity of the attachment framework as applied to religion and spirituality. However, such studies are only relevant to attachment theory insofar as the behavior (e.g., prayer) of individuals in a given religious tradition is directed to some external supernatural figure. In this context, it should also be cautioned that attachment theory cannot, and should not, be about every conceivable aspect of religion and spirituality, but concerns primarily their relational and distress-regulating aspects (see also Kirkpatrick, 2005).

While we do see research that indicates child–God and adolescent–God relationships paralleling attachments to parents and peers, we need more studies on adjustment outcomes to make possible an estimation of whether religious and spiritual changes do in fact promote self-integration and well-being, particularly in insecurely attached individuals.

Although this chapter concerns children and adolescents, it is appropriate here to mention the need for life span studies of attachment and spiritual development. Major life events presumably shift attachment experiences. Attachment is a reciprocal process, and while the infant forms an attachment to the parents, the parents also form an affectional bond to the infant. Once we take a developmental and life span view, new questions about the relationship between attachment and spiritual development arise. These questions still await our research attention, but their answers could have a profound effect on the ways we visualize spiritual development.

NOTE

1. Variances for mothers' and fathers' nurturance and power did not differ in this study.

REFERENCES

Acock, A. C., & Bengston, V. L. (1978). On the relative influences of mothers and fathers: A covariance analysis of political and religious socialization. *Journal of Marriage and the Family, 40*, 519–530.

Ainsworth, M. D. S. (1985). Attachments across the life-span. *Bulletin of the New York Academy of Medicine, 61*, 792–812.

Ainsworth, M. D. S. (1990). Some considerations regarding theory and assessment relevant to attachments beyond infancy. In M. T. Greenberg, D. Cicchetti, & E. M. Cummings (Eds.), *Attachment in the preschool years: Theory, research, and intervention* (pp. 463–488). Chicago: University of Chicago Press.

Ainsworth, M. D. S., Blehar, M. C., Waters, E., & Wall, S. (1978). *Patterns of attachment: A psychological study of the strange situation*. Hillsdale, NJ: Erlbaum.

Allen, J. P., & Land, D. (1999). Attachment in adolescence. In J. Cassidy & P. R. Shaver (Eds.). *Handbook of attachment theory and research* (pp. 319–335). New York: Guilford.

Armsden, G. C., & Greenberg, M. T. (1987). The inventory of parent and peer attachment: Individual differences and their relationship to psychological well-being. *Journal of Youth and Adolescence, 16*, 427–453.

Bartholomew, K., & Horowitz, L. M. (1991). Attachment styles in young adults: A test of a four-category model. *Journal of Personality and Social Psychology, 61*, 226–244.

Birgegard, A., & Granqvist, P. (2004). The correspondence between attachment to parents and God: Three experiments using subliminal separation cues. *Personality and Social Psychology Bulletin, 30*, 1122–1135.

Bowlby, J. (1969). *Attachment*. Vol. 1 of *Attachment and loss*. New York: Basic Books.

Bowlby, J. (1973). *Separation anxiety and anger.* Vol. 2 of *Attachment and loss*. New York: Basic Books.

Bowlby, J. (1980). *Loss*. Vol. 3 of *Attachment and loss*. New York: Basic Books.

Brennan, K. A., Clark, C. A., & Shaver, P. R. (1998). Self-report measurement of adult attachment: An integrative overview. In J. A. Simpson & W. S. Rholes (Eds.), *Attachment theory and close relationships* (pp. 46–76). New York: Guilford.

Cassidy, J. (1994). Emotion regulation. Influences of attachment relationships. In N. A. Fox (Ed.), The development of emotion regulation: Biological and behavioral considerations. *Monographs of the Society for Research in Child Development, 59*(2–3), 228–249.

Cassidy, J., & Shaver, P. R. (Eds.). (1999). *Handbook of attachment theory and research.* New York: Guilford.

Coles, R. (1990). *The spiritual life of children.* Boston: Houghton Mifflin.

De Roos, S. A., Miedema, S., & Iedema, J. (2001). Attachment, working models of self and others, and God concept in kindergarten. *Journal for the Scientific Study of Religion, 40*(4), 607–619.

DeWolff, M. S., & van IJzendoorn, M. H. (1997). Sensitivity and attachment: A meta-analysis on parental antecedents of infant attachment. *Child Development, 68,* 571–591.

Dickie, J. R., Eshleman, A. K., Merasco, D. M., Sherpard, A., Vander Wilt, M., & Johnson, M. (1997). Parent–child relationships and children's images of God. *Journal for the Scientific Study of Religion, 36*(1), 25–43.

Dickie, J. R., Woodall, L. V., Hankamp, J. R., & Nixon, K. M. (2004). *Mother, father, and self: Sources of young adults' God concepts.* Manuscript submitted for publication.

Elkind, D. (1970). The origins of religion in the child. *Review of Religious Research, 12,* 35–42.

Eshleman, A. K., Dickie, J. R., Merasco, D. M., Shepard, A., & Johnson, M. (1999). Mother God, father God: Children's perceptions of God's distance. *International Journal for the Psychology of Religion, 9*(2), 139–146.

Fowler, J. W. (1994). Keeping faith with God and our children: A practical theological perspective. *Religious Education, 89*(4), 543–560.

Fraley, R. C., & Davis, K. E. (1997). Attachment formation and transfer in young adults' close friendships and romantic relationships. *Personal Relationships, 4,* 131–144.

Friedlmeier, W., & Granqvist, P. (2004). *Attachment transfer among German and Swedish adolescents: A prospective longitudinal study.* Submitted for publication.

George, L. K., Ellison, C. G., & Larson, D. B. (2002). Explaining the relationships between religious involvement and health. *Psychological Inquiry, 13,* 190–200.

George, C., Kaplan, N., & Main, M. (1996). *Attachment interview for adults* (3rd ed.). Unpublished manuscript, University of California, Berkeley.

George, C., & Solomon, J. (1999). Attachment and caregiving: The caregiving behavioral system. In J. Cassidy & P. R. Shaver (Eds.), *Handbook of attachment theory and research* (pp. 649–670). New York: Guilford.

Granqvist, P. (2002). Attachment and religiosity in adolescence: Cross-sectional and longitudinal evaluations. *Personality and Social Psychology Bulletin, 28,* 260–270.

Granqvist, P. (2003). Attachment theory and religious conversions: A review and a resolution of the classic and contemporary paradigm chasm. *Review of Religious Research, 45,* 172–187.

Granqvist, P. (in press a). On the relation between secular and divine relationships: An emerging attachment perspective and a critique of the depth approaches. *International Journal for the Psychology of Religion.*

Granqvist, P. (in press b). The study of attachment in the psychology of religion. In D. Wulff (Ed.), *Psychology of religion: Handbook.* New York: Oxford University Press.

Granqvist, P., & Hagekull, B. (1999). Religiousness and perceived childhood attachment: Profiling socialized correspondence and emotional compensation. *Journal for the Scientific Study of Religion, 38,* 254–273.

Granqvist, P., & Hagekull, B. (2001). Seeking security in the new age: On attachment and emotional compensation. *Journal for the Scientific Study of Religion, 40,* 529–547.

Granqvist, P., & Hagekull, B. (2003). Longitudinal predictions of religious change in adolescence: Contributions from the interaction of attachment and relationship status. *Journal of Social and Personal Relationships, 20,* 793–817.

Granqvist, P., Hagekull, B., Broberg, A., & Ivarsson, T. (2004). *Examining relations between attachment, religiosity, and new age spirituality using the Adult Attachment Interview.* Manuscript submitted for publication.

Hazan, C., & Zeifman, D. (1999). Pair bonds as attachments: Evaluating the evidence. In J. Cassidy & P. R. Shaver (Eds.), *Handbook of attachment theory and research* (pp. 336–355). New York: Guilford.

Heller, D. (1986). *The children's God.* Chicago: University of Chicago Press.

Hertel, B. R., & Donahue, M. J. (1995). Parental influences on God images among children: Testing Durkheim's metaphoric parallelism. *Journal for the Scientific Study of Religion, 34*(2), 186–199.

James, W. (1902). *The varieties of religious experience.* New York: Longmans, Green.

Johnson, B. W., & Eastburg, M. C. (1992). God, parent and self concepts in abused and non-abused children. *Journal of Psychology and Christianity, 11*(3), 235–243.

Jones, J. W. (1991). *Contemporary psychoanalysis and religion: Transference and transcendence.* New Haven, CT: Yale University Press.

Kirkpatrick, L. A. (1992). An attachment-theory approach to the psychology of religion. *International Journal for the Psychology of Religion, 2,* 3–28.

Kirkpatrick, L. A. (1995). Attachment theory and religious experience. In R. W. Hood Jr. (Ed.), *Handbook of religious experience* (pp. 446–475). Birmingham, AL: Religious Education.

Kirkpatrick, L. A. (1998). God as a substitute attachment figure: A longitudinal study of adult attachment style and religious change in college students. *Personality and Social Psychology Bulletin, 24,* 961–973.

Kirkpatrick, L. A. (1999). Attachment and religious representations and behavior. In J. Cassidy & P. R. Shaver (Eds.), *Handbook of attachment theory and research* (pp. 803–822). New York: Guilford.

Kirkpatrick, L. A. (2005). *Attachment, evolution, and the psychology of religion.* New York: Guilford.

Kirkpatrick, L. A., & Shaver, P. R. (1990). Attachment theory and religion: Childhood attachments, religious beliefs and conversions. *Journal for the Scientific Study of Religion, 29,* 315–334.

Kobak, R. R., Cole, H. E., Ferenz-Gillies, R., & Fleming, W. S. (1993). Attachment and emotion regulation during mother–teen problem solving: A control theory analysis. *Child Development, 64,* 231–245.

Kobak, R., & Ferenz-Gillies, R. (1995). Emotion regulation and depressive symptoms during adolescence: A functionalist perspective. *Development and Psychopathology, 7,* 183–192.

Kobak, R., Ferenz-Gillies, R., Everhart, E., & Seabrook, L. (1994). Maternal attachment strategies and emotion regulation with adolescent offspring. *Journal of Research on Adolescence, 4,* 553–566.

Kwilecki, S. (in press). There is nothing new under the sun: A case study of contemporary spiritual seeking. In D. Wulff (Ed.), *Psychology of religion: Handbook.* New York: Oxford University Press.

Lapsley, D. K., Rice, K. G., & Fitzgerald, D. P. (1990). Adolescent attachment, identity, and adjustment to college: Implications for the continuity of adaptation hypothesis. *Journal of Counseling and Development, 68,* 561–565.

Londerville, S., & Main, M. (1981). Security of attachment, compliance, and maternal training in the second year of life. *Developmental Psychology, 17,* 289–299.

Main, M., & Cassidy, J. (1988). Categories of response to reunion with the parent at age six: Predictable from infant attachment classifications and stable over a one-month period. *Developmental Psychology, 24,* 415–426.

Main, M., & Hesse, E. (1990). Parents' unresolved traumatic experiences are related to infant disorganized attachment status: Is frightened and/or frightening parental behavior the linking mechanism? In M. T. Greenberg, D. Cicchetti, & E. M. Cummings (Eds.), *Attachment in the preschool years: Theory, research, and intervention* (pp. 161–182). Chicago: University of Chicago Press.

Main, M., Kaplan, N., & Cassidy, J. (1985). Security in infancy, childhood and adulthood: A move to the level of representation. In I. Bretherton and E. Waters (Eds.), Growing points of attachment theory and research. *Monographs of the Society for Research in Child Development, 50,* 66–104.

Marvin, R. S. (1977). An ethological-cognitive model for the attenuation of mother–child attachment behavior. In T. M. Alloway, L. Krames, & P. Pliner (Eds.), *Advances in the study of communication and affect: Vol. 3. Attachment behavior* (pp. 25–60). New York: Plenum Press.

Marvin, R. S., & Greenberg, M. T. (1982). Preschoolers' changing conceptions of their mothers: A social-cognitive study of mother–child attachment. In D. Forbes & M. T. Greenberg (Eds.), *New directions for child development: No. 18. Children's planning strategies* (pp. 47–60). San Francisco: Jossey-Bass.

Myers, B. J., Jarvis, P. A., & Creasey, G. L. (1987). Infants' behavior with their mothers and grandmothers. *Infant Behavior and Development, 10,* 245–259.

Nelson, H. M., & Kroliczak, A. (1984). Parental use of the threat of "God will punish": Replication and extension. *Journal of the Scientific Study of Religion, 23,* 267–277.

Oser, F. (1991). The development of religious judgment. In F. Oser & G. Scarlett (Eds.), Religious development in childhood and adolescence. *New Directions for Child Development, 52,* 47–60.

Pargament, K. I. (1997). *The psychology of religion and coping: Theory, research, practice.* New York: Guilford.

Rice, K. G. (1990). Attachment and adolescence: A narrative and meta-analytic review. *Journal of Youth and Adolescence, 19,* 511–538.

Richters, J. E., & Waters, E. (1991). Attachment and socialization: The positive side of social influence. In M. Lewis & S. Feinman et al. (Eds.), Social influences and socialization in infancy. *Genesis of behavior* series (Vol. 6, pp. 185–213). New York: Plenum.

Rizzuto, A. M. (1979). *The birth of the living God: A psychoanalytical study.* Chicago: Chicago University Press.

Roof, W. C., & McKinney, W. (1987). *American mainline religion: Its changing shape and future.* New Brunswick, NJ: Rutgers University Press.

Rutter, M. R., & O'Connor, T. (1999). Implications of attachment theory for child care policies. In J. Cassidy & P. R. Shaver (Eds.), *Handbook of attachment theory and research* (pp. 823–844). New York: Guilford.

Spilka, B., Hood, R. W., Jr., Hunsberger, B., & Gorsuch, R. (2003). *The psychology of religion: An empirical approach* (3rd ed.). New York: Guilford.

Tamm, M. E. (1996). The meaning of God for children and adolescents: A phenomenographic study of drawings. *British Journal of Religious Education, 19*(1), 33–44.

Tamminen, K. (1994). Religious experiences in childhood and adolescence: A viewpoint of religious development between the ages of 7 and 20. *International Journal for the Psychology of Religion, 4*(2), 61–85.

Weinfield, N. S., Sroufe, L. A., Egeland, B., & Carlson, E. A. (1999). The nature of individual differences in infant–caregiver attachment. In J. Cassidy & P. R. Shaver (Eds.), *Handbook of attachment theory and research* (pp. 68–88). New York: Guilford.

15

COGNITIVE-CULTURAL FOUNDATIONS OF SPIRITUAL DEVELOPMENT

CARL N. JOHNSON

CHRIS J. BOYATZIS

In ancient stories of origin, human beings are often conceived as an amalgam of matter and spirit (Berryman, 1991). Material substance is united with an immaterial spirit that can think and choose its own destiny. Cognitive-developmental research has demonstrated that even young children recognize this duality. From early on, children organize reality in terms of ontological categories, distinguishing physical from mental, animate from inanimate, and natural from supernatural kinds of things. These early capacities have led researchers to conclude that children are prepared equally to think about natural and supernatural possibilities.

This current view differs radically from the traditional Piagetian account in which young children were characterized as fundamentally confused about kinds and causes of things in the world. Described as "adualistic," magical thinkers, children were described as confusing thoughts with things, life with inanimate movement, believing that ordinarily mortals can do supernatural things (Piaget, 1929). The ability to distinguish spiritual kinds of things was considered to be a late developing achievement, dependent on universal stages culminating in abstract, rational thought.

Current cognitive-developmental thinking has been enriched in two interdependent ways. First, we have a better understanding of the rich, intuitive capacities that serve to frame children's understanding from early on. Second, we appreciate how these early cognitive capacities are culturally nurtured and recruited. The present chapter offers a contemporary look at cognitive-cultural foundations of spiritual development. Spiritual practices are considered to be founded on uniquely human cognitive capacities that emerge early in development and depend on cultural support.

The chapter is divided into four major parts. First, we sketch a contemporary cognitive-cultural account of the foundations of religious and spiritual development. Second, we consider how this framework has been applied specifically to the development of supernatural concepts and practices, especially concepts of God, soul, afterlife, and prayer. Third, we look at how nature and culture are intertwined in this development. Finally, we look beyond supernatural

211

concepts, proposing a broader account of the role of cognition in spiritual development.

FOUNDATIONS

Human spiritual activity first appears in human historical record with evidence of ritualized burial practices about 40,000 years ago. Cognitive scientists consider these practices to be the result of a cognitive leap that generally supported the proliferation of carefully fashioned artifacts, including tools, body ornaments, and cave drawings. Mithen (1996) describes this leap as an increase in *cognitive flexibility* with connections being made across previously separate domains of intelligence. Harris (2000b) describes the same change in terms of the emergence of human imagination, an opening of thinking about possibilities beyond the here and now.

Religious and spiritual practices consist of intentional efforts to connect with a higher, deeper, more valued reality beyond what appears to the senses. Historically and developmentally, such practices rest on an intersection of multiple cognitive abilities and propensities. Central are capacities to make adaptive inferences about different properties of ordinary objects, actions, and events. In contemporary cognitive terms, human beings must be guided by intuitive cognitive constraints that frame the boundaries of ordinary reality. Thinking also extends beyond these limitations (Harris, 2000b; Mithen, 1996), generating metaphysical, teleological, theistic ideas (Barrett, 2004; Bering & Bjorklund, 2004; Evans, 2000; C. Johnson, 2000; Kelemen, 2004). Equally, there must be some conscious awareness and concern about one's personal connection to these possibilities of higher value, some "relational consciousness" (Hay & Nye, 1998).

On this basis, we propose five tenets of a cognitive framework for understanding spiritual development. First, spiritual development arises from the same human cognitive capacities that led to the emergence of art, science, and technology. Spiritual development is an integral part of normal, human cognitive-developmental mechanisms and processes. (As such, some scholars have called for recognition of spiritual development as "a core developmental process that

deserves equal standing in the pantheon of universal developmental processes"; Benson, 2004, p. 50.)

Second, these cognitive capacities depend on culture, just as culture depends on these capacities. The historical emergence of technical, artistic, and spiritual artifacts was not precipitated by any immediate change in the anatomy of the human brain. The human brain, as we know it, existed many thousands of years before these artifacts appeared. The change, hence, must have been due to dynamic interplay between culture and cognition. Indeed, the expanded cognitive capacity must have depended on new cultural artifacts and practices, just as the new cultural achievements depended on cognition. The spiritual life of human beings arose as part of a collective, cognitive achievement, as human beings engaged in the creation of collectively interpreted representations and artifacts (see Harris, 2000b).

Third, ontogenetically, the cognitive-cultural foundation for spiritual development is normally established within the first few years of life. The imaginative capacities that spawned human culture 40,000 years ago make their fledgling appearance in the pretend play of toddlers (Harris, 2000b). In the preschool and early school years, children develop capacities to make core ontological distinctions: They come to understand that people are animate beings with internal desires, emotions, and thoughts, whereas rocks and statues are not. In inferring that mental states cause human behavior, they equally appreciate that such states cannot affect reality at a distance. Thus, children distinguish ordinary actions from special, magical powers of wishing or prayer (Woolley, 2000). They come to appreciate that there is a deeper reality behind appearance (Flavell, Green, & Flavell, 1986) and make inferences about imperceptible essences and forces beyond the here and now (Gelman, 2003; Hunt, 1995). Young children's explanations and ontologies extend beyond the ordinary, with inferences about the existence of supernatural agents, theistic creation, and life after death (Barrett & Richert, 2003; Bering & Bjorklund, 2004; Evans, 2000; Kelemen, 2004). Young children are also coming to understand and participate in practices of play, prayer, and narrative that serve to orient and connect them to higher possibilities (Miller, Hengst, Alexander, & Sperry, 2000; Taylor & Carlson, 2000; Woolley, 2000).

Although these capacities establish an intuitive spiritual foundation, the actual building of spiritual development awaits the subsequent recruitment of these capacities with the acquisition of more reflective beliefs and consciously self-directed practices. Development consists of having increasingly reflective ideas about the nature of one's identity in relation to ultimate reality, combined with increasing abilities to orient and strengthen one's personal connections to this reality.

The fourth and final point is that spiritual concerns are propelled by intrinsic links between cognition, emotion, and value. Three such links deserve emphasis. First, human emotion is driven by what we conceive to be the objects of such emotion. As James (1990) so well put it, "All our attitudes, moral, practical or emotional, as well as religious, are due to the 'objects' of our consciousness, the things which we believe exist, whether really or ideally, along with ourselves" (p. 55). Second, human beings are intrinsically attracted to higher order organization, consisting of the unity of differences. On this account, agents that represent the unity of natural and supernatural, material and immaterial, spirit and body are not only attention-getting and memorable (Barrett & Nyhof, 2001; Boyer, 2001; Boyer & Walker, 2000) but also recognized as being of higher value (Nozick, 1981, 1990). Third, spiritual ideas matter because they bear on ultimate existential concerns.

SUPERNATURAL CONCEPTS

Cognitive-developmental theories have caused two waves of research on the development of religious concepts. An initial wave of research was spawned in the 1960s by the application of Piagetian theory to the study of concepts of God, prayer, and faith (e.g., Elkind 1961, 1963, 1970; Fowler, 1981; Goldman, 1964). A second wave of research, beginning in the 1990s, was sparked by new theories of cognitive development that distinctly emphasized the early intuitive, domain-specific nature of knowledge and turned attention to the representation of

distinctively supernatural kinds of agents and actions (Boyer, 1994; Lawson & McCauley, 1990). Despite major theoretical changes, three themes have remained constant. First, religious concepts operate under the same conceptual principles and tendencies of children's everyday cognition. Second, children's acquisition of religious concepts depends on how such concepts are assimilated within developing cognitive frameworks. Third, as of yet, attention has focused on the cognitive basis of religious concepts to the exclusion of broader spiritual issues of meaning and value (see Boyatzis, in press). We take up this third issue in the final section of this chapter. To begin, we focus on the second wave of research, looking at the intuitive foundation of children's understanding of supernatural kinds of agents and actions.

Supernatural Agents

Cognitive research has recently focused on accounting for why human beings so readily attend to, remember, and represent supernatural agents. In simple terms, the claim consists of two parts. First, because of our evolutionary history, human beings readily conceive and overextend inferences about existence of intentional agency. Second, human beings are especially attracted to representations of agents that consist of ordinary, intuitive qualities combined with extraordinary supernatural powers.

As Boyer and Walker (2000, p. 152) put it, "The particular way in which religious ontology develops depends on the wider development of ontological categories." These ontologies are marked by several key features. One is the "counterintuitive" nature of religious ontologies (i.e., they violate ordinary expectations, as in the case of spiritual entities who are immortal, omniscient, or can pass through physical objects). A second is that counterintuitive religious beliefs operate within the implicit backdrop of theory of mind, which provides children with a prepared set of qualities to extend to religious agents they think about (e.g., "My supernatural God has wishes and thoughts and worries [just like all beings with minds do]"). In addition, the combination of such agents' counterintuitiveness with the belief that such agents are *real* makes the religious beliefs all the more *salient* to those who hold them. The salience of such beliefs enhances their likelihood of being transmitted and shared with others.

Another theoretical revision is the claim that children and adults are not so radically different in their thinking. In place of the Piaget-inspired progressive march from the irrational magical thinking child to the rational, scientific thinking adult, multiple thought processes are seen to coexist and compete in the minds of children and adults alike (Subbotsky, 1993; Woolley, 1997). As Woolley (2000) asserted, "Children's minds are not inherently one way or another—not inherently magical nor inherently rational" (pp. 126–127). Children *and* adults sometimes invoke the powers of magic, enact superstitions, and puzzle over boundaries between real and imagined.

Concepts of God. The most studied topic in spiritual and religious cognition is children's concepts of God (e.g., Hyde, 1990). This focus is not surprising, given the centrality of this concept in the monotheistic religions that dominate the modern culture of the researchers.

Traditionally, children have been depicted as having concrete, anthropomorphic notions of God, as a kind of big person in the sky (e.g., Goldman, 1964; Heller, 1986; Pitts, 1976). In contrast, current research suggests that children and adults are not so different. Even adults have an anthropomorphizing tendency, a "fundamental cognitive bias" (Barrett & Keil, 1996, p. 223) that operates by extension of an intuitive folk psychology to supernatural figures (Boyer, 1994, 2001).

Children, like adults, appear to produce God concepts that entail both natural and supernatural properties. Work by Barrett and colleagues challenges the established view that children are unaware of God's distinctly supernatural powers (Barrett & Keil, 1996; Barrett & Richert, 2003). Contrary to claims that children are limited to a concrete, anthropomorphic God, their findings demonstrate that preschoolers recognize that God is a very special kind of agent who, unlike other agents, is not constrained by ordinary laws of nature. On the basis of this work, Barrett has offered a "preparedness" hypothesis that posits that children are prepared conceptually at very early ages to think about God as *unique,* not

humanlike. The preparedness helps explain why children readily distinguish the special status of God (omniscient, omnipotent, . . .) in the absence of explicit religious tuition (Giminez & Harris, 2001), as well as in the presence of explicitly anthropomorphic religious teaching (Johnson & Nyhof, 2003).

Research by Evans (2000, 2001) and Kelemen (2004) points to another way in which children seem prepared to be theists. When children extend their causal explanations beyond the constraints of local objects and events to explain the origins of things (e.g., dinosaurs), they display a natural tendency toward teleological, creationist explanations. Even children from nonreligious families tend toward such explanations. An evolutionary account of origins is a relatively late-emerging, hard-won cultural achievement (Evans, 2000, 2001).

Immaterial Spirit and Afterlife. Researchers have also documented cognitive propensities underlying ideas of immaterial spirit and life after death, which are widespread across cultures (Bering & Bjorklund, 2004; Boyer, 2001). Contrary to traditional claims that young children are completely unable to understand the cessation of bodily function, recent research indicates how afterlife beliefs are connected with an early developing understanding of distinct qualities of minds and bodies (Bering & Bjorklund, 2004). Children readily appreciate that death stops physical/biological functions (such as the working of eyes, ears) but have difficulty imagining that death similarly eliminates mental functions. In other words, a mind–body, immaterial–material distinction appears to arise naturally from children's intuitive understanding of physical and mental behavior. Such thinking is readily recruited in religious beliefs that a spirit or soul exists separately from the body at death. As one preschooler put it, "The spirit goes up but the body gets buried" (Boyatzis, 1997).

A study by Boyatzis (1997) demonstrates how children's developing intuitive understanding of minds may underlie their nascent inferences about which entities have a soul. Young children growing up in Protestant, Roman Catholic, and Mennonite traditions were asked to judge what kinds of entities have souls. Responses of the Protestant and Catholic children appeared to reflect children's intuitive metric of the degree to which they think different entities have mental capacities. Souls were attributed to parents 75% of the time; children, 64%; babies, 48%; cats and dogs, 45%; plants, 40%; and furniture, 20%. These judgments apparently reflect children's own thinking about the subject, not something they've been directly taught. In contrast, the Mennonite children from rural Pennsylvania attributed souls exclusively to parents (100%) and babies (88%), reflecting the tighter constraints of early religious tuition.

Supernatural Actions

Just as young children are distinguishing special qualities of supernatural beings, so too are they distinguishing the special qualities of supernatural actions such as prayers and rituals. Woolley (2000) has demonstrated that young children are generally well aware that desires, words, and thoughts cannot directly affect physical reality. Against this understanding of the limits of ordinary causality, children come to appreciate the special qualities of magical wishes and prayer.

Research is also under way on children's understanding of ritual. Cognitively, ritual actions can be understood as special actions that are framed by an intuitive understanding of ordinary actions. Rituals in this sense are structured like ordinary actions, but include special markers that orient people to the extraordinary power and significance of these actions (see Barrett & Lawson, 2001; Jacobs, 2003).

Nature and Culture

The Piagetian constructivist tradition rightly emphasized the interplay between influences of the environment and the developing cognitive structure of the organism. The concepts children acquire depend on how they can be assimilated into the child's current frame of understanding. Newer to the field, however, are two ideas. First, we better appreciate how the acquisition and spread of concepts depend on the unconscious operation of multivarious, intuitive inferential processes (cf. Barrett, 2004; Boyer, 2001). Culture in this sense rests on the recruitment of natural processes. Second, we have a much richer appreciation of the role of cultural practices and scaffolding in development (cf. Miller & Goodnow, 1995; Rogoff, 1990). In place of the isolated child making sense of the world, attention has turned to the social child participating in cultural practices, including narrative and testimony that embed children in a reality that extends well beyond their own direct experience (Harris, 2002; Miller, Hengst et al., 2002).

The interplay of culture and nature has been particularly well investigated in studies of children's beliefs in creationism. Evans (2000, 2001) has examined children growing up in secular as compared to fundamentalist Christian families who either attended religious schools or were home-schooled. Two findings were striking. First, regardless of religious background, young children (7 to 9 years of age) tended to embrace creationist views. Not until early adolescence did youth in secular homes begin to consistently echo their families' evolutionist cosmologies. Second, children from fundamentalist families never acquired evolutionary ideas, with their parents deliberately guarding them from exposure to evidence such as fossil records. Thus, children appear naturally prone to creationist ideas, even without direct religious training. Such accounts are likely to persist unrevised, absent concerted exposure to relevant scientific evidence.

Another line of investigation has focused on social-cultural factors that influence children's beliefs in mythical characters such as Santa Claus, the Easter Bunny, and the Tooth Fairy. Children's beliefs in such characters are not the result of a general failure to distinguish reality from fantasy (Taylor, 1999; Woolley, 1997). On the contrary, such figures are attractive precisely because of their distinctive supernatural attributes. Beliefs in this case are not simply a matter of being taught or told. Rather, beliefs are elicited by cultural *practices* that provide supporting evidence (such as money left by the Tooth Fairy). Children also differ in their attraction to supernatural phenomena, just as they differ in their exposure to relevant cultural practices as well as competing evidence and claims (such as those coming from older disbelievers). On this account, it is understandable that children's beliefs are not tightly related to their parents' endorsement of such beliefs. For example, Prentice, Manosevitz, and Hubbs (1978) found that of parents who encouraged their children to believe in the Easter Bunny, 23% of their children did *not* believe, and of parents who discouraged children's belief, 47% nonetheless did believe in the Easter Bunny. Stronger correspondence emerged on Santa Claus, likely reflecting more pervasive cultural support for this character in their U.S. sample.

In the first study of its kind, Woolley, Boerger, and Markman (2004) experimentally tested factors influencing children's acquisition of belief in a novel fantasy being. Preschool children were told about the Candy Witch, who brings toys to children in exchange for their Halloween candy. They found that belief in the Candy Witch was greater among older children, greater among children who participated in a Candy Witch ritual (versus being told), and greater among children who were more generally prone to believe in fantastical beings. In other words, belief in this case rested on the development of cognitive capacities in conjunction with individual propensities and cultural practices.

Of course, the development of religious beliefs differs in important ways from beliefs in childhood myths. Santa Claus, the Easter Bunny, and the Candy Witch are isolated actors invoked in terms of highly specified practices on special occasions. Religious deities or spirits, in contrast, are typically invoked in more profound and pervasive ways. Nonetheless, the degree and nature of belief surely depend on how individual minds are engaged in cultural practices.

We need to know more about how different supernatural beliefs are transmitted, acquired, and function in the context of different cultural practices. Within our own culture, children are exposed to widely different practices and beliefs (see Miller et al., 2000; Taylor & Carlson, 2000). In traditional non-Western cultures, such as the Beng of West Africa and the Aboriginal Warlpiri of north-central Australia (DeLoache & Gottlieb, 2000), life is more pervasively infused with multifarious supernatural agents. In some cases, babies and young children are ascribed a kind of "spiritual emissary" status, as the children are believed to have arrived from an ancestral spirit realm. In the Fulani tribe, a nomadic people in West Africa, babies are protected in myriad ways from evil spirits in their midst who wish to steal the babies back to the spirit world (M. Johnson, 2000). Parents give their babies unflattering names, openly insult them, and even roll them in cow dung, all to make them unappealing to the evil spirits.

A cognitive-cultural perspective enables us to better understand why supernatural beliefs are easily acquired and spread. However, supernatural beliefs are neither necessary nor sufficient for spiritual development. Arising from cognitive mechanisms, supernatural beliefs need not be connected with any higher or deeper levels of understanding (Boyer, 2001). Attention needs to turn to developments along this vertical dimension.

MORE REALITY

In his original investigation, William James (1990) concluded that the religious impulse is driven by a desire for "something more": "that union or harmonious relation with that higher universe which is our true end" (p. 435). Cognitive scientists have recently challenged James's focus on exceptionally religious individuals, turning attention to how religious concepts are ordinarily represented and disseminated (Boyatzis, 2001; Boyer, 2001). Instead of looking for the ground of religion in extraordinary spiritual insight, current cognitive research looks for the ground of religious representations in ordinary cognition. As yet, however, there is little account of how ordinary cognition may widely serve to energize a search for higher reality and deeper value (for exceptions, see Bering, 2003; Turiel & Neff, 2000).[1]

Progress in this field has been inhibited by a failure to appreciate that reality is experienced in terms of dimensions and degrees.[2] The philosopher Robert Nozick (1981, 1990) offers the beginnings of such an account. He argues that human beings intrinsically desire their lives to be more *real*. Reality in this sense does not consist of the mere representation of whether or not something exists. Reality enters our experience and understanding in dimensions and degrees. Things are more real insofar as they are more vivid, more intense, more valuable, more important, and so forth. Reality also extends to ideal limits: perfection, omnipotence, and infinitude. (God in this account can be viewed as ultimate reality, a unity of all that is.)

The human pursuit of more reality entails more value and more meaning. Nozick argues that value is intrinsic to reality in the form of organic unity, consisting of "unity in diversity." Organisms, theories, or ecologies are intrinsically more valuable insofar as they consist of a unity of diverse elements. Human beings have high intrinsic value because individuals reflect the integration of mind and matter. Meaning, in turn, "involves transcending limits so as to connect with something valuable; meaning is a transcending of the limits of your own value" (Nozick, 1981, p. 610).

From this standpoint, the exceptional religious spirit, described by James as aspiring for "something more," can be viewed as an extension of a generic human aspiration for more reality, more value, more meaning. Piaget similarly described an intrinsic motive toward higher organization or equilibrium, reflected in his own personal quest to unify knowledge and value (Vidal, 1994). The present proposal, however, offers a more robust view of reality, as it bears on the multiple ways individuals seek to expand meaning and value in their lives.

The intrinsic attraction to more reality can be linked with the flowering of human cognition and culture, described earlier. The profusion of cultural artifacts, tens of thousands of years ago, was enabled by an increase in higher order connections, across different domains of intelligence and beyond the here and now. More than an intellectual leap, this proliferation allowed an expansion in the possibility for more reality, more value, and more meaning. At once, human beings were able to appreciate the limitations of their embodied existence and imagine connections with things of higher value.

Developmentally, children first connect with wider reality as they engage in social practices of pretend and language (Harris, 2000b). Although this development is normally a gradual, multimodal process, the spiritual implications are particularly well illustrated in the case of Helen Keller's sudden discovery of the cultural artifact of naming. Keller marks this discovery as the awakening of her soul. Prior to this point, she describes her experience as like living in a dense fog, functioning from moment to moment with no sense of larger connection or value. Her discovery that everything has a name was the key to meaningfully connecting herself to people and things beyond herself. This discovery, made by every young child, includes an intuitive awareness of invisible links between different kinds of things. Names exist as a unified organization of physical (utterances), social (conventions), and mental (thoughts) properties, thus having high intrinsic value. Remarkably, the connecting power of names opened Keller to wider values. Before her discovery of language, she describes anger and then delight after breaking her doll into pieces. After the discovery, she appreciates the doll in a new way, tries in vain to repair it, and feels repentance and sorrow for the first time (Keller, 1996).

More Knowledge and Value

If spiritual development consists of connecting with more reality and transcending the boundaries of self, its cognitive underpinnings consist of two parts: cognition of more reality, and practices that serve to orient, frame, and connect an individual with this reality. Cognition of reality expands beyond initial intuition to include the hard-won cultural insights of science, religion, the arts, and the humanities. Development includes the scientific insights of vast realities existing beyond our ordinary experience. Equally it includes knowledge of the human condition and possibilities that extend beyond what we know (metaphysical, theological). The engine of this development, however, is not curiosity or the accumulation of facts. It is, rather, the meaningful connection of the self with more valued reality.

While spiritual development commonly aims toward connection with ultimate reality, beyond the limits of human knowledge, this reality need not be conceived as supernatural or religious. Reality and value can grow in height and depth within the presumed constraints of the natural world and even in opposition to religious authority. Developing biological knowledge, for example, includes increasing consciousness about the existence of higher forms of organization (e.g., nervous systems, ecologies), with respect for the intrinsic value of such organization (Holmes, 2003; Kahn & Lourenco, 2002). Equally, as children come to understand the nature of people and institutions, they recognize that these highly unified organizations intrinsically command respect, rights, and obligations, even against the external authority of religion (Turiel & Neff, 2000). What commands respect in the world, what elicits compassion or awe (Nussbaum, 2001), depends on what one takes to exist (whether ecological systems, conscious beings, or souls). Values intrinsically arise from experience and depend on "informational assumptions" about the world (Turiel & Neff, 2000).

Spiritual development in this account depends on normal cognitive-developmental changes in children's conceptions of reality. Three general kinds of changes are relevant. First, development proceeds from intuitive understanding to an increased capacity for reflective ideas (cf. C. Johnson, 2000). While children start out with powerful inference mechanisms for intuitively sorting out what exists in the world, conscious reflection on the nature and origins of the world is a subsequent development. Intuition is not "lost" or outgrown, but is rather guided and integrated with reflective ideas. Second, development consists of developing knowledge and changing "theories" about the nature of reality, including the self. Developing knowledge includes a deepening appreciation of the boundaries of different kinds of things in the world (ranging from subatomic particles to nervous systems), as well as their interdependence. Knowledge not only develops within domains (physical, psychological, biological, social) but also includes potential connections and radical reshuffling across domains. For example, while children begin with intuitions that mental and physical things are essentially different kinds, they may later acquire a deeper understanding of how mental states are tightly linked with the functioning of the physical brain. Finally, cognitive development opens up more reality in terms of discerning higher order organization (intrinsic value) in terms of patterns, processes, and connections.

Developing cognition of more reality must be intertwined with developing participation in cultural-cognitive practices that orient to and connect the self with this realty. Spiritual development arises not from the mere acquisition of knowledge but from meaningful connections of the self to more valued reality. In meaning-making practices, including dialogue, narrative, and prayer, cognition is intertwined with emotions, such as awe and compassion, that reflect higher values.

The culturing of spiritual development is more than the fostering of particular religious beliefs. It can involve engaging children in reflective dialogue on the limitations of the known, confronting the unknowable and ineffable, and discussing ultimate concerns. For example, a diary and survey study of Christian families' communication about religion found that the most common topics were God, Jesus, heaven, and prayer, with conversations marked by a reciprocal exchange of ideas and parents asking many questions without imposing their own beliefs too strongly (Boyatzis, 2004; Boyatzis & Janicki, 2003). Such conversations were more than a matter of belief; they were a communal exploration of higher reality, meaning, and value. Although some have argued (Harris, 2000a, p. 176) that to children themselves, there is "nothing special" about their God questions, religious and spiritual discussions often do grapple with ultimate concerns.

Religious practices potentially serve to create organizations of higher value, unifying diversity in communities that are held together by a common orientation to a transcendent reality (see Rizzuto, 1979). Ideally, practices serve to organize individuals and groups with a valued identity, not only linking individuals in a community, but also linking a deepening appreciation of the self with a widening appreciation of value and reality. The power of such practices is particularly evident in the development of a sense of shared humanity and compassion, variously documented in Haight's (2002) study *African-American Children at Church* and in Youniss and Yates's (1999) description of adults who rescued Jews during World War II.

Although little research has focused on particular religious practices that foster spiritual development and identity,[3] evidence is available on the development of increased depth and value in children's understanding of prayer. Scarlett and Perriello (1991) asked adolescents to write prayers they would make in response to hypothetical challenges described within several vignettes (e.g., a friend was ill with cancer). Analyses of the prayers showed age trends in the content and functions of prayers. The youngest subjects (7th graders) made petitions to God to help the friend get well, 9th graders asked God to give the friend strength for her struggles, and college students expressed a search for meaning amidst doubt. When describing the nature and function of prayer, subjects' responses progressed with age from objective concerns (asking God for things) to subjective issues (coping with feelings) to becoming closer to God. Other analyses revealed that youths' beliefs progressed from thinking of prayer as "talking to" God to "talking with" God, a trend that reflects increased maturity in both the breadth and depth of relationality with a transcendent.

New lines of investigation also point to the way in which emotions may serve to integrate higher levels of understanding, value, and identity. Theoretically, emotions can be viewed as judgments of and physiological responses to external value (Nozick, 1981; Nussbaum, 2001). Judgments of higher value, we have argued, depend on cognition of higher order organization. In this regard, the emotions of awe and compassion appear to reflect a sense both of one's limits and of one's wider connection (see Keltner & Haight, 2003; Neff, 2003; Youniss & Yates, 1999).[4]

Recent cognitive theorizing also indicates how narrative may serve a higher integrative role (Currie & Jureidini, 2004). In contrast to theory-like knowledge, narrative potentially serves to more intensely integrate cognition and emotion, self and others, across time and space. Theories of children's and adolescents' relationality to the transcendent human and divine (e.g., Fowler, 1981) emphasize the centrality of story. For the child and adolescent, stories embody, reconstruct, and link experience of multiple realities—the historically real, or immediate here and now; the possible, lying within a distant future; or the impossible, a playful experimentation with the present, past, or future. In these imagined milieus, either shared with others or confined to one's mind, stories and narrative constitute a cognitive-cultural workshop for spiritual development by exercising images of the self in relation to other agents, entities, and forces that transcend time, place, or reality.

Cognitively, narrative appears to serve an organizing function in the framing of reality, the construction of identity, and the integration of diverse elements. Drawing on the work of the Russian linguist and critic Mikhail Bakhtin, Miller et al. (2000) have described how speech genres provide "ways of seeing," framing the boundaries of reality and value. Habermas and Bluck (2000) have framed the development of identity in terms of cognitive capacities to generate personal life stories.

Insights and Illusions of Spiritual Thinking[5]

In one way or another, spiritual development rests on ordinary cognitive processes that naturally lead thinking beyond given appearances toward higher and deeper levels of reality and value. This stretching beyond the given is a source of enlightenment, empowerment, and unity as well as delusion, repression, and destruction. While it is critical to appreciate and nurture the potential of the human mind, it is equally important to recognize the risks of thought that ventures beyond the constraints of the knowable (see Chinn & Brewer, 2000). As Immanuel Kant (1997) originally indicated, in stretching beyond ordinary boundaries, the human mind is naturally prone to "transcendental illusions," just as it is prone to perceptual illusions. It is critical to consider both the insights and illusions, considering how spirit and knowledge, science and religion, reality and value can be integrated in development (see Piaget, 1972).

Consider, for example, the natural tendency of humans to represent and transmit supernatural concepts. Without some enlightened, scientific constraints, the domain of the spiritual risks becoming the domain of the illusory. Similar risks are evident in the human tendency toward essentialist thinking. Essentialist thinking appears to be a core mechanism that originally serves to help children imagine how apparently different kinds of things share an underlying unifying essence. Potentially such thinking serves an integrative function uniting human differences in a sense of shared humanity (all men and women are created equal). But essentialist thinking may be equally recruited to divide in-groups from out-groups (Silberman, 2003), marginalizing and devaluing certain kinds of people (deemed unclean, unblessed, or otherwise essentially different) (Mahalingham, 2003a, 2003b).

In conclusion, cognitive research leads us to believe that from early on human beings are naturally spiritual, as we are oriented toward expanding our sense of meaning and value in connecting ourselves to a wider reality, beyond the perceptually given. The challenge is to understand how this development is psychologically organized and culturally scaffolded in ways that are both valuable and true.[6]

NOTES

1. Recent cognitive science has well demonstrated that most of human thinking, religious and otherwise, is automatic, unreflective, and shallow (Boyer, 2001; Keil, 2003). Despite this fact, people live under an "illusion of depth," believing that they understand things that they do not (Keil, 2003). The challenge for spiritual development is to understand the motives, practices, and competencies that lead to greater insight and depth.

2. Huston Smith (2001), among others, has pointed out how a scientific worldview has contributed to ignoring dimensions of reality such as height and depth.

3. What personal sense, value, and meaning do children gain from practices such as first communion, confirmation, bar or bat mitzvah, or other ceremonies that mark coming of age? If public support for research on particular religious practices remains limited, evidence on these issues is likely to remain isolated, descriptive, and anecdotal.

4. Compassion, whether directed toward self or others, appears to be linked with the capacity to appreciate one's common humanity. Awe combines perceived vastness with a need for accommodation.

5. This subhead echoes Piaget's (1972) *Insights and Illusions of Philosophy*.

6. In seeking more reality, spiritual development includes deepening respect for the power and human limitations of the institutions of science and religion.

REFERENCES

Barrett, J. L. (2004). *Why would anyone believe in God?* Walnut Creek, CA: AltaMira Press.

Barrett, J. L., & Keil, F. C. (1996). Anthropomorphism and God concepts: Conceptualizing a non-natural entity. *Cognitive Psychology, 31,* 219–247.

Barrett, J. L., & Lawson, E. T. (2001). Ritual intuitions: Cognitive contributions to judgments of ritual efficacy. *Journal of Cognition and Culture, 2,* 183–201.

Barrett, J. L., & Nyhof, M. A. (2001). Spreading non-natural concepts: The role of intuitive conceptual structures in memory and transmission of cultural materials. *Journal of Cognition and Culture, 1,* 69–100.

Barrett, J. L., & Richert, R. A. (2003). Anthropomorphism or preparedness? Exploring children's God concepts. *Review of Religious Research, 44,* 300–312.

Benson, P. L. (2004). Emerging themes in research on adolescent spiritual and religious development. *Applied Developmental Science, 8,* 47–50.

Bering, J. M. (2003). Towards a cognitive theory of existential meaning. *New Ideas in Psychology, 21,* 101–120.

Bering, J. M., & Bjorklund, D. F. (2004). The natural emergence of reasoning about the afterlife as a developmental regularity. *Developmental Psychology, 40,* 217–233.

Berryman, J. (1991). *Godly play: A way of religious education.* San Francisco: Harper.

Boyatzis, C. J. (1997, April). *Body and soul: Children's understanding of a physical-spiritual distinction.* Poster session presented at the biennial meeting of the Society for Research in Child Development, Washington, DC.

Boyatzis, C. J. (2001). A critique of models of religious experience. *International Journal for the Psychology of Religion, 11,* 247–258.

Boyatzis, C. J. (in press). Religious and spiritual development in childhood. In R. Paloutzian & C. L. Park (Eds.), *The handbook of the psychology of religion.* New York: Guilford.

Boyatzis, C. J. (2004). The co-construction of spiritual meaning in parent-child communication. In

D. Ratcliff (Ed.), *Children's spirituality: Christian perspectives, research, and applications* (pp. 182–200). Eugene, OR: Wipf & Stock.

Boyatzis, C. J., & Janicki, D. (2003). Parent-child communication about religion: Survey and diary data on unilateral transmission and bi-directional reciprocity styles. *Review of Religious Research, 44*, 252–270.

Boyer, P. (1994). *The naturalness of religious ideas: A cognitive theory of religion.* Berkeley and Los Angeles: University of California Press.

Boyer, P. (2001). *Religion explained: The evolutionary origins of religious thought.* New York: Basic Books.

Boyer, P., & Walker, S. (2000). Intuitive ontology and cultural input in the acquisition of religious concepts. In K. S. Rosengren, C. N. Johnson, & P. L. Harris (Eds.), *Imagining the impossible: Magical, scientific, and religious thinking in children* (pp. 130–156). Cambridge, UK: Cambridge University Press.

Chinn, C. A., & Brewer, W. F. (2000). Knowledge change in response to data in science, religion, and magic. In K. S. Rosengren, C. N. Johnson, & P. L. Harris (Eds.), *Imagining the impossible: Magical, scientific, and religious thinking in children* (pp. 334–371). Cambridge, UK: Cambridge University Press.

Currie, G., & Jureidini, J. (2004). Narrative and coherence. *Mind and Language, 19*, 409–427.

DeLoache, J., & Gottlieb, A. (Eds.). (2000). *A world of babies: Imagined childcare guides for seven societies.* Cambridge, UK: Cambridge University Press.

Elkind, D. (1961). The child's conception of his religious denomination: I. The Jewish child. *Journal of Genetic Psychology, 99*, 209–225.

Elkind, D. (1963). The child's conception of his religious denomination: III. The Protestant child. *Journal of Genetic Psychology, 103*, 291–304.

Elkind, D. (1970). The origins of religion in the child. *Review of Religious Research, 12*, 35–42.

Evans, E. M. (2000). Beyond Scopes: Why creationism is here to stay. In K. S. Rosengren, C. N. Johnson, and P. L. Harris (Eds.), *Imagining the impossible: Magical, scientific, and religious thinking in children* (pp. 305–333). Cambridge, UK: Cambridge University Press.

Evans, E. M. (2001). Cognitive and contextual factors in the emergence of diverse belief systems: Creation versus evolution. *Cognitive Psychology, 42*, 217–266.

Flavell, J. H., Green, F. L., & Flavell, E. R. (1986). Development of knowledge about the appearance–reality distinction. *Monographs for the Society for Research in Child Development, 51*(1).

Fowler, J. (1981). *Stages of faith: The psychological quest for human meaning.* San Francisco: Harper.

Gelman, S. G. (2003). *The essential child.* New York: Oxford University Press.

Giminez, M., & Harris, P. (2001, April). *Understanding the impossible: Intimations of immortality and omniscience among young children.* Poster session presented at the biennial meeting of the Society of Research in Child Development.

Goldman, R. G. (1964). *Religious thinking from childhood to adolescence.* London: Routledge & Kegan Paul.

Habermas, T., & Bluck, S. (2000). Getting a life: The emergence of the life story in adolescence. *Psychological Bulletin, 126*, 748–769.

Haight, W. L. (2002). *African-American children at church. A sociocultural perspective.* Cambridge, UK: Cambridge University Press.

Harris, P. L. (2000a). On not falling down to earth: Children's metaphysical questions. In K. S. Rosengren, C. N. Johnson, & P. L. Harris (Eds.), *Imagining the impossible: Magical, scientific, and religious thinking in children* (pp. 157–178). Cambridge, UK: Cambridge University Press.

Harris, P. L. (2000b). *The work of the imagination.* Malden, MA: Blackwell.

Harris, P. L. (2002). What do children learn from testimony? In P. Carruthers, S. P. Stich, & M. Siegal (Eds.), *The cognitive basis of science.* Cambridge, UK: Cambridge University Press.

Hay, D., & Nye, R. (1998). *The spirit of the child.* London: HarperCollins.

Heller, D. (1986). *The children's God.* Chicago: University of Chicago Press.

Holmes, R. (2003). Value in nature and the nature of value. In A. Light & H. Rolston III (Eds.), *Environmental ethics. An anthology* (pp. 143–153). Malden, MA: Blackwell.

Hunt, H. T. (1995). *On the nature of consciousness.* New Haven, CT: Yale University Press.

Hyde, K. E. (1990). *Religion in childhood and adolescence: A comprehensive review of the research.* Birmingham, AL: Religious Education Press.

Jacob, L. (1999). *Identity's architect.* New York: Scribner.

Jacobs, M. (2003). *Transforming reality with ritual: Children's understanding of ritual grammar and causality.* Unpublished doctoral proposal, University of Pittsburgh, Pittsburgh, Pennsylvania.

James, W. (1990). *The varieties of religious experience.* New York: Vintage. (Original work published 1902)

Johnson, C. N. (2000). Putting different things together: The development of metaphysical thinking. In K. S. Rosengren, C. N. Johnson, & P. L. Harris (Eds.), *Imagining the impossible: Magical, scientific, and religious thinking in children* (pp. 179–211). Cambridge, UK: Cambridge University Press.

Johnson, C. N., & Nyhof, M. (2003, April). Children's conceptions of God: Cognitive themes and religious variations. Society for Research in Child Development. Preconference on Spiritual Development. Tampa, FL.

Johnson, M. C. (2000). The view from the Wuro: A guide to child rearing for Fulani parents. In J. DeLoache & A. Gottlieb (Eds.), *A world of babies: Imagined childcare guides for seven societies* (pp. 171–198). Cambridge, UK: Cambridge University Press.

Kahn, P. H., & Lourenco, O. (2002). Water, air, and earth: A developmental study in Portugal of environmental moral reasoning. *Environment and Behavior, 34*(4), 405–430.

Kant, I. (1997). *Critique of pure reason.* New York: St. Martin's Press. (Original work published in 1781).

Keil, F. (2003). Folkscience: Coarse interpretations of a complex reality. *Trends in Cognitive Science, 7*(8), 368–373.

Kelemen, D. (2004). Are children "intuitive theists"? Reasoning about purpose and design in nature. *Psychological Science, 15,* 295–301.

Keller, H. (1996). *The story of my life.* Mineola, NY: Dover.

Keltner, D., & Haight, J. (2003). Approaching awe, a moral, spiritual and aesthetic emotion. *Cognition and Emotion, 17*(2), 297–314.

Lawson, E. T., & McCauley, R. N. (1990). *Rethinking religion: Connecting cognition and culture.* Cambridge, UK: Cambridge University Press.

Mahalingham, R. (2003a). Essentialism, culture, and beliefs about gender among the aravanis of Tamil Nadu, India. *Sex Roles, 49,* 489–496.

Mahalingham, R. (2003b). Essentialism, culture, and power: Representations of social class. *Journal of Social Issues, 59,* 733–749.

Miller, P. J., & Goodnow, J. J. (1995). Cultural practices: Toward an integration of culture and development. In J. J. Goodnow, P. J. Miller, & F. Kessel (Eds.), *New Directions for Child Development:* No. 67. *Cultural practices as contexts of development* (pp. 5–16). San Francisco: Jossey-Bass.

Miller, P. J., Hengst, J., Alexander, K., & Sperry, L. L. (2000). Versions of personal storytelling/ versions of experience: Genres as tools for creating alternate realities. In K. S. Rosengren, C. N. Johnson, and P. L. Harris (Eds.), *Imagining the impossible: Magical, scientific, and religious thinking in children* (pp. 212–246). Cambridge, UK: Cambridge University Press.

Mithen, S. (1996). *The prehistory of the mind.* London: Thames & Hudson.

Neff, K. (2003). Self-compassion: An alternative conceptualization of a healthy attitude toward oneself. *Self and Identity, 2*(2), 85–101.

Nozick, R. (1981). *Philosophical explanations.* Cambridge, MA: Harvard University Press.

Nozick, R. (1990). *The examined life.* New York: Simon & Schuster.

Nussbaum, M. (2001). *Upheavals of thought. The intelligence of emotions.* Cambridge, UK: Cambridge University Press.

Piaget, J. (1929). *The child's conception of the world.* New York: Harcourt, Brace.

Piaget, J. (1972). *Insights and illusions of philosophy.* London: Routledge & Kegan Paul.

Pitts, V. P. (1976). Drawing the invisible: Children's conceptualization of God. *Character Potential, 8,* 12–24.

Prentice, N. M., Manosevitz, M., & Hubbs, L. (1978). Imaginary figures of early childhood: Santa Claus, Easter Bunny, and the Tooth Fairy. *American Journal of Orthopsychiatry, 48,* 618–628.

Rizzuto, A.-M. (1979). *The birth of the living God: A psychoanalytic study.* Chicago: University of Chicago Press.

Rogoff, B. (1990). *Apprenticeship in thinking.* New York: Oxford University Press.

Scarlett, W. G., & Perriello, L. (1991). The development of prayer in adolescence. In F. Oser & W. G. Scarlett (Eds.), *New directions for child development:* No. 52. *Religious development in childhood and adolescence* (pp. 63–76). San Francisco: Jossey-Bass.

Silberman, I. (2003). Spiritual role modeling: The teaching of meaning systems. *International Journal for the Psychology of Religion, 13,* 175–195.

Smith, H. (2001). *Why religion matters.* New York: HarperCollins.

Subbotsky, E. (1993). *Foundations of the mind: Children's understanding of reality.* Cambridge, MA: Harvard University Press.

Taylor, M. (1999). *Imaginary companions and the children who create them.* New York: Oxford University Press.

Taylor, M., & Carlson, S. (2000). The influence of religious beliefs on parental attitudes about children's fantasy behavior. In K. S. Rosengren, C. N. Johnson, & P. L. Harris (Eds.), *Imagining the impossible: Magical, scientific, and religious thinking in children* (pp. 247–268). Cambridge, UK: Cambridge University Press.

Turiel, E., & Neff, K. (2000). Religion, culture, and beliefs about reality in moral reasoning. In K. S. Rosengren, C. N. Johnson, and P. L. Harris (Eds.), *Imagining the impossible: Magical,* *scientific, and religious thinking in children* (pp. 269–304). Cambridge, UK: Cambridge University Press.

Vidal, F. (1994). *Piaget before Piaget.* Cambridge, MA: Harvard University Press.

Woolley, J. D. (1997). Thinking about fantasy: Are children fundamentally different thinkers and believers from adults? *Child Development, 68,* 991–1011.

Woolley, J. D. (2000). The development of beliefs about direct mental-physical causality in imagination, magic, and religion. In K. S. Rosengren, C. N. Johnson, & P. L. Harris (Eds.), *Imagining the impossible: Magical, scientific, and religious thinking in children.* (pp. 99–129). Cambridge, UK: Cambridge University Press.

Woolley, J. D., Boerger, E. A., & Markman, A. B. (2004). A visit from the Candy Witch: Factors influencing young children's belief in a novel fantastical being. *Developmental Science, 7,* 456–468.

Youniss, J., & Yates, M. (1999). Youth service and moral-civic identity: A case for everyday morality. *Educational Psychology Review, 11,* 361–377.

16

THE RELATIONSHIP BETWEEN MORAL AND SPIRITUAL DEVELOPMENT

LAWRENCE J. WALKER

KEVIN S. REIMER

Over a century ago, William James (1902), in his seminal and still significant *Varieties of Religious Experience*, explicated the interdependence between moral and spiritual development, arguing that authentic religious experience should be evidenced in mature moral functioning or what he called "the value of saintliness" (especially his Lectures XI-XV). Although James proffered additional criteria (immediate luminousness and philosophical reasonableness), his primary claim was that the authenticity of religious life should be judged on the basis of its results—its "moral helpfulness" (p. 18). While he acknowledged the potentially maladaptive aspects of expressed religiosity, he believed that, in general, religious experience is evinced by "the best things history has to show" (p. 259), and he devoted a significant portion of *Varieties* to an exploration of the range of moral virtues that are the practical extension of an authentic spirituality.

Although James argued convincingly that religious experience is accompanied by moral maturity (and he did present some anecdotal evidence in that regard), the field of moral psychology has generally disregarded or distorted the significance of religion and spirituality in moral functioning. This secular skew is revealed in the tendency either to disregard the importance of religion and spirituality in daily life or to focus on their negative manifestations. Strangely, the skew persists despite the now abundant findings that religious commitment and participation frequently emerge as positive contributors to quality-of-life indicators (Koenig, 1998).

Kohlberg's (1969, 1981, 1984) hugely influential work served to legitimize the study of moral development, setting the agenda for a generation of scholarship and practice. Unfortunately, Kohlberg (1967) perpetuated the secular skew within moral psychology and education with his claim that the moral and religious domains were independent of each other. Perhaps this claim was motivated by the perceived need to establish the scientific legitimacy of his enterprise in the tumultuous intellectual climate of the 1960s and 1970s, a period that embraced secular humanism. Kohlberg's context additionally reflected the

American doctrine of the strict separation of church and state, precluding religious "contamination" of school-based moral and character education programs. Interestingly, Kohlberg (1981) later softened his antagonistic stance toward religion and spirituality by postulating a quasi-mystical moral Stage 7 that was held to undergird Stage 6 principles of justice through appeals to metaethical and religious epistemologies and that served to answer the question, "Why be moral?" Despite this seemingly bold shift, the eventual retrenchment of Stage 6 from Kohlberg's scoring system and the ongoing difficulties in adducing empirical evidence for that stage (Colby & Kohlberg, 1987) meant that scholarly interest in the even more illusory Stage 7 waned completely. Nevertheless, the relationship between morality and spirituality, and the proper role of religion in moral/character education, remain contentious in the field (see, for example, the debate between Kunzman, 2003, and Nucci, 2003).

Controversy regarding the role of faith, religion, and spirituality within moral psychology is particularly surprising given their commonsensical interrelationships. For example, central to the teachings of all religious traditions are moral guidelines for living a good life and for interacting appropriately with others. Furthermore, the pervasiveness of morality in everyday life means that it will intersect with religious and spiritual concerns. Morality, properly understood, has both interpersonal and intrapsychic aspects. The interpersonal aspects of morality regulate our interactions, order our relationships, and adjudicate our conflicts, whereas the intrapsychic aspects reference our fundamental goals and values, lifestyle, and identity. (For an extended discussion of this definition of the moral domain, see Walker, 2003, 2004.) It is not difficult to appreciate that these domains are interconnected in complex ways. Not surprisingly, evidence is now beginning to emerge that indicates the significance of religion and spirituality in moral functioning and development. This chapter will provide an overview of recent research that explores the intersection between moral and spiritual development and will suggest some directions for further research in this area. First, we will review moral and spiritual issues in relation to

psychological functioning. We will then consider ordinary conceptions of moral and spiritual maturity in people's everyday understanding. Finally, we will present preliminary findings from a study that attempts to bridge these two domains of inquiry on the basis of goal systems in young adults working with the developmentally disabled in religious communities.

PSYCHOLOGICAL FUNCTIONING

One obvious issue is whether people reference religion or spirituality in their moral reasoning. Certainly, the common finding within the context of Kohlberg's model and measure (Colby & Kohlberg, 1987) is that people rarely express themes of spirituality in their responses to his hypothetical moral dilemmas (a classic dilemma being: "Should a man steal an overpriced drug in order to save the life of his dying wife?"). But this should not be unexpected given that such dilemmas are constructed on the basis of conflicting values that imply a societal morality (in contrast to the personal morality that is more at the core of many faith traditions). More important, Kohlberg's coding manual is almost completely bereft of criterion judgments that would allow the assessment of moral reasoning with spiritual connotations.

In contrast, Walker and his colleagues have found that religion and spirituality ordinarily loom large in the moral thinking of many people. However, the evidence comes from a different approach to moral reasoning, relying instead on recollections of significant real-life dilemmas from personal experience. Although these actual dilemmas have the obvious methodological challenge of being idiosyncratic, this approach has several advantages, including that it ensures participants regard the problem as a moral one, that it is relevant to their lives, and that it allows a more diverse range of considerations to be expressed regarding the issue. Particularly because of the latter reason, Walker has found that many people spontaneously invoke notions of religion, faith, and spirituality in handling their own real-life moral problems.

Walker, Pitts, Hennig, and Matsuba (1995) prompted a sample of adults to recall and discuss two real-life moral dilemmas from their own experience: a recent conflict along with the most difficult one they had ever confronted. A frequent theme in people's reported handling of these moral problems was their reliance on explicitly religious and spiritual values. The strength of the theme in this sample was somewhat surprising given that the participants were drawn from the Vancouver area, one of North America's most irreligious regions (with regular church attendance at around 5% of the population; Bibby, 1987). For some of these individuals, religious tradition simply provided a reasonably adequate and convenient system of morality. For others, however, their moral framework was firmly entrenched in their faith. Moral decisions were made on the basis of reading holy writings and discerning the relevance of their standards for the issue at hand, and through seeking divine guidance in prayer and meditation.

For these people, morality and spirituality were not really separate and distinct domains; rather their morality was governed and structured by their faith: the source of their values and goals, the resolution of conflicts, and the determination of appropriate social behaviors and interpersonal relationships were all based on religious beliefs and faith commitments. Blasi (1990), Fernhout (1989), and Kunzman (2003) have all similarly argued that morality may only acquire meaning for some people within the context of religion. The sophistication of participants' religious rationales for moral choices varied, ranging (in a developmental progression) from straightforward fear of eternal damnation or anticipation of heavenly rewards, to the importance of a shared faith community, and then to rather principled notions of agape love and forgiveness.

Thus, for many people, moral reasoning is imbued with religious and spiritual considerations. An alternate empirical approach in examining the potential significance of religion and spirituality in morality is through the analysis of the psychological functioning of moral exemplars. A noteworthy study in this regard is Colby and Damon's (1992) case study analysis of a small sample of people who were identified as leading lives of extraordinary moral commitment (based on the nominations of a panel of experts who had derived a set of criteria for

moral excellence). Colby and Damon's qualitative analysis suggested several important processes in the development and maintenance of moral exemplarity, but one process was particularly serendipitous and provocative: about 80% of their sample of exemplars clearly attributed the value commitments underlying their moral action to their religious faith. This was surprising since the nomination criteria formulated by the panel of experts included nothing that was explicitly religious or spiritual in nature. It is important to clarify that the religious affiliations (if any) of these moral exemplars and the substance of their faith both varied considerably, but Colby and Damon did offer the generalization that there was a common "intimation of transcendence: a faith in something above and beyond the self" (p. 311).

Colby and Damon's case study analysis has had obvious heuristic value for the field, but it is limited by its small and select sample, and the lack of both objective methodology and a comparison group. These limitations were addressed in a recent study by Matsuba and Walker (2004), who examined the psychological functioning of a sample of young adults who displayed extraordinary moral action. Participants were identified on the basis of their exemplary moral commitment to social service agencies. A comparison group of young adults was also recruited, matched on the basis of several demographic variables. These participants responded to a battery of questionnaires and were involved in a semistructured interview.

Among the various developmental and personality constructs tapped by these measures was faith development, which was examined in the context of the individual interview. The assessment of faith development was based on Fowler's (1981) stagelike theory. Faith development stages reflect people's processes of meaning making in life and their relatedness to a transcendent being or center; they are conceptually unrelated to either religiosity or religious affiliation. These stages of faith are Stage 1—*intuitive-projective*, Stage 2—*mythical-literal*, Stage 3—*synthetic-conventional*, Stage 4—*individuative-reflective*, Stage 5—*conjunctive*, and Stage 6—*universalizing*. If the exemplars' extraordinary prosocial actions reflect meaning-making values, then those values may form the core of a more complex framework of faith than would be evidenced among the comparison participants who do not have the same level of prosocial commitment.

This hypothesis was supported. Matsuba and Walker found that the young adults in their exemplar group attained a significantly higher level of faith development than did those in the comparison group, despite being closely matched on demographic variables. Beyond faith development, this study assessed several other aspects of psychological functioning, and a subsequent descriptive discriminant analysis was conducted to assess the relative contribution of each of these constructs to the discriminability of the exemplar and comparison groups. Among the other constructs assessed in this study and used in this analysis were personality traits, ego identity status, level of moral reasoning, and adult attachment dimensions. Each of these variables is seemingly relevant for moral action, and indeed all were found to contribute to the discriminant function; however, the variable that emerged as the strongest predictor of group membership was faith development. This finding strongly implies that spirituality and faith commitments can form a foundation for moral functioning.

The approach we have been discussing explores the relation between the moral and spiritual domains by examining the psychological functioning of actual moral exemplars and the religious reasoning of people as they deal with everyday moral problems. Another approach to understanding the relationship between morality and spirituality is to examine people's ordinary conceptions of meaning. Presumably, the evidence regarding people's psychological functioning and the evidence regarding their conceptual understandings will yield mutually informative and convergent depictions of the interrelation of morality and spirituality. It is to that evidence we now turn.

ORDINARY CONCEPTIONS

Perhaps some rationale should be provided as to why ordinary people's somewhat naive conceptions are important to an understanding of the relationships between the moral and spiritual

domains. First, ordinary conceptions of these domains are operative in everyday life and do impact individuals' attitudes and behavior, so it is important to appreciate people's understandings if we are to explain their psychological functioning. Second, people's ordinary conceptions can provide a check on the conceptual skewing inherent in philosophical perspectives. That is not to imply that laypeople's conceptions are necessarily veridical; indeed, they may be badly mistaken. But when there is some divergence between experts and laypeople or between theory and data, it calls for some accounting and alerts us to the possibility that our conceptual framework may be askew.

One study of people's ordinary conceptions by Walker et al. (1995) asked participants to identify two people whom they regarded as highly moral and to justify their nominations. These nominations were not constrained, so choices could be historical figures or someone known only personally. A content analysis of the various types of moral exemplars identified revealed not only the somewhat predictable categories of humanitarians (e.g., Mother Teresa), revolutionaries (e.g., Nelson Mandela), remarkable politicians (e.g., Abraham Lincoln), and social activists (e.g., Andrei Sakharov), but also a large number of people who were not public figures; rather they were simply family members and friends whose character was known intimately. After this category of family members and friends (42% of the nominations), however, the next most common category of moral exemplars (at 18%) was composed of a range of religious leaders and founders of religions (e.g., Jesus, Muhammad). This is perhaps surprising given the explicit instructions to participants to identify *moral* exemplars. It should also be noted that many other explicitly religious people who were identified as moral exemplars (e.g., Mother Teresa, Jean Vanier, Desmond Tutu, Thomas More, Martin Luther King Jr.) were classified in other categories based on participants' rationales for their nominations. Indeed, another content analysis was conducted of the characteristics that participants attributed to these moral exemplars in support of their nominations. Again, consistent with the previous findings, many moral exemplars were identified on the basis of their religious and spiritual attributes, implying that for many people the moral and spiritual domains are overlapping and interdependent.

Another empirical approach that more systematically assesses people's understanding of the moral, religious, and spiritual domains is to analyze their conceptions through the perspective of the five-factor model, which taps the fundamental dimensions of personality (Wiggins & Trapnell, 1997). There are, of course, many theoretical perspectives for analyzing personality, potentially accomplished at different levels (McAdams, 1995). In contemporary psychology, however, the five-factor model has emerged as the dominant framework in the understanding of personality. The model organizes personality traits in terms of five basic and ubiquitous factors: *extroversion, agreeableness, conscientiousness, emotional stability,* and *openness to experience.* Each factor represents a bipolar dimension (with both desirable and undesirable traits; e.g., emotional stability vs. neuroticism). The broad scope of these factors and the traits they entail allow for a comprehensive assessment of personality attributions.

People's implicit personality theory regarding functioning in the moral, religious, and spiritual domains was examined by Walker (1999), using the template of the five-factor model to uncover the similarities and contrasts in personality attributions. A sample of adults was prompted to generate the characteristics and attributes for three types of persons (a highly moral person, a highly religious one, and a highly spiritual one; presented in random order). These attributes, free-listed by participants, were then classified according to which personality factor each represented, using a computer program that matches text to a standard lexicon (derived by experts). This procedure yielded a personality profile for each type of exemplar in the three domains. These profiles were found to have some obvious similarities (indicating overlap in meaning), as well as some striking differences.

Prototypic exemplars in the moral domain were characterized primarily by positive personality traits, particularly those reflecting the classic dimensions of character, namely, conscientiousness and agreeableness. Attributions regarding conscientiousness were expressed largely in terms of traits associated with dependability and integrity, whereas attributions regarding agreeableness were expressed largely in terms of prosocial traits.

The personality of exemplars in the religious domain was characterized somewhat differently. Although conscientiousness was again frequently ascribed, in this case it was expressed more in terms of faithfulness, devotion, and commitment (rather than dependability and integrity). Religious exemplars were also characterized by agreeableness, not only the positive prosocial traits, but also by a substantial proportion of "disagreeable" negative traits (e.g., *authoritarian* and *self-righteous*). Finally, the personality of religious exemplars was also characterized by the negative traits associated with the openness-to-experience factor (e.g., *rigid* and *narrow-minded*).

The personality profile ascribed to exemplars in the spiritual domain was somewhat different from that ascribed to those in the religious domain, despite the shared meaning between the two domains. The personality of spiritual exemplars was described in terms of the positive traits associated with agreeableness and openness to experience, whereas the personality of religious exemplars was described with a significant proportion of negative traits on these two factors. In addition, exemplars in the spiritual domain were characterized by conscientiousness and both the positive and negative traits associated with the extroversion factor, that is, both extroversion (e.g., *joyful, leader, active*) and introversion (e.g., *humble, solitary, quiet*). Notably, the extroversion/introversion dimension is the least evaluative of the five personality factors (McCrae & John, 1992).

Walker's (1999) study indicates that there are remarkable similarities in people's understanding of functioning in the moral, religious, and spiritual domains, especially in terms of the positive aspects of conscientiousness and agreeableness. People also regard other aspects of personality as distinguishing these domains; witness the divergent depictions of the religious and spiritual exemplars on the openness-to-experience dimension, for example. We turn now to other empirical approaches that can further illuminate the nature of the relationship among these domains in people's ordinary conceptions.

One approach that suggests a way to compare these domains is prototype theory (Cantor & Mischel, 1979; Rosch, 1978), a slant on social cognition implying that mental categories are best represented in terms of examples or prototypes identifying the core of the category rather than definitional boundaries (the classical definition of concepts). Walker and Pitts (1998, Study 2) explored the relations in people's understanding among the moral, religious, and spiritual domains using the framework of prototype theory. In their study, the attributes of moral, religious, and spiritual exemplars (generated by participants in Walker's, 1999, study) were distilled into nonredundant descriptor lists for each (using standard judgment rules to group synonyms and delete idiosyncratic responses). Then, participants in Walker and Pitts's (1998) study were asked to rate the prototypicality (i.e., accuracy) of the attributes on each descriptor list in characterizing each type of exemplar.

The critical feature of these descriptor lists in this context was that, across the lists, some attributes were unique (appearing on only a single list), whereas others were shared between or among lists. Prototype theory holds that the pattern of participants' prototypicality ratings can inform our understanding of the relations among these domains. Each list had a sizable number of unique attributes (implying that the domains are not identical), as well as a sizable number of shared attributes (implying that the domains are not completely independent).

The pattern of participants' ratings of the unique and shared attributes suggested that these domains are somewhat related in people's conceptions, albeit in an asymmetrical pattern. For example, the unique attributes for the moral exemplar (e.g., *just*) received higher prototypicality ratings, on average, than did the attributes shared with the religious (e.g., *hard-working*) or spiritual (e.g., *accepting*) exemplar. This indicates that the core moral virtues are relatively independent of religious and spiritual ones; or, in other words, to be a highly moral person one need not manifest the characteristics that are regarded as central to religion and spirituality. In contrast, for both the religious and spiritual exemplars, their shared attributes (with the moral exemplar) received higher prototypicality

ratings than did their unique attributes (e.g., *traditional* for the religious exemplar and *peaceful* for the spiritual exemplar). This result indicates that some manifestation of moral character is indeed central to what it means to be a highly religious or spiritual person, reflecting the earlier observation that moral guidelines for living are a consistent feature of religious teachings and traditions. Finally, it was found that the shared attributes between the religious and spiritual exemplars (e.g., *dedicated*) received higher prototypicality ratings than did their unique attributes, indicating that these two domains are strongly related in people's understanding. Although the core meaning and content of these two domains are closely associated (Bergin, 1991), nuanced differences in psychological profiles have been shown (Walker, 1999). Hence, further research is warranted to clarify the relationships among these domains.

The asymmetrical relation between moral and religious domains has also been reported in a study by Nucci and Turiel (1993), who interviewed children and adolescents from different religious traditions regarding the alterability and generalizability of various moral actions (such as stealing and hitting) and of various religious practices (concerning, for example, the day of worship and dietary regulations). They found that moral guidelines were not simply reducible to religious ones in that participants consistently judged moral rules to be unalterable by religious authorities, not contingent on holy writings, and applicable to people who follow other religions. On the other hand, many religious rules were regarded as alterable by religious authorities and relative to one's own religion.

Another way to understand the relations among the moral, religious, and spiritual domains is to examine the attributes included on the descriptor lists themselves (from Walker & Pitts's, 1998, study) to identify predominant themes, but each list entailed over a hundred descriptors, which presents an immediate challenge in terms of deriving a sensible set of themes that has empirical validity. Thus, Walker and Pitts (1998, Study 3) conducted a subsequent study to discern the underlying dimensions in people's conceptions of these domains. Participants were asked to sort the most prototypic attributes for each of the moral, religious, and spiritual exemplars. This task simply prompted participants to group the attributes in the way that made best sense to them (with as few or as many groups and with as few or as many attributes per group as they thought appropriate). Data reduction using multidimensional scaling was used to discern the latent structure (or dimensions) underlying people's understanding of these three domains.

In the moral domain, two dimensions were found to best capture people's conceptions. The primary dimension (the one weighted more heavily) was labeled a *self–other* dimension wherein themes of agency were balanced by, or perhaps in tension with, themes of communion. This dimension was anchored at the "self" end by attributes reflecting personal agency in moral functioning and at the "other" end by attributes reflecting a moral focus on others. Some version of this dimension consistently arises as central in understandings of interpersonal functioning (Wiggins & Trapnell, 1997). The secondary dimension in the moral domain was labeled an *external–internal* dimension, referencing the tension between adherence to external moral standards and guidelines, on the one hand, and reliance on individual autonomy, internalized values, and conscience, on the other.

In the religious domain, the primary dimension was labeled a *divine–other* dimension, reflecting a vertical–horizontal tension or the dual obligation in religious life between a focus on the divine and a focus on sensitivity to others. The secondary dimension was a *devout–authoritarian* dimension, anchored at one end by attributes reflecting personal religiosity and at the other end by attributes reflecting various negative aspects of personality (as was found in Walker's, 1999, study, which pointed to the preponderance of undesirable traits on the agreeableness and openness-to-experience factors for the highly religious person).

In the spiritual domain, the primary dimension was labeled a *divine–inner* dimension reflecting an emphasis on the divine in contrast to an emphasis on inner awareness. Notably, it is this inner awareness that characterizes the spiritual exemplar but is largely lacking in the religious exemplar. The secondary dimension in the spiritual domain was labeled the *divine–other* dimension, interestingly the same as the primary

dimension in the religious domain and entailing the same contrasting range of attributes.

Scholars and researchers often struggle to distinguish appropriately the religious and spiritual domains because of their shared meaning and content. The findings of the studies discussed here suggest that, in people's ordinary conceptions, the spiritual domain is characterized more typically as some kind of personal affirmation of the transcendent whereas the religious domain is more commonly viewed as the creedal and ritual expression of spirituality associated with institutionalized religion, and an aspect of human functioning that perhaps is more prone to distortion and maladaptive expression.

SPIRITUALITY AND GOALS IN YOUNG ADULT MORAL EXEMPLARS

We have suggested that the relationship between morality and spirituality in development may be considered on the basis of psychological functioning along with people's ordinary (conceptual) understanding of prototypical behaviors and commitments. These two approaches imply a consistent (albeit asymmetrical) relationship between spiritual, religious, and moral domains. Along these lines, Emmons (1999) has argued that prosocial goals or strivings can serve as a kind of nexus for the intersection of psychological functioning, personality, and behavior. Goals reflect ultimate or ideological concerns potentially influential of moral commitment. One direction for research on the developmental intersection between morality and spirituality might include the manner by which personal goals are organized in the interest of sustained moral commitment.

Recently, Reimer and Walker (2004) examined the goal systems of exemplary young adults who care for developmentally disabled individuals in a residential community setting. The idea was to bridge an understanding of psychological functioning in morally exemplary individuals with ordinary conceptions of spirituality from prototype theory. For the study, exemplary moral commitment was considered through the lives of caregiver assistants in L'Arche communities. L'Arche is an international federation of more than 100 communities in 29 countries that cares for persons with developmental disabilities. Widely considered to be living altruists, L'Arche assistants are asked to live in community with the disabled, renouncing material possessions (Post, 2002; Reimer, 2004). In most American L'Arche communities, assistants conduct their work on very small stipends with little financial incentive or reward. Peace, nonviolence, and conflict mediation are emphasized in L'Arche through a detailed charter of community life. Assistants are encouraged to grow deeper in their knowledge and experience of God, supported in many communities by the presence of residential priests, therapists, and spiritual directors.

It is a distinct possibility that goal systems relevant to the psychological functioning of L'Arche assistants are ordered (or potentially reordered) around spiritual concepts influential of moral commitment. The nature and persistence of these changes likely influence assistant longevity, a major issue for L'Arche given attrition approaching 40% within the first year of service. The main purpose of the preliminary study reported here was to ascertain how spirituality might be implicated in the solidification of goals that potentially promote sustainable moral commitment. Of interest was the idiosyncratic organization of goals in L'Arche assistants and the manner by which spiritual concepts and ideology were emphasized in the goal systems of moral exemplars.

One way of considering the role of spirituality in moral goal organization involves the actual words used by caregiver assistants to describe the self and its relation to others. Reimer (2003) found that change associated with moral exemplarity in adolescents was evident where goals were affectively and cognitively reordered on the basis of social criteria. The personal significance of ordinary spiritual concepts is likely evident in the kind of language used by L'Arche assistants to describe themselves in the context of a particular other (such as God), along with the kinds of moral expectations internalized within that context. Indeed, Colby and Damon (1995) noted that for their exemplar sample, goal systems were altered on the basis of the manner by which exemplar selves incorporated the expectations of significant others. Assuming that change is

necessary for longevity in L'Arche, the manner of assistant self-reference in the spiritual domain, along with related affect and thought patterns, may reveal clues to developmental processes associated with moral goal organization.

Linguistic assessment of spiritual self-reference and expectations associated with moral goal organization can be accomplished with the use of a word-counting computer program. Pennebaker, Mehl, and Niederhoffer (2003) noted that personality variables dealing with social context are linked to word usage in participant narratives, accessible through the use of linguistic inquiry and word count analysis (LIWC; Pennebaker, Francis, & Booth, 2001). LIWC counts words in prespecified categories, creating a proportion of usage relative to the total words in participant responses. By specifying different word fields (e.g., self-reference through personal pronouns, affect, thought/cognition), LIWC can be used to explore developmental process associated with goal organization through assistant descriptions of the self and God, along with related moral expectations.

An allied strategy for evaluating how spirituality is reflected in moral goal systems involves the content of actual goals and their organization in cognition. Emmons (1999) notes that personal well-being may be related to the proportion of spiritual goals incorporated into people's goal systems. Yet this argument assumes that goals carry more or less spiritual content. In an overtly spiritual community such as L'Arche it is possible that even apparently mundane goals may be spiritually significant insofar as they contribute to an overall posture of care with the developmentally disabled. The philosophy of L'Arche upholds an "earthy spirituality" of the mundane so that superficially unspiritual concerns (e.g., getting enough sleep) are framed within a religious rubric in order to promote communities of holistic care. In the event that goals carry latent spiritual content or significance in L'Arche, we might consider the organization of assistant goal systems on the basis of how each goal is similar or dissimilar to the ordinary conceptions of spirituality outlined in Walker and Pitts (1998).

To deal with developmental implications of spirituality and moral goal systems, two L'Arche assistant sample groups were identified from American residential communities. The first group was formed on the basis of having 1 year (or less) of service within L'Arche. This group of 28 novice assistants averaged 27 years of age, and most were college educated with a number reporting graduate degrees. Through their recent exposure to L'Arche, novice assistants were presumed to be undergoing some kind of developmental change relative to the organization of a moral goal system. The second group was constructed with the criterion of having had 3 or more years of service within L'Arche communities. This group of 28 experienced assistants averaged 41 years of age, and again, the vast majority were well educated; some had professional experience and advanced degrees. In all probability, experienced assistants had already undergone change to their moral goal systems.

Study 1: Spirituality in Word Usage

The first study sought to explore developmental process associated with moral goal organization where the assistant referenced the self with God. It was hypothesized that the impact of spiritual concepts on moral goal organization would differ by sample group in terms of how assistants described the self with God and what moral expectations were perceived as being spiritually mandated for that individual's behavior. Assistants were given two questions as part of a larger semistructured interview. The first question pertained to self with God/divine ("What kind of person are you with God/divine?"). The second question extended this discussion, centering on perceived expectations of God/divine ("What kind of person does God/divine expect you to be?"). Responses to these questions were collated by sample group and analyzed using LIWC. LIWC was programmed to handle self and social reference through personal pronoun usage (e.g., *I, we, self, you*). Affect was considered on the basis of total emotion words, positive emotion words, positive feelings, optimism, negative emotions, anxiety, anger, and sadness. Thought processes (cognition) were evaluated on the basis of causality, insight, inhibition, tentativeness, and certainty. A complete lexicon of words associated with personal pronoun, affect,

and cognition fields in LIWC can be found in Pennebaker et al. (2001).

Word count proportions were compared between novice and experienced assistant groups for personal pronouns, affect, and cognition with the use of a transformation resulting in z scores. For the first interview question (self with God/divine), no significant differences were observed for personal pronoun usage between groups. However, negative-emotion words were significantly elevated in the responses of experienced assistants. Thought processes related to insight and tentativeness also differed significantly between groups where novice assistants scored higher than experienced assistants. The LIWC lexicon for the insight category included words such as *think, know,* and *consider.* Tentativeness related to words such as *maybe, perhaps,* and *guess.* For the second interview question (perceived moral expectations of God/divine), personal pronouns differed where experienced assistants used more "I" language and novices used more "we" language. Further, experienced assistants used significantly more positive emotion words, anger words, and words that generally related to feeling states than novice assistants.

These findings raise the curtain on a spectrum of individual and social processes that characterize spiritual influence on moral goal organization in L'Arche. First, when considering the self with God/divine, novice assistants were considerably more tentative in the language they used to describe spiritual experience, but also more insight oriented. This makes sense to the extent that young adults are reconciling personal identity with a growing wealth of experience. For novice assistants in L'Arche, powerful spiritual priorities in community life anticipate novel experiences of the divine interpreted more on the basis of concrete rather than abstract dimensions. Certainly, spiritual experience tends to follow a concrete–abstract articulation in development, noteworthy in the faith maturity work of Fowler (1981) and more recently in analyses of children's spiritual narratives (Reimer & Furrow, 2001). For many novice assistants, L'Arche may represent a fresh exposure to spiritual ideology that requires objectification and testing prior to incorporation into an overall goal system with moral objectives.

Second, experienced assistants tended to describe the self with God/divine using negative-emotion language. We can assume that experienced assistants have already undergone a process of goal system change around spiritual and moral concepts. Long-term commitment in L'Arche affirms the importance of the community to the coherence of spiritually oriented moral goals, but also implies collateral depression that may be a developmental artifact. For the perceived moral expectations of God/divine, significantly elevated use of "I" language by experienced assistants is consistent with clinical depression associated with recovery from conflict and trauma (Campbell & Pennebaker, 2003). Such an individualization of spiritual concerns around expectations of the divine suggests a high level of internalized responsibility with regard to prosocial and caring goals. By contrast, novices used significantly more "we" language associated with divine moral expectations, framing spiritual experiences around collective interests. This raises an interesting paradox in which the developmental literature reviewed in this chapter would suggest improved well-being when spiritual concepts are incorporated into people's moral goal systems. Why might this be?

It is possible that the reordering of moral goals around spiritual concerns is only sustainable where the exemplar is able to establish a level of autonomy sufficient to carve out an adaptive, prosocial niche within the community. Brewer and Roccas (2001) outline a theory of optimal distinctiveness patterned around group dynamics. In this theory, individuals form collective social identities based on the interplay of opposing drives of inclusion and differentiation. In powerfully collectivist communities such as L'Arche, high group emphasis on interpersonal intimacy may activate a need for individual uniqueness or distinctness. Novice assistants arrive with fairly individualistic perspectives but move into a period of renegotiation regarding the orientation of moral goals on the basis of the spiritual and collectivist philosophy of the community. In this renegotiation phase, obligations to the group are not yet absolute or reliable. In effect, novice assistants are "hedging bets" with regard to full inclusion in the L'Arche community, maintaining close relations with others outside of L'Arche, resulting in a diverse range of collective selves. With this diminished drive for inclusion comes diminished personal differentiation. By contrast, experienced assistants have bought into the collectivist value orientation of L'Arche. As a consequence, inclusion is achieved within the community, making other groups less significant for the definition of people's collective selves. One cost of maintaining this connection is a heightened need for differentiation, making the range of "optimal identity" a narrow one (Brewer & Roccas, 2001). Thus, the extent to which spirituality is implicated in helping to reorder moral goal systems in assistants relates to identification with the collectivist values of L'Arche, heightening both inclusion and differentiation. Depression may emerge as a developmental confederate in the reconciliation of collectivist spirituality with personal needs to establish and maintain a coherent moral goal system.

Finally, experienced assistants used words related to greater overall affect, positive emotions, and anger than did novice assistants. Reimer (2003) noted the importance of emotion in the process of change to goal systems associated with moral identity formation in adolescence. It may be that where assistants consider the moral import of divine expectations for the self, affect is involved in cementing a realigned goal system. Damasio (1994, 2002) has argued persuasively for somatic markers of affect regulation that are involved in moral reasoning and motivation. Future research should consider the extent to which moral goal systems are established and adaptively sustained where spirituality is experienced on the basis of an array of affect categories.

Study 2: Goal Systems and Prototypical Spiritual Meaning

The second study sought to compare L'Arche assistant goals to prototype descriptors reflecting ordinary conceptions of spirituality (Walker & Pitts, 1998). The objective of this study was to ascertain the organization of goal systems in assistants where the basis of categorization was spiritual. Put another way, this meant that all goals, regardless of explicitly spiritual content, would be considered in spiritual terms. This required a methodology capable of creating a mathematical basis for the comparison of meaning between goals identified by assistants and prototype descriptors. Latent semantic analysis (LSA) is both a knowledge representation theory and a computational method for the extraction of meaning from large text corpora (Laham, 1997; Landauer, Foltz, & Laham, 1998). LSA compares test language corpora to an 11-million-word library of knowledge taken from first-year collegiate readers. By using a matrix decomposition technique similar to factor analysis, LSA is able to compare target words, phrases, or paragraphs to generate an estimate of meaning similarity or dissimilarity (Landauer et al., 1998; Rehder, Schreiner, Wolfe, Laham, Landauer, & Kintsch, 1998). LSA does not make any use of word order; thus, syntax and morphology are not considered in meaning assessment. Instead, the model operates on the principle that the identification of the correct mathematical dimensionality for computerized analysis is analogous to the representation of meaning in human cognition (Landauer et al., 1998). Best known as an "artificial teaching assistant" through its commercial application of grading undergraduate essays, LSA has been successfully applied to unsupervised analysis of goal systems in adolescent moral exemplars and in outlining the social cognition of moral identity (Reimer, 2003; Reimer & Wade-Stein, 2004; details on the LSA computational method may be found at http://lsa .colorado.edu).

For the present study, novice and experienced L'Arche assistants were asked to outline 12–15 personal goals in order of greatest significance (Emmons, 1999). A total of 172 goals was identified from each sample group. The goals from each group were then compared to 98 spiritual prototype descriptors (adjectives) taken from Walker and Pitts (1998). Thus, LSA was used to assess similarity and dissimilarity between assistant goals using ordinary conceptions of spirituality as the basis for comparison. LSA covariance output data were then subjected to hierarchical cluster analysis to determine latent relations indicative of goal systems.

It should be noted that the identification of clusters is a subjective process, in this case

aided by the use of the percentage change in agglomeration schedule procedure (Hair, Anderson, Tatham, & Black, 1999). Using this method, a five-cluster solution was confirmed for novice assistant goals. The first cluster was termed *self-efficacy* (e.g., *ensure I am treated fairly, do my best,* and *do the right thing*). The second cluster was termed *openness* (e.g., *be open minded, make contact with others,* and *consider future directions*). The third cluster was named *differentiation* (e.g., *seek new experiences, be financially independent,* and *seek new relationships*). The fourth cluster was identified in terms of a *theory of mind* (e.g., *take care of people, look good in public,* and *be helpful in stressful situations*). The fifth cluster was noted in terms of *lifestyle* (e.g., *live simply, waste few resources,* and *eat less*).

Using the same procedure, a five-cluster solution was confirmed for experienced L'Arche assistants. The first cluster here was named *balance* (e.g., *find balance between work, prayer, and play,* and *practice patience*). The second cluster was understood in terms of *groundedness* (e.g., *make time to garden, keep in touch with friends,* and *find space to relax*). The third cluster was framed in terms of *self-care* (e.g., *take a nap, go for walks,* and *sit calmly for 20 minutes*). The fourth cluster was identified as *interpersonal responsibility* (e.g., *forgive others who hurt me, maintain good relationship with my staff,* and *give love to those I serve*). The fifth cluster was named *transcendence and ethics* (e.g., *look at stars, live in gratitude,* and *be a godly disciple*).

The clusters identified for each assistant sample group might be considered as goal systems organized on the basis of prototypical (ordinary) conceptions of spirituality. Several observations are pertinent to the goal systems identified in the study. First, when considered on prototypical spiritual meaning, novice assistants orient their goals toward tasks related to identity resolution, including the construction of an increasingly sophisticated theory of mind. As part of this process, novice goals are structured around the cultivation of an interpersonal ethic. Novice goals are powerfully social in orientation but, typical of early adulthood, are geared toward improved self-understanding in a growing range of diverse relationships. Following the personal pronoun findings in Study 1, it appears that novice goals emphasize getting along with others and renegotiating self-understanding amid the collectivist values of the L'Arche community. Novice goals imply a spirituality of action before contemplation, of relationships that reflect a considerable degree of collectivist idealism.

By contrast, experienced assistants evidence more introspective goal systems, demonstrating a marked capacity for self-reflection. Idealism for this group is tempered by recognition of personal limitations and the means by which spiritual insight is coupled with growth through difficult circumstances and situations. When taken as counterfactuals, experienced assistant goals reflect interpersonal and intrapsychic struggles consistent with the depressive and autonomy-oriented findings in Study 1. Clearly, goal systems between these two groups differ along developmental lines. In a general sense, moral functioning appears to be shaped by spirituality in terms of the means by which goals are reordered around caring concerns and in the organization of goal systems. The findings presented in this preliminary study are highly exploratory and suggestive of moral and spiritual interrelatedness within a unique context, that of L'Arche. Given the unique philosophy of L'Arche, it would be unwise to make broad generalizations regarding the nature of developmental convergence in the moral and spiritual domains. However, it is interesting to note that goal systems considered on the basis of prototypical meaning at least in part reflect the very language used by assistants to outline self-reference, affect, and cognition related to the divine. Future research on the relation between moral goals and ordinary conceptions of spirituality might consider the importance of social context and identification with groups or faith communities capable of promoting coherence for the moral self.

CONCLUSIONS

This chapter has explored some recent research regarding the interconnections between moral and spiritual development, domains that have been compartmentalized in our conceptual frameworks for understanding human development and functioning. It was found, for example, that faith and spirituality are apparently foundational for many people in their everyday processes of moral decision making and moral action. Other research, focusing instead on people's conceptions of these domains, revealed a complex pattern of understandings. Here, for example, it was found that different profiles of personality attributions were evident across domains and that different dimensions characterized people's structuring of the attributes in each domain. These personality attributions were generally positive, but some morally questionable aspects of functioning were noted, particularly in the religious domain. This is simply a reminder that most virtues can be distorted, become unbalanced, or taken to excess. One particularly informative set of findings was derived from the prototype-based research that indicated that the moral, religious, and spiritual domains are related, albeit asymmetrically. Moral excellence does not seem to require, at least in most people's understanding, the attributes that are central to religion and spirituality; but religious and spiritual excellence does seem to entail the moral virtues that are at the core of morality. In other words, it seems more probable that someone can be highly moral but irreligious than it is that someone can be authentically religious but characteristically immoral. Certainly this principle appears to be relevant to the work of exemplar assistants in L'Arche communities, particularly as people's goal systems are reordered around sustainable caring commitments framed by spiritual ideology.

The reader will have noticed that the bulk of the research reviewed in this chapter was conducted with samples that were late adolescent and older and that there was relatively little research with children. Simply put, this area of research is in its beginning stages, and although there is plenteous work on the moral development of children and also on the spiritual development of children, there is scant research on the relationships between these two domains in the earlier part of the life span. This area is primed for sustained conceptual and empirical attention.

Finally, it should be acknowledged that the research discussed here is situated in a particular cultural and historical context, and that the nature of the relations among the moral, religious, and spiritual domains may be variable across contexts, as suggested by the work of Shweder and his colleagues (1997) and Jensen (2004). Shweder and Jensen have proposed that there are three ethical frameworks: autonomy, community, and divinity. An ethic of autonomy references notions of individual freedom, well-being, harm, rights, and justice; an ethic of community references notions of duty, hierarchy, interdependence, and concern for the welfare of groups; and an ethic of divinity references notions of natural and sacred order, tradition (authority of holy writings), sin, sanctity, and purity. The three ethical frameworks entail highly diverse moral concepts and structure the relation between the moral and spiritual domains quite differently. The ethic of autonomy is most closely concordant with Western moral philosophy and best characterizes dominant moral thinking in America, but in other cultures there are different hierarchies of ethical frameworks. For example, as indicated by Jensen's (2004) review, in India it has been found that the ethics of community and divinity are much more prevalent. Other research reviewed by Jensen (2004) indicated that even within cultures there are significant differences among groups in the valuing and structuring of these ethics. As an example, for religious conservatives in America the ethic of divinity prevails as the moral framework. Thus, the hierarchical relationships among these ethical frameworks may be structured differently across various contexts. Jensen further proposed that the developmental patterns in the acquisition of the moral concepts inherent in the three ethics will also vary across cultures and groups. Future study of morality and spirituality in development must address the particularities of ethnicity, culture, and language in the interest of forging a more coherent and complete picture of maturity.

Through a review of some recent research, this chapter has explored the relationships between the domains of moral and spiritual development, picking up on William James's (1902) acute observations about the value of saintliness. His primary contention, adduced without the benefit of empirical data, was that authentic religious experience should be clearly evidenced in mature moral functioning. The findings reviewed in this chapter are largely consistent with James's claim of a close association between the domains, but have also revealed other complexities in their relationship, laying the foundation for further research on these domains that for too long have been compartmentalized in our understanding of human development.

REFERENCES

Bergin, A. E. (1991). Values and religious issues in psychotherapy and mental health. *American Psychologist, 46*, 394–403.

Bibby, R. (1987). *Fragmented gods: The poverty and potential of religion in Canada.* Toronto: Irwin.

Blasi, A. (1990). How should psychologists define morality? Or, the negative side effects of philosophy's influence on psychology. In T. Wren (Ed.), *The moral domain: Essays in the ongoing discussion between philosophy and the social sciences* (pp. 38–70). Cambridge, MA: MIT Press.

Brewer, M. B., & Roccas, S. (2001). Individual values, social identity, and optimal distinctiveness. In C. Sedikides & M. Brewer (Eds.), *Individual self, relational self, collective self* (pp. 219–240). London: Taylor and Francis.

Campbell, R. A., & Pennebaker, J. W. (2003). The secret life of pronouns: Flexibility in writing style and physical health. *Psychological Science, 14*, 256–262.

Cantor, N., & Mischel, W. (1979). Prototypes in person perception. In L. Berkowitz (Ed.), *Advances in experimental social psychology* (Vol. 12, pp. 3–52). New York: Academic Press.

Colby, A., & Damon, W. (1992). *Some do care: Contemporary lives of moral commitment.* New York: Free Press.

Colby, A., & Damon, W. (1995). The development of extraordinary moral commitment. In M. Killen & D. Hart (Eds.), *Morality in everyday life: Developmental perspectives* (pp. 343–369). Cambridge, UK: Cambridge University Press.

Colby, A., & Kohlberg, L. (1987). *The measurement of moral judgment* (Vols. 1–2). Cambridge, UK: Cambridge University Press.

Damasio, A. R. (1994). *Descartes' error: Emotion, reason, and the human brain.* New York: Putnam.

Damasio, A. R. (2002). A note on the neurobiology of emotions. In S. Post, L. Underwood, J. Schloss, & W. Hurlbut (Eds.), *Altruism and altruistic love: Science, philosophy, and religion in practice* (pp. 264–271). New York: Oxford University Press.

Emmons, R. A. (1999). *The psychology of ultimate concerns: Motivation and spirituality in personality.* New York: Guilford.

Fernhout, H. (1989). Moral education as grounded in faith. *Journal of Moral Education, 18,* 186–198.

Fowler, J. W. (1981). *Stages of faith: The psychology of human development and the quest for meaning.* San Francisco: Harper & Row.

Hair, J., Anderson, R., Tatham, R., & Black, W. (1999). *Multivariate data analysis* (5th ed.). Saddle River, NJ: Prentice-Hall.

James, W. (1902). *The varieties of religious experience.* New York and London: Longmans, Green.

Jensen, L. A. (2004). *Through two lenses: A cultural-developmental approach to moral psychology.* Manuscript submitted for publication.

Koenig, H. G. (Ed.). (1998). *Handbook of religion and mental health.* San Diego, CA: Academic Press.

Kohlberg, L. (1967). Moral and religious education and the public schools: A developmental view. In T. Sizer (Ed.), *Religion and public education* (pp. 164–183). Boston: Houghton Mifflin.

Kohlberg, L. (1969). Stage and sequence: The cognitive-developmental approach to socialization. In D. A. Goslin (Ed.), *Handbook of socialization theory and research* (pp. 347–480). Chicago: Rand McNally.

Kohlberg, L. (1981). *Essays on moral development: Vol. 1. The philosophy of moral development.* San Francisco: Harper & Row.

Kohlberg, L. (1984). *Essays on moral development: Vol. 2. The psychology of moral development.* San Francisco: Harper & Row.

Kunzman, R. (2003). Religion, ethics, and the implications for moral education: A critique of Nucci's *Morality and religious rules. Journal of Moral Education, 32,* 251–261.

Laham, D. (1997). Latent semantic analysis approaches to categorization. In M. Shafto & P. Langley (Eds.), *Proceedings of the 19th Annual Conference of the Cognitive Science Society* (p. 979). Hillsdale, NJ: Erlbaum.

Landauer, T. K., Foltz, P. W., & Laham, D. (1998). An introduction to latent semantic analysis. *Discourse Processes, 25,* 259–284.

Matsuba, M. K., & Walker, L. J. (2004). Extraordinary moral commitment: Young adults working for social organizations. *Journal of Personality, 72,* 413–436.

McAdams, D. P. (1995). What do we know when we know a person? *Journal of Personality, 63,* 365–396.

McCrae, R. R., & John, O. P. (1992). An introduction to the five-factor model and its applications. *Journal of Personality, 60,* 175–215.

Nucci, L. (2003). Morality, religion and public education in pluralist democracies: A reply to Kunzman. *Journal of Moral Education, 32,* 263–270.

Nucci, L., & Turiel, E. (1993). God's word, religious rules, and their relation to Christian and Jewish children's concepts of morality. *Child Development, 64,* 1475–1491.

Pennebaker, J. W., Francis, M. E., & Booth, R. J. (2001). *Linguistic inquiry and word count (LIWC).* Mahwah, NJ: Erlbaum.

Pennebaker, J. W., Mehl, M. R., & Niederhoffer, K. G. (2003). Psychological aspects of natural language use: Our words, our selves. *Annual Review of Psychology, 54,* 547–577.

Post, S. G. (2002). The tradition of agape. In S. Post, L. Underwood, J. Schloss, & W. Hurlbut (Eds.), *Altruism and altruistic love: Science, philosophy, and religion in dialogue* (pp. 51–64). New York: Oxford University Press.

Rehder, B., Schreiner, M. E., Wolfe, M. B. W., Laham, D., Landauer, T. K., & Kintsch, W. (1998). Using latent semantic analysis to assess knowledge: Some technical considerations. *Discourse Processes, 25,* 337–354.

Reimer, K. S. (2003). Committed to caring: Transformation in adolescent moral identity. *Applied Developmental Science, 7,* 129–137.

Reimer, K. S. (2004). Natural character: Psychological realism for the downwardly mobile. *Theology and Science, 2,* 89–105.

Reimer, K. S., & Furrow, J. F. (2001). A qualitative exploration of relational consciousness in Christian children. *International Journal of Children's Spirituality, 6,* 5–32.

Reimer, K. S., & Wade-Stein, D. (2004). Moral identity in adolescence: Self and other in semantic space. *Identity, 4,* 229–249.

Reimer, K. S., & Walker, L. J. (2004, March). Altruistic love and spirituality in L'Arche assistants for the developmentally disabled. In L. R. Sherrod (Chair), *Youth religiosity and participation in community service.* Symposium conducted at the meeting of the Society for Research on Adolescence, Baltimore.

Rosch, E. (1978). Principles of categorization. In E. Rosch & B. B. Lloyd (Eds.), *Cognition and categorization* (pp. 27–48). Hillsdale, NJ: Erlbaum.

Shweder, R. A., Much, N. C., Mahapatra, M., & Park, L. (1997). The "big three" of morality (autonomy, community, divinity) and the "big three" explanations of suffering. In A. Brandt & P. Rozin (Eds.), *Morality and health* (pp. 119–169). New York: Routledge.

Walker, L. J. (1999). The perceived personality of moral exemplars. *Journal of Moral Education, 28,* 145–162.

Walker, L. J. (2003). Morality, religion, spirituality: The value of saintliness. *Journal of Moral Education, 32,* 373–384.

Walker, L. J. (2004). What does moral functioning entail? In T. A. Thorkildsen & H. J. Walberg (Eds.), *Nurturing morality* (pp. 3–17). New York: Kluwer Academic/Plenum.

Walker, L. J., & Pitts, R. C. (1998). Naturalistic conceptions of moral maturity. *Developmental Psychology, 34,* 403–419.

Walker, L. J., Pitts, R. C., Hennig, K. H., & Matsuba, M. K. (1995). Reasoning about morality and real-life moral problems. In M. Killen & D. Hart (Eds.), *Morality in everyday life: Developmental perspectives* (pp. 371–407). Cambridge, UK: Cambridge University Press.

Wiggins, J. S., & Trapnell, P. D. (1997). Personality structure: The return of the Big Five. In R. Hogan, J. Johnson, & S. Briggs (Eds.), *Handbook of personality psychology* (pp. 737–765). San Diego, CA: Academic Press.

17

THE RELATIONSHIP BETWEEN SPIRITUAL DEVELOPMENT AND CIVIC DEVELOPMENT

THOMAS M. DONNELLY

M. KYLE MATSUBA

DANIEL HART

ROBERT ATKINS

Fundamental to our notion of spirituality is the belief that those who possess this quality view the world differently than those who lack it. It is no easy task to define precisely what makes the spiritual perspective unique, a point to which we return in the next section. It suffices for our purposes here to note that spirituality usually connotes a belief in a transcendent force or a divine entity, the possession of which transforms the understanding of the material world, relationships, values, and institutions. One theme of this handbook is the examination of the effects of spirituality on the acquisition and interpretation of a variety of social concepts.

In this chapter, we take up the intertwining of spirituality with civic development, focusing particularly on the interrelations of these two streams in adolescence. Our goal is to explicate the bidirectional influences between spirituality, on the one hand, and civic behavior and civic attitudes, on the other. For the most part, these influences are positive; however, as we shall elucidate, spiritual development can proceed independently of civic development and can, in fact, detract from it. We begin by exploring some definitional issues, then present a conceptual model of the relation of spiritual development to civic development, and, finally, review lines of research appropriate to the model.

DEFINITIONAL ISSUES

As previous reviewers have noted (e.g., Benson, 2004; King & Boyatzis, 2004), defining

AUTHORS' NOTE: The support of the W. T. Grant Foundation is gratefully acknowledged.

spiritual development is complicated by the elusiveness of the essence of spirituality. William James, America's greatest psychologist, attempted to delineate human experience and devoted considerable effort to understanding the boundaries of spirituality, or what he called religious experience. James suggested that religious experience is constituted of "the feelings, acts, and experiences of individual men in their solitude, so far as they apprehend themselves to stand in relation to whatever they may consider the divine" (1902, pp. 31–32). This definition captures much of what is meant by the notion of spirituality, as most descriptions seem to incorporate connections between the self and "something greater" than the self (see, e.g., King & Boyatzis, 2004). Assuming that these connotations of spirituality track to some extent the essence of the notion, spiritual development is consequently the processes through which this belief in the transcendent is acquired, and the manifestations of this belief in emotion, behavior, and experience. It should be noted in advance, however, that even the broad definition offered by James fails to incorporate all experiences that have been attributed to spirituality. Consequently, our review will necessarily exclude several threads of spiritual development believed important by some.

Spiritual development often occurs in the context of religions, which King and Boyatzis (2004) describe as "cumulative, organized traditions of beliefs, practices, symbols, and polity" (p. 3). Throughout the world, families send their children to religious institutions—churches, mosques, and so on—to receive instruction in spiritual matters and to be initiated into communities that share beliefs concerning the nature of the divine. Unsurprisingly, research has demonstrated that participation in religious communities can deepen spirituality. For example, Wink and Dillon (2002) found that religiosity (e.g., church attendance) in early adulthood predicted the depth of spirituality (e.g., connection with a sacred other) in older age.

However, spiritual development can occur outside traditional religious contexts. A belief in the divine can be acquired or deepened as a result of a vast array of experiences with the physical and social worlds. For example, profoundly beautiful natural sites occasion spiritual

responses among many, as can witnessing genuinely altruistic behavior of individuals. Consequently, spirituality and religiosity are different notions, a fact noted by psychologists (e.g., James, 1902) and by lay individuals (Walker & Pitts, 1998).

In the context of this chapter, the concept of "civic" may be best represented as "civic commitment," referring to adolescents' personal goal of contributing to their country and society (Flanagan, Bowes, Jonsson, Csapo, & Sheblanova, 1998), or as civic engagement (Andolina, Jenkins, Keeter, & Zukin, 2002). The advantage of such a broad definition is that it captures related constructs such as political volunteering (Rosenthal, Feiring, & Lewis, 1998), voting (Walker, 2002), the work of care exemplars (Hart & Fegley, 1995), volunteering (Atkins, Hart, & Donnelly, 2004), and community service (Youniss, Yates, & Su, 1997). In each case, the youth in these studies are contributing in some way to the society of which they are members.

The relationship between spirituality and civic engagement is partly understood through what researchers call social capital. Social capital is a characteristic of social organizations that describes the social networks, social trust, and norms that support individuals in their efforts to work for the mutual benefit of the community. It is an indispensable resource of civil society, and as Smidt (2003) suggested, "the importance of social capital is tied to its capacity to bind together autonomous individuals into communal relationships" (p. 5). Just as financial capital (money and other monetary assets) and human capital (one's available time, effort, and physical ability) can help individuals be productive and succeed in a variety of life areas, social capital is also considered a resource on which the individual can draw to accomplish goals.

We have organized this chapter on the relationship between spirituality and the civic engagement of youth (primarily in the United States) using the model shown in Figure 17.1. According to this framework, spirituality is connected to civic engagement through two pathways. First, as depicted on the left side of the model, spirituality and civic engagement may be connected through involvement in organized religion. As we noted in the previous section,

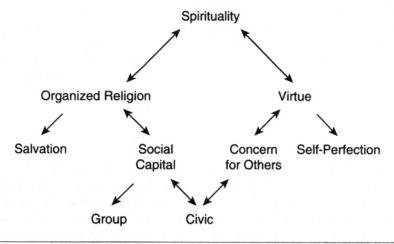

Figure 17.1   Pathways Between Spirituality and Civic Engagement

while spirituality and religiosity are conceptually independent, religious institutions are frequently important in the facilitation of spiritual development. Moreover, immersion in organized religion may be guided (or dictated) by the youth's family (Ellison & Sherkat, 1993). As we shall describe, participation in organized religion generates social capital, and youth with higher levels of religious participation are more likely to become civically engaged as a result of this resource. Depending on the cultural and religious context, increased social capital and religious involvement could also lead to focusing efforts mostly on one's own group, rather than on involvement in the broader community.

Second, as shown on the right side of the model, spirituality can also be connected to civic engagement without direct mediation by religious institutions. As William James noted, profound spirituality, or saintliness, can be organized by "abstract moral ideals, civic or patriotic utopias, or inner visions of holiness," which can be "felt as the true lords and enlargers of our life" (1902, p. 267). Obviously, those for whom "civic utopias" organize their beliefs in the divine are likely to become deeply involved in civic life. More generally, James suggested that all forms of transcendent beliefs produce change in personality, with this change potentially evident in the qualities of asceticism, purity, strength of soul, and charity (1902, pp. 267–268). To the extent that spirituality leads to changes in asceticism, purity, and

strength of soul, we postulate little connection to civic development as these qualities pertain more to self-perfection than they do connection to the social world. This outcome is portrayed on the right side of the model, in which virtue may lead the individual in the direction of self-perfection. On the other hand, if spirituality leads to greater charity—as an individual transcends the self—the needs of others may become more apparent, and a realization of one's obligations to others may become more prominent. This increase in civic attitude can be manifested in civic engagement, such as volunteering. This pathway is also depicted on the right side of the model.

Finally, as indicated in the framework depicted in Figure 17.1, there is some evidence to suggest that the relationship of spirituality to civic engagement is bidirectional (because the evidence for these upward pathways is limited, they are depicted with a different type of arrow). Civic engagement can lead one to an increased concern for others (moving up the right path in the model), possibly by providing experiences in caring for others that may produce a deepening of empathy. This concern for others can lead to virtue and affect one's moral values, which in turn can lead one to higher levels of spirituality. Civic engagement allows for greater socialization with others in the community and can therefore lead to an increase in social capital. This increased level of social capital might lead to an increase in involvement in organized religion, and potentially higher levels of spirituality, because one's newfound social connections may encourage closer ties with religious associations.

PATHWAYS FROM SPIRITUALITY TO CIVIC ENGAGEMENT

Religion and Community Service

One commonly applied measure of civic engagement is community service. Numerous studies have demonstrated a positive relationship between religion and community service. Some of the best-known work in this area comes from Youniss and his colleagues. In a study of high school seniors, Youniss, McLellan, and Yates (1999) found that students who believed religion to be important were nearly three times more likely to perform community service compared to students who did not value religion. This study is limited by two factors. First, only one measure of religion was used to assess the salience of religion in the students' lives. Second, it is still not clear whether religion leads to community service or community service leads to religion.

These limitations were addressed in a study conducted by Donnelly, Hart, Youniss, and Atkins (in preparation) that uses the National Educational Longitudinal Survey (NELS) to investigate the relationship between religion and community service. In these analyses, the community service participation rates of three groups of young adults were compared—those who had done no community service as seniors in high school, those who had done community service outside the context of religious organizations as seniors in high school, and those who had done community service within the context of religious institutions as seniors in high school. After controlling for a range of demographic variables (e.g., gender, ethnicity, family composition, SES, and religious affiliation), the authors found that high school seniors who did community service in the context of religious institutions were 33% more likely to perform community service as young adults than high school seniors who did community service outside the context of a religious institution and 64% more likely to perform community service

as young adults than high school seniors who did no community service. These results provide some support for the assertion that youth involved with religious institutions may be more likely to become civically engaged adults.

Further support for the idea that religion influences community service work comes from analyses of the National Longitudinal Survey of Youth—Child Sample data. Hart and Atkins (2004) compared preadolescents who reported weekly religious participation to preadolescents who reported no religious participation. After controlling for personality, family environment, academic achievement, and club and team memberships, they found that preadolescents who reported weekly religious participation were three times more likely than those who reported no religious participation to be involved in community service 2 years later (Hart & Atkins, 2004).

Together these results lend substantial support to the conjecture that religion, as captured in a diversity of ways, influences future community service participation. What is less clear, however, is how this comes about: How is religion influencing people to perform service? One possibility offered by Youniss, McLellan, et al. (1999) takes an Eriksonian approach. They suggested that religious organizations offer youth a "transcendent system" that provides an ideological base from which youth can derive principles for action. These principles serve as guides for current behavior as well as future, ideal actions, much of which involve community service work. Another way in which religion may influence participation in community service is through social capital. Hart and Atkins (2004) argue that adolescents' religious participation can lead to increased and deeper relationships with peers and adults, and these relationships can become avenues for recruitment into service.

Religion as a Civic Training Ground

For those growing up within a religious community, such an organization may serve an important purpose in leading individuals to community service work. In addition to providing an ideological context, churches, mosques, and temples provide the learning grounds to practice the activities and skills of civic engagement (Flanagan, 2003). These activities include community service work such as participating in soup kitchens and tutoring children in after-school programs; however, members of faith communities may also lead Bible studies, make public announcements to the congregation, and write weekly newsletters. As Smith (2003) aptly noted, these skills are transferable to other domains:

> The community and leadership capacities that American youth learn in religious congregations may serve youth equally well throughout their lives in study groups, student government, sports, neighborhood organizing, political activism, professional activities, business ventures, civic involvement, and beyond. (p. 23)

Moreover, these skills are vitally important to civic engagement. For example, Verba, Schlozman, and Brady (1995) found that civic skills were significantly associated with civic participation. Therefore, religious organizations provide opportunities to participate in civic activities and through these activities practice skills that will be useful in future community service work.

Religion and Civic Orientation

In addition to acting as an incubator for civic engagement through service, religious affiliation may also influence the civic orientation of youth. For example, in a study of 300 students enrolled in private schools in Washington, DC, and the San Francisco Bay areas, Crystal and DeBell (2002) found a significant association between the extent to which participants valued their religion and civic orientation. Religious valuation predicted students' sense of effectiveness regarding their community service activities and their endorsement of values associated with good citizenship. This finding is important in suggesting that youth with more positive civic attitudes may be more likely to become civically engaged as adults than youth with less positive civic attitudes.

Why are youth with stronger connections to faith communities more likely to have a stronger civic orientation than those with weaker connections to faith communities? Crystal and

DeBell (2002) reasoned that at least three factors present in religious settings contribute to this answer. First, youth with stronger connections to faith communities are more likely to be socialized to participate in associational life. Second, issues of public concern are often discussed and requests for volunteers are often made in places of worship. And finally, faith communities often promote values indispensable to civic involvement, such as charity. Sullivan and Transue (1999) argued that a fundamental element of a democratic community is that citizens share certain attitudes and values regarding democratic principles. In the case of faith communities, similarity in values that prescribe community service-oriented attitudes and work may be important in facilitating civic engagement.

Religion and Social Capital

Finally, in understanding the connection between religion and community service, one needs to consider religion as a source of social capital, especially in light of the fact that in countries such as the United States, religion generates more social capital than any other institution (Coleman, 2003). There is evidence to suggest that social networks, a facet of social capital, are associated with increased civic engagement of youth. For example, Yates and Youniss (1998) examined essays from alumni of an urban Catholic school who had participated in a yearlong service-learning course. They found that the students' social network influenced their likelihood to volunteer after high school. Compared to alumni who were not volunteering, alumni who were volunteering indicated that a higher percentage of their families and friends were currently volunteering. In sum, there is evidence that the civic orientation of youth is enhanced through access to social capital. Unfortunately, there is evidence to suggest that stores of social capital are dwindling and in danger of not being replenished (see Putnam, 2000). Furthermore, some studies have found that young people have less trust in the political system than previous generations and are not gaining in trust (Putnam, 2000). These two trends may contribute to an explanation for why some youth do not feel a sense of obligation to participate in the civic community (Bennett & Bennett, 1990).

In the face of these trends, religious institutions may be able to help make up for the declines in social capital in society. A growing body of work suggests that religious participation increases the amount of social capital available to youth. In a study of nearly 1,400 students at a public high school in a large metropolitan area, King and Furrow (2004) found that youth reporting regular religious participation had access to higher levels of social capital (e.g., frequency of social interactions, trusting relationships, and shared values with others) than their less religious counterparts. Moreover, social capital served as a mediator between religion and altruism. Religious organizations provide communities of supportive trusting relationships between people who share the same values, and this facilitates a more civic-minded orientation.

Although the research presented in the preceding sections provides clear evidence that religion and spirituality play an important role in facilitating civic engagement, the processes underlying this connection are still unclear. Based on preliminary data and conjectures, many religious organizations provide a set of shared core values that are civic-oriented, such as charity and compassion. This is especially important for youth during the period of identity exploration. In addition, these values are prescriptive in calling them to action and providing opportunities for them to get involved in service work. Finally, these actions are often accomplished by youth with the help of a supportive community of "like-minded" individuals who serve as resources in encouraging and sustaining the youth in their work over time.

Religion and Politics

Flanagan and Faison (2001) draw a clear distinction between the concepts of *civic* and *political*. For them, civic has a broader meaning and is associated with membership within the polity. Political has a narrower meaning, which is encompassed by civic and is associated with the affairs of the state or government. Walker (2002) highlights differing pathways by which youth may become involved politically.

Traditional political engagement includes involvement with governmental institutions through voting, lobbying, political party membership and service, and running for elected positions. There are also alternative forms of involvement such as participation in civil rights and political protests. In this section we explore the ways in which youth are politically engaged, and the role religion and spirituality plays in this form of engagement.

Religion and Voting. One of the most common ways in which older youth can be politically involved within democratic societies is through voting. Although voter turnout is generally lower among youth in the United States (McLeod, 2000) and Canada (Pammett, 1991) relative to other age cohorts, some researchers have found that religious individuals are more likely to vote than less religious individuals (Taylor & Thornton, 1993; Verba et al., 1995). Few researchers have examined the influence of religious participation during childhood and adolescence on adult voting patterns. However, the results of our analyses on the NELS data set suggest that, after controlling for demographic variables, youth who had higher levels of religious involvement as high school seniors were more likely to vote 8 years later. This finding suggests that religious institutions do have a role in promoting voting among youth.

Religion and Protest Participation. An alternate form of political involvement is engaging in protests. Results from studies by Sherkat and Blocker (1994, 1997) suggested that religion does influence protest participation among youth. Sherkat and Blocker used a socialization model as a framework to explain protest participation, focusing on the role that parents and religious institutions play. These institutions influence the likelihood of activism by providing an ideological orientation that is supportive of or opposed to a particular protest movement. Drawing on data from the Youth–Parent Socialization Panel Study, Sherkat and Blocker collected information on high school students during the 1960s, dividing students into those who were actively involved in protest movements (i.e., antiwar, student, civic rights movements), and those who were not. They also assessed students on measures of religious socialization, which included the frequency of church attendance and beliefs regarding the Bible. In addition, the researchers separated groups into specific denominations (conservative Protestants, Catholics, and Jews). Sherkat and Blocker reported that there were significant differences between the protesters and nonprotesters. The nonprotesters were more likely to be conservative Protestants who held strong biblical beliefs. In contrast, the protesters were more likely to be Catholic or Jewish, and did not hold as strong biblical beliefs. Overall, these results are important in illustrating that religion may contribute to the socialization of youth toward specific forms of civic engagement.

Finally, depending on their historical and current context, some religious institutions are reluctant to become involved in the political realm. For example, during the first few decades following World War II, Italian Catholic Church leaders discouraged civic engagement by members (Putnam, 1993). Putnam found that the Catholic Church had a privileged political position in Italian society and feared that involvement by Catholics in political issues might endanger this status. Hence, the influence of religion on youth political involvement needs to be understood within the particular cultural and historical context.

Based on the research reviewed thus far, a substantive case can be made that religious and spiritual experiences among youth influence their level of involvement in various forms of civic engagement. While there is plenty of evidence in support of this connection, less is known about the underlying processes of how this happens. The reviewed research does provide evidence to speculate on the possible pathways. Religious institutions are important avenues by which youth develop an ideological basis that will help guide their attitudes and behaviors. Moreover, these organizations provide opportunities to engage in behaviors consistent with the ideological beliefs of the institution, as well as a supportive community. Interestingly, these pathways seem to be the same whether the outcome is community service or protest movements.

Spirituality and Community Service

While spirituality and religion can lead to civic engagement in the ways we have discussed, spirituality, apart from organized religion, can also lead one to increased virtue (down the right path of the model depicted in Figure 17.1). By *virtue* we mean a motivation to follow a set of ethical and spiritual principles that may lead one to (a) become more concerned with the needs of others and/or (b) seek out self-perfection.

Spirituality and Concern for Others. There is some empirical evidence that links spirituality to civic engagement outside organized religion. One study conducted by Hart and Fegley (1995) explored the relationship between adolescent care exemplars, youth nominated for their involvement in their community, and how they defined their selves in semantic space. Hart and Fegley found that these extremely compassionate and civically engaged youth were more likely than matched controls to be connected to their moral principles and to a transcended self. Similarly, Matsuba and Walker (2004) studied the life narratives of a group of young adult moral exemplars. These moral exemplars were youth who had been involved with numerous social organizations and were nominated as moral exemplars. In comparison to more typical youth, the moral exemplars were more likely to mention empowerment themes when recounting past significant episodes in their lives. In addition, the moral exemplars' life narratives were found to show a greater ideological depth relative to the comparison group. Finally, for both groups of participants, their past transcendent experiences were positively correlated with the depth of their current ideological beliefs. This finding suggests that their transcendent experiences may have helped shape their ideological beliefs. Such an interpretation is consistent with the findings from Youniss, McLellan, Su, and Yates (1999) and Youniss, McLellan, et al. (1999) that suggested that religious or spiritual experiences may be important in shaping youths' ideological beliefs, which may orient them toward community service work.

There is some evidence that spirituality may contribute to youth thriving separately from religiosity. Dowling et al. (2004) analyzed a sample of 1,000 youth in order to examine the contribution of religiosity (e.g., the role of faith in one's life) and spirituality (e.g., orientation to do good and toward helping others rather than oneself) on thriving (e.g., presence of a moral compass and having personal values). Using structural equation modeling for cross-sectional data, they found evidence for unique effects of spirituality and religiosity on thriving. Although their study did not employ longitudinal data, their analysis suggests a need to examine religiosity and spirituality as separate constructs in that each has a substantial and different effect on thriving.

While the studies reviewed here have been described in terms of how spirituality, apart from organized religion, can influence civic engagement, it is not clear whether spirituality influences civic identity, or civic identity influences spirituality. However, later we consider the former directional influence.

Spirituality and Self-Perfection. The growing popularity of spiritual practices and activities such as meditation, yoga, chanting, and tai chi suggests that many individuals are interested in optimizing their spiritual potential in an effort to achieve self-betterment, which often includes a concern for world peace and the environment (Mickleburgh, 2004). Although most of these spiritual practices originate from ancient religious or philosophical traditions, practitioners often do not follow or identify with these traditions in any great depth. For the most part, this area of spiritual development remains relatively unexplored. In addition, the influence of spirituality on self-perfection is of peripheral concern here.

PATHWAYS FROM CIVIC ENGAGEMENT TO SPIRITUALITY

Civic engagement can be a catalyst for an increase in one's spirituality. For example, through volunteering, an individual may become more aware of social problems, may develop a greater empathy with those in need of help, and may feel connected with other volunteers. This awareness and connection to others may compel an individual to transcend the self and adopt moral and ethical principles that emphasize concern for others, which can lead to increased spirituality. While a large body of evidence exists demonstrating the influence of religion and spirituality on civic development, as previously discussed, there is less evidence suggesting that civic engagement can lead to increased spirituality.

Community Service and Spirituality

To begin with, there have been a few studies reporting a relationship between community service and the virtue of compassion as measured by the concern for others. For instance, Astin, Sax, and Avalos (1999) collected survey data from more than 12,000 undergraduate participants during freshman and senior years, and another follow-up survey four years after college. They found that the frequency of community service during college predicted volunteering and increased civic attitudes and values 4 years after college. This study provides some evidence that performing community service in college can lead to an increase in concern for others, which in turn may lead to volunteering after graduation. In another study, Hamilton and Fenzel (1988) analyzed data from 44 adolescents who participated in youth volunteer projects in New York. They examined pretest and posttest scores on a social responsibility scale and found an increase in virtue after participation in the volunteer project, suggesting that civic engagement can lead to increased concern for others.

Other studies have reported a link between community service and measures of spirituality. Serow and Dreyden (1990) examined survey data on 965 undergraduates collected at one time point. They found a positive association between community service participation and both spirituality and the value placed on community service. Although that study cannot determine whether community service participation is the cause or the effect of one's values, our review suggests that each influences the other. Further, Hofer (1999) analyzed data on 76 German adolescents, half volunteers and half matched controls (nonvolunteers). Transcendence scores were calculated from responses to fictitious scenarios. They found that the volunteers had higher transcendence scores and were more likely to be classified into a higher stage of identity development. Inasmuch as one's identity status and transcendence score reflect higher levels of spirituality, this study suggests that there is a positive relationship between civic engagement and spirituality, although again it is not clear in this study whether civic engagement is influencing spirituality, or vice versa.

Youniss, McLellan, Su, et al. (1999) took advantage of the Monitoring the Future data set, which measured high school seniors on community service and religion. They hypothesized that community service would predict religiosity. Controlling for a number of demographic factors, the frequency of community service was found to be a significant predictor of religious attendance, as well as the importance of religion in respondents' lives. However, the design of this study does not allow one to determine the directionality of influence.

To further explore this topic, we analyzed the NELS data to determine the extent to which volunteering in high school influences future religious service attendance 8 years after high school while controlling for gender, ethnicity, family composition, SES, religious orientation, and church attendance in high school. Based on a sample of 5,789 participants, we found that adolescent volunteering was a significant, although weak ($\beta = 0.044$), predictor of the frequency of adult religious service attendance in days per month. Based on this analysis, those who volunteer as adolescents are predicted to attend church services in young adulthood about 4 days a year more than those who did not volunteer in high school. Therefore, because this a longitudinal study, this result provides some support for the contention that community service impacts one's future spiritual development broadly defined, but further study in this area is needed.

Service-Learning and Transcendence

When high school and college students perform community service as part of a course, it is called service-learning. The idea behind this type of course is that pairing service with formal reflection and discussion of that service can increase civic knowledge, as well as civic values. Giles and Eyler (1994) examined survey data from 72 undergraduates taking a community service laboratory. Data were collected at the beginning of the class, midway in the semester, and at the end of performing community service. Many of the students stated that the service changed their perceptions to a more positive view of the recipients of the service. In addition, participating in the community service lab increased the students' commitment to performing service the next semester. Although there is no direct evidence, the analyses imply that this increase in community service commitment was in part due to an increase in participants' concern for others.

Yates and Youniss (1998) analyzed data from high school juniors in an urban Catholic school participating in a yearlong religious course on social justice that included performing community service (at a soup kitchen) and reflecting on the service. The students' essays and discussions suggested that the course stimulated their reflection on social problems and instilled a sense of responsibility to their community. Their reflections on service and commitment to future service deepened over the yearlong course (Yates & Youniss, 1996; Youniss and Yates, 1997), suggesting that civic engagement in combination with active reflection and discussion within an ideological framework may lead to a deepening morality and spirituality. When another set of essays from alumni of the same high school were examined, several themes were prominent, including an awakening to social problems, having made contact with people from different backgrounds, feeling a sense of responsibility for others, and the ability to think critically about political and moral questions.

Conrad and Hedin (1982) examined the effects of service-learning courses on a variety of outcomes. They found that service-learning adolescents showed an increase in their sense of civic competence and performance, and in social efficacy and sense of duty, while the control groups showed no change in these civic attitudes and values. Conrad and Hedin suggested that "changes in behavior often precede rather than follow changes in attitude." (p. 66).

In another study, Leming (2001) analyzed surveys and essays on ethical dilemmas from three groups of high school seniors: those in a community service program with a structured ethical reasoning component, those in a community service program with a limited reflection component, and those not involved in community service. Leming found that both community service groups had increased feelings of social responsibility within their schools and were more likely to indicate a commitment to future service than the control group based on the survey data; however, he also found that students in the structured ethical reasoning group were higher in being aware of ethical issues and were more likely to accept responsibility for an ethical issue than the other two groups based on the scores on the ethical dilemma essays. This study suggests that community service participation, regardless of the context of structured reflection, can lead to increased commitment toward the community, but it also suggests that service in the context of a structured reflection course may be most effective in increasing moral reasoning skills.

Unfortunately, little is known about the underlying processes that move youth to develop spiritually. For some individuals, the opportunities to be actively involved in community service may result in their developing perspectives beyond the self, thereby realizing that they can be a part of something larger, whether it is a religious, social, or spiritual movement. Further research is needed in this area.

Protest Participation and Religion

While Sherkat and Blocker's (1994) study of protest participation focused on events happening in the 1960s in the United States, more recent published work has considered youth protests in the Middle East. Unlike many Western nations in which only a minority of youth are ever involved in protest movements (Cairns, 1996), in Gaza and the West Bank a majority of youth were involved in Palestinian intifada (the Arabic word for *uprising*) experiences from 1987 to 1993. Underlying the political tension in this region is the religious tension between Islam and Judaism.

Barber (1999, 2001) has been studying Palestinian youth from the intifada for the past decade. As part of his research, Barber (2001) considered the association between youth involvement in the intifada and their integration within different social contexts, including religion. To explore this relationship, Barber tapped into the Palestinian Family Study data set that surveyed students in ninth grade in the West Bank, East Jerusalem, and the Gaza Strip on a wide range of topics. Included in the measure were questions on their experience in the intifada, as well as reflections on their participation and victimization experienced in the movement. In addition, youth were assessed on their level of integration into their respective religious institutions through items such as perceived religiosity, religious behavior, and salience of religion in their lives. Through structural equation analyses, Barber found a positive association between youths' reported retrospective intifada experience and their current reported religious integration. That is, for youth, participation in the intifada may lead to greater affiliation with the Muslim faith. Moreover, religious integration was found to serve as a buffer between the intifada experience and antisocial behavior. Hence, for some Palestinian youth, it appears that involvement in protest is leading them to draw closer to their religion. Although the study was cross-sectional with one data collection, youth who participated in the intifada did so prior to the study; thus, participation information was attained through retrospective self-reports.

CONCLUSIONS AND FUTURE RESEARCH

Overall, the current research presented provides evidence suggesting a bidirectional influence of spirituality and civic engagement. A sufficiently large number of research papers have reported results demonstrating a positive relationship between spirituality/religiosity and positive outcome measures including civic engagement, such that there is a growing confidence that this is a robust finding. Moreover, as our model suggests, there are at least two pathways connecting spirituality and civic engagement. Along one path, people's spirituality develops within the context of an organized religious tradition. Here a substantial amount of research shows that increased involvement in organized religion can increase one's civic skills and strengthen one's social capital. In turn, these increases can lead to the greater likelihood of becoming involved in civic activities, the development of new civic skills, and a greater receptivity to remaining active in the community.

Less research has charted the right-hand path depicted in Figure 17.1. Nevertheless, the little research that we were able to uncover suggests that increased spirituality can lead to a number of positive outcomes that include a deepening of beliefs and moral commitments. This spiritual and moral growth allows one to think beyond the immediate and beyond the self, which may lead to more civic engagement.

Our review also found evidence that participation in community service may influence spiritual development. Service often challenges youths' current perspectives and encourages them to think more broadly and feel more deeply about others in the world. This shifting in perspective can aid adolescents in their identity development by encouraging them to ponder spiritual or religious issues.

Research on the relationship between civic engagement and spirituality is generally positive. There are some examples in which religions have played an important role in suppressing forms of civic engagement such as protest movements. These pieces of research are reminders of the importance of taking into account the cultural and historical context when studying the complex and dynamic relationship between spiritual and civic development.

Some limitations to the research reviewed should be noted. Most studies have been on Western societies and with Christian-Judeo religions. Therefore, the results reported here may not parallel results in Eastern religions and indigenous cultures. Also, many studies have focused on religion rather than spirituality and on civic engagement rather than the development of one's civic identity and involvement. While some of the research supports the notion that increased spirituality leads to increased civic engagement, and vice versa, the mechanism for this bidirectional influence has not been fully explicated. As a result, many exciting avenues of research remain to be explored pertaining to the relationship between civic and spiritual development.

REFERENCES

Andolina, M. W., Jenkins, K., Keeter, S., & Zukin, C. (2002). Searching for the meaning of youth civic engagement: Notes from the field. *Applied Developmental Science, 6,* 189–195.

Astin, A. W., Sax, L. J., & Avalos, J. (1999). Long-term effects of volunteerism during the undergraduate years. *Review of Higher Education, 22,* 187–202.

Atkins, R., Hart, D., & Donnelly, T. M. (2004). *The association of childhood personality type with volunteering during adolescence.* Manuscript submitted for publication.

Barber, B. K. (1999). Political violence, family relations, and Palestinian youth functioning. *Journal of Adolescent Research, 14,* 206–230.

Barber, B. K. (2001). Political violence, social integration, and youth functioning: Palestinian youth from the intifada. *Journal of Community Psychology, 29,* 259–280.

Bennett, L. L. M., & Bennett, S. E. (1990). *Living with Leviathan.* Lawrence: University Press of Kansas.

Benson, P. L. (2004). Emerging themes in research on adolescent spiritual and religious development. *Applied Developmental Science, 8,* 47–50.

Cairns, E. (1996). *Children and political violence.* Cambridge, UK: Blackwell.

Coleman, J. A. (2003). Religious social capital: Its nature, social location, and limits. In C. Smidt (Ed.), *Religion as social capital: Producing the common good.* Waco, TX: Baylor University Press.

Conrad, D., & Hedin, D. (1982). The impact of experiential education on adolescent development. In D. Conrad & D. Hedin (Eds.), Youth participation and experiential education [Special issue]. *Child and Youth Services, 4,* 57–76.

Crystal, D. S., & DeBell, M. (2002). Sources of civic orientation among American youth: Trust, religious valuation, and attributions of responsibility. *Political Psychology, 23,* 113–132.

Donnelly, T. M., Hart, D., Youniss, J., & Atkins, R. (2004). *Factors in adolescence that promote civic engagement in young adulthood.* Manuscript submitted for publication.

Donnelly, T. M., Hart, D., Youniss, J., & Atkins, R. (in preparation). *Adolescent volunteering in a religious context predicts adult community service.*

Dowling, E. M., Gestsdottir, S., Anderson, P. M., Eye, A. v., Almerigi, J., & Lerner, R. M. (2004). Structural relations among spirituality, religiosity, and thriving in adolescence. *Applied Developmental Science, 8,* 7–16.

Ellison, C. G., & Sherkat, D. E. (1993). Obedience and autonomy: Religion and parental values reconsidered. *Journal for the Scientific Study of Religion, 32,* 313–329.

Flanagan, C. (2003). Trust, identity, and civic hope. *Applied Developmental Science, 7,* 165–171.

Flanagan, C. A., Bowes, J. M., Jonsson, B., Csapo, B., & Sheblanova, E. (1998). Ties that bind: Correlates of adolescents' civic commitments in seven countries. *Journal of Social Issues, 54,* 457–475.

Flanagan, C., & Faison, N. (2001). Youth civic development: Implications of research for social policy and programs. *Social Policy Report, 15*(1).

Giles, D. E., & Eyler, J. (1994). The impact of a college community service laboratory on students' personal, social, and cognitive outcomes. *Journal of Adolescence, 17,* 327–339.

Hamilton, S. F., & Fenzel, L. M. (1988). The impact of volunteer experience on adolescent social development: Evidence of program effects. *Journal of Adolescent Research, 3,* 65–68.

Hart, D., & Atkins, R. (2004). Religious participation and the development of moral identity in adolescence. In T. Thorkildsen, J. Manning, & H. Walberg (Eds.), *Nurturing morality* (pp. 157–172). New York: Kluwer.

Hart, D., & Fegley, S. (1995). Prosocial behavior and caring in adolescence: Relations to self-understanding and social judgment. *Child Development, 66,* 1346–1359.

Hofer, M. (1999). Community service and social cognitive development in German adolescents. In M. Yates & J. Youniss (Eds.), *Roots of civic identity: International perspectives on community service and activism in youth.* Cambridge, UK: Cambridge University Press.

James, W. (1902). *The varieties of religious experience.* New York: Random House.

King, P. E., & Boyatzis, C. J. (2004). Exploring adolescent spiritual and religious development: Current and future theoretical and empirical perspectives. *Applied Developmental Science, 8,* 2–6.

King, P. E., & Furrow, J. L. (2004). Religion as a resource for positive youth development: Religion, social capital, and moral outcomes. *Developmental Psychology, 40,* 703–713.

Leming, J. S. (2001). Integrating a structured ethical reflection curriculum into high school community service experiences: Impact on students' sociomoral development. *Adolescence, 36,* 33–45.

Matsuba, M. K., & Walker, L. J. (2004). *Young adult moral exemplars: The making of self through stories.* Manuscript submitted for publication.

McLeod, J. M. (2000). Media and civic socialization of youth. *Journal of Adolescent Health, 27,* 45–51.

Mickleburgh, R. (2004, April 19). First and foremost, a spiritual leader. *Globe and Mail,* p. A4.

Pammett, J. H. (1991). Voting turnout in Canada. In H. Bakvis (Ed.), *Voter turnout in Canada: Vol. 15* (pp. 33–60). Toronto: Dundurn Press.

Putnam, R. D. (1993). *Making democracy work: Civic traditions in modern Italy.* Princeton, NJ: Princeton University Press.

Putnam, R. D. (2000). *Bowling alone: The collapse and revival of American community.* New York: Simon & Schuster.

Rosenthal, S., Feiring, C., & Lewis, M. (1998). Political volunteering from late adolescence to young adulthood: Patterns and predictions. *Journal of Social Issues, 54,* 477–493.

Serow, R. C., and Dreyden, J. I. (1990). Community service among college and university students: Individual and institutional relationships. *Adolescence, 25,* 553–567.

Sherkat, D. E., & Blocker, T. J. (1994). The political development of sixties' activists: Identifying the influence of class, gender, and socialization on protest participation. *Social Forces, 72,* 821–842.

Sherkat, D. E., & Blocker, T. J. (1997). Explaining the political and personal consequences of protest. *Social Forces, 75,* 1049–1076.

Smidt, C. (2003). Introduction. In C. Smidt (Ed.), *Religion as social capital: Producing the common good.* Waco, TX: Baylor University Press.

Smith, C. (2003). Theorizing religious effects among American adolescents. *Journal for the Scientific Study of Religion, 42,* 17–30.

Sullivan, J., & Transue, J. (1999). The psychological underpinnings of democracy: A selective review of research on political tolerance, interpersonal trust, and social capital. *Annual Review of Psychology, 50,* 625–650.

Taylor, R. J., & Thornton, M. C. (1993). Demographic and religious correlates of voting behavior. In J. S. Jackson, L. M. Chatters, and R. J. Taylor (Eds.), *Aging in Black America.* London: Sage.

Verba, S., Schlozman, K. L., & Brady, H. E. (1995). *Voice and equality: Civic voluntarism in American politics.* Cambridge, MA: Harvard University Press.

Walker, T. (2002). Service as a pathway to political participation: What research tells us. *Applied Developmental Science, 6,* 183–188.

Walker, L. J., & Pitts, R. C. (1998). Naturalistic conceptions of moral maturity. *Developmental Psychology, 34,* 403–419.

Wink, P., & Dillon, M. (2002). Religiousness, spirituality, and psychosocial functioning in late adulthood: Findings from a longitudinal study. *Psychology and Aging, 18,* 916–924.

Yates, M., & Youniss, J. (1996). A developmental Perspective on community service in adolescence. *Social Development, 5,* 85–112.

Yates, M., & Youniss, J. (1998). Community service and political identity development in adolescence. *Journal of Social Issues, 54,* 495–512.

Youniss, J., McLellan, J. A., Su, Y., & Yates, M. (1999). The role of community service in identity development: Normative, unconventional, and deviant orientations. *Journal of Adolescent Research, 2,* 248–261.

Youniss, J., McLellan, J. A., & Yates, M. (1999). Religion, community service, and identity in American youth. *Journal of Adolescence, 22,* 243–253.

Youniss, J., & Yates, M. (1997). *Community service and social responsibility in youth.* Chicago: University of Chicago Press.

Youniss, J., Yates, M., & Su, Y. (1997). Social integration: Community service and marijuana use in high school seniors. *Journal of Adolescent Research, 12,* 245–262.

18

THE RELATION BETWEEN SPIRITUAL DEVELOPMENT AND IDENTITY PROCESSES

JANICE L. TEMPLETON

JACQUELYNNE S. ECCLES

In this chapter we take a journey that weaves together spiritual development and identity processes. First, we explore what is known about identity and how we define a spiritual identity. Then, we discuss spiritual identity development as a universal human experience. Next, we examine the developmental processes underlying spiritual identity development. Finally, we suggest future research options related to spiritual identity development.

BACKGROUND ISSUES

Collective and Personal Identity Distinction

Like several other identity theorists (e.g., Tajfel, 1981; Turner, Hogg, Oakes, Reicher, & Wetherell, 1987), we believe the self system contains both collective and personal identities. Collective identity refers to that part of an individual's self-concept that derives from his or her knowledge of and attitudes toward membership in a social group coupled with the value and emotional significance attached to that membership. Unlike personal identities, which distinguish a person from other individuals, collective identities are that part of the collective self that defines the individual in terms of shared similarities with members of certain social groups. Collective identities include those that are socially ascribed (race and gender), as well as those that emanate from group memberships of choice. Different collective identities may vary in salience over time and as a function of various social situations.

All people have multiple collective and personal identities to which they are committed; the salience of these identities may differ across contexts and situations (Brewer, 1991; Deaux & Martin, 2003; Ethier & Deaux, 1994). In addition, identities may manifest in the form of social roles such as student, friend, son/ daughter, and leader, as well as more individual or group characteristics (Goffman, 1959; Oyserman & Markus, 1998). Finally, Ashmore, Deaux, and McLaughlin-Volpe (2004) believe both personal and collective identities include a cognitive component (e.g., beliefs, ideological positions, and stereotypic traits shared by members of the category), an affective component (e.g., value, importance, perceived value of others, commitment and closeness to members of the category), and a behavioral component (e.g., religious service attendance for a religious identity).

Whether a particular identity is personal or collective depends on its function to the individual. Personal identities are those identity components or characteristics people believe are more unique to themselves rather than shared with a group. In contrast, a collective identity (similar to the social psychological concept of social identity) is shared by a group of people with some characteristic(s) in common, for example, native language, country of origin, or religion (Ashmore et al., 2004; Côté, 1996). It includes category membership, shared beliefs, perceived closeness to other members of the group, and behavioral enactments such as meeting attendance.

Based on this distinction, we define a religious identity as a collective identity. Religion is defined as "an organized system of beliefs, practices, rituals and symbols designed (a) to facilitate closeness to the sacred or transcendent (God, higher power or ultimate truth/reality) and (b) to foster an understanding of one's relationship and responsibility to others living together in a community" (Koenig, McCullough, & Larson, 2001, p. 18). Individuals with a religious identity believe they are members of a religious group; their identity can vary in terms of their acceptance of belief systems, and their endorsement of the importance of religious values, commitment to the religious group, and practices associated with the religion.

In contrast, we define a spiritual identity as a personal identity because it consists of spiritual characteristics unique to the individual rather than shared with a group and because a spiritual identity is not associated directly with feelings of belonging to a valued religious group. Thus, based on this distinction, a particular identity could be either religious or spiritual or both.

For example, being Muslim can be either a collective identity or a personal identity, depending upon the function of being Muslim for the individual. If the identity function is primarily associated with being a member of the Islamic community, then being Muslim is a collective identity. On the other hand, if the identity function is not about group membership, but about characteristics unique to the individual, and based on thoughtful commitment to the tenets of this faith, then being Muslim is a personal identity. Creating this conceptual distinction between personal and collective identity allows us to explore the different functions a spiritual identity serves for the individual.

Religiousness as a Collective Identity

Often when people hear the word *spirituality,* religion comes to mind. Because perceived membership in a religious group, a collective religious identity, can be a powerful contextual influence on spiritual identity development, let's take a closer look at what we know about collective identities. One's perceived membership in a social group may be based on assigned or chosen characteristics (Grotevant, 1992). Race, national origin, and gender are examples of assigned characteristics because they are components of identity over which individuals have little choice, but around which they must construct meaning (Grotevant, 1992). On the other hand, chosen collective identity components arise from choices afforded in the social context of the individual, such as being a member of a football team or a political party.

Where does a religious identity fall on the spectrum of *assigned* versus *chosen?* This is not an easy question to answer. A young child growing up in an actively practicing Catholic family is likely to develop a Catholic identity without any reflection or conscious commitment. Such a religious identity is closer to an assigned than a chosen collective identity. The line between a chosen and assigned religious identity becomes more blurred in adolescence, however. For example, imagine an adolescent who is given the freedom and opportunity to explore outside of his or her familial religious tradition and in the end chooses to become a member of a different religious community (e.g., Methodist). This adolescent's religious identity is closer to the chosen end of the continuum. In contrast, imagine an adolescent who does not explore alternate religious belief systems or who does, but then does not change his childhood religious affiliation. Is his collective religious identity still assigned? If it is chosen, at what developmental point did the change from assigned to chosen take place? Does it become chosen at a developmental turning point, such as when the individual is free to choose whether or not she attends religious services? Even when the individual is allowed to make a choice not to attend religious services, are the social norms regarding religion in the family and community so strong that the individual's identity continues to be more assigned than chosen? Or has the individual simply internalized the prescriptive belief system? Eriksonian theory suggests that a conscious evaluation of, and subsequent commitment to, the religious group is key to the distinction between assigned versus chosen collective identities.

Spirituality as a Personal Identity

Clearly, having a collective religious identity is one possible pathway to a spiritual identity, but it is not the only pathway. We conceive of a spiritual identity as a chosen personal identity that may or may not include collective identity components. We define spiritual identity as a personal identity that mirrors the individual's personal reflection about the role of spirituality in her or his life.

Other researchers suggest that many people distinguish between spirituality and religiosity in similar terms in that people emphasize the personal and chosen nature of a spiritual identity in contrast to the group membership nature of a religious identity. For example, in Mattis (2000) African American women described spirituality as an "internalization and consistent expression of key values" and religiousness as "an individual's embrace of prescribed beliefs and ritual practices related to God" (p. 114). Religious values and practices were described as the means to achieve spirituality. "Spirituality was variously conceptualized as one's relationship with God, self and/or transcendent forces, including nature" (p. 115). O'Brien (1996) described spirituality as an "enduring and integrating core" providing the foundation to

answer questions such as "Who am I?" "Where did I come from?" "What is the meaning of my life?" and "Where am I going?"

Similarly, in a study of people who respond "none" in surveys asking "What is your religious preference?" Vernon (1968) found that some people who reject membership in formal religious groups have a strong sense of spirituality and both a moral and ethical identity. More recently Kosmin, Mayer, and Keysar (2001) found that the proportion of people in the United States responding "none" to the question "What is your religion, if any?" had grown from 8% (14.3 million) in 1990 to more than 14% (29.4 million) in 2001. Interestingly, only 900,000 of the 29.4 million labeled themselves atheists, and almost half of the 29.4 million strongly endorsed the view that God exists. Although it is possible that the spiritual but not religious individuals have some other nonreligious but spiritual group affiliation, we believe it is likely that many of these individuals have a personal spiritual identity without a collective religious or spiritual component.

We categorize such a spiritual identity as a personal identity that is grounded in one's personal beliefs, behaviors, and values concerning the transcendent. We are interested in the developmental pathways associated with the emergence of these personal identity components of one's spiritual identity. For example, when, how, and why do individuals develop personal spiritual identities that they perceive as uniquely theirs? We believe an important developmental mechanism in spiritual identity development is personal experience with the transcendent. Because opportunities for such personal experiences often occur through religious participation, a personal spiritual identity often coexists with a collective religious identity. But this is not always the case; alternative pathways to a personal spiritual identity are possible.

Like other identities, we believe spiritual identities are multidimensional in nature, with cognitive, affective, and behavioral dimensions. Koenig et al. (2001) defined spirituality as "the personal quest for understanding answers to ultimate questions about life, about meaning and about relationship to the sacred or transcendent, which may (or may not) lead to or arise from the development of religious rituals and the formation of community" (p. 18). We believe this definition well describes spiritual identity formation, and as it implies, a prerequisite for a spiritual identity is the belief that one is embedded in something greater than oneself. Along with this belief comes the desire for, and commitment to, self-transcendence and connection with a greater force. Individuals can express these beliefs and desires through a variety of behaviors, such as attending religious services, picking up trash in the park, private prayer and meditation, volunteering in the community, and spending time in nature.

We also propose that religious and spiritual identities vary in maturity based on individual differences and sociocultural influences. Allport (1950) coined the term *mature religion* to refer to religiousness characterized by complex and critical reflection on religious issues, by a dynamic nature that is responsive to new information and by heuristics that provide direction in life. In contrast, individuals with a foreclosed (Marcia, 1980) collective religious identity may simply accept handed-down prescriptive religious values and beliefs. We believe personal meaning making is at the core of mature personal spiritual identities. Corbett (2000) suggested that the opportunity to develop a more "mature" spiritual identity emerges when traditional religious beliefs and images from childhood no longer offer comfort from suffering or provide adequate reasons for injustices in the world. This mature personal spiritual identity usually develops in private as individuals give new personal meaning to traditional religious beliefs or seek out what is personally sacred in other ways. Such a spiritual developmental journey will produce varying degrees of resonance with different religious figures (e.g., Jesus, Allah, Buddha), different spiritual locations (churches, temples, mosques, natural areas), and different spiritual practices (e.g., prayer, meditation).

FOUNDATIONS OF SPIRITUAL IDENTITIES

Spiritual development is a "process of growing the intrinsic human capacity for self-transcendence, in which the self is embedded in something greater than the self, including the sacred" (Benson, Roehlkepartain, & Rude, 2003). Benson and colleagues (2003) proposed that humans have intrinsic motivation to search for purpose, meaning, contribution, and self-transcendence and that spiritual development takes place both inside and outside religious traditions, beliefs, and practices. We propose that the search for self-transcendence, which may take the form of a search for purpose, meaning, connection, and contribution, results in the development of a personal spiritual identity. The claim by Benson and colleagues (2003) that humans in general possess intrinsic spiritual motivation suggests a universal human phenomenon. In the following subsections we review research focused on supernatural beliefs, teleological reasoning, dream concepts, and connection needs that supports the universal propensity to develop a spiritual identity.

Supernatural Beliefs

False belief tasks, commonly used to assess whether children know that other people hold beliefs different from their own, suggest that humans begin believing in the supernatural at a very young age. For example, in a study in which American children from religious families predicted other individuals' knowledge of the contents of a closed box, Barrett, Richert, and Driesenga (2001) found that most 3- to 4-year-olds attributed true beliefs (e.g., knowing what is in the box) to mother, God, a bear, an elephant, a snake, and a tree; however, by 5 years of age true beliefs were only attributed to God. Only God was assumed to know that the closed box held rocks rather than crackers.

Similarly, in another false belief task, American children from religious families evaluated whether God, a girl named Maggie, a monkey, and a special kitty with night vision could see a block in a blackened box. Most 3-year-olds assumed all could see in the dark. In contrast, most 5-year-olds believed only God (81.8%) and the special kitty (90.9%) could see in the dark; only 36.3% reported that Maggie could see the block.

In a cross-cultural replication, 4-year-old Yukatek children in Mexico believed God and humans could see the box contents, whereas 5-year-olds believed only God could see the contents (Knight, Sousa, Barrett, & Atran, 2004). In addition, Yukatek children 5 years old and older applied a supernatural hierarchy to true belief attributions; the most "true" beliefs were attributed to God, followed by the sun and forest spirits, then minor spirits and, last, people. That children across cultures readily distinguish between supernatural agents and human agents at young ages suggests fertile ground for spiritual identity development.

Teleological Reasoning and Dream Concepts

Studies of teleological reasoning (propensity to reason about biological and nonbiological things and events in terms of their purpose) also suggest that humans seek meaning and purpose to explain the world around them. Work by Kelemen (2003) suggests that children have a strong tendency to find purposefulness in the shape of natural things. For example, Kelemen asked 7-, 8-, and 10-year-old American and British children to choose between a teleological and physical explanation of properties for living and nonliving things. When the American children were asked "why are rocks so pointy?" 7- and 8-year-olds preferred the explanation that "rocks are pointy so that animals wouldn't sit on them and smash them"; the 10-year-olds preferred the choice that "they were pointy because little bits of stuff piled up on top of one another over a long time" (Kelemen, 1999).

Kelemen (2003) replicated these findings in a British sample. Because the results were evident in both a sample of children from the United States, one of the most religious industrialized nations, and a British sample, one of the least religious industrialized countries, Kelemen concluded that young children are predisposed to teleological reasoning. She also suggested the decline in teleological reasoning after 9 years of age may reflect exposure to a formal science curriculum at school.

Young children also think that their dreams are real events rather than mental images (Piaget, 1928). Kohlberg's (1966) work indicates that the change in beliefs over the childhood years is very similar across cultures. American middle-class children around 5 years of age recognize that dreams are not real, by age

6 they believe that dreams take place inside themselves, and by age 7 they believe that dreams are thoughts caused by themselves rather than by God or other supernatural agents. The progression of beliefs about dreams among boys of the Atayal, a Taiwanese aboriginal tribe, was similar to although slower than among American boys, even though the adults in this cultural group believe that dreams are real. However, the developmental patterns diverge at age 11, when the Atayal boys were exposed to the dream ideology of the adults in their community; at this point the boys again endorsed the belief that dreams are real and come from deities. Kohlberg's dream concept work is important for two reasons: It supports the idea of a universal predisposition to believe in the supernatural, and it shows that contextual influences can exert a powerful influence on developmental changes in supernatural beliefs.

Evidence also demonstrates contextual influences on developmental changes in the endorsement of supernatural versus physical explanations for natural phenomena. Evans (2001) found that 8- to 10-year-old American children, regardless of whether they attended a Christian fundamentalist school, embraced creationist explanations over evolutionary explanations for the origins of life. In contrast, by 11–12 years of age, children endorsed the dominant explanations in their community and home, whether creationist or evolutionist.

The Need for Connection

We propose that humans are intrinsically motivated to develop a spiritual identity in order to satisfy their need for connection. Several research and spiritual communities stress a universal need for connection. Within the research community, this need has been studied by scholars interested in attachment (Bowlby, 1969), belonging (Baumeister & Leary, 1995; Maslow, 1954), the minimal group paradigms and social identities (Tajfel, Flament, Billig, & Bundy, 1971; Turner et al., 1987), and terror management (Greenberg, Pyszczynski, Solomon, & Rosenblatt, 1990).

Attachment and belonging needs refer to the need for connection with other individuals. Bowlby (1969) stressed the fact that early interactions with one's mother have long-term consequences for the satisfaction of this need. If the mother–infant attachment system is dysfunctional, the child will develop an avoidant attachment style. Maslow (1954) placed love and belonging needs second only to basic survival needs such as food and safety. In addition, Baumeister and Leary (1995) proposed that the need to belong includes needs for frequent, affectively pleasant interactions with at least a few other people in the context of stable relationships based on mutual caring and concern to satisfy their need to belong.

Religion is one place individuals can turn to have their attachment and belonging needs met. Stark and Bainbridge (1985) concluded from their review of the literature that the need to belong may be a stronger driver in religious participation than religious ideology. For example, they found that movement into and out of religious groups depends more on social bonds than ideological belief. In a religious community, belonging and attachment needs may be satisfied by an individual's relationship with the religious leader (e.g., pastor, rabbi, priest) and other members of the religious group. Kirkpatrick (1998) proposed that people with avoidant attachment styles would be more prone to religious conversion than other attachment styles because adult attachment to God may compensate for lack of secure parental attachment in childhood.

Evidence also suggests that humans gravitate to groups. According to self-categorization theory (Turner et al., 1987), human beings have an automatic cognitive tendency to divide the world into social categories and to place themselves in the category they perceive most similar to themselves. Tajfel and colleagues (1971) demonstrated through the minimum group paradigm that arbitrary labeling of two groups (such as overestimators and underestimators) was sufficient to elicit in-group favoritism among study participants. Turner (1999) proposed that feeling part of a group provides a meaningful collective identity powerful enough to trigger in-group behavior (e.g., favoritism, loyalty, adherence to group norms). Membership in a religious community provides a powerful setting to fulfill these needs. It also has the potential to foster and reinforce intolerance toward other religious groups.

The need to manage the potential terror resulting from people's awareness of their own mortality is the core of terror management theory (Greenberg et al., 1990). Being a member of a religious group is a very effective way to manage this awareness because many religious belief systems stress one form or another of immortality. But when coupled with in-group/out-group psychological processes, terror management theory (TMT) also helps explain intolerance. TMT experiments show that thoughts of death increase attraction to those who validate one's own cultural worldview and decrease attraction to those who threaten these beliefs (Greenberg et al., 1990). For example, when Christian participants were reminded of their mortality, they made more positive evaluations of an in-group member (a Christian) and more negative evaluations of an out-group member (a Jew) than participants who were not reminded of their mortality.

Atran and Norenzayan (in press) contend that belief in supernatural agency provides a unique buffer against the terror of death that supersedes the need to maintain a cultural worldview. When mortality was salient for mostly Christian American undergraduates, they reported stronger belief in the power of Buddhist prayer than the nonmortality salient group. In addition, Christians with strong religious beliefs were more likely to believe in the power of the Buddhist prayer than other Christians. Atran and Norenzayan (in press) contend that the cultural worldview buffer against terror management is not adequate to explain this finding; however, prayer itself, rather than religious affiliation, may be the core component of the cultural worldview that these undergraduates invoked to buffer against their fear of death.

Thus, it seems likely that individuals are motivated to develop spiritual and/or religious identities in order to fulfill connection needs. Religious organizations provide the opportunities for connection to other individuals and belonging to a group likely to result in a collective religious identity. Likewise, a personal spiritual identity can develop from personal connection with the transcendent (God, higher power, universal energy, etc.). Unlike human relationships, which the other person may leave for a number of reasons, one's relationship with the transcendent is not vulnerable to dissolution except by the choice of the individual. This is true even in death, which is described in many spiritual traditions as a return to, or ultimate connection with, the transcendent.

SPIRITUAL IDENTITY DEVELOPMENT

Childhood to Emerging Adulthood: Developmental Processes

One could claim that if the goal of spiritual development is self-transcendence, newborns are inherently spiritual beings. Many theories in psychology, such as attachment and ego psychology, imply that newborns do not differentiate self from other and thus exist in a state of "oneness." Children move out of the state of undifferentiated oneness as they begin to categorize their world. They place themselves into gender, race, and other religious social categories based on assigned or biologically determined characteristics. They also choose social categories based on the cultural opportunities available to them, such as being a soccer player or a ballet dancer. Unlike chosen social categories, children often perceive the behaviors and values associated with assigned identities as immutable (Martin, Ruble, & Szkrybalo, 2002). They learn the power of social and group conformity norms and what it means to be included or excluded from a group (Dishion, McCord, & Poulin, 1999).

Children categorize themselves based on the concrete categories available in their social worlds, for example, the religion of their parents or primary caregivers. When parents include their children in religious activity participation and/or stress the importance of their religion, children may accept a religious identity much like an assigned identity rather than a chosen identity. Children not only accept their categorical membership in a religious group, they also accept the beliefs, values, and behaviors that are normative for the religious group. In other words, my parents are Catholic, so I'm a Catholic, and this is how a Catholic thinks and behaves.

An atheist friend, Tom, grew up in a religious family. During a discussion about spirituality, he surprised me by saying that it takes just as much faith to be an atheist as it does to believe in God. He recalls walking around the corner at the age of 8 or 9 and looking back to his house. His view was blocked by other houses and yet he believed the house was still there. Tom started thinking about how he knew the house was still there even though he couldn't see it, and this led him to question how one knows that God exists when you can't walk back around the corner and verify God's existence. He resolved his conflict regarding the existence of things that you can't see or experience with the five senses by deciding God does not exist.

Tom's story demonstrates a turning point in religious identity development concurrent with cognitive and social maturational changes that begin to occur around age 10. During adolescence, individuals begin to develop a new set of cognitive resources described by Piaget and Inhelder (1969) as the formal operations stage. These cognitive resources include an increased ability to think abstractly, to use more sophisticated information-processing strategies, to conceptualize many different perspectives on a problem at once, and to reflect on oneself (Byrnes, 2001). On a social level, adolescents have increased perspective-taking abilities and better developed social skills (Harter, 1999). These cognitive changes move the young child's hedonistic orientation to the world, from concern with approval and disapproval of others in late elementary years, to a more self-reflective and empathetic orientation in adolescence (Eisenberg, 1998). In early adolescence, individuals also begin to become more focused on the psychological as well as to introspect more about their inner life (Damon & Hart, 1982). These maturational changes bring new meaning to the question, "Who am I?" and may trigger questioning of the youth's current religious, or lack of religious, identity similar to what Tom experienced as a child.

Erikson (1968) would describe Tom's loss of belief in God as a turning point, "a crucial period of increased vulnerability and heightened potential, and therefore, the ontogenetic source of generational strength and maladjustment" (p. 96). Development, as conceptualized by Riegel (1975), progresses along four interdependent dimensions: the inner-biological, the individual-psychological, the cultural-sociological, and the outer-physical. When the progression of events along each of these four dimensions loses synchronicity, conflict or crisis is assumed to be the result. Through the process of restoring balance, the individual matures and is internally strengthened.

In this perspective, development is assumed to proceed through a hierarchical series of crisis formations and resolutions. By attaining new levels of synchrony across the four dimensions and by successfully adapting to each new context, individuals gradually broaden their repertoire of cognitive schemas and become increasingly capable of dealing with more complex situations. Exposure to more complex situations and to maturational and social changes, in turn, can produce new crises and new resolutions (Eccles & Bryan, 1994). The nature and direction of this sequential hierarchy have been described in similar terms by different cognitive and ego stage theorists (e.g., Kohlberg, Erikson, and Loevinger). These theorists describe a graduated, dialectical process of inner psychological growth, mediated by active individual/environment interaction, culminating in autonomous levels of functioning in which the individual integrates once conflicting and differentiated aspects of personality to satisfy self-realized needs. Furthermore, each of these theorists points to adolescence as a critical period in the formation and solidification of a postconventional identity—an identity reflecting one's own goals and experiences rather than being based on socially prescribed roles. Because Erikson has so directly influenced thinking about identity development, we will discuss his work and identity theories derived from his perspective.

Erikson (1968) conceptualized development as a series of stages, each representing a crisis created by the individual's level of development and the socialization demands faced. Optimal growth depends on the successful resolution of each of these crises. Unsuccessful resolution can lead to stagnation and continuing functional preoccupation with that particular level. Important here is that this process reflects dialectical growth, in which the individual is able to incorporate factors of lower stages into current schemas, even while forming newly transcendent ones.

Erikson (1968) believed identity formation to be the primary developmental task of adolescence. Erikson's stages of development can be conceptualized as turning points in development. The eight stages are marked by crises created when an individual's current stage of development no longer matches demands in the social context (Erikson, 1968). Although identity growth can continue to occur after adolescence, future growth will be easier in adulthood if the identity crisis is dealt with well during adolescence. Erikson's Identity versus Role Confusion stage is particularly relevant for our understanding of spiritual identity development. During this stage the individual may develop a stable spiritual identity that can guide subsequent goals, behaviors, and personal experience choices. The length and depth of the "crisis" in this stage depend on the individual and on the sociocultural context.

The potential importance of adolescence as a gateway to spiritual transcendence is made even more salient if one assesses it within the context of Riegel's dialectical model. Viewed from this crisis resolution model, adolescence has to be seen as a period in which the simultaneous changes occurring at all levels create a stage with great potential for rapid growth. On the inner-biological level, adolescence brings rapid brain changes, hormonal changes, and physical changes. The changes in adolescent brains in particular may lead to increases in exactly the kind of reasoning needed to take on the identity tasks occurring at the individual-psychological level (Spear, 2000).

On the individual-psychological level, one's assigned religious identity from childhood, or lack therefore, may be questioned and synchrony lost. Newly acquired reasoning skills may lead to questions about previously unquestioned beliefs from childhood, such as God's existence or the assumed superiority of one's assigned religion over other religions. Religious belief systems regarding what is right and wrong, good and bad, may be challenged as adolescents explore new peer groups and romantic relationships and seek balance between new biological drives and what constitutes a meaningful intimate relationship.

In gradually resolving this crisis, adolescents may seek a renewed balance between their spiritual identity, socially ascribed beliefs and values, and other personal and collective identities. Individuals may still consider themselves part of a particular religious group, but they may not question some of the beliefs advocated by the group. Negotiating a spiritual identity may mean dealing with conflict between overlapping collective identities. For example, imagine that an adolescent female, who considers herself very religious, realizes she is a lesbian, yet homosexuality is not accepted in the doctrines of her faith. If she accepts the lesbian identity, she must deal with the ideological conflict produced by her religious and homosexual collective identities colliding. If she finds a way to reconcile the conflict and maintains both collective identities, her personal spiritual identity will reflect a new facet representing the resolution of the conflict. If she doesn't resolve the conflict, she may suffer negative mental health outcomes. Another individual's spiritual identity may look much like a patchwork quilt, including bits and pieces of many different religious belief systems without identifying with any one of them. Such a person may not accept any collective identity as part of his or her spiritual identity.

Parents also play a critical role in the spiritual identity development of their children. Fuligni and Flook (in press) propose that family membership provides a social identity for adolescents that helps them interpret and make sense of larger social categories such as ethnicity or religion. The quality of the relationship with parents influences the effectiveness of parental religious socialization. Ream and Savin-Williams (2003) found adolescents were more likely to accept their parents' religion if they had a positive relationship with their parents and were securely attached. On the other hand, if the affective tone of the relationship was less positive and if the youth were not securely attached to their parents, they are more likely to disaffiliate or convert to another spiritual tradition. If adolescents who are close to their parents are more likely to accept their parents' religion, does this mean they continue to have an assigned collective religious identity that may also imply a foreclosed religious identity? And likewise, if the relationship is not positive, are adolescents more likely to develop a personal spiritual identity? We do not have answers to these questions, but they highlight the importance of context in spiritual identity development.

Adolescent adaptation in the context of spirituality expands beyond parents and peer groups into the perceived cultural milieu. Adolescents are concerned with shaping their rapidly developing identity into socially acceptable roles. On the sociocultural level, spiritual identity may or may not be a major determinant of acceptability during this period. Marcia (1983) suggested that cultures that allow for choice in social, ideological, and vocational roles are best suited to the resolution of the identity crisis. The current cultural environment in the United States presents many opportunities for spiritual exploration. Not only is it the most religious industrialized country, it is also the most religiously diverse industrialized country (Eck, 2001). American adolescents are exposed to more opportunities than ever before to explore spiritual connections beyond the religious and spiritual roles and social groups they identified with as children.

Thus, we believe the periods of adolescence and emerging adulthood can serve as a gateway to a spiritual identity that transcends, but does not necessarily exclude, the assigned religious identity from childhood. Most of our attention has focused on adolescence because it is a unique universal transition time when individuals evaluate childhood identities and begin making the transition to new adult identities. However, spiritual identity development is a lifelong process not bound to a specific critical period, nor does it unfold in an easily understandable or predictable pattern.

Transcendent Spiritual Identity

Normally, people will follow the path that rises from the plains of their own civilization; those who circle the mountain, trying to bring others around to their paths, are not climbing. . . . It is possible to climb life's mountain from any side, but when the top is reached the trails converge. At base, in the foothills of theology, ritual, and organizational structure, the religions are distinct. Differences in culture, history, geography and collective temperament all make for diverse starting points.

—Huston Smith (1991), *The World's Religions: Our Great Wisdom Traditions*

It is easier to name the summit of the mountain (e.g., mature religion, Allport, 1950; universalizing faith, Fowler, 1981) than to identity the pathways that lead there. Equifinality (Cicchetti & Rogosch, 1996) describes the developmental complexity of diverse pathways that lead to the same destination. For example, adults who consider themselves spiritual but not religious may come from a variety of religious and spiritual family backgrounds. They may have grown up in families actively engaged in their religion and religious community, or in families engaged in community service and civic issues, or in families who spent lots of time outdoors and were very active in conservation efforts. The end point of particular interest to us is the transcendent spiritual identity. Our term, *transcendent spiritual identity,* is paradoxical because transcendent implies, by intention, rising above personal and collective identities to reach a state of oneness with the universe.

To use the artist's technique of defining the negative space around the object of interest, let us first say what a transcendent spiritual identity is *not.* It is not a foreclosed (Marcia, 1980) religious identity in which one accepts and internalizes the doctrines, values, and roles offered by parents or other authority figures without exploring other options. It is also not related to the conventional level of moral reasoning (Kohlberg, 1984) where respect for rules and authority dictates one's moral reasoning. It is not an assigned identity that maintains consistent behavior (such as church attendance) or beliefs (such as abortion is a sin) from childhood without question. A transcendent spiritual identity also can't be measured solely by individual outcomes because more global concerns (such as social justice and environmental issues) are at stake as well.

We believe the mountain summit, a transcendent spiritual identity, is seldom attained because it is difficult to continue climbing the mountain once the three types of connection needs described earlier are met. Grotevant (1992) suggests that those who are satisfied with

their identity are unlikely to be motivated to explore other identities. Individuals who stop climbing the mountain may be functioning very well because they have attained a state of equilibrium or synchrony; from a global needs perspective, however, they have neither moved beyond in- or out-group prejudice nor gained commitment to solving critical social and ecological issues.

Earlier in this chapter, we proposed that a transcendent spiritual identity provides a potential gateway to positive social change and better stewardship of our planet. Imagine a world in which humans did not see themselves as separate or different from other humans and other life-forms. Imagine a world in which group cooperation was not in the service of competition as some argue (Dawkins, 1976). What if we could find a way to encourage people to develop spiritual identities that transcend not only the self but also the boundaries that separate individuals from those who appear to be different, including other religious groups, other ethnic groups, and other nonhuman life-forms? First, we would need to understand more fully the developmental processes that encourage such a spiritual identity.

Adolescence and emerging adulthood in modern culture, marked by exposure to changing life circumstances coupled with both exposure to many worldviews and the leisure time needed to explore these worldviews, may encourage people to explore their relationship with the transcendent. Loevinger (1976) described such challenging life events as "pacers." Pacers are defined as complex interpersonal situations that can stimulate movement to a higher level of ego functioning. This movement requires increasing complexity in one's perspective on events, and a search for meaning and purpose in one's life. Pacers may motivate adolescents to reflect on and develop a spiritual identity as they struggle to make meaning and find purpose in life. Thus because challenging life experiences can induce a state of disequilibrium or loss of synchrony, they may provide motivation to deepen one's connection with the transcendent.

But what else is necessary for spiritual development? Think back for a moment to the example of Tom, who, after pondering whether to believe in something whose existence he could not prove, consciously decided to become an atheist. What if Tom had felt a breeze on his face and had looked up to see the leaves on the trees gently moving in the wind? He might have experienced a sense of oneness with the natural world that reaffirmed rather than undermined his faith in the existence of a transcendent presence in the universe. This simplistic example illustrates the importance of both what we attend to and our emotional reactions to these cognitive experiences when we are in a state of disequilibrium. Disequilibrium merely provides the opportunity for developmental change. The exact nature of that change will depend on what else we experience and feel at that time.

Spiritual development can also be stimulated by family and community practices and beliefs. Exposure to such spiritual practices as meditation, contemplative education, vision quests, and intense experience of nature may encourage individuals to seek a deeper connection with the sacred. Much more needs to be understood about contexts that promote development of a transcendent spiritual identity.

WHERE DO WE GO FROM HERE?

Future investigations should examine the search, formation, and negotiation of spiritual identities across time, situations, and social contexts with a particular focus on how spiritual identity relates to individuals' attitudes and behaviors across a range of domains. We believe spiritual identities are multidimensional and expect variation even within seemingly homogeneous religious groups, but this needs to be verified by empirical studies. We also need to learn more about the role of parent, peers, religious institutions, and cultural practices in facilitating spiritual identity development.

We assume adolescence and early young adulthood are crucial times for exploration and development of a spiritual identity and that spiritual identity work in adolescence can lay the foundation for future spiritual identity development. Some youth take on the complex task of integrating a wide variety of religious and spiritual messages; some youth build a spiritual identity from their assigned religious identity; some youth develop a spiritual identity while

rejecting religious messages; and still others do not develop a spiritual or religious identity at all. We know very little about developmental outcomes related to diverse spiritual identities, little about how youth act as agents in the construction and maintenance of their spiritual identities, and even less about mechanisms that influence spiritual identity pathways. Given the potential of transcendent spiritual identities to address individual and social concerns, we believe increased understanding of these issues is a worthwhile, if not essential, endeavor.

We also know little about the nature of spiritual development across the life span. Erikson suggested that older adulthood may also be a prime time for spiritual development. Similarly, major pacer events throughout adulthood may stimulate renewed attention to one's spiritual development. Future research agendas should address multiple aspects of spiritual identity development. First, a better understanding of the content of spiritual identities is needed. Content includes the subjective meanings, ideologies, behavioral attributes, attitudes, beliefs, values, and cultural traditions that underlie and make up an individual's spiritual identity. Next, we need to know more about the structural properties underlying a spiritual identity: Are spiritual and religious identities experienced by individuals as distinct from one another? We also need to know more about the relation of spiritual identities to individuals' other identities. In addition, we should learn more about continuity and discontinuity of spiritual identity across contexts and across time. What are the stable and dynamic properties of spiritual identities across situations and time? Does a spiritual identity become more salient under certain conditions and situations? Which types of events or situations increase spiritual identity salience and promote growth toward spiritual transcendence? More attention should also be given to the socialization of spiritual identities.

Finally, more information is needed about the developmental and societal outcomes related to various types of spiritual identities. Does a spiritual identity predict individuals' attitudes and behaviors in other domains and in daily life? When do spiritual identities protect individuals against the adverse psychological effects of negative and uncontrollable events and daily experiences of discrimination and stress? Are some types of spiritual identities more effective in promoting well-being of self, others, and our planet? Finally, what role do spiritual identities play in individuals' attitudes and behavior toward other groups? In other words, do spiritual identities promote tolerance, intolerance, or both?

REFERENCES

Allport, G. W. (1950). *The individual and his religion: A psychological interpretation.* New York: Macmillan.

Ashmore, R. D., Deaux, K., & McLaughlin-Volpe, T. (2004). An organizing framework for collective identity: Articulation and significance of multidimensionality. *Psychological Bulletin, 130*(1), 80–114.

Atran, S., & Norenzayan, A. (in press). Religion's evolutionary landscape: Counterintuition, commitment, compassion, communion. *Behavioral and Brain Sciences.*

Barrett, J. L., Richert, R. A., & Driesenga, A. (2001). God's beliefs versus mother's: The development of nonhuman agent concepts. *Child Development, 72*(1), 50–65.

Baumeister, R. F., & Leary, M. R. (1995). The need to belong: Desire for interpersonal attachments as a fundamental human motivation. *Psychological Bulletin, 117*(3), 497–529.

Benson, P. L., Roehlkepartain, E. C., & Rude, S. P. (2003). Spiritual development in childhood and adolescence: Toward a field of inquiry. *Applied Developmental Science, 7*(3), 205–213.

Bowlby, J. (1969). *Attachment and loss.* New York: Basic Books.

Brewer, M. B. (1991). The social self: On being the same and different at the same time. *Personality & Social Psychology Bulletin, 17*(5), 475–482.

Byrnes, J. P. (2001). *Minds, brains, and learning: Understanding the psychological and educational relevance of neuroscientific research.* New York: Guilford.

Cicchetti, D., & Rogosch, F. A. (1996). Equifinality and multifinality in developmental psychopathology. *Development & Psychopathology, 8*(4), 597–600.

Corbett, L. (2000). A depth psychological approach to the sacred. In D. P. Slattery & L. Corbett (Eds.), *Depth psychology: Meditations in the field* (pp. 73–86). Carpinteria, CA: Pacifica Graduate Institute.

Côté, J. E. (1996). Sociological perspectives on identity formation: The culture-identity link and identity capital. *Journal of Adolescence, 19*(5), 417–428.

Damon, W., & Hart, D. (1982). The development of self-understanding from infancy through adolescence. *Child Development, 53*(4), 841–864.

Dawkins, R. (1976). *The selfish gene.* New York: Oxford University Press.

Deaux, K., & Martin, D. (2003). Interpersonal networks and social categories: Specifying levels of context in identity processes. *Social Psychology Quarterly, 66*(2), 101–117.

Dishion, T. J., McCord, J., & Poulin, F. (1999). When interventions harm: Peer groups and problem behavior. *American Psychologist, 54*(9), 755–764.

Eccles, J. S., & Bryan, J. (1994). Adolescence and gender-role transcendence. In M. Stevenson (Ed.), *Gender-roles across the life span: A multidisciplinary perspective* (pp. 111–148). Muncie, IN: Ball State University Press.

Eck, D. L. (2001). *A new religious America: How a "Christian country" has now become the world's most religiously diverse nation.* San Francisco: Harper.

Eisenberg, N. (1998). The socialization of socioemotional competence. In D. Pushkar & W. M. Bukowski (Eds.), *Improving competence across the lifespan: Building interventions based on theory and research* (pp. 59–78). New York: Plenum.

Erikson, E. H. (1968). *Identity, youth, and crisis.* New York: Norton.

Ethier, K. A., & Deaux, K. (1994). Negotiating social identity when contexts change: Maintaining identification and responding to threat. *Journal of Personality & Social Psychology, 67*(2), 243–251.

Evans, E. M. (2001). Cognitive and contextual factors in the emergence of diverse belief systems: Creation versus evolution. *Cognitive Psychology, 42*(3), 217–266.

Fowler, J. W. (1981). *Stages of faith: The psychology of human development and the quest for meaning.* San Francisco: Harper & Row.

Fuligni, A. J., & Flook, L. (in press). A social identity approach to ethnic differences in family relationships during adolescence. In R. Kail (Ed.),

Advances in child development and behavior (Vol. 33). New York: Academic Press.

Goffman, E. (1959). *The presentation of self in everyday life.* Garden City, NY: Doubleday.

Greenberg, J., Pyszczynski, T., Solomon, S., & Rosenblatt, A. (1990). Evidence for terror management theory II: The effects of mortality salience on reactions to those who threaten or bolster the cultural worldview. *Journal of Personality & Social Psychology, 58*(2), 308–318.

Grotevant, H. D. (1992). Assigned and chosen identity components: A process perspective on their integration. In G. R. Adams & T. P. Gullotta (Eds.), *Adolescent identity formation* (pp. 73–90). Newbury Park, CA: Sage.

Harter, S. (1999). *The construction of the self: A developmental perspective.* New York: Guilford.

Kelemen, D. (1999). Why are rocks pointy? Children's preference for teleological explanations of the natural world. *Developmental Psychology, 35*(6), 1440–1452.

Kelemen, D. (2003). British and American children's preferences for teleo-functional explanations of the natural world. *Cognition, 88*(2), 201–221.

Kirkpatrick, L. A. (1998). God as a substitute attachment figure: A longitudinal study of adult attachment style and religious change in college students. *Personality & Social Psychology Bulletin, 24*(9), 961–973.

Knight, N., Sousa, P., Barrett, J. L., & Atran, S. (2004). Children's attributions of beliefs to humans and God: Cross-cultural evidence. *Cognitive Science, 28*(1), 117–126.

Koenig, H. G., McCullough, M. E., & Larson, D. B. (2001). *Handbook of religion and health.* New York: Oxford University Press.

Kohlberg, L. (1966). Cognitive stages in preschool education. *Human Development, 9,* 5–17.

Kohlberg, L. (1984). *The psychology of moral development: The nature and validity of moral stages.* San Francisco: Harper & Row.

Kosmin, B. A., Mayer, E., & Keysar, A. (2001). *American religious identification survey.* New York: The Graduate Center of the City University of New York.

Loevinger, J., & Blasi, A. (1976). *Ego development: Conceptions and theories.* San Francisco: Jossey-Bass.

Marcia, J. E. (1980). Identity in adolescence. In J. Adelson (Ed.), *Handbook of adolescent psychology* (pp. 159–187). New York: Wiley.

Marcia, J. E. (1983). Some directions for the investigation of ego development in early adolescence. *Journal of Early Adolescence, 3*(3), 215–223.

Martin, C. L., Ruble, D. N., & Szkrybalo, J. (2002). Cognitive theories of early gender development. *Psychological Bulletin, 128*(6), 903–933.

Maslow, A. H. (1954). *Motivation and personality.* New York: Harper & Row.

Mattis, J. S. (2000). African American women's definitions of spirituality and religiosity. *Journal of Black Psychology, 26*(1), 101–122.

O'Brien, M. (1996). Spirituality and older women: Exploring meaning through story telling. *Journal of Religious Gerontology, 10*(1), 3–16.

Oyserman, D., & Markus, H. R. (1998). Self as social representation. In U. Flick (Ed.), *Psychology of the social* (pp. 107–125). Cambridge, UK: Cambridge University Press.

Piaget, J. (1928). *The child's conception of the world.* New York: Harcourt Brace.

Piaget, J., & Inhelder, B. (1969). *The development of physical number concepts in children: Maintenance and atomism.* Stuttgart, Germany: Ernst Klett.

Ream, G. L., & Savin-Williams, R. C. (2003). Religious development in adolescence. In G. R. Adams & M. D. Berzonsky (Eds.), *Blackwell handbook of adolescence* (pp. 51–59). Malden, MA: Blackwell.

Riegel, K. F. (1975). Toward a dialectical theory of development. *Human Development, 18*(1), 50–64.

Smith, H. (1991). *The world's religions: Our great wisdom traditions.* San Francisco: Harper.

Spear, L. P. (2000). The adolescent brain and age-related behavioral manifestations. *Neuroscience & Biobehavioral Reviews, 24*(4), 417–463.

Stark, R., & Bainbridge, W. S. (1985). *The future of religion: Secularization, revival, and cult formation.* Berkeley and Los Angeles: University of California Press.

Tajfel, H. (1981). *Human groups and social categories: Studies in social psychology.* Cambridge, UK: Cambridge University Press.

Tajfel, H., Flament, C., Billig, M. G., & Bundy, R. P. (1971). Social categorization and intergroup behaviour. *European Journal of Social Psychology* (1), 149–178.

Turner, J. C. (1999). Some current issues in research on social identity and self-categorization theories. In N. Ellemers, R. Spears, & B. Doosje (Eds.), *Social identity: Context, commitment, content* (pp. 6–34). Oxford, UK: Blackwell.

Turner, J. C., Hogg, M. A., Oakes, P. J., Reicher, S. D., & Wetherell, M. S. (1987). *Rediscovering the social group: A self-categorization theory.* New York: Blackwell.

Vernon, G. M. (1968). Religious nones: A neglected category. *Journal for the Scientific Study of Religion, 7*(2), 219–222.

19

PERSONALITY AND SPIRITUAL DEVELOPMENT

TERESA T. KNEEZEL

ROBERT A. EMMONS

William James (1902), more than 100 years ago, wrote extensively on the unifying force of religion in personality. Drawing from empirical narrative data, James concluded that "to be converted, to be regenerated, to receive grace, to experience religion, to gain an assurance, are so many phases which denote the process, gradual or sudden, by which a self hitherto divided, . . . becomes unified" (p. 160). Although James focused heavily on religious conversion in *The Varieties of Religious Experience,* religious experience in general has real, examinable effects on one's personality. Likewise, one's personality colors religious experience. Conversions are plentiful in adolescence (Gillespie, 1991), and personality development is a primary task of the young person; yet, developmental researchers have not devoted significant time and resources to the study of religious experience and personality development. Considering that the influence of religion on the lives of people of all ages is undeniable (Smith, 2003), the dearth of research on religious and spiritual issues for the developing personality understates this influence.

We argue that those aspects of personality most relevant to spiritual development constantly evolve to incorporate new life experiences. During childhood and adolescence, one's motivation to perform certain behaviors and hold specific beliefs has the potential to change dramatically as new demands and challenges are presented. Children and adolescents, as intentional beings, can also alter and shift their everyday goals as they develop. Finally, we contend that these changes in motivation and goals are manifested in the life narratives and stories children and adolescents tell of their lives.

Self-determination theory (SDT; Deci & Ryan, 1985), a theory of motivation and personality, proposes that people strive toward structure and coherency between one's self and one's experiences. Spirituality may provide meaning and structure to a developing person's sense of self by offering a global interpretation of one's everyday experience, and may be a powerful catalyst for personality development; therefore, SDT is an ideal theory from which to approach the study of spirituality and personality development. We begin with an overview of SDT, then interpret the existing research on personality and spiritual development from the perspective of SDT, and offer new directions for religious and spiritual research in developmental psychology.

An Overview of
Self-Determination Theory

Self-determination theory argues that people intrinsically strive toward integration and differentiation of the self (Ryan & Deci, 2002). Incorporating one's various and diverse experiences with the environment and with others into one's sense of self or identity is the process of integrating the self, or creating a unified, coherent self. Differentiation occurs as the individual attains a sense of structure within the self that respects the complexities of a mature self. Integration and differentiation of the self, then, refer to the process by which the self becomes increasingly complex yet whole. The self intrinsically strives toward integration and differentiation through action and therefore influences the social world; yet the social world also impacts the extent to which the self develops.

The autonomous and intrinsic process toward integration and differentiation of the self is facilitated by social contexts that support the three basic needs of autonomy, relatedness, and competence posited by SDT (Ryan & Deci, 2002). Autonomy, relatedness, and competence are innate and universal needs, and each will be addressed separately.

Autonomous actions are fully self-endorsed and personally valued (Ryan & Deci, 2000). When one feels his or her actions are more controlled, however, one is more driven by internal or external pressures into action; controlled behaviors are not congruent with one's self, but are imposed upon it. Intrinsic motivation emanates from the self, yet intrinsic motivation can be undermined by rewards that are used to elicit behavior. Rewards undermine behaviors performed for intrinsic reasons, or just for "the fun of it," by placing the control of the action outside of the self to external forces (Lepper, Greene, & Nisbett, 1973; Ryan, Mims, & Koestner, 1983).

The methods parents and teachers use to motivate children in school-related activities can also undermine intrinsic motivation. Parents and teachers can be more or less autonomy-supportive socializers, and more or less warm toward their child or student. Autonomy-supportive parents and teachers use minimal pressure and control, and value their child's interests and perspectives, though autonomy-supportive caregivers are not uninvolved with their children. Instead, autonomy-supportive caregivers provide guidance and structure to their child, but do so while respecting the child's interests through conversation and negotiation about rules and choice of activities. Controlling parents and teachers tend not to value children's own perspectives and are less autonomy supportive, valuing "obedience and conformity, solv[ing] children's problems for them, tak[ing] the lead in interactions" (Grolnick & Apostoleris, 2002, p. 161).

Children with parents who are nurturing and warm, autonomy supportive, and involved in their child's life are more autonomously self-regulated, are more competent, and have higher grades in school than children with controlling parents (Grolnick & Ryan, 1989). Similarly, children in classrooms with teachers who are autonomy supportive are more interested in learning and have higher levels of mastery motivation and perceived competence than children in classrooms with controlling teachers (Deci, Schwartz, Scheinman, & Ryan, 1981).

Relatedness is the feeling of being loved by others and of loving others, feeling supported by others and supporting others, and feeling a sense of belonging with others and with one's community (Ryan & Deci, 2002). Competence is one's sense of effectiveness in interactions with the environment and social world (Ryan & Deci, 2002). The integral notion of competence is the perceived sense of efficacy one has, not one's actual ability to be successful in all endeavors.

According to SDT, when the three needs of autonomy, relatedness, and competence are consistently met, personality can adequately develop; the self is able to become more organized and coherent. The organismic, core self posited by SDT develops through a process of action that begins in infancy. The self proceeds toward organization and its expression is truly authentic. This core self is not to be confused with the self-concept often discussed in developmental psychology. The self-concept is formed through the interpretation of others' views of the individual. Rather, the core self is formed through an intrinsic, self-directed process of internalizing and integrating actions and beliefs that reflect the fundamental needs of the self for autonomy, relatedness, and competence.

SDT has been successfully applied to research in numerous domains, such as the academic setting (Reeve, 2002), the workplace (Baard, 2002), the sports and exercise arena (Frederick-Recascino, 2002), and healthcare (Williams, 2002). SDT has also productively expanded its research program to include religion and spirituality (Baard, 2002; Kneezel & Ryan, 2004; Ryan, Rigby, & King, 1993).

SDT AND SPIRITUAL DEVELOPMENT

Self-determination theory is a broad theory that treats the person as a whole being, and provides a foundation for researchers intent on developing a comprehensive theory of religious and spiritual development. Insofar as spiritual development is a search for "connectedness, meaning, purpose, and contribution" (Benson, Roehlkepartain, & Rude, 2003, pp. 206–207), it is clearly a search for integration in which one's thoughts, motivations, and actions are pointed toward self-transcendence. A religious or spiritual outlook on life can provide one with an overarching theme or goal that helps to unify the person's entire self. A person also strives for relatedness and integration of the self with others. In addition to a sense of relatedness with parents and other loved ones, integration with others might also include unity with a higher being such as God (i.e., relatedness to God) or the sacred.

It is within this framework of SDT that we will approach the relationship of spiritual development and personality. A spirituality that promotes autonomy and relatedness with others and with God will facilitate the development of an integrated and authentic self. A child's or adolescent's own motivation for engaging in religious and spiritual practices may also influence the youth's positive spiritual development (Kneezel & Ryan, 2004; Strahan & Craig, 1995).

Motivation for behaving in certain ways is not easily differentiated into autonomous or controlled motivation. Intrinsic motivation, although the most preferred type of autonomous motivation, becomes increasingly rare as children develop. With the commencement of

school and other responsibilities, children have to meet the demands of parents, teachers, peers, and even of themselves, and many of the behaviors associated with different demands may not be intrinsically motivated. For example, not many children intrinsically want to do math homework after school; instead, they may prefer to play with their friends or engage in other enjoyable activities. However, extrinsically motivated actions, beliefs, and values can become internalized and integrated into the self. SDT distinguishes between four types of internalization, shown in Table 19.1 as a continuum from non-self-determined to more self-determined regulations.

Introjection and identification, two of the types of internalization, are of interest to the study of spirituality in developing persons. Introjected internalization is an internally controlling state in which a person performs a behavior to attain social approval and to avoid anxiety and the loss of self-esteem (Deci & Ryan, 1985). Introjection is associated with poorer psychological adjustment than is a higher form of internalization, identification, which occurs when a person feels that his or her beliefs and behaviors are important and personally chosen. Therefore, this type of internalization is felt to be more self-determined and is associated with better psychological adjustment (Grolnick & Ryan, 1989; Vallerand & Bissonnette, 1992). Psychological adjustment is indicative of personality development: A self that is fragmented will experience more negative symptoms than a more unified self. An individual who acts in accord with his self is acting authentically and genuinely, and this type of behavior leads to better psychological adjustment, including a feeling of vitality and happiness (Ryan & Deci, 2000).

The reasons *why* a child or adolescent engages in religious practices and has religious and spiritual beliefs provide rich information about personality development. Developmentally, the internalization and integration of external regulations into the self is a process. Individuals increasingly tend to internalize external regulations as they age, lending support to the notion that the developing self strives to become more autonomous (Chandler & Connell, 1987). It might be expected that as

Behavior	Non-self-determined					Self-determined
Type of motivation	Amotivation	Extrinsic motivation (Internalization processes)				Intrinsic motivation
Regulatory styles	Nonregulation	External regulation	Introjection	Identification	Integration	Intrinsic regulation
Regulatory processes	Non-intentional, nonvaluing, no control	External rewards and punishments, external control	Internal rewards, punishments, and self-control	Personal importance and value	Self-awareness, incorporation within Self	Interest, Intrinsic satisfaction

Figure 19.1   Internalization of Extrinsic Regulations on the Self-Determination Continuum

NOTE: From R. M. Ryan & E. L. Deci (2000), "Self-determination theory and the facilitation of intrinsic motivation, social development, and well-being," *American Psychologist, 55,* 72. Copyright 2000 by the American Psychological Association. Adapted with permission

children grow, they also are more able to internalize their religious beliefs, values, and behaviors at higher, more self-determined levels. James Fowler's stages of faith (1981) point to this increasing propensity for internally motivated religious and spiritual beliefs. Moving to a higher stage of faith requires development in cognitive abilities, and can aid the explanation as to why children have less mature faiths than adolescents and adults. One might expect that, like Fowler's stages of faith, children and adolescents will be more able to internalize religious and spiritual beliefs and behaviors as they age, given that they are socialized in a warm, autonomy-supportive environment. Religious internalization has yet to be examined in children, but there is a growing literature on adolescent religious internalization.

Religious beliefs, values, and practices are internalized to different degrees. Ryan et al. (1993) developed a scale measuring the religious internalization of Christians. The Christian Religious Internalization Scale measures the perceived reasons why a person endorses a belief or practice, and captures how self-determined and autonomous one feels about one's religious beliefs and values. The Religious Internalization Scale differentiates between religious introjection and religious identification. Religious introjection involves a partial internalization of beliefs, values, and practices. However, the individual perceives the religious beliefs and practices to be internally or externally controlled, resulting in one's feeling pressured to conform

to internal and social demands and in conflict between one's own authentic self and one's beliefs. Religious identification involves the internalization of a religious regulation because one personally chooses and values the belief or behavior. For example, several items in the scale measure the reasons a Christian attends church. An individual who is high in religious introjection would attend church "because others would disapprove if I didn't" and "because one is supposed to go." An individual high in religious identification attends church "because by going I learn new things."

RELIGIOUS ORIENTATION AND RELIGIOUS INTERNALIZATION

Religious orientation, another construct related to religious internalization, has been extensively studied using Allport and Ross's (1967) intrinsic and extrinsic religious orientations, as well as Batson and Ventis's (1982) formulation of Religion as a Means, Religion as an End, and Religion as a Quest. However, Ryan et al. (1993) argue that both the Religious Orientation Scale and the Religious Life Inventory blend religious motivation with measures of orthodoxy. In addition, they argue that the Religious Internalization Scale measures the reasons why a person endorses a belief or practice without confounding his or her religious commitment, which some items in the Religious Orientation Scale and Religious Life Inventory do. The

Religious Internalization Scale captures how autonomous one feels about one's religious beliefs and values. It does not intend to replace the other religious orientation scales; rather, it is more specific in its purpose and is theoretically distinct from the other scales.

To develop the Religious Internalization Scale, Ryan et al. (1993) examined a nonsecular undergraduate sample and a sample of Christian adolescents participating in a summer evangelical project in New York. The two groups were given the Religious Internalization Scale, as well as measures of psychological adjustment. The General Health Questionnaire (Goldberg & Hillier, 1979) was used to detect somatic, depressive, and anxious symptoms in the individual. Global self-esteem, identity integration (O'Brien & Epstein, 1987), and self-actualization (Jones & Crandall, 1986), a measure of one's ability to reach one's potential, were also used to assess psychological adjustment. In the university sample, religious introjection was related to higher levels of anxiety, depression, and somatic symptoms, and to lower levels of global self-esteem, identity integration, and self-actualization. Conversely, religious identification was positively associated with self-esteem, identity integration, and self-actualization, and negatively related to anxiety, depression, and somatization. In the sample of Christian youths who were involved in a summer missionary project in New York, religious identification was positively related to global self-esteem, identity integration, and self-actualization; religious introjection was not significantly related to these well-being constructs. In addition, there were age-related differences on religious introjection and identification such that older adolescents were higher in religious identification than younger adolescents. In a recent study of Christian late adolescents (Kneezel & Ryan, 2004), religious identification was positively associated with self-esteem and vitality, and was negatively associated with depression. Religious introjection was positively related to depressive symptoms.

The results of the two studies examining religious internalization suggest that the *ways* in which youth are religious are related to psychological functioning and self-development. Youth who personally value and choose their religious beliefs and values appear to feel less conflict between their own desires and religious convictions, and this harmony is evident in positive psychological adjustment. Also, more autonomous forms of religious internalization were evident in older youth, supporting the idea that the increasing propensity for the internalization of regulatory processes is a developmental process.

INTERNALIZATION OF SPIRITUALITY AND RELATEDNESS

The motivation for religious practices and beliefs is important to psychological functioning and personality integration. It is thus necessary to study the socialization of religious motivation and internalization. Research needs to address how, and under what conditions, religious motivation to behave and think in certain ways becomes more or less integrated with one's self. Developmental psychologists no longer favor transmission models of socialization, which viewed children as passive receptacles who simply absorb parental values taught to them. Instead, researchers are beginning to look at bidirectional, transactional models of religious socialization processes, whereby parent and child simultaneously influence each other (Boyatzis & Janicki, 2003; Flor & Knapp, 2001; Kuczynski, 2003).

Internalization and Relatedness to Parents

Self-determination theory also recognizes the intricacies of parent–child interactions. Instead of only focusing on how parenting behavior can either foster or hinder authentic self-development, SDT also views the child as an agentic being striving toward autonomy. The child is constantly striving to meet his or her own needs of autonomy, relatedness, and competence, and so expresses his or her own beliefs, values, and behaviors in parent–child exchanges. The parent's behavior toward his or her child will be influenced by the extent to which the child feels related to the parent and autonomous. Yet the extent to which the child feels autonomous in his or her actions and connected to the parent is affected by the quality of parenting. Both the parent and the child bring different beliefs, values, and actions to their interactions, making the study of parent–child exchanges essential for an understanding of religious internalization.

Illustrating the importance of autonomy-supportive and warm parenting for the socialization of religious beliefs, Okagaki, Hammond, and Seamon (1999) showed that parental nurturance, composed of warmth, autonomy support, and parental monitoring, predicted agreement between parent's and child's religious beliefs. Goodnow's socialization theory posits that children are active in the socialization process (Goodnow, 1992). Okagaki et al.'s research (1999) expands Goodnow's research into the religious domain and shows that children's perceptions of their parents' religious beliefs and the accuracy of these perceptions influence the acceptance of these beliefs. Children who have accurate perceptions and perceive strong agreement between the parents about the religious beliefs tend to adopt beliefs similar to those of their parents.

Flor and Knapp (2001) also emphasized the importance of parents who support their adolescent child's basic needs of autonomy, relatedness, and competence, and acknowledged the contributions of the child to the socialization process. Their study revealed that dyadic parent–child conversations about religion predicted greater importance of religion to the child and more child religious behavior.

These studies point to the importance of both the parent and the child in the socialization of religious beliefs, yet until recently, there has been little research examining the relationship between the parent's religious internalization and the child's religious internalization. The parent's religious internalization may affect how the parent socializes his or her child, which could in turn affect the child's religious internalization.

Strahan and Craig's (1995) study of religious internalization and socialization in Seventh-Day Adventists showed that parents high in religious identification scored higher on expressiveness and lower on negative affect directed toward their children than parents high in religious introjection. Interestingly, highly religiously identified parents tended to have children who also had high identification of their religious values. A parent high in religious identification who gains enjoyment and satisfaction from his or her religion may pass this type of religious internalization down to the child by fostering self-determined behavior. The lack of volition a parent high in religious introjection feels with regard to religious actions may inhibit the parent's encouragement of self-determined behavior in his or her child. The child may then develop an introjected internalization of religion as well. Indeed, in Strahan and Craig's study, religious introjection in parents was associated with religious introjection in children.

Similarly, Kneezel and Ryan (2004) found an association between mother's religious identification and child's religious identification in a study of Christian late adolescents and between father's religious introjection and child's religious introjection. As assessed by the adolescent, perceived autonomy support from the father was negatively related to the child's religious introjection, and perceived maternal warmth was marginally associated with the child's religious identification. Perceived parenting style did not mediate the relationship between parent and child religious internalization. These studies suggest, however, that parents who have high levels of religious identification are likely both to have discussions with their children about religion and to have children who also have high levels of religious identification and who value religion.

Central to this issue of reciprocal parent–child influence is the idea that youth have changing needs for relatedness and autonomy. As children develop, they feel as though parents need to allow them more autonomy, especially in issues they deem to concern a personal choice (Smetana & Daddis, 2002). Religion and spirituality may be one of the areas adolescents consider to be a personal choice. Parents who attempt to discipline this domain may be met with resistance instead of compliance. The study of these changing needs of youth from childhood to adolescence must be incorporated into research designs of spiritual and religious studies.

Internalization and Relatedness to Others

As children grow and develop, they spend increasingly more time with their peers, and more particularly, with their friends. During childhood, friends are usually chosen based on similarities in observable characteristics, such as appearance and personality (Rubin, Coplan, Nelson, Cheah, & Lagace-Seguin, 1999), but during adolescence, friends are also chosen based on similarities in attitudes. Similarity of spiritual beliefs and attitudes between friends may be more important to adolescents than to children. During adolescence, relatedness with friends may play an increasingly important role in the internalization of spiritual and religious beliefs and practices. One study showed that peers and the target adolescent had similar levels of religious orthodoxy and similar religious practices (de Vaus, 1983). However, the study did not look at religious motivation, nor did it investigate why this association might exist. In addition to selecting friends who are similar in religious beliefs, both religious and nonreligious peer groups may influence one's religious beliefs, either fostering or hindering the internalization process.

The influences of clergy, religious teachers, and other organized religion socialization agents also might affect the internalization of religion in youth. Children who experience a warm, autonomy-supportive church environment may be more likely to be religiously identified than children who experience a cold, controlling religious environment, even if the children have nurturing parents. With the exception of a literature on religious and well-being outcomes of children of Christian pastors (Brousson Anderson, 1998; Lee, 1992), there is an absence of work on the relationship between one's religious environment and personality. Socialization of lay children in religious settings is potentially strong and needs to be examined.

However the internalization process occurs, an integral concern remains: Do youth with identified religious beliefs, values, and practices have more developed, coherent personalities than children who are introjected in their religious internalization, or who are not religious or spiritual? This question remains unanswered, but we might hypothesize that spiritual beliefs and practices felt to be controlled and foreign to the self will not be integrated into the self. Instead of promoting personality development, an introjected child may experience fragmentation of the self.

SDT argues that internalizing and integrating regulations into the self produces a person who is more unified and less conflicted about his or her daily thoughts and actions. However, this hypothesis needs to be examined in the religious context. Spiritual beliefs and values can provide ultimate meaning and explanation to one's life, and the internalization of these values may affect regulation of other value and behavioral systems. Insofar as religious and spiritual beliefs are central to one's daily life, religious introjection may adversely affect personality development more so than controlling regulations of other "secular," nonultimate beliefs and behaviors. An individual with religious beliefs that are congruent to her sense of self may be better able to develop her personality.

Finally, socialization of religious beliefs and practices may greatly differ among diverse religious traditions. Most of the studies on parental influences in the religious domain have focused on Christian families. Parents involved in religions with a focus on orthopraxy, or right practice, such as Judaism and Islam, may use different parenting techniques than parents who adhere to a religion with a focus on orthodoxy, or right belief, such as Christianity. Indeed, a parenting style that is successful for the socialization of religious beliefs and practices in one religion may not be successful for another religion. However, regardless of the tradition, we theorize that more self-determined internalization of religious beliefs will be associated with autonomy-supportive parenting that allows the child to identify his or her religious practices as personally chosen.

Internalization of Spirituality and Relatedness to God

A child or adolescent feels relatedness not only toward the parents and extrafamilial others but also toward God. Relatedness to God (King, Lynch, & Ryan, 1989), or how safe and loved by God an individual feels, as well as how loving one feels toward God, may also influence personality development in youth. A more positive, warm, supporting relationship with God should facilitate autonomy in the child and lead to more internalized beliefs about God; the child will be more likely to engage in religious behavior because he enjoys it and feels it is important in his life. In contrast, a person who feels that God is critical of her or feels dissatisfied with her relationship with God may practice religious behaviors due to external pressures felt from God. This idea is not trivial; relatedness to God can facilitate or thwart personality development. An individual will feel conflicted about their spirituality if they feel externally controlled by God. Their actions will not emanate from their core self, but will instead be externally driven, suppressing the development of an authentic self.

A more developed concept than relatedness to God, attachment to God (Kirkpatrick & Shaver, 1992) is a construct measuring how safe and secure one feels in one's relationship to God. In adults, anxious attachment to God is related to neuroticism and negative affect (Rowatt & Kirkpatrick, 2002), suggesting that personality and one's relationship with God are linked. Attachment theory and SDT might be productively combined to study the reciprocal effects of one's relationship with God and personality (see Granqvist & Dickie, chapter 14, this volume, for a thorough discussion of religion and attachment theory).

PERSONALITY AS TRAITS AND SPIRITUAL DEVELOPMENT

According to SDT, the positive development of a youth's identity, or sense of self, is either facilitated or thwarted depending on the relative satisfaction of the youth's three basic psychological needs. Spirituality can play a role in self-development. However, the study of personality traits—stable individual differences that predispose people to act consistently over time and across situations—can provide some insight into what types of children and adolescents are more likely to be spiritual or religious, and how these people fare psychologically.

Personality research has reached a consensus that the five-factor model (McCrae & Costa, 1999) can describe the major trait dimensions of personality (openness to experience, conscientiousness, extraversion, agreeableness, and neuroticism). Many studies have established positive links between religiousness and two of the Big Five traits, agreeableness and conscientiousness (Kosek, 1999; MacDonald, 2000; McCullough, Tsang, & Brion, 2003; Taylor & MacDonald, 1999). In McCullough et al.'s longitudinal study, openness to experience in adolescence and religiousness in early adulthood were linked. The study also found an association between emotional stability and religious upbringing, in that adolescents low in emotional stability who had a strong religious upbringing were more likely to be religious in adulthood than the emotionally stable adolescents. Emotionally unstable individuals may adhere to religious beliefs and practices in an effort to maintain closeness with their parents' ideals, thus avoiding the associated conflict and negative emotions adolescents experience when there are discrepancies between parents' values and the child's values. Also, emotionally unstable, or neurotic, individuals may use their childhood beliefs as a way to cope with stress. In any case, at least one personality trait, neuroticism or emotional instability, is affected by religious socialization during childhood and adolescent development.

Research on the effects of personality traits, and perhaps more important, the interaction of personality traits and socialization, on spirituality, can aid in our understanding of the types of individuals who may be drawn to or deterred from religious and spiritual traditions. Understanding how the relationship between personality traits and spirituality is moderated by socialization can inform parents and religious leaders about religious and spiritual upbringing strategies. In addition, longitudinal studies may reveal changes in personality due to changes in one's spiritual life; likewise, developing and changing personality traits in children and adolescents may lead to subsequent spiritual changes.

There are several significant limitations to the study of personality traits as predictors of religious and spiritual outcomes. Virtually all of the studies on personality traits and their significance for religion, with the exception of the McCullough et al. (2003) study, have been cross-sectional. Prospective, longitudinal studies are necessary to examine how traits interact with developmental processes and spirituality. In addition, religiousness is only one outcome of different personality traits. Other constructs, such as religious orientation, religious internalization, religious fundamentalism, spiritual transcendence, and attachment to God, might be associated with different personality traits.

Also, like most research on religious issues, the majority of personality trait studies have primarily focused on Christianity, leading to a dearth of knowledge on the association of personality traits with other religious traditions and personal forms of spirituality. Perhaps youth low in agreeableness tend to adhere to less traditional forms of religion and more to their own personal form of spirituality. Neurotic youth may be more reluctant to try novel or different forms of spirituality, fearing the interpersonal conflict that might arise from the experimentation.

In addition, personality traits explain little unique variance of differences in religiousness (3% of the variance of religiousness in the McCullough et al., 2003, study; 4% of the variance of the relationship with God in the Kosek, 1999, study). Personality traits have little predictive power, then, on religiousness. Traits may be most helpful to the psychology of religion and spirituality as base measures that interact with socialization processes such as religious teaching and parental involvement in religious upbringing. Additional units of analysis beyond traits are needed to examine more fully the relationship between personality and spiritual development. Indeed, Kosek's (1999) study of middle school students showed that religious orientation accounted for 35% of the variance of one's relationship with God, contrasted with just 4% of the variance explained by the Big Five personality traits.

Personality describes the entire person and is arguably best examined at three different levels: personality traits, motivation and goals, and identity and life narrative (McAdams, 1995). From both an empirical and a theoretical viewpoint, personality and spirituality development need to be studied using a broad theory of motivation and personality development, such as SDT, that looks at the person not only as having personality traits but also as a being with agency, and as a being that exists in a social world. SDT also provides a framework for the interpretation of one's life story (Bauer & McAdams, 2000), and is well complemented by a study of personality traits as an important source of individual differences in spirituality. Unlike some of the Big Five personality traits, spiritual and religious traditions often encourage the development of traits of virtue, and their inclusion into research may offer meaningful insights about spirituality's role in personality development.

Personality and Virtue: The Case of Gratitude

The study of virtue, long ignored in psychology, appears to be making a valiant comeback (Emmons & Paloutzian, 2003; Snyder & McCullough, 2000). Virtues are strengths of character that contribute to effective functioning in life. One of the strengths that have been the subject of recent research and theory is gratitude (Emmons & McCullough, 2004). Gratitude is the habit of being thankful and appreciative of one's blessings in life, and it also entails acknowledging one's debt to others. Across cultures and time spans, experiences and expressions of gratitude have been treated as both basic and desirable aspects of human personality and social life. From the perspectives of moral philosophy and theology, gratitude is seen as a human strength that enhances one's personal and relational well-being and is beneficial for society as a whole (Simmel, 1950).

Developmental theorists from Melanie Klein to the present have considered gratitude a capacity present from birth that develops as the child's cognitive and emotional systems mature. Klein (1957) viewed gratitude as a developmental achievement and hallmark of emotional maturity that "underlies the appreciation of goodness in others and in oneself" (p. 187). Psychological research has shown that children's comprehension of gratitude develops over several years. Although children are encouraged by their parents to write thank-you notes, gratitude does not appear to occur regularly in response to receiving benefits until middle childhood. It appears that the link between attributions of responsibility for positive outcomes, the experience of gratitude, and the desire to do good to one's benefactor probably is solidified between ages 7 and 10 (see Weiner & Graham, 1988, for a review). Klein was especially interested in the processes that thwart or facilitate the achievement of gratitude. From the perspective of SDT, environments that are autonomy supportive are more likely to facilitate gratefulness than environments that are more controlling and less nurturing. In autonomy-supportive environments, a sense of thankfulness for life is less likely to be viewed as an obligation and, over time, is more likely to be incorporated into the self.

Little is known about the crucial role played by interpersonal relations and by spirituality in the emergence, development, and maintenance of gratitude. In this regard, programmatic, developmental research stands out as a critical priority. We do not know when gratitude becomes a stable personality trait or whether it is stable in childhood and adolescence. Valid, age-appropriate measures of gratitude need to be constructed. What are the best ways of measuring gratitude in children? In research with adults, there is no standardized, agreed-upon method of measuring gratitude—gratitude has been measured in a multitude of different ways and forms. Measurements of gratitude are generally of the self-report variety, but they can also be behavioral (Emmons, McCullough, & Tsang, 2003). Behavioral measures may be most appropriate with young children, and some researchers have looked at grateful behavior. It is often difficult, however, for researchers to know whether they are actually measuring gratitude, a form of politeness, or some other construct. Therefore, a combination of behavioral and self-report measures of gratitude might be the most useful.

We can easily envision a productive research program on gratitude, its antecedents and social correlates. Some of the following questions might appear on a research agenda: How is parenting associated with children's gratitude? SDT would predict that an autonomy-supportive family environment would facilitate the development and internalization of grateful traits. Do families vary in their "gratitude climate" that might promote or impede the child's capacity to feel grateful for life? Might relatedness to others and to God facilitate a consistent feeling of gratitude? Conversely, would an intervention to increase a child's personal sense of gratefulness (Emmons & McCullough, 2003) have positive personal and interpersonal (e.g., family functioning) benefits? One consequence of a gratitude intervention might be a greater feeling of relatedness toward close others and the community. Finally, how do religious and spiritual rituals influence socialization mechanisms in the cultivation of gratitude?

CONCLUSIONS

Virtually all of the research described in this chapter has used Judeo-Christian religious samples, and most of these samples are from Western nations. Religions with a personally transcendent god such as Judaism, Christianity, and Islam, as opposed to religions without personally transcendent gods, such as Hinduism and Buddhism, may influence personality development in diverse ways. However, believers in Hinduism and Buddhism often form very personal relationships with Hindu deities or with the Buddha, respectively. These types of relationships can also be examined using SDT. SDT is a broad theory that works well cross-culturally and offers researchers a model of personality through which to study religious and spiritual development.

In cross-cultural theoretical models, individualism and collectivism are often dichotomized. However, the research presented in this chapter points out that dependence on another human being is not necessarily detrimental, but is actually beneficial for spiritual development. SDT argues that individuals can thrive in both a collectivist culture and in an individualistic culture if they can live autonomously, competently, and feel a sense of relatedness with others. The psychological definition of the interdependent, collective model of self that is prevalent in Eastern cultures argues that "persons are not independent, autonomous entities but are instead fundamentally interdependent with one another" (Markus & Kitayama, 1998, p. 69). Autonomy, according to SDT, is not synonymous with independence and individualism. Relationality, the concern for being a part of the group and for improving relations between the self and what is expected in the group, can be an internalized belief. Both reflective action sensitive to others' feelings and an active concern for upholding social expectations can be volitional and originate within the self. Relatedness with others is thus seen as an extremely important part of the self's organization and worth, and as such, the individual strives to maintain and improve relatedness with others. Several studies exploring the cultural generality of SDT have found that individuals in Eastern cultures do feel autonomous in their beliefs and actions, and at the same time are interdependent on one another (Ryan et al., 1999). Far from being a theory confined to individualistic cultures, SDT can be used to study diverse religious traditions, including those rooted in collectivist cultures, and offers researchers a theoretical framework applicable to both Western and non-Western populations.

Religious and spiritual variables and their relationship to personality development are understudied. The field is expanding, though, and more research is produced each year dealing with religious issues in youth. Personality psychologists are beginning to look at the developing youngster in complex ways, studying more than simply the personality traits exhibited. Motivation and prosocial behaviors, such as gratitude and forgiveness, are important pieces of personality. These constructs, in conjunction with the Big Five personality traits, provide psychologists with rich research possibilities.

So far as religion and spirituality affect integration of the self, these processes must be studied developmentally. An autonomy-supportive spirituality can provide an interpretation of one's experiences and provide an overarching and transcendent structure to one's sense of self. Relatedness to God enables youth to feel connected and loved, and relationships with others in the same spiritual tradition provide social support and nurturance to developing youth. The needs of children and adolescents for adequate personality development change as individuals grow cognitively, emotionally, and spiritually; these changing needs must be reflected in the research conducted with youth.

Today's psychologists need to continue their search for innovative ways to tap into religious constructs in children. William James's remarkable insight into psychological and religious processes led to his subsequent reliance on autobiographical documents and interviews; these methodological tools will prove to be very powerful in current research with youth. Listening to and analyzing prayers of children for evidence of need satisfaction and self-development, talking extensively with youth about religious beliefs and values, and role playing are all similar to James's approach in the 19th century. Coupled with experimental designs and longitudinal investigations, the study of the development of spirituality and personality can be greatly enhanced.

REFERENCES

Allport, G. W., & Ross, J. M. (1967). Personal religious orientation and prejudice. *Journal of Personality and Social Psychology, 5,* 432–443.

Baard, P. P. (2002). Intrinsic need satisfaction in organizations: A motivational basis of success in for-profit and not-for-profit settings. In E. L. Deci & R. M. Ryan (Eds.), *Handbook of self-determination research* (pp. 255–275). Rochester, NY: University of Rochester Press.

Batson, C. D., & Ventis, W. L. (1982). *The religious experience: A social-psychological perspective.* New York: Free Press.

Bauer, J. J., & McAdams, D. P. (2000). Competence, relatedness, and autonomy in life stories. *Psychological Inquiry, 11,* 276–279.

Benson, P. L., Roehlkepartain, E. C., & Rude, S. P. (2003). Spiritual development in childhood and adolescence: Toward a field of inquiry. *Applied Developmental Science, 7,* 205–213.

Boyatzis, C. J., & Janicki, D. (2003). Parent–child communication about religion: Survey and diary data on unilateral transmission and bi-directional reciprocity styles. *Review of Religious Research, 44,* 252–270.

Brousson Anderson, C. (1998). The experience of growing up in a minister's home and the religious commitment of the adult child of a minister. *Pastoral Psychology, 46,* 393–411.

Chandler, C. L., & Connell, J. P. (1987). Children's intrinsic, extrinsic and internalized motivation:

A developmental study of children's reasons for liked and disliked behaviours. *British Journal of Developmental Psychology, 5,* 357–365.

de Vaus, D. A. (1983). The relative importance of parents and peers for adolescent religious orientation: An Australian study. *Adolescence, 18,* 147–158.

Deci, E. L., & Ryan, R. M. (1985). *Intrinsic motivation and self-determination in human behavior.* New York: Plenum.

Deci, E. L., Schwartz, A. J., Sheinman, L., & Ryan, R. M. (1981). An instrument to assess adults' orientations toward control versus autonomy with children: Reflections on intrinsic motivation and perceived competence. *Journal of Educational Psychology, 73,* 642–650.

Emmons, R. A., & McCullough, M. E. (2003). Counting blessings versus burdens: Experimental studies of gratitude and subjective well-being in daily life. *Journal of Personality and Social Psychology, 84,* 377–389.

Emmons, R. A., & McCullough, M. E. (Eds.). (2004). *The psychology of gratitude.* New York: Oxford University Press.

Emmons, R. A., McCullough, M. E., & Tsang, J. (2003). The measurement of gratitude. In S. Lopez & C. R. Snyder (Eds.), *Handbook of positive psychology assessment* (pp. 327–341). Washington, DC: American Psychological Association.

Emmons, R. A., & Paloutzian, R. F. (2003). The psychology of religion. *Annual Review of Psychology, 54,* 377–402.

Flor, D. L., & Knapp, N. F. (2001). Transmission and transaction: Predicting adolescents' internalization of parental religious values. *Journal of Family Psychology, 15,* 627–645.

Fowler, J. W. (1981). *Stages of faith: The psychology of human development and the quest for meaning.* San Francisco: Harper & Row.

Frederick-Recascino, C. M. (2002). Self-determination theory and participation motivation research in the sport and exercise domain. In E. L. Deci & R. M. Ryan (Eds.), *Handbook of self-determination research* (pp. 277–294). Rochester, NY: University of Rochester Press.

Gillespie, V. B. (1991). *The dynamics of religious conversion: Identity and transformation.* Birmingham, AL: Religious Education Press.

Goldberg, D. P., & Hillier, V. F. (1979). A scaled version of the General Health Questionnaire. *Psychological Medicine, 9,* 139–145.

Goodnow, J. J. (1992). Parents' ideas, children's ideas: Correspondence and divergence. In I. E. Sigel, A. V. McGillicuddy-DeLisi, & J. J. Goodnow (Eds.), *Parental belief systems: The psychological consequences for children* (2nd ed., pp. 293–317). Hillsdale, NJ: Erlbaum.

Grolnick, W. S., & Apostoleris, N. H. (2002). What makes parents controlling? In E. L. Deci & R. M. Ryan (Eds.), *Handbook of self-determination research* (pp. 161–181). Rochester, NY: University of Rochester Press.

Grolnick, W. S., & Ryan, R. M. (1989). Parent styles associated with children's self-regulation and competence in school. *Journal of Educational Psychology, 52,* 890–898.

James, W. (1902). *The varieties of religious experience.* London: Longmans.

Jones, A., & Crandall, R. (1986). Validation of a short index of self-actualization. *Personality and Social Psychology Bulletin, 12,* 63–73.

King, K. M., Lynch, J. H., & Ryan, R. M. (1989). *The relatedness to God scale.* Unpublished manuscript, University of Rochester, Rochester, NY.

Kirkpatrick, L. A., & Shaver, P. R. (1992). An attachment-theoretical approach to romantic love and religious belief. *Personality and Social Psychology Bulletin, 18,* 266–275.

Klein, M. (1957). *Envy and gratitude: A study of unconscious sources.* New York: Basic Books.

Kneezel, T. T., & Ryan, R. M. (2004, May). *Not just a reflection of parents: God as a source of support and nurturance.* Paper presented at the International Conference on Self-Determination Theory, University of Ottawa, Canada.

Kosek, R. B. (1999). Adaptation of the Big Five as a hermeneutic instrument for religious constructs. *Personality and Individual Differences, 27,* 229–237.

Kuczynski, L. (2003). Beyond bidirectionality: Bilateral conceptual frameworks for understanding dynamics in parent–child relations. In L. Kuczynski (Ed.), *Handbook of dynamics in parent–child relations* (pp. 3–24). Thousand Oaks, CA: Sage.

Lee, C. (1992). *PK: Helping pastors' kids through their identity crisis.* Grand Rapids, MI: Zondervan.

Lepper, M. R., Greene, D., & Nisbett, R. E. (1973). Undermining children's intrinsic interest with extrinsic rewards: A test of the "overjustification" hypothesis. *Journal of Personality and Social Psychology, 28,* 129–137.

MacDonald, D. A. (2000). Spirituality: Description, measurement, and relation to the five factor model of personality. *Journal of Personality, 68*, 153–197.

Markus, H. R., & Kitayama, S. (1998). The cultural psychology of personality. *Journal of Cross-Cultural Psychology, 29*, 63–87.

McAdams, D. P. (1995). What do we know when we know a person? *Journal of Personality, 63*, 365–396.

McCrae, R. R., & Costa, P. T. (1999). A five-factor model of personality. In L. A. Pervin & O. P. John (Eds.), *Handbook of Personality: Theory and research* (pp. 139–153). New York: Guilford.

McCullough, M. E., Tsang, J., Brion, S. (2003). Personality traits in adolescence as predictors of religiousness in early adulthood: Findings from the Terman Longitudinal Study. *Personality and Social Psychology Bulletin, 29*, 980–991.

O'Brien, E. J., & Epstein, S. (1987). *The multidimensional self-esteem inventory.* Odessa, FL: Psychological Assessment Resources.

Okagaki, L., Hammond, K. A., & Seamon, L. (1999). Socialization of religious beliefs. *Journal of Applied Developmental Psychology, 20*, 273–294.

Reeve, J. (2002). Self-determination theory applied to educational settings. In E. L. Deci & R. M. Ryan (Eds.), *Handbook of self-determination research* (pp. 183–203). Rochester, NY: University of Rochester Press.

Rowatt, W. C., & Kirkpatrick, L. A. (2002). Two dimensions of attachment to God and their relation to affect, religiosity, and personality constructs. *Journal for the Scientific Study of Religion, 41*, 637–651.

Rubin, K. H., Coplan, R. J., Nelson, L. J., Cheah, C. S. L., & Lagace-Seguin, D. G. (1999). Peer relationships in childhood. In M. H. Bornstein & M. E. Lamb (Eds.), *Developmental psychology: An advanced textbook* (4th ed., pp. 451–501). Mahwah, NJ: Erlbaum.

Ryan, R. M., Chirkov, V. I., Little, T. D., Sheldon, K. M., Timoshina, E., & Deci, E. L. (1999). The American dream in Russia: Extrinsic aspirations and well-being in two cultures. *Personality and Social Psychology Bulletin, 25*, 1509–1524.

Ryan, R. M., & Deci, E. L. (2000). Self-determination theory and the facilitation of intrinsic motivation, social development, and well-being. *American Psychologist, 55*, 68–78.

Ryan, R. M., & Deci, E. L. (2002). Overview of self-determination theory: An organismic dialectical perspective. In E. L. Deci & R. M. Ryan (Eds.), *Handbook of self-determination research* (pp. 3–33). Rochester, NY: University of Rochester Press.

Ryan, R. M., Mims, V., & Koestner, R. (1983). Relation of reward contingency and interpersonal context to intrinsic motivation: A review and text using cognitive evaluation theory. *Journal of Personality and Social Psychology, 45*, 736–750.

Ryan, R. M., Rigby, S., & King, K. (1993). Two types of religious internalization and their relations to religious orientations and mental health. *Journal of Personality and Social Psychology, 65*, 586–596.

Simmel, G. (1950). *The sociology of Georg Simmel.* Glencoe, IL: Free Press.

Smetana, J. G., & Daddis, C. (2002). Domain-specific antecedents of parental psychological control and monitoring: The role of parenting beliefs and practices. *Child Development, 73*, 563–580.

Smith, C. (2003). *Moral believing animals.* New York: Oxford University Press.

Snyder, C. R., & McCullough, M. E. (2000). A positive psychology field of dreams: "If you build it, they will come . . ." *Journal of Social and Clinical Psychology, 19*, 151–160.

Strahan, B. J., & Craig, B. (1995). *Marriage, family and religion.* Sidney, Australia: Adventist Institute of Family Relations.

Taylor, A., & MacDonald, D. A. (1999). Religion and the five factor model of personality: An exploratory investigation using a Canadian university. *Personality and Individual Differences, 27*, 1243–1259.

Vallerand, R. J., & Bissonnette, R. (1992). Intrinsic, extrinsic, and amotivational styles as predictors of behavior: A prospective study. *Journal of Personality, 60*, 599–620.

Weiner, B., & Graham, S. (1988). Understanding the motivational role of affect: Life-span research from an attributional perspective. *Cognition and Emotion, 3*, 401–419.

Williams, G. C. (2002). Improving patients' health through supporting the autonomy of patients and providers. In E. L. Deci & R. M. Ryan (Eds.), *Handbook of self-determination research* (pp. 233–254). Rochester, NY: University of Rochester Press.

PART IV

THE ECOLOGIES OF
SPIRITUAL DEVELOPMENT

Introduction to Part IV

The intention of this section is to provide an overview of the complex contexts in which spiritual development occurs. As noted in the introduction, this volume draws upon a developmental systems approach to argue that spiritual development should not focus solely on individual transformation, but must also take seriously the transactions between the individual and the many systems in which they live. Consequently, the authors of the following four chapters examine how spiritual development is embedded within multilayered systems.

Part IV begins with a macrosystemic analysis of religion and spirituality as cultural phenomena, and considers the role of ethnicity and culture in spiritual development. Jacqueline S. Mattis, Muninder K. Ahluwalia, Sheri-Ann E. Cowie, and Aria M. Kirkland-Harris examine the ways in which socially constructed group identities (e.g., race, ethnicity, culture) shape the form, content, and trajectory of people's religious and spiritual development. They do so by taking into account important differences in societies that assume a separation of sacred and secular domains of life and those in which religiosity and spirituality are perceived as inextricably bound and interwoven.

The next three chapters look closely at different microsystems. First, Chris J. Boyatzis, David C. Dollahite, and Loren D. Marks discuss how spiritual development takes place within a family context, examining how families may help or hinder the promotion of transcendence of the self. They consider different models of religious and spiritual influence in families; the role of narrative epistemology and ritual in family life; the role of mothers, fathers, and siblings in children's religious growth; generative spirituality; and unhealthy spirituality in families. In the process, they demonstrate the intricate relationship between spirituality, religion, and family life.

Extending beyond the family, Kelly Dean Schwartz, William M. Bukowski, and Wayne T. Aoki explore peer, mentor, and guru (e.g., sage, youth director, spiritual director) microsystems. They also examine the powerful ways in which extrafamilial relationships can be complementary or compensatory in spiritual development. These investigators establish the significance of reciprocal influences between children and adolescents and their social context and weigh the existing theoretical and empirical evidence for the unique influences of peers, mentors, and gurus.

In the final chapter of this section, Eugene C. Roehlkepartain and Eboo Patel consider how religious congregations potentially serve as rich contexts of spiritual transformation. They emphasize that congregations represent a unique focal point for exploring the dynamic interplay of numerous forces and processes in spiritual development, such as personal agency, self-reflection, moral guidance, intergenerational relationships, rituals, traditions, and practices that build bridges to the sacred and transcendent. Roehlkepartain and Patel illustrate the dynamic ecologies of congregations through the case study of a young Ismaili Muslim in London.

Part IV demonstrates the considerable theoretical and empirical growth within the field of spiritual development and at the same time acts as a signpost for the extent to which further study is needed. Early approaches to spiritual, religious, or faith development underscore individual change or transformation. The authors in this section provide evidence that the field is *beginning* to shift its focus from individuals to transactions between individuals and the various contexts in which they function. Although each chapter documents the work begun in each of these areas and points to additional areas for research, surely other contexts such as schools (both faith-based and public), camps, after-school programs, and health care providers merit investigation.

20

ETHNICITY, CULTURE, AND SPIRITUAL DEVELOPMENT

Jacqueline S. Mattis

Muninder K. Ahluwalia

Sheri-Ann E. Cowie

Aria M. Kirkland-Harris

It generally is accepted that religiousness and spirituality are cultural-level phenomena (see Geertz, 1973). However, most studies in the United States that endeavor to explore the relationship between religiosity, spirituality, ethnicity, and culture do so by examining racial differences in patterns of religiousness (e.g., in patterns of service attendance, prayer, or religious salience). Although these race-based studies purport to reveal group differences in religious and spiritual experience, they do little to explicate the ways in which socially constructed group identities (e.g., race, ethnicity, culture) shape the form, content, and trajectory of people's religious and spiritual development. We assert that any serious efforts to use ethnicity, culture, or race as analytic devices must lead

us to interrogate, rethink, and recast the most basic tenets of our thinking about religious and spiritual life. Analyses that attend seriously to ethnicity and race must force confrontations with questions that seem at once simplistic and profound: Who, from a global perspective, is a child? Are childhood and adolescence universal concepts? When does selfhood/beingness, and therefore spiritual life, begin? For whom and in what contexts do the concepts of religiosity, spirituality, and spiritual development make sense? How are religiosity and spirituality shaped by the social, political, and economic ecologies in which young people live?

As a point of entry into our exploration of the links between ethnicity, culture, race, religiosity, and spirituality in the lives of youth, we first

---

AUTHORS' NOTE: The authors wish to thank the following individuals for their contributions to the content of this manuscript: Dr. Daljit Singh Ahluwalia, Devinder Kaur Ahluwalia, Mouhamed Diop, Zerish Mattis Easton, Monica Hall, Rev. Dr. Cedric Kirkland-Harris, Rev. Dr. Linda Kirkland-Harris, Shelia Powell-Porteous, and Beryl Watson.

offer definitions of these core constructs. Importantly, our review of definitions of ethnicity and culture, and of extant literature on the link between ethnicity, culture, and spirituality, suggests a need to problematize a number of culture-bound assumptions that undergird existing social science scholarship. First, we note that Western (i.e., mainstream European American) philosophical systems assume a division between sacred and secular domains of life. This perspective exists in direct contrast with cultural tenets that imagine religiosity and spirituality as inextricably bound to and interwoven with all aspects of life. This latter cultural perspective on spirituality raises challenging considerations about the meaning and social scientific study of spiritual development. More specifically, these differences in perspectives highlight the point that bounded notions of spirituality have led mainstream European and European American social scientists to construct and study spiritual development in terms of a fairly distinct set of content areas (e.g., beliefs about the divine) and practices (e.g., participation in formal worship activities). However, for those cultures that embrace a more integrative perspective on spirituality, all aspects of life (psychological, physical, cognitive, social, and political) are imbued with spiritual content and are relevant in any discourse on spiritual development. For example, some cultures believe that children are reincarnations of ancestral spirits. In such contexts, a child's physical features, behavior, personality style, luck, and fate (e.g., vocation in life) are inextricable from the life of the spirit that he or she inherited. Indeed, these aspects of a child's life may serve as evidence of the reincarnation. In other cultures, each child is imagined as a unique and new entity whose development is shaped exclusively by his or her experiences in the world. In these latter communities, discussions of a child's physical features, personality, behavior, and fate would likely focus primarily on issues of genetics, subjective experiences of attachment, reinforcements, personal motivations, and individual choice.

Second, we note that Western psychologists tend, in general, to privilege the independent self (i.e., the individual) as the principal unit of analysis in studies of development. In these cultural contexts, the self denotes a being that is contained and separable, and that can be imagined outside of the context of community or relationship. Further, the "spirit" is understood as that ephemeral aspect of the living self that is distinct from one's body. This construction of the self stands in direct contrast with cultural constructions in which it is understood that beings are indexical (i.e., communally situated), and that beingness/selfhood cannot exist outside of the context of community. Finally, Western social science has constructed youth and youth development in ways that privilege chronological time over "social time," and that assume that childhood and adolescence are periods of development that exist universally and have universal meaning. On a practical level, these culture-bound notions of spirituality and religion, beingness/selfhood, and of time, have led Western social scientists to conceptualize religious and spiritual development in ways that highlight subjective endorsement of beliefs and practices that are assumed to be religious (rather than secular), and that assume a link between chronology and spiritual maturity. In this chapter we explore and challenge contemporary approaches to the study of the relationship between ethnicity, culture, and spirituality. We also advance a set of recommendations regarding future studies of the links between these constructs.

On Ethnicity, Culture, and Race

Much of the research in the United States that attends to religious and spiritual development in the lives of youth focuses on "race" rather than on ethnicity and culture (e.g., Regnerus, Smith, & Fritsch, 2003; Smith, Faris, Denton, & Regnerus, 2003). In some instances, the terms *race* and *ethnicity* are used interchangeably. For example, in their seminal paper on adolescent religiosity, under the heading of "Race/Ethnicity," Donahue and Benson (1995) wrote:

The Monitoring the Future (MtF) study invariably shows large differences in attendance and self-rated importance of religion favoring African American over "white" (non-Hispanic) high school seniors. . . . MtF does not analyze data from other ethnic groups because of concerns about the unrepresentativeness of their samples. (p.149)

The reference to African Americans and Whites as ethnic groups, although common in social science literature, is erroneous. For example, the label African American/Black is broadly applied to Blacks born in the United States, Afro-Caribbeans (e.g., Jamaicans, Haitians), and Blacks of Central American, European, and continental African ancestry. Because the label groups people on the basis of physical characteristics (e.g., darker skin and genetic history that includes people of Black African ancestry), *African American* is a racial rather than an ethnic label.

Many studies that focus on race attempt to explain the complex functioning of religion and spirituality in the lives of youth of diverse backgrounds by deploying race or ethnicity as a unidimensional independent variable in models that seek to explain key social and psychological outcomes (e.g., substance use and academic outcomes). Although many social science researchers do not explicitly endorse ideas of biological race, our uncritical use of labels such as *Black, White,* and *Asian* reinforces Stone's (1995) point that beliefs about biologically determined races continue to operate in sociological arguments. Indeed, race, as conceptualized in many Western nations, is a biologized social construct (i.e., a construct that is believed to be tied to biology, particularly to genes), and differences that emerge from the studies that deploy race as a predictor variable are presumed to reveal important and meaningful differences between groups. However, studies that purport to reveal group differences in religiosity and spirituality typically fail to attend to at least three key points. First, these studies fail to consider that race is not a universally meaningful social construct. The concept of race does not exist in all communities. Further, relatively few non-Western nations and communities use race as a way of organizing the social world. Second, studies that use race fail to unpack the complexities associated with lumping vast and disparate groups of people under discrete racial categories that are based on similarities in phenotype (e.g., skin color, hair texture). Finally, these studies

fail to account for the reality that race often serves as a proxy for complex historical relationships (i.e., relationships of power and domination) as well as a proxy for other indices of social location (e.g., class) and social identity (e.g., ethnicity and cultural identity).

In contrast to the focus on race in mainstream social science scholarship in the United States, scholars in other nations and communities have paid greater attention to *ethnicity* and *culture* as constructs of interest. The term ethnicity is used by social scientists to refer to "distinctions based on national origin, language, religion, food and other markers" (Frable, 1997, p. 142). In the 1960s, the word ethnicity was emphasized as a tool for discussing the ways in which "groups and entities arise and define themselves as against others also engaged in the process of development and self-definition" (Wolf, 1994, p. 6). This usage suggests that ethnicity is interactive in that it is shaped by the relations between and among groups based on religion, original heritage, politics, economics, and geographic territory (Modood, Berthoud, & Nazroo, 2002). Although, from a sociological perspective, ethnicity is used to refer to "concerns of community culture, kinship and power" (Abraham, 2001, p. 981), in contemporary scholarly discourses the term is often used to explain histories of conflict between people. In sum, ethnicity serves as a political fault line in the modern world (Rothchild & Alexander, 1995). Phinney asserts that in psychology, the word ethnicity, also referred to as ethnic identity, is used inconsistently. The word is used by some authors to mean "self-identification (self-definition, self-labeling), others emphasize attitudes and feelings (group belonging, commitment, and pride), and yet others stress cultural aspects (knowledge of ethnic language, behavior, and values; involvement with group members and practices)" (as cited in Frable, 1997, p. 141).

Ethnicity is often used as a synonym for culture. The words have distinct meanings, however. Culture, Geertz writes, "denotes a historically transmitted pattern of meanings embodied in symbols, a system of inherited conceptions expressed in symbolic forms by means of which men communicate, perpetuate, and develop their knowledge about and attitudes toward life"

(Geertz, 1973, p. 89). Kroeber and Kluckhohn (1963) add that *culture* refers to "patterns, explicit and implicit, of and for behavior acquired and transmitted by symbols, constituting the distinctive achievement of human groups, including their embodiments of artifacts; the essential core of culture consists of traditional (i.e., historically derived and selected) ideas and especially their attached values; culture systems may, on the one hand, be considered as products of actions, on the other as conditioning elements of further action" (p. 357). At the level of ideology, culture shapes people's notions of the nature of the sacred, the nature of God, and the nature of "beingness" (i.e., selfhood).

In order to transcend the conceptual fuzziness created by overlaps in scholarly definitions of these two terms, we ground our usage of these two terms in the following anthropological definition of ethnicity proffered by Wolf (1994). Wolf notes that among anthropologists, there has been a shift toward conceptualizing ethnicity as "the idea of common descent as a transgenerational vehicle for the transmission of an authentically rooted culture" (1994, p. 6). In sum, we conceptualize ethnicity in terms of common descent and common national origins. We conceive of ethnicity's relation to culture in terms of its utility as a means of transmitting cultural content (shared meanings, beliefs, values, symbolic and material traditions, patterns of social organization, etc.).

Religiosity and spirituality are domains of culture that have garnered particular interest in the social sciences. Wulff (1991) notes that the word *religiosity* is derived from the Latin word *religio* and refers to a belief in the existence of a divine or superhuman force, and to one's adherence to the beliefs and public and private ritual practices that signify reverence for this divine or superhuman force (see also James, 1999; Mattis, 2000; Zinnbauer et al., 1997). *Spirituality,* derived from the Latin word *spiritus,* which means "breath of life" (Berdyaev, 1939; MacQuarrie, 1972), simultaneously denotes a belief in a transcendent dimension of life, the intimate relationship between humans and the divine, and one's quest toward goodness and righteousness that resulted from that relationship (Mattis, 2000; Zinnbauer et al., 1997). However meaningful these definitions may be

in reflecting U.S. perspectives on religiosity and spirituality, we must remain mindful that these definitions do not necessarily reflect the perspectives of people worldwide.

ETHNICITY, CULTURE, AND THE CONCEPT OF SPIRITUAL DEVELOPMENT

Ethnicity (i.e., ethnic identity) is often invented and imposed in response to external interventions (e.g., colonialism), and political and religious conflict (war, genocide). For example, the nation of Hercegovina was created as means of resolving political and religious conflicts between Catholic ethnic Bosnians (e.g., Serbians and Croatians) and their Muslim counterparts (Sells, 2003). Similarly, India's division into India and Pakistan reflected political and religious divisions (between India's largely Hindu community and the Muslims who were segmented into the nation that is now Pakistan) that occurred with and in response to independence from British colonial rule. Importantly, as national lines are (re)drawn, and as people are reconfigured into new ethnic and religious communities, young people find themselves having to construct new political, ethnic, and religious identities—identities that in many cases are distinct from those held by their older siblings, peers, and their families. For example, a 9-year-old Yugoslavian child born to parents who were atheists, but who had a Muslim last name, could have awakened one day to find that, by fiat, she and her family had been redefined as Hercegovinian Muslims (see Sells, 2003). A child in such a position would have to negotiate a new national and ethnic identity (e.g., Hercegovinian of Yugoslavian ancestry) that is tied inextricably to a religious identity and tradition (e.g., a Muslim in a nation of Muslims) with which she is ideologically unfamiliar.

In many contexts, national identity, ethnic identity, and religious identity are inextricably intertwined. In these contexts, religious and spiritual identity may be determined exclusively by one's national and ethnic identities (i.e., to be Malay is to be Muslim). In most communities, a young person's religious identity is determined by the religious and cultural identity of one or both of the parents. For example, a child whose mother is Jewish is considered to be Jewish, and that child may be raised either as a religious or as a secular Jew.

In religiously and ethnically pluralistic societies, young people may have the freedom to determine how to construct and negotiate their religious and spiritual identities. For example, in England, a child whose father is Catholic and whose mother is Anglican might worship with friends at a local synagogue, and may adopt a religious and spiritual framework that is a synthesis of Christianity, Judaism, and Eastern religions (e.g., Hinduism). In these latter contexts, religious identity does not stand in opposition to ethnic identity.

In some contexts, interethnic, intercultural, and interracial unions further complicate religious and spiritual development. Importantly, throughout the world there are youth who live under the rubric of more than one ethnic label/identity and who, consequently, live under the rubric of more than one set of spiritual and religious influences. For example, there are places (e.g., Tanzania) where young people often describe themselves as Christian, Muslim, and traditional adherents. While such identity descriptions may seem ideologically contradictory, they point to the complex ways in which people transcend ideological boundaries in the service of constructing coherent identities for themselves. The ways in which, and the extent to which, these blended religious and spiritual identities inform religious practice are topics worthy of examination. Certainly, anthropological research demonstrates that some communities symbiotically blend various religious ideologies and practices in ways that result in entirely new religions (see Brandon, 1993; Desmangles, 1992; Stewart, 1999). For example, Haitian Catholicism resulted from the unique blend of African religions, African, European, and indigenous Carib Indian cultural practices, and European Catholicism. We certainly cannot lose sight of the reality that anthropological and historical studies of religious syncretism or religious symbiosis tend to account for the ways in which entire religious communities are shaped by decades or centuries of contact. When such blends are studied cross-sectionally, at the individual level, and among adolescents, social science researchers may be tempted to imagine that blended identities reflect a point of unresolved religious and spiritual searching. Such a perspective would be erroneous since it would fail to account for the complex ways in which macrolevel religious and spiritual movements manifest in the everyday lives of young people.

INFLUENCES OF RELIGION AND SPIRITUALITY ON DEVELOPMENTAL MARKERS AND TRAJECTORY

Any effort to explore spiritual development necessarily entails critical thought concerning the way in which ethnic and cultural groups resolve fundamental questions about the inception and the evolution of life: At what point does life begin? At what point do children have a spiritual life? And at what point and through what processes do young people become members of their religious/spiritual communities?

Spiritual Development and Ritual Processes Pre- and Postbirth

In some cultural contexts it is understood that spiritual development begins prior to birth. In communities in which reincarnation and transmigration of the soul are accepted, people believe that children inherit their spirit/soul from individuals who have died. According to Magesa (1997), "The life force of the deceased comes to inhabit, protect, and shape the character of the child" (p. 89). Because conception and childbirth mark the return of a deceased ancestor, the child is thought, therefore, to have spiritual powers. In African American, Caribbean, and some African communities, people speak of children who are "old spirits" or "old souls." These old souls are children whose wisdom, character, and/or physical appearance give evidence that they have been through this life before, and that they have brought existing knowledge and experience into this life. Old souls, in sum, are children who have entered the world with a particular level of spiritual maturity that distinguishes them from their peers.

In instances where spiritual development is thought to begin before birth, families and communities also are intimately aware of the spiritual vulnerability of young people, and they engage in practices that are intended to protect the spirit of unborn children and of neonates. The spiritual vulnerability of children is evident in cultural beliefs about the impact of the evil eye on newborns and infants. The evil eye (*mal de ojo; maldjo,* Grenada; *mal-yeux,* Haiti; *maljoe,* Trinidad; *nazar,* India) occurs when a person excessively admires a child, for some length of time, with a direct and insistent look, or with lavish praise and compliments (Burleigh, Dardano, & Cruz, 1990). A belief in the evil eye is widely held, not only in Latin American and Caribbean countries, but also in countries in Northern Africa, Europe, the Mediterranean (Leach & Fried, 1972; Obermeyer, 2000), and South Asia (Babb, 1975).

In some African cultures, individuals believe that ancestors assist in protecting unborn children and neonates from malevolent forces (Magesa, 1997). In some contexts, families and community members may create a matrix of care for the unborn child through prayer, spiritual rituals, or the use of spiritual symbols and objects. Among Hindus in India, for example, a pregnant woman wears charms and amulets to protect her from the glance of the evil eye. Women may keep iron nearby in order to ward off *jadu-tona* or witchcraft and *bhut-pret* or malevolent ghosts (Babb, 1975). In some Latin American communities, if the infant or the mother is already a victim of the evil eye, a family member or a trusted person (e.g., a *curandero,* or healer) will conduct a *limpia* (spiritual cleansing) using herbs and/or by passing an egg over the body to absorb the negative influence of the evil eye. In Haiti, a *Houngan* (shaman-priest) also performs a cleansing by bathing the infant and feeding her or him leaves designed to make the infant's blood bitter and thus less appetizing in taste and smell to the spirits. After birth, Hindu rituals often use the color black in a deliberate attempt to put a visible "flaw" on infants to ward off the evil eye (Babb, 1975). In short, kajal or lampblack is placed on the baby's body or around the eyes, a black string may be tied around the baby's wrist, or an amulet may be worn.

Certain conditions (e.g., *susto,* fright, and *muinas,* anger) and events may also mark points of vulnerability in a young person's early spiritual development. *Susto,* also known as *espanto* (being frightened), *pasmo* (sluggishness), or *pérdida de sombra* (loss of one's shadow), is a condition experienced by mothers in several countries in the Caribbean, Latin America, and Asia (Rubel, O'Nell, & Collado Ardán, 1992). In infants, *susto* may occur after a fall or after witnessing something frightening (Villaseñor-Bayardo, 1994). When this happens the future mother's or the baby's "good fortune" (soul) is believed to abandon their body. To cure *susto,* a *curandero* or shaman conjures the "soul" (state of well-being or good luck) to return to the person's body through prayers and herbal remedies (Maduro, 1983). In the effort to ensure the appropriate development of a child's spirit, the family often prevents the mother from receiving bad news or being exposed to episodes of rage.

In other cultural contexts, life and spiritual development begin not at the point of conception or birth, but with the naming of a child. Magesa (1997) notes that a child's name, particularly the child's ancestral name, binds him or her to a spiritual community, and marks the beginning of moral character and development as a member of that community. The meanings attached to a child's name have implications for a child's destiny, for the values he or she will embody, and for the physical attributes he or she will manifest. The name signifies that the transmission of life is completed (Magesa, 1997). The process by which names are assigned to children varies from one cultural and religious context to another. In the Sikh religion in India and elsewhere, when a baby is born, the family turns to the religious text, the Guru Granth Sahib. The text is opened to a random page and the first letter of the first passage becomes the first letter of the baby's first name. The last (or, in some cases, the middle) name of the child is then given "by the gurus" to symbolize equality across castes and gender; boys receive the name Singh, meaning "lion," and girls receive the name Kaur, meaning "princess" or "lioness." In Hinduism, the name-giving ceremony is dictated by caste (Babb, 1975). Birth is considered a highly polluting event; the pollution falls over the entire household, and ridding the household of it requires many rituals. Among lower castes, the name of the baby is given on *chaati* day, which is 6 days after the birth of the baby and is the day on which the mother begins rituals to remove the pollution associated with giving birth. Among the higher castes, *namkaran,* a special name-giving ceremony, is conducted by a Brahman priest 12 days after the baby's birth.

While naming plays a role in the earliest phases of spiritual development, it can also play an important role in the latter stages of spiritual development. Nicknames are given to a child by peers. These nicknames may describe beauty or prowess. Nicknames may indicate a new stage in life and a new point in the process of spiritual development.

Cultural beliefs about *susto,* the evil eye, and other maladies reinforce a number of important points. First, the earliest stages of a child's development are highpoints of spiritual vulnerability. Second, malevolent and benevolent supernatural forces can exist in and act through members of the child's social network as well as the broader community. These forces can affect every aspect of a child's life (e.g., physical health, physical features, emotional well-being, and destiny). Finally, children's survival and healthy development depend on parents' and community members' ability to protect them from spiritual harm. Traditional healing techniques, the wearing of protective objects (e.g., amulets, crosses), and the deliberate choice of names are among the many strategies that communities employ in the effort to provide spiritual protection and to secure positive life outcomes for their children.

Membership in Spiritual and Religious Communities

In some cultural and religious communities, rituals of confirmation such as baptism, christening, a bris, or the assignment of godparents are the activities that mark the child's inclusion and membership in a particular community. In most Christian communities, the priest or religious leader pours water on the baby's forehead to symbolize the moment that the spirit of Christ cleanses the child of sin. This moment of baptism is a moment of sacred rebirth. In Ghana, babies are given a handful of water to drink because the water becomes an external conductor of the communication between humans and spirits (Gottlieb, 2003).

In Swazi nations, the ceremonial burial of the umbilical cord marks an important starting point for membership in the community. After a child is born, the child and mother are isolated to protect them from impurities. When the umbilical cord falls off, the father makes a mixture of bark and medicine with which the baby is washed. The mixture and the cord are then buried outside of the door of the space in which the mother and child have resided since the child's birth. After this rite is completed, the baby is qualified to be a human with a name (M'Passou, 1998).

Many ethnic and cultural communities have rituals and rites of passage that ensure incorporation into religious and ethnic community, and/or that signal the passage into adulthood (or personhood). Bar and bat mitzvahs, confirmations, and turban ceremonies serve such functions. In the Sikh religion, boys wear their hair in a joora, a topknot, and they wear a patka, a cloth covering, on top of the joora. As they get older, boys have a turban ceremony in which their family helps them tie their first turban in the presence of the holy book and the community. There is no equivalent spiritual ceremony for girls. In some contexts in which formal religious practices are distinct from indigenous spiritual practices, children may go through multiple rites of transition. For example, in Haitian and Haitian American communities, children may go through Catholic rites of baptism as well as rites of protection and passage related to vodun (voodoo).

In sum, religion and spirituality inform each community's ideas about when and by what process youth obtain an identity and gain membership into the community. For some communities rituals of transition may celebrate a child's membership in the community or may be the means by which children gain access to community. In other cultural contexts (e.g., in the religions of many African peoples), religion is "lived" and not "doctrinal." In many such contexts, youth are not involved in formal ceremonies of induction. Instead, members are born into the religious/spiritual community and learn the values and tenets of the community through experience and socialization (Magesa, 1997).

CULTURE, COMMUNITY AGENTS, AND SPIRITUAL DEVELOPMENT

The means by which transitions occur are important. Equally important, however, is the social context in which these transitions take place. A substantial amount of empirical attention has been paid to the role of biological parents in the religious socialization of young people. Less attention has been paid to the role of non-blood-related kin in the developmental process. Within every community, however, there are significant figures (family, religious leaders, community members, peers) and institutions (schools, temples) that participate in children's spiritual development. These social agents play crucial roles in organizing and enacting the activities (bar/bat mitzvahs, baptisms) that mark critical periods in the path toward spiritual maturity. They may also participate in informal public and private activities that have significance for young people's religious and spiritual development (Mattis, in press).

In Latin American countries such as El Salvador, Paraguay, Nicaragua, Bolivia, and Ecuador, as well as in the Caribbean (e.g., Dominican Republic) and Mexico, godparent-hood (*compadrazgo*) is an important relational context for supporting the spiritual development of youth (Weil, 1973). Godparents assist in the spiritual development of the child through prayers and by modeling appropriate religious behavior. Godparents are also necessary for incorporation into the Santeria community. Santeria (the worship of saints) is an Afro-Cuban religion that has its origins in the Yoruba people of Nigeria. Santeras (priestesses) and Santeros (priests) become the godparents and provide guidance for the child. In some traditions, godparents are chosen at baptism, confirmation, and/or marriage, thus making them a fixture at each major stage of the life cycle (e.g., birth, puberty, marriage).

Institutions (whether religious or secular) may also play crucial roles in the cultural, ethnic, and spiritual development of youth. These institutions provide children with contexts for socializing with in-group members, and for learning crucial lessons about what it means to be a member of the ethnic and religious community (Johnson & Stanford, 2002). Institutions serve as contexts for ideological and social support. In these spaces, youth are exposed to the systems of meaning, the texts, and the symbols that are central to their ethnic, cultural, and spiritual communities.

Although they are generally ignored in American social science research, griots, artists, and popular cultural icons also play important roles in shaping the spiritual lives of young people. In India, for example, filmmakers use the film industry, "Bollywood," as a means to transmit messages of the sacred, mysticism, and transcendence to youth and adults alike. In African American communities musicians (e.g., gospel singers and hip-hop gospel artists), many of whom are adolescents and young adults, also play significant roles in articulating important messages about spiritual life to youth.

Attention to the role of popular culture, art, and artists in spiritual socialization highlights the importance of attending to the content of the texts that these figures produce. Folk theories and narratives exist in the private and public domains of life, and serve as powerful assets in the religious and spiritual socialization of youth. In communities worldwide there are folk theories and folk narratives that represent childhood as a powerful, transformational moment (e.g., stories of the Buddha, Christ as a teen, the Dalai Lama, Krishna, Guru Har Krishan Ji). The folk stories that are common to a given culture also contain crucial information about that cultural community's laws, social rules, core beliefs, and moral mandates (e.g., Ma'at, the Beatitudes).

Sacred as well as secular music and poetry ("spoken word") are also important sites where many adolescents and young adults articulate spiritually relevant narratives. Music and poetry may serve as particularly ideal sites for expressing important yet transgressive ideas and concerns. For example, in his 1997 song "I Wonder If Heaven Got a Ghetto," hip-hop artist, poet, and singer Tupac Shakur observes:

It ain't a secret don't conceal the fact
The penitentiary's packed, and it's filled with blacks
I wake up in the morning and I ask myself

Is life worth living should I blast myself
I'm tired of being poor and even worse I'm black
My stomach hurts so I'm lookin' for a purse to snatch
Cops give a damn about a ne-gro
Pull a trigger kill a nigger he's a hero . . .
Let the Lord judge the criminals
If I die, I wonder if heaven got a ghetto

Shakur's text articulates a complex set of reflections about the unjust social arrangements that are evident on earth, and about the transgressive thoughts and actions that emanate from living with brutal oppression. He raises concerns about the extent to which the utopia (i.e., traditional notions of heaven and salvation) to which we aspire may replicate those same unjust arrangements. Although these concerns may seem vulgar, blasphemous, or outrageous to adults, they are meaningful to young people worldwide who must craft their spirituality in the context of everyday realities marked by injustice, extreme poverty, war, and oppression.

Taken together, these points suggest that as we consider the link between culture, ethnicity, religion, and spirituality, we must pay attention to the content of the stories told *about* children as well as those that are told *to* children. We must pay attention to the forms these stories take and the way in which they are shaped by culture. Attention to and knowledge of these stories can inform scholars about the experiences, beliefs, and behaviors that are key in a community's efforts to socialize young people. Further, if we are to gain access to young people's spiritual lives, our scholarship about adolescent spiritual development must also include critical analyses of the film, music, art, and poetry that they produce.

ETHNIC IDENTITY AND SPIRITUAL DEVELOPMENT

For many young people, the effort to construct and negotiate ethnic and religious identity is complicated by nationally legislated secularism, and/or by state sanctioned religious and ethnic preferences. For example, the French government,

claiming a tradition of secularism, has suspended and/or expelled Muslim youth who wear hijabs, Sikh youth who wear turbans, and Jewish children who wear yarmulkes to school. Youth in these contexts must attempt to forge their ethnic and spiritual identities in spaces that are hostile to them, and that force them to make decisions that undermine the integrity of their cultural, ethnic, racial, religious, and spiritual values and traditions.

It is important to note that race, skin color, religious dress, and other public markers of identity (e.g., last names) can be used to (mis)-identify young people as members of particular ethnic and religious communities. In certain settings, these public markers of identity can be perceived as threatening, and can be used to label individuals as outsiders and to target them for discrimination. For example, immediately after the 9/11 attacks in the United States, many Muslim men (including Muslim youth) were harassed and or incarcerated because of their affiliations with and support of religious and/or religious/political/ethnic organizations that were assumed to be linked to terrorism. Also, in the post-9/11 United States, Sikh youth and men wearing turbans were (and are) often misidentified as Muslim, and continue to be targeted for acts of discrimination and violence (Ahluwalia, 2004).

Religious and ethnic identity and the conflicts that arise in relation to these identities can serve as foundations for crafting mature spirituality. Youth growing up in political contexts and in historical moments in which ethnicity and religious identity serve as the foundations for discrimination or state-sanctioned pogroms ("ethnic cleansings") will, without doubt, be forced to grapple with questions of faith that may distinguish them from their peers who live in politically stable, accepting, and "secure" environments. For example, these youth may directly confront questions about the problem of evil, the relevance of forgiveness, and the meanings and limits of peace and freedom. Youth who confront such questions, and those who are faced with pressures from their peers to behave in ways that violate key spiritual norms (e.g., to engage in drug use or sexual activity), may use these experiences as launch points for clarifying their faith. Scholars who are interested in adolescent spiritual development must explore the nature of the ethnically determined conflicts young people encounter, the meanings they construct about these conflicts, and the impact of these consequences on their faith lives.

CULTURE, THE PHYSICAL BODY, AND SPIRITUAL MATURITY

The transition from childhood into adulthood is signified by a young person's physical as well as moral maturity. In sum, as children transition into adolescence, the developing body becomes a powerful and intimate space on which to inscribe and enact key spiritual and religious themes. Through their bodies, children and adolescents learn crucial lessons about culturally salient concepts such as humility and purity. In some cultural contexts, the inscribing of ethnic-spiritual markers happens through objects that are worn on the body. For example, for Hindus who are *dvija* (twice-born), a ceremony (Upanayana) occurs in which male members are invested with the janeu, the sacred thread that is worn over the left shoulder and the right hip. This thread is considered a source of pride as well as a burden, and those who are entitled to wear it are granted with a "clear superiority over the general run of men" (Babb, 1975, p. 78).

Many African communities use the body to impart important lessons regarding the sacredness of life and the importance of spiritual community. Children may be involved, for example, in processes of induction into certain groups and societies through blood friendships (Magesa, 1997). These unions, which are metaphorized in embodied space, teach young people about the importance of societal cohesion, and about the vital, intimate, and enduring nature of spiritual connections.

In circumcision and scarification rites, indicators of spiritual maturity are literally written on the bodies of youth. These rituals are always deliberately and intensely painful. The pain both instills fear and evokes courage in the moral character of the adolescent (Magesa, 1997). The physical elements of initiation, such as pain and scarring, are used to instill lessons about courage, self-sacrifice, and communal cooperation,

without which the culture and spiritual community will not survive. By submitting to physical pain, the young person metaphorically and literally acknowledges the harsh realities of life, and asserts a particular willingness to endure these costs in the service of the community's survival.

Changes in the body can signal a young person's entry into a new phase of religious and spiritual development. In Swazi nations, for example, the change from childhood to adulthood is marked by the physical commencement of puberty. Initiation rites associated with this transition take place in the bush, which is the home of spirits with transforming powers (Chakanza, 1998). These rituals of initiation signify the ever-present connection and interaction between ancestral spirits and human life. For males, the initiation process often begins with the first ejaculatory experience (i.e., "wet dream"), after which the young man is taught lessons regarding sexuality and male responsibility. For females, the initiation begins with her first menstruation, after which she participates in a rite of passage into womanhood (M'Passou, 1998).

The link between culture, ethnicity, physicality, and religious and spiritual development finds one of its most profound manifestations in youth martyrdom. In some communities, the willingness of youth to sacrifice their bodies (and lives) serves as the ultimate signal of moral, psychological, and spiritual maturity. The narrative traditions of various communities highlight this point. For example, when the 5- and 7-year-old sons of Guru Gobind Singh Ji (the 10th Sikh guru) refused forcible conversion to Islam, a brick wall was built to entomb them, thus ensuring their death. This act of sacrifice marked them as role models and leaders in the community.

Although body space is an important site for enacting themes and stages of spiritual development, communities also use geographic and social spaces to achieve these ends. In many cultural contexts, for example, the process of "spiritual" development includes initiation, seclusion from, and reincorporation into the community. In many African religions, young initiates are physically removed from society and they are not allowed contact with the people of their communities (Magesa, 1997). Magesa argues that through the process of seclusion and rein-corporation "the community is telling them in a very radical way that without membership in a community, a person is nothing" (p. 96). The initiates learn duties, responsibilities, and rights required for communal living through ancestral, religious, and community wisdom. Once the process has been completed, the initiates are reintegrated and reincorporated into the community. The reunion signifies physical, moral, and spiritual maturity.

We must note here that physicality need not be the sole or most salient marker of spiritual maturity. In some cultures, youth who are seen as spiritually mature can emerge as leaders of religious and ethnic communities. Maturity and preparedness for leadership may be determined through pre-established patterns of ascendancy, including lineage. Alternatively, youth may demonstrate their legitimacy as leaders through precocious wisdom, or through mastery of religious and spiritual principles.

Together these points suggest the need for scholarly attention to the mechanisms by which communities mark young people's transitions toward spiritual maturity. It is critical that scholars take an ecological approach to studies of spiritual maturity—one that accounts for shifts in the ways in which youth (and communities) negotiate their relationships to their bodies and to the broader community, as well as ways that account for wisdom, courage, sensitivity to others, and mastery of principles of faith.

CONCLUSIONS

Ethnicity and culture describe systems of thought and social organization that are transmitted historically, and that have enduring impact on the way people experience and make meaning about their world. However, the danger that looms over every serious discourse regarding ethnicity and culture is that these domains of identity will be treated as auxiliary rather than central. We believe that because religion and spirituality are cultural systems (see Geertz, 1973), any serious study of religiosity and spirituality must use culture and ethnicity as analytic devices. This belief leads us to several key considerations, each of which will have implications

for future research on adolescent spirituality and religion.

First, scholars must appreciate that culture is, by definition, a system of meaning making. As such, any serious cultural analysis of spiritual development must shift away from a social science of surveillance in which we limit our work to those aspects of life that are observable and easily quantifiable (e.g., behavior), and toward a study of religion and spirituality that is meaning centered. We must attend not simply to the *ascribed* meanings of events, objects, identities, and experiences but also to the *processes* by which meanings evolve. In achieving this latter end, researchers need to pay attention to both content (e.g., metaphors) and process (e.g., narrative styles). Further, we must employ methodologies (e.g., ethnography, conversational analysis) that will allow us to examine meaning making as well as the link between meaning and behavior.

Second, we must interrogate the assumptions that undergird the term *spiritual development*. Spiritual development, as conceptualized in Western (i.e., U.S.) social science, is rooted in a perspective that distinguishes between the spiritual/sacred and the secular, and in a very particular notion of self (i.e., body as distinct from spirit). This term suggests that we can understand and study the development of the spiritual domains of life in isolation from life's secular components. Magesa (1997) points out, however, that some ethnic and cultural communities make no distinctions between the secular and the spiritual. In those communities spiritual life involves the whole of life. As such, to study spiritual development is to study development. This point has practical implications for scholars. For example, research on spiritual development need not embrace narrow ideas about what outcomes and processes are spiritual and secular. We must, instead, acknowledge that young people's "spiritual" and "religious" values and ideologies are embedded in and inextricable from their relationships, academic life, psychological well-being, and health practices.

Third, for many communities the self is "indexical"—that is, the self emerges in relationship and does not exist outside of community. Social scientific work that is grounded in a preoccupation with the individual will inevitably fail to capture the reality of more communal cultural perspectives on spiritual development. As such, researchers must interrogate the assumptions behind the methods we use and the questions we ask. We must understand, for example, that implicit in many of our questions about religious and spiritual life is an assumption that faith is a matter of personal choice, and that key concepts such as worship, honor, salvation, grace, forgiveness, and love are relevant to individuals rather than entire families and communities. We will need to develop language and methodologies that are rooted in an appreciation of the fact that young people come to know God in and through relationships, and that their spiritual lives and identities are bound to the lives and identities of significant others (e.g., families and communities).

Fourth, given the inextricable link between ethnicity (e.g., national identity), cultural identity, and spirituality, our empirical examinations must attend to the way in which political, economic, and social forces influence spiritual development. For example, we might take note that in many communities children serve as soldiers, others bear witness to or are victims of police brutality, and some benefit from the spoils of war and oppression. We need to study the interplay between notions of ethnic pride, racial privilege, wealth, poverty, neocolonialism, war, patriotism, and young people's experience of faith. We must also explore what happens to the religious development of youth when role models (e.g., parents and siblings) and key religious leaders are removed from the community. Removal of religious models through arrest and deportation or through the placement of youth in alternative settings (e.g., foster homes) means that a crucial extension necessary to religious development has been severed. Greater attention to these points will, without doubt, advance our current knowledge about the development of spirituality among youth in the national and global landscape.

Fifth, given the complex ways in which people construct their identities, we must recognize and allow for interethnic and interreligious identifications. For example, some adolescents endorse religious identities that have multiple components (e.g., a part Muslim and a part Protestant). As such, researchers need to be mindful that forced-choice religious selections do not transport well across ethnic and cultural boundaries. As we account for the complex consequences of multiculturalism and globalization, we will need to be mindful of the ways in which diverse religious and spiritual practices and icons get transported and become incorporated into the belief systems of individuals and cultures.

Sixth, we need to grapple with questions about what constitutes legitimate text for the critical study of adolescent religiosity and spirituality. In particular, we must attend to the content and the structure (e.g., narrative style) of folk stories, parables, film, visual art, and music. We must explore the meanings that these cultural products reveal about the links between ethnicity, culture, race, religiosity, and spiritual development. In particular, there will be value in exploring what these products reveal about young people's spiritual beliefs and dilemmas.

Finally, researchers, particularly those in the United States, should be mindful to avoid the common trap of assuming that ethnicity and culture are constructs that have meaning only when they are applied to "people of color" or to international communities. Scholars have a responsibility to unpack racial labels such as *White*, and explore the meaning and functional significance of ethnicity and culture for those whose identities are subsumed under such labels. We also must resist efforts to use culture and ethnicity to exoticize the faith experiences of adolescents. If we attend critically to the meanings of culture and ethnicity, we stand to gain immeasurable insights into the religious and spiritual lives of youth worldwide.

References

Abraham, S. (2001). The shifting sources of racial definition in Trinidad and Tobago, and Guyana: A research agenda. *Ethnic and Racial Studies, 24,* 979–997.

Ahluwalia, M. K. (2004). *Sikh men post 9/11: Misidentification, discrimination, and masculinity in an era of violence.* Unpublished manuscript.

Babb, L. A. (1975). *The divine hierarchy.* New York: Columbia University Press.

Berdyaev, N. (1939). *Spirit and reality.* London: Centenary Press.

Brandon, G. (1993). *Santeria from Africa to the New World: The dead sell memories.* Bloomington: Indiana University Press.

Burleigh, E., Dardano, C., & Cruz, J. R. (1990). Colors, humors, and evil eye; Indigenous classification and treatment of childhood diarrhea in highland Guatemala. *Medical Anthropology, 12,* 419–441.

Chakanza, J. (1998). Unfinished agenda: Puberty rites and the response of the Roman Catholic Church in Southern Malawi. In J. Cox (Ed.), *Rites of passage in contemporary Africa* (pp. 1901–1994). Cardiff, UK: Cardiff Academic Press.

Desmangles, L. (1992). *The faces of the gods: Vodou and Roman Catholicism in Haiti.* Chapel Hill: University of North Carolina Press.

Donahue, M. J., & Benson, P. L. (1995). Religion and the well-being of adolescents. *Journal of Social Issues, 51* (2), 145–160.

Frable, D. E. S. (1997). Gender, racial, ethnic, sexual, and class identities. *Annual Review of Psychology, 48,* 139–162.

Geertz, C. (1973). *Interpretations of culture.* New York: HarperCollins.

James, W. (1999). *The varieties of religious experience: A study in human nature.* New York: Modern Library. (Original work published in 1902)

Johnson, R. L., & Stanford, P. (2002). *Strength for their journey: Five essential disciplines African American parents must teach their children and teens.* New York: Harlem Moon.

Kroeber, A. L., & Kluckhohn, D. (1963). *Culture: A critical review of concepts and definitions.* New York: Vintage.

Leach, M., & Fried, J. (Eds.). (1972). *Funk & Wagnalls standard dictionary of folklore, mythology and legend.* San Francisco: Harper.

MacQuarrie, J. (1972). *Paths in spirituality.* London: SCM Press.

Maduro, R. (1983). Curanderismo and Latino views of disease and curing. *Western Journal of Medicine, 139,* 868–74.

Magesa, L. (1997). *African religion: The moral traditions of abundant life.* Maryknoll, NY: Orbis Books.

Mattis, J. S. (2000). African American women's definitions of spirituality: A qualitative analysis. *Journal of Black Psychology, 26,* 101–122.

Mattis, J. S. (2004). Spirituality and religiosity. In C. Peterson & M. Seligman (Eds.), *Character strengths and virtues: A handbook and classification* (pp. 599–622). London: Oxford University Press.

Mattis, J. S. (in press). Religion in African American family life. In K. Dodge, V. C. McLoyd, & N. E. Hill (Eds.), *African American family life in 21st century America: Changes, challenges, and opportunities.* New York: Guilford.

Modood, T., Berthoud, R., & Nazroo, J. (2002). "Race," racism and ethnicity: A response to Ken Smith. *Sociology, 36,* 419–427.

M'Passou, D. (1998). The continuing tension between Christianity and rites of passage in Swaziland. In J. L. Cox (Ed.), *Rites of passage in contemporary Africa* (pp. 15–33). Cardiff, UK: Cardiff Academic Press.

Obermeyer, C. M. (2000). Pluralism and pragmatism: Knowledge and practice of birth in Morocco. *Medical Anthropology Quarterly, 14,* 180–201.

Regnerus, M., Smith, C., & Fritsch, M. (2003). *Religion in the lives of American adolescents: A review of the literature* (Rep. No. 3). Chapel Hill: University of North Carolina, National Study of Youth and Religion.

Rothchild, D., & Alexander, J. G. (1995). Pathological dimensions of domestic and international ethnicity. *Political Science Quarterly, 110,* 69–82.

Rubel, A. J., O'Nell, C. W., & Collado Ardán, R. (1992). Introducción al susto [Introduction to fright]. In R. Campos (Ed.), *La antropologia médica en Mexico* [Medical anthropology in Mexico] (pp. 105–120). Mexico City: Universidad Autónoma Metropolitana.

Sells, M. (2003) Crosses of blood: Sacred space, religion, and violence in Bosnia-Hercegovina. *Sociology of Religion, 64,* 285–410.

Shakur, T. (1997). I wonder if heaven got a ghetto. On *R U still down* [CD]. New York: Amaru/Jive Records.

Smith, C., Faris, R., Denton, M. L., & Regnerus, M. (2003). Mapping American adolescent subjective religiosity and attitudes of alienation toward religion: A research report. *Sociology of Religion, 64,* 111–133.

Stewart, R. (1999). Religion in the Anglophone Caribbean: Historical overview. In J. Pulis (Ed.), *Religion, diaspora, and cultural identity: A reader in the Anglophone Caribbean* (pp. 13–35). Amsterdam: Gordon and Breach.

Stone, J. (1995). Race, ethnicity, and Weberian legacy. *American Behavioral Scientist, 38,* 391–406.

Villaseñor-Bayardo, S. J. (1994). Ébauche d'ethno-psychiatrie nahua (Outline of Nahuatl Ethno-psychiatry). *Annales Médicales-Psychologiques, 152,* 589–599.

Weil, T. E. (1973). *Area handbook for Ecuador.* Washington, DC: U.S. Government Printing Office.

Wolf, E. R. (1994). Perilous ideas: Race, culture, people. *Current Anthropology, 35,* 1–7.

Wulff, D. (1991). *The psychology of religion: Classic and contemporary views.* New York: Wiley.

Zinnbauer, B. J., Pargament, K. I., Cole, B., Rye, M. S., Butter, E., Belavich, T. G., et al. (1997). Religiousness and spirituality: Unfuzzying the fuzzy. *Journal for the Scientific Study of Religion, 36,* 549–564.

21

THE FAMILY AS A CONTEXT FOR RELIGIOUS AND SPIRITUAL DEVELOPMENT IN CHILDREN AND YOUTH

CHRIS J. BOYATZIS

DAVID C. DOLLAHITE

LOREN D. MARKS

Our chapter addresses how the family promotes or hinders transcendence of the self in children, that is, how the family is a context in which spiritual development occurs. Due to space limitations, our emphasis is on socialization and interaction processes within the family and not on other issues such as psychodynamic processes (e.g., Rizzuto, 1979) or faith development (e.g., Fowler, 1981). There are many motivations to explore family socialization of religious and spiritual development. One, family spirituality and religiosity are linked with many desirable outcomes and inversely with negative outcomes in children and youth. (Other chapters in this volume examine these issues.) Two, therapists and family life educators are increasingly addressing spirituality and religion (Richards & Bergin, 1997). Three, religion is an important, even central force in many families (Dollahite, Marks, & Goodman, 2004).

In America, religion is in some ways a family affair, as 95% of married couples and parents report a religious affiliation (Mahoney, Pargament, Swank, & Tarakeshwar, 2001), and about 90% of parents desire religious training for their children (Gallup & Castelli, 1989). Thus, the widespread significance of religion to so many families compels scholars to examine the family as a locus of religious and spiritual development (RSD). Although religion (and spirituality) has been examined by sociology (e.g., Durkheim, 1897/1986) and psychology (e.g., James, 1902/1896) for more than a century, these disciplines have only recently begun to address RSD in connection with *family*. (In contrast, organized religions have a long tradition of emphasizing the family as the crucial context for RSD; e.g., Bunge, 2001.)

Family scholars exploring spirituality have frequently described it as a type of *transcendence* that can involve going beyond the limits of materiality and the physical tendencies of humanity (Bahr & Bahr, 1996). Anderson and Worthen (1997) suggest that "every human relational event can be viewed as spiritual" (p. 5), and we believe this is particularly true for intergenerational family relationships. Spirituality permeates human relationships and is often, though not necessarily, associated with religious belief and practice. Spiritual and religious development are similar though distinct processes that often influence each other, and most people are concerned about both at some level (Miller & Thoresen, 2003); for this reason, we will often alternate between these terms. At the outset, we encourage family scholars to investigate how families themselves define and conceptualize spirituality.

FAMILY AND RELIGIOUS AND SPIRITUAL DEVELOPMENT

In this section, we highlight topics that illuminate RSD of youth and children in the family: (a) religion and family in America; (b) family interaction and parent–child communication; (c) models of religious and spiritual influence in families; (d) narrative epistemology and ritual in family life; (e) the role of mothers, fathers, and siblings in children's religious growth; (f) conservative Protestant parenting; and (g) unhealthy spirituality in families.

Religion and Family in America

The majority of data in this chapter are drawn from U.S. samples. We unfortunately know much less about religion and family in non-Western faiths and cultures—in other words, about most of the families of the earth—as well as non-Christian families in America (see Boyatzis, 2003). We recognize that our focus on the nuclear family is a limitation but this is due in large part to the focus by researchers on the nuclear family.

Recent empirical studies report positive connections between parents' religiosity and higher parental warmth (Bartkowski & Wilcox, 2000), closer parent–child relationships (Dollahite et al., 2004; Mahoney et al., 2001), and different

aspects of parent functioning (Brody, Stoneman, & Flor, 1996; Gunnoe, Hetherington, & Reiss, 1999). Further, parental religiosity is associated positively with various desirable child outcomes and inversely with negative outcomes (Mahoney et al., 2001) and protects adolescents (Brody et al., 1996; Regnerus, 2003). In sum, family religiosity is a positive factor in development, though it can also be an unhealthy force in families, which we address later.

Even if it takes a village to raise a child, the family is surely "the first village" of RSD. Parents' practices and beliefs constitute a personal religious community (Cornwall, 1987), and the family functions as "interpreters of religious ideology" (Heller, 1986, p. 32). On many measures, particularly behavioral indicators such as worship attendance, children's religiosity appears consistent with their parents' religiosity (e.g., Acock & Bengston, 1978; Bao, Whitbeck, Hoyt, & Conger, 1999; Dudley & Dudley, 1986; Hoge, Petrillo, & Smith, 1982; King, Furrow, & Roth, 2002). The pressing question concerns *how* the family influences spiritual development.

Family Interaction and Parent–Child Communication

It is likely that parents influence their children's RSD as they do other realms, that is, through verbal communication and induction and indoctrination of beliefs, disciplinary tactics, rewards and punishments, and behavioral modeling. "Spiritual modeling" and spiritual observational learning are important mechanisms (Bandura, 2003; Silberman, 2003). For example, work from England has underscored the power of parental modeling of specific behaviors such as praying in children (Francis & Brown, 1990) and adolescents (Francis & Brown, 1991). Families also engage in activities that can promote children's RSD, such as saying rote mealtime prayers, engaging in devotions at home, and performing religiously motivated charity for others. Retrospective reports from religious adults confirm that these kinds of "embedded routines"—regular family rituals—were frequent in their families in childhood and helped form the narrative structure of religious meaning in family life (Wuthnow, 1999).

Dollahite and Marks (2005) created a conceptual model from narrative analyses of in-depth interviews conducted in the homes of 74 highly religious Jewish, Christian, Mormon, and Muslim families from various regions in the United States. The framework suggests the contexts, processes, and outcomes at work in highly religious families as they strive to fulfill the sacred purposes suggested by their faith—chief among them passing on religious and spiritual meaning and practice to their children. Dollahite and Marks identified 10 central processes families used to facilitate RSD among family members, including: relying on God or God's word for support and guidance; sanctifying the family by living religion at home, including religious traditions; resolving conflict with prayer, repentance, and forgiveness; loving and serving others in the family, faith community, and wider community; overcoming challenges and trials through shared faith; abstaining from proscribed activities and substances; sacrificing time, money, comfort, and convenience for religious/spiritual reasons; nurturing spiritual observance and growth in family members through teaching, example, and discussion; obeying God, prophets, parents, or commandments; and putting faith or family ahead of personal or secular interests. Narratives from children and youth (ages 10–20) indicated, for example, that religiously inspired service to people in the faith community and wider community allowed children and youth to develop positive qualities: greater concern and empathy for others; abstention from proscribed activities and substances and making sacrifices for religious/spiritual reasons, which encouraged youth to develop ego strength and a sense of uniqueness through being different from their peers; and a religiously motivated emphasis on honoring their parents, which fostered more respect and less contention between youth and parents. Children and youth indicated that their spiritual development was facilitated primarily through their parents' teaching, example, and through parent–child discussions of spiritual/religious issues (often initiated through children's questions and concerns). Although this sample consisted of highly religious families, this study identifies religious and spiritual socialization processes that may operate in many families.

Another study has examined parent–child discussion about religion. Boyatzis and Janicki (2003) asked a small sample of Christian families with children ages 3 to 12 to complete a survey on parent–child communication and keep a diary of all conversations about religious and spiritual issues. In diaries, God was discussed in one out of two conversations. Data from surveys and diaries demonstrated that in such conversations children are active: They initiate and terminate about half of family conversations about religion, they speak as much as parents do, and they ask questions and offer their own views. Parents asked many more open-ended questions than test questions (e.g., "What do you think heaven is like?" vs. "Who built the Ark?"). In this study, parents did not impose their own beliefs too strongly. One measure was a "conviction rating," as parents indicated on a 5-point scale in each diary the degree to which their comments reflected their actual beliefs about the topic. The average rating was 3.7, suggesting that parents were not strongly stating their own views, or that parents "watered down" their statements to help their children better understand their views. (Another interpretation is that parents were not sure of their own beliefs.) The diary and survey data support the notion that most families' conversations about religion have a mutual give-and-take with reciprocal influence. This is consistent with two different but compatible models.

Models of Religious and Spiritual Influence in Families

A sociocultural model emphasizes the role of knowledgeable adults who use scaffolding and guided participation in culturally meaningful practices to help the child move to higher understandings (Vygotsky, 1978). Thus, parents have the important task of helping children maneuver toward higher competencies in their zone of proximal development. A second model, consistent with but building on the first, is a transactional model of development that posits that children and parents influence each other (P← →C) in recurrent reciprocal exchanges (Kuczynski, 2003). This characterization of family interaction contrasts sharply with a unilateral P→C "transmission" model that has dominated socialization research for decades. Bidirectional transactional models differ from the unilateral transmission model in key ways (Kuczynski, 2003). First, transmission models assume a static asymmetry of power between parent and child; in transactional models, there is an interdependent asymmetry. Transactional models presume that causes and effects are recursive and indeterminate, so it is difficult to determine when parent influence ends and child influence begins. Inherent in this view is that child → parent influence occurs, but unfortunately few scholars have examined this dynamic. It is likely (see Boyatzis, 2004) that in some families there is a distinct "parent as mentor, child as apprentice" role structure; in other families, there may be more fluidity between these roles as parent and child can function as teacher and student to the other. Finally, in some families the child may be viewed as something of a "spiritual savant" with full spiritual status. This perspective seems common in many indigenous cultures (e.g., the Beng of West Africa, the Warlpiri Aboriginals of north-central Australia), which view babies as having recently come to the living from a realm of ancestral spirits (see DeLoache & Gottlieb, 2000); this view is shared to some extent in Latter-day Saint (Mormon) doctrine, which posits that children exist in spirit form prior to birth, and newborns come to a family immediately and directly from being in the presence of God (Dollahite, 2003). We mention these different parent–child roles and views of children to expand our conceptions of the child's spiritual place in the family.

Research must address the degree to which parent–child communication actually *influences* children's and parents' spiritual growth. Although Boyatzis and Janicki (2003) did not measure this impact, in other studies sustained discourse on religion between parents and adolescents strongly related to how the adolescents felt about religion, whereas poor communication inhibited transmission of beliefs and values (Flor & Knapp, 2001). Adults' retrospective reports suggest that religious views were shaped by conversations about religion in childhood (e.g., Dudley & Wisbey, 2000; Wuthnow, 1999). A longitudinal study on adolescents' moral reasoning found that moral reasoning was enhanced when parents asked questions about the child's opinions and discussed the child's reasoning (Walker & Taylor, 1991). Research on other topics reveals that parents' speech influences children's maturity. For example, the more parents use words when talking with their toddlers that describe mental states (e.g., think, believe, wonder), the more the children later use such mental-state terms when they are preschoolers (Jenkins, Turrell, Kogushi, Lollis, & Ross, 2003). Do such patterns emerge in family discourse about religious or spiritual issues?

Parents and children have distinct conversational styles (e.g., Beaumont, 2000). Parents know that some children have a high tolerance for ambiguity, and their spirituality may grow best in a milieu of ongoing open-ended exchanges that prioritize questions and ruminations over answers and certainty. Other children prefer closure and may find the didactic transmission of information most helpful. Does growing up with a particular family communication style predict specific religious beliefs and faith orientations later in life? Are communication styles in childhood nascent forms of religious orientations that continue into adulthood? Longitudinal work is needed to answer these questions, but it is likely that family discourse about religious and spiritual issues creates a milieu in which children construct spiritual meaning and understanding. Parents' views can serve as cognitive anchors (Ozorak, 1989) for children's beliefs, and the reciprocal dynamic in conversation allows parent and child to co-construct meaning (Boyatzis, 2004).

Given the role that such communication might have, would there be stronger *correspondence* or *independence* between children's and parents' religious and spiritual beliefs? The correspondence position is that children's beliefs would be strongly similar to their parents' beliefs; we might expect this given the ample evidence of similarity between children's and parents' religiosity (e.g., Acock & Bengston, 1978; Bao et al., 1999). However, these studies have focused on religious behavior more than beliefs and attitudes, and in some studies there is greater correspondence between parent and child religious behavior than belief (e.g., Francis & Gibson, 1993), though in some cases, as in a study of Conservative Jewish families

(Parker & Gaier, 1980), there is strong similarity in religious belief as well. In general, we might also expect considerable independence between parent and child beliefs because it has become a truism in developmental and cognitive psychology (see Johnson & Boyatzis, chapter 15, this volume) that children actively construct their reality. While many studies show that both correspondence and independence occur (see Boyatzis, in press), the image of the child as an active creator of his or her own spiritual belief is most illuminating theoretically because it challenges the venerable (and limited) model of one-way P→C transmission of belief.

Consider work by Evans (2000), who analyzed beliefs about the origins of species and the world in children growing up in families that were either distinctly secular or Christian fundamentalist. Evans found that 7- to 9-year-old children from *both* family types—fundamentalist and secular—were likely to have Creationist views of the origin of species and view the natural world as the product of a nonhuman supernatural being. Not until early adolescence did youth in secular homes begin to embrace their families' evolutionist views. Important evidence is emerging that children's religious belief is less related to their parents' (self-reported) beliefs than to the children's perceptions of the parents' religious views (e.g., Bao et al., 1999; Okagaki & Bevis, 1999). Thus, what parents do and believe may matter less than what *children think* parents do and believe. Studies of family socialization must account for children's intuitive belief systems and active construction of input around them.

Narrative Epistemology and Ritual in Family Life

Narrative is a fundamental epistemology for humans, and family narratives are a major embodiment of meaning. One reason why religions are so prevalent as worldviews is that they offer descriptive, explanatory stories about their adherents' place in the world and in relation to each other and to a transcendent divinity. Indeed, religious narratives map onto human thinking naturally, particularly with children, as story plays a central role in children's thinking (see Johnson & Boyatzis, chapter 15, this

volume). Even though family-centered data have emerged over the past decades, the majority of studies have used survey data. Although valuable, such data paint broad but often shallow images that fail to capture the human capacity and need for narrative. Narrative is at the heart of familial and personal meaning making, and hence it is integral to spirituality/religion. For example, a recent narrative-based study (Dollahite & Clifton, 2005) of 45 adolescents from highly religious Jewish, Christian, and Muslim families indicated that religion offered and promoted a sense of purpose and direction, stronger connections to family and others, a unique identity as a religious person, and enhancement of confidence. The adolescents also offered rich illustrations and explanations of the interface between religious and family life, which would be difficult to tap with quantitative methods.

Narrative methods can also provide scholars with firsthand accounts of what it is like to be raised with spiritual or religious expectations and experiences as well as be a parent trying to facilitate a child's or adolescent's spiritual development in a culture or circumstance that makes that difficult. However, few researchers have examined personal and family narratives as a way of understanding spirituality and religion.

Another topic requiring attention is children's enactment and understanding of ritual. Ritual is an integral feature in many world religions and has an important place in family traditions. Some questions researchers could address include these: How are Jewish children affected by their central role in opening the Passover seder? How do Muslim children experience their obligation to pray to Allah five times a day? How are children in sacramental Christian traditions affected by first communion or confirmation? These kinds of issues are at the heart of faith traditions and social scientists should address them.

In a recent study of the influence of sacred rituals in families, Marks (2004) offers qualitative reports from parents regarding why sacred practices and rituals are influential and meaningful to Christian, Jewish, and Muslim parents. Parents indicated several motivations for family rituals, including a desire "to transmit religious beliefs of parents to children," consistent with the traditional view of socialization discussed previously. Two other parental motivations were to "teach" and "provide an example" for their children. These findings indicate that parents may be influenced to influence their children; thus, a transactional influence seems to occur. A final motivation for sacred ritual was that less eager parents reported engaging in sacred rituals because their children "push or pull them into it" (Marks, 2004, p. 221). This is the type of "bottom–up," child → parent influence that has been rarely captured in the past. Unfortunately, this study did not include views from children or adolescents in the family. Anecdotal data speak to the import of family rituals in childhood (Wuthnow, 1999), but systematic research should describe the form, frequency, meaning, and influence of children's religious rituals.

The Role of Mothers, Fathers, and Siblings

Within the family, many individuals have the potential to affect and be affected by children's religious and spiritual growth. Based on research, it is axiomatic to say that in most families the mother is the primary figure in children's religiosity. This finding has emerged in the United States (e.g., Acock & Bengston, 1978; Okagaki & Bevis, 1999; Strommen & Hardel, 2000), England (Francis & Gibson, 1993), and Australia (Hunsberger & Brown, 1984), and the mother's prominence has been confirmed in Jewish intermarriages (Silberman, 1985) and other religious groups (Brodsky, 2000). Even in interfaith families, children's denominational affiliation is more similar to the mothers' than the fathers' (Nelsen, 1990), especially when the mother is Catholic.

Why do mothers have such an influential role, and what mechanisms are at work? Women are more religious than men and attend worship services more often (e.g., Spilka, Hood, Hunsberger, & Gorsuch, 2003), and adults recall seeing their mothers pray more than their fathers did (Wuthnow, 1999). In general, mothers speak with their children more than fathers do (e.g., Leaper, Anderson, & Sanders, 1998) and in conversations about religion mothers are much more involved than fathers are. In one study using a diary method, mothers participated in all diary conversations in almost 90% of families,

whereas fathers did not appear in any diary entries in almost half of the families (Boyatzis & Janicki, 2003). In a national study, 3,000 mainline Protestant youth reported they had regular dialogue about faith issues with their mothers almost 2.5 times more often than with their fathers (Benson & Eklin, 1990).

Mothers talk about emotions more than fathers do (e.g., Kuebli, Butler, & Fivush, 1995) and, perhaps consequently, most children rate their mothers higher than fathers as a confidante and self-disclosure partner (Buhrmester & Furman, 1987). The personal nature of many religious and spiritual issues could put the more communicative and intimate parent in the crucial role for discussing religion and thereby serve as "cognitive anchors" (Ozorak, 1989) for the child's spiritual views. We recognize that in some families the father will be the more communicative partner for the child.

Research is beginning to acknowledge the role of religion in fathers' lives and the impact of fathers' religiosity on their parenting (e.g., Dollahite, 1998, 2003). Marks and Dollahite (2001) found that religion may promote greater commitment to children and greater father involvement; religion may strengthen marriage, which, in turn, may promote father involvement. Father involvement is linked with children's positive outcomes (Doherty, Kouneski, & Erickson, 1998). For many fathers, religious faith plays a central role in their construction of the father role and fosters their involvement (King, 2003; Latshaw, 1998). Involvement in a religious community reduces the likelihood of adolescent boys becoming fathers outside of marriage (Hendricks, Robinson-Brown, & Gray, 1984).

Other recent work has found that compared to religiously unaffiliated fathers, affiliated fathers are more likely to be engaged with their children (e.g., one-on-one talks) and be involved with youth activities (Wilcox, 2002). On another measure of paternal involvement— having dinner with one's family—conservative Protestant fathers score higher than unaffiliated fathers (Wilcox, 2002). A study of Jewish families (Herzbrun, 1993) found that fathers who were warmer and communicated more with their adolescents tended to have adolescents who shared their religious views. Dollahite and colleagues have found that religious belief, practice, and community are particularly salient in helping fathers of children with special needs meet the ordinary and extraordinary challenges associated with being a parent of such a child (Dollahite, 2003; Dollahite, Marks, & Olson, 2002; Marks & Dollahite, 2001).

Siblings represent another potential influence in the religious life of a child's family, but unfortunately this role has been rather ignored. Religious belief and practice can draw families together in challenging times, such as when children pray for their siblings who have disabilities (Marshall, Olsen, Mandelco, Allred, & Sansom, 2003). We point to research on other, nonreligious topics to suggest that siblings could be important influences on children's religiosity. For example, compared to children without siblings, children with siblings develop a more sophisticated understanding of how people's minds work, for example, how one's beliefs and desires relate to one's behaviors and experiences (Perner, Ruffman, & Leekam, 1994). Preschoolers with older siblings talk more about mental states than do preschoolers without older siblings, probably because as toddlers they are exposed to more mental-state terms from their older siblings (Jenkins et al., 2003). Because older siblings help younger ones understand the minds of other people, future research should examine whether older siblings seem to help younger ones understand the mind of God and other religious issues. Siblings can offer each other religious and spiritual input and modeling, as well as serve as valuable communication partners who can expand and enrich each other's linguistic maturity and conceptual understanding of spiritual issues. As others have argued (Jenkins et al., 2003), siblings contribute to the amount of talk other children hear in the family about specific topics, and this exposure enhances the children's ability to comprehend and produce such language. This competence then brings the child deeper into the family system's construction of spiritual meaning.

Although our chapter has emphasized parent–child exchange as an engine for spiritual growth, children's beliefs undergo many "secondary adjustments" through so-called third-party discussions, and siblings are a major source of such discussions and adjustments (Kuczynski, 2003). These third-party exchanges are probably common in family life and must be studied for a fuller understanding of spiritual growth in children and families.

Conservative Protestant Parenting

Much empirical work has examined conservative Protestant parents. At the outset it seems fair to say that conservative Protestant parenting is more complicated than some critiques (e.g., Greven, 1990) have suggested. While parents with conservative Protestant affiliations often endorse spanking as a child-rearing technique and feel that it will not harm children (Gershoff, Miller, & Holden, 1999), they are less likely than other parents to yell at their children (Bartkowski & Wilcox, 2000) and they typically have a warm, expressive style in nondisciplinary situations (Bartkowski & Xu, 2000).

Parents' views and behaviors are related not simply to their denominational affiliation but to their endorsement of particular beliefs. For example, theologically conservative ideology (of biblical literalism and fundamentalist beliefs) mediates between parents' denomination and their views and use of corporal punishment (Gershoff et al., 1999). In addition, disciplinary tactics are mediated by the degree to which parents sanctify their role, that is, see parenting as a sacred and holy duty (Mahoney, Pargament, Murray-Swank, & Murray-Swank, 2003). For example, parents who sanctified their roles and who had more liberal biblical views used less corporal punishment, but corporal punishment by theologically conservative parents was not related to their sanctification of parenting (Murray-Swank, Mahoney, & Pargament, 2004). Another study found that sanctification of parenting in conservative Christian parents in Appalachia was not related to their endorsement of spanking (Boyatzis & Tunison, 2002). Together, these studies demonstrate that parents' beliefs are associated with parenting behaviors. Other work has indicated that some parents engage in child-rearing practices that appear to be influenced by their religious faith and that have unhealthy consequences for child development. We now briefly discuss this issue.

Unhealthy Spirituality in Families

Some forms of family religiosity can distort, misunderstand, or misapply religious teaching in ways that are harmful to children. This could include acts done in the name of religion—such as withholding needed medical treatments or forms of spiritual or physical abuse (Mahoney et al., 2003; Silberman, 2003). Arterburn and Felton (2001) offer case studies from ministry and therapy illustrating what they term "toxic faith," the use of religion by parents to "justify" their abusive parenting. Some parents form a "coalition with God" as a disciplinary tactic, threatening children that "God will punish" if they do not obey parents (e.g., Nelsen & Kroliczak, 1984). In such families, this work has found, children are likely to view God as malevolent.

In addition, some families (perhaps due to influences in their broader culture) promote values that seem inimical to spirituality, including racism, religious bigotry, materialism, consumerism, individualism, and hedonism. Recent work has found that adolescents who highly value financial success and material goods have mothers who were less nurturing than did other adolescents who highly valued relationships and helping the community (Kasser, Ryan, Zax, & Sameroff, 1995). Related work has shown that adolescents higher in materialism view their parents as less likely to listen to their views or recognize their feelings (Williams, Cox, Hedberg, & Deci, 2000). Although causality is difficult to establish, these studies indicate that parent–child relationships that appear low in warmth and authenticity are associated with the youth having more hedonistic and self-centered values. In short, these topics become increasingly complex as researchers move from the individual to the familial level of analysis (see Dollahite et al., 2004). In addition, a necessary step to understanding "toxic religion" in families is to have more participant-observer work to balance the typical "outsider" vantage in this research. Qualitative data will illuminate parents' religious beliefs and motivations for child-rearing behaviors that may be deemed by outsiders as unhealthy for their children.

GENERATIVE SPIRITUALITY

There has been conceptual and empirical work connecting Erikson's concept of generativity (1982) with spirituality (Dollahite, 2003). Snarey and Dollahite (2001) argue that a generative perspective is uniquely suited to give conceptual coherence to the study of religiosity and family life. A generative approach to spirituality in children and youth can provide scholars with important concepts and processes. One approach is "generative spirituality" (Dollahite et al., 2002; Dollahite, Slife, & Hawkins, 1998). Generative spirituality is a transcendent connection with the next generation that flows from and encourages convictions of abiding care for that generation.

For many families and family members, religious belief encourages their generative commitment, and religious practice and community support their generative actions. Dollahite et al. (1998) argued that generative action is inherently spiritual because it "involves transcending selfishness, the demands of the present, and the attractions and distractions of one's own generation" (p. 469). Generative spirituality involves adult family members, in concert with others and individually, abiding by their deep convictions to maintain transcendent connections with the next generation. For many families and family members, religious belief, practice, and community encourages generative action, although many generative individuals and families do not define themselves as religious or even spiritual.

There are three aspects of generative spirituality for families: shared spiritual paradigm (common transcendent beliefs), shared spiritual practices (meaningful rituals and traditions), and shared spiritual community (a congregation of care).

Shared Spiritual Paradigm. Pargament (1997) suggested that the essential definition of religion is a process that involves "a search for significance in ways related to the sacred" (p. 32). Eliade's (1959) concept of an *axis mundi* as adapted by Latshaw (1998) and Marks and Dollahite (2001) relates to the core religious meanings through which a person or family perceives and acts upon the world. For highly religious families, beliefs, practices, and communities serve as the "core worldview" around which other parts of life revolve. Consistent with these assertions, religious parents are likely influenced by their beliefs in how they view their parenting, the appropriateness of physical punishment, and the degree of warmth they exhibit toward children (Mahoney et al., 2003).

Shared Spiritual Practices. Several studies have shown a connection between joint religious practices and marital happiness. Mahoney et al. (1999) found that spouses who share involvement in religious activities (praying, attending worship) and who perceived marriage as having a spiritual character also had better functioning across many aspects of marriage (adjustment, less conflict and verbal aggression, greater use of collaborative problem solving).

Shared Spiritual Community. Generative spirituality cannot occur without involvement of parent and child in some larger community. In other words, it takes a faith community to raise a child to generative and spiritual maturity. If a child only has parents and neighbors (a local village, if you will), the child will likely lack a broader community of caring that addresses important issues in a coherent way and enacts a set of beliefs and practices that may help the child become more fully human—that is, connected in a caring way to what is beyond the self.

Generative spirituality, then, focuses on encouraging significant, sustained, and sacred consideration of the needs of the next generation. A spiritual approach to generativity emphasizes the benefits (blessings) of faith to adults and children and to relationships (marital, horizontal, intergenerational). The generative spirituality framework highlights "responsible religion" (i.e., religious beliefs and practices that support intergenerational commitment) and "faithful family life" (i.e., committed marital and parent–child relationships infused with spiritual meaning and transcendence). In sum, generative spirituality is developmental in nature and encourages relational, moral, and spiritual growth over the life span; links psychological variables (e.g., meaning), social variables (e.g., community support), and spiritual factors (e.g., prayer, ritual); focuses on strengthening links between generations; encourages responsible parenting; and generates constructive solutions to intergenerational problems.

Generative spirituality thus focuses on how parents, in concert with others and individually,

abide by their convictions to maintain transcendent connections with the next generation. A spiritual dimension can encourage families and adult family members to create connections and convictions that can help them transcend intergenerational distance or conflict. This approach suggests that intergenerational relationships should be viewed as *sacred* and *enduring:* sacred because they are singular, related to the holy, highly significant, and, to some extent, capable of helping one transcend the mundane concerns of the self; enduring because they have a boundless quality to them, both in terms of time and importance.

Generative Spirituality and Research on RSD. This section discusses how the construct of generative spirituality might influence research on family and RSD. A generative spirituality approach would involve researchers asking questions such as the following: (a) What are your deepest and strongest spiritual beliefs that pertain to helping your children and youth grow spiritually? (b) In what ways do these beliefs influence your relations with your children? (c) When your child faces challenging circumstances, are there ways you try to help your child develop spiritual resources to address the situation? (d) How has your child influenced you religiously and spiritually? (e) How has your relationship with your child influenced how you have addressed challenges to you as a parent? (f) What kinds of sacrifices have your spiritual or religious beliefs or practices influenced you to make for your child? (g) What sacrifices have you asked your child to make for religious or spiritual reasons?

CONCLUSIONS

The family is probably the most potent influence—for better or for worse—on children's spiritual and religious development, but we still have much to learn about this context. One, we still know too little about specific mechanisms through which family life influences RSD. For the most part, the extant literature speaks only obliquely to the processes and mechanisms of spiritual growth in families. Two, a more valid conceptualization of the complexity of family interaction and influence is needed. We must directly examine the child's active role, including how the child can influence parents' spiritual growth, and measure more precisely the differential contributions of mothers, fathers, and siblings, not to mention extended family members. We suspect all family members play roles, albeit different ones. We cite here a recent provocative finding to illustrate the unique contributions of mothers and fathers: Schoolchildren's willingness to forgive others for their transgressions is related positively to their mothers' modeling of forgiveness at home but, surprisingly, to their fathers' being *low* on forgiveness and on empathy at home (Denham, Neal, & Bassett, 2004). Three new topics, designs, and methods must be explored (see Boyatzis & Newman, 2004, on methodological issues). We have highlighted briefly two of these here—children's religious ritual and unhealthy spirituality in families. We also know too little about the construction and use of shared narratives in family life. Researchers will need to employ qualitative methods to probe the deep structure and meanings of such narratives and to fully explore the generative spirituality as laid out above. To understand the long-term impact of childhood experience in the family, longitudinal designs are needed. Finally, the relative paucity of knowledge about non-Christian families in the United States and families in other parts of the world should compel social scientists to study the diversity of families in many countries. We close by noting that progress in all of these areas will be facilitated by a broader professional recognition and respect among social scientists for the potential power of religion and spirituality in family life and children's development.

REFERENCES

Acock, A. C., & Bengston, V. L. (1978). On the relative influence of mothers and fathers: A covariance analysis of political and religious socialization. *Journal of Marriage and Family, 40,* 519–530.

Anderson, D. A., & Worthen, D. (1997). Exploring a fourth dimension: Spirituality as a resource for the couple therapist. *Journal of Marital and Family Therapy, 23,* 3–12.

Arterburn, S., & Felton, J. (2001). *Toxic faith.* Colorado Springs, CO: Waterbrook.

Bahr, H. M., & Bahr, K. S. (1996). A paradigm of family transcendence. *Journal of Marriage and the Family, 58,* 541–555.

Bandura, A. (2003). On the psychosocial impact and mechanisms of spiritual modeling. *International Journal for the Psychology of Religion, 13,* 167–174.

Bao, W.-N., Whitbeck, L. B., Hoyt, D., & Conger, R. C. (1999). Perceived parental acceptance as a moderator of religious transmission among adolescent boys and girls. *Journal of Marriage and the Family, 61,* 362–374.

Bartkowski, J. P., & Wilcox, W. B. (2000). Conservative Protestant child discipline: The case of parental yelling. *Social Forces, 79,* 265–290.

Bartkowski, J. P., & Xu, X. (2000). Distant patriarchs or expressive dads? The discourse and practice of fathering in conservative Protestant families. *Sociological Quarterly, 41,* 465–485.

Beaumont, S. L. (2000). Conversational styles of mothers and their preadolescent and middle adolescent daughters. *Merrill-Palmer Quarterly, 46,* 119–139.

Benson P. L., & Eklin, C. H. (1990). *Effective Christian education: A national study of Protestant congregations: A summary on faith, loyalty, and congregational life.* Minneapolis, MN: Search Institute.

Boyatzis, C. J. (2003). Religious and spiritual development: An introduction. *Review of Religious Research, 44,* 213–219.

Boyatzis, C. J. (2004). The co-construction of spiritual meaning in parent-child communication. In D. Ratcliff (Ed.), *Children's spirituality: Christian perspectives, research, and applications* (pp. 182–200). Eugene, OR: Wipf & Stock.

Boyatzis, C. J. (in press). Socialization and cognitive processes in children's religious development: Where we have been, where we must go. In R. F. Paloutzian & C. L. Park (Eds.), *The handbook of the psychology of religion.* New York: Guilford.

Boyatzis, C. J., & Janicki, D. (2003). Parent-child communication about religion: Survey and diary data on unilateral transmission and bi-directional reciprocity styles. *Review of Religious Research, 44,* 252–270.

Boyatzis, C. J., & Newman, B. (2004). How shall we study children's spirituality? In D. Ratcliff (Ed.), *Children's spirituality: Christian perspectives, research, and applications* (pp. 166–181). Eugene, OR: Wipf & Stock.

Boyatzis, C. J., & Tunison, S. (2002, August). *Religiosity and interpersonal aggression and corporal punishment in Appalachian parents and children.* Paper presented at the annual meeting of the American Psychological Association, Chicago.

Brodsky, A. E. (2000). The role of religion in the lives of resilient, urban, African American, single mothers. *Journal of Community Psychology, 28,* 199–219.

Brody, G. H., Stoneman, Z., & Flor, D. (1996). Parental religiosity, family processes, and youth competence in rural, two-parent African American families. *Developmental Psychology, 32,* 696–706.

Buhrmester, D., & Furman, W. (1987). The development of companionship and intimacy. *Child Development, 58,* 1101–1113.

Bunge, M. J. (Ed.). (2001). *The child in Christian thought.* Grand Rapids, MI: Eerdmans.

Cornwall, M. (1987). The social bases of religion: A study of factors influencing religious belief and commitment. *Review of Religious Research, 29,* 44–56.

DeLoache, J., & Gottlieb, A. (2000). *A world of babies: Imagined childcare guides for seven societies.* Cambridge, UK: Cambridge University Press.

Denham, S. A., Neal, K., & Bassett, H. H. (2004, April). *"You hurt my feelings pretty bad": Parents' and children's emotions as contributors to the development of forgiveness.* Paper presented at the biennial Conference on Human Development, Washington, DC.

Doherty, W. J., Kouneski, E. F., & Erickson, M. F. (1998). Responsible fathering: An overview and conceptual framework. *Journal of Marriage and the Family, 60,* 277–292.

Dollahite, D. C. (1998). Origins and highlights of the special issue on fathering, faith, and spirituality. *Journal of Men's Studies, 7,* 1–2.

Dollahite, D. C. (2003). Fathering for eternity: Generative spirituality in Latter-day Saint fathers of children with special needs. *Review of Religious Research, 44,* 237–251.

Dollahite, D. C., & Clifton, C. (2005). *Religion as source of identity, purpose, connection, and strength in Jewish, Christian, Muslim, and Mormon youth.* Unpublished manuscript.

Dollahite, D. C., & Marks, L. D. (2005). How highly religious families strive to fulfill sacred purposes. In V. L. Bengtson, D. Klein, A. Acock, K. Allen, & P. Dilworth-Anderson (Eds.), *Sourcebook of family theory and research* (pp. 533–537). Thousand Oaks, CA: Sage.

Dollahite, D. C., Marks, L. D., & Goodman, M. (2004). Families and religious beliefs, practices, and communities: Linkages in a diverse and dynamic cultural context. In M. J. Coleman & L. H. Ganong (Eds.), *The handbook of contemporary families: Considering the past, contemplating the future* (pp. 411–431). Thousand Oaks, CA: Sage.

Dollahite, D. C., Marks, L. D., & Olson, M. M. (2002). Fathering, faith, and family therapy: Generative narrative therapy with religious fathers. *Journal of Family Psychotherapy, 13,* 263–294.

Dollahite, D. C., Slife, B. D., & Hawkins, A. J. (1998). Family generativity and generative counseling: Helping families keep faith with the next generation. In D. P. McAdams & E. de St. Aubin (Eds.), *Generativity and adult development: How and why we care for the next generation* (pp. 449–481). Washington, DC: American Psychological Association.

Dudley, R. L., & Dudley, M. (1986). Transmission of religious values from parents to adolescents. *Review of Religious Research, 28,* 3–15.

Dudley, R. L., & Wisbey, R. L. (2000). The relationship of parenting styles to commitment to the church among young adults. *Religious Education, 95,* 39–50.

Durkheim, E. (1951). *Suicide.* Glencoe, IL: Free Press. (Original work published 1897)

Eliade, M. (1959). *The sacred and the profane: The nature of religion.* New York: Harcourt Brace Jovanovich.

Erikson, E. H. (1982). *Identity and the life cycle.* New York: Norton.

Evans, E. M. (2000). Beyond Scopes: Why creationism is here to stay. In K. S. Rosengren, C. N. Johnson, & P. L. Harris (Eds.), *Imagining the impossible: Magical, scientific, and religious thinking in children* (pp. 305–333). Cambridge, UK: Cambridge University Press.

Flor, D. L., & Knapp, N. F. (2001). Transmission and transaction: Predicting adolescents' internalization of parental religious values. *Journal of Family Psychology, 15,* 627–645.

Fowler, J. (1981). *Stages of faith: The psychology of human development and the quest for meaning.* New York: HarperCollins.

Francis, L. J., & Brown, L. B. (1990). The predisposition to pray: A study of the social influence on the predisposition to pray among eleven-year-old children in England. *Journal of Empirical Theology, 3,* 23–34.

Francis, L. J., & Brown, L. B. (1991). The influence of home, church and school on prayer among sixteen-year-old adolescents in England. *Review of Religious Research, 33,* 112–122.

Francis, L. J., & Gibson, H. M. (1993). Parental influence and adolescent religiosity: A study of church attendance and attitude toward Christianity among adolescents 11 to 12 and 15 to 16 years old. *International Journal for the Psychology of Religion, 3,* 241–253.

Gallup, G., Jr., & Castelli, J. (1989). *The people's religion.* New York: Macmillan.

Gershoff, E. T., Miller, P. C., & Holden, G. W. (1999). Parenting influences from the pulpit: Religious affiliation as a determinant of corporal punishment. *Journal of Family Psychology, 13,* 307–320.

Greven, P. (1990). *Spare the child: The religious roots of punishment and the psychological impact of physical abuse.* New York: Vintage Books.

Gunnoe, M. L., Hetherington, E. M., & Reiss, D. (1999). Parental religiosity, parenting style, and adolescent social responsibility. *Journal of Early Adolescence, 19,* 199–225.

Heller, D. (1986). *The children's God.* Chicago: University of Chicago Press.

Hendricks, L. E., Robinson-Brown, D. P., & Gray, L. E. (1984). Religiosity and unmarried black adolescent fatherhood. *Adolescence, 19,* 417–424.

Herzbrun, M. B. (1993). Father-adolescent religious consensus in the Jewish community: A preliminary report. *Journal for the Scientific Study of Religion, 32,* 163–168.

Hoge, D. R., Petrillo, G. H., & Smith, E. I. (1982). Transmission of religious and social values from parents to teenage children. *Journal of Marriage and the Family, 44,* 569–580.

Hunsberger, B., & Brown, L. B. (1984). Religious socialization, apostasy, and the impact of family background. *Journal for the Scientific Study of Religion, 23,* 239–251.

James, W. (1986). *The varieties of religious experience.* New York: Penguin. (Original work published 1902)

Jenkins, J. M., Turrell, S. L., Kogushi, Y., Lollis, S., & Ross, H. S. (2003). A longitudinal investigation of the dynamics of mental state talk in families. *Child Development, 74,* 905–920.

Kasser, T., Ryan, R. M., Zax, M., & Sameroff, A. J. (1995). The relations of maternal and social environments to late adolescents' materialistic and prosocial values. *Developmental Psychology, 31,* 907–914.

King, V. (2003). The influence of religion on fathers' relationships with their children. *Journal of Marriage and the Family, 65,* 382–395.

King, P. E., Furrow, J. L., & Roth, N. (2002). The influence of families and peers on adolescent religiousness. *Journal of Psychology and Christianity, 21,* 109–120.

Kuczynski, L. (2003). Beyond bidirectionality: Bilateral conceptual frameworks for understanding dynamics in parent-child relations. In L. Kuczynski (Ed.), *Handbook of dynamics in parent-child relations* (pp. 3–24). Thousand Oaks, CA: Sage.

Kuebli, J., Butler, S., & Fivush, R. (1995). Mother-child talk about past emotions: Relations of maternal language and child gender over time. *Cognition and Emotion, 9,* 265–283.

Latshaw, J. S. (1998). The centrality of faith in father's role construction: The faithful father and the axis mundi paradigm. *Journal of Men's Studies, 7,* 53–70.

Leaper, C., Anderson, K. J., & Sanders, P. (1998). Moderators of gender effects on parents' talk to their children: A meta-analysis. *Developmental Psychology, 34,* 3–27.

Mahoney, A., Pargament, K. I., Jewell, T., Swank, A. B., Scott, E., Emery, E., et al. (1999). Marriage and the spiritual realm: The role of proximal and distal religious constructs in marital functioning. *Journal of Family Psychology, 13,* 321–338.

Mahoney, A., Pargament, K. I., Murray-Swank, A., & Murray-Swank, N. (2003). Religion and the sanctification of family relationships. *Review of Religious Research, 44,* 220–236.

Mahoney, A., Pargament, K. I., Swank, A., & Tarakeshwar, N. (2001). Religion in the home in the 1980s and 90s: A meta-analytic review and conceptual analysis of religion. *Journal of Family Psychology, 15,* 559–596.

Marks, L. D. (2004). Sacred practices in highly religious families: Christian, Jewish, Mormon, and Muslim perspectives. *Family Process, 43,* 217–231.

Marks, L. D., & Dollahite, D. C. (2001). Religion, relationships, and responsible fathering in Latter-day Saint families of children with special needs. *Journal of Social and Personal Relationships, 18,* 625–650.

Marshall, E. S., Olsen, S. F., Mandelco, B. L., Allred, K. W., & Sansom, N. (2003). "This is a spiritual experience": Perspectives of Latter-Day Saint children with disabilities. *Qualitative Health Research, 13,* 57–76.

Miller, W. R., & Thoresen, C. E. (2003). Spirituality, religion, and health: An emerging research field. *American Psychologist, 58,* 24–35.

Murray-Swank, A. B., Mahoney, A., & Pargament, K. I. (2004). *Sanctification of parenting: Links to corporal punishment and parental warmth among biblically conservative and liberal mothers.* Manuscript submitted for publication.

Nelsen, H. M. (1990). The religious identification of children of interfaith marriages. *Review of Religious Research, 32,* 122–134.

Nelsen, H. M., & Kroliczak, A. (1984). Parental use of the threat "God will punish": Replication and extension. *Journal for the Scientific Study of Religion, 23,* 267–277.

Okagaki, L., & Bevis, C. (1999). Transmission of religious values: Relations between parents and daughters' beliefs. *Journal of Genetic Psychology, 160,* 303–318.

Ozorak, E. W. (1989). Social and cognitive influences on the development of religious beliefs and commitment in adolescence. *Journal for the Scientific Study of Religion, 28,* 448–463.

Pargament, K. I. (1997). *The psychology of religion and coping.* New York: Guilford.

Parker, M., & Gaier, E. L. (1980). Religion, religious beliefs, and religious practices among Conservative Jewish adolescents. *Adolescence, 15,* 361–374.

Perner, J., Ruffman, T., & Leekam, S. R. (1994). Theory of mind is contagious: You catch it from your sibs. *Child Development, 65,* 1228–1238.

Regnerus, M. D. (2003). Linked lives, faith, and behavior: Intergenerational religious influence on adolescent delinquency. *Journal for the Scientific Study of Religion, 42*(2), 189–203.

Richards, P. S., & Bergin, A. E. (1997). *A spiritual strategy for counseling and psychotherapy.* Washington, DC: American Psychological Association.

Rizzuto, A.-M. (1979). *The birth of the living God: A psychoanalytic study.* Chicago: University of Chicago Press.

Silberman, C. E. (1985). *A certain people: American Jews and their lives today.* New York: Summit.

Silberman, I. (2003). Spiritual role modeling: The teaching of meaning systems. *International Journal for the Psychology of Religion, 13,* 175–195.

Snarey, J. R., & Dollahite, D. C. (2001). Varieties of religion-family linkages. *Journal of Family Psychology, 15,* 646–651.

Spilka, B., Hood, R. W., Jr., Hunsberger, B., & Gorsuch, R. (2003). *The psychology of religion: An empirical approach* (3rd ed.). New York: Guilford.

Strommen, M. P., & Hardel, R. A. (2000). *Passing on the faith: A radical new model for youth and family ministry.* Winona, MN: Saint Mary's Press.

Vygotsky, L. S. (1978). *Mind in society.* Cambridge, MA: Harvard University Press.

Walker, L. J., & Taylor, J. H. (1991). Family interaction and the development of moral reasoning. *Child Development, 62,* 264–283.

Wilcox, W. B. (2002). Religion, convention, and paternal involvement. *Journal of Marriage and Family, 64,* 780–792.

Williams, G. C., Cox, E. M., Hedberg, V. A., & Deci, E. L. (2000). Extrinsic life goals and health risk behaviors in adolescents. *Journal of Applied Social Psychology, 30,* 1756–1771.

Wuthnow, R. (1999). *Growing up religious: Christians and Jews and their journeys of faith.* Boston: Beacon.

22

MENTORS, FRIENDS, AND GURUS: PEER AND NONPARENT INFLUENCES ON SPIRITUAL DEVELOPMENT

KELLY DEAN SCHWARTZ

WILLIAM M. BUKOWSKI

WAYNE T. AOKI

Much has been explored and written about the nature of familial relationships and their influence on spiritual development during childhood and adolescence (Altemeyer & Hunsberger, 1997; Cornwall, 1989; de Vaus, 1983; Hood, Spilka, Hunsberger, & Gorsuch, 1996). Although extrafamilial relationships may not have the primacy of experiences with parents and siblings, relationships with nonfamily members can also be powerful in ways that can be complementary or compensatory to those with family members. In this chapter we examine three types of extrafamilial social relationships—mentors, friends, and gurus—and consider the theoretical and empirical support for their association to spiritual development. Thus, our goal is to discuss how the spiritual development of the individual is related to these forms of social relationship, either as an antecedent or as a consequence.

Consistent with the view that there is reciprocal influence between individuals and the social or personal context in which they are situated, we aim to show that (a) aspects of spiritual development are well represented in the social experiences of children and adolescents, and (b) that experiences with friends, mentors, and other nonfamilial gurus can influence spiritual development. For our purposes, the term *spiritual development* will be inclusively used to describe both spirituality—the human experience of discovering universal meaning—and religion (or religiosity)—the social, organizational, and practical expression of said spiritual beliefs. The terms *spirituality* and *religiosity* will be used only when they identify unique aspects of the spiritual development process. It is within the parameters of these definitions that we begin the exploration of the role of mentors, friends, and other gurus, respectively, as they shape and are shaped by spiritual development during childhood and adolescence.

MENTORS AND SPIRITUAL DEVELOPMENT

The importance of spiritual development is well documented but not fully appreciated by the North American scholarly community. Regnerus and colleagues (Regnerus, Smith, & Fritsch, 2003) make the illuminating comparison that among adults, weekly religious participation has the same positive effects on health as a pack of cigarettes a day have negative effects on health. The positive effects of religion on youth and adolescents are also well documented (e.g., Donahue & Benson, 1995; Muller & Ellison, 2001). While 76% of adolescents believe in a personal God (Gallup & Bezilla, 1992) and 30% of high school seniors indicate that religion is "very important" (Johnston, Bachman, & O'Malley, 1999), little is documented on the effective nurturance of that religiosity.

If the spiritual development of our youth is robust in its correlation with both positive and healthy development, then one needs to better understand the factors that contribute to that development. A promising line of research has focused on the role of mentors and their influence as nonparental adults on youth. For our purposes, a mentor is defined as an older, more experienced person who seeks to further the development of character and competence in a younger person (Hamilton, 1990). The goal of the following discussion is to review the empirical data supporting mentoring of youth as beneficial for their well-being. This will be followed by a discussion of the dynamics of the mentor bond and how it fosters positive development, particularly spiritual development.

Mentoring as Developmental Context for Spiritual Development

Mentoring has long been a social mechanism found in cultures to facilitate the development of young people into adulthood (Levinson, 1978). Mentors have typically been nonparental adults who often are kin, including aunts, uncles, grandparents, and older siblings (Zimmerman, Bingenheimer, & Notaro, 2002). In today's society, however, with fractured and stressed familial bonds, teachers, coaches, youth workers, and programmatically assigned mentors are augmenting the social and parental tasks of transitioning youth into adulthood. According to the Save the Children National Mentoring Database, there are more than 1,700 mentor programs (Save the Children, 1999).

Adolescents naturally seek out adults as mentors in their social development (Beam, Chen, & Greenberger, 2002). Rhodes and colleagues (Rhodes, Bogat, Roffman, Edelman, & Galasso, 2002) differentiate these naturally sought-out mentor bonds from programmatically assigned mentor bonds organized by Big Brothers Big Sisters of America, one of the best-known mentoring programs in the United States. Natural mentors are often relatives and part of a youth's extended family. These relationships provide instrumental support such as job skills and social networking (Zimmerman et al., 2002). In addition, they provide emotional and psychological encouragement and support to help the young person meet life challenges. Beam et al. (2002) conclude that in addition to being a naturally occurring part of adolescent development, these relationships are meaningful because of the support and mutuality that characterize the mentor bonds.

Mentoring has demonstrated multiple benefits to adolescent development. Expanding on our definition, a mentor has been described as one who supports and provides access to resources (Rhodes, Ebert, & Fischer, 1992), acts as a transitional figure to adulthood (Levinson et al., 1978), and provides a relationship of support, guidance, and inspiration to a mentee (Zimmerman et al., 2002). These mentor relationships have shown a significant correlation with a variety of decreased risk factors as well as increased protective factors. For example, students with mentors showed increased rates of school attendance compared to students without mentors (LoScuito, Rajala, Townsend, & Taylor, 1996; Tierney, Grossman, & Resch, 1995). In a small sample of 20 mothers, Zippay (1995) found that the girls attributed the choice to remain in high school to their mentor relations. In another sample of teen mothers, those with a mentor relationship over 2 years (postpartum) were more likely to remain in school and graduate than teen mothers without a mentor (Klaw, Rhodes, & Fitzgerald, 2003). Similarly, Slicker and Palmer (1993) found mentor relationships reducing dropout rates for at-risk teens, though only for those with quality mentor relationships as measured by frequency and quantity of contacts.

There is evidence that mentor relations generalize to enhance a youth's interpersonal relationships. Using self-reports, adolescents have attributed successful conflict resolution to their mentors (Rhodes, 1994). Youths with a Big Brother or Big Sister reported more emotionally supportive peer relations as compared to those without a mentor. These mentor relations provided a buffer effect for other peer relations and even in relationships with parents (Tierney et al., 1995).

Drug and alcohol use has also been designated as an outcome variable, responsive to the mentor relationship. Several studies have documented either decreased usage or delayed onset of alcohol and drug use as a correlate of the mentor–mentee relationship (LoScuito, Rajala, Townsend, & Taylor, 1994; Rhodes, 1995). Nevertheless, Greenberger, Chen, and Beam (1998) have also found that an older, nonparental adult influenced engagement in illegal activities, including alcohol use among adolescent boys. Mentor adults function as gatekeepers, and antisocial adults may easily model antisocial behaviors and attitudes.

Enhanced academic performance, rewarding interpersonal relations, and decreased drug and alcohol use are some of the documented positive outcomes for mentor relationships with youth and adolescents. The dynamics of this relationship are now being more closely evaluated (Rhodes et al., 2002). Youths are generally impacted in a prosocial direction. They are more engaged with the community (LoScuito et al., 1994) and demonstrate greater resiliency against life stressors.

Contrary to sweeping positive effects of such initiatives, DuBois, Holloway, Valentine, and Cooper (2002), in their meta-analysis of mentor programs, found only modest support for mentoring interventions. They point out the variability in program implementation and therefore the difficulty in making generalizations. Variations included different evaluation designs, program features such as mentor selection criteria, different quality measures of the relationship, and assessment of the outcomes. They conclude with the recommendation that mentor programs follow best-practice guidelines for program implementation, such as screening of mentors,

mentor training, structured activities, and parent involvement. When programs followed best-practice guidelines, effect sizes were .20 and .22 for fixed and random effects compared to .04 and .07, respectively, for programs that did not follow best-practice guidelines. Furthermore, mentoring worked best as a secondary prevention program for at-risk youth (DuBois, Holloway, et al., 2002).

Mentoring and Spiritual Development: Empirical Evidence

Several different lines of reasoning have been offered for the mechanisms by which mentoring may be effective for spiritual development. Most primarily, the mentor bond helps to reinforce social and religious norms, clarify values, and establish expectations for behavior. It is not surprising that better outcomes were demonstrated in those mentor relations that were more enduring and satisfying to the mentee. The social influence factor can be understood from the perspective of previous work done on the effects of modeling and observational learning. Citing the work of Albert Bandura (1986) as foundational to their paradigm, Oman and Thoresen (2003) address this dynamic as it relates to spiritual development: "The people with whom one regularly associates, either through preference or imposition, delimit the behavioral patterns that will be repeatedly observed, and hence, learned most thoroughly" (p. 150). Crucial to the role of mentoring on spiritual development is the extent of engaged contact between mentor and mentee. DuBois, Neville, Parra, and Pugh-Lilly (2002) found that only when mentors were perceived as significant to the mentee over an extended period of time did the mentees show positive psychological and behavioral outcomes.

Central to understanding mentors as spiritual models is the appreciation that spiritual development is the acquisition of a complex set of skills, attitudes, and behaviors. Spirituality is therefore difficult to teach and is better understood as embodied or exemplified (Bandura, 2003). Religious traditions will cite the images of exemplars such as Jesus, Buddha, Gandhi, and Mother Teresa as examples to follow in belief, values, and behaviors. Modeling is instructive through the process of observational learning, which requires attention, retention, reproduction, and motivation. Oman and Thoresen (2003) argue that these components of observational learning have been intuitively used throughout the histories of the world religions as the means for teaching both spirituality and religiosity. It is therefore suggestive that the relational process of the mentor–mentee bond promotes spiritual development through this observational learning.

The components of observational learning have their parallels in several religious practices. Meditation, for example, purposely focuses a person's attention, one of the components of modeling and observational learning. Retention is encouraged through the repetition of story, song, and sacred readings as reminders in collective memory of exemplars. Reproduction is taught as doing what is right and as imitating exemplars. The universal virtues of charity, truthfulness, and humility are deeds and not just words. The role of the exemplar and by implication the value of a mentor is a demonstration of how these virtues look in real life. And finally, motivation is rich in many religious traditions by modeling the benefits of tranquillity, belonging, and the satisfaction of our need for transcendence. Oman and Thoresen (2003) therefore argue that these practices of observational learning have always been part of religious training.

While mentoring may have a strong instrumental influence in the sense of social networking and access to resources, there may also be a source of strong modeling of restraint and social control, reinforcement of social norms, and the tacit appreciation for the importance of familial, communal, and social obligation (Erickson, Crosnoe, & Dornbusch, 2000). The mentor gives of his or her time, wisdom, and skills, because together, mentor and mentee are part of the community. The mentor provides to the child or adolescent what a parent would otherwise feel obligated to do, without the emotional complexities of the family. This altruistic act reinforces the relational connection of the individual to the greater community (Lerner & Benson, 2001; Youniss, McLellan, & Yates, 1999). It reinforces the fact that the individual's identity goes beyond the "self." That is, we have an identity within the community that transcends our individualism. The mentor therefore serves the important task of connecting the child or adolescent to the larger whole and enables the youth to identify a transcendent self, a spiritual self, mediated through the mentor relationship (see Hamel, Leclerc, & Lefrancois, 2003).

There is modest support for mentoring as supportive of the maturing spiritual development of adolescents and young adults. The investigation conducted by Cannister (1999) on first-year college students suggested that young adults who established a formal mentoring relationship with professors who were intent on nurturing spiritual development reported enhanced spiritual growth. These first-year students were compared to a randomly assigned group who were not matched with a mentor. This is one of the few studies that directly correlated mentoring with self-reported spiritual growth, the conclusions of which may or may not follow to the child and adolescent populations.

Cook (2000) evaluated African American, Haitian, and Latino youth who were actively involved with their church and found that mentoring was one mechanism by which these youth demonstrated increased resilience to the stresses and strains of inner-city life. Both churched and nonchurched youth relied on nonparental adult mentors for managing life. Nevertheless, while both groups endorsed having adult mentors, the churched youth demonstrated fewer externalized behavioral problems. Decreased behavioral problems may be important, but in the long term may be less important than the development of prosocial attitudes and values. The internalization of such prosocial perspectives, while not directly measured, may have been supported in the spiritual and religious context as mediated by their mentors (Cook, 2000; Krause, Ellison, Shaw, Marcum, & Boardman, 2001).

Adolescence is a time for the development of one's identity, not just who one is but also who one wants to become. This theme is important to adolescents because of their maturing cognitive capacity and the ability of adolescents to take multiple perspectives (Selman, 1980). Parents are clearly the most influential in laying a foundation for religious beliefs (Bao, Whitbeck, Hoyt, & Conger, 1999; Ozorak, 1989). Nevertheless, the adolescent's ability to entertain different beliefs and try on new, imaginative selves makes the social environment especially important as it provides multiple examples of possible selves. Nonparental affirmation, through the mentor relationship, can provide the social and cultural context for youth to experience their spiritual selves. An experience of the transcendent may come from a relationship with a significant other (Crystal & DeBell, 2002; Hamel et al., 2003) because it is in relationships that adolescents explore the significance and meaning of life (King & Boyatzis, 2004). Few relationships are more significant than those we consider in the next section: childhood and adolescent friendships.

Friendships and Spiritual Development

The association between friendship and spiritual development can be approached from several perspectives. The approach we adopt concerns the characteristics and processes of friendship during childhood and adolescence (Schwartz, in press b). This description is based on the broad empirical literature about friendship as a developmental context (e.g., Berndt, 2002; Bukowski & Hoza, 1989; Bukowski & Sippola, 1996; Newcomb, Bukowski, & Bagwell, 1999; Rubin, Bukowski, & Parker, 1998, in press). It will be discussed that friendship possesses many characteristics related to spirituality and that some of the basic processes underlying friendship can also be found in religious practices. We derive from this approach a set of theoretical and empirical premises regarding the view that the association between friendship and spiritual development is best conceptualized as one of bidirectional effects. In this way spirituality and religion can influence friendship *and* they can be influenced by it. We discuss each of these four premises at the end of this section.

Friendship as Developmental Context for Spiritual Development

It is necessary to first distinguish friends from a peer or peer group, as friends differ from other pairs of peers in many ways. A meta-analysis of research on differences between pairs of friends and nonfriends (Newcomb & Bagwell, 1995) showed that children are more

likely to behave in positive ways with friends than with nonfriends, and that in their interactions with friends, relative to interaction with nonfriends, children show higher levels of affect regulation. Consistent with the arguments of Parker and Gottman (1989), friendship during middle childhood appears to be an important context for learning about the display and regulation of emotions. For example, friends are more concerned about achieving an equitable resolution to conflicts that will preserve or promote the continuity of their relationship. That is, friendship leads a child away from her- or himself in order to develop a view of the world that works for and promotes the larger social context. In this way friendship helps children move beyond their own individual needs and views and to develop a sense of how they fit and function within the social world.

During childhood and adolescence, friends engage in many mutual activities that allow them to explore and become sensitive to the needs of others and to feel a strong attachment to others (Gottman, 1983). Friends talk to each other and share matters they do not disclose to others; they encourage each other, teach each other, listen to each other's worries and hopes, share each other's secrets, and tolerate each other's faults. They fight and make up, compete with each other, challenge each other, tease one another (good-naturedly), protect each other from the wiles of their enemies, and help each other in more ways than one can count. Friends know each other deeply, not superficially. They are kind in each other's sorrows, glad in each other's successes, and firm in times of adversity. It is in friendship that one learns how to relate to others and to have a deep sensitivity and union with them, a transcendent experience in embryonic form that may provide the foundation for the spiritual development of children and adolescents.

An important aspect of children's understandings of friendship is the recognition that friendship is something that exists between two people (Rubin et al., in press). In this way, each friend contributes to the friendship, but neither of them owns it; it exists between them, and each is responsible for nourishing and maintaining it. The development of children's thoughts about friendships has been compared to

Aristotle's model of friendship that conceptualized friendship according to pleasure, utility, and goodness (Bukowski & Sippola, 1996). Whereas young children see friendship according to the pleasure or utility that it provides, the mature view of friendship seen among older children and adolescents emphasizes friendship as a form of goodness. By this it is meant that they see friendship as an opportunity to make a positive contribution to (i.e., to promote goodness in) the life of one's friend. These essential characteristics of friendship, specifically its transcendent quality and its link with goodness, make it easy to see how friendship and spiritual development go together for children and adolescents.

Friendship and Spiritual Development: Empirical Evidence

In spite of the remarkable paucity of empirical research focused specifically on the association between friendship and child or adolescent spiritual development, evidence suggests that these associations are at least bidirectional and certainly multifaceted. Our first claim is that religion or religiosity (which includes religious traditions, behavior, and experience) contributes to friendship. We defend this claim by showing that there is a special place for friendship in the basic writings of major religions and that this emphasis may promote the development of the concept of friendship in children. We also argue that religiosity provides a context for friendship and promotes friendship formation by facilitating common ground activities and shared belief systems. As outlined earlier in the special characteristics of friendships, our second claim reiterates the links between friendship and spirituality (which does not necessarily include religiosity), showing that these constructs are intertwined.

Religiosity Contributes to Friendship and Friendship Contributes to Religiosity. One can speculate that spiritual development as expressed in religious traditions promotes friendship in two ways. First, most religions teach children how to be a responsible and effective friend. Specifically, the emphasis in most religious traditions on equality, regulation, charity, compassion, understanding, and humility gives children the tools

needed to be competent and effective friends. Foundational axioms like that found in the Christian Bible (e.g., "Love your neighbor as yourself," Mark 12:31) provide children and adolescents with the spiritual impetus to acknowledge and practice friendships. Second, religion provides opportunities for meaningful interactions and shared experience. We discussed earlier that friendship is based on common ground experiences (Gottman, 1983). Children are more similar to their friends than they are to other peers. Moreover, a critical component of the process of friendship formation is finding areas of agreement in terms of activity preferences, values, and ideas. Insofar as coparticipation in practices that nurture spirituality (e.g., sharing, compassion, companionship) or are associated with religion (e.g., church, mosque, or synagogue attendance, catechism) is likely to provide opportunities for shared activities and shared meanings, it is likely to promote opportunities for friendship (e.g., Ozorak, 1989).

Coming from the alternative direction, it is also likely that friendship promotes religiosity. In a previous section we made clear that friendship is given a special, if variable, role in most religions. The features that religion associates with friendship often bear a strong resemblance to the features that children, especially children in the West, ascribe to friendship. From a young age children are familiar with what friendship means and the basic processes it relies on and requires. Nearly all children have experience with friendship, and they recognize the benefits and challenges that peer relations present. For example, empathy and forgiveness experienced within friendships are prominent in learning about both human and transcendent relationships and have strong ties to spiritual development (e.g., McCullough, Thoresen, & Pargament, 2001).

Regardless of whether children bring these ideas and experiences with them to their experiences in religious traditions, or develop them in parallel, this confluence between one's social-cognitive understanding of friendship with the emphasis on friendship in religion is likely to facilitate one's participation in a religion. For example, Hoge and Petrillo's (1978) early study found that friends have at least moderate influence on religious practice (e.g., participation in the church youth group, enjoyment of that participation), though no measure was taken to assess their influence on religious belief. Additionally, friends have been found to add unique variance over and above that of parental influence in adolescents' experience of God and importance of religion (King, Furrow, & Roth, 2002; Schwartz, 2005). For example, Schwartz (2005) found that not only did friends' faith modeling and faith dialogue account for more variance in adolescent religious belief and commitment, but the modeling of and dialogue with friends about faith actually mediated the influence of parents on religiosity. Thus, friendship may become an organizing principle by which children come to involve themselves with the meaning and practices inherent in religious tradition.

Another way in which friendship promotes religiosity is by providing opportunities for social belonging and interaction with others, the activities associated with religion satisfy human needs for interdependence and social embeddedness. King and Furrow (2004) found that religious youth reported high levels of positive social interaction, trust, and shared values with their closest group of friends compared to their less religious peers. In other words, the human need for belonging and friendship may motivate religious children and adolescents to participate in activities that result in the experience of human relationship at a deeper level than that experienced by their nonreligious peers.

Friendship Contributes to Spirituality and Spirituality Contributes to Friendship. The experience of friendship as a form of goodness is most notably intertwined with spirituality. Involvement with friends enhances one's understanding of others and facilitates a transcendent connection with the larger social group. Participating in friendships and peer groups provides the opportunity to become connected to something bigger than oneself and to have compassion and affection for the other. In friendship one learns about others and learns to have affection for others. Insofar as friendship requires us to see and to appreciate the thoughts, feelings, and ideas of others, it forces us to see outside ourselves. Supporting the findings of others (e.g., Martin, White, & Perlman, 2001), Schwartz (2005) found that having friends who both

modeled and verbally shared about their spirituality was associated with higher self-reported belief and commitment compared to those with friends who did not model or dialogue about their faith. Thus, having a friend, particularly one who shares in this quest for meaning and authentic development, signifies that one is part of "something" outside the self. This something (i.e., the friendship) does not belong exclusively to either of the friends but is a shared property (Sroufe & Fleeson, 1986).

Part of friendship is the recognition that belonging to a relationship requires that one nurture both the friend and the relationship. It also means that one needs to be open to nurturing from the friend. In these ways, friendship requires transcendence. Shelton (1983) accurately points out that identity acquisition often finds support in close interpersonal relationships with one or more friends, and that such relationships often provide reinforcement for the personal spiritual questioning that the adolescent experiences. A friendship needs to look beyond the self and see the self's position in something larger than it. As a result, this quest may lead the child or adolescent to be placed under the guidance of spiritual directors separate from the mentoring and friendship relationship we have reviewed thus far.

GURUS, SAGES, AND OTHER SPIRITUAL DIRECTORS

Moving away from the friend and mentoring relationships recognized as influencing both children's and adolescents' spiritual development, there exist several other sources of relationship that have historically been known to exert great influence on a young person's religious development. The guru–devotee relationship, whether recognized by the child or not as such a relationship, has played a crucial role in the practice of many religious traditions, including Hinduism, Buddhism, Christianity, and Islam. This is particularly true in religions of India, where teachers (e.g., Ramana Maharshi) are widely considered to be self-realized masters and embodiments of the divine (Martignetti, 1998). In this relationship, followers of such teachers often treat this as the principal focus of their lives: "They consider their gurus not only to be the means but as the ones who bear the obligation to lead their followers to the 'freedom' or 'liberation' that lies at the end of the Hindu or Buddhist view of the religious life" (Martignetti, 1998, p. 128). The relationship with the guru is expressed in acts of devotion or service, often simply in the act of sitting in the guru's presence.

Hindu gurus have become familiar sights outside of India, but their work remains a mystery to most people in the West. The guru is responsible for the spiritual development of followers, and initiation into a religious community "at the feet of the guru" involves a willingness to follow his guidance. Not uncommonly, the guru becomes involved in the intimate affairs and problems of those in the community, serving as pastoral counselors for followers. The guru is expected to impart truth in such a way that he becomes a mediator between God and the followers. As will be discussed later, North American examples of youth pastors and/or religious educators may serve much the same function and role for youth.

For Western religions—Christianity, Islam, and Judaism—the archetype of spiritual modeling has been the emulation of God as much as it is the emulation of the spiritual guide. For example, Judaism recommends strongly associating with righteous role models, called sages, in order to learn their ways and be influenced by their good deeds (Schochet, 1990). Jewish sources emphasize that such spiritual role models must be people whose scholarship is clearly reflected both in their private and public conduct. The ideal sage is described as a person who is great in wisdom and strong in character traits, who sanctifies himself, constantly dedicates himself to God, purifies himself from the dust of materialism, and improves himself with every decent character trait (Surasky, 1982).

The Talmud further teaches that the young devotee can learn as much from the private lives of sages as from their teachings in the study hall (Scherman, 1995). Righteous people, accordingly, can serve as "role models by allowing others to watch them in their everyday lives" (Silberman, 2003, p. 177). Unlike gurus, sages can also serve their young seekers even when they cannot be observed, through hearing or

reading stories about their lives. For example, books can impart to students characteristics such as courage, spiritual strength and perseverance under difficult circumstances, self-control, self-sacrifice, concern and compassion for others, generosity, forgiveness and peace seeking, hopefulness and serenity, the ability to see only good in the world, humility, honesty, and fairness (Surasky, 1982). Indeed, past and recent history has shown some positive impact of exemplary figures of faith, such as Moses, Saint Francis of Assisi, and Martin Luther King Jr. (Silberman, Higgins, & Dweck, in press). Silberman (2003) further states that the role of sages, alive or remembered, is to inspire and elevate young learners to spiritual heights and attach them to God: "They represent the personification of the ideal of sanctifying every aspect of one's life, even the physical and material ones such as eating, sleeping, engaging in business, and so forth" (p. 178). The hope therefore is that early contact with wise and holy sages will promote, in some small measure, the absorption of their exemplary characteristics (Oman & Thoresen, 2003).

As one might expect, empirical evidence supporting the value of gurus and sages on the spiritual development of children and adolescents is either nonexistent or unreported. Quantitative or qualitative measurement of spiritual growth has always been a debatable and contentious issue, as the subjective impact of such development is usually evaluated retrospectively and/or with weak methodological rigor (e.g., a single question on frequency of church attendance). When they are studied, guru–devotee relationships are often exhumed to investigate their dangerous and even pathological consequences, usually in the form of cultlike behavior. In one of the few studies looking at this domain, Martignetti (1998) explored whether Hindu-based guru-devoted followers were more likely than other followers (i.e., Unitarian Universalist Church adherents and employees of a computer company) to idealize or mirror their gurus based on the parenting style all participants experienced as children. The findings indicated that there were no differences among the groups in their idealization or mirroring of their leaders, nor did the type of parenting style interact to produce differences in the level of devotion to the identified leaders. The author concluded that the study "empirically demonstrated that, despite conventional notions of disciples of gurus [as] pathologically inclined or as unfortunate, emotionally-disadvantaged dupes, devotees exhibit equivalence in important self sectors and in a significant aspect of their developmental experiences as compared with others in groups and settings which are not guru-devoted and which are not viewed negatively" (Martignetti, 1998, p. 136). Such findings seem to support the assessment of others (e.g., Hardcastle, 2001) that the spiritual connections between a sage or guru and his or her protégé result in heightened potential to witness the exchange of integrity, wisdom, compassion, and the ability to inspire others.

Empirical Evidence from Youth Ministry

Although the term *guru* or *sage* would seldom be used to describe their role and position, youth ministers in the North American and other Western contexts serve much the same function within more mainstream Judeo-Christian traditions. The task of nurturing the faith development of children and youth is taken seriously by thousands of adult youth workers across hundreds of denominations, Catholic and Protestant. In a recent survey of more than 2,400 youth ministers, the nurturing of adolescents' spiritual development was ranked number one in terms of both perceived importance and how well it was being achieved (Strommen, Jones, & Rahn, 2001). This study also found that those youth ministers who placed a high priority on the spiritual development of their youth had a clear youth ministry philosophy and mission, enabled youth to "own" their youth ministry program, and related well to youth.

Other research has indicated that the work of youth ministers results in the development of numerous spiritual outcomes for youth: personal relationship with God, moral responsibility, hopeful and positive attitudes, and engaging in mission and service, to name a few (Strommen & Hardel, 2000). Youth ministers and their youth are reported to experience a bond that is both relationally intentional and spiritually focused, resulting in spiritual development that

contributes to growth in cognitive, behavioral, and interpersonal maturity. Such findings support the value of youth ministers who assist adolescents in their "need to be paced with and then led by spiritual caregivers who are able to perceive and engage in whole-life spirituality" (Dunn, 2001, p. 59).

It is apparent from the research cited here that religious ministers have a significant role in the spiritual development of the youth under their tutelage. Little investigation, however, has been completed to date on the specific qualities of the youth and other religious ministers that have the greatest impact on that development. In a recent study by Schwartz (2003), more than 3,000 Christian adolescents (age 13–18) were asked to rate the importance of various characteristics of both their youth minister and the senior pastor at their church. The specific relationship qualities included perceived expertise in religious instruction, strength of Christian example, provision of opportunities to learn, and being known by that youth minister or pastor. Participants were also asked to complete measures of religious belief and commitment, rate the importance of selected Christian beliefs (e.g., living a holy life, avoidance of sin), and provide estimates of participation in at-risk (e.g., drug and alcohol use, cigarette use) and religious behavior (e.g., praying for others, church attendance). Results indicated that as perceived qualities of both youth ministers and church pastors increased, so did the participants' ratings of their religious belief and commitment, importance of religious beliefs, and Christian behavior. Somewhat surprisingly, there were no significant relationships between the adolescents' ratings of these pastoral qualities and their participation in at-risk behaviors. Thus, although not predictive of behavior outside of religious and spiritual development, it was apparent that strong religious instruction, spiritual modeling, and being known (i.e., intimacy) by adult youth ministers contributed significantly to youths' perceptions of their own spiritual development.

Strommen et al.'s (2001) study also revealed that youth ministers' perceptions of their effectiveness in giving spiritual direction to their youth is not uniform across male and female youth ministers. The effectiveness in achieving spiritual development in youth for male youth workers in the study was influenced by three factors: size of youth group, the stance of their denomination, and the physical location of their church. For example, the authors articulated that the more evangelical and conservative the denomination or organization (e.g., Assembly of God, Youth for Christ), and the larger the city in which the church or organization was located, the greater the male youth workers' estimate of their effectiveness, whereas for male youth workers in more mainline denominations (e.g., United Methodist, Presbyterian), and/or in smaller cities or towns, the opposite was true. For female youth ministers, the conservative denominational affiliation also resulted in higher estimates of achieving spiritual development in their youth; females also serving as ministers for up to 15 years and who were ministers in churches with more than 40 children and adolescents in the youth group also had higher effectiveness estimates; church location was not a factor for female youth ministers. Confirming the power of expectations of youth ministers in influencing spiritual development, Schwartz (2001) also found that adolescents in church youth groups with fewer than 20 members rated their religious beliefs and commitment lower than did those in larger youth groups (e.g., over 100). These analyses suggest that, both from the perspective of youth ministers and the youth under their direction, the spiritual development of children and adolescents takes place within the context of diverse and enriching social contexts, a fact not lost in the findings of the significant contributions that adolescents' involvement in a religious institution makes to their development (Benson, 1997).

SUMMARY AND CONCLUSIONS

As the preceding discussion has articulated, the domain of childhood and adolescent spiritual development is clearly and critically associated with mentors, friendship, and spiritual directors (e.g., gurus, sages, youth ministers). Not only are such relationships seen as having value as a manifestation of one's spirituality, but all are ascribed a critical role in steering someone toward spiritual growth within a religious tradition.

Mentors, gurus, and other nonparental spiritual influences were presented as having a potentially significant effect on children and adolescents' spirituality and religiosity. The preceding discussion suggests that such openness to these peer and nonparental sources of spiritual and religious influence (e.g., Fowler, 1981; Schwartz, in press a) is not by accident. Rather, it is very likely that their place in the developmental trajectory (i.e., cognitive development, identity, physical maturation) may actually increase their seeking of and responsiveness to these important sources of spiritual nurture.

There are several key places where this investigation into peer and nonparental influences requires further exploration. For example, further research is needed to firmly establish the role of mentors in adolescent spiritual development. For example, Cannister's (1999) work needs replication to further substantiate the direct effects of mentoring on spiritual development. The meta-analytic work of DuBois, Holloway, et al. (2002) points to the need for collaboration between researchers and program administrators to better define mentoring practices and the development of measurable outcomes directly related to spiritual consequences. In addition, it is clear that not all mentors are equal. That is, some mentors are better able to nurture and develop meaningful relationships with youth. Similar to studies of friends and families, research is needed to better define those qualities of effective mentors. Also challenging is that youth themselves are not equally responsive to nonparental adult influences. The nature of both the mentor–mentee and guru–disciple bond is therefore complex, but given the importance youth attach to spirituality, further research is warranted.

Perhaps most important, spiritual development appears to value friendship, whether in its own right or as a means to increased spirituality or religiosity. Sadly, although the theoretical rationale supporting the association between social development and spiritual development is more than sound, the empirical evidence necessary to ratify these theoretical underpinnings is quite fragile. As noted earlier, Schwartz (2005) attempted to explore the nature and qualities of adolescent friendship as they predict religious belief and commitment, leading to conclusions that the internalization of beliefs that was initially nurtured by parents evolves to include and be represented by meaningful and deepening friend relationships. More studies are needed to elucidate the qualities (e.g., compassion), individual differences (e.g., age, gender), and contextual factors (e.g., peer group versus close friends) most significantly responsible for predicting and being influenced by spiritual and religious development. Future studies would also do well to explore how the experience of spirituality and religiosity in childhood and adolescence changes the experience of friendships, possibly heightening the dynamics of those relationships as has been found in the case of families (e.g., Mahoney, Pargament, Murray-Swank, & Murray-Swank, 2003). Notwithstanding what we already know about the influence of parents on childhood and adolescent spiritual development, also ignored in the literature is the impact of sibling and intergenerational sources (i.e., grandparents) in this domain of functioning.

Gurus, sages, and other spiritual directors have a rich history in nurturing childhood and adolescent spiritual development, but religious entities have been hesitant to pursue or allow empirical investigation of the outcomes associated with such intentional relationships. The recent positive youth development initiatives have found overwhelming evidence that children and adolescents who are involved with church and/or faith-based youth groups not only are more likely to avoid at-risk behaviors but actually thrive in their development (e.g., Lerner, Dowling, & Anderson, 2003). As North American churches and denominations lose thousands of child and adolescent attendees and members every year, research is needed to explore the nature and dynamics of the relationships that exist between those charged with the task of spiritual direction (i.e., youth ministers) and the youth. In a church culture swamped with curricular and programmatic ministries, there still appears to be no substitute for a close, caring mentoring or gurulike relationship in a child's or adolescent's spiritual development.

As we stated at the outset, the goal of this chapter was to explore the antecedent and consequent associations between childhood and adolescent spiritual development and three sources of peer and nonfamilial relationship.

Rather than assume that there is a confirmed directionality of influence between social and spiritual development, the best conclusion may be that there is, as opposed to even a bidirectional or transactional relationship, a transformational relationship between these two sources. That is, not only do relationships with friends, mentors, and gurus change one's spiritual development, but one's spirituality and religiosity also have an impact on the health and success of one's relationships with these same persons. Add to this the context within which social and spiritual development coexists—family, school, neighborhood, faith community—and one begins to conceive of the complexity inherent in understanding even one ecology of spiritual development. For children and adolescents, however, the social world of friends and other adult figures grows increasingly wider, as does their capacity for experiencing a spiritual world that transcends even those they hold most closely. It is the vitality of this untapped capacity that demands a continued diligence in exploring that which we call childhood and adolescent spiritual development.

REFERENCES

Altemeyer, B., & Hunsberger, B. (1997). *Amazing conversions: Why some turn to faith and others abandon religion.* Amherst, NY: Prometheus Books.

Bandura, A. (1986). *Social foundations of thought and action.* Englewood Cliffs, NJ: Prentice Hall.

Bandura, A. (2003). On the psychosocial impact and mechanisms of spiritual modeling. *International Journal for the Psychology of Religion, 13,* 167–174.

Bao, W. N., Whitbeck, L. B., Hoyt, D. R., & Conger, R. D. (1999). Perceived parental acceptance as a moderator of religious transmission among adolescent boys and girls. *Journal of Marriage and the Family, 61,* 362–374.

Beam, M. R., Chen, C., & Greenberger, E. (2002). The nature of adolescents' relationships with their "very important" non-parental adults. *American Journal of Community Psychology, 30*(2), 305–325.

Benson, P. L. (1997). *All kids are our kids: What communities must do to raise caring and responsible children and adolescents*. San Francisco: Jossey-Bass.

Berndt, T. J. (2002). Friendship quality and social development. *Current Directions in Psychological Science, 11,* 7–10.

Bukowski, W. M., & Hoza, B. (1989). Popularity and friendship: Issues in theory, measurement, and outcomes. In T. Berndt & G. Ladd (Eds.), *Peer relations in child development* (pp. 15–45). New York: Wiley.

Bukowski, W. M., & Sippola, L. K. (1996). Friendship and morality: (How) Are they related? In W. M. Bukowski, A. F. Newcomb, & W. W. Hartup (Eds.), *The company they keep: Friendship during childhood and adolescence* (pp. 238–261). Cambridge, UK: Cambridge University Press.

Cannister, M. W. (1999). Mentoring and the spiritual well-being of late adolescents. *Adolescence, 34,* 769–779.

Cook, K. V. (2000). "You have to have somebody watching your back, and if that's God, then that's mighty big": The church's role in the resilience of inner-city youth. *Adolescence, 35,* 717–730.

Cornwall, M. (1989). The determinants of religious behavior: A theoretical model and empirical test. *Social Forces, 68*(2), 572–592.

Crystal, D. S., & DeBell, M. (2002). Sources of civic orientation among American youth: Trust, religious valuation, and attributions of responsibility. *Political Psychology, 23*(1), 113–132.

De Vaus, D. A. (1983). The relative importance of parents and peers for adolescent religious orientation: An Australian study. *Adolescence, 18,* 147–158.

Donahue, M. J., & Benson, P. L. (1995). Religion and the well-being of adolescents. *Journal of Social Issues, 51,* 145–160.

DuBois, D. L., Holloway, B. E., Valentine, J. C., & Harris, C. (2002). Effectiveness of mentoring programs for youth: A meta-analytic review. *American Journal of Community Psychology, 30,* 157–197.

DuBois, D. L., Neville, H. A., Parra, G. R., & Pugh-Lilly, A. O. (2002). Testing a new model of mentoring. *New Directions for Youth Development, 93,* 21–57.

Dunn, R. (2001). *Shaping the spiritual life of students.* Downers Grove, IL: InterVarsity Press.

Erickson, K. G., Crosnoe, R., & Dornbusch, S. M. (2000). A social process model of adolescent deviance: Combining social control and differential association perspectives. *Journal of Youth and Adolescence, 29,* 395–425.

Fowler, J. W. (1981). *Stages of faith: The psychology of human development and the quest for meaning.* San Francisco: HarperCollins.

Gallup, G., & Bezilla, R. (1992). *The religious life of young Americans.* Princeton, NJ: George H. Gallup International Institute.

Gottman, J. M. (1983). How children become friends. *Monographs of the Society for Research in Child Development, 48* (3, Serial No. 201).

Greenberger, E., Chen, C., & Beam, M. R. (1998). The role of "very important" non-parental adults in adolescent development. *Journal of Youth and Adolescence, 27,* 321–343.

Hamel, S., Leclerc, G., & Lefrancois, R. (2003). A psychological outlook on the concept of transcendent actualization. *International Journal for the Psychology of Religion, 13,* 3–15.

Hamilton, S. F. (1990). *Apprenticeship for adulthood.* New York: Free Press.

Hardcastle, B. (2001). Spiritual connections: Protégés' reflections on significant mentorships. *Theory Into Practice, 40*(2), 201–208.

Hoge, D. R., & Petrillo, G. H. (1978). Development of religious thinking in adolescence: A test of Goldman's theories. *Journal for the Scientific Study of Religion, 17,* 359–379.

Hood, R. W., Spilka, B., Hunsberger, B., & Gorsuch, R. (1996). *The psychology of religion: An empirical approach.* New York: Guilford.

Johnston, L. D., Bachman, J. G., & O'Malley, P. M. (1999). *Monitoring the future: Questionnaire responses from the nation's high school seniors.* Ann Arbor: University of Michigan, Institute for Social Research.

King, P. E., & Boyatzis, C. J. (2004). Exploring adolescent spiritual and religious development: Current and future theoretical and empirical perspectives. *Applied Developmental Science, 8,* 2–6.

King, P. E., & Furrow, J. L. (2004). Religion as a resource for positive youth development: Religion, social capital, and moral outcomes. *Developmental Psychology, 40*(5), 703–713.

King, P. E., Furrow, J. L., & Roth, N. (2002). The influence of families and peers on adolescent religiousness. *Journal of Psychology & Christianity, 21,* 109–120.

Klaw, E. L., Rhodes, J. E., & Fitzgerald, L. F. (2003). Natural mentors in the lives of African-American adolescent mothers: Tracking relationships over time. *Journal of Youth and Adolescence, 32,* 223–232.

Krause, N., Ellison, C. G., Shaw, B. A., Marcum, J. P., & Boardman, J. D. (2001). Church-based social support and religious coping. *Journal for the Scientific Study of Religion, 40,* 637–656.

Lerner, R. M., & Benson, P. L. (Eds.). (2001). *Developmental assets and asset-building communities: Implications for research, policy, and practice.* New York: Kluwer Academic/Plenum.

Lerner, R. M., Dowling, E. M., & Anderson, P. M. (2003). Positive youth development: Thriving as the basis of personhood and civil society. *Applied Developmental Science, 7*(3), 172–180.

Levinson, D. (1978). *The seasons of a man's life.* New York: Ballantine.

LoScuito, L., Rajala, A. K., Townsend, T. N., & Taylor, A. S. (1996). An outcome evaluation of Across Ages: An intergenerational mentoring approach to drug prevention. *Journal of Adolescent Research, 11,* 116–129.

Mahoney, A., Pargament, K. I., Murray-Swank, A., & Murray-Swank, N. (2003). Religion and the sanctification of family relationships. *Review of Religious Research, 44*(3), 220–236.

Martignetti, C. A. (1998). Gurus and devotees: Guides or God? Pathology or faith? *Pastoral Psychology, 47*(2), 127–144.

Martin, T. F., White, J. M., & Perlman, D. (2001). Religious socialization: A test of the channeling hypothesis of parental influence on adolescent faith maturity. *Journal of Adolescent Research, 18*(2), 169–187.

McCullough, M. E., Thoresen, C. E., & Pargament, K. I. (2001). *Forgiveness: Theory, research, and practice.* New York: Guilford.

Muller, C., & Ellison, C. G. (2001). Religious involvement, social capital, and adolescents' academic progress: Evidence from the National Longitudinal Study of 1988. *Sociological Focus, 34,* 155–183.

Newcomb, A. F., & Bagwell, C. (1995). Children's friendship relations: A meta-analytic review. *Psychological Bulletin, 117,* 306–347.

Newcomb, A. F., Bukowski, W. M., & Bagwell, C. L. (1999). Knowing the sounds: Friendship as a developmental context. In W. A. Collins & B. Laursen (Eds.), *The Minnesota Symposia on Child Psychology: Vol. 30. Relationships as developmental contexts* (pp. 63–84). Mahwah, NJ: Erlbaum.

Oman, D., & Thoresen, C. E. (2003). Spiritual modeling: A key to spiritual and religious growth? *International Journal for the Psychology of Religion, 13,* 149–165.

Ozorak, E. W. (1989). Social and cognitive influences on the development of religious belief and commitment in adolescence. *Journal for the Scientific Study of Religion, 23,* 448–463.

Parker, J. G., & Gottman, J. M. (1989). Social and emotional development in a relational context: Friendship interaction from early childhood to adolescence. In T. J. Berndt & G. W. Ladd (Eds.), *Peer relations in child development* (pp. 95–131). New York: Wiley.

Regnerus, M., Smith, C., & Fritsch, M. (2003). *Religion in the lives of American adolescents: A review of the literature* (Research report No. 3 of the National Study of Youth and Religion). Chapel Hill: University of North Carolina, Odum Institute for Research in Social Science.

Rhodes, J. E. (1994). Older and wiser: Mentoring relationships in childhood and adolescence. *Journal of Primary Prevention, 14,* 187–196.

Rhodes, J. E., Bogat, G. A., Roffman, J., Edelman, P., & Galasso, L. (2002). Youth mentoring in perspective: Introduction to the special issue. *American Journal of Community Psychology, 30,* 149–155.

Rhodes, J. E., Ebert, L., & Fischer, K. (1992). Natural mentors: An overlooked resource in the social networks of young African American mothers. *American Journal of Community Psychology, 20,* 445–461.

Rubin, K. H., Bukowski, W. M., & Parker, J. G. (1998). Peer interactions, relationships and groups. In W. Damon (Series Ed.) and N. Eisenberg (Vol. Ed.), *The handbook of child psychology* (5th ed., pp. 619–700). New York: Wiley.

Rubin, K. H., Bukowski, W. M., & Parker, J. G. (in press). Peer interactions, relationships and groups. In W. Damon (Series Ed.) and N. Eisenberg (Vol. Ed.), *The handbook of child psychology* (6th ed.). New York: Wiley.

Save the Children. (1999). *Overview of Save the Children's National Mentoring Database.* Retrieved May 21, 2004, from www.savethechildren.org/mentors/

Scherman, N. (Ed.). (1995). *The ethics of the fathers.* New York: Mesorah.

Schwartz, K. D. (2001, March) *Predicting adolescent belief and commitment: Social and developmental factors.* Paper presented at the meeting of the Society for the Study of Psychology and Wesleyan Theology, Pasadena, CA.

Schwartz, K. D. (2003, August). *Adolescent belief and commitment: Perceived support of parents, friends, church, and youth group.* Paper presented at the Fourth International Conference on Children's Spirituality, Victoria, BC, Canada.

Schwartz, K. D. (2005). *Transformations in parent and friend faith support predicting adolescents' religious belief and commitment.* Manuscript submitted for publication.

Schwartz, K. D. (in press a). The adolescent as theologian. In E. M. Dowling and W. G. Scarlett (Eds.), *Encyclopedia of spiritual development in childhood and adolescence.* Thousand Oaks, CA: Sage.

Schwartz, K. D. (in press b). Peer and friend influences on adolescent faith development. In E. M. Dowling and W. G. Scarlett (Eds.), *Encyclopedia of spiritual development in childhood and adolescence.* Thousand Oaks, CA: Sage.

Selman, R. (1980). *The growth of interpersonal understanding.* New York: Academic Press.

Shelton, C. M. (1983). *Adolescent spirituality: Pastoral ministry for high school and college youth.* New York: Crossroad.

Silberman, I. (2003). Spiritual role modeling: The teaching of meaning systems. *International Journal for the Psychology of Religion, 13,* 175–195.

Silberman, I., Higgins, E. T., & Dweck, C. S. (in press). Religion and openness to change. *Journal of Social Issues.*

Slicker, E. K., & Palmer, D. J. (1993). Mentoring at-risk high school students: Evaluation of a school-based program. *School Counselor, 40,* 327–334.

Sroufe, L. A., & Fleeson, J. (1986). Attachment and the construction of relationships. In W. W. Hartup & Z. Rubin (Eds.), *Relationships and development.* Hillsdale, NJ: Erlbaum.

Strommen, M. P., & Hardel, R. A. (2000). *Passing on the faith: A radical new model for youth and family ministry.* Winona, MN: Saint Mary's Press.

Strommen, M. P., Jones, K., & Rahn, D. (2001). *Youth ministry that transforms: A comprehensive analysis of the hopes, frustrations, and effectiveness of today's youth workers.* Grand Rapids, MI: Zondervan.

Surasky, A. (1982). *Giants of Jewry* (Vol. 2). Lakewood, NJ: Chinuch.

Tierney, J. P., Grossman, J. B., & Resch, N. L. (1995). *Making a difference: An impact study of Big Brothers Big Sisters.* Philadelphia: Private/ Public Ventures.

Youniss, J., McLellan, J. A., & Yates, M. (1999). Religion, community service, and identity in American youth. *Journal of Adolescence, 22,* 243–253.

Zimmerman, M. A., Bingenheimer, J. B., & Notaro, P. C. (2002). Natural mentors and adolescent resiliency: A study with urban youth. *American Journal of Community Psychology, 30,* 221–243.

Zippay, A. (1995). Expanding employment skills and social networks among teen mothers: Case study of a mentor program. *Child and Adolescent Social Work Journal, 12,* 51–69.

23

Congregations: Unexamined Crucibles for Spiritual Development

Eugene C. Roehlkepartain

Eboo Patel

Participation in a faith community is consistently found to have a positive impact on young people's development in multiple domains of life, from reduction in high-risk behaviors to increases in resiliency and thriving, physical health, and overall development (part V of this volume). Furthermore, congregations represent a unique crucible or focal point for exploring the dynamic interplay of numerous forces and processes in spiritual development: family, peer, personal agency, self-reflection, moral guidance, and intergenerational relationships—not to mention the rituals, traditions, and practices that build bridges to the sacred and transcendent.

Although the vast majority of the research utilizes religious participation as a primary indicator for examining the role of religion and spirituality in adolescence (Benson, Scales, Sesma, & Roehlkepartain, 2005; King & Furrow, 2004; Smith, Denton, Faris, & Regnerus, 2002; Wagener, Furrow, King, Leffert, & Benson, 2003), little is known about how the dynamics of participation interact with and affect young people's spiritual development, or about the self-transcendent process that propels young

people's search for connectedness, meaning, purpose, and contribution. Although spiritual development is shaped both within and outside of religious traditions, beliefs, and practices, congregations remain a vital socializing institution for many young people. Based on a theoretical understanding of congregational dynamics, as well as the impact that congregational involvement and dynamics are known to have on multiple youth outcomes, this chapter makes the case that congregations should be seen—and studied—as important crucibles for spiritual development in childhood and adolescence.

The chapter begins by exploring the available research on congregations related to faith, maturity, healthy development (developmental assets), and social capital.[1] It then proposes a theoretical model for understanding congregations not simply as deliverers of programs but as complex, dynamic ecologies conducive to spiritual development, illustrating the potential through a case study of a young Ismaili Muslim in London. The chapter concludes by highlighting issues for future research that integrates congregational studies with spiritual development.

THE CHALLENGE OF TERMINOLOGY

It is important, first, to clarify terminology. We use *congregation* in its generic sense to refer to a church, parish, or cathedral (Christian), synagogue (Jewish), masjid/mosque (Muslim), temple (Buddhist, Hindu, Jewish), ward (Latter-day Saint), gurdwara (Sikh), assembly (Baha'i), or other group that represents "the smallest, relatively autonomous membership unit with a religious organization" (Stark & Finke, 2000, p. 154). Congregations may be formally organized and highly institutionalized, or they may be loosely organized gatherings. While some number their participants in the thousands, most are quite small.

Even when used broadly, the term congregation is less than ideal, given the world's diverse rituals, practices, and structures. Adding to the complexity, congregations range from the formalized structures of major temples, cathedrals, mosques, and megachurches to the indigenous groupings in which culture, religious, and community life are interwoven and seamless. Across these vast differences, people in most religious traditions (as well as some "spiritual" groups that do not consider themselves "religious") regularly gather for worship, prayers, rituals, festivals, rites of passage, spiritual nurture, transmitting doctrine and sacred texts, social support, fulfillment of obligation or disciplines, and charity or social action (Schwartz, Scheckner, & Kotler-Berkowitz, 2002; Wind & Lewis, 1994). For many people, congregations are also carriers of their culture's basic wisdom, traditions, and practices.

Although temples, mosques, and other institutions are sometimes dedicated exclusively or primarily to religious rituals, prayer, and worship, these institutions tend to become multifaceted centers of community life, particularly when located in more religiously pluralistic, Westernized societies (Levitt, 2002; Thompson & Gurney, 2003; Warner & Wittner, 1998; Waugh, 1991; Wind & Lewis, 1994) or when the religious community faces oppression based on race, class, culture, or belief (Billingsley, 1999). Because of the centrality of congregations to most religious traditions, and because of the impact congregations have in many dimensions of people's lives, congregations merit exploration as critical ecological contexts for spiritual development.

CURRENT RESEARCH IN CONGREGATIONS

Despite their potential, congregations have generally not been adequately examined in studies of spirituality or, more specifically, in studies of child and adolescent spirituality. Many factors may contribute to this lack of attention, including a perception among some scholars that congregations represent "the dark side of religious experience" (Demerath, Hall, Schmitt, & Williams, 1998, p. v). Moreover, the burgeoning field of congregational studies has focused primarily on institutional growth and decline, paying little attention to children and adolescents in these environments (Ammerman, Carroll, Dudley, & McKinney, 1998; Mercer, Matthews, & Walz, 2004; Regnerus, Smith, & Smith, 2004; Roehlkepartain, 2003).

However, several recent studies offer insights into the roles congregations may play in child and adolescent spiritual development. It is important to note that none of these studies focuses on spiritual development per se, as defined by the editors of this volume. Rather, their emphasis is on faith development, resiliency, healthy development, and social capital. Furthermore, the dynamics identified in these studies in the United States may not be relevant to understanding dynamics in other cultures (Hendriks, 2004; Norris & Inglehart, 2004). Thus these studies' findings point toward, but do not adequately examine, the interactions between congregational life and young people's spiritual development.

Mapping Young People's Congregational Involvement

In a massive effort to map the scope of the religious and spiritual lives of adolescents in the United States, Smith (2005) reports on findings from a nationally representative study that involved telephone surveys of parents and teenagers followed by 267 personal, in-depth interviews with a subsample of the telephone survey. The samples were racially/ethnically, socioeconomically, and religiously diverse, offering unparalleled insights into their experiences, beliefs, and practices, including their congregational participation.

As expected, the study found considerable variability in types of religious involvement by adolescents across the religious spectrum. For example, 38% of U.S. teenagers (ages 13–17) indicate that they are currently involved in a religious youth group. However, this percentage is about three times higher for Latter-day Saint youth (72%) than for Catholic youth (24%) or Jewish youth (27%), with mainline and conservative Protestants in between (55% and 56%, respectively). The study distinguishes among four levels of engagement among adolescents:

- The devoted, who attend at least weekly, engage in personal faith practices regularly, and have strong religious beliefs;
- The regulars, who attend two to three times per month, but whose beliefs and practices vary;
- The sporadic, who attend services only a few times per year and whose beliefs and practices are inconsistent; and
- The disengaged, who rarely or never participate or engage in spiritual practices.

The researchers find important differences among young people based on their place in this typology. Those who are most engaged (the devoted) are least likely to participate in a range of risky behaviors, and they are more likely to have a sense that they are cared for by others, that their life has meaning and purpose, and that they have more positive relationships with family and nonparent adults. They also tend to be more concerned about social justice issues, even after controlling for demographic differences (gender, age, race/ethnicity, region of residence, parental marital status, parent's education, and family income). Although this study only begins to examine congregational dynamics, it highlights the variability in levels and types of congregational engagement that moderate the congregation's influence in a young person's life.

Congregational Factors Related to "Faith Maturity"

In the early 1990s, Search Institute completed a major study of Protestant Christian congregations in the United States that examined the relationships between congregational dynamics, religious education, and faith maturity, using a scale that measures "the degree to which a person embodies the priorities, commitments, and perspectives characteristic of vibrant and life-transforming faith" (Benson, Donahue, & Erickson, 1993, p. 3; also see Tisdale, 1999). Whereas spiritual development emphasizes the process of self-transcendence and meaning making, faith maturity can be seen as one of many potential outcomes of healthy spiritual development within a faith tradition (in this case, mainline Protestant Christian).

The study found that a wide range of congregational factors were associated with self-reported growth in faith maturity, including learner-centered educational practices (such as openness to questions and interactive teaching), caring and effective leaders, a climate of warmth and caring, a thinking climate, support for families, engagement in life issues as well as the religious tradition, and opportunities to serve others (Benson & Eklin, 1990; Roehlkepartain, 1993). Similar studies have identified similar themes in other Christian faith traditions, including Seventh-Day Adventists (Rice & Gillespie, 1992), Catholics (Kelly, Benson, & Donahue, 1986), and the Lutheran Church–Missouri Synod (Benson, Roehlkepartain, & Andress, 1995).[2]

Congregations as Sources of "Developmental Assets"

Through secondary analyses of a large data set, another quantitative study involved looking at the developmental resources at play in a congregation that may contribute to positive outcomes for young people. Using a subsample of 20,020 randomly selected 6th- to 12th-grade students from Search Institute's aggregate data set of 99,462 students surveyed in public and alternative schools in the United States during the 1996–1997 school year, Wagener et al. (2003) tested whether religiousness has an independent relationship with positive or negative outcomes, and whether the effects are mediated by other developmental resources identified in Search Institute's framework of developmental assets that may also be present as an integral part of young people's religious commitment or involvement.

The analyses showed that religious importance (viewing faith or spirituality as very important in life) and participation (attending activities in a religious institution) explained about 10% of the variation in thriving behaviors and varying degrees of variation on engagement in high-risk behaviors. However, the relationship between religiousness and youth outcomes is much weaker (explaining 1% of the variation), after controlling for developmental assets, which are 40 positive relationships, opportunities, experiences, and personal characteristics associated with reductions in high-risk behaviors and increased positive outcomes (see Benson & Leffert, 2001; Scales & Leffert, 2004).

Although religious variables do have some independent effect on some risk behaviors (for example, delinquency for boys), the researchers found that the positive benefits of religion are at least partially mediated by developmental assets. They conclude: "Religious influence is better understood within the network of supportive relationships, personal obligations, and shared values common to religious communities. Participation in religious life results in greater exposure to developmental assets and this in turn is reflected in the positive relationships found between religious variables and developmental assets" (Wagener et al., 2003, p. 281).

Congregations as Sources of Social Capital

King (2000) deepens the understanding of the socializing influence of religious importance and participation by using social capital theory as a conceptual model for understanding how positive developmental outcomes are mediated through congregations and other socializing settings (also see King & Furrow, 2004). Social capital refers to the actual and potential resources that a person can access through her or his network of affiliations and relationships. Thus, social capital provides a conceptual link between an individual and her or his immediate social context—in this case, a congregation.

Through a quantitative study of 1,524 ethnically and religiously diverse high school students in Los Angeles, King found that religiously engaged youth benefit from more social capital resources than less active youth, including social interaction and shared vision (mutually held beliefs, values, and goals). She also found that religiousness appears to influence moral outcomes indirectly through these social capital resources. Particularly important qualities of social capital were parent-shared values, social interaction with peers, and adult trust.

It is important to note that this study did not examine relationships within a congregation per se, but compared the relationships (and outcomes associated with these relationships) to which religious and less religious youth had access. Although these relationships can be hypothesized to have occurred within the congregation, that aspect was not explicitly assessed. In addition, a follow-up replication of the study in South Korea (where religious institutions are not as woven into the fabric of society) did not show the same strength of relationships between religious participation and social capital (King, 2004). This comparison underscores the critical need for research grounded in settings other than North America before drawing conclusions about congregational dynamics associated with spiritual development.

An Ecological Understanding of Congregations

Each of these studies points to the multiple dynamics that potentially converge in congregations, making them unique crucibles of spiritual development. At their heart, churches, mosques, synagogues, temples, and other congregations are cultures, ecologies, and communities within which spirituality is (or could be) intentionally nurtured. Although most offer programs and services for children and youth, their potential can only be understood and tapped when they are recognized as complex, dynamic, and multifaceted ecologies or systems in which spiritual development is influenced through a web of relationships, rituals, expectations, and other interactions and processes across time.

In focusing on congregations as crucibles for spiritual development, it is important to shift the focus from seeing them as primarily deliverers of child and youth programs and services toward recognizing them as vibrant cultures that shape young people's socialization and that are

**A. The Congregation's
Context and Culture**

**B. Congregational
Dynamics and Settings**

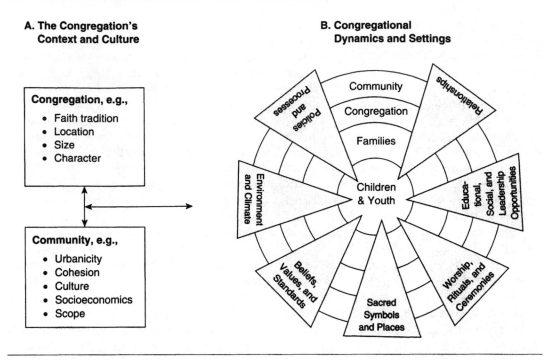

Figure 23.1   Congregations as Complex Ecologies for Spiritual Development: A Preliminary,
Multidimensional Model

shaped by young people's participation. Ammerman (1997) argues that congregations represent a community's moral order and values while also offering a sense of transcendence:

> Congregations are not just places to be reminded of what one ought to do. They are spaces where "ought" is put in cosmic perspective. While people may encounter transcendent realities in all sorts of places, congregations bear the weight of cultural expectation. The spaces and rituals of congregational life invite transcendence. We expect to meet God—at least on occasion—when we go to church or synagogue or mosque. . . . As places of religious ritual, congregations are potential sites for social and personal transformation. (p. 368)

Building on frameworks of congregational dynamics grounded in the disciplines of congregational studies (e.g., Ammerman et al., 1998), we propose a theoretical model for examining core processes that influence young people's spiritual development (Figure 23.1). Whereas others have focused on the developmental processes that may be at work through young people's congregational engagement (e.g., King & Furrow, 2004; Smith, 2003b; Wagener et al., 2003), this model emphasizes ecological dynamics and interactions. Here we briefly review each of the key elements in this framework.

Context and Culture

Congregations' cultures are shaped by their context, history, faith heritage, values, beliefs, location, size, member demographics, facilities, and other factors that might be considered "givens," although they change slowly in response to both internal and external dynamics. Ammerman and colleagues (1998) note that theological and denominational traditions—coupled with expectations from the culture, class, ethnicity, and similar factors—are shaped into "a unique creation, constructed out of their interaction together over time" (p. 82).

A congregation's identity, history, and worldview have important bearings on how it engages with children and adolescents. For example, those with a history and orientation that emphasize orthodoxy and conformity will likely have much different attitudes toward youth empowerment, dialogue, and teaching methods than those that emphasize self-discovery and faith exploration. Thus, understanding a congregation's national, cultural, religious, socioeconomic, and ideological context—and how these factors interact with individuals' own beliefs, values, and spiritual journey—would yield insight into the person–environment interaction in spiritual development.

Dynamics and Settings

The right side of the model articulates a variety of crosscutting settings or points of contact (in the circles) and dynamics (in the triangles) within congregations that potentially influence child and adolescent spiritual development.

Points of Contact. Congregations potentially influence, directly or indirectly, young people's spiritual development through multiple points of contact. These certainly include age-specific opportunities for children and youth (religious education, youth groups, service projects, etc.), but they also extend to include the congregation's engagement with families, intergenerational engagement, and broader community involvement through the congregation's public leadership, service, and action on behalf of children, adolescents, and others in society. In addition, congregations also can plan a role in young people's spiritual nurture by building the capacity and sense of responsibility among everyone in the congregation (leaders, parents, other adults, peers) to be attentive to nurturing the spiritual lives of children and adolescents— not only through their leadership in congregational programs, but also through their informal interactions throughout congregational life, in families, and in the community. Indeed, much of congregations' potential capacity to socialize young people spiritually may, in fact, lie beyond child and youth programming, as suggested by the relatively small size of the child and youth programming circle in the diagram.

Congregational Dynamics. A number of dynamics occur across all of these points of contact that have the potential to enrich understanding

of the processes by which congregations may influence young people's spiritual development. The following elements likely shape these processes:

- *Sacred symbols and space*—At the center of most religious traditions are sacred symbols, such as the cross for Christians, the Torah for Jews, the Qur'an for Muslims, and altars or shrines in many religious traditions. Congregations convey the importance of these symbols and provide a space for the faith community to convene in reverence of these symbols. Furthermore, the "sacred spaces" of congregations—from austere meetinghouses to ornate cathedrals and shrines—are an important part of the sense of transcendence and sacredness within religious life (Williams, 2002).

- *Relationships*—Meaningful relationships may be the primary vehicle through which congregations influence young people's spiritual development. Within congregations, people of all generations can come together for mutual support, sharing of values, vision, and beliefs, and shared action and practices. Children and adolescents have opportunities to build sustained relationships with "sages of faith" and to form positive, supportive peer relationships (Maton, in press; Regnerus et al., 2004; Schwartz, Bukowski, & Aoki, chapter 22, this volume). Through relationships, the faith community transmits its values, beliefs, and practices, and young people have the opportunity to "structure relational networks that facilitate more informal and effective oversight and control of youth by adults who care about them" (Smith, 2003a, p. 260).

- *Environment and climate*—What a congregation "feels like" plays an important, if intangible, role in its spiritual nurture of children and adolescents. Congregations are more likely, for example, to nurture faith when they have a climate that is warm and caring, encourages thinking, expects service to others, and has minimal conflict (Benson & Eklin, 1990; Mercer et al., 2004). On the other hand, one can easily name negative climate attributes (e.g., mistrust, a lack of intellectual openness or honesty, uninviting space) that suppress, misdirect, or even derail spiritual development.

- *Beliefs, values, and standards*—The overall vision that permeates congregational life plays an important role in how the congregation nurtures spiritual development. That vision—connected to the faith tradition's idea of the transcendent and nurtured through a range of rituals, ceremonies, and other congregational activities—becomes integral to the congregation's identity. Identity development is often considered a primary function of religious involvement in childhood and adolescence (Erikson, 1968; King, 2003; Smith, 2003b), and young people are likely to have their identity impacted by this process. Furthermore, a shared moral vision is integral to the building of social capital within a congregational context (King & Furrow, 2004). In addition, through their educational and formative experiences, congregations translate these beliefs, values, and standards into worldviews, language, and stories that answer ultimate questions of meaning, purpose, and vocation.

- *Worship, rituals, and ceremonies*—At the heart of most congregations is worship or other forms of connection to the transcendent. From daily prayers, music, services, devotional practices, and other religious acts (e.g., sacraments) to once-in-a-lifetime ceremonies, pilgrimages, and rites of passage, rituals "define the congregation and the people who participate in them" (Ammerman et al., 1998, p. 86). Through their patterning, sequencing, and repetition, worship and other rituals separate the sacred from the profane, creating new cognitive schemas and profound emotional meaning (Alcorta & Sosis, in press; Eliade, 1959). Rituals also socialize both children and adolescents into their tradition's narratives, beliefs, and practices, giving them the language, form, and structure needed to understand experiences of transcendence (Smith, 2003b; Yust, 2003).

- *Educational, social, and leadership opportunities*—Congregations provide a wide range of programs and activities that involve children and/or adolescents. Structured learning (religious education); social service, or missions; and recreational activities provide significant contexts for nurturing spiritual development. Although each program may have a different focus and structure, many provide young people with opportunities to learn spiritual disciplines, build relationships, develop personal competencies, and contribute to the community—all of which can be formative in spiritual development. Crucially, congregational youth programs often have high levels of youth participation and leadership. By becoming involved, young people not only grow and develop, they also gain immediate opportunities to have an impact on their immediate congregation, and on the wider world through their congregation.

- *Policies and processes*—To understand how congregations can or do nurture spiritual development, one must understand the ways in which policies and processes either facilitate or inhibit the nurturing of spiritual growth. Congregational policies and processes involve both formal and informal ways things happen in a congregation, including how decisions are made; how adults are equipped to guide young people; resources used in religious education; how young people are protected from harm; and many other dynamics. Each of these processes and policies can have either a positive or negative impact on spiritual nurture.

CASE STUDY: A YOUNG MUSLIM'S EXPERIENCE

The preliminary model outlined above is, by definition, abstract. We hypothesize that it would be manifested in very different ways, depending on context, tradition, and many other variables. In some cases (such as in developing countries or settings and traditions in which congregations do not play a central socializing role), dynamics may be dramatically different from what is proposed.

It is important to emphasize that different components are more salient for some young people than others, highlighting the person–context interactions of this ecological model. Thus some young people may be particularly engaged through leadership and service opportunities, while others may find the greatest meaning through the rituals and music, the care received, or the social interactions among peers and across generations. By recognizing the multiple, interlocking dynamics, the model begins to offer a tool for examining these individual differences as well as similarities and differences across cultures, contexts, and traditions.

To begin the dialogue, we present an ethnographic case study of how one young Ismaili Muslim's spiritual development was nurtured by the *jamat* (Ismaili community) in London during his childhood, and how he decided as a young adult that he needed to be connected to that religious community for his spiritual development. In the process, the discussion concretely illustrates how many of the named dynamics can play out in the specifics of one young person's life.

The case study comes from a larger examination of the nexus between religious education, *jamati* (or congregational) life, and youth within an Ismaili Muslim community in London (Patel, 2002). The study applied what Denzin (1989) calls the "interpretive biographical method," which consists of collecting personal histories, or the "reconstructions of [lives] based on interviews, conversations and self- and personal-experience stories" (p. 38).

The Ismailis are the second-largest Shia community after the Twelvers in the Muslim world. They live in more than 20 countries of Asia, Africa, Europe, and North America. Like all Muslims, Ismailis believe in one God and Muhammad (peace be upon him) as his messenger. Along with the broader Shia community, Ismailis believe that Muhammad (pbuh) appointed his son-in-law, Ali, as the leader of the Muslim community. All Shia further believe that Ali was endowed with the unique ability to interpret God's message and thus was the best guide for the Muslim community. This spiritual gift is passed down by appointment from the Imam (the title of the Shia leader, not to be confused with the imam as prayer leader) to a member of his family.

The Ismailis are distinct from other major Muslim communities in claiming to have a living and present Imam (the Twelver Shia believe the true Imam is in occultation), known as "Hazir Imam." The current Ismaili Imam is Karim al-Husseini, known more generally by his title, Aga Khan IV. In accordance with Ismaili tradition, the Aga Khan guides both the spiritual and material lives of Ismailis. Ismailis have a different prayer practice and community culture than most other Muslim communities because of the guidance of the Imam. In his 50 years as Imam, Karim Aga Khan has emphasized women's rights, education, Muslim arts, social service, and poverty alleviation efforts.

Aly was an Ismaili in his late 20s. He wore a gold hoop in each ear, a goatee, and a ponytail. Aly did computer-related work for a bank in London, but his real passion was being an Ismaili youth educator. He taught 13- and 14-year-olds at Baital-ilm (the Ismaili religious education school for youth ages 5 to 15, which takes place on Saturday mornings at various venues around London), and was involved in other religious education programs for Ismaili adolescents. He attended Ismaili worship services several times a week and spent a lot of his social time with other Ismailis. Aly was close to many teenagers in the *jamat;* he would stand around chatting with them after *jamat khana* (the place Ismailis worship and hold other congregational activities), or during the lunch break of a religious education program.

Being a youth religious educator was an extension of the volunteer work Aly had been doing in the *jamat* since he was a child. Aly's father was very involved with the *jamat,* and he required his son to participate. "I would say the first time I was really involved in voluntary service, I was seven," Aly recalls. "I was there whenever my dad would go to *khana.* He would stay late, so I would help him clean the *khana.* It was very much like a second nature I was building up in myself without knowing it" (personal interview, May 23, 2000).

Only after graduating from university and taking a job in Luxembourg did Aly begin to realize how formative those experiences had been for him. He recalls:

> I was starting to lose my balance, a balance I was not aware of. I grew up in an environment where *jamat khana* is there, [taken for] granted. Go say your *du'a* [prayers], do your voluntary service, come back home and do whatever you have to do. So there was some kind of balance. . . . And that balance was not there in Luxembourg. I might have had everything I needed . . . except for a supportive environment for my personal development in terms of my spiritual journey. (personal interview, May 23, 2000)

Although his job was excellent and he found Luxembourg a pleasant place, Aly felt like he was "starting to lose his balance." He harkened back to a time when going to *jamat khana* and doing voluntary service was part of his routine, and claimed he reached "some kind of balance" through that. In the next quotation, Aly relates that he asked for a transfer to a city where he could do voluntary service and restore his balance:

> I was saying my prayers morning and evening— all these things we call rites and ceremonies. But . . . there was this aspect in my life that was missing in Luxembourg. This voluntary service, this sense of belonging, this sense of satisfaction of doing something for someone else. . . . I wanted to go to a place where there is a *jamat khana*, a structure where I can carry on my voluntary service. [The company] offered me a position in London and I said, "Bingo, that's for me." . . . A month after I arrived, I got involved in Baital-ilm. (personal interview, May 23, 2000)

When he moved to London, Aly visited a class of teenagers at Baital-ilm. He said they were talking about what being an Ismaili meant in their lives. Aly had a personal interest in these kinds of discussions, and he wanted to help younger Ismailis develop an understanding of the faith that was meaningful to them. So he began teaching teenagers and soon got involved in other youth religious education programs as well.

Aly's story illustrates how crucial congregations can be for the spiritual development of an individual along the journey from childhood to young adulthood. Aly remembers being brought into the *jamat* through his father, and how the *jamat* provided a context that strengthened that relationship. Aly recalls his participation in the *jamat*—from saying prayers to doing volunteer work to just spending time there with his father— as providing "some kind of balance" for his life.

This statement underscores the cumulative influence of multiple dimensions of a congregation's ecology—from its worship rituals to its methods for involving young people to the relationships its climate nurtures—on a child's spiritual development. Aly realizes that the congregation itself plays a central role in his spiritual development only when he goes away as a young adult. In Luxemborg he continues to pray and be a devoted Ismaili, but he feels something is missing. That thing is a congregation—Aly wants to convene with a group of people around the symbols of the faith. Furthermore, he feels his spiritual development is partially dependent on taking responsibility for nurturing other people in their faith, which he believes can only happen in the context of a congregation.

TOWARD AN EXPANDED RESEARCH AGENDA

The proposed framework, illustrated by Aly's experience, points toward a potentially rich, though unexplored, research agenda focused on organizational dynamics that may be at play within congregations that may either enhance or diminish the congregation's capacity to be optimally effective in nurturing healthy spiritual development. If congregations are indeed important ecologies for spiritual development, then theoretical and empirical research (both quantitative and qualitative) is needed to understand the dynamics that occur at both a micro level within particular congregations, traditions, and cultures, and at a macro level that explores patterns, similarities, and differences among congregations, traditions, and cultures. Below are some proposed themes to be considered for future research.

Diversity of Young People

As noted several times, a major gap in current research is its domination, with few exceptions, by studies of Caucasian Christian adolescents in the United States. Such a narrow picture misses dramatic variability in congregational involvement and young people's spiritual pathways around the world (Lippman & Keith, chapter 8, this volume). Even within the United States, for example, what processes lead to significantly higher participation in congregational life among African American youth (Benson et al., 2005), as well as significant variations in religious participation by religious tradition (Smith, 2005)? The complexity of these questions only increases as they are asked from a more international perspective.

There is also a pressing need to understand the person–context interaction across the developmental trajectory from early childhood through adolescence. Few studies have focused on young children, and no identified studies have sought to trace patterns across the first two decades of life. Such questions are vital, particularly given the widespread (though not universal) pattern of disengagement of young people from congregational life during early adolescence across different faith traditions and cultures (Benson et al., 2005; Lippman & Keith, chapter 8, this volume; Saxe, Kelner, Kadushin, & Brodsky, 2000; Smith, 2005; Smith et al., 2002).

Variability in Culture, Tradition, Nationality, and Institutional Dynamics

Basic questions on variability in religious institutions also need extensive study. What are similarities and differences in congregational dynamics across religious, cultural, and national boundaries? What roles do congregational size, structure, climate, and other variations play in either stimulating or thwarting spiritual development? And what specific and unique socialization roles do congregations play in different cultures, traditions, and contexts?

All this being said, it is important to be cautious about presuming that any framework for studying congregations can be adequate—as illustrated by King's (2004) finding that social capital dynamics identified in U.S. research were not well replicated in a Korean sample. Indeed, H. Jurgens Hendriks of Stellenbosch University in South Africa cautions against any effort to find models that may be relevant across diverse continents. After years of observing many congregations in southern Africa, he has concluded that "one cannot really compare the continents on the same level or playing field" (personal e-mail correspondence, August 6, 2004; see also Hendriks, 2004). Among factors that come into play are the traditional religious practices, such as initiation rites, that have no parallel in Western culture (see Gottlieb, chapter 11, this volume; Inglehart, Basáñes, Díez-Medrano, Halman, & Luijkx, 2004).

Interactions With Other Contexts and Influences

Just as important as understanding the dynamics and processes at work within congregations are questions about the connections between congregations and other socializing systems, including families, schools, neighborhood,

social services, and government. Indeed, a congregation's socializing role in spiritual development is, at its best, working in tandem with families, schools, and other influences in young people's lives (see Alexander & Carr, chapter 6, this volume; Regnerus et al.; 2004). Important questions need to be addressed about whether and how congregations' socializing influence reinforces or conflicts with other socializing systems in young people's lives. Such a line of inquiry builds on Erickson's (1992) study of the interaction of family, peer, and congregational influences, as well as Rice and Gillespie's (1992) finding that family, school, and congregation, when aligned, have a cumulative impact on young people's development.

The Need for Multiple Methods

No single study or method can adequately address the range of issues and questions raised here or that would be contemplated by other observers, scholars, and practitioners. There is a clear need for a diverse array of scholars to use a wide range of methodologies in a wide range of contexts, cultures, and traditions. We would propose the need for qualitative and quantitative studies that go both deep and wide.

Like Haight's (2002) ethnographic study of children in African American churches, deep studies might delve into the processes, practices, dynamics, and other factors that are at work in shaping spiritual development among a particular group of children and adolescents. On the other hand, integrative studies are needed to create broad maps of congregational life, young people's participation through childhood and adolescence, relationships among individual, congregation, and community variables, and similar questions. Together, these kinds of studies can yield both the specific insights that offer nuanced understandings as well as broad, integrative patterns that highlight similarities and differences. Interactions between different methodologies and units of analysis will, ultimately, profoundly enrich both research and practice.

CONCLUSIONS

A crucible is a "place or situation in which concentrated forces interact to cause or influence change or development" (*Merriam-Webster's Online Dictionary,* 1993). Churches, mosques, synagogues, temples, and other congregations can, in fact, be that kind of crucible for child and adolescent spiritual development. In a time of growing pluralism and fragmentation, congregations may actually be significant resources for spiritual development. But for such a focus to emerge, important theoretical and empirical research is needed. Such research would not only deepen and broaden understanding of congregations and their role in spiritual development, but also point toward practices that could be employed across and within diverse faith traditions and cultures to nurture young people's spirituality in ways that cultivate meaning and purpose, and call them to acts of compassion, service, and justice.

Notes

1. There are many other types of religious institutions, including national and international religious bodies or denominations; paracongregational youth programs and organizations; faith-based social services, camps, schools, and other educational institutions; health care providers; connectional networks; and many other faith-based organizations. These institutions also play roles in young people's spiritual development, but an examination of their dynamics lies beyond the scope of this chapter. (See Kerestes and Youniss, 2003.)

2. At the time of this writing, the Study of Exemplary Congregations in Youth Ministry is under way, led by Roland Martinson of Luther Seminary, St. Paul, Minnesota. The study is examining Lutheran, Catholic, Southern Baptist, Evangelical Covenant, Assemblies of God, Presbyterian (USA), and United Methodist congregations in the United States, with initial results being released in 2005. The study, which builds on Search Institute's research on faith maturity, seeks to identify dynamics in congregations that nurture young people's faith. (For more information, visit www.exemplarym.com.)

References

Alcorta, C. S., & Sosis, R. (in press). Ritual, emotion, and sacred symbols: The evolution of religion as an adaptive complex. *Human Nature.*

Ammerman, N. T. (with Farnsley, A. E.). (1997). *Congregation and community.* New Brunswick, NJ: Rutgers University Press.

Ammerman, N. T., Carroll, J. W., Dudley, C. S., & McKinney, W. (Eds.). (1998). *Studying congregations: A new handbook.* Nashville, TN: Abingdon.

Benson, P. L., Donahue, M. J., & Erickson, J. A. (1993). The Faith Maturity Scale: Conceptualization, measurement, and empirical validation. *Research in the Social Scientific Study of Religion, 5,* 1–26.

Benson, P. L., & Eklin, C. H. (1990). *Effective Christian education: A national study of Protestant congregations: A summary on faith, loyalty, and congregational life.* Minneapolis, MN: Search Institute.

Benson, P. L., & Leffert, N. (2001). Developmental assets in childhood and adolescence. In N. J. Smelser & P. G. Baltes (Eds.), *International encyclopedia of the social and behavioral sciences* (pp. 1690–1697). Oxford, UK: Elsevier.

Benson, P. L., Roehlkepartain, E. C., & Andress, I. S. (1995). *Congregations at crossroads: A national study of adults and youth in the Lutheran Church–Missouri Synod.* Minneapolis, MN: Search Institute.

Benson, P. L., Scales, P. C., Sesma, A., Jr., & Roehlkepartain, E. C. (2005). Adolescent spirituality. In K. A. Moore & L. H. Lippman (Eds.), *What do children need to flourish? Conceptualizing and measuring indicators of positive development* (pp. 25–40). New York: Kluwer Academic/Plenum.

Billingsley, A. (1999). *Mighty like a river: The Black church and social reform.* New York: Oxford University Press.

Bowker, J. (Ed.). (1997). *The Oxford dictionary of world religions.* New York: Oxford University Press.

Demerath, N. J., III, Hall, P. D., Schmitt, T., & Williams, R. H. (1998). Preface. In N. J. Demerath III, P. D. Hall, T. Schmitt, & R. H. Williams (Eds.), *Sacred companies: Organizational aspects of religion and religious aspects of organizations* (pp. iii-xiii). New York: Oxford University Press.

Denzin, N. K. (1989). *Interpretive biography.* Newbury Park, CA: Sage.

Eliade, M. (1959). *The sacred and the profane: The nature of religion.* New York: Harcourt Brace Jovanovich.

Erickson, J. A. (1992). Adolescent religious development and commitment: A structural equation model of the role of family, peer group, and educational influences. *Journal for the Scientific Study of Religion, 31*(2), 131–152.

Erikson, E. (1968). *Identity: Youth and crisis.* New York: Norton.

Haight, W. (2002). *African-American children at church: A sociocultural perspective.* Cambridge, UK: Cambridge University Press.

Hendriks, H. J. (2004). *Studying congregations in Africa.* Wellington, South Africa: Lux Verbi.

Inglehart, R., Basáñez, M., Díez-Medrano, J., Halman, L., & Luijkx, R. (Eds.). (2004). *Human beliefs and values: A cross-cultural sourcebook based on the 1999–2002 values surveys.* Mexico City: Siglo XXI Editores.

Kelly, F. D., Benson, P. L., & Donahue, M. J. (1986). *Toward effective parish religious education for children and young people: A national study.* Washington, DC: National Catholic Education Association.

Kerestes, M., & Youniss, J. E. (2003). Rediscovering the importance of religion in adolescent development. In R. M. Lerner, F. Jacobs, & D. Wertlieb (Eds.), *Handbook of applied developmental science: Vol. 1. Applying developmental science for youth and families—Historical and theoretical foundations* (pp. 165–184). Thousand Oaks, CA: Sage.

King, P. E. (2000). *Adolescent religiousness and moral behavior: A proposed model of social capital resources and moral outcomes.* Unpublished doctoral dissertation, Fuller Theological Seminary, Graduate School of Psychology, Pasadena, CA.

King, P. E. (2003). Religion and identity: The role of ideological, social, and spiritual contexts. *Applied Developmental Science, 7,* 196–203.

King, P. E. (2004). Communities of character: Religion in the moral development of American and Korean youth. In H. A. Alexander (Ed.), *Spirituality and ethics in education: Philosophical, theological, and radical perspectives* (pp. 112–129). Brighton, UK: Sussex Academic Press.

King, P. E., & Furrow, J. L. (2004). Religion as a resource for positive youth development: Religion, social capital, and moral outcomes. *Developmental Psychology, 40,* 703–713.

Levitt, P. (2002). Two nations under God? Latino religious life in the United States. In M. Suárez-Orozco & M. M. Páez (Eds.), *Latinos: Remaking America* (pp. 150–164). Berkeley and Los Angeles: University of California Press.

Maton, K. I. (in press). Mobilizing adults for positive youth development: Lessons from religious congregations. In E. G. Clary & J. Rhodes (Eds.), *Mobilizing adults for positive youth development.* New York: Kluwer Academic/Plenum.

Mercer, J. A., Matthews, D. L., & Walz, S. (2004). Children in congregations; Congregations as contexts for children's spiritual growth. In D. Ratcliff (Ed.), *Children's spirituality: Christian perspectives, research, and applications* (pp. 249–265). Eugene, OR: Cascade Books.

Merriam-Webster's online dictionary (10th ed.). (1993). Springfield, MA: Merriam-Webster. Retrieved July 20, 2004, from www.m-w.com

Norris, P., & Inglehart, R. (2004). *Sacred and secular: Religion and politics worldwide.* Cambridge, UK: Cambridge University Press.

Patel, E. (2002). *Ismaili religious education and modernity.* Unpublished doctoral thesis, Oxford University, Oxford, UK.

Regnerus, M. D., Smith, C., & Smith, B. (2004). Social context in the development of adolescent religiosity. *Applied Developmental Science, 8*(1), 27–38.

Rice, G., & Gillespie, V. B. (1992). Valuegenesis: A megastudy of faith maturity and its relationship to variables within the home, school, and church. *Journal of Research on Christian Education, 1*(1), 49–67.

Roehlkepartain, E. C. (1993). *The teaching church: Moving Christian education to center stage.* Nashville, TN: Abingdon.

Roehlkepartain, E. C. (2003). Building strengths, deepening faith: Understanding and enhancing youth development in Protestant congregations. In R. M. Lerner, F. Jacobs, & D. Wertlieb (Eds.), *Handbook of applied developmental science: Vol. 3. Promoting positive youth and family development* (pp. 515–534). Thousand Oaks, CA: Sage.

Saxe, L., Kelner, S., Kadushin, C., & Brodsky, A. (2000). Jewish adolescents: American teenagers trying to "make it." *Agenda: Jewish Education, 13,* 3–7.

Scales, P. C., & Leffert, N. (2004). *Developmental assets: A synthesis of the scientific research on adolescent development* (Rev. ed.). Minneapolis, MN: Search Institute.

Schwartz, J., Scheckner, J., & Kotler-Berkowitz, L. (2002). Census of U.S. synagogues, 2001. In D. Singer & L. Grossman (Eds.), *American Jewish Yearbook 2002* (pp. 112–150). New York: American Jewish Committee.

Smith, C. (with Denton, M. L.). (2005). *Soul searching: The religious and spiritual lives of American teenagers.* New York: Oxford University Press.

Smith, C. (2003a). Religious participation and network closure among American adolescents. *Journal for the Scientific Study of Religion, 42*(2), 259–267.

Smith, C. (2003b). Theorizing religious effects among American adolescents. *Journal for the Scientific Study of Religion, 41*(1), 17–30.

Smith, C., Denton, M. L., Faris, R., & Regnerus, M. (2002). Mapping American adolescent religious participation. *Journal for the Scientific Study of Religion, 41*(4), 597–612.

Stark, R., & Finke, R. (2000). *Acts of faith: Explaining the human side of religion.* Berkeley and Los Angeles: University of California Press.

Thompson, N. E., & Gurney, A. G. (2003). "He is everything": Religion's role in the lives of immigrant youth. *New Directions for Youth Development, 100,* 75–90.

Tisdale, T. C. (1999). Faith Maturity Scale. In P. C. Hill & R. W. Hood Jr. (Eds.), *Measures of religiosity* (pp. 171–174). Birmingham, AL: Religious Education Press.

Wagener, L. M., Furrow, J. L., King, P. E., Leffert, N., & Benson, P. L. (2003). Religious involvement and developmental resources in youth. *Review of Religious Research, 44*(3), 271–284.

Warner, R. S., & Wittner, J. G. (1998). *Gatherings in Diaspora: Religious communities and the new immigration.* Philadelphia: Temple University Press.

Waugh, E. H. (1991). North America and the adaptation of the Muslim tradition: Religion, ethnicity and the family. In E. H. Waugh, S. M. Abu-Laban, & R. B. Qureshi (Eds.), *Muslim families in North America* (pp. 68–95). Edmonton: University of Alberta Press.

Williams, R. H. (2002). Religion, community, and place: Locating the transcendent. *Religion and American Culture, 12,* 249–263.

Wind, J. P., & Lewis, J. W. (Eds.). (1994). *American congregations* (Vols. 1 & 2). Chicago: University of Chicago Press.

Yust, K. M. (2003). Toddler spiritual formation and the faith community. *International Journal of children's spirituality, 8,* 133–149.

PART V

DEVELOPMENTAL OUTCOMES OF SPIRITUAL DEVELOPMENT

Introduction to Part V

I n the realm of spiritual development, perhaps the area of scholarship that has generated the most scientific study is the exploration of spirituality and religion and their developmental correlates. The consistent positive relationships between religion and developmental benefits have captured the attention of the public and the academy as indicated in the growing body of literature evident in this volume. Perhaps it is the scientific validation of the benefits of religion and spirituality that has made understanding its formation in youth an important developmental and public concern.

Although there is a significant amount of outcome-related research, the scope is limited. To date the majority of the studies have included adolescents, not children. Most of the measures have focused on religion rather than on spiritual development per se. In fact, all too often the operationalization of religious variables has been restricted to religious attendance and religious salience. In addition, until recently most of the outcome variables have pertained to risk-taking behaviors and, with the exception of academic achievement, have almost entirely ignored positive developmental outcomes. As the following chapters note, these trends are beginning to change, but there is much room for further study.

The authors in part V take on the task of reviewing and building on the existing theoretical and empirical literature in the traditional developmental sciences. In doing so they offer insight into the developmental impact of spirituality and religion in the lives of young people. They also reflect theoretically on the role spiritual development and religion play.

Annette Mahoney, Sara Pendleton, and Heidi Ihrke focus on the understudied realm of spiritual development and coping in children and adolescents. Drawing on more established discussions of religious coping in adolescents and in adulthood, Mahoney and colleagues make a strong case for the importance of spirituality in coping for children and adolescents.

Emily Crawford, Margaret O'Dougherty Wright, and Ann S. Masten provide evidence that spirituality is related to resilience for children and adolescents who are experiencing adverse life circumstances. They examine the relationship between spirituality and resilience within a developmental and multisystems perspective, paying particular attention to the mechanisms through which spirituality appears to affect resilience. They consider the potential roles of social support, active peer engagement, a comforting relationship with God, spiritual practices, positive faith community mentors, and a framework of coherence and meaning for life.

Although higher rates of religiousness and spirituality are related to lower levels of delinquency, Ronnie Frankel Blakeney and Charles David Blakeney make a provocative case for understanding adolescent delinquency as a quest for spiritual and moral meaning. Through presenting existing research and theory they argue that when spirituality and religion provide a supportive environment and enable youth to accomplish their necessary developmental tasks, then spiritual transformation can take place and give youth a sense of developmental integrity.

Empirical and theoretical literatures suggest a strong relationship between spirituality and adolescent well-being or thriving. Using the framework of positive youth development, Pamela Ebstyne King and Peter L. Benson look at how spirituality and religion enable youth to thrive. In addition to serving as a potentially important resource for developmental assets, religion and spirituality provide a rich context in which to wrestle with issues of meaning, purpose, vocation, relationships, and identity that are particularly salient during adolescence.

In this section's final chapter, Doug Oman and Carl E. Thoresen examine links between health and spiritual development for ages ranging from prenatal through late adolescence. Oman and Thoresen present the available empirical research and review theoretical considerations suggesting that family and child spiritual development may influence child health outcomes through a variety of mechanisms, such as improved prenatal environment, more secure attachment relationships, better parental supervision, improved health behaviors, and transmission of adaptive personal goals and strivings and effective coping strategies.

Although the chapters in this section offer an optimistic view toward spirituality and developmental outcomes, they do not do so blindly. The authors prudently uncover potential deleterious consequences of spirituality on development—ranging from involvement with religious sects that cause the violation of human rights, to child abuse by clergy, to ideologically oppressive denominations. In addition, these authors call forth important areas of further research that will enable scholars and practitioners to better understand how spirituality may help or hinder the developmental journey.

24

Religious Coping by Children and Adolescents: Unexplored Territory in the Realm of Spiritual Development

Annette Mahoney

Sara Pendleton

Heidi Ihrke

R ecent surveys (1991–2003) indicate that 90%-95% of American adolescents believe in God or a universal spirit, 69% view themselves to be religious, 30%-50% participate in weekly worship services or religious youth activities, 42% pray alone frequently, and 24% read scriptures weekly (George Gallup International Institute, 1999; Smith, Denton, Faris, & Regnerus, 2003). Also, 65% of Caucasian families with young children participate in religious services at least monthly (Mahoney et al., 1999), and 90% of all parents desire religious education for their children (Gallup & Castelli,1989). These figures paint a vivid picture of the general importance of religion in the lives of children and adolescents. Yet, unlike the rapidly burgeoning theory and research on religious coping by adults (Pargament & Ano, in press), social scientists have directed little attention to how youth proactively use their faith to cope with stressful events. To encourage more scientific investigation of this topic, this chapter presents a theoretical framework about religious coping by youth, supplemented by empirical findings when available.

We begin this chapter by setting forth key definitions, followed by a critique of empirical research on religious coping by youth. We then delineate two sets of constructs under the broad rubric of religious coping that may pertain to youth: primary religious appraisals and religious coping processes. Along the way, we discuss adaptive and maladaptive variations within both categories and describe their possible outcomes. Given the developmental focus of this handbook, we speculate about how the impact of religious coping on adjustment may vary across middle childhood and adolescence. However, we leave it to others to discuss the possible predictors and developmental course of religious coping (Pendleton, Benore, Norwood, Jonas, & Herrmann, 2004).

DEFINITIONS

Over the past two decades, scientific research on the interface between religion and coping by adults has skyrocketed (Pargament & Ano, in press). This literature provides a useful stepping-off place to begin exploring the largely uncharted territory of religious coping by youth. In particular, we rely on Pargament's widely used theoretical framework on religious coping. Pargament (1997) proposed a model that integrates religion into Lazarus and Folkman's (1984) classic tripartite theory of coping consisting of primary and secondary appraisals of a stressor; cognitive or behavioral strategies to deal with the event; and sought-after outcomes of coping. Specifically, Pargament (1997) theorized that life events can be interpreted in religious terms (i.e., religious coping appraisals), that religion offers people of all ages unique religious pathways to cope with stress (i.e., religious coping processes), and that religion can imbue with sacred significance the destinations that people strive to reach by means of coping processes.

In Pargament's model, "religious coping" is a broad construct, defined as "a search for significance in times of stress in ways related to the sacred" (Pargament, 1996, 1997). This elegant, deceptively simple definition integrates the unique dimension of religion, namely, "the sacred," with other central psychosocial constructs involved in coping. In this definition, the term *stress* corresponds to negative life events. The term *search* highlights that humans engage in proactive, intentional processes to appraise and come to terms with stressful events. The term *significance* refers to the hoped for outcomes sought when negative events challenge status quo functioning, with the two major options of either conserving or transforming the ends/goals that are perceived as being of ultimate importance. The term *the sacred* highlights what makes religion unique. The core of the sacred consists of concepts of God, the divine, and the transcendent, but virtually any object can become part of the sacred through its association with, or representation of, divinity

(Pargament & Mahoney, in press). And, unlike other personal and social institutions, religion connects the search for significance during times of stress with higher powers and beliefs, experiences, rituals, and institutions associated with supernatural forces. In this frame of reference, "spirituality" is conceptualized as the heart of religion and defined as "the search for the sacred" (Pargament & Mahoney, 2002). Although formal religious institutions may promote nonspiritual ends (e.g., social conformity) and nonreligious pathways to reach goals (e.g., social networking), the primary function of traditional as well as noninstitutional manifestations of spirituality is to facilitate an individual's search for the sacred. In short, in this chapter, religion and spirituality are treated as overlapping constructs. Also, "religious coping" and "spiritual coping" are viewed as synonymous, given the theoretical framework used and the lack of empirical evidence thus far available to make distinctions between the two terms.

CURRENT EMPIRICAL RESEARCH ON RELIGIOUS COPING AND YOUTH

Review of Empirical Studies

Although it is reasonable to assume that, like adults, children and adolescents may often turn to religious faith to cope with stressful life events, empirical studies directly addressing this topic are surprisingly scarce. For example, in April 2004, we conducted an extensive literature search to locate studies published in journals on religious coping and youth (under age 18). We searched PsycINFO, the Social Sciences Citation Index, and Medline using the key phrases *religious coping* and *spiritual coping* as well as combinations of the terms *religion, spirituality, children,* and *adolescents*. We also inspected reference lists of recent literature reviews on religion and youth (e.g., Barnes, Plotnikoff, Fox, & Pendleton, 2000; Benson, Roehlkepartain, & Rude, 2003; Donahue & Benson, 1995; Regneus, 2003). Of the studies we located, only a handful (i.e., $N = 14$) directly assessed some type of religious coping. The largest group ($N = 7$) were brief, descriptive accounts using unstandardized measures and small samples. These studies centered on the emergence of religious concerns and the frequency of religious activity by youth during stressful medical situations, including hospitalization (Ebmeier, Lough, Huth, & Autio, 1991; Silber & Reilly, 1985), a cancer diagnosis (Friedman et al., 1997; Spilka, Zwartjes, & Zwartjes 1991; Tebbi, Mallon, Richards, & Bigler, 1987), sibling death (Batten & Oltjenbruns, 1999), or fears (Mooney, Graziano, & Katz, 1985). One qualitative study provides more systematic insights into children's religious coping in a medical context (Pendleton, Cavalli, Pargament, & Nasr, 2002) and is highlighted in more detail later.

Six quantitative studies were found that linked religious coping variables to adolescent adjustment in community samples experiencing high risk or stressful life circumstances. In two studies (Pearce, Jones, Schwab-Stone, & Ruchkin, 2003; Wills, Yaeger, & Sandy, 2003), items assessing religious coping behaviors were combined with more general items on religious beliefs or practices. Although this measurement approach confounds the effects of religious coping with other aspects of religious functioning, higher scores on these omnibus indices were linked to lower rates of substance abuse (Wills et al., 2003) and serious conduct problems in response to difficult life situations (Pearce, Jones, et al., 2003). Using factor analyses, Dubow, Pargament, Boxer, and Tarakeshwar (2000) identified three distinct coping strategies used by Jewish early adolescents: seeking God's support, seeking support from Jewish culture/social network, and experiencing spiritual struggles. All three variables covaried with higher rates of ethnic-related stressors, such as restrictions on social life due to religious duties and exposure to anti-Semitism, but links to youths' psychosocial adjustment were not examined. Using a community sample, Pearce, Little, and Perez (2003) combined adolescents' responses to two items about whether their religious congregation would offer help if they became sick or support in difficult situations. After controlling for demographic and global religious variables, adolescents' speculations of receiving interpersonal religious support were related to lower levels of current depressive symptoms. In contrast, scores from two items that assessed

whether the congregation was generally demanding or critical of teens correlated with more depression. This study hints at possible differential effects of positive versus negative religious coping resources, but it is limited by the fact that adolescents were not queried about other people's responses in the context of an actual stressful event. In a national survey, Heath et al. (1999) found that the less adolescents said they relied on religious beliefs to deal with day-to-day living, the more they used alcohol or tobacco after controlling for ethnicity, family socioeconomic level, family religious affiliation, and church attendance. But no such links emerged for two items that directly assessed religious coping (i.e., rely on religious teaching when a problem occurs; turn to prayer when facing personal problem). Finally, Vaughn and Roesch (2003) employed a four-item scale of religious coping as 1 of 15 types of coping used by low-income, college-bound high schoolers from historically underrepresented ethnic groups. After controlling for other types of coping, religious coping predicted Mexican American and Asian American (but not African American) students' retrospective reports of more personal growth (e.g., learning to be nicer to others) as a result of experiencing a stressor in the past year.

Critique of Empirical Literature

Overall, the handful of studies above offers tantalizing glimpses into religious coping by children and adolescents. Although this research is intriguing, current evidence about the variety, pervasiveness, or importance of specific ways that youth rely on religion to cope is neither extensive nor conclusive. Further, the bulk of research typically cited in support of the idea that youth use and benefit from religious coping employs global markers of religiousness (e.g., affiliation, frequency of prayer or religious attendance). Comprehensive reviews do document that global religious variables are consistently tied to lower rates of teenage delinquency, smoking, alcohol use, drug use, premarital sexuality, and pregnancy (e.g., Donahue & Benson, 1995), as well as to more positive psychosocial functioning (e.g., Regneus, 2003). These findings imply that religion may play an important and distinctive role in how some youth cope with stressful events. Such inferences, however, need to be verified with rigorous investigations grounded in conceptually based, well-delineated measures of religious coping for several reasons.

First, global indices of religiousness cannot be assumed to reflect actual use of religious coping to deal with a stressful event. For example, items about religious affiliation, attendance rates, frequency of prayer, and self-rated religiousness do not assess whether or how individuals engage in religiously grounded beliefs or behaviors to cope with stressful events. Global religious variables are especially likely to yield uninformative and imprecise information about religious coping by children and adolescents because youth may often endorse such items simply because they are pressured by family members to be nominally religiously active.

Second, global items about religion fail to reveal whether religion offers unique resources to youth that are not otherwise available. Although religious coping processes clearly offer adults unique physical and mental health benefits in stressful circumstances after controlling for other coping resources (Pargament & Ano, in press), such evidence is not available for children and adolescents. In-depth assessment of religious coping is necessary to resolve debates as to whether religion offers something to youth that is special, either theoretically or practically (Smith, 2003).

Third, relying on brief, global indices of religiousness in the context of distressing events does not adequately distinguish between helpful and harmful forms of religious coping. Failure to do this can lead to seemingly contradictory findings about religious coping. On one hand, for example, single items on the importance of religion have been linked to more resiliency by female adolescents who have suffered sexual abuse (Chandy, Blum, & Resnick, 1996) and lower levels of violence by at-risk urban youth (Powell, 1997). Likewise, greater church attendance has been tied to less internalization of negative racial stereotypes by African American adolescents (Brega & Coleman, 1999). On the other hand, in a rare longitudinal study, greater church attendance by unmarried adolescents during pregnancy was linked to higher levels of postbirth depression, particularly for those affiliated with certain religious groups (Sorenson, Grindstaff, & Turner, 1995). These conflicting findings are likely to be rooted in the fact that religion can present both unique resources and burdens in the face of stressful events. This reality can be obscured without careful assessment of both positive and negative manifestations of religious coping, which predict opposing outcomes in research with adults (Pargament & Ano, in press).

A related fourth issue is that research on religious coping by youth needs to attend to the type of stressor being faced. In particular, it is important to distinguish between stressors that are typically perceived as falling outside versus inside human control. Working with adults dealing with a wide range of life stressors, Pargament and his colleagues have identified distinct styles of religious coping, which have diverse implications for mental health, depending on "fit" between the type of stressor and religious coping style (Pargament, 1996, 1997; Pargament, Smith, Koenig, & Perez, 1998). Thus, although religion may facilitate youths' adjustment to uncontrollable events (e.g., medical problems, racial discrimination), opposite effects may occur for stressors that fall under the perceived control of the child (e.g., pregnancy), family members (e.g., divorce, domestic violence), or peers (e.g., interpersonal betrayals).

Finally, although systematic empirical research has only just begun to assess religious coping methods used by adults affiliated with non-Christian world religions (e.g., Judaism, Buddhism, Islam), social scientists have successfully developed reliable and valid measures that yield a fine-grained picture of a wide variety of religious coping strategies adults employ within and across different Christian groups. Such work advances an understanding of the role religion plays in coping well beyond what is revealed by traditional religious affiliations. We believe similar work can fruitfully be done with youth in predominantly Christian samples. Furthermore, future researchers should strive to develop theory and assessment tools that apply to people of all ages in cultures and ethnic groups not dominated by Christianity.

In sum, more in-depth research is needed on specific ways that youth use religion to cope with stressors and how different religious coping strategies affect psychosocial adjustment, even after taking into account other coping strategies. Without such evidence, it can be argued that religion does not offer youth unique coping mechanisms, but merely reflects their access to social and personal resources available in both religious and nonreligious contexts (Smith, 2003).

EXTENDING ADULT RELIGIOUS COPING CONSTRUCTS TO YOUTH

In the past decade or so, theoretical models of religious coping by adults have been developed and validated with extensive empirical research. In this section, we discuss key constructs found within this literature and how these concepts may extend to youth. Naturally, only time will tell whether the distinctive types of religious coping uncovered in adult samples generalize to younger samples, and care must be taken to make necessary adaptations in theory and measures to accommodate developmental issues. However, we believe the adult literature on religious coping offers useful stepping-off points to generate more in-depth research with youth.

Primary Religious Appraisals: Religiously Based Initial Interpretations of Events

Overview. According to Lazarus and Folkman's (1984) theory, one central aspect of coping involves an individual making sense of an event, especially with regard to its threatening implications to a person's core values and needs (i.e., primary appraisal). This is accompanied by an appraisal of resources available to manage the stressor (i.e., secondary appraisal). Together, these appraisals shape the degree to which an event is experienced as distressing. Recent studies have identified four religious constructs that closely adhere to Lazarus and Folkman's conception of primary appraisals that occur in the first stage of coping. These include one religious appraisal that could minimize the distress provoked by an event (sanctification) and three that would heighten distress (desecration, sacred loss, and demonization of the perpetrator).

Sanctification. Sanctification refers to perceiving an aspect of life as having divine character and significance (Mahoney et al., 1999; Pargament & Mahoney, in press). Two such processes have been highlighted in previous studies. Theistic sanctification refers to experiencing an aspect of life as being a manifestation of one's images, beliefs, or experience of God. Nontheistic sanctification occurs without reference to a specific deity and takes place when an aspect of life is imbued with divine qualities such as timelessness, ultimate value, and transcendence. Thus, the marriage of a child's parents can be a sacred covenant with God, a football game can become a holy battleground, a career can become a God-given vocation, and sexual abstinence can become saintly. The process of sanctification extends the realm of the sacred beyond concepts of God, the divine, and transcendence to include a wide range of aspects of life. Several studies indicate that adults sanctify many aspects of life, either by seeing God as being manifest in the domain (e.g., God is present in marriage, parenting, or life goals) or imbuing it with sacred qualities (e.g., holy, blessed, sacred; Pargament & Mahoney, in press). Further, people invest more energy as well as work harder to preserve and protect sanctified aspects of life (Pargament & Mahoney, in press; Mahoney, Pargament, Murray-Swank, & Murray-Swank, 2003).

Conceptually, sanctification reflects a religiously based interpretation of life events. Like adults, children or adolescents could view virtually any aspect of life through this spiritual frame of reference, including stressful events. Moreover, the sanctification of stressful events could be conceptualized as a potentially helpful religious coping appraisal. For example, youth could view the divorce of violent parents, the death of an abusive parent, or the departure of a sibling from the household as an answer to prayers. Negative events perceived in this manner would presumably be less stressful and thus less likely to trigger subsequent coping processes. To date, the empirical study of sanctification has not focused on the initial appraisal of stressors. Some research has, however, been conducted on interpreting negative events as a violation or loss of a sanctified aspect of life. We now turn our attention to these two religious appraisals.

Desecration and Sacred Loss. "Desecration" is one type of primary religious appraisal that would presumably heighten a youth's sense of distress. This construct refers to perceiving a sanctified aspect of life as having been violated (Pargament, Magyar, Benore, & Mahoney, 2004). An example of desecration beliefs is "a part of my life that God made sacred was attacked." "Sacred loss" is another negative primary religious appraisal of an event rooted in sanctification (Pargament et al., 2004). This construct is defined as the loss of an aspect of life that has previously been viewed as a manifestation of the divine and/or invested with sacred qualities. An example of a sacred loss belief is "something I held as sacred is no longer present in my life." Three initial studies with adults indicate that desecration is linked to psychological distress. For example, the more college students experienced a betrayal in a romantic relationship as a desecration, the more psychological distress they reported (Magyar, Pargament, & Mahoney, 2000). Likewise, the more college students living in both New York City and Ohio viewed the 9/11 attacks as a desecration, the more anxiety and anger they felt about the attacks. In a third study, adults from the community reported the extent they viewed their most negative life event in the past two years as a desecration as well as a sacred loss (Pargament et al., 2004). Higher levels of both constructs were related to more intrusive thoughts. Further, sacred loss was uniquely related to depression, whereas desecration was uniquely related to greater anger.

In light of this initial research with adults, youths' reactions to stressors might be expected to intensify, depending on the degree to which they appraise events as being a desecration or sacred loss. Such hypotheses are consistent with the idea that desecration and sacred loss represent two primary religious appraisals that challenge critical ingredients of the individual's worldview (Pargament & Mahoney, 2002). Thus, the suicide of a high school friend, the end of one's parents' marriage, or the experience of sexual abuse may be terribly traumatic to a child, not only because these stressful events damage the child's emerging sense of benevolence, justice, and self-worth, but also because the events compromise the development of his or her spiritual system of meaning. In addition, desecrations and sacred losses may often contradict the spiritual narrative lens that children are taught to use to organize their thinking about their own personal life story and other people's behavior. Events that disrupt these sacred storylines may be especially upsetting. Finally, youth may feel more distress when a sacred aspect of life is violated or lost because they, like adults, have more invested in and derive greater personal benefits from things in life that reflect a connection to the divine.

Demonization of the Perpetrator. A third primary religious appraisal that may exacerbate a child's sense of threat associated with a negative event is the demonization of the individual(s) who are seen as the perpetrator of a trauma. One type of demonization is the belief that a perpetrator is operating under the influence of supernatural evil forces. For example, in the 9/11 study (Mahoney et al., 2002), approximately 50%–60% of college students endorsed the following items about the terrorists: The devil is at work in these people's actions; these people are confusing God's work with the devil's work; and these people are on the devil's side. The more students endorsed such appraisals, the more they felt threatened and experienced posttraumatic symptoms. In a similar manner, children and adolescents may be prone to demonizing other people's behavior, particularly if such beliefs are encouraged by authority figures. For example, divorcing parents may encourage the demonization of each other during or after divorce proceedings. While likely to be rare, such negative primary religious appraisals may greatly heighten a child's confusion and distress, and undermine family relationships.

Religious Coping Processes: Religiously Based Responses to a Perceived Stressor

Using a 100-item, multidimensional measure of religious coping, the RCOPE, Pargament and others have reliably discriminated 21 specific religious coping strategies employed by adults. Pargament conceptually sorts these strategies into religious reappraisals and four sets of religious coping processes used to achieve certain goals (Pargament et al., 1998). To facilitate more in-depth research with youth, we describe the religious coping strategies found with adults using this framework, highlight available evidence as to whether youth employ similar strategies, and discuss the likely impact of these strategies on youths' psychosocial adjustment.

Overview. Four of the 21 religious coping strategies identified by Pargament and colleagues consist of religious reappraisals that give spiritual meaning to a negative event. Notably, Pargament has labeled these constructs as "reappraisals" of a stressor, not "appraisals" per se. This scientific terminology accommodates Lazarus and Folkman's (1984) proposition that coping occurs in a sequential, two-stage manner. First, an individual evaluates the level of threat that an event poses when it occurs and the resources available to respond, which are labeled primary and secondary appraisals, respectively. If these initial perceptions generate sufficient alarm, a second stage ensues wherein the individual proactively engages in intentional efforts to overcome the stressor. In Pargament's framework, a religious reappraisal is viewed as a "reframe" of a threatening event already viewed as threatening in order to cope. In contrast, the primary appraisals discussed earlier help shape the degree to which, if any, an event is experienced as a threat.

Benevolent Religious Reappraisal and Reappraisal of God's Powers. "Benevolent religious reappraisals" occur when an individual uses a spiritual lens to reinterpret a stressor in a positive, potentially beneficial light. For example, an adolescent might try to view her parents' divorce as a way that God is trying to strengthen her or as part of God's plan. Based on responses to semistructured interview questions, Pendleton et al. (2002) found that 26% of children ($N = 23$) with cystic fibrosis used this kind of appraisal to understand their illness. Children who made benevolent religious reappraisals emphasized what could be learned spiritually from their illness. Further, unlike some ill adults, none of the children interpreted their illness as being part of God's will. In addition, in this qualitative study, children's benevolent reappraisals were grouped with appraisals reflective of the idea that God may not be all-powerful. This latter notion corresponds to

a distinct religious coping factor found in adult samples that has been labeled "reappraisal of God's powers." Here a stressful event is viewed as evidence that things are not fully under God's control. For adults, benevolent religious reappraisals have clearly been linked to lower levels of psychological and spiritual distress, but the opposite is true for reappraisal of God's power. More research is needed to untangle the impact of these two religious coping appraisals for youth. For example, adolescents who report higher levels of "religious doubting" in general (not necessarily triggered by a stressor) also report more adverse life events, conflictual family patterns, and emotional distress (Kooistra & Pargament, 1999). Of course, it is possible that only adolescents, not younger children, may be able to distinguish these religious reappraisals.

Punishing God and Demonic Reappraisals. In college and adult samples, Pargament and other researchers have also identified two religious interpretations that cast a stressor in starkly dark, sinister terms. Namely, individuals may view an event as a punishment from God for their sins (i.e., punishing God reappraisal) or as an act of the devil (i.e., demonic reappraisal). Although the base rates of such reappraisals by adults are fairly low (around 15%), higher levels of such negative religious cognitions have been linked to greater mental, physical, and spiritual distress both cross-sectionally and longitudinally (Pargament & Ano, in press). Anecdotal accounts of children interpreting negative events as divine punishment are substantiated in Pendleton et al.'s (2002) study, which found that about 17% of elementary children make such appraisals when confronted with a serious illness. In addition, 27% of school-aged children from the midwestern United States have reported that at least one parent told them God will punish them if they are bad (Nelsen & Kroliczak, 1984). Viewing a negative event as divine punishment would presumably exacerbate youths' psychological distress as it does for adults.

Religious Coping Processes Reflective of Particular Goals

Conceptually, Pargament has sorted the 17 religious coping processes other than reappraisals into four categories, based on the ultimate goal an individual appears to be pursuing while responding to a stressor. We discuss each of these categories below, along with specific religious coping processes within each category that have been identified in child samples.

Religious Coping Processes With the Goal to Gain Control. One set of religious coping methods identified within adult samples deals with efforts to gain control of a situation by spiritual means. These methods include (a) collaborative religious coping, defined as seeking control through a partnership with God; (b) active religious surrender, defined as intentionally giving up control to God as a way to cope; (c) passive religious deferral, defined as passively waiting for God to control the situation; (d) pleading for direct intercession wherein control is sought indirectly by pleading with God for a miracle or divine intercession; and (e) self-directing religious coping, defined as seeking control alone and without God's help. In most situations, the first two strategies are adaptive for adults over the long run, whereas the next two approaches are not. The effect of the last approach depends on the type of stressor, with poorer adjustment for uncontrollable events, such as terminal illnesses.

In Pendleton et al.'s (2002) qualitative study of 23 medically ill children's responses to open-ended questions about coping activities, 26% reported collaborative religious coping as a means to gain control. Also, 17% of children declaratively stated that God does or would heal someone if asked. While this theme reflects the tendency of children to think in concrete, literal terms, such beliefs could be interpreted as children seeking control over a stressor indirectly by assuming divine intervention will occur. It is unclear from available research how often youth engage in other religious problem-solving styles, such as active surrender or passive deferral, and how different approaches of using religion to control the outcomes of stressors impact youth.

Religious Coping to Gain Spiritual Comfort. Another set of religious coping processes found with adults reflects the goal of gaining comfort from and closeness to God. Four of these processes are adaptive for adults over the long

run: (1) seeking spiritual support, defined as searching for comfort and reassurance from God's love and care; (2) religious focus, defined as engaging in religious activities or rituals to shift internal focus away from a stressor; (3) religious purification, defined as searching for spiritual cleansing through religious actions; and (4) spiritual connection, defined as experiencing a sense of connectedness with forces that are transcendent. Two of the strategies in this category reflect obstacles to obtaining spiritual comfort and exacerbate maladjustment. They are spiritual discontent, defined as expressing confusion and dissatisfaction toward God about the stressor; and marking religious boundaries, defined as rigidly demarcating and remaining within perceived boundaries of acceptable religious behavior.

In Pendleton et al.'s (2002) study, 65% of medically ill children reported a firm belief in God's help/support. Such beliefs overlap with the religious coping constructs of seeking spiritual support from God and feeling a spiritual connection. Further, 48% of these children made prayer requests to God to ask for help getting well and not dying, as well as for their families. Also, 39% reported engaging in religious rituals/activities, such as going to church or reciting religious phrases. These activities are consistent with the adult religious coping method labeled "religious focus." As reviewed earlier, links between the frequency rates of prayer and church attendance and better psychosocial adjustment in youth imply that these forms of religious coping by youth are adaptive. Again, however, in-depth studies on youth who are suffering a stressor are still needed. In terms of negative religious coping, 9% of children in Pendleton et al.'s study (2002) reported thoughts and feelings that match the construct of "spiritual discontent." An example is "God's going down in the room so He can make me feel better, but it didn't work." Presumably, such beliefs would undermine youths' adjustment.

Interpersonal Religious Coping. A third set of religious coping strategies found in adult samples centers on engaging in interpersonal activities with fellow believers during times of crisis. This includes (a) seeking support from clergy or fellow believers, (b) providing religious help to others; and (c) experiencing discord and rejection with a religious community. The first two strategies facilitate long-term adjustment of adults, while the third experience has been linked to more distress. With regard to ill children, Pendleton et al. (2002) combined children's comments about the first two positive religious coping methods and found that 72% of medically ill children either sought spiritual support for self from other people (e.g., asking others for prayers) or gave spiritual support to others (e.g., praying for others). Direct research on the extent and effects of youth experiencing positive and negative interactions with religious communities when coping with stressors does not appear to be available. As highlighted earlier, Pearce, Little, et al. (2003) found that adolescents who anticipated greater support from fellow believers in the event of an illness or problem reported lower current depressive symptoms, whereas the reverse was true for perceiving one's religious community as generally demanding or critical. This study implies that adolescents may commonly encounter interpersonal religious support or strife when negative life events occur, but studies are still of youth who are, in fact, struggling with a stressor. The potential value of such research is underscored by the fact that Pearce, Little, et al.'s (2003) findings emerged using only a few religious coping items and after controlling for demographics, self-rated religiousness, religious attendance, and private religious practices.

Transformative Religious Coping. A fourth set of coping strategies found in adult samples concern individuals' efforts to achieve a life transformation through coping processes, and these strategies generally appear to be adaptive. They include seeking religious direction, religious conversion, and religious forgiveness as a means to come to terms with a stressor. Although these three topics have each received some attention within college student samples, we were unable to locate controlled studies that directly examined such phenomena with children and adolescents. Given the importance of youths' ability to recover from interpersonal violations within a family and peer context, we believe that religious forgiveness especially merits further attention. For example, youth and their families

may often turn to their faith to facilitate forgiveness of one another, particularly for actions that are perceived as desecrations (Mahoney, Rye, & Pargament, 2004).

Positive Religious Coping and Negative Religious Coping

In addition to distinguishing between 21 specific forms of religious coping by adults, Pargament and colleagues have identified two higher order constructs of "positive" and "negative" religious coping. These broadband constructs have consistently emerged as factors with the RCOPE and have been linked respectively to better and worse psychosocial adjustment for adults. Further, given its growing popularity, it should be noted that a 14-item measure of religious coping, the Brief RCOPE, has been derived from the original 100-item version of the RCOPE (Pargament et al., 1998) as an efficient way to assess these two factors.

Published quantitative research on positive and negative religious coping by youth is restricted to Dubow et al.'s (2000) study of Jewish adolescents. Using factor analysis on 17 items drawn from the RCOPE and revised for Judaism, two factors emerged that correspond well to the constructs of "positive" and "negative" religious coping. A third factor also tapped into seeking support from Jewish practices and social ties. Specifically, these five items dealt with interacting with rabbi/fellow believers and engaging in Jewish religious rituals. This suggests that the broadband constructs of "positive" and "negative" religious coping found in Christian groups also fit for Jewish adolescents, and that these young religious believers also relied on narrowband religious coping methods found with longer measures of religious coping. This study did not report links of these religious coping factors with psychosocial adjustment.

Other efforts to develop a quantitative measure of youths' positive and negative religious coping include two unpublished studies in which some RCOPE items were adapted to create a tool called the Children's Religious Coping Scale. Both studies used samples of predominantly Caucasian, Christian pediatric patients (ages 8 to 18) suffering from chronic asthma ($N = 87$, Benore, 2004; $n = 62$, Ezop,

2002). Youth responded to 20 items about positive religious coping and 9 items about negative religious coping. In both studies, youth reported using positive religious coping strategies fairly often, whereas negative religious coping methods were rare. For example, in Ezop (2002), 65% of youth used at least one positive religious coping strategy, whereas only 25% used at least one negative strategy. Based on cross-sectional data analyses, Ezop (2002) and Benore (2004) found that both positive and negative religious coping were correlated with poorer psychological adjustment of ill youth, after controlling for demographic and general religiousness. Whereas findings about negative religious coping are expected, the link between higher positive religious coping and greater maladjustment highlights a key complexity in studying religious coping. Namely, in many cases, greater suffering is likely to mobilize greater positive religious coping as a means to cope, thereby yielding positive cross-sectional correlations between religious coping and distress. Thus, longitudinal designs are needed to determine whether positive religious coping is, in fact, adaptive over the long haul with youth as is the case for adults. Benore (2004) obtained 1-month follow-up data and found positive religious coping to be tied to greater spiritual growth, but null results emerged for psychological outcomes. Clearly, more studies are needed to judge the ultimate impact on youth of positive versus negative religious coping for different types of stressors.

In sum, efforts have begun to develop psychometrically sound measures of religious coping methods by youth. To date, this research has involved brief measures to assess the broadband constructs of "positive" and "negative" religious coping. More in-depth measures are needed to determine whether more specific forms of religious coping apply either to children or to adolescents. Because the "fit" between the type of stressor and form of religious coping is so important for adults, more detailed tools may likewise be valuable for youth. But, of course, distinctions between many forms of religious coping may only emerge for adolescents who have more advanced cognitive abilities relative to children. In addition, researchers should be aware that negative religious coping reappraisals

(e.g., feeling punished by God) and processes (e.g., interpersonal religious conflict) could be conceptualized as obstacles to coping, rather than coping per se. Along these lines, Pargament (1997) also refers to negative religious coping processes as "spiritual struggles." This term highlights that negative religious coping processes reflect religious beliefs or practices that become problems in and of themselves. As research is pursued with youth, this conceptual issue deserves recognition.

FAMILY-BASED RELIGIOUS COPING CONSTRUCTS

Thus far, research with adults and youth on religious coping has focused primarily on an individual's spiritual functioning, such as one's relationship to God, one's appraisals of stressors, and religious resources that are under one's sole control. Given the centrality of the family to children's functioning, another set of potentially powerful but unstudied religious coping strategies is those that tap directly into religiously based perceptions of family relationships or interactions between family members. For example, the primary religious appraisals of sanctification, desecration, and sacred loss discussed above may enter into family dynamics during times of crisis (e.g., family conflicts, divorce, domestic violence, child abuse; Mahoney et al., 2003; Mahoney, in press). Below we highlight three other family-based religious constructs that deserve attention as potential methods of interpersonal religious coping.

Theistic Mediation. Theistic mediation involves the belief that God is a "third person" who can actively participate in and facilitate adaptive interpersonal dynamics (Mahoney, in press). This construct is derived from clinicians' observations of how some couples draw God into the marital system to cope adaptively with marital conflict (e.g., Butler & Harper, 1994; Rotz, Russell, & Wright, 1993). Namely, theistic mediation occurs when both parties in a dyadic family relationship, and presumably even larger units of a given family system, view God as (a) being intensely interested in maintaining a compassionate relationship with each party,

(b) taking a neutral stance about each person's "side" of the story, and (c) insisting that each person take responsibility for constructive change in the relationship. Based on these assumptions, theistic mediation by youth and their parents should facilitate the quality of family relationships, assuming that expectations for the child's responsibility are developmentally appropriate. Accordingly, findings from a recent dissertation involving college students and their parents indicated that theistic mediation (e.g., turning to God to maintain objectivity and the ability to listen to the other party) was tied to fewer arguments, better communication skills, and higher overall quality of parent–child relationships (Yanni, 2003).

Theistic Triangulation. Theistic triangulation is a construct also rooted in the belief that God is a "third" person who can be drawn into relationship dynamics, but here God is viewed as being aligned with one party against the other party to cope noncollaboratively with a relationship problem. Some clinicians have observed that couples sometimes maladaptively triangulate God into the marital system when conflict emerges (Butler & Harper, 1994). Specifically, God can be drawn into three types of counterproductive triangles that block effective interpersonal problem solving: coalition (God takes one party's side), displacement (adversity is God's fault), or substitution (each party seeks God's support but avoids dealing directly with the conflict). Hypothetically, theistic triangulation by either youth or parents would be expected to exacerbate relationship distress. Indeed, in an initial study on this topic, Yanni (2003) found that higher rates of theistic triangulation between college students and their parents were related to more relationship conflict and distance between the parties.

Positive Conjoint Religious Coping Activities. Finally, family members may engage in overt religious activities together as a unit to cope with stressful events. Examples include intentional efforts to pray together silently or aloud, attending religious services as a family unit, and seeking family counseling from clergy or spiritual counselors as a means to come to terms with stressors. To be effective, such activities

would presumably depend on a fairly high level of agreement between individual family members about religious values and practices. In fact, the level of similarity on global religious variables (e.g., affiliation, church attendance, self-rated importance of religion) between youth and their parents has been found to be longitudinally predictive of positive adolescent outcomes and better parent–child relationships (Regnerus, 2003). However, there does not appear to be systematic research on the frequency or effects of conjoint religious activities by families specifically to cope with stressful events.

DIRECTIONS FOR FUTURE RESEARCH

Given the early stage of religious coping research among youth, we propose eight goals to guide future research:

- Develop theoretical models and corresponding detailed operational definitions of specific religious coping mechanisms used by children and adolescents;
- Refine and evaluate existing measures of youths' personal religious coping (Benore, 2004; Dubow et al., 2000; Ezop, 2002) and develop new measures that are sensitive to how religious coping constructs differ as a function of developmentally relevant factors (i.e., changes over time due to differential impact of cognitive capabilities, peer and family influences, religious beliefs and community, role of ethnicity and culture);
- Assess family-based religious coping constructs among youth;
- Take care not to confound psychosocial outcomes with individual or family religious coping items themselves;
- Attend to both adaptive and maladaptive manifestations of religious coping by individuals or within family relationships;
- Evaluate religious coping constructs both cross-sectionally and longitudinally to assess for possible stress mobilization effects, and detect short-term and long-term outcomes;
- In line with the development of general coping models among youth (Compas, Connor-Smith, Saltzman, Thomsen, & Wadsworth, 2001), determine the uniqueness of religious coping

processes beyond secular coping processes and how the nature of stressors may moderate these outcomes; and

- Develop and test developmentally appropriate interventions aimed at maximizing positive religious coping and minimizing negative religious coping.

In conclusion, despite the high prevalence of religious beliefs and practices among American youth, surprisingly little research has evaluated the impact of religiousness on youths' coping with life stressors. The research on adult religious coping provides a strong theoretical base from which to launch further exploratory research among youth. This adult model elucidates four types of primary religious appraisals: sanctification, desecration, sacred loss, and demonization of the perpetrator. Research with adults has also reliably identified 21 specific coping strategies that encompass religious reappraisals and four other sets of coping processes that depend on the goals sought (i.e., gaining control, gaining comfort and closeness to God, managing interpersonal relations, and achieving a life transformation). Although preliminary evidence hints that youth may employ many of these strategies, much more work is needed to understand religious coping by youth. Along the way, care must be taken by researchers and clinicians to address both positive and negative effects of religious coping on youth in order to promote optimal adjustment. Additionally, the roles of family-based religious coping constructs, such as theistic mediation, theistic triangulation, and positive conjoint religious coping activities, represent rich areas for future research with youth. Given the well-established power of religious coping for adults, far more attention should be devoted to this topic in the lives of youth.

REFERENCES

Barnes, L. L., Plotnikoff, G. A., Fox, K., & Pendleton, S. (2000). Spirituality, religion, and pediatrics: Intersecting worlds of healing. *Pediatrics, 104,* 899–908.

Batten, M., & Oltjenbruns, K. A. (1999). Adolescent sibling bereavement as a catalyst for spiritual development: A model for understanding. *Death Studies, 23,* 529–546.

Benore, E. (2004). *Religious coping and pediatrics.* Unpublished master's thesis, Bowling Green State University, Bowling Green, Ohio.

Benson, P. L., Roehlkepartain, E. C., & Rude, S. P. (2003). Spiritual development in childhood and adolescence: Toward a field of inquiry. *Applied Developmental Sciences, 7,* 205–213.

Brega, A. G., & Coleman, L. M. (1999). Effects of religiosity and racial socialization on subjective stigmatization in African-American adolescents. *Journal of Adolescence, 22,* 223–242.

Butler, M. H., & Harper, J. M. (1994). The divine triangle: God in the marital system of religious couples. *Family Process, 33,* 277–286.

Chandy, J. M., Blum, R. W., & Resnick, M. D. (1996). Female adolescents with a history of sexual abuse: Risk outcome and protective factors. *Journal of Interpersonal Violence, 11,* 503–518.

Compas, B. E., Connor-Smith, J. K., Saltzman, H., Thomsen, A. H., & Wadsworth, M. E. (2001). Coping with stress during childhood and adolescence: Problems, progress, and potential in theory and research. *Psychological Bulletin, 127,* 87–127.

Donahue, M., & Benson, P. L. (1995). Religion and the well-being of adolescents. *Journal of Social Issues, 51,* 145–160.

Dubow, E. F., Pargament, K. I., Boxer, P., & Tarakeshwar, N. (2000). Initial investigation of Jewish early adolescents' ethnic identity, stress, and coping. *Journal of Early Adolescence, 20,* 418–441.

Ebmeier, C., Lough, M. A., Huth, M. M., & Autio, L. (1991). Hospitalized school-age children express ideas, feelings, and behaviors toward God. *Journal of Pediatric Nursing, 6,* 337–349.

Ezop, S. J. (2002). *Religious and spiritual coping in children with chronic illness.* Unpublished dissertation, Bowling Green State University, Bowling Green, Ohio.

Friedman, T., Slayton, W. B., Allen, L. S., Pollock, B. H., Dumont-Driscoll, M., Mehta, P., & Graham-Pole, J. (1997). Use of alternative therapies for children with cancer, *Pediatrics, 100,* E1.

Gallup, G., Jr., & Castelli, J. (1989). *The people's religion: American faith in the 90s.* New York: Macmillan.

George Gallup International Institute. (1999). *The spiritual life of young Americans: Approaching the year 2000.* Princeton, NJ: Author.

Heath, A. C., Madden, P. A., Grant, J. D., McLaughlin, T. L., Todorov, A. A., & Bucholz, K. K. (1999). Resiliency factors protecting against teenage alcohol use and adolescent female twin study. *Twin Research, 2,* 145–155.

Kooistra, W., & Pargament, K. I. (1999). Predictors of religious doubting among Roman Catholic and Dutch Reformed high school students. *Journal of Psychology and Theology, 27,* 33–42.

Lazarus, R., & Folkman, S. (1984). *Stress, appraisal, and coping.* New York: Springer.

Magyar, G. M., Pargament, K. I., & Mahoney, A. (2000, August). *Violating the sacred: A study of desecration among college students.* Paper presented at the annual meeting of the American Psychological Association, Washington, DC.

Mahoney, A. (in press). Religion and conflict in family relationships. *Journal of Social Issues.*

Mahoney, A. M., Pargament, K. I., Ano, G., Lynn, Q., Magyar, G., McCarthy, S., Pristas, E., & Wachholtz, A. (2002, August). *The devil made them do it? Demonization and the 9/11 attacks.* Paper presented at the annual meeting of the American Psychological Association, Washington, DC.

Mahoney, A., Pargament, K. I., Jewell, T., Swank, A. B., Scott, E., Emery, E., & Rye, M. (1999). Marriage and the spiritual realm: The role of proximal and distal religious constructs in marital functioning. *Journal of Family Psychology, 13,* 1–18.

Mahoney, A., Pargament, K. I., Murray-Swank, A., & Murray-Swank, N. (2003). Religion and the sanctification of family relationships. *Review of Religious Research, 40,* 220–236.

Mahoney, A., Rye, M. S., & Pargament, K. I. (2004). *When the sacred is violated: Desecration as a unique challenge to forgiveness.* Manuscript under review.

Mooney, K. C., Graziano, A. M., & Katz, J. N. (1985). A factor analytic investigation of children's nighttime fear and coping responses. *Journal of Genetic Psychology, 146,* 205–215.

Nelsen, H. M., & Kroliczak, A. (1984). Parental use of the threat "God will punish": Replication and extension. *Journal for the Scientific Study of Religion, 23,* 267–277.

Pargament, K. I. (1996). Religious methods of coping: Resources for the conservation and transformation of significance. In E. P. Shafranske (Ed.), *Religion and the clinical practice of psychology* (pp. 215–239). Washington, DC: American Psychological Association.

Pargament, K. I. (1997). *The psychology of religion and coping: Theory, research, practice.* New York: Guilford Press.

Pargament, K. I., & Ano, G. (in press). Empirical advances in the psychology of religion and coping. In K. W. Schaie (Ed.), *Religious influences on health and well-being in the elderly.* New York: Springer.

Pargament, K. I., Magyar, G. M., Benore, E., & Mahoney, A. (2004). *Sacrilege: A study of sacred loss and desecration and their implications for health and well-being in a community sample.* Manuscript under review.

Pargament, K. I., & Mahoney, A. (2002). Spirituality: Discovering and conserving the sacred. In C. R. Snyder (Ed.), *Handbook of positive psychology* (pp. 646–675). Washington, DC: American Psychological Association.

Pargament, K. I., & Mahoney, A. (in press). Sacred matters: Sanctification as vital topic for the psychology of religion. *International Journal for the Psychology of Religion.*

Pargament, K. I., Smith, B. W., Koenig, H. G., & Perez, L. (1998). Patterns of positive and negative religious coping with major life stressors. *Journal of the Scientific Study of Religion, 37,* 711–725.

Pearce, M. J., Jones, S. M., Schwab-Stone, M. E., & Ruchkin, V. (2003). The protective effects of religiousness and parent involvement on the development of conduct problems among youth exposed to violence. *Child Development, 74,* 1682–1696.

Pearce, M. J., Little, T. D., & Perez, J. E. (2003). Religiousness and depressive symptoms among adolescents. *Journal of Clinical Child and Adolescence, 32,* 267–276.

Pendleton, S. M., Benore, E., Norwood, W., Jonas, K., & Herrmann, C. (2004). Spiritual influences in helping children cope with life stressors. In D. Ratcliff (Ed.), *Children's spirituality: Christian perspectives, research, and applications* (pp. 358–382). Portland, OR: Wipf & Stock.

Pendleton, S. M., Cavalli, K. S., Pargament, K. I., & Nasr, S. Z. (2002). Religious/spiritual coping in childhood cystic fibrosis: A qualitative study. *Pediatrics, 109,* 1–11.

Powell, K. B. (1997). Correlates of violent and nonviolent behavior among vulnerable inner-city youths. *Family & Community Health, 20,* 38–47.

Regnerus, M. D. (2003). Religion and positive adolescent outcomes: A review of research and theory. *Review of Religious Research, 44,* 394–413.

Rotz, E., Russell, C., & Wright, D. (1993). The therapist who is perceived as "spiritually correct": Strategies for avoiding collusion with a "spiritually one-up" spouse. *Journal of Marital and Family Therapy, 19,* 369–375.

Silber, T. J., & Reilly, M. (1985). Spiritual and religious concerns of the hospitalized adolescent. *Adolescence, 20,* 217–224.

Smith, C. (2003). Theorizing religious effects among American adolescents. *Journal for the Scientific Study of Religion, 42,* 17–30.

Smith, C., Denton, M. L., Faris, R., & Regnerus, M. (2003). Mapping American adolescent subjective religiosity and attitudes of alienation toward religion: A research report. *Sociology of Religion, 64,* 111–133

Sorenson, A. M., Grindstaff, C. F., & Turner, R. J. (1995). Religious involvement among unmarried adolescent mothers—a source of emotional support. *Sociology of Religion, 56,* 71–81.

Spilka, B., Zwartjes, W. J., & Zwartjes, G. M. (1991). The role of religion in coping with childhood cancer. *Pastoral Psychology, 39,* 295–304.

Tebbi, C., Mallon, J. C., Richards, M. E., & Bigler, L. R. (1987). Religiosity and locus of control of adolescent cancer patients. *Psychological Reports, 61,* 683–696.

Vaughn, A. A., & Roesch, S. C. (2003). Psychological and physical health correlates of coping in minority adolescents. *Journal of Health Psychology, 8,* 671–683.

Wills, T. A., Yaeger, A. M., & Sandy, J. M. (2003). Buffering effect of religiosity for adolescent substance use. *Psychology of Addictive Behavior, 17,* 24–31.

Yanni, G. (2003). *Religious and secular dyadic variables and their relation to parent–child relationships and college students' psychological adjustment.* Unpublished doctoral dissertation, Bowling Green State University, Bowling Green, Ohio.

25

RESILIENCE AND SPIRITUALITY IN YOUTH

EMILY CRAWFORD

MARGARET O'DOUGHERTY WRIGHT

ANN S. MASTEN

Stories of individuals who overcome adversity to succeed in life have circulated for many centuries in diverse cultures around the world, yet the systematic study of resilience dates back only a few decades (Masten, 2001). Research on resilience emerged from the study of children at risk for psychopathology as investigators searched for the origins of behavioral and emotional problems and disorders. A group of pioneering researchers realized that many young people whose lives were burdened with adversity or disadvantage nonetheless managed to do well in life. These scientists also realized that a full understanding of such resilience had the potential to guide efforts to promote positive development and outcome among youth whose lives were threatened by similar risky conditions and experiences. Thus began the study of resilience—a search for knowledge about the processes that could account for positive adaptation and development in the context of adversity and disadvantage.

Early in the history of resilience research, the role of organized and personal religion, faith, or spirituality was noted, both in quantitative studies of variables associated with good outcomes among individuals at risk for problems due to negative life circumstances and in case reports about resilience in individual lives (e.g., Anthony & Cohler, 1987; Garmezy & Rutter, 1983; Werner & Smith, 1982). The implicit and explicit protective functions of religion, religious practices, and faith in these accounts took many forms, ranging from deeply personal beliefs and feelings to the counseling, rituals, activities, and supports provided by organized religions. Reviews of this early literature noted in passing that protective factors associated with religion and spirituality paralleled in multiple ways the protective processes implicated in general studies of resilience at the individual, family, school, and community level (e.g., Masten, Best, & Garmezy, 1990). Yet this parallel was not examined in detail nor was it given much attention in the resilience research until recently, when religion and spirituality became more prominent themes of research in the social sciences.

356 DEVELOPMENTAL OUTCOMES OF SPIRITUAL DEVELOPMENT

The purpose of this chapter is to provide a conceptual framework for understanding the functional significance of religion and spirituality in promoting resilience in youth, drawing when possible on the empirical literature on resilience. The empirical literature linking religion and spiritual behavior to resilience remains sparse. Nonetheless, we believe that there are important clues about the nature of the protective processes provided by religious systems and beliefs suggesting that religion functions through the operation of the same fundamental adaptive systems implicated in the general literature on resilience in children, adolescents, and young adults.

This chapter is organized in four sections. The first section provides a working definition of resilience for the consideration of religion and spirituality as protective processes. In the second section, we examine four major ways in which religion and spirituality may function to facilitate resilience. In the third section, we examine the possibility that religion and spirituality may sometimes function in negative roles as risks, adversities, and vulnerabilities. In the final section, we first discuss what is missing in our knowledge of how religion and spirituality promote positive adaptation and development in children whose lives are burdened with risk and then consider future directions for research.

It should also be noted that in the following discussion, we rarely differentiate among the numerous distinctive aspects of the complex set of constructs denoted by "spirituality and religion." Although spirituality, religiousness, and religion are typically regarded as distinct, interrelated constructs (Miller & Thorenson, 2003; Pargament, 1997), often they are not differentiated in the literature reviewed here.

DEFINING RESILIENCE

Two Judgments

Resilience refers to positive patterns of adaptation or development manifested by individuals who have experienced a heavy burden of risky or adverse conditions. Thus, to evaluate whether individuals or groups of individuals have shown resilience, two types of judgments are required: (1) that the individuals are doing "OK" in whatever ways one expects them to be doing well and

(2) that there has been significant adversity or risk to overcome (Masten, 2001). Developmental scientists typically decide whether people are doing well or not in life according to their competence in the *developmental tasks* expected of people at a given age, gender, or period of development in a particular cultural and historical context (Masten & Coatsworth, 1998). For example, in many societies today, school-age children are expected to get along with other children, do well in school, listen to adults, and follow the rules of the society for behavior. Older youth are expected to make closer friends and eventually form romantic relationships, as well as complete their education, explore the world of work, and in time establish themselves in careers and families. Other investigators have focused on internal well-being or the absence of mental illness as the criterion by which resilience is judged. With regard to the second part of judging resilience, researchers have studied a wide variety of adverse rearing conditions and negative life experiences, including poverty, war, divorce, child abuse, and many other adversities (Luthar, 2003; Masten et al., 1990; Masten & Coatsworth, 1998; Rutter, 2000).

Empirical studies of resilience have focused on identifying the correlates and predictors of resilience, in the child, family, or larger context, that may reflect the causal processes accounting for good functioning during or following adversity (Masten & Reed, 2002). *Assets, promotive* and *compensatory factors* are terms used to describe the positive attributes of persons or contexts generally associated with better adaptation or development at nearly every level of adversity, high as well as low. For example, competence in children is generally associated with good cognitive schools and effective parenting in many cultures and situations. *Protective factors* play a special role under high-adversity conditions, ameliorating or preventing the full negative impact of adversity, analogous to child safety seats in a car accident or a good immune system during flu season.

Fundamental Protective Systems Implicated in Resilience Research

Despite variety in the definitions of resilience across studies, a remarkably similar list of promotive and protective factors associated with competence under difficult circumstances has emerged (Masten, 2001; Masten & Coatsworth, 1998). While there may be many ways in which resilience is achieved, particularly in different contexts, the convergence of the evidence from diverse studies of resilience suggests that basic and powerful human adaptational systems may have evolved over the course of biological and cultural evolution to facilitate adaptation under a wide variety of conditions. These include attachment, self-regulation, motivation for learning and engaging successfully with the environment, beliefs that life has meaning and hope, a sense of belonging, opportunities to learn from prosocial peers and adults, social support, and the benefits afforded by social order and cohesion.

The adaptive capacity represented by human involvement in all these systems is profound. Masten (2001) has argued that children are most damaged by types of adversity (e.g., malnutrition, neglect or abuse, chronic stress) that specifically threaten or harm these systems. Similarly, resilience is most likely when multiple efforts are made to maintain and/or restore these systems. Children who experience massive trauma, such as those exposed to war, political oppression, or chronic community violence, often are deeply affected precisely because the cultural systems (e.g., family, religious organizations, neighborhoods, and schools) that normally function to support and protect their development have been severely damaged or destroyed (Wright, Masten, Northwood, & Hubbard, 1997).

PROCESSES THROUGH WHICH SPIRITUALITY AND RELIGION MAY PROMOTE RESILIENCE

Religious faith or affiliations often appear on lists of protective factors in the resilience literature (e.g., Masten 2004; Wright & Masten, 2005). However, religion is a broad umbrella for many human endeavors that may operate in multiple ways and at multiple levels as protective processes, tapping into a variety of biopsychosocial systems from the molecular or cognitive level within the individual to the many levels of ecological systems in which human life is embedded (Bronfenbrenner, 1979). Protection

could be afforded through diverse self-regulatory processes, the microsystem functions of relationships, families, peer groups, or schools, or the macrosystem processes of much larger human organizations, including mass media, government, or cultural groups.

Adaptive systems implicated in the resilience literature, we suggest, are reflected in religious beliefs, practices, and organizations and how they work to protect individuals, families, and communities in overcoming adversity. A preliminary list of the ways religion or spirituality might operate in resilience is shown in Table 25.1. We have grouped these in four major categories, although there are undoubtedly many other ways to organize this list.

Attachment Relationships

God has said, "Never will I leave you; never will I forsake you." So we say with confidence, "The Lord is my helper; I will not be afraid. What can man do to me?"

—Hebrews 13:5–6

Namastè! I honor the place in you in which the entire universe dwells. I honor the place in you of love, of truth, of light, of peace. When you are in that place in you and I am in that place in me, we are One.

—Ancient Sanskrit blessing

Relationship With a Spiritual Being. One of the most prominent elements of religion is the formation of a relationship with a spiritual entity or divinity. This relationship has the potential to provide a profound sense of security and well-being. People who experience such a relationship with the divine, particularly in the form of a caring and compassionate figure, can experience strength and confidence in life and appear to cope better in stressful situations as a result (Hill & Pargament, 2003). In his classic book *Childhood and Society,* Erikson (1963) wrote about the link between faith in parents and faith in religion: "Trust born of care is, in fact, the touchstone of the actuality of a given religion. . . . [A]ll religions have in common the periodical childlike surrender to a Provider or providers" (p. 250). Attachment research suggests

Table 25.1   Processes by Which
Religion and Spirituality
May Promote Resilience

Attachment Relationships

Relationships with the divine
Marital relationship and family cohesion
Prosocial peers
Prosocial mentors

Social Support

Sense of community belonging
Rituals for birth, marriage, death, and burial
Prayers for the sick, the traveler, the bereaved
Visits when sick
Bringing food in troubled times
Counseling
Support groups
Political sanctuary, sanctuary from persecution

Guidelines for Conduct and Moral Values

Integrity
Compassion
Forgiveness
Empathy
Altruism
Kindness/love

Personal Growth and Development,
Transformational Opportunities

Regulation of affect and arousal
Prayer
Meditation
Liturgy and music of worship, celebration,
comfort
Reinforcement of family values and rules
Provision of meaning and a philosophy of life
Reframing of trauma
Acceptance of God's will
Conversion and transformation

---

that through secure attachment to a parent, a child learns to trust others and gains a sense of self-worth. However, there are various reasons why youth and their parents may fail to establish a secure attachment. In some cases, a relationship with a higher power seems to offer security in the form of a substitute attachment figure for such youth. For example, a child who experiences the death of a parent may find comfort in the spiritual belief that the deceased parent is in heaven with God, and therefore able to continue in a parental role, guiding and protecting them (Angell, Dennis, & Dumain, 1998; Lovinger, Miller, & Lovinger, 1999). There is also evidence that adolescents who are insecurely attached to their caregivers and who feel insecure about themselves are more motivated to seek out a relationship with a higher power and to view this relationship as an attachment relationship. However, developing this relationship may be more difficult for them than for those who have had secure attachment relationships (Kirkpatrick, 1998).

Supernatural religious figures often are conceptualized as someone who loves unconditionally. It is not difficult to imagine why this is comforting for youth who have not experienced unconditional acceptance, or who feel that they are unable to meet other people's conditions of worthiness. Even when there are conditions for love, most religions have specific and concrete descriptions of how to meet these conditions, such as through prayers and rituals. This may be one reason why victims of torture among adult Bhutanese refugees in Nepal who were Buddhist experienced less anxiety and depression than those torture survivors who were not religious. Many of the Buddhist refugees viewed their trauma as a result of bad karma and believed that practicing regular rituals would convince their offended gods to restore a favorable relationship with them. Such beliefs provided a sense of control and rituals that offered hope for the future, which may have encouraged these survivors to persevere in the face of severe adversity (Shrestha et al., 1998).

The ability to find hope and remain optimistic in the midst of violent ethnic conflict is remarkable yet common. Muslim refugees from Kosovo and Bosnia who used positive patterns of religious coping, such as seeking God's help in letting go of their anger, were more likely to report feelings of optimism about their future (Ai, Peterson, & Huang, 2003). It is important to note that these findings do not support that religiousness per se contributes to optimism, but rather that only those refugees who experienced a higher power in a *positive* way, by seeking comfort, guidance, and support, benefited from their religious beliefs.

The sense that a divine power can work through one's own and others' prayers adds a unique element of comfort not found in nonspiritual sources of social support. Some mothers living in an environment characterized by violence noted that the belief that God answers our prayers provided their children with a sense of protection and hope in an environment where they otherwise felt helpless—some mothers even described how praying with their children in the midst of nearby gunfire helped to comfort their children (Brodsky, 2000).

> *A cord of three strands is not quickly broken.*
>
> —Ecclesiastes 4:12

Family Relationships. In addition to offering a relationship with a divine being, spirituality and religion may strengthen family relationships by supporting marriage, providing child care support, and teaching moral virtues. Adolescents in families who attend church, pray, and partake of other religious activities tend to have stronger family relationships than those who are in nonreligious families (Smith & Kim, 2003). Spirituality and religion may serve a particular protective function when the family faces significant adversity, such as poverty, chronic health problems in a family member, the death of a family member, or other traumatic experiences. In times of difficulty, turmoil, or crisis, religious practices and beliefs can provide intrinsic benefits as well as enhance the support available to the family (Walsh, 1998).

Having an intact family may be one important protective factor for at-risk youth (Repetti, Taylor, & Seeman, 2002), since there is substantial correlational evidence that children in two-parent families fare better than those growing up with a single parent (Waite & Gallagher, 2000). However, recent research highlights that this positive effect holds true only for marriages that both partners find satisfying. Marriages with high levels of conflict between the parents place children at risk for adverse outcomes and are not more advantageous than cohesive single-parent families (Cowan & Cowan, 2002). Children who live in "risky families" (either intact or single-parent homes) are exposed to numerous factors that can adversely impact their physical and mental health. These factors include conflict, aggression, estranged, distant, or hostile relationships between their parents and/or other members of the family, neglect, abuse, and lack of emotional support and appropriate supervision (Repetti et al., 2002).

Since spirituality and religion are positively correlated with marital satisfaction and marital stability (Larson & Swyers, 2002; Weaver et al., 2002), they may serve as protective factors for families. Married couples who attend church regularly report fewer marital problems and are less likely to divorce than are those couples who attend church less often (Larson & Swyers, 2002). In addition, married couples who perceive marriage as spiritually significant report greater marital satisfaction, more investment in marriage, and less marital conflict than couples who do not view their marriage as having a spiritual component (Mahoney et al., 1999). When marital conflict does occur, spouses who perceive their marriages as spiritual in some way are more likely to remain committed to the marriage. Furthermore, many religions offer guidelines through scripture for how to handle such conflict, and also offer support in the form of pastoral counseling (Mahoney, Pargament, Murray-Swank, & Murray-Swank, 2003).

Parents who perceive the role of parenting as spiritually significant report less verbal aggression and more consistent discipline with their children than do other parents (Pargament & Mahoney, 2002). Religion also conveys messages to children that their role in the parent–child relationship has spiritual significance, such that they ought to honor their parents (Mahoney et al., 2003). Indeed, research suggests that religion plays an important role in increasing adolescents' commitment to their families. More specifically, adolescents who attend church tend to be more involved with their families, hold profamily attitudes, and report satisfaction with their family life (Smith, 2003).

Positive Peer Engagement. Children's peers may also communicate with one another that religious faith is positive and acceptable, may model appropriate behavior, and may provide a social life within the church (Erickson, 1992). Some religious classes actively encourage children to engage with each other in responding to the lessons, thus fostering peer relationships

(Haight, 1998). Religious organizations and activities may also provide an alternative path to identity development for teens susceptible to searching for identity through riskier means, such as drinking, drug use, early initiation of sexual activity, or gang membership. Congregations often offer youth groups, summer camps, festivals, and other events that encourage at-risk youth to refrain from these risky behaviors and allow them to engage in activities that foster positive relationships with other peers (Cook, 2000; Hodge, Cardenas, & Montoya, 2001). These positive influences may counteract other peer pressures to engage in high-risk behaviors and result in spending more time in social settings where activities are closely supervised (Hodge et al., 2001). Bergin and colleagues found that such peer modeling can enable adolescents to more effectively resist peer pressures that oppose church standards (Bergin, Stinchfield, Gaskin, Masters, & Sullivan, 1988).

Positive Mentors. Religious community is one of the few remaining social institutions that is less stratified by age, providing youth with opportunities to interact with older generations (Smith, 2003). Thus, congregations may serve an important protective factor by modeling positive adult–child relationships (Haight, 1998). For example, Brega and Coleman (1999) suggest that religion promotes destigmatization among African American adolescents by providing models of powerful and respected African American adults, and the message of acceptance and love from God (which may encourage the adolescent to question negative feedback from others). Positive religious mentors may also encourage African American teenagers from low-income households to continue their education and aspire to better jobs by providing an example that it is possible to transcend dire circumstances. Cook (2000) found that teenagers who attended church were more likely to have a job compared to teenagers who did not attend church.

It also appears that spiritual counselors improve health among refugees by offering companionship, support, and a sense of hope that someone is praying for them during difficult times, as well as hope for divine companionship and comfort. Such counselors also may communicate a genuine desire to listen during a time when the refugee's sense of connectedness with others may be very low (Spiegel, 2004).

General Social Support

Individuals and Families. Data from a national health survey (Ellison & George, 1994) indicate that participants who attended religious services often were more likely to report having larger social networks, more contact with network members, more types of social support, and that they perceived themselves as having a higher quality of social relationships than those participants who attended less often. In addition, many participants who attended services on a regular basis reported feeling valued and cared for as part of a network of nurturing support. During times of trouble, such as bereavement within a family, or chronic illness, religious communities often provide substantial support in the form of visits, bringing meals, praying for and with each other, and providing child care assistance. There are also often specific rituals for coping with highly stressful life events, such as death and burial, which provide a communal form of support during such crises.

A supportive network of child care is offered by many clergy and members to those in need of support (Smith, 2003). For example, African American single mothers who raised young children in an inner-city neighborhood characterized by high crime rates, drug abuse, poor access to resources, and low income were identified as resilient based on elementary school informants who saw these women as positive community role models and good mothers. Many of these resilient mothers, when interviewed about how they coped with stress, spontaneously discussed the role of religion in alleviating stress and enabling them to be resilient. The mothers who appreciated attending church described the support of the clergy during difficult emotional and financial times (Brodsky, 2000).

Groups Within the Community. Religious support may provide a unique form of social support. Even when the people change in a person's support system, individuals with a religious or spiritual framework for life report a sense of continuity in support over the life span from like-minded individuals who share similar values and worldviews (Hill & Pargament, 2003).

As an example, the African American church has established itself as a haven for many African American children and adolescents who experience racial discrimination in their communities. Experiences with racial discrimination can be very stressful, leading to feelings of injustice, frustration, rage, and alienation (Szalacha et al., 2003). Treatment that is demeaning and/or degrading can result in considerable psychological distress, particularly feelings of anxiety, depression, and physical distress (Landrine & Klonoff, 1996). The role of religion in the lives of many African American youth likely serves many different functions, but one particularly important one may be that it buffers young people against the stress of discrimination or exclusion from the dominant society (Scott, 2003). The church has been described as a place where these children can learn about their heritage from other African Americans who care for and nurture them. A sense of connection to the African American community is likely to be protective by fostering a sense of self-worth and pride for children who feel otherwise alienated from the larger community (Haight, 1998; Markstrom, 1999).

Similarly, refugees in new host countries often congregate with other refugees to begin to restore their lost community and culture (Marsella, Bornemann, Ekblad, & Orley, 1994). This often occurs through celebration of cultural traditions, establishment of temples or other religious organizations, and establishment of educational programs to teach children about their cultural heritage. Kinzie and colleagues (1986) observed in their study of Cambodian refugees that the cultural and spiritual values the Khmer Rouge had tried to destroy in Cambodia played a major role in recovery for these refugee families after the war. Cambodian culture, which is characterized by a long tradition of Buddhism, places a high value on acceptance of fate, harmony and peacefulness, family and community support, avoidance of conflict, suppression of painful memories, and an ethic of hard work (Kinzie, Sack, Angell, Manson, & Rath, 1986). The philosophy of Buddhism likely provided strong support to Cambodian families as they attempted to recover from the horrendous experiences and losses they had endured in Cambodia (Wright et al., 1997). Finally, religious communities may provide political sanctuary, and sanctuary from persecution for those who have been forced to flee their homeland.

Guidelines for Conduct and Moral Values

The thought manifests as the word; the word manifests as the deed; the deed develops into habit; and habit hardens into character. So watch the thought and its ways with care, and let it spring from love born out of concern for all beings.

—The Buddha

The merciful are shown mercy by the All-Merciful. Show mercy to those on earth and God will show mercy to you.

—The Prophet Muhammad

People with a religious or spiritual framework for life may be empowered by a sense of persevering to meet transcendent goals, and thus may be more apt to cope with life stress by practicing certain virtues (i.e., compassion, forgiveness, gratitude, honesty, integrity, and hope) that have themselves been associated with better physical and mental health (Hill & Pargament, 2003). Many researchers have suggested that religious involvement appears to help teens develop self-regulatory abilities by offering a standard for behavior, or a guide for right and wrong that may prevent some at-risk teens from engaging in risky behaviors (Cook, 2000).

Parents, by communicating a worldview, can make use of religion/spirituality to help their children cope with life's difficulties (Erickson, 1992). Some mothers in the Brodsky (2000) study noted the importance of religion in instilling important values, both because being spiritual themselves encouraged the mothers to work hard to teach their children values, and also because Bible school teachers directly provided their children with valuable lessons. These lessons included being grateful for what you are blessed to have because there are others who have less, and being forgiving and loving toward other children who make hurtful comments.

Holding on to anger is like grasping a hot coal with the intent of throwing it at someone else; you are the one who gets burned.

—The Buddha

Forgiveness. Forgiveness has received prominent attention in many spiritual teachings and religious practices. Acts of betrayal, violence, injustice, or victimization violate fundamental moral and social norms, and such incidents typically lead to righteous indignation and an impulse to punish the transgressor. Such responses likely have an adaptive evolutionary basis since mutual cooperation, respect, and adherence to rules or norms for conduct are essential for maintenance of social order (Finkel, Rusbult, Kumashiro, & Hannon, 2002). However, victims may seek vengeance or demand retribution or atonement; in addition, they may be overcome by negative affect (e.g., sadness, anger, anxiety, self-blame), may ruminate about the event(s), or engage in other negative processing of the event and their own role in it. Healthy long-term adaptation, thus, often hinges on "moving beyond this constellation of negative affect, cognition, and behavior" (Finkel et al., 2002, p. 958). The religious teaching that people have been forgiven by God and therefore should forgive others is common to many religions (McCullough & Worthington, 1999), although religious traditions often differ on how to define forgiveness.

One definition of forgiveness found in empirical literature is "a prosocial change in a victim's thoughts, emotions, and/or behaviors toward a blameworthy transgressor" (McCullough & van Oyen Witvliet, 2002, p. 447). As such, forgiveness may be an important component in fostering resilience because it allows the individual to move past potentially crippling negative emotion and despair. For example, adolescents who forgave their parents for perceived love deprivation had higher self-esteem, better attitudes toward their parents, lower levels of anxiety and depression, and more hope than adolescents who had not forgiven their parents (Almabuk, Enright, & Cardis, 1995). Also, it has been shown that female incest survivors who were able to forgive their offender (i.e., let go of feelings of resentment and instead feel compassion toward their offender) suffered from less anxiety

and depression and were more hopeful than those survivors who were not as forgiving (Freedman & Enright, 1996).

Children and adolescents who are able to forgive, rather than seek vengeance, and/or become consumed with negative affect, might be able to better overcome adversity for a number of reasons—forgiveness may allow them to let go of or be released from their pain, resentment, and anger; they may develop compassion for themselves as well as for others; they may have been successful in reframing the experience; and the act of forgiveness may have strengthened their relationships with others. Individuals who exude a forgiving, prosocial attitude may elicit more social support than those who display a bitter attitude toward others. Such forgiveness does not mean excusing, condoning, or diminishing the impact of the abuse, nor does it need to imply reconciliation with the perpetrator, although it might. Rather, the process of healing forgiveness acknowledges the severity of the injury and its impact on the individual, and also focuses on the processes that one must go through to find positive benefits from the act of forgiving (Freedman, 1999).

Personal Growth and Development

The spark of divinity is in all of us and can be released in our own lives by meditation, prayer, and daily spiritual practice.

—Eknath Easwaran

Regulation of Affect and Arousal. Spirituality and religion may also promote positive well-being in at-risk youth by offering important coping and social skills. Religious worship often encourages the ongoing experience of positive emotions and rest, meditation, and quiet reflection, all of which are associated with good mental and physical health (Powell, Shahabi, & Thoresen, 2003). As a result of prayer, meditation, and reflection, important self-regulatory skills (e.g., focused concentration) and mindfulness qualities (e.g., acceptance, patience, gratitude, nonjudgmental attitude, openness, letting go) can be acquired and used to promote healing and personal development (Shapiro, Schwartz, & Santerre, 2002).

Research also suggests that urban African American male adolescents' use of religion and spirituality as coping mechanisms is important in their development of a healthy sense of self and self in relation to others. More specifically, these males report better emotional well-being, more positive feelings about the future, feelings of being valued by others, and perceived popularity with peers (Spencer, Fegley, & Harpalani, 2003).

Children and adolescents who actively participate in religious activities are afforded many opportunities to improve their community and leadership skills (by helping with charity drives, counseling peers or younger children in youth groups, and so on), in addition to cultural and musical competency (e.g., biblical history, participation in church choirs or pageants) (Smith, 2003). Meaningful social roles are provided through the act of helping, and helping others appears to bolster feelings of personal control and to lower feelings of depression. Congregations may thus strengthen a sense of self-worth, the importance of which cannot be overstated, particularly for teenagers at risk for depression and suicide. For example, faith communities often teach that as children of a loving and powerful God, everyone has a purpose to fulfill, or special gifts to offer. Perhaps this is one reason why, among rural adolescents, parochial high school students were found to have lower risk for suicide than public high school students (Greening & Dollinger, 1993).

Meaning Making. Human beings typically hold several fundamental assumptions about the world and their place in it. These assumptions— that the world is a benevolent and meaningful place and that others and the self are good and worthy people—form the structures of meaning from which we operate on a day-to-day basis (Janoff-Bulman & Frantz, 1997). Traumatic events can shatter these beliefs, and people often must work to rebuild them. This process of making meaning following trauma can lead to changes in the person's faith and trust in a loving and benevolent higher power. Falsetti, Resick, and Davis (2003) explored the impact of trauma on religious beliefs in young adults and found that religious beliefs either became stronger or weaker following a single traumatic

event. Surprisingly, experiencing more than one traumatic event was associated with stronger, as opposed to weaker, religious beliefs. While the precise reasons for these relationships were unclear, the researchers proposed that strengthening intrinsic religious beliefs might function to reduce anxiety and make life more meaningful for those who undergo multiple traumas (Falsetti et al., 2003). Their study highlighted several factors that need to be considered when assessing how one copes with a specific trauma. Future research is needed to help clarify why some people's faith is strengthened while others' faith can be shattered. For those whose faith is strengthened, spirituality and religion may offer a way to make meaning out of the adversity by encouraging a different way of understanding the reason for the trauma, by teaching the importance of accepting God's will, and by providing relief from the fear of death.

But we also rejoice in our sufferings, because we know that suffering produces perseverance; perseverance, character; and character, hope.

—Romans 5:3–4

Reframing Trauma. The belief that a loving God is in control, even though we may not always understand God's will, may allow some youth to reframe trauma. Many biblical lessons promise rewards for suffering as well as ultimate fair judgment for good and evil. Also, Buddhism teaches that life is characterized by suffering but that no suffering is permanent (Canda & Furman, 1999). Youth who have faith in a just God who gives strength to those who suffer may find comfort in the belief that all things happen for a reason, and that where God's will takes them God's grace will also follow. Such beliefs inspire hope that despite the adverse events that have happened, as long as one follows God's plan, nothing can deter the individual from achieving the ultimate goal, for example, that of paradise with God. Faith, hope, and belief in God's love, thus, serve as motivating and inspiring factors for intrinsic believers that they will be able to find the pathway leading to an eventual positive outcome (Snyder, Rand, & Sigmon, 2002).

Your kingdom come, your will be done on earth as it is in heaven.

—Matthew 6:10

Acceptance of God's Will. African American youth who are confronted with discrimination appear to be more capable of coping with the hurt and anger they experience if they believe in a higher power (Scott, 2003). Children and adolescents who suffer from racial discrimination in their community are susceptible to low self-esteem and a decreased motivation to succeed academically. Predominately African American churches may serve as a refuge from discrimination, where such children are taught that God created people in different colors because God values variety (Haight, 1998). The mothers in the Brodsky (2000) study found church to be a source of positive messages to pass on to their children, such that God created and loves all races of people. In addition, some of the mothers reported that religion reminded them and their children that life has a larger purpose, and that all that matters in the end is the Lord's will. These reminders were believed to provide hope of a better place and a better future with God in heaven, and this hope, in turn, may have made their children less apt to succumb to peer pressure. Spiritual beliefs also offer relief from fear of death. Many religions promise a way to transcend death, such as through eternal life or through reincarnation.

A comprehensive longitudinal study by Werner and Smith (1992) followed a large birth cohort into adulthood, including more than 200 high-risk children. These children had been born into poverty, experienced prenatal stress, and lived in troubled families characterized by chronic discord, parental alcoholism, or mental illness. One third of these children were identified by age 18 as resilient because of their academic and interpersonal successes. Spirituality was identified among the most important protective factors associated with resilience in this study. Nearly half of the resilient women and one in five of the resilient men relied on prayer and faith for security and comfort during difficult times. Religious faith was not confined to a specific denomination; the Hawaiian Islanders studied included individuals embracing many religious beliefs, from the beliefs of the indigenous Hawaiians, to Catholicism, Buddhism, and many Protestant denominations. Werner and Smith suggested that spiritual faith aided these children in the development of a sense of purpose and meaning in their lives, as well as security in an otherwise troubled environment, and provided them with a sense of control over their fate.

SPIRITUALITY AND RELIGION AS RISK FACTORS

There are many ways through which spirituality and religion may foster positive adaptation. Like other powerful adaptive systems, however, these may also have the potential for harm in the lives of children, because they can be misdirected or manipulated to achieve ends that are unhealthy for development. Thus, children can be harmed by wars or destructive cultural practices perpetrated in the name of religion. Terrible events can also threaten the sense of security and belonging that faith provides. Thus, it is important to note that there are mechanisms through which spirituality and religion can have a negative effect and can function as risk factors. For example, when trauma or adversity shatters a belief in a supreme being, or results in a condemning relationship with this higher power, resilience may be less likely to follow adversity. Also, some religious mentors exploit those who place their trust in them. Finally, religious beliefs can lead to prejudice and persecution of others who hold different beliefs.

Trauma Shatters Religious Beliefs

Child sexual abuse appears to be one trauma that leaves survivors struggling with spiritual questions. Abusive experiences may lead to despair and anger toward God: "What kind of God would let this happen?" (Ganje-Fling & McCarthy, 1996; Wright, Crawford, & Sebastian, 2004). Children who have survived trauma such as sexual abuse may find it very difficult to make meaning out of their experience, and may even alter their belief systems to reflect a disbelief in God, or a perceived lack of meaning in life. Sexual abuse perpetrated by a trusted leader or mentor in a religious organization has the potential to be particularly damaging in this regard.

Condemning Relationship With a Higher Power

When people understand religion and spirituality as frameworks for life, they may perceive many aspects of life as sacred (i.e., the body as a temple, sense of self, meaning in life). Thus, the loss of the sacred as experienced through trauma can be particularly devastating (Hill & Pargament, 2003). For example, childhood sexual abuse survivors often blame themselves for the abuse, believing that they should have prevented their perpetrator(s) from abusing them. Deep shame may hinder a survivor's ability to feel worthy of God's love. Sexual abuse survivors who find it difficult to forgive their perpetrator(s) may experience guilt if they believe that God expects them to forgive. It may also be difficult for childhood sexual abuse survivors to trust God when, as is often the case, it was an authority figure who violated their trust or exploited their vulnerability (Ganje-Fling & McCarthy, 1996).

Negative Religious Mentors

People who view God as harsh, punitive, or distant report higher levels of distress (Pargament, Smith, Koenig, & Perez, 1998). There are instances in which clergy or other church members encourage youth to view God in this manner. Youth who may be particularly susceptible to experiencing God in this way are those who are struggling with their sexual orientation. In addition to being at risk for discrimination and violence from the larger community, such youth may not find comfort in their religious community. Some religious communities view homosexuality as a sin to be punished, and may even attempt to drive homosexuals out of the community. In extreme cases, individuals who are gay, lesbian, or transgendered may be publicly harassed and labeled deviant criminals or immoral sinners (Canda & Furman, 1999). It is certainly conceivable that youth who do not receive social support but are instead shunned by their religious communities are at risk for feeling isolated as well as internalizing feelings of shame and self-hatred.

Children who have been raised in a religious community that emphasizes the sanctity of marriage may experience heightened psychological distress should their parents separate or divorce. Children who feel responsible for their parents' divorce may experience a great deal of anxiety and guilt, accompanied by a sense of spiritual failure. Children whose religion condemns the breach of marriage because marriage is also a union with God may experience their parents' divorce as a separation from God (Mahoney et al., 2003). Thus, ironically, some religious beliefs that may be intended to support the family may have an adverse effect during times when the family is experiencing a great deal of distress.

Some childhood sexual abuse survivors have reported that their religious community either ignored them when they reported that they were being abused or even supported the abuse by teaching that a child must submit to adults who are in authority (Ganje-Fling & McCarthy, 1996). Furthermore, there are a growing number of alleged sexual abuse cases by clergy members themselves. Restoring faith in a religious community following a severe violation of trust is undoubtedly a difficult task in which some survivors simply choose not to engage (Ganje-Fling & McCarthy, 1996).

Ethnic and Religious Differences Can Lead to War and Regional Violence

Finally, ethnic and religious conflicts are responsible for producing a majority of the many millions of refugees and displaced persons in the world, half of whom are children (Marsella et al., 1994). Internal, regional, and international conflicts have resulted in tremendous devastation, violence, and civil unrest throughout history, and have been extremely prevalent throughout the 20th and 21st centuries (e.g., the Holocaust, Hindu–Muslim conflict on the Indian subcontinent, Palestinian–Israeli conflict, Catholic–Protestant conflict in Northern Ireland, Bosnian–Croatian conflict in the former Yugoslavia, and war throughout many countries in Africa, Southeast Asia, Latin America, and the Middle East). There was a significant change in the phenomenon of war over the course of the 20th century. Whereas past "conventional" wars focused primarily on military targets, the trend in more recent wars has been to target civilian populations directly, with significant disruption of medical, social, educational, and housing services. In contemporary wars many civilians are killed, children are targeted directly and even actively incorporated into the military, and rape, ethnic cleansing, and torture and mutilation are often employed (UNICEF Special Session on Children, 2002). Children and families are extremely vulnerable in such situations, and such conflicts have profound and deleterious effects. The cumulative effect of these conflicts, which are often prolonged, diminishes opportunities for resilience, since war and continuing political and religious oppression often result in the destruction of essential community and cultural support systems.

CONCLUSIONS

This chapter has highlighted the diverse roles that religion and related processes may play in the lives of children at risk due to adversity or disadvantage. Spirituality and religion may foster resilience through a number of fundamental human adaptive systems, including attachment relationships, rules and rituals for living, arousal and affect regulation, motivation, and sense of coherence. Spirituality and religion appear to provide a unique form of social support, strengthen family relationships, improve personal growth and development, and encourage a framework of meaning through which youth can make sense of their adversity or trauma. There is also good reason to believe that spirituality and religion can sometimes have negative influences in the lives of children and youth. Yet, despite many indications that spirituality and religion play important roles in adaptation and development for children and youth at risk due to adversity, trauma, or disadvantage, there are many gaps in the literature, reflecting a surprising neglect of an important domain of potential protective processes in human development.

Major Gaps in the Literature on Spirituality, Religion, and Resilience

The most striking gaps in the literature pertain to developmental issues. As noted in several chapters of this volume (see parts III and V for in-depth discussions of developmental outcomes of spiritual development), many aspects

of religious behaviors show a developmental course. In early development, religion is most likely to have an impact on young children indirectly through its effects on their caregivers, families, and communities. As children gain cognitive skills, their capacity for direct experiences and comprehension of religion and faith will expand. Interest in religion and a personal search for religious identity and a philosophy of life are more common among youth than young children. Religious conversions are often reported in adolescence or the emerging adulthood years, a time also characterized by an intensive search for meaning and personal identity. Many religions have a sequence of developmentally meaningful rituals and learning experiences reflecting expected developmental changes, including rites of passage into adult status within the religious community (e.g., bar and bat mitzvahs; Native American coming-of-age ceremonies).

The functions of spirituality and religion in the resilience of children would be expected to change as individuals develop and contexts change. Yet little is known about changing risk, vulnerability, or protective functions of religious faith, practices, or organizations in the lives of children and how these relate to developmental or contextual changes. When do various protective roles of spirituality or religion become possible in the lives of children? How do religious protective processes change with development? Theoretical attention to such questions is needed, with a solid foundation in developmental science and the normative course of religious and spiritual behavior, followed by prospective and longitudinal designs suited to the study of change and development over time.

Religion is also in many ways a social process, embedded in relationships and practiced in groups. Some of the protective (and damaging) potential of religious beliefs and practices relates to the interplay of social development, families, and the unique vulnerabilities and opportunities in adolescent development in relation to peers, risk taking, and the management of emotions and desires (Dahl & Spear, 2004). Peers play an important role in the transition to adolescence and adulthood, particularly with regard to identity and autonomy processes, romantic relationships, and risk-taking behaviors.

Yet, once again, little is known about the role of religion with respect to peer relations in development or resilience, though it is clear that parents encourage the positive and fear the negative influences of peer groups. It is apparent that some young people actively seek the protection of religious peer organizations that meet their social needs and provide a secure base away from home as they navigate their way into adulthood. However, peer processes related to risks and protections afforded by religion or spirituality need closer examination.

Closer attention to the *specificity* of religious and spiritual processes in adaptation among children and youth is also necessary. In some situations, the power attributed to faith or religious organizations for overcoming adversity may actually be the result of an unnoticed causal and correlated influence that is producing both better adaptation and also religiosity or faith. Examples of such influential factors might include a disposition to experience positive affect, extraversion, good parenting, or psychosocial advantages of many other kinds. Rare in the current literature is any attempt to test alternative causal models either statistically or through experimental designs.

Although a developmental neuroscience of resilience is just getting under way (Curtis & Cicchetti, 2003), as of yet very little attention has been focused on the biology of religious behavior and protective processes in the literature on resilience, particularly in children. Many aspects of religious experience seem particularly well suited to such study. Meditation, prayer, conversion, chanting, singing, speaking in tongues, healing, near-death experiences, and many other religious activities and phenomena associated with health and positive well-being suggest that powerful regulatory systems in the human organism are influenced by religious beliefs and practices. While there has been a recent resurgence in attention to spirituality, religion, and health (Miller & Thoresen, 2003; Seeman, Dubin, & Seeman, 2003), little direct research has explored the evidence for biological pathways in children and youth, and such work is needed.

Finally, the relative neglect of religion and spirituality in developmental research on resilience reflects the broader neglect of culturally based protective systems and ethnic diversity in existing resilience research (Luthar, 2003; Werner & Smith, 1992), as well as the hesitance on the part of the scientific community to approach the spiritual dimension as a subject of study. It is critical that systems-oriented researchers broaden their focus of study to include the belief systems embraced by diverse cultural groups, which provide meaning, purpose, and solace in times of distress (Walsh, 1998). Suffering and adversity are spiritual concerns, and our understanding of what will promote recovery and foster resilience will be more comprehensive when we incorporate "spiritual" processes into the biopsychosocial approach. It is time for a far more systematic and detailed theoretical and empirical examination of the multifaceted functions of religion and spirituality in the development of children at risk. Perhaps this handbook will serve as a harbinger of a new wave of scholarship focused on the role of religion and spirituality in resilience.

REFERENCES

Ai, A. L., Peterson, C., & Huang, B. (2003). The effect of religious-spiritual coping on positive attitudes of adult Muslim refugees from Kosovo and Bosnia. *International Journal for the Psychology of Religion, 13*(1), 29–47.

Almabuk, R. H., Enright, R. D., & Cardis, P. A. (1995). Forgiveness education with parentally love-deprived late adolescents. *Journal of Moral Education, 24,* 427–444.

Angell, G. B., Dennis, B. G., & Dumain, L. E. (1998). Spirituality, resilience, and narrative: Coping with parental death. *Families in Society, 79,* 615–630.

Anthony, E. J., & Cohler, B. J. (Eds.). (1987). *The invulnerable child.* New York: Guilford.

Bergin, A. E., Stinchfield, R. D., Gaskin, T. A., Masters, K. S., & Sullivan, C. E. (1988). Religious life-styles and mental health: An exploratory study. *Journal of Counseling Psychology, 35,* 91–98.

Brega, A. G., & Coleman, L. M. (1999). Effects of religiosity and racial socialization on subjective stigmatization in African-American adolescents. *Journal of Adolescence, 22,* 223–242.

Brodsky, A. E. (2000). The role of religion in the lives of resilient, urban, African American, single mothers. *Journal of Community Psychology,* 28(2), 199–219.

Bronfenbrenner, U. (1979). *The ecology of human development: Experiments by nature and design.* Cambridge, MA: Harvard University Press.

Canda, E. R., & Furman, L. D. (1999). *Spiritual diversity in social work practice: The heart of helping.* New York: Free Press.

Cook, K. V. (2000). "You have to have somebody watching your back, and if that's God, then that's mighty big": The church's role in the resilience of inner-city youth. *Adolescence, 35*(140), 717–730.

Cowan, P. A., & Cowan, C. P. (2002). Interventions as tests of family systems theories: Marital and family relationships in children's development and psychopathology. *Development and Psychopathology, 14,* 731–759.

Curtis, W. J., & Cicchetti, D. (2003). Moving research on resilience into the 21st century: Theoretical and methodological considerations in examining the biological contributors to resilience. *Development and Psychopathology, 15,* 773–810.

Dahl, R. E., & Spear, L. P. (Eds.). (2004). *Annals of the New York Academy of Sciences: Vol. 1021. Adolescent brain development: Vulnerabilities and opportunities.* New York: New York Academy of Sciences.

Ellison, C. G., & George, L. K. (1994). Religious involvement, social ties, and social support in a southeastern community. *Journal for the Scientific Study of Religion, 33*(1), 46–61.

Erikson, E. H. (1963). *Childhood and society* (2nd ed.). New York: Norton.

Erickson, J. A. (1992). Adolescent religious development and commitment: A structural equation model of the role of family, peer group, and educational influences. *Journal for the Scientific Study of Religion, 31*(2), 131–152.

Falsetti, S. A., Resick, P. A., & Davis, J. L. (2003). Changes in religious beliefs following trauma. *Journal of Traumatic Stress, 16*(4), 391–398.

Finkel, E. J., Rusbult, C. E., Kumashiro, M., & Hannon, P. A. (2002). Dealing with betrayal in close relationships: Does commitment promote forgiveness? *Journal of Personality and Social Psychology, 82,* 956–974.

Freedman, S. R. (1999). A voice of forgiveness: One incest survivor's experience forgiving her father. *Journal of Family Psychotherapy, 10,* 37–60.

Freedman, S. R., & Enright, R. D. (1996). Forgiveness as an intervention goal with incest survivors. *Journal of Consulting and Clinical Psychology, 64*(5), 983–992.

Ganje-Fling, M. A., & McCarthy, P. (1996). Impact of childhood sexual abuse on client spiritual development: Counseling implications. *Journal of Counseling and Development, 74,* 253–258.

Garmezy, N., & Rutter, M. (1983). *Stress, coping, and development in children.* New York: McGraw-Hill.

Greening, L., & Dollinger, S. J. (1993). Rural adolescents' perceived personal risks for suicide. *Journal of Youth and Adolescence, 22,* 211–217.

Haight, W. L. (1998). "Gathering the spirit" at First Baptist Church: Spirituality as a protective factor in the lives of African-American children. *Social Work, 43*(3), 213–221.

Hill, P. C., & Pargament, K. I. (2003). Advances in the conceptualization and measurement of religion and spirituality. *American Psychologist, 58*(1), 64–74.

Hodge, D. R., Cardenas, P., & Montoya, H. (2001). Substance use: Spirituality and religious participation as protective factors among rural youths. *Social Work Research, 25*(3), 153–161.

Janoff-Bulman, R., & Frantz, C. M. (1997). The impact of trauma on meaning: From meaningless world to meaningful life. In M. Power & C. R. Brewin (Eds.), *The transformation of meaning in psychological therapies* (pp. 75–89). New York: Wiley.

Kirkpatrick, L. A. (1998). God as a substitute attachment figure: A longitudinal study of adult attachment style and religious change in college students. *Personality and Social Psychology Bulletin, 24,* 961–973.

Kinzie, J. D., Sack, W., Angell, R., Manson, S., & Rath, B. (1986). The psychiatric effects of massive trauma on Cambodian children: I. The children. *Journal of the American Academy of Child Psychiatry, 25,* 370–376.

Landrine, H., & Klonoff, E. A. (1996). The schedule of racist events: A measure of racial discrimination and a study of its negative physical and mental health consequences. *Journal of Black Psychology, 22,* 144–168.

Larson, D. B., & Swyers, J. P. (2002). Do religion and spirituality contribute to marital and individual health? In J. Wall, D. Browning, W. J. Doherty, & S. Post (Eds.), *Marriage, health, and the professions* (pp. 283–304). Grand Rapids, MI: Eerdmans.

Lovinger, S. L., Miller, L., & Lovinger, R. J. (1999). Some clinical applications of religious development in adolescence. *Journal of Adolescence, 22,* 269–277.

Luthar, S. S. (Ed.). (2003). *Resilience and vulnerability: Adaptation in the context of childhood adversities.* Cambridge, UK: Cambridge University Press.

Mahoney, A., Pargament, K. I., Jewell, T., Swank, A. B., Scott, E., Emery, E., & Rye, M. (1999). Marriage and the spiritual realm: The role of proximal and distal religious constructs in marital functioning. *Journal of Family Psychology, 13*(3), 321–338.

Mahoney, A., Pargament, K. I., Murray-Swank, A., & Murray-Swank, N. (2003). Religion and the sanctification of family relationships. *Review of Religious Research, 44*(3), 220–236.

Markstrom, C. A. (1999). Religious involvement and adolescent psychosocial development. *Journal of Adolescence, 22,* 205–221.

Marsella, A. J., Bornemann, T., Ekblad, S., & Orley, J. (1994). *Amidst peril and pain: The mental health and well-being of the world's refugees.* Washington, DC: American Psychological Association.

Masten, A. S. (2001). Ordinary magic: Resilience processes in development. *American Psychologist, 56*(3), 227–238.

Masten, A. S. (2004). Regulatory processes, risk, and resilience in adolescent development. In R. E. Dahl & L. P. Spear (Eds.), *Annals of the New York Academy of Sciences: Vol. 1021. Adolescent brain development: Vulnerabilities and opportunities* (pp. 310–319). New York: New York Academy of Sciences.

Masten, A. S., Best, K. M., & Garmezy, N. (1990). Resilience and development: Contributions from the study of children who overcome adversity. *Development and Psychopathology, 2,* 425–444.

Masten, A. S., & Coatsworth, J. D. (1998). The development of competence in favorable and unfavorable environments: Lessons from research on successful children. *American Psychologist, 53,* 205–220.

Masten, A. S., & Reed, M.-G. J. (2002). Resilience in development. In C. R. Snyder & S. J. Lopez (Eds.), *Handbook of positive psychology* (pp. 74–88). New York: Oxford University Press.

McCullough, M. E., & van Oyen Witvliet, C. V. (2002). The psychology of forgiveness. In C. R. Snyder & S. J. Lopez (Eds.), *Handbook of positive psychology* (pp. 446–458). New York: Oxford University Press.

McCullough, M. E., & Worthington, E. L., Jr. (1999). Religion and the forgiving personality. *Journal of Personality, 67,* 1141–1164.

Miller, W. R., & Thoresen, C. E. (2003). Spirituality, religion, and health. *American Psychologist, 58,* 24–35.

Pargament, K. I., & Mahoney, A. (2002). Spirituality: Discovering and conserving the sacred. In C. R. Snyder & S. J. Lopez (Eds.), *Handbook of positive psychology* (pp. 646–659). London: Oxford University Press.

Pargament, K. I., Smith, B. W., Koenig, H. G., & Perez, L. (1998). Patterns of positive and negative religious coping with major life stressors. *Journal for the Scientific Study of Religion, 37*(4), 710–724.

Powell, L. H., Shahabi, L., & Thoresen, C. E. (2003). Religion and spirituality: Linkages to physical health. *American Psychologist, 58*(1), 36–52.

Repetti, R. L., Taylor, S. E., & Seeman, T. E. (2002). Risky families: Family social environments and the mental and physical health of offspring. *Psychological Bulletin, 128,* 330–366.

Rutter, M. (2000). Resilience reconsidered: Conceptual considerations, empirical findings, and policy implications. In J. P. Shonkoff & S. J. Meisels (Eds.), *Handbook of early intervention* (2nd ed., pp. 651–681). Cambridge, UK: Cambridge University Press.

Scott, L. D. (2003). Cultural orientation and coping with perceived discrimination among African American youth. *Journal of Black Psychology, 29*(3), 235–256.

Seeman, T. E., Dubin, L. F., & Seeman, M. (2003). Religiosity/spirituality and health: A critical review of the evidence for biological pathways. *American Psychologist, 58,* 53–63.

Shapiro, S. L., Schwartz. G. E. R., & Santerre, C. (2002). Meditation and positive psychology. In C. R. Snyder and S. J. Lopez (Eds.), *Handbook of positive psychology* (pp. 632–645). New York: Oxford University Press.

Shrestha, N. M., Sharma, B., Van Ommeren, M., Regmi, S., Makaju, R., Komproe, I., Shrestha, G. B., & Jong, J. T. V. M. (1998). Impact of torture on refugees displaced within the developing world: Symptomatology among Bhutanese refugees in Nepal. *Journal of the American Medical Association, 280*(5), 443–448.

Smith, C. (2003). Theorizing religious effects among American adolescents. *Journal for the Scientific Study of Religion, 42*(1), 17–30.

Smith, C., & Kim, P. (2003). *Family religious involvement and the quality of parental relationships for families with early adolescents.* Chapel Hill, NC: National Study of Youth and Religion.

Snyder, C. R., Rand, K. L., & Sigmon, D. R. (2002). Hope theory: A member of the positive psychology family. In C. R. Snyder & S. J. Lopez (Eds.). *Handbook of positive psychology* (pp. 257–276). New York: Oxford University Press.

Spencer, M. B., Fegley, S. G., & Harpalani, V. (2003). A theoretical and empirical examination of identity as coping: Linking coping resources to the self processes of African American youth. *Applied Developmental Science, 7*(3), 181–188.

Spiegel, A. (2004). *Spirituality and the immigration and naturalization service: Conceptualizing the counseling of detainees.* Available at http://www.hds.harvard.edu/cswr/research/RHHI/rhhi_pubs_fieldreports.html.

Szalacha, L. A., Erkut, S., Coll, C. G., Fields, J. P., Alarcón, O., & Ceder, I. (2003). Perceived discrimination and resilience. In S. S. Luthar (Ed.), *Resilience and vulnerability: Adaptation in the context of childhood adversities* (pp. 414–435). Cambridge, UK: Cambridge University Press.

UNICEF Special Session on Children. (2002). *Building a world fit for children.* Available at http://www.unicef.org/specialsession/index.html

Waite, L. J., & Gallagher, M. (2000). *The case for marriage: Why married people are happier,*

healthier, and better off financially (1st ed.). New York: Doubleday.

Walsh, F. (1998). *Strengthening family resilience.* New York: Guilford.

Weaver, A. J., Samford, J. A., Morgan, V. J., Larson, D. B., Koenig, H. G., & Flannelly, K. J. (2002). A systematic review of research on religion in six primary marriage and family journals: 1995–1999. *American Journal of Family Therapy, 30,* 293–309.

Werner, E. E., & Smith, R. S. (1982). *Vulnerable but invincible: A study of resilient children.* New York: McGraw-Hill.

Werner, E., & Smith, R. S. (1992). *Overcoming the odds: High risk children from birth to adulthood.* Ithaca, NY: Cornell University Press.

Wright, M. O., Crawford, E., & Sebastian, K. (2004, April). *What promotes positive resolution of childhood sexual abuse experiences? The role of coping, benefit finding, and meaning making.* Paper presented at the annual meeting of the Midwestern Psychological Association, Chicago.

Wright, M. O., & Masten, A. S. (2005). Resilience processes in development: Fostering positive adaptation in the context of adversity. In S. Goldstein & R. Brooks (Eds.), *Handbook of resilience in children,* pp.17–37. New York: Kluwer Academic/Plenum.

Wright, M. O., Masten, A. S., Northwood, A., & Hubbard, J. J. (1997). Long-term effects of massive trauma: Developmental and psychobiological perspectives. In D. Cicchetti & S. L. Toth (Eds.), *Developmental perspectives on trauma: Theory, research, and intervention* (pp. 181–225). Rochester, NY: Rochester University Press.

26

Delinquency: A Quest for Moral and Spiritual Integrity?

Ronnie Frankel Blakeney

Charles David Blakeney

The connection between adolescent misbehavior and spiritual development captures the public's imagination. Research reports that young people who are religiously connected are less likely to get trapped in delinquency than their disconnected peers. Nevertheless, even good children reared in religious families break rules. When Eve broke G-d's commandment and ate the "forbidden" fruit, she became the first delinquent. When Adam also ate of the fruit, he and Eve became the first delinquent peer group. Recent research (Benda & Corwyn, 1997; Furrow, King, & White, 2004; Larson & Johnson, 1998) suggests that religiousness/spirituality support a positive developmental trajectory in adolescence in part by creating a sanctuary where moral values are maintained and transmitted. Higher rates of religiousness are associated with lower rates of delinquency (Johnson, Jang, Li, & Larson, 2000). But 25%-50% of youth who consider themselves religious or spiritual, who grow up in families that practice their faith, and who themselves attend religious services regularly report delinquent behavior during adolescence. Conversely, 25%-40% of adjudicated delinquents report growing up in religious families and/or placing importance on their own spiritual beliefs (Wetzels, 2003).

What, then, is the connection between spirituality and delinquency? Researchers have asked whether and how religiousness/spirituality protect (Johnson, Li, Larson, & McCullough, 2000), buffer (Wills, Yaeger, & Sandy, 2003), mediate (Pearce, Jones, Schwab-Stone, & Ruchkin, 2003), and immunize (Blakeney & Blakeney, in press) youth who are at risk for delinquency and substance use/abuse. This assumes that delinquency and religiousness are alternate (mutually exclusive) paths. The latter protects youth from the former. Maybe we've been asking the wrong question. Perhaps delinquent behavior can be construed as missteps. In the same way that toddlers stumble and fall as they learn to walk, adolescents misbehave as they struggle to figure out who they are, where they belong, what is right and wrong, and what is ultimately meaningful. Learning from mistakes is a part of development (Oser & Spychiger, 2005). The question isn't, "How does spirituality protect youth from delinquency?" But rather, "How does spirituality help young people learn from their mistakes and not get stuck on a delinquent trajectory?"

In this chapter we attempt to untangle the complicated paths that tie religiousness/spirituality to moral development and to delinquent behavior in adolescence. First, we review research that examines the role of delinquency and spirituality in adolescent development generally. This research suggests that most teenagers misbehave, and most question what is ultimately meaningful in life. It also suggests that youth who have a connection to something meaningful and larger than themselves misbehave less than those who are lost in transition. Then, we review the literature about the role of spirituality in cases of high-risk youth. Here we find a paradoxical relationship in that in cases of moderate risk, a spiritual connection seems to serve as what Isaac Newton (1687/1995) referred to as an unknowable elastic Spirit, holding youth on course; and in cases of the highest risk, spiritual connection provides meaning outside conventional morality. Third, we review research on the role of spirituality in recovering integrity after long-term, serious misbehavior. Here we suggest that leaps of faith may indicate a way in which spirituality functions to help people find their way back from a delinquent trajectory. Finally, we propose a program of research to examine the proposition that delinquency and spirituality are not so much separate paths as interwoven ways of searching for autonomy, belonging, and meaning in adolescence.

This chapter takes as basic assumptions that delinquency includes both "normal" teenage misbehavior (cutting school, disobeying parents, smoking, drinking, sex) and serious misbehavior (fighting, stealing, rape). Further, we think of spirituality as the transformative capacity to find goodness and meaning. Since adolescence is a time of potential and transformation, and since delinquency is a misstep in the adolescent struggle to be good, then spirituality is the capacity that helps youth transform misbehavior into the potential to be good. If our formulation is correct, we will find that (1) for most youth, delinquent misbehavior is self-correcting; that is, there is a natural recovery or a maturing. (2) For youth who are stuck in a delinquent trajectory, or who are at higher risk, spiritual connection is supportive of developmental transformation. (3) For adults who began a pattern of delinquent misbehavior in adolescence, but who didn't "grow out of it," the development of a spiritual connection can be a path to recovering developmental integrity.

At the turn of the 20th century two Harvard scholars proposed two different theories about the connection between delinquent behavior and spiritual beliefs. Psychologist William James (1902/1961) noted the role of religious conversion experiences in transforming delinquent trajectories. Sociologist W. E. B. Du Bois (1899/1996) noted that social conditions for Negro youth would improve when the churches were more welcoming than the pool halls. James attended to the *developmental flow*, that is, the times and states when flow was constrained, and the way in which spirituality supports a leap of faith that jump-starts development.[1] Du Bois attended to the *fit* between young people and the sociomoral environment in which they grow up, especially when community and larger society create undue stress for youth. Recent studies, too, rely on theories that can be loosely grouped into (a) those that attend to the natural process, the developmental flow that characterizes learning, growth, and change; and (b) those that attend to the fit (and misfit) between vulnerable youth, social context, and moral norms.

DELINQUENCY, SPIRITUALITY, AND TRANSFORMATION

The Nature of Developmental Transformation

Among high school seniors, regardless of religiousness or spirituality, family structure or socioeconomic status, misbehavior peaks at about age 16 and declines steadily thereafter (Allen, Moore, & Kuperminc, 1997; Marsh, McFarlane, Allen, McElhaney, & Land, 2003; McNamara, 2001). Although more than 50% of adolescents in Western Europe and North America are likely to commit delinquent acts in any given year, nevertheless, most nonviolent delinquency is a time-limited adolescent phenomenon (Moffitt, 1993). Fewer than 10% of 12-year-olds report having lied to a teacher, committed vandalism, been truant from school, used drugs, gotten drunk, stolen something from a store, or gotten in trouble with the law in the prior year. By their midteens, as many as 60% in any given sample have admitted to a range of delinquent behavior, and by their mid-20s, most youth have "matured out" of delinquent misbehavior (Johnson, Li, et al., 2000). Recognizing that misbehavior is a common characteristic of adolescence is critical to formulating hypotheses about the connection between delinquency and spirituality. Religious conversion, delinquency, and declining church attendance are all typical of American adolescents. Longitudinal studies show that from one year to the next, young people change in their reported religiousness just as they change their behavior, their friends, and the color of their hair. Regnerus and Elder (2003) found that 33% of American adolescents reported changes in the personal importance of religion from one year to the next. Spiritual salience decreases between ages 12 and 18 in both Europe and the United States, but by the time they reach young adulthood, 81% of American young adults surveyed in Monitoring the Future (Johnson, Li, et al., 2000) rank spiritual beliefs as important or very important in their lives. Further, spiritual awakening, religious calling, and spiritual/religious commitment are more common in late adolescence than at any other time of life (Gorsuch, 1988).

Adolescence is a time of particularly turbulent developmental flow across and through bio-psycho-social-spiritual systems (Curtis, 2003). Just when adolescents become their most awkward, pimply-faced, voice-changing, hips-spreading, gangly-armed selves, they suddenly have the cognitive and social capacity to see themselves through the eyes of others (Edelstein, 1996; Selman, 2003). Just when the pressure of biological maturation overwhelms an emotional system subject to hormone-related fluctuations of self-regulation, the adolescent is aware of a longing for meaning, personal ideals, and connection to something greater than the self (Lerner, Brentano, Dowling, & Anderson, 2002). New neural growth and the closing of the corpus callosum allow for the proliferation of abstract thinking, a new consistency in emotional self-regulation, the integration of social perspective taking, moral judgment, and moral behavior (Damasio, 1998), as well as conversion experiences, revelations, and spiritual transformations

(King & Boyatzis, 2004; Reimer, 2003; Streib, 2003). These new developmental capacities come with an increased risk of emotional upheaval, moral misbehavior, meaninglessness, despair, and disintegration.

Transforming Beliefs

Developmental theories of religion, spirituality, and faith describe adolescence as a time of major questioning, rediscovery, and recommitment. Adolescents typically leave behind a conception of G-d and the Ultimate as One who can answer prayers, reward, and punish, and with whom one can negotiate, in favor of a conception of G-d and religiousness in which G-d has G-d's domain and I (or we humans) have ours (Fowler, 1981; Oser & Gmünder, 1991). Young people don't just give up their earlier, simple beliefs, however. They spend several years questioning what's true and how to know. According to Oser and Gmünder, the adolescent transition "presents a major shock which negates the previous patterns of reasoning and simultaneously initiates the acceptance of new elements and dimensions" (p. 73). In early adolescence, a youth "must try living without God, without a supernatural being" (p. 73). This is equally true of changes in moral judgment development in adolescence (Gregg, Gibbs, & Basinger, 1994; Hamil-Luker, Land, & Blau, 2004; Kerner, Holger, & Wegel, 2003). The transition from one moral and religious stage to another leaves youth vulnerable to mistakes as they test for what is good and who knows best, and are easily influenced by peers, media, and other factors. The developmental transition that characterizes adolescent religious and moral development may explain why—even in the presence of a moral community and a religious family with regular attendance and family religious practices—many youth do not appreciate the importance or personal relevance of moral norms (Benda & Corwyn, 2000).

Developmental Tasks of Adolescence

Autonomy, a Declaration of Independence. Many authors suggest that autonomy striving is related to baseline delinquency (Regnerus, 2003; Regnerus & Elder, 2003). Delinquency at this age can be a way of establishing one's own identity, one's right to choose, one's autonomy, and one's moral agency (Erikson, 1968; Markstrom-Adams & Spencer, 1994). "It's my body, and I can pierce it if I want to." Failure to question parental values and expectations, to merely adopt them as one's own, is said to be an unhealthy form of identity foreclosure (Marcia, 1996). In a longitudinal study of adolescent development, Miller and Stark (2002) found that adults who had violated the law moderately as teenagers had higher rates of well-being and social adjustment than either those who frequently violated the law as youth (including excessive drug and alcohol use), or those who were abstinent as teens.

People have assumed that adolescent rebellion, if unpleasant, was at least normal and healthy. In a series of qualitative and quantitative research projects, however, Marsh and colleagues (2003) demonstrated that developing a sense of autonomy and an independent identity does not imply rejecting parental values and expectations, but rather struggling within the context of a secure relationship. The Allen group videotaped moral dilemma discussions in family contexts and found that teens who have secure attachments to their parents, although they are likely to argue, disagree, and misbehave in early adolescence, are most likely, by midadolescence, to develop a stable, autonomous sense of self. An autonomous self in turn is associated with developing integrity—a sense of meaning that is often associated with spirituality—in early adulthood (Baltes, Glück, & Kunzmann, 2002; Blakeney, Blakeney, & Reich, 2005; Dowling et al., 2004; Elder & Conger, 2000; Pardini, Plante, Sherman, & Stump, 2000).

Belonging. Young people who are plagued by questions about the finite and the infinite find answers in both traditional and nontraditional groups (Roof, 2000). Youniss and his colleagues (Kerestes, Youniss, & Metz, 2004; Youniss, McLellan, & Yates, 1999) found that youth who participate in prosocial activities as members of a religious group have "transcendent" experiences that contribute to positive well-being and identity development. According to Streib

(1999), the growth of nontraditional religious participation may have its roots in the same developmental need to fit in as delinquency, sports teams, and civic involvement. The need to belong to a group that has a higher purpose may be an attraction of fundamentalism and alternative spiritually based groups among Christians, Muslims, and Jews. This hypothesis demands further testing.

DELINQUENCY, SPIRITUALITY, AND MORAL COMMUNITY

Much of the research on spirituality/religiousness looks at its ability to protect vulnerable youth, or change their developmental trajectory. This research suggests that spiritual attachment *and/or* a strong belief in G-d may strengthen or replace social, institutional, and normative connections for young people growing up in disintegrated families, neighborhoods, or societies (Hüsler, Egon, & Blakeney, 2003). Hirschi and Stark (1969) have argued that this was particularly true where religious institutional norms are embedded in a moral community with shared spiritual beliefs, such as Salt Lake City, Utah (Bainbridge, 1992; Stark & Bainbridge, 1997; Tittle & Welch, 1983; Van Fleet, Cockayne, & Fowles, 1999). That is, a personal spiritual connection that is consistent with the community's moral norms protects youth from long-term delinquency. However, religious affiliation alone without consistent moral community or spiritual connection does not deter adolescent misbehavior (Hirschi & Stark, 1969). Having religious peers, families, and role models is statistically associated with reduced likelihood of delinquency, but the direction of causation and the mechanisms are difficult to sort out (Beyers, Bates, Pettit, & Dodge, 2003; Kuntsche & Kuendig, 2003; Larson & Johnson, 1998; Markstrom, 1999).

Hirschi and Stark's important conclusion in their article "Hellfire and Delinquency" (1969) may help explain the strength of religious participation in African American communities. Johnson and his colleagues (Johnson, Jang, et al., 2000) examined neighborhood disorganization, religious participation, and delinquent activity among the 525 African American youth in their sample of 1,725 at-risk youth. They found that those youth from highly disorganized, high-crime neighborhoods who participated in religious institutions were less likely to become involved in delinquency than those youth who participated less or not at all. The more disorganization there was in the neighborhood, the more protective religion was. In general, African American youth who are religiously involved are less likely than their nonaffiliated peers to get in trouble with the law, get pregnant, or drop out of school (Ahmed & Toro, 2002; Markstrom, 1999).

How does religious involvement help? According to social control theory, African American religious institutions provide social, emotional, and material support, and thus integrate members—including neighborhood youth—into a supportive network within which there are mutual obligations and expectations (Durkheim, 1897/1951). Connection to the social network "constrains" the individual to act within a set of shared norms. Without social bonds—that is, without a sense of belonging—children engage in antisocial behavior (Chung, 2004; Chung, Hill, Hawkins, Gilchrist, & Nagin, 2002). Moral constraint is a traditional function of religious communities and institutions, but is there anything inherently spiritual about this constraining role, or is it a function of institutional belonging, regardless of the nature of the social institution?

Spiritual Connection Alters a Negative Trajectory

Although few studies directly examine spirituality *and* religiousness in relation to delinquent behavior, some research suggests that the two don't operate in the same way. In neighborhoods with high rates of social disorganization (crime, poverty, unemployment, drugs, "broken families," bad schools, and inadequate health care), religious attachments may provide critical mediating social networks (Chase-Lansdale, Gordon, Brooks-Gunn, & Klebanov, 1997; Chase-Lansdale, Gordon, Coley, Wakschlag, & Brooks-Gunn, 1999). Religious attachments can include both attachment to a religious institution (as in social control theory) and attachment to G-d or a Higher Power that gives life its ultimate meaning. In a study of 1,703 U.S. adolescents in

high-risk urban neighborhoods, Pearce et al. (2003) examined the ability of religious and spiritual values to mediate the likelihood that young people in high-crime neighborhoods would repeat the cycle of violent crime to which they were exposed. Youth for whom religion was important were less likely to get sucked into the intergenerational vortex of violence.

Religiousness, family relationships, exposure to violence, and conduct problems were measured at two time points. Youth who were exposed to the highest levels of violence and who had high levels of personal religious practice had less of an increase in conduct problems between Time 1 and Time 2. Under low and moderate exposure to violence, high levels of spirituality as well as good family relations lowered the rates of increased conduct problems. Good family relationships alone did not mitigate exposure to the highest levels of community violence. Paradoxically, at the highest levels of exposure and the highest levels of spirituality, there was an *increase* in conduct disorder. Finally, youth who had the highest rates of victimization were *less* likely to victimize others when they had high rates of personal prayer and reading religious literature, but were *more* likely to victimize others when they had high levels of spirituality (i.e., belief in the transcendent and one's interaction with the transcendent). That is, the most spiritual victims of violence had increased levels of violent behavior between the two testing points. Why?

Oppression, Exclusion, and a Spiritual Mission

From the point of view of social control theory, family and religious norms don't make sense in the face of unmitigated evil. Nearly half the youth in the Pearce et al. (2003) study witnessed shootings, knifings, and other acts of violence in the previous year, and about a third were threatened by or were victims of violence. The connection between high levels of spirituality, high levels of oppression, and acts of violence is not limited to inner-city American youth, Catholic youth in Northern Ireland, or Muslim fundamentalist youth. We can imagine that the same is true for adolescents in much of the Middle East, central Africa, and the former

Yugoslavia. Perhaps youth who are the most serious victims of violence delegitimize normative institutions that fail to protect them. People who see themselves as dis-integrated or outside the larger societal framework, including, for example, African American and Latino youth in the United States (Blakeney & Blakeney, 1991, 1992), and North African, Turkish, and Eastern European youth in Western Europe (Rommelspacher, 2002; Wetzels, 2003), may find that religious affiliation provides an alternate sociomoral network to that of the larger society from which they feel excluded (Nasir, 2004; Ogbu, 2003; Riegel, 2003). Spiritual beliefs offer hope, identity, and belonging (Streib, 1999)—but they limit delinquent behavior only to the extent that religious norms and societal norms are consistent. When societal norms don't protect minority or excluded youth from violence and oppression, spirituality may offer comfort (Hathaway & Pargament, 1990; Hill & Pargament, 2003). Alternately, however, spirituality may justify a mission as an agent of divine justice or retribution.

The increase in violent behavior among the most spiritual victims of violence in the Pearce et al. (2003) study and elsewhere might relate to divine retribution. Religious zeal may offer a transcendent path to young people who live in conditions of violent oppression (e.g., young fundamentalist suicide bombers). One way to make sense of bad things happening to good people is to "heed a calling" to see oneself as an agent of divine will, and thus justify revenge. In light of the history of youth involvement in religious crusades and current concerns with spiritual and moral justifications for intergroup violence and self-destructive behavior, this potential link between spirituality, moral meaning, and adolescent "misbehavior" demands further exploration.

Spirituality as Resilience: Coping with Stress and Strain

Three important recent studies illuminate the ability of spiritual beliefs to change negative trajectories (downward spirals) of at-risk youth. Wills et al. (2003), in a sample of 1,182 early adolescents at risk, found that spiritual beliefs had a buffering effect for young people. In the face of stressful life events, youth who were high on the religious/spiritual dimensions were

somewhat less likely to use drugs and alcohol than those who were low on the religious/spiritual dimensions. Pearce et al. (2003) tested 1,703 sixth- and eighth-grade youngsters who had been exposed to or were victims of serious violence. Youth who prayed more were less likely to be violent in the subsequent year. Regenerus and Elder (2003) found that personal religiousness (spirituality) was associated with a change in developmental trajectories for the most vulnerable middle-class, protected youth, as well.

While all three studies found that spirituality at Time 1 was associated with decreased likelihood of delinquent behavior at Time 2, the question of causation remains unanswered. There are several plausible hypotheses that merit careful testing. (1) Youth who are most vulnerable are those for whom the transition from childhood to adolescence is particularly tumultuous (Kegan, 1982), entirely apart from spirituality. (2) Troubled early adolescents may have had a revelation or an awakening that changed the course of their behavior. (3) Having changed the course of their behavior, youth felt "saved," redeemed, grateful, and thus became more spiritually faithful. (4) An outside factor (e.g., change in family or classroom environment) could have influenced both changes simultaneously.

In sum, these studies suggest that spiritual meaning offers a way to transcend the turbulence of adolescence, especially for drug-using inner-city youth, youth from disorganized neighborhoods, and protected but vulnerable middle-class youth. Further, in areas of highest crime, even moderate religious participation provides a sanctuary. Youth who are most vulnerable to delinquent trajectories, who are less likely to learn from their mistakes, experience high levels of stress. The inability to regulate stress is related to continued patterns of problem behavior and to the development of moral disorder (Blakeney & Blakeney, 1992). More research is needed to determine how spiritual transcendence and moral sanctuaries interact to transform delinquent trajectories, especially in morally disordered communities. This issue is particularly important because, as we have seen, not all delinquent young people manage to transform their lives—even those who have strong faith.

What is known about the spiritual and moral meaning of resistant patterns of misbehavior in adolescence?

No Fit, No Flow, No Transformation

One way to better understand the intimate relationship between moral development and spirituality is by looking at youth in whom the two are not integrated. Young people with early onset, resistant misbehavior tend to be more aggressive than other teens, have fewer social skills (Beyers et al., 2003; Thornberry, Ireland, & Smith, 2001), and are more resistant to intervention. The habitual patterns of misbehavior of seriously troubled teens (e.g., fighting, stealing, running away) are structurally and functionally related to predictable disturbances in moral reasoning (Blakeney, 1984; Blakeney & Blakeney, 1996). Resistant patterns of moral misbehavior act out unresolved moral claims of caring, autonomy, fairness, and truthfulness. Troubled young people get stuck because they rely on *either* thinking or feeling; *either* self-regard or other regard (Selman, 2003). Some use "logical thinking" to justify their misbehavior ("It was dumb of him to leave the keys in the car. I was just trying to teach him a lesson"). Others use their feelings ("I was mad, that's why I hit her. You get mad. Everybody gets mad"). The two domains are not integrated, so there is no feedback loop and, hence, no learning from mistakes (Bandura, Barbaranelli, Caprara, & Pastorelli, 1996; Oser & Spychiger, 2005) and therefore no transformation. Moral development depends on the integration of feeling and thinking in the social context. A moral split or stuckness affects (and can be affected by) spiritual connection.

In sum, in the face of high levels of disorganization in the family (Hanlon, Bateman, Simon, O'Grady, & Carswell, 2004) and community (Pearce et al., 2003)—in other words, where there is a problem of "fit"—problems in the flow of moral development help explain the potential for spiritual connection and spiritual transcendence to alter a delinquent trajectory (Piedmont, 2004).

Recovering Developmental Integrity: Leaps of Faith

There is very little quantitative research on the role of spirituality in changing a delinquent trajectory, but faith-based treatment programs provide fertile ground for generating hypotheses about the way spirituality works in recovery among adults. Blakeney and colleagues (2003, 2004) found that 75% of the residents at Beit T'Shuvah, a faith-based alcohol and drug treatment program, exhibited developmental splits between religious, moral, and affective development. After 6 weeks in treatment, there is a regression in moral judgment, accompanied by the loss of an antisocietal moral orientation. Within 4 months, social and/or spiritual aspects of religiousness increased, and after 4 to 6 months, moral judgment and affective development became increasingly integrated with and transformed by ultimate meaning. In other words, spirituality worked to recover moral functioning by integrating cognitive moral judgment and emotional self-regulation that has been observed both neurologically and behaviorally (Adolphs, Tranel, & Damasio, 2003) so that residents could act in ways consistent with their own highest levels of moral judgment. The role of faith in recovery is consistent with findings in a faith-based prison experiment in Brazil (Johnson, 2002), as well as with findings in faith-based recovery programs such as Alcoholics Anonymous (Avants, Marcotte, Arnold, & Margolin, 2003; Miller, 1998; Pardini et al., 2000).

Summary

A Theory of Delinquency, Spirituality, and Adolescent Transformation

We come, at last, to applying the theory of developmental integrity to our proposed model of delinquency as spiritual missteps. Like social control and social learning theories, the model takes into account the youth's fit within family, cultural community, and nation-state. Like developmental flow models, it attends to developmental stage, state, and tasks. Most important, the model attends to moral development and spiritual transformation on the micro (individual) and macro (social) levels.

Flow. We have said that both delinquency and spirituality characterize adolescent development. Development is a process of reciprocal interweaving. Like making a woven bread (whether it is called challah or tresse or zopf), ingredients (parents, genes) are mixed and the dough is kneaded and left to rise (family, culture, community). From the raised dough, three ropes are formed—call them three strands of development. They are braided together and left to rise again. Put in the oven at the proper temperature for the right amount of time, the strands rise again, integrate, and bake together into a single, solid, shapely whole. The outside retains the image of the original strands, but sliced open, the loaf has substantial integrity. Early adolescents have adultlike thoughts, feelings, questions, desires, but they are still rising, not yet whole and integrated. Paradoxically, delinquent misbehavior may represent the developmental leavening through which youth rise.

Fit. Delinquent behavior increases when there is a problem of fit between the adolescent and her or his family, community, society. Attachment to religious institutions and to spiritual meaning may provide a compensatory holding environment, a potential space where young people can grow spiritually. Some children grow up in families and/or neighborhoods that do not provide basic nurturing needs. This includes communities where children are not protected from physical danger, where their basic needs for survival are not met or are not met equitably; where certain children are excluded, not wanted either as individuals or because of the group to which they belong; where they are caught between two sets of cultural norms, either explicit or implicit; and so on. It also includes middle-class, protected youth, for whom stress may come from within as well as without. There is also the possibility that children from some groups experience conflicts between the norms and values of their group, and those of the larger society and its laws (e.g., Turkish youth in Germany). This includes the recognition, in adolescence, that the public norms do not apply in family, community, societal practice—or are unfairly applied.

Three Delinquent Trajectories, Three Spiritual Connections

Spirituality, particularly as embodied in religious practice, helps young people fit in and find a meaningful place for themselves, with a set of moral values and norms that (1) serve as a guide and (2) yoke them to a larger, higher purpose and meaning. There are three developmental trajectories wherein spirit may function in three slightly different ways.

The Testing Trajectory. For the range of "normal" teens, delinquent behavior is a way of testing what is true, what is good, who I am, and what is ultimately meaningful. Rates of moral, religious, and faith development vary between and within adolescents, who are, at the same time subject to fits and starts of emotional self-regulation. These developmental changes affect adolescents' ability to apply their own best judgment to their behavior from moment to moment. The potential to learn from mistakes and be "better" reflects what some refer to as the spiritual capacity for transformation.

Stuck at the Crossroads. If adolescent misbehavior persists, it signals the inability to integrate thinking, feeling, and behavior in a particular social context. There is no feedback loop, no learning from mistakes. When a child is stuck in a repeated pattern of misbehavior, she becomes demoralized. It is as if her spirit is trapped. Many such children struggle throughout their adolescence, yet eventually find meaning and connection in their lives.

Split. If youth become truly demoralized (as is the case with drug addiction, clinical depression, severe abuse and intractable social conflicts, for example), their developmental systems lose their elasticity, their ability to bounce back. Nevertheless, the human spirit being what it is, the self-system adapts by strengthening one domain over another. In these cases, a leap of faith in adulthood may reignite development and the potential to recover integrity, albeit later in life.

DIRECTIONS FOR FURTHER RESEARCH

There is increasing evidence that a spiritual connection, a sense of ultimate meaning, is itself a developmental project in adolescence, yet there is little research that examines *how* spirituality helps youth integrate moral norms and a sense of self, *how* spirituality and delinquent behavior interact in the process of development. The next area of inquiry for a spiritual theory of delinquency is to understand this process of transformation. This will help us understand how personal religiousness (prayer, faith, spirituality, a commitment to something larger than the self, meaningfulness) alters developmental trajectories in the ways that we have seen. It also helps to account for the paradoxical and troubling findings that the most spiritual victims of severe violence are more prone to violence than less intensely spiritual victims; that some youth have resistant patterns of habitual moral misbehavior regardless of spiritual and religious exposure; and that spirituality is a better bridge to moral behavior for African American than for Euro-American youth. The three trajectories outlined earlier suggest alternate paths to the Sacred: the positive, *Testing,* trajectory, in which young people learn from their mistakes, and correct themselves along the way, in line with the good (this trajectory is reflected in general surveys showing that church and prayer give kids an edge against delinquency); the negative, *Stuck at the Crossroads,* trajectory, in which young people only learn what is good by getting stuck in the bad and then actively seeking the alternative (this trajectory fits studies showing that for the most vulnerable youth a connection to the Divine, to something greater than the self, gives them something to hang on to through the storm); and the *Split,* divided soul, who doesn't learn from mistakes or seek an alternative, but is stuck in the split until awakened from his or her stupor, sometimes through a head-on collision with the self. In the case of divided souls, a spiritual awakening creates a safe place where emotions and cognition, who I am and what I believe is right, true, and good, can be brought together, through such transformative paths as redemption, return, and forgiveness. Given our conjecture about the way in which spirituality helps us understand delinquency, there are three recommendations to guide further research.

First, qualitative, cross-cultural, longitudinal research is needed to test the hypothesis that the relationship between spirituality and delinquency can be illuminated by attending to the three outlined developmental trajectories. Initially, hypotheses can be refined through cross-sectional research that examines critical points in developmental trajectories where crossroads, stuckness, and awakenings are likely to occur.

Second, we need an overarching construct that can operationalize cross-domain integrity, including the relationship between moral, affective, and spiritual development. A measure of developmental integrity allows us to account for, and attend to, apparent developmental anomalies, to integrate recent neurological and psychological findings, and to examine spirituality across a range of social, cultural, and religious contexts.

Third, we need a theory and construct that attend to macro as well as micro levels. On the individual, micro, level, delinquent behavior is "noise" that signals that something in the developmental self-system needs correcting. Youth who learn from their mistakes renorm their behavior (Oser & Spychiger, 2005). This creates the opportunity for transformation. Similarly, on the macro level, adolescent delinquency is a wake-up call to society, signaling normative problems that need inspection and perhaps renorming. When half the youth in a given sample regularly violate particular norms it may point to corruption in the social system. An epidemic of cheating, for example, suggests an imbalance between goals and means. An increase in youth violence and bullying may reflect an unspoken but apparent societal norm that sanctions the misuse of power and violence. What is the spiritual state of a society in which half the school-age youth smoke marijuana and drink alcohol? What of a society where adolescents enthusiastically volunteer for war and terror? On the macro level, we need to ask ourselves what message is being shouted by the graffiti on the wall.

If we attend to the individual child in the contexts of family, community, and society through a lens that looks at the developmental process as the progressive transformation and integration of affect, cognition, and ultimate meaning, we can see delinquent behavior in a more differentiated and helpful way. Delinquent behavior can be the way a teen asks what is good and what is true, as well as "who cares?" "Who am I?" and "How should I be?" Delinquent behavior can also signal the stuck places where a child needs help in sorting out identity, morality, and ultimate meaning. Finally, delinquent behavior can signal a split between a teenager's day-to-day behavior and her or his spiritual path. Social science can illuminate much of how delinquency functions on the spiritual journey of adolescence, and reciprocally, a spiritual focus may help account for the indirect and anomalous relationship between adolescent misbehavior and moral development.

As the hip-hop artist Shia B has written (Oser, 2004), "The devil is complex. In a contest with God, the devil may be God's accomplice."

NOTE

1. Developmental flow is not to be confused with Czikszentmihalyi's conception of "flow," which is related to creativity and characterized by a more integrated process. Developmental flow is a process of integrating that includes periods of stability and calm, and periods of rapid change. For more on "flow" see Czikszentmihalyi (1995).

REFERENCES

Adolphs, R., Tranel, D., & Damasio, A. R. (2003). Dissociable neural systems for recognizing emotions. *Brain and Cognition, 52*(1), 61–69.

Ahmed, S., & Toro, P. A. (2002). *Religiosity and ethnicity as moderators of substance abuse in at-risk adolescents.* Retrieved January 7, 2004, from http://sun.science.wayne.edu/~ptoro/swjpsp1a.pdf

Allen, J. P., Morre, C. M., & Kuperminc, G. P. (1997). Developmental approaches to understanding adolescent deviance. In S. S. Luthar (Ed.), *Developmental psychopathology: Perspectives on adjustment, risk and disorder* (pp. 548–567). Cambridge, UK: Cambridge University Press.

Avants, S. K., Marcotte, D., Arnold, R., & Margolin, A. (2003). Spiritual beliefs, world assumptions, and HIV risk behavior among heroin and cocaine users. *Psychology of Addictive Behaviors, 17*(2), 159–162.

Bainbridge, W. S. (1992). Crime, delinquency and religion. In J. F. Schumaker (Ed.), *Religion and mental health.* New York: Oxford University Press.

Baltes, P. B., Glück, J., & Kunzmann, U. (2002). Wisdom: Its structure and function in regulating successful life span development. In C. R. Snyder & S. J. Lopez (Eds.), *Handbook of positive psychology* (pp. 327–347). Oxford, UK: Oxford University Press.

Bandura, A., Barbaranelli, C., Caprara, G. V., & Pastorelli, C. (1996). Mechanisms of moral disengagement in the exercise of moral agency. *Journal of Personality and Social Psychology, 71,* 364–374.

Benda, B. B., & Corwyn, R. F. (1997). A test of a model with reciprocal effects between religiosity and various forms of delinquency using 2-stage least squares regression. *Journal of Social Service Research, 22,* 27–52.

Benda, B. B., & Corwyn, R. F. (2000). A test of the validity of delinquency syndrome construct in a homogeneous sample. *Journal of Adolescence, 23,* 497–511.

Beyers, J. M., Bates, J. E., Pettit, G. S., & Dodge, K. A. (2003). Neighborhood structure, parenting processes, and the development of youths' externalizing behaviors: A multilevel analysis. *American Journal of Community Psychology, 31*(1/2), 35–53.

Blakeney, C. D. (1984). *Moral judgement disturbance and moral misbehavior.* Unpublished doctoral dissertation, Harvard University, Cambridge, MA.

Blakeney, C. D., & Blakeney, R. F. (1991). Pluralism and the dilemma of discordance among Blacks and Jews. In F. C. Power & D. K. Lapsley (Eds.), *The challenge of pluralism* (pp. 65–102). Notre Dame, IN: Notre Dame University Press.

Blakeney, R. F., Blakeney, C.D., & Maiello, C. (2003, October). *Recovering developmental integrity in addiction treatment.* Paper presented at the 10th International Conference on Treatment of Addictive Behaviours, Heidelberg, Germany.

Blakeney, C. D., Blakeney, R. F., & Reich, K. H. (2005). Leaps of faith: The role of spirituality in recovering integrity among Jewish alcoholics and drug addicts. *Mental Health, Religion & Culture, 8*(1), 63–77.

Blakeney, R. F., & Blakeney, C. D. (1992). Growing pains: Toward a theory of stress and moral conflict. *Journal of Counseling and Values, 36,* 162–177.

Blakeney, R. F., & Blakeney, C. D. (1996). A therapeutic just community for troubled girls. Reclaiming children and youth. *Journal of Emotional and Behavioral Problems, 5,* 163–166, 172.

Blakeney, R. F. & Blakeney, C. D. (in press). Adolescent spirituality and resistance to alcohol and drug use. In E. M. Dowling & W.G. Scarlett (Eds.), *Encyclopedia of spiritual and religious development in childhood and adolescence.* Thousand Oaks, CA: Sage.

Blakeney, C. D., Rihs-Middel, M., & Blakeney, R. F. (2004). *Recovering developmental integrity: A test of the addictive syndrome hypothesis. Gambling and addictions: Common causes, managing consequences.* Harvard Medical School, Institute for Research on Pathological Gambling and Related Disorders, Division on Addictions.

Chase-Lansdale, P. L., Gordon, R. A., Brooks-Gunn, J., & Klebanov, P. K. (1997). Neighborhood and family influences on the intellectual and behavioral competence of preschool and early school-age children. In G. Brooks-Gunn, J. Duncan, & J. L. Aber (Eds.), *Neighborhood poverty: Vol. 1. Context and consequences for children* (pp. 79–118). New York: Russell Sage Foundation.

Chase-Lansdale, P. L., Gordon, R. A., Coley, R. L., Wakschlag, L. S., & Brooks-Gunn, J. (1999). Young African-American multigenerational families in poverty: The contexts, exchanges, and processes of their lives. In E. M. Hetherington (Ed.), *Coping with divorce, single parenting, and remarriage: A risk and resiliency perspective* (pp. 165–191). Mahwah, NJ: Erlbaum.

Chung, I.-J. (2004). A conceptual framework for understanding the relationship between poverty and antisocial behavior: Focusing on psychosocial mediating mechanisms 1. *Journal of Primary Prevention, 24*(3), 375–400.

Chung, I.-J., Hill, K. G., Hawkins, J. D., Gilchrist, L. D., & Nagin, D. (2002). Childhood predictors of offense trajectories. *Journal of Research in Crime and Delinquency, 39,* 60–90.

Curtis, J. W., & Cicchetti, D. (2003). Moving research on resilience into the 21st century: Theoretical and methodological considerations in examining the biological contributors to resilience. *Development and Psychopathology, 15,* 773–810.

Czikszentmihaly, M. (1995). *Flow: Das Geheimnis des Glücks.* Stuttgart, Germany: Klett-Cotta.

Damasio, A. R. (1998). Emotion in the perspective of an integrated nervous system. *Brain Research Reviews, 26,* 83–86.

Dowling, E., Gestsdottir, S., Anderson, P., von Eye, A., Almerigi, J., & Lerner, R. M. (2004). Structural relations among spirituality, religiosity, and thriving in adolescence. *Applied Developmental Science, 8*(1), 7–16.

Du Bois, W. E. B. (1996). *The Philadelphia Negro: A social study. Together with a special report on domestic service by Isabel Eaton.* Philadelphia: University of Pennsylvania Press. (Original work published 1899)

Durkheim, E. (1951). *Suicide: A study in sociology.* Glencoe, IL: Free Press. (Original work published 1897)

Edelstein, W. (1996). The social construction of cognitive development. In G. C. Noam & K. W. Fischer (Eds.), *Development and vulnerability in close relationships* (pp. 91–112). Mahwah, NJ: Erlbaum.

Elder, G. H. Jr., & Conger, R. D. (2000). *Children of the land: Adversity and success in rural America.* Chicago: University of Chicago Press.

Erikson, E. H. (1968). *Identity, youth and crisis.* New York: Norton.

Fowler, J. W. (1981). *Stages of faith: The psychology of human development and the quest for meaning.* New York: Harper & Row.

Furrow, J. L., King, P. E., & White, K. (2004). Religion and positive youth development: Identity, meaning, and prosocial concerns. *Applied Developmental Science, 8*(1), 17–26.

Gorsuch, R. L. (1988). Psychology of religion. *Annual Review of Psychology, 39,* 201–221.

Gregg, V. R., Gibbs, J. C., & Basinger, K. (1994). Patterns of developmental delay in moral judgment by male and female delinquents. *Merrill-Palmer Quarterly, 40,* 538–553.

Hamil-Luker, J., Land, D. C., & Blau, J. (2004). Diverse trajectories of cocaine use through early adulthood among rebellious and socially conforming youth. *Social Science Research, 33,* 300–321.

Hanlon, T. E., Bateman, R., Simon, B. D., O'Grady, K. E., & Carswell, S. B. (2004). Antecedents and correlates of deviant activity in urban youth manifesting behavioral problems. *Journal of Primary Prevention, 24*(3), 285–309.

Hathaway, W. L., & Pargament, K. (1990). Intrinsic religiousness, religious coping, and psychosocial competence: A covariance structure analysis. *Journal for the Scientific Study of Religion, 29,* 423–441.

Hill, P. C., & Pargament, K.I. (2003). Advances in the conceptualization and measurement of religion and spirituality: Implications for physical and mental health research. *American Psychologist, 58,* 64–74.

Hirschi, T., & Stark, R. (1969). Hellfire and delinquency. *Social Problems, 17,* 202–213.

Hüsler, G., Egon, W., & Blakeney, R. F. (2003). *Morbidity and co-morbidity in a Swiss sample of youth at risk.* Report to the Bundesamt für Gesundheit, Bern, Switzerland.

James, W. (1961). *The varieties of religious experience.* New York: Collier. (Original work published 1902)

Johnson, B. R. (2002). Assessing the impact of religious programs and prison industry on recidivism: An exploratory study. *Texas Journal of Corrections* (February), 7–11.

Johnson, B. R., Jang, S. J., Li, S. D., & Larson, D. B. (2000). The invisible institution and black youth crime: The church as an agency of local social control. *Journal of Youth and Adolescence, 29,* 479–498.

Johnson, B. R., Li, S. D., Larson, D. B., & McCullough, M. (2000). A systematic review of the religiosity and delinquency literature. *Journal of Contemporary Criminal Justice, 16,* 32–52.

Kegan, R. (1982). *The evolving self.* Cambridge, MA: Harvard University Press.

Kerestes, M., Youniss, J., & Metz, E. (2004). Longitudinal patterns of religious perspective and civic engagement. *Applied Developmental Science, 8*(1), 39–46.

Kerner, H.-J., Holger, S., & Wegel, M. (2003). Erziehung, Religion und Wertorientierungen bei jungen Gefangenen. *Zeitschrift für Jugendkriminalrecht und Jugendhilfe, 3,* 233–240.

King, P. E., & Boyatzis. C. J. (2004). Exploring adolescent spiritual and religious development: Current and future theoretical and empirical perspectives. *Applied Developmental Science, 8*(1), 2–6.

Kuntsche, E., & Kuendig, H. (2003, October). *What is worse? A hierarchy of family related risk factors predicting alcohol use in adolescence.* Paper presented at the Schweizerische Gesellschaft für Psychologie, Bern, Switzerland.

Larson, D. B., & Johnson, B. R. (1998). *Religion: The forgotten factor in cutting youth crime and saving at-risk urban youth* (Jeremiah Project Report 98–2). New York: Manhattan Institute for Policy Research.

Lerner, R. M., Brentano, C., Dowling, E. M., & Anderson, P. M. (2002). Positive youth development: Thriving as the basis of personhood and civil society. *New Directions for Youth Development, 95,* 11–34.

Marcia, J. E. (1996). Development and validation of ego-identity status. *Journal of Personality and Social Psychology, 3,* 551–558.

Markstrom, C. A. (1999). Religious involvement and adolescent psychosocial development. *Journal of Adolescence, 22,* 205–221.

Markstrom-Adams, C., & Spencer, M. B. (1994). A model for identity intervention with minority adolescents. In S. Archer (Ed.), *Interventions for adolescent identity development* (pp. 84–102). Thousand Oaks, CA: Sage.

Marsh, P., McFarland, F. C., Allen, J. P., McElhaney, K. B., & Land, D. (2003). Attachment, autonomy, and multifinality in adolescent internalizing and risky behavioral symptoms. *Development and Psychopathology, 15,* 451–467.

McNamara, P. (2001). Religion and the frontal lobes. In J. Andresen (Ed.), *Religion in mind: Cognitive perspectives on religious belief, ritual, and experience* (pp. 237–256). Cambridge, MA: Harvard University Press.

Miller, A., & Stark, R. (2002). Gender and religiousness: Can socialization explanations be saved? *American Journal of Sociology, 107*(6), 1399–1423.

Miller, W. R. (1998). Researching the spiritual dimensions of alcohol and other drug problems. *Addiction, 93,* 979–990.

Moffitt, T. E. (1993). Adolescence-limited and life-course-persistent antisocial behavior: A developmental taxonomy. *Psychological Review, 100,* 674–701.

Nasir, N. S. (2004). Halal-ing the child: Re-framing identities of resistance in an urban Muslim School. *Harvard Educational Review, 74*(2), 153–174.

Newton, I. (1995). *The principia.* Amherst, MA: Prometheus. (Original work published 1687)

Ogbu, J. (2003). *Black American students in an affluent suburb: A study of academic disengagement.* Mahwah, NJ: Erlbaum.

Oser, F. (2004). On becoming moral: How negative experience can inspire the moral person. In W. Veugelers & F. Oser (Eds.), *Teaching in moral and democratic education* (pp. 15–42). Bern: Peter Lang.

Oser, F., & Gmünder, P. (1991). *Religious judgment: A developmental approach.* Birmingham, AL: Religious Education Press.

Oser, F., & Spychiger, M. (2005). *Lernen ist Schmerzhaft: Zur Theories des Negativen Praxis der Fehlerkultur.* Munich: Beltz.

Pardini, D. A., Plante, T. G., Sherman, A., & Stump, J. E. (2000). Religious faith and spirituality in substance abuse recovery. *Journal of Substance Abuse Treatment, 19,* 347–354.

Pearce, M. J., Jones, S. M., Scwab-Stone, M. E., & Ruchkin, V. (2003). The protective effects of religiousness and parent involvement on the development of conduct problems among youth exposed to violence. *Child Development, 74*(6), 1682–1696.

Piedmont, R. L. (2004). Spiritual transcendence as a predictor of psychosocial outcome from an outpatient substance abuse program. *Psychology of Addictive Behaviors, 18*(3), 213–222.

Regnerus, M. (2003). Linked lives, faith, and behavior: Intergenerational religious influence on adolescent delinquency. *Journal for the Scientific Study of Religion, 42*(2), 189–203.

Regnerus, M. D., & Elder, G. H. (2003). Religion and vulnerability among low-risk adolescents. *Social Science Research, 32,* 633–658.

Reimer, K. S. (2003). Committed to caring: Transformation in adolescent moral identity. *Applied Developmental Science, 7,* 129–137.

Riegel, C. (2003). *Im Kampf um Zugehörigkeit und Anerkennung: Orientierungen und Handlungsformen von jungen Migrantinnen. Eine qualitativ-empirische Untersuchung.* University of Tübingen, Germany.

Rommelspacher, B. (2002). *Annerkennnung und Ausgrenzung.* Frankfurt, Germany: Campus Verlag.

Roof, W. C. (2000). *Spiritual marketplace: Baby boomers and the remaking of American religion.* Princeton, NJ: Princeton University Press.

Selman, R. L. (2003). *The promotion of social awareness.* New York: Russell Sage Foundation.

Stark, R., & Bainbridge, S. (1997). *Religion, deviance, and social control.* New York: Routledge.

Streib, H. J. (1999). Off-road religion? A narrative approach to fundamentalist and occult orientations of adolescents. *Journal of Adolescence, 22,* 255–267.

Streib, H. J. (2003). Variety and complexity of religious development: Perspectives for the 21st century. In P. H. M. P. Roelofsma, J. M. T. Corveleyn, & J. W. Van Saane (Eds.), *One hundred years of psychology of religion: Issues and trends in a century long quest* (pp. 123–138). Amsterdam: Vrije Universiteit University Press.

Thornberry, T., Ireland, T., & Smith, T. A. (2001). The importance of timing: The varying impact of childhood and adolescent maltreatment on multiple problem outcomes. *Development and Psychopathology, 13,* 957–979.

Tittle, C. R., & Welch, M. R. (1983). Religiosity and deviance: Toward a contingency theory of constraining effects. *Social Forces, 61,* 653–682.

Van Fleet, R. K., Cockayne, J., & Fowles, T. R. (1999). *Examining religion as a preventive factor to delinquency.* Salt Lake City: State of Utah, Department of Justice.

Wetzels, P. (2003, October). *Religion and criminality.* Paper presented at the Third Conference on Migration, Culture Conflict, and Crime, Istanbul, Turkey.

Wills, T. A., Yaeger, A. M., & Sandy, J. M. (2003). Buffering effect of religiosity for adolescent substance use. *Psychology of Addictive Behaviors, 17*(1), 24–31.

Youniss, J., McLellan, J. A., & Yates, M. (1999). Religion, community service, and identity in American youth. *Journal of Adolescence, 22,* 243–253.

27

SPIRITUAL DEVELOPMENT AND ADOLESCENT WELL-BEING AND THRIVING

PAMELA EBSTYNE KING

PETER L. BENSON

Perhaps one of the reasons adolescent spirituality has begun to capture the attention of the public and the academy is the growing body of research associating spirituality and religion with positive adolescent development (Bridges & Moore, 2002; Eccles & Gootman, 2002; Scales & Leffert, 2004). Empirical and theoretical literatures suggest a strong relationship between spirituality and adolescent well-being or thriving. Spirituality and religion have not only been associated with positive physical health (see Oman & Thoresen, chapter 28, this volume), the reduction of risk behaviors (see Blakeney & Blakeney, chapter 26, this volume), and the increase in resiliency (see Crawford, Wright, & Masten, chapter 25, this volume), but also with the presence of indicators of positive development. This chapter summarizes existing theoretical and empirical work that offers insight into the relationship between spiritual development and adolescent well-being.

Within this chapter spirituality and religion are considered as independent but overlapping constructs. *Spirituality* refers to a universal human capacity or a quality of a person's character, personality, or disposition with tendencies toward transcendence or connectedness beyond the self. It is often related to a manner of living that is carried out with a deep awareness of self, others, and the divine (John E. Fetzer Institute, 1999). This awareness yields a sense of meaning or purpose in life that provides direction or guidance, often at an existential level (King, 2003). *Spiritual development* can thus be defined as "the process of growing the intrinsic human capacity for self-transcendence, in which the self is embedded in something greater than the self, including the sacred. It propels the search for connectedness, meaning, purpose, and contribution. It is shaped both within and outside of religious traditions, beliefs, and practices" (Benson, Roehlkepartain, & Rude, 2003, p. 207).

Spirituality is often described in personal or experiential forms, whereas religiousness includes personal beliefs as well as institutional beliefs and practices. Borrowing from Koenig, McCullough, and Larson (2001), we refer to religion as an organized system of beliefs, practices, rituals, and symbols that facilitates closeness to the sacred or transcendent (God, higher power, or ultimate truth/reality) and fosters an understanding of an individual's relationship and responsibility to others in living together in community. As such, *religiousness* refers to the extent to which an individual has a relationship with a particular institutionalized doctrine about a supernatural power, a relationship that occurs through affiliation with an organized faith and participation in its prescribed rituals (Reich, Oser, & Scarlett, 1999). *Religious development,* then, is the growing relationship between an individual and a particular institutionalized doctrine and tradition related to a divine being, supernatural other, or absolute truth.

Interest in positive adolescent development has gained momentum in the past decade (Benson, 1990; Damon, 2004; Eccles & Gootman, 2002; Lerner, 2004). Consequently, scholars have pursued research in positive developmental outcomes such as well-being and thriving. Well-being is often used as an indicator of general mental health and can refer to positive affect, happiness, and life satisfaction or to positive functioning (Keyes & Haidt, 2003). For our use within this chapter *well-being* refers to general positive outcomes in childhood and adolescence.

Thriving, on the other hand, is a specific term that refers to more than positive functioning. Presumed in an understanding of thriving is the notion of contribution to the common good. A thriving young person not only grows and flourishes as an individual but also contributes to family, community, and/or society (Benson, 1997a; King et al., in press; Lerner, Dowling, & Anderson, 2003; Scales, Benson, Leffert, & Blyth, 2000). As such, thriving refers to positive development that is characterized over time by a pattern of functioning indicative of the individual's ability to adapt to environmental opportunities, demands, and restrictions in a way that best satisfies the individual's needs and also benefits society. Thriving youth show evidence not only of the absence of negative behaviors but also of indicators of positive development, such as school engagement, commitment to helping others, positive adult relationships, self-esteem, overcoming adversity, and valuing diversity (Scales et al., 2000).

Berger and Berger (1983) contend that religious congregations serve as mediating institutions that promote responsible individuals who sustain democratic society. This is not surprising given the prosocial values typically present within religion. Religions provide an environment in which youth can experience the "self" embedded within a larger context that enables the "caring, compassion, and variants of 'we' [to] temper the rampant pursuit of 'me'" (Benson, 1997b, p. 8). Faith communities embody a prosocial worldview that values the sanctity of individual and communal life. They provide exemplars and experiences that enable youth to internalize a sense of self that is defined in relation to other. They provide youth with an environment of intergenerational support that can foster values, meaning, identity, and a sense of belonging and connectedness beyond themselves. As such, religion serves as what Garbarino (1995) refers to as spiritual anchors, "institutions of the soul that connect children and teenagers to the deeper meanings of life and provide solid answers to the existential questions: Who am I? What is the meaning of life?" (p. 150). Youth need contexts in which to grapple with the spiritual issues of understanding their purpose in life, what they believe, and their place in the world. Religion and spirituality may provide a distinct context in which a young person can explore these issues that are critical to commitment to well-being and thriving.

THEORETICAL APPROACHES

Although empirical research generally documents a positive relationship between spirituality/religion and well-being, theoretical formulations of this association are scattered at best (King & Furrow, 2004; Smith, 2003). This section reviews existing conceptual explanations of the relationships between spirituality and religion and well-being.

Religious Experience and Conversion

In the early days of the study of the psychology of religion, religion was understood to bring about a positive reordering in the lives of adherents either through religious experiences or conversion. James (1902/1958) recognized that an individual's experiences with religion might bring about resolve, understanding, and positive change in the life of the individual. He understood that an individual's subjective experience with religion, occurring in such feelings as solemnity, seriousness, and transcendence, had reordering powers on the individual that in turn gave him or her new resolution and understanding.

Several early pioneers in the field used the concept of conversion to explain how religion promoted well-being in young people. In his defining text *Adolescence,* Hall (1904) devoted an entire chapter to religious awakenings in adolescents because he believed that religious conversion was a "natural, normal, universal, and necessary" part of adolescence (p. 301). Starbuck (1899) found that for converts "the joy, the relief, and the acceptance are qualities of feelings, perhaps, which give the truest picture of what is going on in conversion—the free exercise of new powers, an escape from something, and the birth into Larger life" (p. 122). Since then, research has found that conversion is related to increased openness, better relationships with others, greater emotional responsivity, a heightened sense of personal satisfaction and happiness, and positive identity formation (Spilka, Hood, Hunsberger, & Gorsuch, 2003). Smith (2003) argues that spiritual experiences such as conversion or answers to prayer often legitimate or reinforce their religious moral order for adolescents. Research suggests that within adult populations, converts appear to be better adjusted than nonconverts (see Hood, Spilka, Hunsberger, & Gorsuch, 1996, for a systematic review of this literature).

Religion, Spirituality, Identity, and Thriving

More recently, a developmental systems perspective offers insight on how spirituality motivates young people to contribute to something greater than themselves and is therefore at the core of the thriving process (see Lerner, Alberts, Anderson, & Dowling, chapter 5, this volume). According to developmental systems theory, youth whose interactions with their contexts are adaptive commit to a sense of identity that yields fidelity to an ideology that promotes reciprocity with their family, community, and society. This signifies the integration of moral and civic identities and promotes a commitment to contribute to the good of others and society (Furrow, King,

& White, 2004; King & Furrow, 2003; Youniss, McLellan, & Yates, 1999). Young people thrive when their moral and civic identities involve them in valuing and taking action that contributes to a world beyond themselves. Such awareness and responsibility are described as transcendent or spiritual sensibilities.

In this sense, spirituality is recognized as an orientation that involves the transcendence of self, fueling or motivating the development of a commitment to contributing to others and institutions beyond self in time and place (Lerner et al., 2003). Such an understanding of spirituality is beyond a feeling of transcendence, but a motivational force that propels individuals to care for self and others and contribute to something greater than themselves. As such, spirituality nurtures a sense of thriving in young people by providing the awareness of responsibility and the passion to initiate and sustain commitment to agency.

Religion has been recognized as offering a potentially fertile environment to nurture this sense of prosocial identity. Specifically, religion has been recognized for rich ideological, social, and spiritual contexts that may promote identities that transcend the self (King, 2003). Religious traditions often provide a worldview composed of beliefs and values embedded within social relations that seek to embody and model ideologies, histories, and traditions that in turn can sustain a young person with a sense of identity, purpose, and belonging (Erikson, 1959). This sense of belonging strengthens a young person's commitment to a broader collective who share similar beliefs, providing motivation for service and identity formation (Erikson, 1964, 1965; King, 2003; Youniss et al., 1999).

Religious involvement potentially provides a rich ideological context in which identity can take shape. Young people strive to make sense of the world and to assert their place in it. The beliefs, worldview, and values of religious traditions provide an ideological context in which a young person can generate a sense of meaning, order, and place in the world that is crucial to identity formation (Erikson, 1968; Loder, 1998). Religion intentionally offers beliefs, moral codes, and values from which a young person can build a personal belief system. Smith

(2003) asserts that American religions promote specific *moral directives* that are grounded in the authority of long historical traditions and narratives. These aspects of one's worldview form the cornerstone of a young person's individual sense of uniqueness and are an important facet of his or her identity (Damon, 1983; Erikson, 1968).

In addition to providing an ideologically rich context, religion offers a social context helpful for identity development. Not only does religion provide a transcendent worldview, but religious tradition exemplifies these principles and behavioral norms in actual historical events and in the lives of fellow believers. During adolescence personal integration is facilitated by the embodiment of these ideologically based principles and behavioral norms (Erikson, 1968). Religions often provide opportunities for young people to interact with peers and role models as well as build intergenerational relationships (see Schwartz, Bukowski, & Aoki, chapter 22, this volume; Smith, 2003).

In addition, religion may offer a spiritual context in which a young person can explore issues related to identity development. Religions are generally concerned with the transcendent and address ultimate questions about life's meaning, with the assumption that there is more to life than what we can see or fully understand. Engaging in the spiritual provides connectedness with divine, human, or natural other, giving a young person an opportunity to experience him- or herself in relationship to God, a community of believers, or nature, for example. This moving beyond the self provides the opportunity for the search for meaning and belonging that is central to the task of identity exploration (Benson, 1997b; Hill et al., 2000). Awareness that stems from this search provides the ultimate answers and perspective in the larger issues of life that are crucial to the resolution of the adolescent identity crisis (Erikson, 1964, 1965).

Furthermore, religions can offer a profound sense of connection to a divine or human other that has great implications for self-concept. Religious doctrine offers an understanding of self-worth. For example, within Judeo-Christian traditions, believers experience themselves as being in a special relationship with God—as sons or daughters of God (Galatians 3:26) or

as the covenant people of God (Furman, 1987). These traditions both teach and provide opportunities through ritual whereby believers not only learn about their sense of belonging to God but also experience themselves in relationship to God. Understanding oneself as a beloved or chosen one of the Creator may have profound implications for identity. Spiritual experiences, such as experiencing the love of God or an answered prayer, also provide devotion and commitment to one's ideological commitments (Smith, 2003).

In addition, youth may find a profound sense of belonging as members of a faith community. As young people participate in congregations, they can locate themselves as members of a historic tradition. Religion provides both a previous community of believers who have gone before them and a present body of believers that live alongside them, giving youth a sense of being a part of something greater than themselves. One way religion promotes a sense of belongingness is through religious rituals (Erikson, 1965). For example, a bar or bat mitzvah recognizes a boy or a girl in transition to manhood or womanhood as members of a synagogue, confirming their unique place in the body of believers. Such religious rites of passage are unique events that intentionally celebrate and affirm young people's sense of identity as believers, as well as recognize their place within their faith community. Ongoing worship rituals also confirm one's place in a community. For instance, one of the foremost religious practices within Islam is *salat,* or prayer. According to this tradition, believers pray at five specific times a day. In this repetitive act, believers experience themselves in solidarity with other Muslims prostrating themselves toward Mecca.

In sum, religion potentially offers an ideologically, sociologically, and spiritually rich context for identity formation. Religion is seen as affording a potent milieu for identity development through providing explicitly prosocial worldviews, values, and morals; fellow participants as models or sources of encouragement, teaching, or inspiration; and spiritual experiences and environments that help youth internalize and integrate a sense of belonging and meaning. Identity consolidation is central to adolescent well-being and thriving—giving young people a sense of self and a sense of fidelity that motivate them to contribute to the greater good. Integrated into this other-aware identity is a spiritual sensitivity. In this regard, spirituality nurtures thriving in young people by providing the awareness of responsibility and the passion to initiate and sustain commitment to agency.

The Mediating Role of Developmental Resources

Synergistic with Smith's (2003) formulation of the constructive social influences of religion is a growing account of resources available to youth through religion. The most prominent approaches to understanding these resources are through the frameworks of (1) developmental assets and (2) social capital.

Developmental assets refer to internal and external resources that serve as the building blocks of development. (For a review of developmental assets—support, empowerment, boundaries and expectations, constructive use of time, commitment to learning, positive values, social competencies, and positive identity—see Benson, 1997a; Benson, Leffert, Scales, and Blyth, 1998; Scales and Leffert, 2004; and, linked to the religious context, Roehlkepartain, 1998, 2003a.)

A fairly recent line of inquiry supports the hypothesis that developmental assets mediate the influence of religion. That is, religious contexts can offer the kind of asset-building resources—such as intergenerational relationships, prosocial norms, and adult role models—known to facilitate positive development. Recent analysis of a large ($N = 20,020$) database on adolescents provides strong evidence that religious engagement enhances the developmental asset landscape (Furrow & Wagener, 2000; Wagener, Furrow, King, Leffert, & Benson, 2003). A related study provides strong evidence that frequency of attendance enhances positive engagement with adults outside of one's family (Scales, 2003). Such networks of adult relationships can be powerful influences on protecting youth from high-risk behaviors as well as promoting positive attitudes and behaviors (Scales & Leffert, 1999, 2004). Several recent publications building on this research

suggest strategies for enhancing the developmental impact of religious communities within multiple faith traditions (Roehlkepartain, 1998, 2003a, 2003b).

Social capital also serves as a conceptual framework for understanding the influence of religion on young people. This perspective suggests that religion's constructive influence on young people may be accounted for by the relationships—and the benefits associated with them—available through the religious social context. Through religious involvement young people have access to intergenerational relationships that are recognized as rich sources of social capital (King & Furrow, 2004; Putnam, 1995; Smith, 2003). Few other social institutions afford the opportunity to build trustworthy cross-generational relationships and link youth to sources of helpful information, resources, and opportunities. In addition, congregations may promote *network closure* through the provision of relatively dense networks of relationships within which youth are embedded and through which oversight of and information about youth can be supplied to their parents and other individuals positioned to discourage negative behaviors and promote positive life practices among young people (Smith, 2003).

Social capital not only suggests that relationships may positively influence individuals but provides guidance in understanding what kinds of relationships are most beneficial. King and Furrow (2004) found that relationships characterized by social interaction, trust, and shared values are most strongly related to positive youth outcomes. These structural, relational, and cognitive dimensions (Tsai & Ghoshal, 1998) of social capital provide a conceptual lens for explaining how relationships available through the religious social context might influence positive development.

The *structural* aspect of social capital pertains to social interaction and is concerned with the location and frequency of contacts in social structure. Presence and frequency of interaction with family members are common measures in social capital studies involving youth (Coleman, 1988; Furstenberg, Cook, Eccles, Elder, & Sameroff, 1999; Furstenberg & Hughes, 1995). Indicative of the *relational* dimension, trust describes the quality of a relationship. Trust is a primary construct in the assessment of social capital (Fukuyama, 1995; Putnam, 1995) and creates the opportunity for a give-and-take system of interdependence of obligations and expectations to exist (Coleman, 1988; Furstenberg & Hughes, 1995; Portes, 1998). The *cognitive* dimension refers to having a shared vision or a shared code or paradigm that facilitates common understanding of collective goals and expectations of acting in a social system. Relationships characterized by mutual understanding, shared social norms, and effective sanctions are associated with positive outcomes (Coleman, 1988; Portes, 1998).

Specifically, structural, relational, and cognitive social capital resources are associated with being religious and are a more effective determinant of moral behavior than general religiousness alone, revealing that the religious social context plays an important role in development (King & Furrow, 2004). This approach suggests that the social support available through religion is particularly effective for promoting adolescent thriving and also that the support is most effective when constituted of trusting, interactive, mutual relationships—dynamic relationships that include communication, time spent together, trust and respect, and mutually held beliefs and values.

EMPIRICAL EVIDENCE

A growing body of literature documents the role of religious factors associated with various elements of well-being and thriving. Generally, this research establishes a dual role of religion: as a protective factor inhibiting risk-taking behavior (see Blakeney & Blakeney, chapter 26, this volume; Crawford et al., chapter 25, this volume) as well as a factor that promotes positive developmental outcomes, including prosocial behavior and academic achievement. Several syntheses of this literature have been published (Benson, Donahue, & Erickson, 1989; Benson, Masters, & Larson, 1997; Benson et al., 2003; Bridges & Moore, 2002; Smith, 2003; Smith & Faris, 2003; Spilka et al., 2003).

In the existing research, spirituality and religion are rarely distinguished, making it difficult to discern the unique effects of these different factors. Religious variables dominate the current literature. An exception is made by Dowling and colleagues, in whose work spirituality and religiosity were distinctly operationalized. They found that spirituality and religiousness are both associated with thriving (Dowling et al., 2004). Secondary analysis of Search Institute's (Benson, Williams, & Johnson, 1987) Young Adolescents and Their Parents data set (8,165 youth; 10,467 parents) found that spirituality (defined as experiencing transcendence, understanding self in relationship to others, and having genuine concern for others) and religion (defined as institutional affiliation and participation with a religious tradition and doctrine) both had direct effects on thriving (defined as a concept incorporating the absence of problem behaviors and the presence of healthy development). In addition, religion mediated the effects of spirituality on thriving. These findings suggest that spirituality and religiousness may both play unique roles in the development of thriving. Although most existing research confirms the positive role of religion, this study demonstrated that spirituality may have an influence on youth thriving beyond that of religion. Clearly, further research is needed to continue to discern the unique effects of spirituality and religiousness.

Health

A number of studies suggest that religion is a constructive resource for enabling youth, whether they are physically ill or well, to cope with problems (Balk, 1991; Mahoney, Pendleton, & Ihrke, chapter 24, this volume; Shortz & Worthington, 1994). Church attendance has been found to be a key factor in promoting health-enhancing behaviors, such as exercise, diet, dental hygiene, and seat belt use (Jessor, Turbin, & Costa, 1998). Using a large nationally representative sample of high school seniors, another study demonstrated that religious youth are more likely to take care of themselves through proper nutrition, exercise, and rest, and less likely to engage in health-compromising behaviors such as carrying weapons, fighting, and drinking and driving. Mutlivariate analyses found that these relationships remain even after controlling for demographic factors (Wallace & Forman, 1998).

Academic Achievement

A newer line of inquiry extends to the arenas of school performance and academic achievement, with positive but modest correlations with church attendance and religious importance (Benson, Scales, Sesma, & Roehlkepartain, 2005; Muller & Ellison, 2001; Regnerus, 2000). Regnerus and Elder (2003) offer an important explanation for this relationship, particularly for youth in urban, low-income neighborhoods. They suggest that church attendance functions as a protective mechanism in high-risk neighborhoods, generating relationships, values, and sanctions that build "a transferable skill set of commitments and routines" (p. 646) useful for promoting success.

Civic Engagement and Altruism

Research appears to support that religion plays a prominent role in thriving. Several studies indicate a positive relationship between religion and such indicators as community service and altruism. In several studies, Youniss and colleagues found that religious youth were more involved in community service compared to those adolescents reporting little religious activity (Kerestes, Youniss, & Metz, 2004; Youniss et al., 1999; Youniss & Yates, 1997). In fact, based on Monitoring the Future data, Youniss et al. (1999) reported that students who believe that religion is important in their lives were almost three times more likely to participate in service than those who do not believe that religion is important. Tracking religious development from the sophomore year to the senior year, Kerestes and colleagues (2004) found that civic integration, measured by participation in civic activities such as working on a political campaign and demonstrating for a cause, and willingness to perform volunteer service, was positively associated with stable or upward religious developmental trajectories among a sample of predominately white, mid- to upper-class students. Religious salience (Crystal & DeBell, 2002) and religious values (Serow & Dreyden, 1990) have both been shown to be associated with various forms of civic engagement. As previously discussed, although King and Furrow (2004) found that religious salience and religious attendance were correlated with altruism and

empathy, structural equation models revealed that social capital resources of having trusting, interactive, mutual relationships with parents, friends, and an adult mediated the effects of religion on adolescent altruism and empathy. This suggests that the relationships available to religious youth are an important component of religion's potential influence on moral development.

In several studies, gender differences have been noted that suggest that religion may influence thriving through different psychological mechanisms for different individuals. One study of urban youth revealed that religious identity was positively associated with personal meaning and a prosocial concern for others (Furrow et al., 2004). Structural equation models found gender differences in the relationship of personal meaning and prosocial personality. For boys personal meaning mediated the effect of religious identity on prosocial concerns, whereas significant direct effects of religious identity on personal meaning and prosocial concerns were found for girls. These findings potentially suggest that for girls their religious self-understanding is more relational and integrated with prosocial concerns, compared to the less personal and generic conceptualization of personal meaning that was found for boys. In efforts to understand what aspects of religion influence adherents to participate in volunteer service, a study of college undergraduates revealed that the best predictor of intention to repeat volunteer service was intrinsic motivation to volunteer, which was associated with prayer styles and a personal relationship with God. Reporting belief in God was a strong predictor for men but not for women. These findings suggest that religion is a multidimensional construct that can influence individuals differently.

Studies of individuals nominated for moral excellence also note religious themes as distinctive among many nominees. Colby and Damon (1992) found that most of the moral exemplars in their study claimed that faith commitments played a significant role as a foundation for their moral action. The authors suggested that religion acts as a unifying construct in the lives of those with a salient moral identity, promoting the integration of personal goals and moral concerns. Hart and Fegley (1995) made a similar observation, noting the positive role of religion in the lives of youth recognized for their remarkable commitment to caring and contributions to others. An important finding in these studies is the unique relationships among identity, religion, and prosocial commitments. For many, caring values, attitudes, and behaviors were not independent of their spirituality; rather all aspects of their morality were governed by their religious beliefs and experience, which informed their goals of service and care and were closely related to their identity.

Developmental Assets

As previously discussed, a growing body of literature conceptualizes religion's constructive influence on adolescent development as providing access to internal and external developmental resources that contribute to risk reduction and well-being and thriving. Religious youth report higher levels of developmental assets than do their less religious peers. Additionally, those youth who are more active participants in religious institutions or who value being religious or spiritual report lower levels of risk behaviors, such as substance abuse and violence (Furrow & Wagener, 2000; Wagener et al., 2003). Structural equation models suggest that these developmental resources mediate the effects of religion on risk outcomes. Again, King and Furrow (2004) found that social capital resources (e.g., interactive, trustworthy, and mutual relationships with parents, friends, and adults) mediated the effects of religion on adolescent moral outcomes.

Identity

The resolution of identity is a key developmental task of adolescence (see Templeton & Eccles, chapter 18, this volume) and plays a significant role in promoting adolescent well-being and thriving. As discussed by numerous contributors to this volume, religion and spirituality may prominently contribute to well-being and thriving by directly influencing identity development. Several studies support the argument that religion can function as a resource in positive identity development among youth. Tzuriel (1984) found that religiously involved youth reported higher levels of commitment and

purpose when compared to less religiously engaged youth. Fulton (1997) noted that intrinsic forms of religiousness were more likely linked to identity achievement than extrinsic or utilitarian forms of religiousness. Markstrom-Adams, Hofstra, and Dougher (1994) examined the relationship of religious participation to Marcia's (1966) identity commitments. Although they found that identity commitments of foreclosure and achievement were related to church attendance, later studies have not always replicated these findings (Markstrom, 1999). In another study, Markstrom-Adams and Smith (1996) found that intrinsic religiosity correlated with the Marcia stage of identity achievement. Hunsberger, Pratt, and Pancer (2001) found only weak associations between identity achievement and religious commitment. In turn, identity diffusion has also been associated with lower levels of importance of church/temple participation, orthodoxy of Christian beliefs, and intrinsic religious commitment (Hunsberger et al., 2001; Markstrom-Adams et al., 1994).

Meaning

Given that identity commitment has been found to result in fidelity, it is not surprising that initial evidence of a positive relationship between religion and meaning exists in the current literature. Fidelity, an abiding commitment or loyalty to others, ideologies, and roles, enhances a sense of meaning and purpose among youth who have reached identity achievement (Erikson, 1964; Markstrom & Kalmanir, 2001). Fidelity signifies a commitment that in turn provides direction and belonging to those who have an established identity, and as a result we would expect that ideological commitments specifically would promote personal meaning and purpose. Francis (2000) found a positive association between meaning and purpose in life and religiosity. Youth participating in religious communities are more likely to report having a sense of purpose indicative of a commitment to a personal philosophy (Markstrom, 1999). Religion has been shown to have a positive impact on personal meaning (Chamberlain & Zika, 1992). Showalter and Wagener (2000) found among youth attending a Christian summer camp that religion served as a productive source of meaning.

Although the current research suggests that religion and spirituality are associated with positive developmental outcomes in young people, drawing specific and generalizable conclusions is difficult. The different methodologies, in particular the many ways in which religiousness is operationalized, reflect the complexity of the multidimensional constructs of religiousness and spirituality and make it premature to generalize findings, but do point to clear avenues of further research.

SPIRITUALITY AND OTHER DEVELOPMENTAL RESOURCES

Do spirituality and religion act differently from other areas of adolescent engagement? Many societies provide a rich tapestry of opportunities for youth to engage and explore. Youth today have myriad options both for finding a sense of belonging and for affirming a unique sense of self. Young people participate in families, sports, entrepreneurial enterprises, employment opportunities, philanthropy, and different forms of civic engagement; in addition, through technology they have access to real and virtual environments through which to explore identity. Personal pursuits such as art, academics, and spirituality also offer pathways for well-being and thriving. Does spirituality or religion play a unique role in this social fabric? If so, how do they differ from other opportunities and experiences available to young people in today's multifaceted world?

The theoretical and empirical work addressed in this chapter suggests that spirituality and religion may offer unique opportunities for the development of well-being and thriving. Clearly, the empirical evidence available today is highly suggestive of the potential positive influence of religious and spiritual involvement. Adolescence is a developmentally rich stage during which the brain undergoes a dramatic growth spurt, cognitive capacities increase, hormones intensify emotional experience, and questions of identity are explored with angst. Religious and spiritual environments may serve as a rich milieu for this complex stage of development. As discussed, they provide an intentional and coherent worldview that offers prosocial values and behavioral norms that are grounded in an ideology. In particular, religions intentionally teach these values, and adherents may embody these ideals and values and serve as role models. In addition, the faith community provides an intergenerational network of enduring, caring relationships through which youth may wrestle with issues pertinent to identity exploration as well as offer experiences in which they can test personal gifts. Finally, spiritual environments enable youth to transcend their daily concerns and encounter a supernatural other and a faith community in a meaningful way through ritual, spiritual practices (e.g., worship, meditation), and nature.

Given the advances in cognitive functioning that occur during adolescence, young people seek out opportunities to generate forms of meaning and order. With the onset of formal operational thought, adolescents are capable of abstract reasoning and thinking. Religion and spirituality provide meaningful opportunities for young people to exercise their new intellectual powers to reason critically and skeptically about previously held beliefs (Markstrom, 1999). Religion and spirituality can provide opportunities for youth to use their analytical capacities to think through and question beliefs and values, which may be especially helpful in the consolidation of identity.

Although other institutions and activities offer a wide range of opportunities for youth to explore identity, they rarely offer the breadth and depth of developmental resources that foster factors central to adolescent well-being and thriving. Religious and spiritual contexts do at their best. Theory and research suggest that spirituality and religion are positively related to identity formation, meaning making, developmental resources, civic engagement, altruism, and the reduction of dangerous behaviors. Rarely do organizations intentionally offer ideological cohesiveness; an intergenerational social network that nurtures and sustains beliefs, meaning, and values; and provide opportunities for sacred and communal transcendence. These contributions enable religious involvement to serve as a potentially fertile ground for identity formation and the emergence of fidelity. In particular, religion and spirituality provide an environment in which youth can experience the self embedded within a larger context that simultaneously validates the inherent value of the self as well as promotes a sense of belonging and connectedness beyond the self. The young person can gain a sense of self as a unique individual, as well as a self that is a contributing member to a larger whole.

SPIRITUALITY GONE AWRY

This chapter has suggested that spirituality and religion may serve as potent resources for development, and we acknowledge that they may have deleterious consequences as well. Although Wagener and Malony (chapter 10, this volume) look at spiritual pathology in depth, it would be remiss to discuss spirituality and thriving without addressing the negative potential of these transcendent domains. As the theories and studies reviewed in this chapter suggest, spirituality and religion are especially productive in the promotion of thriving when they nurture a solid sense of identity and a sense of transcendence that promote prosocial connectedness, the care of and respect for others. However, religion—either as it is taught by institutions or processed by individuals—contains the possibility of pathology. In a major review of the costs and benefits of religiousness, Pargament (2002) suggests that the answer to the question of whether religion is helpful or harmful is that it depends. Among the factors that can inform both sides of the ledger are the espoused content of a religion, the social context, and the degree to which "the various elements of religious life are well-integrated into the person's life" (p. 169). In certain combinations of these factors, religious engagement can become dysfunctional, as has been shown in such areas as child abuse or partner abuse (Capps, 1995) and prejudice (Hunsberger, 1995).

Not only may religion or spirituality hinder or jeopardize the healthy development of an individual, but they may bring harm, even extreme harm, to others. Religious groups that have an "in-group" mentality and that discriminate against racial groups or other religious groups do not promote thriving in individuals or society. For example, White supremacist groups, which might have a spirituality at their core and who actively suppress members of other races, do not promote thriving in their adherents.

Although a particular religious group might point to certain behaviors as indicators of thriving from within that group's perspective, when those behaviors bring harm to the self or others, we as social scientists do not recognize it as thriving. For example, as Silberman (2003) points out, the September 11, 2001, attacks on the United States can be viewed very differently within different religious meaning systems. According to one religious system, the attacks were carried out by religiously motivated men who were leaders or exemplars within their spiritual or religious tradition and were most likely considered as evidence of thriving. From a Judeo-Christian, Western worldview the attacks were seen as criminal assaults on innocent civilians. These differing views of religion and the use of violence have fueled (and justified) an endless array of national and international conflicts. Former Secretary of State Madeleine Albright (2004) recently captured a prime example:

> I am especially wary when God is invoked as a teammate in the clash of one nation against another, particularly when the nations involved have different religious traditions. When I was secretary of state, I confronted Yugoslav dictator Slobodan Milosevic about his heinous policy of ethnic cleansing in the Balkans. He said he was merely preserving his country's historic role as the protector of "Christian Europe" from the Muslims. I told Milosevic I would be proud to help "Christian Europe" and the rest of NATO protect the world from him. (p. 6)

ADVANCING THE FIELD

A growing body of solid theoretical formulations and empirical evidence substantiates important relationships among spirituality, religion, and adolescent thriving. Both spirituality and religion are multifaceted constructs and are recognized as potentially rich resources for the development of factors central to well-being and thriving—prosocial behaviors, civic engagement and altruism, identity, meaning, and the reduction of risk behaviors. In addition, spiritual development may be a central and universal domain of human development. It has been argued, for example, that the sphere of human action having to do with the domains of religion and spirituality is transhistorical and transcultural. And to the extent that spiritual development is understood as the process of "growing the intrinsic human capacity for self-transcendence" (Benson et al., 2003, p. 207), it is a core and universal dimension of human development. Viewed in this way, the study of spiritual development belongs at the center of academic inquiry.

The resurgence of theory and research—as documented in this volume—is a hopeful sign that scholarship in this arena is gaining importance. Nevertheless, it is a field that in many ways is still in its infancy. Many scholars in this reemerging field unite in calling for needed advances in definitions of religion and spirituality, measurement, and attention to cultural and religious diversity. Much of the extant research has used samples of Christians in fairly conventional (i.e., institutional) settings. Much less is known scientifically about spiritual or religious development in other cultures and traditions (see Boyatzis, 2003; Bridges & Moore, 2002). Accordingly, many of the efforts to measure deeper themes and dimensions use items and scales tailored to these samples. If there is any trend that describes the global spiritual/religious landscape, it is the growth and spread of new religious beliefs, practices, forms, and movements (Eck, 2001). Hence, a critical measurement issue has to do with how to capture this rich diversity of spiritual and religious energy.

In addition, little is known about religious and spiritual development within the United States other than in the European American culture. For example, Mattis and Jagers (2001) noted that the vast majority of conceptualization and research in the area of spirituality has stressed the individual "quest" rather than the social and relational context of spiritual development. This individual focus has, for example, "failed to situate African American religiosity and spirituality in an explicitly relational context" (Mattis & Jagers, 2001, p. 523), which they find to be integral to the African American experience of spiritual and religious development.

The topic of this chapter—spiritual development and thriving—is a relatively new formulation ready for significant advances in theory and research. As argued by Benson and colleagues (2003), the concept of spiritual *development* adds an important dimension to an exploration of spirituality. Spiritual development introduces an emphasis on spiritual change, transformation, growth, or maturation. Through most of the 20th century, spiritual (or, more often, religious) development or change was viewed through stage theory (e.g., Fowler, 1981) or was dominated by nondevelopmental approaches (see Oser & Scarlett, 1991; Paloutzian, 1996; Reich et al., 1999). In the same way that developmental psychology has moved beyond stage theory (e.g., Overton, 1998), spiritual development must also move beyond an overreliance on stage theory, which "implies a certain amount of discontinuity in religious [and spiritual] development, whereas it may actually be a reasonably continuous process" (Hood et al., 1996, p. 55).

Consistent with a developmental systems perspective (Lerner, 2002), we posit that individuals are active agents in shaping their spiritual development. As evidence, one need only note that, even within strong, centralized religious traditions, there are wide individual differences among adherents in how they select, integrate, and attend to a tradition's messages (Benson & Spilka, 1973). This dynamic interaction between ecological influences and personal agency suggests that the individual and the culture in which he or she is embedded are coauthors in creating one's life story (Reker & Chamberlain, 2000). This bidirectional approach to spiritual development needs to become more prominent in future research.

Although some scholars have argued that spirituality only emerges in adolescence or early adulthood (e.g., Helminiak, 1987; Irwin, 2002), examination of spiritual development may be particularly germane to child and adolescent development. Issues of meaning, purpose, vocation, relationships, and identity are particularly salient during adolescence, and many observers note that major identity transformations occur during these years (Gorsuch, 1988; Paloutzian, 1996). Furthermore, work by Coles (1990), Nye (1999), and others (e.g., Reimer & Furrow,

2001) raises important possibilities about the emergence of spirituality during early childhood.

REFERENCES

Albright, M. K. (2004). The mighty and the Almighty: United States foreign policy and God. *Reflections, 91*(2), 4–9.

Balk, D. (1991). Sibling death, adolescent bereavement, and religion. *Death Studies, 15,* 1–20.

Benson, P. L. (1990). *The troubled journey.* Minneapolis, MN: Search Institute.

Benson, P. L. (1997a). *All kids are our kids: What communities must do to raise caring and responsible children and adolescents.* San Francisco: Jossey-Bass.

Benson, P. L. (1997b). Spirituality and the adolescent journey. *Reclaiming Children and Youth, 5*(4), 206–209.

Benson, P. L., Donahue, M. J., & Erickson, J. A. (1989). Adolescence and religion: A review of the empirical literature 1970–1986. *Social Scientific Study of Religion, 1,* 153–181.

Benson, P. L., Leffert, N., Scales, P. C., & Blyth, D. A. (1998). Beyond the "village" rhetoric: creating healthy communities for children and adolescents. *Applied Developmental Science, 2*(3), 138–159.

Benson, P. L., Masters, K. S., & Larson, D. B. (1997). *Religious influences on child and adolescent development: Vol. 4. Varieties of development.* New York: Wiley.

Benson, P. L., Roehlkepartain, E. C., & Rude, S. P. (2003). Spiritual development in childhood and adolescence: Toward a field of inquiry. *Applied Developmental Sciences, 7*(3), 204–212.

Benson, P. L., Scales, P. C., Sesma, A., Jr., & Roehlkepartain, E. C. (2005). Adolescent spirituality. In K. A. Moore & L. H. Lippman (Eds.), *What do children need to flourish? Conceptualizing and measuring indicators of positive development* (pp. 25–40). New York: Kluwer Academic/Plenum.

Benson, P. L., & Spilka, B. (1973). God image as a function of self-esteem and locus of control. *Journal for the Scientific Study of Religion, 12,* 297–310.

Benson, P. L., Williams, D., & Johnson, A. (1987). *The quicksilver years: The hopes and fears of early adolescence.* San Francisco: Harper & Row.

Berger, B., & Berger, P. (1983). *The war over the family: Capturing the middle ground.* Garden City, NY: Anchor.

Boyatzis, C. J. (2003). Religious and spiritual development: An introduction. *Review of Religious Research, 44,* 213–219.

Bridges, L. J., & Moore, K. A. (2002). *Religion and spirituality in childhood and adolescence.* Washington, DC: Child Trends.

Capps, D. (1995). *The child's song: The religious abuse of children.* Louisville, KY: Westminster/John Knox Press.

Chamberlain, K., & Zika, S. (1992). Religiosity, meaning in life, and psychological well-being. In J. F. Schumaker (Ed.), *Religion and mental health* (pp. 138–148). New York: Oxford University Press.

Colby, A., & Damon, W. (1992). *Some do care: Contemporary lives of moral commitment.* New York: Free Press.

Coleman, J. S. (1988). Social capital in the creation of human capital. *American Journal of Sociology, 94*(Suppl.), S95–S120.

Coles, R. (1990). *The spiritual life of children.* Boston: Houghton Mifflin.

Crystal, D. S., & DeBell, M. (2002). Sources of civic orientation among American youth: Trust, religious valuation, and attributions of responsibility. *Political Psychology, 23*(1), 113–132.

Damon, W. (Ed.). (1983). *Social and personality development.* New York: Norton.

Damon, W. (2004). What is positive youth development? *Annals of the American Academy of Political and Social Science, 591,* 13–24.

Dowling, E. M., Gestsdottir, S., Anderson, P. M., von Eye, A., Almerigi, J., & Lerner, R. M. (2004). Structural relations among spirituality, religiosity, and thriving in adolescence. *Applied Developmental Science, 8*(1), 7–16.

Eccles, J. S., & Gootman, J. A. (2002). *Community programs to promote youth development.* Washington, DC: National Academy Press.

Eck, D. L. (2001). *A new religious America: How a "Christian country" has become the world's most religiously diverse nation.* San Francisco: HarperSanFrancisco.

Erikson, E. H. (1959). *Identity and the life cycle: Selected papers.* New York: International Universities Press.

Erikson, E. H. (1964). *Insight and responsibility.* New York: Norton.

Erikson, E. H. (1965). Youth: Fidelity and diversity. In E. H. Erikson (Ed.), *The challenges of youth* (pp. 1–28). Garden City, NY: Anchor.

Erikson, E. H. (1968). *Identity: Youth and crisis.* New York: Norton.

John E. Fetzer Institute. (1999). *Multidimensional measurement of religiousness/spirituality for use in health research.* Kalamazoo, MI: Author.

Fowler, J. W. (1981). *Stages of faith: The psychology of human development and the quest for meaning.* San Francisco: HarperCollins.

Francis, L. J. (2000). The relationship between Bible reading and purpose in life among 13–15 year olds. *Mental Health, Religion, & Culture, 3*(1), 27–36.

Fukuyama, F. (1995). *Trust: The social virtues and the creation of prosperity.* New York: Free Press.

Fulton, A. S. (1997). Identity status, religious orientation, and prejudice. *Journal of Youth and Adolescence, 26*(1), 1–11.

Furman, F. K. (1987). *Beyond Yiddishkeit: The struggle for Jewish identity in a Reform synagogue.* Albany: State University of New York Press.

Furrow, J. L., King, P. E., & White, K. (2004). Religion and positive youth development: Identity, meaning, and prosocial concerns. *Applied Developmental Science, 8,* 17–26.

Furrow, J. L., & Wagener, L. M. (2000). Lessons learned: The role of religion in the development of wisdom in adolescence. In W. S. Brown (Ed.), *Understanding wisdom: Sources, science, and society* (pp. 361–391). Philadelphia: Templeton Foundation Press.

Furstenberg, F. F., Cook, T. D., Eccles, J., Elder, G. H., & Sameroff, A. (1999). *Managing to make it: Urban families and successful youth.* Chicago: University of Chicago Press.

Furstenberg, F. F., & Hughes, M. E. (1995). Social capital and successful development among at-risk youth. *Journal of Marriage & the Family, 57*(3), 580–592.

Garbarino, J. (1995). *Raising children in a socially toxic environment.* San Francisco: Jossey-Bass.

Gorsuch, R. L. (1988). Psychology of religion. *Annual Review of Psychology, 39,* 201–221.

Hall, G. S. (1904). *Adolescence: Its psychology and its relations to physiology, anthropology, sociology, sex, crime, religion, and education.* New York: Appleton.

Hart, D., & Fegley, S. (1995). Prosocial behavior and caring in adolescence: Relations to self-understanding and social judgment. *Child Development, 66*(5), 1346–1359.

Helminiak, D. A. (1987). *Spiritual development: An interdisciplinary study.* Chicago: Loyola University Press.

Hill, P. C., Pargament, K. I., Hood, R. W., McCullough, M. E., Swyers, J. P., Larson, D. B., et al. (2000). Conceptualizing religion and spirituality: Points of commonality, points of departure. *Journal for the Theory of Social Behavior, 30*(1), 52–77.

Hood, R. W., Spilka, B., Hunsberger, B., & Gorsuch, R. (1996). *The psychology of religion: An empirical approach* (2nd ed.). New York: Guilford.

Hunsberger, B. (1995). Religion and prejudice: The role of religious fundamentalism, quest, and right-wing authoritarianism. *Journal of Social Issues, 51*(2), 113–129.

Hunsberger, B., Pratt, M., & Pancer, S. M. (2001). Adolescent identity formation: Religious exploration and commitment. *Identity: An International Journal of Theory and Research, 1*(4), 365–386.

Irwin, R. R. (2002). *Human development and the spiritual life: How consciousness grows toward transformation.* New York: Kluwer Academic/Plenum.

James, W. (1958). *The varieties of religious experience: A study in human nature.* Cambridge, MA: Harvard University Press. (Original work published 1902)

Jessor, R., Turbin, M., & Costa, F. (1998). Risk and protection in successful outcomes among disadvantaged adolescents. *Applied Developmental Science, 2,* 194–208.

Kerestes, M., Youniss, J., & Metz, E. (2004). Longitudinal patterns of religious perspective and civic integration. *Applied Developmental Science, 8*(1), 39–46.

Keyes, C. L. M., & Haidt, J. (Eds.). (2003). *Flourishing: Positive psychology and the life well-lived.* Washington, DC: American Psychological Association.

King, P. E. (2003). Religion and identity: The role of ideological, social, and spiritual contexts. *Applied Developmental Sciences, 7*(3), 196–203.

King, P. E., Dowling, E. M., Mueller, R. A., White, K., Schultz, W., Osborn, P., et al. (in press). Thriving in adolescence: The voices of youth-serving practitioners, parents, and early and late adolescents. *Journal of Early Adolescence.*

King, P. E., & Furrow, J. L. (2003). *Adolescent religiousness and civic engagement.* Paper presented at the Biennial Meeting of the Society for Research on Child Development, Tampa, FL.

King, P. E., & Furrow, J. L. (2004). Religion as a resource for positive youth development: Religion, social capital, and moral outcomes. *Developmental Psychology, 40*(5), 703–713.

Koenig, H. G., McCullough, M. E., & Larson, D. B. (2001). *Handbook of religion and health.* London: Oxford University Press.

Lerner, R. M. (2002). *Concepts and theories of human development* (3rd ed.). Mahwah, NJ: Erlbaum.

Lerner, R. M. (2004). *Liberty: Thriving and civic engagement among America's youth.* Thousand Oaks, CA: Sage.

Lerner, R. M., Dowling, E. M., & Anderson, P. M. (2003). Positive youth development: Thriving as the basis of personhood and civil society. *Applied Developmental Sciences, 7*(3), 171–179.

Loder, J. E. (1998). *The logic of the Spirit: Human development in a theological perspective.* San Francisco: Jossey-Bass.

Marcia, J. E. (1966). Development and validation of ego-identity status. *Journal of Personality & Social Psychology, 3*(5), 551–558.

Markstrom, C. A. (1999). Religious involvement and adolescent psychosocial development. *Journal of Adolescence, 22,* 205–221.

Markstrom, C. A., & Kalmanir, H. M. (2001). Linkages between the psychosocial stages of identity and intimacy and the ego strengths of fidelity and love. *Identity: An International Journal of Theory and Research, 1*(2), 179–196.

Markstrom-Adams, C., Hofstra, G., & Dougher, K. (1994). The ego-virtue of fidelity: A case for the study of religion and identity formation in adolescence. *Journal of Youth and Adolescence, 23*(4), 453–469.

Markstrom-Adams, C., & Smith, M. (1996). Identity formation and religious orientation among high school students from the United States and Canada. *Journal of Adolescence, 19*(3), 247–261.

Mattis, J. S., & Jagers, R. J. (2001). A relational framework for the study of religiosity and spirituality in the lives of African Americans. *Journal of Community Psychology, 29,* 519–539.

Muller, C., & Ellison, C. (2001). Religious involvement, social capital, and adolescents' academic progress: Evidence from the National Longitudinal Study of 1988. *Social Focus, 34,* 155–183.

Nye, R. M. (1999). Relational consciousness and the spiritual lives of children: Convergence with children's theory of mind. In K. H. Reich, F. K. Oser, & W. G. Scarlett (Eds.), *The case of religion: Vol. 2. Psychological studies on spiritual and religious development* (pp. 57–82). Lengerich, Germany: Pabst.

Oser, R., & Scarlett, W. G. (1991). *Religious development in childhood and adolescence.* San Francisco: Jossey-Bass.

Overton, W. F. (1998). Developmental psychology: Philosophy, concepts, and methodology. In W. Damon (Series Ed.) & R. M. Lerner (Vol. Ed.), *Handbook of child psychology: Vol. 1. Theoretical models of development* (5th ed., pp. 107–188). New York: Wiley.

Paloutzian, R. F. (1996). *Invitation to the psychology of religion* (2nd ed.). Needham Heights, MA: Allyn & Bacon.

Pargament, K. I. (2002). The bitter and the sweet: An evaluation of the costs and benefits of religiousness. *Psychological Inquiry, 13*(3), 168–181.

Portes, A. (1998). Social capital: Its origins and applications in modern sociology. *Annual Review of Sociology, 24,* 1–24.

Putnam, R. D. (1995). Bowling alone: America's declining social capital. *Journal of Democracy, 6,* 65–78.

Regnerus, M. (2000). Shaping schooling success: Religious socialization and educational outcomes in metropolitan public schools. *Journal for the Scientific Study of Religion, 39,* 363–370.

Regnerus, M. D., & Elder, G. H. (2003). Staying on track in school: Religious influences in high- and low-risk settings. *Journal of the Scientific Study of Religion, 42*(4), 633–649.

Reich, K. H., Oser, F. K., & Scarlett, W. G. (1999). *The case of religion: Vol. 2. Psychological studies on spiritual and religious development.* Lengerich, Germany: Pabst.

Reimer, K. S., & Furrow, J. L. (2001). A qualitative exploration of relational consciousness in Christian children. *International Journal of Children's Spirituality, 6,* 7–23.

Reker, G. T., & Chamberlain, K. (2000). *Exploring existential meaning: Optimizing human development across the life span.* Thousand Oaks, CA: Sage.

Roehlkepartain, E. C. (1998). *Building assets in congregations: A practical guide for helping youth grow up healthy.* Minneapolis, MN: Search Institute.

Roehlkepartain, E. C. (2003a). Building strengths, deepening faith: Understanding and enhancing youth development in Protestant congregations. In R. M. Lerner, F. Jacobs, & D. Wertlieb (Eds.), *Handbook of applied developmental science: Promoting positive child, adolescent, and family development through research, policies, and programs: Vol. 3. Promoting positive youth and family development: Community systems, citizenship, and civil society* (pp. 515–534). Thousand Oaks, CA: Sage.

Roehlkepartain, E. C. (2003b). Making room at the table for everyone: Interfaith engagement in positive child and adolescent development. In R. M. Lerner, F. Jacobs, & D. Wertlieb (Eds.), *Handbook of applied developmental science: Promoting positive child, adolescent, and family development through research, policies, and programs: Vol. 3. Promoting positive youth and family development: Community systems, citizenship, and civil society* (pp. 535–563). Thousand Oaks, CA: Sage.

Scales, P., Benson, P., Leffert, N., & Blyth, D. A. (2000). The contribution of developmental assets to the prediction of thriving among adolescents. *Applied Developmental Science, 4,* 27–46.

Scales, P. C. (with Benson, P. L., Mannes, M., Roehlkepartain, E. C., Hintz, N. R., & Sullivan, T. K.). (2003). *Other people's kids: Social expectations and American adults' involvement with children and adolescents.* New York: Kluwer Academic/Plenum.

Scales, P. C., & Leffert, N. (1999). *Developmental assets: A synthesis of the scientific research on adolescent development.* Minneapolis, MN: Search Institute.

Scales, P. C., & Leffert, N. (2004). *Developmental assets: A synthesis of the scientific research on adolescent development* (2nd ed.). Minneapolis, MN: Search Institute.

Serow, R. C., & Dreyden, J. I. (1990). Community service among college and university students: Individual and institutional relationships. *Adolescence, 25*(99), 553–566.

Shortz, J., & Worthington, J. (1994). Young adults' recall of religiosity, attributions, and coping in parental divorce. *Journal for the Scientific Study of Religion, 33,* 172–179.

Showalter, S. M., & Wagener, L. M. (2000). Adolescents' meaning in life: A replication of DeVogler and Ebersole (1983). *Psychological Reports, 87*(1), 115–126.

Silberman, I. (2003). Spiritual role modeling: The teaching of meaning systems. *International Journal of Psychology of Religion, 13*(3), 175–195.

Smith, C. (2003). Theorizing religious effects among American adolescents. *Journal for the Scientific Study of Religion, 42*(1), 17–30.

Smith, C., & Faris, R. (2003). *Religion and American adolescent delinquency, risk behaviors and constructive social activities.* Chapel Hill: University of North Carolina, National Study of Youth and Religion.

Spilka, B., Hood, R. W., Jr., Hunsberger, B., & Gorsuch, R. (2003). *The psychology of religion: An empirical approach* (3rd ed.). New York: Guilford.

Tsai, W., & Ghoshal, S. (1998). Social capital and value creation: The role of intrafirm networks. *Academy of Management Journal, 41*(4), 464–476.

Tzuriel, D. (1984). Sex role typing and ego identity in Israeli, Oriental, and Western adolescents. *Journal of Personality and Social Psychology, 46,* 440–457.

Wagener, L. M., Furrow, J. L., King, P. E., Leffert, N., & Benson, P. L. (2003). Religion and developmental resources. *Review of Religious Research, 44*(3), 271–284.

Wallace, J. M., Jr., & Forman, T. A. (1998). Religion's role in promoting health and reducing risk among American youth. *Health Education & Behavior, 25*(6), 721–741.

Youniss, J., McLellan, J. A., & Yates, M. (1999). Religion, community service, and identity in American youth. *Journal of Adolescence, 22*(2), 243–253.

Youniss, J., & Yates, M. (1997). *Community service and social responsibility in youth.* Chicago: University of Chicago Press.

28

RELIGION, SPIRITUALITY, AND CHILDREN'S PHYSICAL HEALTH

DOUG OMAN

CARL E. THORESEN

Scientific studies of physical and mental health effects from religious and spiritual factors, or "RS" factors, have gained prominence over the past decade (Miller & Thoresen, 2003). Most empirical studies of RS factors have focused on adults (Dehaven, Hunter, Wilder, Walton, & Berry, 2004; Koenig, McCullough, & Larson, 2001). Adolescents have also been the focus of many studies (e.g., Wallace & Forman, 1998). Infants and preteen children, by contrast, have been the focus of relatively few empirical studies of RS–health linkages (e.g., Comstock & Lundin, 1967). Recently, pediatric and child health journals have become interested in these relationships (e.g., Barnes, Plotnikoff, Fox, & Pendleton, 2000; McEvoy, 2000).

Overall, religious and spiritual factors have been associated with positive health effects among both children and adults in empirical research. Morbidity and mortality *outcomes,* however, have been neglected in published studies in preadult age groups. That is, most RS–health research on children documents RS relationships with *risk and protective factors,* such as smoking, alcohol consumption, and social networks. Seldom has research examined

specific disease outcomes, such as infant mortality, asthma, or sexually transmitted diseases.

We believe that failure to document relationships, positive and negative, between RS factors and health has led to ignorance, neglect, and misunderstanding by both health care practitioners and researchers (Koenig et al., 2001). This situation is now receiving attention with regard to adult health (e.g., Koenig et al., 2001; Miller & Thoresen, 2003). Compared to adults, however, the differing developmental capacities and life situations of adolescents, and especially of preteen children and infants, demand theoretical and empirical approaches tailored to these age groups. Such studies represent an emerging frontier for several fields, including medicine, nursing, public health, social work, psychology, and sociology.

Many conditions make spirituality and health among children a timely topic with important practical implications. One positive condition concerns developmental approaches focused on identifying *developmental assets,* such as RS factors, that may foster healthy psychosocial growth in children and adolescents. Such assets include RS factors (Benson, Leffert, Scales, & Blyth, 1998; Oman et al., 2004). Developmental perspectives are part of an increasing trend in the health sciences to examine salutary rather than pathogenic factors in descriptive and intervention studies (Snyder & Lopez, 2002). Developmental approaches also resonate well with the longstanding epidemiologic concept of host resistance (Levin, 1996).

Lending urgency to greater understanding of RS factors in child and adolescent health have been studies persuasively documenting the positive roles of RS factors in *adults* (Miller & Thoresen, 2003). For example, a recent meta-analysis of more than 40 independent samples found that active religious involvement significantly predicted greater longevity (McCullough, Hoyt, Larson, Koenig, & Thoresen, 2000). A recent large, well-controlled study followed a representative sample of more than 20,000 U.S. adults over 8 years. It found a life expectancy benefit of greater than 7 years for persons attending religious services more than once weekly, compared to those never attending, a finding "similar to the female-male and white-black gaps in U.S. life expectancy" (Hummer, Rogers, Nam, & Ellison, 1999, p. 277). Among African Americans, the life expectancy benefit associated with frequent religious attendance was nearly 14 years. Even after adjusting for demographics, socioeconomic status, health status, health behaviors, and social ties, mortality risk was still strongly associated with nonattendance (50% higher rate of death, i.e., relative hazard [RH] = 1.50). Such a difference is close to that for heavy smoking (63% elevation, RH = 1.63). An expert panel assembled by the National Institutes of Health concluded that evidence of frequent religious attendance (i.e., once weekly or more) predicting longevity, independent from other well-established risk factors, was "persuasive" (Powell, Shahabi, & Thoresen, 2003). Relationships between RS factors and health have also been drawing growing interest in the popular media, as reflected by recent cover stories in magazines, such as *Newsweek* (November 10, 2003). This interest appears to be part of a larger trend in American popular culture regarding health, religion, and spirituality (Miller & Thoresen, 2003).

Previous reviews have either touched briefly on possible mechanisms that could explain health outcomes (Barnes et al., 2000) or have focused solely on adolescents (Smith, 2003b; Wallace & Williams, 1997). In this chapter, we review empirical literature and proposed mechanisms of RS–health relationships for ages from prenatal through adolescence, up to about age 18. In doing so we note relevance of findings for later (adult) health. We focus mostly on implications for the prevention of physical illness, and only briefly discuss mental health outcomes (see Crawford, Wright, & Masten, chapter 25, this volume, regarding mental health). Other important outcomes that may be influenced by RS factors, often favorably, include educational attainment, violence, and delinquency (Blakeney & Blakeney, chapter 26, this volume).

Most studies to date have been done in the United States or other Western countries, leaving open the extent to which theoretical models and empirical findings can generalize, with modification, to non-Western and developing societies. Finally, we give little attention to denominational differences in health (e.g., Protestant versus Catholic children), although evidence suggests such differences do exist in both adults and children. Available adult and child data tend to suggest, however, that involvement in most denominations is associated with superior average risk profiles and health outcomes, when compared to absence of religious involvement (Koenig et al., 2001). These patterns suggest that religious denominations may foster broadly similar health-protective mechanisms that vary somewhat between denominations in their specific intensity.

CHILDHOOD SPIRITUALITY AND RELIGION

Many challenges confront a researcher trying to formulate a broadly generalizable definition of religion or spirituality (Zinnbauer & Pargament, in press; see also Hay, Reich, & Utsch, chapter 4, this volume). Religion and spirituality may each be viewed as multidimensional with latent features (i.e., having some features not directly observable; see Miller & Thoresen, 2003). Religion is often seen as institutionally oriented, while spirituality is viewed as more personally oriented. Some warn, however, that this approach risks oversimplification and polarization

(Zinnbauer & Pargament, in press). Increasingly, data collection is now designed purposefully to bring understanding of how religion and spirituality relate to physical health. Thus, clarity about definitions is becoming much more important. Strengths and weaknesses of various approaches in defining religion and spirituality have been discussed elsewhere (e.g., Zinnbauer & Pargament, in press). In this chapter, we view spirituality and religion, especially religiousness, as highly related, yet each possessing some unique features (e.g., one can be spiritually active but not involved in any recognized religious organization). We comment briefly from time to time on how particular studies have measured RS dimensions.

Children's and adolescents' experiences of spirituality and religiousness differ from adults' owing to developmental differences in life experience, cognitive capacities, and other factors (Johnson & Boyatzis, chapter 15, this volume). Nevertheless, unequivocal evidence indicates that children and adolescents do have spiritual and religious experiences and interests (Coles, 1990; Hart, chapter 12, this volume; Johnson & Boyatzis, chapter 15, this volume). Despite many sociocultural changes in recent decades, much of this interest continues to be accompanied in youth by involvement in organized religion. Several key indicators suggest that religiousness tends to be stable over time. For example, findings from the Monitoring the Future Study (a longitudinal, nationally representative annual survey of American high school students) indicate that 12th graders' belief in the importance of religion has been stable since 1975 (Smith, Faris, Denton, & Regnerus, 2003). Since then, about one third of these adolescents have viewed their faith as "very" important, one third as "pretty" important, and one third as "a little" important. Only about 10% have reported that religion is "not important." In 1996, among more than 14,000 12th graders surveyed, two thirds (67%) reported that their religious beliefs were "mostly" or "very" similar to the religious beliefs of their parents, and only 21% reported them to be "mostly" or "very" different. After examining all the available indicators, Smith and colleagues (2003) reported finding "no notable, consistent trend in these data reviewing the last quarter of the 20th Century of any increase in alienation or antagonism toward organized religion among American youth" (p. 127). However, given the dramatic increases in materialistic values among first-year college students, doubts persist that the apparent stability may be an artifact of how religiousness is measured, or may apply only to certain facets of religiousness (Astin, 1998).

In what follows, we will construe "childhood religious and spiritual factors" broadly, as referring not only to the child's *personal* interest or experience of religion and spirituality but also to the influence of RS factors in structuring the child's biopsychosocial environment through family, peers, and community. That is, RS factors may potentially be measured at levels ranging from the individual, family, congregation, and community, to the society. RS factors measured at different levels may vary in their salience depending on the age group and health outcome under study. Most recent adult research, often based on national samples, has concentrated on effects from RS factors assessed at the level of the individual (e.g., Powell et al., 2003). Other adult studies have also examined RS factors measured at the level of the family (e.g., same-faith versus mixed-faith marriage, the former termed denominational homogamy; Ellison, Bartkowski, & Anderson, 1999) or the county (Dwyer, Clarke, & Miller, 1990).

In contrast, among very young children, assessing individual child-level RS measures seems neither feasible nor clearly meaningful (for a review of childhood RS measures see Gorsuch & Walker, chapter 7, this volume). For infants and the unborn, measuring *maternal* or *family* RS factors is more practical and may better predict health outcomes (e.g., Najman, Williams, Keeping, Morrison, & Andersen, 1988). As children grow older, they acquire the neurological and experiential basis for increasingly mature forms of spirituality and religious faith (Fowler & Dell, chapter 3, this volume). For example, in adolescence they "begin to establish their autonomy with regard to decisions . . . pertaining to religious commitments and beliefs" (Wallace & Williams, 1997, p. 462). Many who study adolescents have relied heavily on individual-level RS measures, such as adolescent self-reports of subjective religiosity and frequency of attendance at services. Some have examined county-level measures (Regnerus,

Smith, & Smith, 2004). Schapman and Inderbitzen-Nolan (2002) demonstrate, however, that we might also measure the extent to which adolescents experience themselves as *forced* to participate in religious activities. These and other age-related developmental considerations must be taken into account when theorizing and operationalizing relationships between specific RS measures and the underlying, often latent, multidimensional RS *constructs* they aim to assess (Miller & Thoresen, 2003).

CHILDHOOD HEALTH

Children's health is an important national public health priority in the United States, as reflected in listings in many categories in the Healthy People 2010 objectives (see U.S. Department of Health and Human Services, 2000, pp. 16–18 to 16–23 and 16–52 to 16–54). Most preadult mortality beyond 1 month of age is judged preventable. In the United States, major preventable causes of infant mortality include preterm birth, low birth weight, sudden infant death syndrome, injuries, and homicide. Major preventable causes of death among preteen children and adolescents are unintentional accidents and injuries (including motor vehicle crashes, drowning, fires, burns, and firearms), as well as homicides, suicides, and AIDS.

Compared to death, morbidity in childhood is much more difficult to characterize, and estimates of the prevalence of childhood chronic conditions have varied according to definitions and methods. One nationally representative study estimated that 31% of American children under age 18 were affected by chronic conditions that included respiratory allergies (9.7%), repeated ear infections (8.3%), and asthma (4.3%) (Newacheck & Taylor, 1992). About one third of chronic conditions were moderate or severe, resulting in limitations of activity. In the early 1990s, approximately 6.5% of U.S. children experienced a disabling chronic condition, resulting in a long-term reduction in ability to conduct social role activities, such as school or play (Newacheck & Halfon, 1998).

Adolescent health behaviors, such as exercising, using seat belts, smoking, drinking alcohol, using other drugs, and risky sexual behaviors, have been a focus of much research interest (Wallace & Forman, 1998). The prevalence of being overweight among children and adolescents has increased dramatically in recent years, echoing adult obesity patterns now viewed as epidemic in magnitude (Wadden, Brownell, & Foster, 2002). Health behaviors established in childhood are known in many cases to predict adult health behaviors. Other infant, childhood, and adolescent factors, such as low birth weight, lower socioeconomic status or poverty, parental divorce, and personality factors (e.g., conscientiousness or chronic mood disorders), have also been linked to youth or adult health outcomes (Friedman, 2000; Petrou, Sach, & Davidson, 2001; Schwartz et al., 1995). One may distinguish a variety of causal pathways by which early childhood experience may affect later health, including cumulative advantage effects, pathway effects (fostering of a lifestyle trajectory), and latent effects (unmediated by intervening experiences). These latent effects can be quite powerful: Animal research suggests that an organism's prenatal experiences can be transmitted to several subsequent generations, even in the absence of additional external stressors (McEwen, 1999).

EFFECTS ON MORBIDITY AND MORTALITY: DIRECT EVIDENCE

Literally hundreds of empirical studies have examined linkages between adult RS factors and mortality, morbidity, and health outcomes. These include heart disease, stroke, cancer, physical disability, pain, exercise, diet, smoking, alcohol and other substance abuse, psychosis, anxiety, depression, and suicide (Koenig et al., 2001). Evidence is now deemed "persuasive" that frequent attendance at religious services is protective against all-cause mortality among large population samples but not necessarily among those suffering from major diseases. This relationship still holds when other well-established risk factors are considered (Powell et al., 2003). Meditative practices are also associated with better patient outcomes (Seeman, Dubin, & Seeman, 2003). However, there is strikingly little empirical research focused on direct links to mortality and morbidity outcomes from *preadult* RS factors.

A rare study of physical health was conducted by Comstock and Lundin (1967), who examined mortality rates of infants under 1 month old (neonates). In families with smoking mothers and uneducated fathers, they reported a strong but nonsignificant trend toward higher death rates among infants whose mothers seldom attended religious services.

For mental health outcomes, one study found that lower rates of psychological distress were significantly associated with several dimensions of Catholic high school students' personal religiosity, especially feelings of closeness to God and perceptions that one's relationship with God influences one's thoughts, feelings, and behavior (Mosher & Handal, 1997). Self-esteem has been positively and significantly correlated with measures of religiosity (e.g., combining subjective importance and service attendance), both in a large U.S. adolescent data set and among adolescents in each of several cities in Germany, Spain, and the United States (Donahue & Benson, 1995; Smith, Weigert, & Thomas, 1979).

Lower rates of suicide, attempted suicide, and suicide ideation have also been linked to religiosity in numerous studies among both adults and adolescents (see Koenig et al., 2001, pp. 531–535). For example, a recent nationally representative study of more than 15,000 adolescents in grades 7–12 found that private but not public religiosity (e.g., prayer but not attending services) was associated with fewer suicide attempts and less suicidal ideation (Nonnemaker, McNeely, & Blum, 2003). Another survey of approximately 30,000 adolescents in grades 6–12 demonstrated that a compound religious involvement index was associated with less suicidal ideation and fewer suicide attempts (Donahue & Benson, 1995). Others have used population-level analyses to demonstrate that lack of religious affiliation is statistically associated with higher suicide rates among both young men and young women (e.g., Trovato, 1992).

Finally, several studies have reported that personal devotion, frequency of religious activities, and other dimensions of religiosity are associated with significantly less depression among adolescents (e.g., Schapman & Inderbitzen-Nolan, 2002). An exception was found among pregnant adolescents, who may feel they have transgressed against religious teachings (Sorenson, Grindstaff, & Turner, 1995). Finally, weekly attendance at religious services by schoolchildren in Scotland correlated favorably with self-esteem and reduced depression among Catholics but unfavorably among Protestants. This could be in part because weekly attendance among Protestants was not the norm for children and subjected a child to teasing (Abbotts, Williams, Sweeting, & West, 2004).

MECHANISMS: WHAT MIGHT EXPLAIN RELATIONSHIPS?

Religious and spiritual factors may influence childhood health through a variety of mechanisms, many similar to how RS factors appear to foster better health in adults. A variety of protective mechanisms have been hypothesized to explain how RS factors foster health in adults. Most fall into five broad categories: (1) improved health behaviors, (2) improved psychological states, (3) improved coping resources, (4) improved social support, and (5) "superempirical" mechanisms (Levin, 1996; Oman & Thoresen, 2002).

Health behaviors, such as getting enough exercise, eating nutritious food, and refraining from smoking, influence physical health by mechanisms that are fairly well understood (Koenig et al., 2001). Similarly, improved psychological states (e.g., less anxiety, less hostility) may translate into enhanced physical health by reducing stress or "allostatic load," the overall chronic burden on organ systems from trying to adapt to perceived environmental challenges (Johnston-Brooks, Lewis, Evans, & Whalen, 1998; McEwen, 1999).

Coping strategies, understood as ways to deal with stressful events and situations, have long been studied as predictors of health outcomes (Arnold, 1990; Pargament, 1997). Individuals have different approaches they use to cope (e.g., problem-focused versus emotion-focused coping orientation). Unhealthy orientations may compromise physical health by fostering poor health behaviors (e.g., abusing drugs to cope) or by undermining one's ability to control one's emotions (e.g., chronic anger), thus increasing allostatic load.

Higher levels of social support have been empirically well established as a health-protective factor among adults, although the mechanisms that explain this remain unclear (Cohen, Underwood, & Gottlieb, 2000). Some have suggested that social support may be conceived as assistance in coping. This view might explain why different dimensions of social support (e.g., perceived emotional support versus material support) are protective among different groups of people with varying resources and experiences (Thoits, 1986).

Some have suggested that RS–health relationships may take place because RS factors can function from a distance (sometimes termed "distant healing"), without any physical contact or even knowledge by the person being supported. For example, praying for sick persons may engender health through previously unknown "superempirical" or even "supernatural" mechanisms. To date the empirical evidence for the health efficacy of prayer remains mixed and inconclusive (Oman & Thoresen, 2002). Still, the fact that a few well-controlled studies have found supportive empirical evidence suggesting a "superempirical" explanation remains noteworthy.

Among children, theorists of RS–health relationships have proposed analogous mechanisms, although conceptualizations must be adapted to the childhood context. Compared to adults, for example, infants and children typically experience relatively less control over some health-relevant domains of living (e.g., diet), but may experience advantages in other areas (e.g., freedom from hazards related to paid employment). At different ages, children spend time in varying peer, school, and neighborhood environments, engage in differing activities, and experience different developmental needs. Children of each age may experience universal yet culturally shaped developmental needs that, if thwarted, can result in distress (for example, needs for "autonomous relatedness," Allen, Philliber, Herrling, & Kupermine, 1997). Thus, health risk and protective factors may operate unequally over time as a child encounters different stages of development. For example, low socioeconomic status, a robust and well-studied predictor of poorer health in adults, appears associated with childhood health outcomes in different ways at different ages (e.g., being associated with elevated injury rates especially at younger ages, and with elevated smoking rates only at older ages, Chen, Matthews & Boyce, 2002).

In childhood as in adulthood, RS factors do not act alone to foster positive psychosocial development and health, but act in concert with a multiplicity of other protective factors. Such factors, often termed developmental assets, include close ties to caring adults, community involvement, positive peer role models, and future aspirations (Benson et al., 1998; King & Benson, chapter 27, this volume; Lerner, Alberts, Anderson, & Dowling, chapter 5, this volume; Oman et al., 2004; Wagener, Furrow, King, Leffert, & Benson, 2003). Each individual developmental asset may facilitate gains or losses in other specific developmental assets. Patterns of reciprocal causation are involved (one factor influences and is influenced by another factor). Multiple developmental assets often appear to be additive in their protective effects. For example, in one study, compared to youths possessing fewer assets, those possessing all of the significantly protective assets were 4.4 and 5.4 times less likely to report using alcohol and drugs, respectively (Oman et al., 2004). Evidence also suggests that psychosocial environmental factors may sometimes interact with biological factors, such as genotype and stress reactivity (Boyce, in press).

Several researchers offer detailed accounts of mechanisms by which RS factors can affect adolescent physical and mental health. The socialization influence model of Wallace and Williams (1997) describes pathways by which religious involvement can influence adolescent health-compromising behaviors. In this framework, the family is viewed as the primary source of socialization into the norms and values of the larger society. Religion is seen as operating as a key secondary socialization influence, assisting parents in fostering certain beliefs, values, and desired lifestyle patterns in their children. "Parents for whom religion is particularly important may seek to shape the other domains of socialization to fit with their religious convictions" (Wallace & Williams, 1997, p. 462). Through family, schools, peers, the media and other social influences, religious norms and attitudes (or the lack of them) influence value and identity formation, as well as offer social support and social control (see also Schwartz, Bukowski, & Aoki and Roehlkepartain & Patel, chapters 22 and 23 in this volume, respectively). Religion is seen as influential not only by constraining possibly unhealthy behaviors but also by prescribing behaviors that may be healthy, such as encouragement to eat nutritious foods or obtain proper rest and exercise.

A different and somewhat more broadly formulated model for salutary influences from religion on adolescents has been offered by Smith (2003b). Nine factors were described and grouped into three broad domains. The domains were "moral order": moral directives, spiritual experiences, and role models (see also Oman & Thoresen, 2003); "learned competencies": community and leadership skills, cultural capital, and coping skills (see Mahoney, Pendleton, & Ihrke, chapter 24, this volume); and "social and organizational ties": social capital, network closure, and extracommunity links (see King & Furrow, 2004; Youniss, McLellan, & Yates, 1999).

Wallace and Williams (1997) and Smith (2003b) offer guidance for thinking about possible mediating factors between RS factors and physical health that can be assessed. Each theory provides detailed accounts of multiple mechanisms by which RS factors might influence recognized health behaviors, such as smoking and alcohol consumption. Each theory also describes mechanisms by which RS factors can enhance social ties and social support, also commonly cited as explanations for how RS factors protect adult health. Smith's (2003b) theory offers rich detail about the types of potentially measurable ties that might be influential (e.g., "by moving youth out of local contexts," extracommunity links provided by religion may present youth "with new experiences and challenges," p. 26). Finally, each theory notes that RS factors may enhance coping skills and resources.

These theories, however, fail to recognize that effective coping skills may influence physical health *independently* of changes in overt health behaviors (e.g., refraining from smoking). That is, theoretical approaches supported by empirical findings in biomedical research suggest that improved coping skills might lead to reduced childhood/adolescent morbidity and mortality by reducing psychological distress and chronic physiological arousal (McEwen, 1999; Pargament, 1997).

We now describe in greater detail a variety of factors and partially overlapping mechanisms that have been proposed to mediate relationships between religion, spirituality, and health outcomes. We summarize available evidence that these mediating factors may be fostered by RS factors, and may also lead to enhanced physical health in childhood or later in adulthood. We emphasize novel insights or perspectives offered by the evidence for each factor.

Improved Family and Social Environments

Empirical evidence supports the claim that RS factors are associated with improved social environments. Physically and mentally healthier children tend to grow up more often in caring families that are free from conflict, coldness, aggression, or neglect (Repetti & Wood, 1997). Reviewing 94 studies on religion and marital or parental functioning, Mahoney, Pargament, Tarakeshwar, and Swank (2001) found that greater religiousness appeared to decrease the risk of divorce and facilitate marital functioning. Some studies also suggested relationships with more positive parenting and with better child adjustment. Ellison and Anderson (2001) found that increased attendance at services correlated with less perpetration of domestic violence (spousal abuse) among both men and women, a finding that persisted when partner report data were substituted for self-reports. This finding held up after controlling for social integration, social support, alcohol and substance abuse, low self-esteem, and depression. Among college students, involvement in church and religious activities has been associated with fewer reports of childhood sexual abuse by nonrelatives (Stout-Miller, Miller, & Langenbrunner, 1997).

More recently, Smith (2003a) analyzed a nationally representative sample of more than a thousand 10- to 18-year-old youth and found that more frequent attendance at religious services was associated with greater expectations about refraining from sex, drugs, alcohol, fighting, and truancy. Also found among frequent attenders was increased parental supervision as reflected in regulation of TV watching and knowing at all times the child's location and how to contact him or her. The findings persisted when adjusting for demographic and family variables, including age of child and parents, number of siblings, parent's education, and income, marital status, and community context (urban, suburban, rural). Other studies have found that fathers who were active in their religion or experienced spiritual support were more likely to involve themselves in the lives of infants and small children (Roggman, Boyce, Cook, & Cook, 2002).

Regarding socialization influences outside the family, few empirical studies appear to have explicitly focused on whether the child's own internalized religiosity, or religious parents' efforts to foster favorable influences, results in healthier peer and community networks. One study, however, reports that adolescents whose mothers attended religious services more frequently felt greater support from friends (Varon & Riley, 1999). The likelihood of nonpeer positive community influences also seems high (see Schwartz et al., chapter 22, this volume). Smith (2003b) notes that "American religion is one of the few, major American social institutions that is not rigidly age stratified . . . providing youth with personal access to other adult members in their religious communities" (p. 25).

Although in most cases social relationships inside and outside the family appear to be positive, reports of child and adolescent physical and sexual abuse by siblings, parents, relatives, and clergy demonstrate that such relationships may also at times be damaging (Plante, 2004; Stout-Miller et al., 1997). In addition to immediate physical and mental damage, such abuse may result in psychological traumatization as well as later physical and mental health difficulties, including irritable bowel syndrome, chronic pelvic pain, headache, pain syndromes, eating disorders, and somatization (Berkowitz, 2000).

Improved Prenatal and Neonatal Environments

Religious and spiritual influences may begin in the womb (Fedor-Freybergh, 2002). The unborn child's well-being is affected by maternal health behaviors such as nutrition, alcohol consumption, and smoking, and may also be affected by maternal stress levels (Huizink, Mulder, & Buitelaar, 2004; Sable & Wilkinson, 2000). As noted earlier, evidence suggests that among adults, marital harmony as well as most health-related behaviors are positively associated with RS factors, although only a few RS-to-behavior associations have been specifically confirmed among pregnant women (e.g., Cornelius, Taylor, Geva, & Day, 1995). Higher levels of RS factors may also foster positive interpretations (framing) of pregnancy experience in ways that reduce maternal stress, thereby fostering positive infant health. Some argue that high levels of Latina religiosity and spirituality, including veneration of the Virgin Mary as an exemplary mother (a spiritual model), may explain the well-established but "paradoxical" finding that despite Latinas' low socioeconomic status, their birth outcomes are equal to those of non-Hispanic whites and superior to outcomes experienced by other disadvantaged ethnic minorities (Magaña & Clark, 1995). In a rare study that empirically examined birth outcomes and intensity of religious involvement, Najman and colleagues (1988) found that more intense RS involvement was associated with better health behaviors, stronger social networks, and higher birth weight after adjusting for sociodemographic characteristics.

Evidence also suggests the possibility that prenatal influences might predispose a child toward salutary spiritual goals or religious coping. For example, religiously or spiritually devout mothers in many cultures participate in frequent singing of spiritual songs or chanting of a holy or divine name, a practice encouraged in some traditional cultures (Oman & Driskill, 2003). Repeated exposure to such stimuli could condition the developing fetal nervous system positively toward the specific holy names or songs, thereby indirectly predisposing the child toward the associated spiritual ways of life. Prenatal auditory experience has been shown to influence postnatal auditory preferences in animal species ranging from chickens and guinea pigs to sheep. Human newborns even demonstrate statistically significant preferences for hearing their mothers recite stories that have been recited prenatally, in comparison to other stories (DeCasper & Spence, 1986).

After birth, evidence from Jewish and Muslim samples suggests that neonates and infants born into religious families may be more likely to be breastfed, a well-established beneficial health practice (Azaiza & Palti, 1997; Birenbaum, Vila, Linder, & Reichman, 1993). Similarly, more religious American undergraduates have been found more likely to endorse breastfeeding as desirable (Magnussen & Kemler, 1969).

Secure Attachment Relationships

Infants and children in high-RS families might experience more secure social and emotional attachment relationships with their parents (Granqvist & Dickie, chapter 14, this volume). This possibility is suggested by the tendency, described earlier, of high-RS families to manifest positive parenting and other salutary qualities. RS and attachment relationships have not yet been empirically tested, although some studies have found that RS factors are significantly correlated with more secure romantic attachment among adults (Kirkpatrick, 1999). If children in high-RS families do experience more secure attachments, evidence suggests that they might experience improved physical health by means of behavioral and psychobiological mechanisms (Maunder & Hunter, 2001).

Adaptive Goals, Strivings, and Coping

As the child in a high-RS family matures, he or she may be socialized not only into norms regarding conventional or antisocial behaviors but also into more adaptive personal goals and strivings, as well as more effective coping strategies (Emmons, 1999; Mahoney et al., chapter 24, this volume). Pargament (1997) recently synthesized research on religious coping, finding that it helped predict better adjustment to stressful life events beyond secular measures of coping. Religious coping "complements nonreligious coping . . . by offering responses to the limits of personal powers" (p. 310). For example, persons adopting a "collaborative" coping orientation with the divine, viewing God as a working partner, experienced better outcomes than persons using either a primarily "deferring" coping style (involving a

passive "it's in God's hands" attitude toward problems) or a primarily "self-directive" ("do it myself") coping style (p. 294). Similarly, Emmons (1999) describes work on "spiritual strivings," seen as personal action commitments that appear to foster mental health and reduce conflict and stress. Examples of spiritual strivings might include "volunteer my time and talent in my church" or "be more Christlike in character" (p. 102).

Being socialized to use RS coping and striving may occur through family, peer, congregational, or media influences (Smith, 2003b; Wallace & Williams, 1997). Spiritual strivings and religious coping may be learned from parents or others serving as models or "living exemplars." The psychological processes involved include attention, retention, reproduction in behavior, and motivation (Bandura, 2003; Oman & Thoresen, 2003). Compared to research on adults, far fewer studies have examined RS coping or striving in children and adolescents. But existing work does indicate, for example, that RS coping has explanatory power beyond other types of coping by children (Shortz & Worthington, 1994), and that RS coping can be helpful in dealing with chronic health conditions and hospitalization (Ebmeier, Lough, Huth, & Autio, 1991; Pendleton, Cavalli, Pargament, & Nasr, 2002). Theoretical and pastoral perspectives both suggest that RS coping and striving could be very important in the health of children and adolescents (Feudtner, Haney, & Dimmers, 2003; Frank & Kendall, 2001).

Virtues

Virtues, or "classical human strengths," have been proposed as mediators of RS–health relationships. Evidence, mostly among adults, indicates that RS factors are positively associated with such tendencies as conscientiousness, forgiveness, and volunteering (McCullough & Worthington, 1999; Saroglou, 2002; Youniss et al., 1999). Other evidence links these virtues with improved physical health indicators or outcomes, perhaps through mechanisms such as reduced self-focus, enhanced social support, more effective coping, and improved health behaviors (Friedman, 2000; Oman & Thoresen, in press).

Improved Health Behaviors

As noted in other reviews, much evidence shows that religiously involved adolescents, like religiously involved adults, are more likely to engage in positive health behaviors (Donahue & Benson, 1995; Smith, 2003b; Wallace & Williams, 1997; individual studies before 2000 are indexed in Koenig et al., 2001, pp. 539–545, 569–572). More specifically, adolescent religious involvement has been associated with several health indicators: reduced smoking, drinking, using other drugs, risky sexual behaviors, and risky use of motor vehicles. Many of these findings have been replicated in numerous studies that controlled for variables such as race, age, sex, rural versus urban residence, region, education and income of parents, family stability, number of siblings, and the presence of a father or male guardian in the household.

Findings about body weight are more unclear. Religious adults are more at risk for being overweight than are less religious adults, according to several studies. These studies primarily used measures of organizational religiosity (e.g., attendance at worship services). This unfavorable RS–overweight relationship stands in contrast to the favorable profiles of religious adults on other health behaviors, including exercise (Koenig et al., 2001, p. 569). We do not know at present if unfavorable RS–overweight relationships generalize to children and adolescents. One study reported that more highly religious adolescents engaged more frequently in vigorous exercise, and ate better diets as measured by frequency of consuming breakfast, green vegetables, and fruit (Wallace & Forman, 1998). Other recent work links RS factors such as spiritual well-being, perceiving the body as sacred, and belief in God to improved body images and reduced disordered eating among adolescent females (see Boyatzis et al., 2003). However, no published studies have examined relationships between RS factors and adolescent or child overweight status. Given the growing epidemic of obesity in children and youth, this strikes us as a high priority research area.

Intriguing evidence regarding adolescent sexual behaviors is beginning to emerge from the developing world (Green, 2003). Evidence is suggesting that faith-based organizations can sometimes effectively promote healthy sexual behavior across populations. In contrast, most professionally administered public health efforts to prevent the spread of AIDS have focused almost exclusively on disseminating and promoting the use of condoms. Tragically, other epidemiologic indicators of equal or greater importance, such as rates of fidelity to a single partner and age of sexual debut, have been largely ignored and almost entirely unmeasured by USAID and other major international agencies. As Green (2003) notes, "If no impact indicators exist, it is safe to conclude that there are no associated programs" (p. 13). Yet "conventional" public health efforts focusing on condom use have met with very limited success in reducing HIV infection rates in many parts of the developing world. Recently, campaigns with large participation by faith-based organizations for sexual restraint, as a more "primary" form of behavioral change, have brought unprecedented reductions in HIV infection rates in developing countries (e.g., Senegal, Jamaica, and especially Uganda). In Uganda, nationwide HIV seroprevalence rates peaked at about 15% in 1991 and fell to 5% as of 2001, with some reductions "most pronounced among younger age cohorts," including those 15–19 years old (Green, 2003, pp. 141, 144). These efforts may have succeeded partly because persons who maintain celibacy or abstain from extramarital sex serve as behavioral models. Such models are believed to contribute to what epidemiologists term "herd immunity," a social condition in which low case-retransmission rates of a disease lead to its elimination from a population (Levin, 1996; Oman & Thoresen, 2003).

Improved Physiological Measures

Insight into RS–health relationships sometimes comes from studying measurable indicators of physiological processes that may operate as mediators. Overweight status and HIV seroprevalence, both potential mediators discussed earlier, are essentially unstudied in their relationships to individual-level child and adolescent RS measures. But other physiological indicators have been studied, albeit modestly. These include birth weight (discussed earlier), tuberculin status, and cholesterol. An early study by Kuemmerer and Comstock (1967) found that the proportion of junior high school and high school students who tested positively for tuberculosis exposure was higher when parents attended religious services less often. More recently, Friedlander, Kark, and Stein (1987) found that greater religious observance in a sample of 673 Jewish 17- to 18-year-olds was inversely associated with plasma levels of cholesterol, triglyceride, and low-density lipoprotein. These associations were independent of sex, country of origin, social class, body mass, and season.

Health Services Utilization

Several studies have examined relationships between adult RS factors and health services utilization. Existing evidence is not conclusive but suggests that higher RS levels are related to better adherence to treatments, and that clergy and chaplain interventions can reduce length of hospital stay and costs of services. Still, this evidence fails to clarify at a more specific level which features of religiousness or spirituality might be involved. Theoretical models exist that try to explain adult RS–health services utilization relationships (e.g., Koenig et al., 2001, p. 431). Similar patterns might apply to children, but this is largely untested by empirical studies (Koenig et al., 2001, pp. 574–576).

Evidence also demonstrates that harm can result to children of members of religious denominations that emphasize faith healing to the exclusion of modern medical procedures such as blood transfusions or vaccinations. Using referral and record search, Asser and Swan (1998) identified 140 children who would have had over 90% chance of survival under medical treatment, but died between 1975 and 1995 of religiously motivated medical neglect. Causes of death (rarely fatal in the U.S.) included dehydration, appendicitis, labor complications, antibiotic-sensitive bacterial infections, vaccine-preventable disorders, or hemorrhagic disease of the newborn. Children were from 34 states and 23 denominations, including most commonly Faith Assembly ($n = 64$), Christian Science ($n = 28$), Church of the First Born ($n = 23$), Faith Tabernacle ($n = 16$), and End Time Ministries ($n = 12$). The authors suggest that

many more fatalities may have occurred during the study period because deaths of children in faith-healing groups are often recorded as attributable to natural causes, with the contribution of neglect minimized or not investigated. Methods precluded computation or comparison of overall denomination-specific mortality rates. Significantly, not all members of some of these denominations strictly avoid modern medical care. For example, nationally, similar proportions of Christian Scientist (74%) and non–Christian Scientist (78%) adults with "common principal medical conditions" report having used conventional medicine, that is, hospital admissions, physician visits, or prescribed medications in the past 12 months (Benson & Dusek, 1999).

Spiritual Practices

Many children engage in spiritual and religious practices, such as prayer, festivals, and attendance at worship services. Some of these practices may have health effects, and research on adults is attempting to identify the short- and long-term effects on health from specific RS practices. As noted elsewhere, attendance at worship services is a multifaceted activity that often embraces a host of more specific practices and experiences, such as prayer, singing, spiritual fellowship, and listening to spiritual discourses and narratives (Thoresen, Oman, & Harris, 2004). Many of these practices, as noted, appear to facilitate observational or vicarious learning of spiritual ways of living from exemplars of virtue and compassion (Bandura, 2003; Oman & Thoresen, 2003). Also as noted earlier, among adults, the practice of attendance at worship services is a reliable predictor of health outcomes, especially longevity (Powell et al., 2003). Attendance at services, sometimes combined with other items into religiosity scales, has predicted improved adolescent health behaviors (Nonnemaker et al., 2003; Wallace & Forman, 1998). However, no studies have examined relationships between morbidity or mortality outcomes or predictors, and attendance at services by younger, preadolescent children.

Another common practice by children of all ages is prayer. Many studies have examined prayer and health among adults, with mixed findings (Thoresen et al., 2004). Prayer, typically assessed with questions about its frequency, can be viewed as a coping method (Mahoney et al., chapter 24, this volume; Pargament, 1997). The overwhelming majority of prayer and health studies have been cross-sectional and have focused on mental health outcomes. These have included well-being, depression, anxiety, marital adjustment, and fear of death. Relationships of most forms of prayer and health have rarely if ever been studied among children. Some evidence shows that frequency of prayer is associated with improved health behaviors among adolescents (Nonnemaker et al., 2003). Controlled experimentally designed studies are rare, if they exist.

Meditation, viewed as a contemplative form of prayer in many traditions (Goleman, 1988), has been clearly linked among adults to physical health benefits, such as reduced physiological arousal and improved outcomes among patients (Seeman et al., 2003). Experimental studies have confirmed some of these findings among adolescents: Compared to controls, high school students trained in meditation experience improved self-esteem, lower systolic and diastolic ambulatory blood pressure, lower resting blood pressure, decreased heart rates, and reduced cardiovascular reactivity (Barnes, Treiber, & Johnson, 2004; Benson, Kornhaber, Kornhaber, & LeChanu, 1994).

CLOSING COMMENTS

We have examined theories and published empirical findings regarding relationships between spiritual and religious factors and childhood health. The likelihood of positive relationships between RS factors and physical health among children is strongly suggested by the existence of many plausible, scientifically supportive mechanisms, and by empirically established positive RS–health relationships among adults. Our review also identified occasions when religious and spiritual factors have been associated with negative health effects, for example, with regard to withholding of medical treatments, and clerical sexual abuse. Furthermore, findings among adults suggest that

negative religious images, such as appraisals of God as punishing, may be associated with poorer outcomes such as depression (Koenig et al., 2001). Such "religious harm" merits much more investigation.

The finding of broadly beneficial patterns of positive RS–health factor associations suggests that RS factors deserve much more study in childhood health interventions for prevention and treatment. To date, some studies have explored the relevance of RS factors to specific treatment contexts and populations, including patients in traditional and developed societies, and pediatric cancer survivors (e.g., Reynolds, 1996; Zebrack & Chesler, 2002). Others have suggested specific spiritual interventions that might be used with even very young children, and have offered guidelines for incorporation of RS factors into pediatric health maintenance visits, pediatric palliative care, and family therapy (Barnes et al., 2000; Davies, Brenner, Orloff, Sumner, & Worden, 2002; McEvoy, 2000; Oman & Driskill, 2003; Walsh, 1999). Naturally, all attempts to incorporate spirituality and religion into pediatric treatment must scrupulously attend to novel ethical issues, largely ignored to date, that may arise in interventions directed toward children (Barnes et al., 2000).

This review makes it abundantly clear that a full understanding of childhood RS–health relationships will require much additional research. Excluding adolescent health behavior studies, empirical work on RS factors and childhood health remains remarkably sparse. Urgently needed is exploration of how existing findings may generalize beyond the primarily American and Judeo-Christian populations studied to date. Deeper, more specific, and more reliable insight will also require diverse research designs and assessments (e.g., multiwave longitudinal or qualitative designs, experience sampling, diaries). Among the many open childhood RS–health questions, some topics especially meriting exploration include:

- How do RS factors relate to childhood asthma, one of the most rapidly growing health problems among U.S. children? Note that multiple studies have reported that religious attendance independently predicts reduced respiratory disease mortality among U.S. adults (Powell et al., 2003).

- Do children raised in high-RS families develop less attention deficit/hyperactivity disorder, perhaps because RS families engage in more praying, storytelling, scriptural reading, and other activities that involve mental focus? Or because they discourage television watching, a practice shown to predict later attention problems, and in some cases aggressive behaviors and attitudes (Christakis, Zimmerman, DiGiuseppe, & McCarty, 2004)?

- Are RS factors among adolescents cross-sectionally or prospectively associated with lower rates of sexually transmitted diseases?

- How do RS factors relate to overweight status and its health sequelae among children and adolescents?

- Do children raised in RS-active families demonstrate lower allostatic load, as measured by indices such as childhood cardiovascular reactivity (Boyce, in press)?

- Are positive RS–birthweight and RS–breast-feeding associations, observed among specific populations, generalizable across many societies and cultures?

- To what extent are better health outcomes associated with RS-sanctioned child-rearing practices that exist at present primarily in non-Western cultures? (For a useful introduction see DeLoache and Gottlieb, 2000.)

A solid foundation for exploring these questions has been provided by recent progress in understanding psychosocial influences on health. The concept of health has moved beyond the limits of pathology and biomedical perspectives. We suspect that religious and spiritual beliefs and practices hold great potential to foster health and well-being in children and youth. However, that suspicion requires that we proceed carefully with the needed sensitivity and modesty. Scientific inquiry as currently practiced has limits in what it can discover about religious and spiritual beliefs and practices. Mindful of the many limitations, we remain optimistic that current research methods can be effectively used to clarify many of the questions involved. As we learn, we will grow wiser about science's capacities and limits, as well as about

connections between spirituality, religion, and health in children and youth.

REFERENCES

Abbotts, J. E., Williams, R. G. A., Sweeting, H. N., & West, P. B. (2004). Is going to church good or bad for you? Denomination, attendance and mental health of children in west Scotland. *Social Science and Medicine, 58,* 645–656.

Allen, J. P., Philliber, S., Herrling, S., & Kuperminc, G. P. (1997). Preventing teen pregnancy and academic failure: Experimental evaluation of a developmentally based approach. *Child Development, 68,* 729–742.

Arnold, L. E. (Ed.). (1990). *Childhood stress.* New York: Wiley.

Asser, S. M., & Swan, R. (1998). Child fatalities from religion-motivated medical neglect. *Pediatrics, 101,* 625–629.

Astin, A. W. (1998). The changing American college student: Thirty-year trends, 1966–96. *Review of Higher Education, 21,* 115–135.

Azaiza, F., & Palti, H. (1997). Determinants of breastfeeding among rural Moslem women in Israel. *Families, Systems, & Health, 15,* 203–211.

Bandura, A. (2003). On the psychosocial impact and mechanisms of spiritual modeling. *International Journal for the Psychology of Religion, 13,* 167–174.

Barnes, L. L., Plotnikoff, G. A., Fox, K., & Pendleton, S. (2000). Spirituality, religion, and pediatrics: Intersecting worlds of healing. *Pediatrics, 106,* 899–908.

Barnes, V. A., Treiber, F., & Johnson, M. H. (2004). Impact of transcendental meditation on ambulatory blood pressure in African-American adolescents. *American Journal of Hypertension, 17,* 366–369.

Benson, H., & Dusek, J. A. (1999). Self-reported health and illness and the use of conventional and unconventional medicine and mind/body healing by Christian Scientists and others. *Journal of Nervous and Mental Disease, 187,* 539–548.

Benson, H., Kornhaber, A., Kornhaber, C., & LeChanu, M. N. (1994). Increases in positive psychological characteristics with a new relaxation-response curriculum in high school students. *Journal of Research & Development in Education, 27,* 226–231.

Benson, P. L., Leffert, N., Scales, P. C., & Blyth, D. A. (1998). Beyond the "village" rhetoric: Creating healthy communities for children and adolescents. *Applied Developmental Science, 2,* 138–159.

Berkowitz, C. D. (2000). The long-term medical consequences of sexual abuse. In R. M. Reece (Ed.), *Treatment of child abuse: Common ground for mental health, medical, and legal practitioners* (pp. 54–64). Baltimore: Johns Hopkins University Press.

Birenbaum, E., Vila, Y., Linder, N., & Reichman, B. (1993). Continuation of breast-feeding in an Israeli population. *Journal of Pediatric Gastroenterology and Nutrition, 16,* 311–315.

Boyatzis, C. J., McConnell, K. M., Baranik, L., Pietrocarlo, K., Walsh, J., & Zuluaga, A. (2003, August). *God in the bod: Women's body image and eating disorders.* Paper presented at the annual meeting of the American Psychological Association, Toronto.

Boyce, W. T. (in press). Biology and context: Symphonic causation and the origins of childhood psychopathology. In Dan Keating (Ed.), *Conference proceedings of the millennium dialogue on early child development.* Toronto: University of Toronto.

Chen, E., Matthews, K. A., & Boyce, W. T. (2002). Socioeconomic differences in children's health: How and why do these relationships change with age? *Psychological Bulletin, 128,* 295–329.

Christakis, D. A., Zimmerman, F. J., DiGiuseppe, D. L., & McCarty, C. A. (2004). Early television exposure and subsequent attentional problems in children. *Pediatrics, 113,* 708–713.

Cohen, S., Underwood, L., & Gottlieb, B. H. (2000). *Social support measurement and intervention: A guide for health and social scientists.* New York: Oxford University Press.

Coles, R. (1990). *The spiritual life of children.* Boston: Houghton Mifflin.

Comstock, G. W., & Lundin, F. E., Jr. (1967). Parental smoking and perinatal mortality. *American Journal of Obstetrics and Gynecology, 98,* 708–718.

Cornelius, M. D., Taylor, P. M., Geva, D., & Day, N. L. (1995). Prenatal tobacco and marijuana use among adolescents: Effects on offspring gestational age, growth, and morphology. *Pediatrics, 95,* 738–743.

Davies, B., Brenner, P., Orloff, S., Sumner, L., & Worden, W. (2002). Addressing spirituality in pediatric hospice and palliative care. *Journal of Palliative Care, 18,* 59–67.

DeCasper, A. J., & Spence, M. J. (1986). Prenatal maternal speech influences newborns' perception of speech sounds. *Infant Behavior & Development, 9,* 133–150.

Dehaven, M., Hunter, I. B., Wilder, L., Walton, J. W., & Berry, J. (2004). Health programs in faith-based organizations: Are they effective? *American Journal of Public Health, 94,* 1030–1036.

DeLoache, J. S., & Gottlieb, A. (2000). *A world of babies: Imagined childcare guides for seven societies.* Cambridge, UK: Cambridge University Press.

Donahue, M. J., & Benson, P. L. (1995). Religion and the well-being of adolescents. *Journal of Social Issues, 51,* 145–160.

Dwyer, J. W., Clarke, L. L., & Miller, M. K. (1990). The effect of religious concentration and affiliation on county cancer mortality rates. *Journal of Health and Social Behavior, 31,* 185–202.

Ebmeier, C., Lough, M. A., Huth, M. M., & Autio, L. (1991). Hospitalized school-age children express ideas, feelings, and behaviors toward God. *Journal of Pediatric Nursing, 6,* 337–349.

Ellison, C. G., & Anderson, K. L. (2001). Religious involvement and domestic violence among U.S. couples. *Journal for the Scientific Study of Religion, 40,* 269–286.

Ellison, C. G., Bartkowski, J. P., & Anderson, K. L. (1999). Are there religious variations in domestic violence? *Journal of Family Issues, 20,* 87–113.

Emmons, R. A. (1999). *The psychology of ultimate concerns: Motivation and spirituality in personality.* New York: Guilford.

Fedor-Freybergh, P. G. (2002). Prenatal and perinatal psychology and medicine: New interdisciplinary science in the changing world. *Journal of Prenatal & Perinatal Psychology & Health, 16,* 305–321.

Feudtner, C., Haney, J., & Dimmers, M. A. (2003). Spiritual care needs of hospitalized children and their families: A national survey of pastoral care providers' perceptions. *Pediatrics, 111,* E67–72.

Frank, N. C., & Kendall, S. J. (2001). Religion, risk prevention and health promotion in adolescents:

A community-based approach. *Mental Health, Religion & Culture, 4,* 133–148.

Friedlander, Y., Kark, J. D., & Stein, Y. (1987). Religious observance and plasma lipids and lipoproteins among 17-year-old Jewish residents of Jerusalem. *Preventive Medicine, 16,* 70–79.

Friedman, H. S. (2000). Long-term relations of personality and health: Dynamism, mechanisms, tropisms. *Journal of Personality, 68,* 1089–1107.

Goleman, D. (1988). *The meditative mind: The varieties of meditative experience.* New York: Tarcher.

Green, E. C. (2003). *Rethinking AIDS prevention.* Westport, CT: Praeger.

Huizink, A. C., Mulder, E. J. H., & Buitelaar, J. K. (2004). Prenatal stress and risk for psychopathology: Specific effects or induction of general susceptibility? *Psychological Bulletin, 130,* 115–142.

Hummer, R. A., Rogers, R. G., Nam, C. B., & Ellison, C. G. (1999). Religious involvement and U.S. adult mortality. *Demography, 36,* 273–285.

Johnston-Brooks, C. H., Lewis, M. A., Evans, G. W., & Whalen, C. K. (1998). Chronic stress and illness in children: The role of allostatic load. *Psychosomatic Medicine, 60,* 597–603.

King, P. E., & Furrow, J. L. (2004). Religion as a resource for positive youth development: Religion, social capital, and moral outcomes. *Developmental Psychology, 40,* 703–713.

Kirkpatrick, L. A. (1999). Attachment and religious representations and behavior. In J. Cassidy & P. R. Shaver (Eds.), *Handbook of attachment: Theory, research, and clinical applications* (pp. 803–822). New York: Guilford.

Koenig, H. G., McCullough, M. E., & Larson, D. B. (2001). *Handbook of religion and health.* New York: Oxford University Press.

Kuemmerer, J. M., & Comstock, G. W. (1967). Sociologic concomitants of tuberculin sensitivity. *American Review of Respiratory Disease, 96,* 885–892.

Levin, J. S. (1996). How religion influences morbidity and health: Reflections on natural history, salutogenesis and host resistance. *Social Science and Medicine, 43,* 849–864.

Magaña, A., & Clark, N. M. (1995). Examining a paradox: Does religiosity contribute to positive birth outcomes in Mexican American populations? *Health Education Quarterly, 22,* 96–109.

Magnussen, M. G., & Kemler, W. M. (1969). Infant feeding preference as related to personality test scores. *Journal of Clinical Psychology, 25,* 258–260.

Mahoney, A., Pargament, K. I., Tarakeshwar, N., & Swank, A. B. (2001). Religion in the home in the 1980s and 1990s: A meta-analytic review and conceptual analysis of links between religion, marriage, and parenting. *Journal of Family Psychology, 15,* 559–596.

Maunder, R. G., & Hunter, J. J. (2001). Attachment and psychosomatic medicine: Developmental contributions to stress and disease. *Psychosomatic Medicine, 63,* 556–567.

McCullough, M. E., Hoyt, W. T., Larson, D. B., Koenig, H. G., & Thoresen, C. (2000). Religious involvement and mortality: A meta-analytic review. *Health Psychology, 19,* 211–222.

McCullough, M. E., & Worthington, E. L. (1999). Religion and the forgiving personality. *Journal of Personality, 67,* 1141–1164.

McEvoy, M. (2000). An added dimension to the pediatric health maintenance visit: The spiritual history. *Journal of Pediatric Health Care, 14,* 216–220.

McEwen, B. S. (1999). Lifelong effects of hormones on brain development: Relationship to health and disease. In L. A. Schmidt & J. Schulkin (Eds.), *Extreme fear, shyness, and social phobia: Origins, biological mechanisms, and clinical outcomes* (pp. 173–192). New York: Oxford University Press.

Miller, W. R., & Thoresen, C. E. (2003). Spirituality, religion, and health: An emerging research field. *American Psychologist, 58,* 24–35.

Mosher, J. P., & Handal, P. J. (1997). The relationship between religion and psychological distress in adolescents. *Journal of Psychology and Theology, 25,* 449–457.

Najman, J. M., Williams, G. M., Keeping, J. D., Morrison, J., & Andersen, M. J. (1988). Religious values, practices and pregnancy outcomes: A comparison of the impact of sect and mainstream Christian affiliation. *Social Science and Medicine, 26,* 401–407.

Newacheck, P. W., & Halfon, N. (1998). Prevalence and impact of disabling chronic conditions in childhood. *American Journal of Public Health, 88,* 610–617.

Newacheck, P. W., & Taylor, W. R. (1992). Childhood chronic illness: Prevalence, severity, and impact.

American Journal of Public Health, 82, 364–371.

Nonnemaker, J. M., McNeely, C. A., & Blum, R. W. (2003). Public and private domains of religiosity and adolescent health risk behaviors: Evidence from the national longitudinal study of adolescent health. *Social Science and Medicine, 57,* 2049–2054.

Oman, D., & Driskill, J. D. (2003). Holy name repetition as a spiritual exercise and therapeutic technique. *Journal of Psychology and Christianity, 22,* 5–19.

Oman, D., & Thoresen, C. E. (2002). "Does religion cause health?": Differing interpretations and diverse meanings. *Journal of Health Psychology, 7,* 365–380.

Oman, D., & Thoresen, C. E. (2003). Spiritual modeling: A key to spiritual and religious growth? *International Journal for the Psychology of Religion, 13,* 149–165.

Oman, D., & Thoresen, C. E. (in press). Religion and spirituality: Do they influence health? In R. F. Paloutzian & C. Park (Eds.), *The handbook of the psychology of religion.* New York: Guilford.

Oman, R. F., Vesely, S., Aspy, C. B., McLeroy, K. R., Rodine, S., & Marshall, L. (2004). The potential protective effect of youth assets on adolescent alcohol and drug use. *American Journal of Public Health, 94,* 1425–1430.

Pargament, K. I. (1997). *The psychology of religion and coping: Theory, research, practice.* New York: Guilford.

Pendleton, S. M., Cavalli, K. S., Pargament, K. I., & Nasr, S. Z. (2002). Religious/spiritual coping in childhood cystic fibrosis: A qualitative study. *Pediatrics, 109,* E8.

Petrou, S., Sach, T., & Davidson, L. (2001). The long-term costs of preterm birth and low birth weight: Results of a systematic review. *Child: Care, Health & Development, 27,* 97–115.

Plante, T. G. (2004). *Sin against the innocents: Sexual abuse by priests and the role of the Catholic Church.* Westport, CT: Praeger.

Powell, L. H., Shahabi, L., & Thoresen, C. E. (2003). Religion and spirituality: Linkages to physical health. *American Psychologist, 58,* 36–52.

Regnerus, M. D., Smith, C., & Smith, B. (2004). Social context in the development of adolescent religiosity. *Applied Developmental Science, 8,* 27–38.

Repetti, R. L., & Wood, J. (1997). Families accommodating to chronic stress: Unintended and unnoticed processes. In B. H. Gottlieb (Ed.), *Coping with chronic stress* (pp. 191–220). New York: Plenum Press.

Reynolds, P. (1996). *Traditional healers and childhood in Zimbabwe.* Athens: Ohio University Press.

Roggman, L. A., Boyce, L. K., Cook, G. A., & Cook, J. (2002). Getting dads involved: Predictors of father involvement in Early Head Start and with their children. *Infant Mental Health Journal, 23,* 62–78.

Sable, M. R., & Wilkinson, D. S. (2000). Impact of perceived stress, major life events and pregnancy attitudes on low birth weight. *Family Planning Perspectives, 32,* 288–294.

Saroglou, V. (2002). Religion and the five factors of personality: A meta-analytic review. *Personality & Individual Differences, 32,* 15–25.

Schapman, A. M., & Inderbitzen-Nolan, H. M. (2002). The role of religious behaviour in adolescent depressive and anxious symptomatology. *Journal of Adolescence, 25,* 631–643.

Schwartz, J. E., Friedman, H. S., Tucker, J. S., Tomlinson-Keasey, C., Wingard, D. L., & Criqui, M. H. (1995). Sociodemographic and psychosocial factors in childhood as predictors of adult mortality. *American Journal of Public Health, 85,* 1237–1245.

Seeman, T. E., Dubin, L. F., & Seeman, M. (2003). Religiosity/spirituality and health: A critical review of the evidence for biological pathways. *American Psychologist, 58,* 53–63.

Shortz, J. L., & Worthington, E. L. (1994). Young adults' recall of religiosity, attributions, and coping in parental divorce. *Journal for the Scientific Study of Religion, 33,* 172–179.

Smith, C. (2003a). Religious participation and parental moral expectations and supervision of American youth. *Review of Religious Research, 44,* 414–424.

Smith, C. (2003b). Theorizing religious effects among American adolescents. *Journal for the Scientific Study of Religion, 42,* 17–30.

Smith, C., Faris, R., Denton, M. L., & Regnerus, M. (2003). Mapping American adolescent subjective religiosity and attitudes of alienation toward religion: A research report. *Sociology of Religion, 64,* 111–133.

Smith, C. B., Weigert, A. J., & Thomas, D. L. (1979). Self-esteem and religiosity: An analysis of Catholic adolescents from five cultures. *Journal for the Scientific Study of Religion, 18,* 51–60.

Snyder, C. R., & Lopez, S. J. (Eds.). (2002). *Handbook of positive psychology.* New York: Oxford University Press.

Sorenson, A. M., Grindstaff, C. F., & Turner, R. J. (1995). Religious involvement among unmarried adolescent mothers: A source of emotional support? *Sociology of Religion, 56,* 71–81.

Stout-Miller, R., Miller, L. S., & Langenbrunner, M. R. (1997). Religiosity and child sexual abuse: A risk factor assessment. *Journal of Child Sexual Abuse, 6,* 15–34.

Thoits, P. A. (1986). Social support as coping assistance. *Journal of Consulting & Clinical Psychology, 54,* 416–423.

Thoresen, C. E., Oman, D., & Harris, A. H. S. (2004). The effects of religious practices: A focus on health. In W. R. Miller & H. D. Delaney (Eds.), *Judeo-Christian perspectives on psychology: Human nature, motivation, and change* (pp. 205–226). Washington, DC: American Psychological Association.

Trovato, F. (1992). A Durkheimian analysis of youth suicide: Canada, 1971 and 1981. *Suicide & Life-Threatening Behavior, 22,* 413–427.

U.S. Department of Health and Human Services. (2000). *Healthy people 2010.* Washington, DC: Author.

Varon, S. R., & Riley, A. W. (1999). Relationship between maternal church attendance and adolescent mental health and social functioning. *Psychiatric Services, 50,* 799–805.

Wadden, T. A., Brownell, K. D., & Foster, G. D. (2002). Obesity: Responding to the global epidemic. *Journal of Consulting & Clinical Psychology, 70,* 510–525.

Wagener, L. M., Furrow, J. L., King, P. E., Leffert, N., & Benson, P. (2003). Religious involvement and developmental resources in youth. *Review of Religious Research, 44,* 271–284.

Wallace, J. M., Jr., & Forman, T. A. (1998). Religion's role in promoting health and reducing risk among American youth. *Health Education and Behavior, 25,* 721–741.

Wallace, J. M., Jr., & Williams, D. R. (1997). Religion and adolescent health-compromising behavior. In J. Schulenberg, J. L. Maggs, & K. Hurrelmann (Eds.), *Health risks and developmental transitions during adolescence* (pp. 444–468). Cambridge, UK: Cambridge University Press.

Walsh, F. (1999). *Spiritual resources in family therapy.* New York: Guilford.

Youniss, J., McLellan, J. A., & Yates, M. (1999). Religion, community service, and identity in American youth. *Journal of Adolescence, 22,* 243–253.

Zebrack, B. J., & Chesler, M. A. (2002). Quality of life in childhood cancer survivors. *Psycho-Oncology, 11,* 132–141.

Zinnbauer, B. J., & Pargament, K. I. (in press). On defining religiousness and spirituality. In R. F. Paloutzian & C. Park (Eds.), *The handbook of the psychology of religion.* New York: Guilford.

PART VI

TOWARD THE FUTURE IN
PRACTICE, POLICY, AND RESEARCH

Introduction to Part VI

T
he first five sections of this handbook offer a rich and multifaceted exploration of the complex issues and dynamics of spiritual development in childhood and adolescence. This final section asks: If spiritual development is an integral or integrating dimension of human development, how is it to be addressed in future practice, policy, and research?

As one reflects on the present state of practice in spiritual development, there is a sense in which current and emerging scientific research has had relatively little impact on policy or numerous areas of practice, including education, religious formation, clinical practice, public health, child and youth care institutions, and other settings. For many scholars and practitioners, spirituality is too private, too "optional," or too ephemeral to merit sustained, thoughtful exploration as a serious domain of study or practice. Among those practitioners who do take it seriously, too many design programs and implement strategies based on superficial or narrow understandings of child and adolescent spiritual development. Such realities undermine the effectiveness of the people and institutions that play vital roles in young people's development in nurturing or addressing this dimension of life.

The first three chapters in this section examine these issues in application and practice. First, Lisa Miller and Brien Kelley focus on clinical work with children and adolescents, looking at the relationship between spiritual development and mental illness, psychopathology, or suffering. Their research and practice work lead them to call for a child-centered view of spiritual psychotherapy that holds children "inherently awake to spirituality."

Next, Dean Borgman discusses religious institutions and religious youth workers, highlighting the challenges in bridging the gap between researchers and practitioners in this field, and noting that practitioners in general and faith-based practitioners in particular often have antipathy toward scientific developmental theory. He advocates true collaboration among scholars, practitioners, and those served by religious institutions wherein all parties are engaged in the whole process of learning, application, and reflection.

Whereas Borgman underscores the gap between the academy and those he describes as "in the trenches," Daniel G. Scott and Douglas Magnuson focus on specific practices that are needed to address the spiritual dimension of life among children and adolescents who are placed in child and youth care programs and institutions. They contend that spirituality must be grounded both in the individual lives of child and youth care workers and in the practices of their institutions.

It should be noted that many other disciplines and institutional settings could appropriately have been represented in this section. For example, not included here is the important field of spirituality in education, the implications for families and family-serving organizations, or for health care.* Thus, rather than being the final word, the chapters presented here provide a starting point for extensions of the discussion into their areas of expertise as well as related disciplines and fields.

In addition to the challenges to and opportunities for applying spiritual development to disciplines of practice, there has been only limited attention to this domain in broader social policy and society. Steve Hornberger, Roberta Furtick Jones, and Robert L. Miller Jr. lay out wider ranging issues for civil society and public policy. Noting that spiritual development is grounded in our common humanness, they call for public policy that promotes sustainability and the strengthening of civil society to work toward meeting the developmental and spiritual needs of children and adolescents.

Finally, although a solid foundation of research has emerged, numerous questions and methodological issues remain inadequately addressed, suggesting the ongoing need for research in this domain. Two chapters are directed toward the research agenda. Donald Ratcliff and Rebecca Nye highlight recent developments in the field of childhood spirituality and urge new rigor in order to gain acceptance for this domain of study.

Peter L. Benson concludes the section and the handbook by proposing an integrated framework for future theory and research on child and adolescent spiritual development that seeks to create coherence for future research in this complex phenomenon, suggesting the dynamic interaction of multiple forces and constructs in shaping young people's engagement in the search for meaning, purpose, and contribution.

If spirituality is central to what it means to be human, societies must find ways to promote young people's spiritual development at many levels and in many settings. This will require ongoing dialogue, exploration of political and philosophical barriers and differences, and best practices needed for spiritual development to become an integral accent and emphasis in how individuals, families, institutions, and communities nurture their young to be thriving members of families, communities, societies, and the world.

---

*Alexander and Carr raise important issues for education in Part I. Boyatzis, Dollahite, and Marks articulate key issues for families in Part IV. Oman and Thoresen address important issues for medicine in Part V, building on a growing field of integrating spirituality in health care.

29

Spiritually Oriented Psychotherapy With Youth: A Child-Centered Approach

Lisa Miller

Brien Kelley

Scholarly books have been written revealing the profundity of childhood spiritual experience, including Robert Coles, *The Spiritual Life of Children* (1990), and Tobin Hart, *The Secret Spiritual Lives of Children* (2003). To date, little if any has been written in the clinical treatment literature to foster a process of spiritual growth—the gaining of spiritual awareness and an integration of that level of awareness into the fullness of experience for the child. Child-centered spiritual psychotherapy supports the spiritual development of the child through acknowledging the primacy of childhood spiritual experience and encouraging the child to lead with this inherent understanding. Spiritual understanding emanates from the child's naturally present inclinations and only needs cultivating in terms of understanding the unfolding human experience from the perspective of a sacred path.

Clinical psychology has evolved over the past 10 to 15 years to embrace spirituality as present in our clients, essential to healing, and a topic for research on the nature of mental illness. Most national conferences now include research presentations and discussion on spirituality, and the topic is often part of graduate student training (Brawer, Handal, Fabricatore, Roberts, & Wajda-Johnston, 2002). As a field, however, we now must face the next challenge of more deeply understanding the confluence between spirituality and the course of mental illness, as well as how to expand treatment models to support spiritual growth and healing for the amelioration of mental distress. A dearth of discussion exists most egregiously on the integration of spirituality into psychotherapy with youth.

Hathaway, Scott, and Garver (2004) recently polled psychotherapists at four leading mental health clinics in the United States on their perceptions of spiritual issues in treatment. The overwhelming majority of psychotherapists saw a spiritual contribution to some forms of mental illness, but did not clearly understand the spiritual component in these illnesses, nor did they feel prepared to address the spiritual issues in treatment. Advances in our understanding of spirituality and mental health might more fully be integrated within the broader field of practice by considering the needs of psychotherapists and clinical researchers. To frame this endeavor, we might consider answering two important and fruitful questions that might be posed by an interested psychotherapist: How might much of what I now know about the course of mental illness be integrated with a spiritual perspective? And, if I can see the spiritual contribution to a mental disorder, what should I do to help my young client who is spiritual in nature?

COURSE OF SPIRITUAL DEVELOPMENT

Just as psychopathology has a lifetime etiological course, so too does spirituality have a lifetime course, generally understood theoretically as spiritual development. As a risk or resilience factor, therefore, spirituality cannot be understood as a static entity. Spirituality grows, changes, and develops, such that examination of the association between spirituality and mental health involves two moving targets.

The changing nature of spirituality might be followed through the consideration of leading theories of spiritual development, such as those put forth by Fowler (1981), Kegan (1983), Helminiak (1987), and Wilber (1999) (see Sperry, 2001, for a review of academic theories of spiritual development). These theories share fundamental tasks within each age-related developmental window, as follows: We are born with a natural spirituality, which seeks expression. In childhood we assemble and integrate the spiritual meaning in the world around us, from parents, peers, and community. In adolescence we delve into a searching individuation process through which we grow to own our spiritual experience. In early adulthood we continue to evolve spiritually such that our faith comes to lead our life's work, social relationships, and choices. Ultimately, in later life we reach a universal consciousness, through which we regard the sanctity of all people and spiritual faiths. This would be considered the "ideal" trajectory, with deviations possibly leading to a stunted spirituality or even a greater likelihood of suffering from mental illness.

This path of spiritual development shares much in common with dominant (mostly Piagetian) theories of moral and social development (Erikson, 1968; Kohlberg, 1984; Stillwell, 1996): assimilation of social norms in childhood, followed by individuation in adolescence, and finally a mature awareness of belonging to a greater body of humanity throughout adulthood. It makes sense that processes of development might carry similarities across domains, given that our various faculties (social, moral, cognitive) progress in balance across the life span. The distinguishing feature of spiritual development from other similar processes is the emphasis on transcendence (Sperry, 2001).

Case studies and theoretical work show that throughout the developmental path our spiritual life may flourish, inclusive of periods of spiritual struggle, or it may be profoundly eclipsed by the destructive conduct of those entrusted with our welfare, such as parents, mentors, and friends. From within several Asian religious traditions, spiritual eclipse is associated with mental illness, and spiritual vitality is associated with mental health and well-being (Dalai Lama, 2001). The uniqueness of spiritual development as understood within many religious traditions (Richards & Bergin, 2000), compared with disruptions in the course of other risk and resilience factors, is that its very nature is renewal and regeneration (Richards & Bergin, 1997). In other words, unfettered spiritual development is teleological. There exists in every human being an inherent tendency toward growth and flourishing through spiritual experience and understanding. Hence, unlike many other dimensions of human experience, our spirituality consistently can heal and be healing, even in the face of the most damaging risk factors and circumstances. The resilient and renewing quality of spirituality allows challenges to our spiritual life to enhance spirituality, rather than depleting our spiritual potential.

From a clinical perspective, theorists have posited that disruptions in each chapter of spiritual development contribute in specific forms of psychopathology or suffering (Cortright, 1997; Walsh, 1999; Wilber, 1999). Explicating most clearly on this notion is Ken Wilber, who casts spiritual development strongly within a school of ego development. Wilber posits three broad levels of psychopathology depending on our level of ego development: (1) Disruptions at the "prepersonal" level are associated with core personality disorders and psychosis, to which the present authors would add substance abuse, as substance abuse is highly comorbid with the Axis II personality disorders (Kessler, 1994) and shares characteristics in severity of debilitation, interpersonal style, and views of the self (Kus, 1995); (2) disruptions at the "personal" level are associated with affective Axis I disorders such as anxiety or depression and concern coping with episodic life events; and (3) at the transpersonal level, struggles in the phase of universal consciousness are associated not with DSM-IV type psychopathology but rather with forms of suffering that generally carry a spiritual name (such as "dark night of the soul"). In keeping with his formulations, Wilber (1999) suggests that psychotherapy at each of the three levels, respectively, be structured as follows: At the prepersonal level, the use of directive and supportive restructuring work; at the personal level, treatment along the lines of psychodynamic or cognitive therapy; and at the transpersonal level, meditation or other contemplative spiritual practice would be used. Recently, clinical psychologist Judith Miller (2005) has posited a method of conducting psychospiritual psychotherapy that hinges on spiritual developmental theory. Miller views the development and ultimate dissolution of the psychological ego as part and parcel of the spiritual path. Alongside interpersonal or psychological events, spiritual experience is used as directive and informative in sessions. Clients heal by acknowledging the deeper spiritual meaning in their fortune, misfortune, and current psychosocial surroundings.

While it appears plausible that broadly speaking the window of development informs the face of related illness, the authors challenge Wilber's assertion that spiritual development only informs pathology at higher levels of development. Given that spiritual development appears to proceed in pace with other fundamental social faculties, and because child and adolescent clients often incorporate religious or spiritual beliefs into their own interpretations of mental disorder, it may be that suppression or deprivation in early phases of spiritual growth also contributes to the etiology of psychopathology, suggesting a conceptual and practical need for the integration of spiritual life into our understanding of mental illness.

IMPLICATIONS FOR NATURE AND TAXONOMY OF DISORDERS

The empirical data suggest that spiritual development might be tightly woven into the course of mental illness, specifically substance abuse and depression, starting in childhood (e.g., Miller, Weissman, Gur, & Greenwald, 2002). From a theoretical perspective, transcendence exists in the path of spiritual development among children in Fowler's assimilative phase (Wilber's prepersonal phase), and among adolescents in Fowler's individuative phase (Wilber's personal phase) (Fowler, 1981; Wilber, 1999). It is argued that the obstruction, obfuscation, or mishandling of potential transcendence in spiritual development may partially account for the childhood and adolescent contributions to the lifetime course of certain psychopathologies. To the extent that spiritual development interweaves with etiology and course of disorder, we might start to consider the notion of spiritual disorder (or spiritual struggle) as fundamental to mental illness. Spirituality is not just another thing that suffers in the path of mental illness; it is central to its very onset, course, and treatment.

It is essential that a model of spiritual disorder need not be contrary to the reams of existing literature on secular risk factors, including social functioning, cognitive style, and family and community context. A strong spiritual contribution to disorder does not mean that secular variables are not important to the onset and treatment of mental illness. Rather, these well-researched secular variables have been shown to correlate with spiritual orientation, including personal devotion and social spiritual support (Oetting, Donnermeyer, Trimble, & Beauvais, 1998; Sethi & Seligman, 1994). However, the authors raise the possibility that the contribution of spirituality to mental illness is more fundamental than that of secular variables. As a model, cognitive style or interpersonal patterns may be the functioning expression, something of a fingerprint rather than the essential core, of mental disorder. Some empirical evidence for the essential spiritual contribution to mental illness is the relatively far greater magnitude of the protective qualities of personal devotion and spiritual social support against mental illness than that found for secular variables of cognitive style and social functioning (Miller, Davies, & Greenwald, 2000; Miller & Greenwald, 1998; Miller & Gur, 2002). For instance, a strong sense of personal devotion is 80% protective against depression among adolescents at high risk (Miller & Greenwald, 1998), and 65% protective against onset of heavy substance use in adolescence (Miller et al., 2000), far exceeding the magnitude of 10%-30% found for social functioning and cognitive style (Hammen, 1992; Reivich & Gillham, 2003).

The current state of clinical science tends to endorse treatments derived from empirical evidence on risk and resilience factors. Research on secular risk factors informs treatments such as cognitive therapy (Leahy, 2003) and interpersonal psychotherapy (Weissman, Markowitz, & Klerman, 2000), and these modalities have generally proved effective over a series of large-scale clinical trials. However, in light of evidence on the robust protective qualities of spirituality against depression and substance abuse, it is worth considering whether some psychotherapeutic techniques may in part be helpful because they are inculcating a spiritual stance in living, or draw us closer to living in accordance with spiritual truths, even while remaining explicitly silent on spiritual matters. For instance, hope and optimism for the future, along with a strong sense of community and the skills to connect with others, are natural byproducts of both these popular psychotherapies and of the practices of spiritual traditions. Whether the spiritual reality is *most* fundamental, or merely a significant contributor to mental health and illness, it is likely that extant, empirically validated methods of treatment would be even more effective with spiritual clients if they were to directly address spiritual issues and development. Pioneering work in this direction has begun and is reported in a new edited volume by Sperry and Shafranske (2004), whose rich anthology represents a broad array of perspectives, including consideration of spiritually informed psychodynamic, humanistic, cognitive behavioral, and interpersonal psychotherapy.

The field of clinical psychology generally draws on a gradational approach toward understanding mental illness. When viewing a disorder, the tendency is to evaluate the contribution of risk and resilience factors along several "levels of analysis": genetic, the contribution of pathogens at a physiological level, psychological experience, problems in living, and social-cultural strata. Among other obstructions to health, those that interfere with spiritual life and growth have yet to be fully considered and integrated into mainstream understanding of mental illness. In that the field relies on an already diverse causational perspective, it is well poised to incorporate spiritual understanding into our layered conceptualization of mental illness and multimodal treatments.

Just as spiritual growth might enrich a multimodal treatment, spiritual growth is likely to be enhanced by treatment at all levels. For instance, schizophrenic patients have expressed the pain of not being able to pray clearly; such patients might be helped by medication. Depressives with a strong spiritual life may benefit from relieving the choke of the ego through basic psychodynamic or object relations–style work. This notion is also quite germane to clinical psychology, as expressed in the well-worn aphorism "Etiology does not predict presentation or treatment." The way we dig ourselves into the hole of an illness does not predict the view upward from the bottom of the hole, nor does it predict which ladder is best equipped for the climb toward health.

IMPLICATIONS FOR NEW DIRECTIONS IN TREATMENT

As the field comes to understand the lifetime course of psychopathology as involving distortion or obfuscation of spiritual development in youth, treatment must expand to facilitate spiritual development. Recently, seminal books have opened the path toward broadening treatment to embrace assisting our clients on the spiritual path (Richards & Bergin, 1997, 2000; Shafranske, 1996; Sperry, 2001). Across these innovative analyses of the possibilities for treatment emerge two major approaches: integration of the client's religious and spiritual beliefs into treatment, and the introduction of pan-denomination or nondenominational spiritual truths in treatment. In the former method, therapists seek knowledge on the beliefs and practices of our client's religious denomination and work within our client's religious beliefs. Or, therapists work from a religious perspective only with those clients who adhere to religious traditions they know well, such as their own. This approach has proved successful, as it may involve prayer, religious readings, and teachings of spiritual growth, which have been shown to serve specific purposes with great effectiveness (Budd, 1999; Richards & Potts, 1995). The latter method also carries nearly endless possibility as it points to practices that open our spiritual awareness, capacity for spiritual growth, and wisdom. Richards and Bergin (1997) posit an extremely helpful rubric for understanding spiritual wisdom beyond specific denominations, the Spirit of Truth. The Spirit of Truth refers to the sacred, powerful force with which we are in dialogue through our actions and choices. Much as gravity pulls at our physical body, this ultimate force responds to our choices and actions in living. Universal laws of living are secular equivalents of the workings of the Spirit of Truth: For instance, cultivating kinship and honoring commitments are laws of living through which we thrive. As noted in all religions, there are inherent consequences to living with or against the Spirit of Truth, most predominant of which is our happiness or psychological suffering. Of course, this ecumenical formulation of the spiritual lifestyle may be inappropriate for those of specific faiths that prescribe different behaviors, but the humanistic bent of the Spirit of Truth can be recognized by and beneficial for many spiritual patients, and even those secular patients unwilling to wholly accept a particular creed or orientation.

The topic in work with children then includes the advent of awareness of these universal laws governing human experience and interaction. The child is working to weave together an understanding of a unified reality, where consequences and intentions interact with a dynamic, sacred universe. Might we be of help to the child by listening with care and supporting this crucial process?

THE SPIRITUAL PATH AS CENTRAL TO SPIRITUALLY BASED PSYCHOTHERAPY

Private psychological experience may be the touchstone that guides us along our spiritual path, but it is not the paramount focus of a spiritually oriented treatment. Within this view, the universe is very much alive and guiding us, and we are in constant, if not continually conscious, dialogue with its influences (Becvar, 1997). Ideally, we make choices in consort with the workings of the universe, hoping to realize our spiritual path through living a meaningful and fulfilled life.

Psychological symptoms are, from within this perspective, interpreted as signals of a spiritual challenge. Depression, anxiety, and interpersonal strife are to be viewed as opportunities for spiritual growth, not merely as symptoms to be eradicated. Depression may signal an awakening spiritual understanding or capacity, a new level at which we are called to evolve spirituality. Anxiety may suggest that we sense that we have strayed from our calling, and on a deep, spiritual level are uncomfortable with our lives. Relationships, replete with their inherent challenges, are designed spiritual gifts and openings for growth. Just the right person comes along at just the right time to help us evolve. Ultimately, the psychological pain or crisis that brings our clients to treatment signals a spiritual announcement of opportunity. This view, or very closely related views, span several contemporary spiritually oriented psychotherapies that take the spiritual reality to be most fundamental in the human journey, although to date most of these clinically applied theories focus exclusively on adult treatment (Griffith & Griffith, 2002; Sperry & Shafranske, 2004).

In our clinical work with children and adolescents we have found that the child finds quite natural the notion that suffering comes from living against spiritual truths. In the case of adolescents making deep soulful decisions about approaches to living, which often influence a full lifetime, the spiritual reality underlying moral decision making is of enormous personal interest and imperative to healthy problem solving. A lack of consideration for ultimate concerns and values makes little sense to adolescents, a predilection that could account for much of what is typically considered the rebelliousness and angst of adolescence. As such, a spiritually oriented psychotherapy can be extremely helpful, indeed crucial, with youth. In many cases, it has been the only effective approach and the only level on which work seems intuitive and natural to the young client. Avoidance of dogmatic coercion is quite possible through adopting a child-centered perspective. This entails allowing the spiritual path of the child to unfold, working explicitly with the concepts and truths the client presents, and providing the therapist's (and others') personal experiences or beliefs only as examples, rather than as ideals or exclusive methods.

In almost any modality of treatment with youth, psychotherapy both targets the present problem and lays a foundational direction for growth. The inchoate seeds of the child germinate in any treatment. In this sense, intervention is inevitably treatment *and* prevention. By ignoring spiritual development in times of suffering and transition, the therapist is fostering in the youth an understanding of the world that does not embrace or validate the sacred dimension of human experience. The youth is left with depleted ways of coping, connecting, and ultimately evolving. From a spiritual perspective, a therapy unwilling to address the highest potentials within the child can divert an individual from his or her life's work and may perpetuate suffering by disavowing the client's inherent dialogue with the universe.

A CHILD-CENTERED VIEW

A child-centered view of spiritual psychotherapy holds as central that children are inherently awake to spirituality. As such, they are considered to be present to the universe through being naturally more curious and aware, or mindful, in their orientation to the world. The alert child hears the teachings in nature, perhaps instantiated in animals and trees, a process still given credence in most indigenous cultures, and still found in the fairy tales that continue to enthrall the young. The child has intimate access to the sacred, or to personalized notions of the Creator, a close relationship that is not mitigated in authenticity or power for lack of abstraction. This later gift of transcendence through communication with the divine is described in the empirical literature as personal devotion (Kendler, Gardner, & Prescott, 1997; Miller & Gur, 2002).

The method of spiritually oriented treatment for children supports the child's firsthand experience and understanding of the world. Rather than dismissing or revising the child's understanding of the universe, the child is heard and encouraged to use intuition, experience, and contemplation as methods for making life choices and interpreting suffering. The love or teachings received in nature, the guidance, comfort, or illumination in their relationship with G-d, are present to the child, whether or not an adult deafness belies such reality. For instance, children frequently identify signs from the world that an adult might understand with the Jungian notion of synchronicity (Jung, 1952/1960). Specifically, Jung wrote of the enormous information suggested by two nonmechanistically related, contiguous events (far too improbable to have occurred by chance). Synchronicity suggests an underlying continuity to the universe, and is interpreted in unique and enormously powerful ways by our young clients. Kaitlin, a 9-year-old girl, noticed: "I was mean to my brother and rude to my mom. Suddenly I stubbed my toe and I realized that I was wrong. So, I apologized." Kaitlin did not think that she was being punished, but merely directed.

Jody, now a woman, reflects on a poignant synchronicity that has enriched her since she was 12 years old:

As a child I lived in an apartment in New York City, where my bedroom window faced a fire escape. As long as I can remember nothing has lived there, until one spring a bird made a nest right in the corner outside my room. I watched the mother lay eggs and then the birds hatched. Then one day, I went outside and looked down to see that the baby bird had fallen all the way down to the pavement, laying dead. I had never encountered death and did not know death until that day. That was the season my only sibling, my brother, died. I feel that the bird was there for me to learn about death, to prepare me in some way for my brother's death. My parents were too grieved to discuss [it]. Nobody talked about his death. I would not have understood at all had it not been for the birds.

However the child or adolescent connects with or conceives of their spirituality, the therapist supports the client in absorbing the teaching and recasting current struggles from the perspective of spiritual growth. The ultimate goal of treatment is that the child embraces his or her own spiritual path through connection with and guidance from the sacred dimension of life. The current challenges, and those yet to come, are viewed as gifts and callings from a loving universe, and spiritual growth in service of personal satisfaction and health is of paramount concern.

Child as Teacher: The Centrality of the Child in Spiritual Family Treatment

A child-centered view applies equally well to work with younger children, adolescents, and families. In the case of family work, oftentimes the child can become the spiritual teacher for the entire family. Many have found that a child can express exactly what the family needs at the fortuitous moment to inspire change. Parents may feel annoyed or pushed by children, but these "disturbances" can also be taken as an opportunity to listen closely to the child's words and observe the child's actions in order to best align the family toward happiness. In a unique and precious way, the child can be a spiritual inspiration for the family. This notion reflects the specific deeper assumption that humans are born close to the Creative source. Our childhood sensibilities reflect more than our atomistic drives and needs as organisms. Spiritual guidance emerges through the raw unadulterated behavior and words of the child, as the child acts out of spiritual connection and awareness without censorship. Although a broad range of alternative perspectives on the innate human composition in childhood certainly exists, that of the inherently spiritual child does not preclude the simultaneous understanding of the child as driven by sexuality, or by the need to connect or balance security with wonderment and curiosity.

Psychotherapy with a child is most often a family treatment. The child lives under the emotional "weather" of the family system, and therefore it only makes sense to address the overarching reality of the child's daily life by incorporating the parents and family into treatment.

Unfortunately, despite advances in the integration of spirituality into individual adult psychotherapy, child and family treatment (at least as commonly discussed in academic and professional circles) remains fairly devoid of a spiritual perspective. The case of Sophie highlights one way that a spiritual orientation can be integrated into child-family treatment.

Sophie was a 7-year-old Caucasian girl living in an affluent suburb in the northeastern United States. Her father, a lawyer, and her mother, a writer, were graduates of an Ivy League college. The oldest of three siblings, Sophie attracted her parents' hopes and aspirations for a bright future. She engaged and delighted her parents when she made a clever or witty remark, showed potential talent in the arts, or succeeded in school. On the other hand, when Sophie showed social awkwardness or signs of academic trouble, her parents homed in with a great deal of concern. The latter issue brought the family to psychotherapy.

Sophie attended a neighborhood elementary school in which most of the students were children of accomplished parents. The culture of the school reflected the culture of the community in that achievement and performance garnered applause and respect from fellow students and parents. By first grade, the community had with interest flagged "smart" kids, who might even skip a grade, and reading early and being quick in math were the currency of success for a 7-year-old. Within this atmosphere, Sophie had hit a barrier. Although a very intelligent girl, she was having problems learning to read. She read more slowly than other classmates and selected books that were less advanced. In this community of single-minded aggressive achievement, Sophie was quick to notice the disparity. Worse, her troubles had been noticed by fellow students and their parents.

Sophie's mother contacted a family therapist in a great deal of distress. She and her husband felt heartbroken for Sophie over her failure and drop in social regard, and were now fearful for her future. They wanted to discuss with a family psychotherapist how they might explain to Sophie her deficits. In treatment, the family therapist was understanding of their disappointment, formulating their surprise as a feeling of loss. She suggested that the parents support

Sophie by explaining that she is "great and smart" but just needs to work on the circumscribed area of reading. The therapy also took on a problem-focused approach through which the family investigated changing schools to one that offered more direct assistance and a smaller student-to-teacher ratio.

Clearly this therapy was predicated on the values of the community. Achievement and performance remained the central goals in living. Notably absent from the treatment, as often is the case in family therapy, was any consideration of the deeper meaning of the event for the family, parents, and the child. What opportunity might be present vis-à-vis the child's growth and evolution? Despite a lack of deeper perspectives in treatment, upon consultation it became clear that within the parents had begun an evolutionary process. The mother had started to embrace the need to tutor her daughter in reading as an opportunity for them to spend time together. Knowing that her daughter loved the theater, she searched the Internet for children's plays. Of greatest significance, the mother began to describe the situation as an opportunity rather than a trauma for Sophie and for their relationship.

Given the awakening of a more spiritual process in the mother, as a therapist I joined with her around understanding the crisis as an opportunity. From this place, we explored the events as a new beginning for her, her family, and, most saliently, for Sophie. She readily acknowledged the overemphasis on achievement and extreme outcome orientation of her community, as a way of peeling back the context surrounding her previous stance. She enthusiastically grabbed hold of the notion that the current troubles in reading, and all that might come of these troubles, were part of Sophie's path. Regardless of her professional outcome, however, the mother's greatest hope for Sophie was that she fulfill her journey and calling from a spiritual perspective. Essentially, this meant that Sophie's benefit from the current situation included a deepened awareness of her own calling and unique personal qualities.

A spiritual approach is entirely compatible and consistent with helping to ameliorate developmental problems, such as reading or other learning difficulties, or socioemotional challenges.

The point was not to ignore the reading difficulties, but rather to treat the social and psychological fallout surrounding the academic crisis as a creative opportunity to allow Sophie to align with her path.

Crisis can be treated as a gift, a chance for a new beginning. Therapists rarely view family work from this perspective, and even more rarely view the resolution as embedded within the sacred current that courses through the child and family. Critical to a spiritually oriented family therapy is the conception of the family as a collective in which the parents and the child walk a spiritual path together. This shared living journey involves interaction (whether through prayer, listening to nature, meditation, attention to synchronicity or some form of awareness) with the vital guidance of the client's personal interpretation of the sacred. The therapist in a spiritual psychotherapy might be most helpful in highlighting ways in which the family has already started to listen to the universe, and supporting the family in responding to the spiritual call. The job of the therapist is to help the family engage this sacred process. The guidance that comes to the family will point the way out of the crisis, meaning that the therapist does not provide a direct strategy for "improvement."

Many families do not trust family therapists out of a fear that the therapist will try to guide or change the family. A child-centered view locates the capacity to engage the path in the clients themselves. Locating authority where it truly resides, in the individuals and the sacred, immediately surmounts the usual clinical issues of race, class, and social disadvantage in explanatory depth and personal meaning. Therapists do not teach ways of parenting or structuring the home; instead, therapists listen to the family, as the family members learn to listen to their spiritual lives.

Youth's Direct Experience and a Naturalistic Spiritual Therapy With Adolescents

Treatment with adolescents usually involves identity work, including the formation of a personal way of belonging in the world. From a spiritual perspective, adolescence marks a time of spiritual awakening (Groeschel, 1983). Just as the young child holds inherent spiritual awareness, the adolescent burgeons with a metacognitive quest for the experience of good and evil, the yearning for transcendence, the integration of spiritual experience into Self, and a close intimate relationship with the Creator.

Identity and social belonging, understood from a spiritual perspective, radically differ from the way of understanding offered through a secular lens. The work of a spiritually informed psychotherapy with adolescents, therefore, calls for an active spiritual stance. The case of Gillian highlights the role of a spiritual foundation in adolescent development, and the great benefit offered by recasting the developmental challenges of adolescence in naturalistic spiritual terms.

Gillian was a 14-year-old middle-class Caucasian girl with feelings of anxiety and social rejection concerning school. Recently Gillian had left her more intimate middle school, where she had known her classmates since early elementary school, and entered high school. Now she was faced with a much broader and more diverse circle of classmates, who were organized into cliques that were interpreted along a hierarchy of appeal and popularity. Gillian was enormously anxious about fitting into a popular clique. She feared that invitations to parties, boyfriends, and all-around social appeal hung on her acceptance by the popular girls. Gillian simultaneously faced concerns about her aptitudes and talents now that she was in a "tougher league" of high school. She always had been a solid student and adequate athlete, but now she noticed that some students were much more successful in these domains. Gillian for the first time felt like her worth was hanging on her abilities, which for the moment were under fire from the competition surrounding her. Overall, Gillian presented as a girl whose confidence had recently plummeted, leaving her with a sense of identity confusion and fostering a forced and awkward style of social interaction.

Despite her dislocation, Gillian had a strong spiritual life. When not plagued by anxiety at school, she relished long moments in nature. Her favorite time of day was the morning before school when she would walk outside in her own backyard. Here in the early morning she interacted with animals and birds. The smell of spring, she explained, brought her "happiness" and "reassurance." In her backyard she prayed each morning that all her immediate family, her extended family, and all children of the Creator be blessed that day. The extreme palpability of her spiritual experience suggested that despite her current experience with school, she could bring her spiritual bearings into her daily life. The goal of treatment was the integration of Gillian's deep personal spirituality into school life. From a spiritual perspective, all of her pressing concerns regarding identity and social interaction appeared in a different light.

Gillian acknowledged feeling "knocked off her block" when she was at school. She identified on her own that she needed to reconnect to the "Source" in her day at school. Working toward spiritual identity development, we first recentered her consciousness through her own personal prayer life (provided by her, not the therapist). Gillian found it extremely helpful to reorient herself before walking into the building at the start of the day, and frequently throughout the day as she started to feel the anxiety rise within her chest. Anxiety came to be viewed as an empty space that could be filled by re-establishing her connection to the Creator.

From a social perspective, Gillian noticed that seeing her classmates from a spiritual stance altered her view of them and made her less reactive to the dominant social order. Rather than seeing people based on their talents or accomplishments, she was reminded that we are all "children of G-d." Unpopular, unathletic, or nonacademic teenagers were just as significant as "winners." Gillian also noticed that she enjoyed joking and befriending people from many groups and cliques. She seemed to feel more connected to the person behind the persona of athlete, drama queen, or scholar. Of greatest significance was that she felt more at home in her own skin. Her forced and awkward social interactions gave way to genuine enjoyment of other people, and presumably her peers felt more comfortable and accepted around her. Over time, Gillian developed the reputation of an uncommonly kind girl, and people from different cliques liked her. Although she was not always included in parties and gatherings within each clique, she did not feel rejected or on tenterhooks emotionally.

Of profound difference, Gillian's view of herself shifted from one of having traits to one of service to her calling. "You have to figure out what you do well and do it as part of your calling," she once explained. Her identity was not formulated on the superiority of her talents, but on the purpose of her skills and self-understanding. Any skill with which she was endowed carried value commensurate to its applicability within her new, broader self-conception. She was no longer a middling athlete or above average student; she was embarking on her path, her identified calling, as a "teacher of love."

It is worth emphasizing that in both the cases of Sophie and Gillian, the therapist did not provide an understanding of the sacred, of divinity, or a formula for spiritual connection. The spiritual journey has a life of its own. The therapist must only support and regard with proper awe the course of the trajectory. The unfolding spiritual path of the client is located in each person's own intimate relationship with our living universe. In this sense, the spiritual approach taken with youth is child centered.

A CONTEMPLATIVE CHILD-CENTERED APPROACH

Both Sophie's and Gillian's cases illustrate the importance of accessing and understanding one's deep, spiritual nature and purpose. Gillian needed time alone to pray and contemplate in order to reconnect with her happiness and with the world, and she found that consciously centering herself made her better able to relate with her peers and maintain a cheerful demeanor. The authors argue that this contemplative "space" is critical to spiritual development, and that its cultivation through meditation (or prayer) can be an easy and useful adjunct to all types of spiritual and secular psychotherapies.

Many fine books have been written comparing and conjoining Buddhist psychology with Western approaches, from psychoanalysis to cognitive-behavioral treatments (Epstein, 1995, 2002; Rubin, 1996; Segal, Williams, & Teasdale, 2002), but very few contemporary thinkers from either camp, the "West" or the "East," have examined Buddhist contemplative or meditative practices with children. The main purposes of psychotherapy and meditation are the same: to deepen knowledge about the self, alleviate psychological suffering, and increase the happiness in an individual's life. The child is at the beginning of that life, and learning from an early age to center and calm oneself through contemplation and stillness only increases the likelihood of living a full and mentally healthy life.

The Buddhist prescription for psychological betterment, both for adults and for children, involves three fundamental assumptions: The person is responsible for his or her own improvement and psychological state; the person has the capacity to understand and change that state; and ultimately, it is one's responsibility to do so, both for one's own happiness and for the sake of others. This stance is entirely coherent with the child-centered spiritual approach described in this chapter, and therefore it seems supplementary to both spiritual development and psychotherapy to include the contemplative practices of such a congruent system in the therapeutic world of the willing child.

Throughout the life span, it is thought that negative thought patterns, fueled by desire and egotism, are the driving force behind psychological suffering, and that through meditation one can become aware of how those patterns maintain themselves, thereby slowly cultivating the ability to disengage from automatically reacting to harmful thoughts and feelings. It is argued here, and has been for millennia, that a deep understanding of one's unique nature and role in the world is critical, if not necessary, to achieving happiness and relief from psychological turmoil. Contemplative practices used with youth provide an increasingly rare opportunity to calmly sit and explore the self and its relation to everything else. They provide confidence in one's spiritual nature, either confirming the prescriptive teachings of organized traditions or providing a sense of meaningful and sacred connection that might otherwise have been missing.

By examining the foundations of Buddhist ideas of being a person, it is possible to adopt a stance toward freedom and responsibility that is in no way applicable only to adults. Gross (1998) focuses on *tathagatagarbha,* or the inherent and benevolent core of Buddha-nature that exists in all people. This entails that all children (and adults) are completely unique in their sanctity, and to expect children to conform uniformly to social conventions of success and development can be to deny that inherent uniqueness, and the life one's talents and interests encourage one to live. From this perspective, the therapist's role is to remain open and compassionate in order to let the child's deepening relationship with his or her spirituality guide the process of psychotherapy and self-discovery. This type of compassionate concern in no way patronizes or disempowers a child; rather, the agency of the patient to effect change from within is balanced by a framework of interdependence and an acknowledgment of the potency of spiritual practice on mental health.

There are several ways, not offensive or contrary to a typical monotheistic Western patient (or his or her parents), in which the contemplative, Buddhist conception of child development and mental health can be adopted by the modern Western psychotherapist. The use of meditation to buttress physical and mental health is now a popular and secular auxiliary to many Western techniques. Meditation can also be used with children. Children can be extraordinarily open to novelty and are often inclined toward more experiential and proactive ways of learning, factors that come in handy when encouraging a child or preteen to sit still and focus for longer than 5 minutes. A child seems more present, fresher in his or her own senses, and it is exactly this characteristic that makes mindfulness so natural to children.

The use of meditation with children has precedence both within Buddhism (although it is rare outside of a monastic context) and increasingly within modern Western psychotherapy and education. The most common technique used is a variation of *vipassana* meditation, which has been adopted and recast as "mindfulness" in ecumenical psychological parlance, but which has not been systematically tried and tested with children nearly enough. Jon Kabat-Zinn (1994) defines mindfulness as "paying attention in a particular way: on purpose, in the present moment, and nonjudgmentally" (p. 4), and the development of this present-focused orientation has been found to be beneficial for children as well as adults (Chang & Hiebert, 1989; Linden, 1973; and

Kabat-Zinn & Kabat-Zinn, 1997, for a description of mindful parenting). Baer (2003) provides an excellent conceptual and empirical overview of the use of mindfulness meditation in psychological research and practice, so we will restrict our discussion to children and adolescents. Astin (1997) found that a mindfulness program used with college undergraduates was very successful (mean rate 9.3 of 10) in effecting changes of "lasting value and importance." Since negative attentional and attributional habits become stronger and more entrenched over time and use, and mindfulness meditation addresses those issues proactively, it only makes sense to attempt to reach youth as early as possible, at the root of their potentially depressogenic thought patterns. Moreover, neurophysiological and clinical research suggests that even short trials of mindfulness can increase neural activity in areas linked to emotional well-being and happiness, and that these changes are correlated positively with more efficient immune functioning and decreases in compulsive behaviors in those with OCD (Davidson et al., 2003; Schwartz & Begley, 2002). Given the fundamental plasticity of the child's brain, and the continuation of neurological development, specifically in the prefrontal cortex, well into adolescence, it also stands to reason that interventions utilizing mindfulness could have increased beneficial psychological sequelae when used with youth.

In lieu of the clinical vignettes presented for the theistic and naturalistic orientations, some recent research on mindfulness with children should help elucidate what a Buddhist-flavored contemplative approach to therapy with children might look like. A small pilot study was recently conducted through Teachers College, Columbia University, in which 5 anxious children (ages 7 and 8) were given an age-modified program of mindfulness that lasted 6 weeks (Semple, Reid, & Miller, in press). Short meditation periods focused awareness on present perceptual modalities, including sound, touch, and taste, and were augmented by engaging exercises that emphasized the implementation of these new attentional skills in daily experience, and by group discussions in which the children discussed their experiences and the subsequent cognitive and emotive attributions. All of the children showed improvement in at least one domain of functioning (academic performance, internalizing or externalizing problems), and 4 of 5 reported enjoying the program. A controlled, randomized study of 24 low-SES, minority children aged 9–12, selected because of reading difficulties, has shown similar results: after 12 weeks of mindfulness practice (adapted from Kabat-Zinn's Mindfulness-Based Stress Reduction program, MBSR), the ability to concentrate and maintain attention was increased in a majority of the students, and this was substantiated by an increase in school performance and standardized reading scores. Interestingly, the benefits were maintained upon 12-week follow-up, regardless of further mindfulness practice, indicating that the children had changed substantially and positively through the experience (Semple, Lee, & Miller, 2004).

Gross (1998) maintains that formal meditation halls and retreats are antithetical to children's priorities, concerns, and attentional abilities. This is most likely true in austere and ritual-infused monastic settings, or within the context of a lengthy retreat, but there is ample anecdotal evidence to suggest that children enjoy and can benefit from meditation conducted in warm, comfortable, and engaging environments, and with full cognizance of the transience of a child's focus (Fontana & Slack, 1997; Kabat-Zinn, 2000; R. A. F. Thurman, personal communication, February 26, 2004). Compared to adults, the child is inherently more present through (at the very least) the five senses (Reid, Semple, & Miller, in press). Learning to live in full awareness is a journey on which children are *better* equipped to embark, having been subjected to fewer years of continual distraction, desire, and potential psychological distress. The overwhelming popularity and success of Kabat-Zinn's MBSR program speak to the degree of acceptance within American culture of alternative forms of physiological and psychological betterment, especially as stress contributes negatively to many deadly health conditions, and our children grapple daily with the ramifications of uncontrollable impulses and wandering minds.

Sitting in meditation, however, requires a sense of psychological and personal responsibility, and personal effort, two components of treatment that hopefully show signs of reemerging among American adults, but are rarely imposed on children and teens (apart from school success and all of the extracurricular activities that requires). There is no 10-milligram dose of mindfulness, nor is there a way that parents can control their child's attributional style or mental habits. A contemplative therapeutic stance places responsibility for spiritual growth and, ultimately, personal happiness on the efforts and unique skills of the individual patient. By utilizing spiritual truths and practices in psychotherapy, we are expanding our treatment targets and scope to include the most fundamental and meaningful parts of a child or adolescent's life. Honoring the *source,* or the core, of health and suffering is a necessary and enlightening journey for both the youth and the therapist, through which lasting happiness can be discovered and maintained.

REFERENCES

Astin, J. A. (1997). Stress reduction through mindfulness meditation. Effects on psychological symptomatology, sense of control, and spiritual experiences. *Psychotherapy and Psychosomatics, 66*(2), 97–106.

Baer, R. A. (2003). Mindfulness training as a clinical intervention: A conceptual and empirical review. *Clinical Psychology: Science and Practice, 10*(2), 125–143.

Becvar, D. S. (1997). *Soul healing: A spiritual orientation in counseling and therapy.* New York: Basic Books.

Brawer, P. A., Handal, P. J., Fabricatore, A. N., Roberts, R., & Wajda-Johnston, V. A. (2002). Training and education in religion/spirituality within APA-accredited clinical psychology programs. *Professional Psychology: Research and Practice, 33*(2), 203–206.

Budd, F. C. (1999). An Air Force model of psychologist–chaplain collaboration. *Professional Psychology: Research and Practice, 30*(6), 552–556.

Chang, J., & Hiebert, B. (1989). Relaxation procedures with children: A review. *Medical Psychotherapy: An International Journal, 2,* 163–176.

Coles, R. (1990). *The spiritual life of children.* Boston: Houghton Mifflin.

Cortright, B. (1997). *Psychotherapy and spirit: Theory and practice in transpersonal psychotherapy.* Albany: State University of New York Press.

Dalai Lama. (2001). *An open heart: Practicing compassion in everyday life.* Boston: Little, Brown.

Davidson, R. J., Kabat-Zinn, J., Schumacher, J., Rosenkranz, M., Muller, D., Santorelli, S. F., et al. (2003). Alterations in brain and immune function produced by mindfulness meditation. *Psychosomatic Medicine, 65*(4), 564–570.

Epstein, M. (1995). *Thoughts without a thinker: Psychotherapy from a Buddhist perspective.* New York: Basic Books.

Epstein, M. (2002). *Going on being: Buddhism and the way of change.* New York: Broadway Books.

Erikson, E. H. (1968). *Identity: Youth and crisis.* New York: Norton.

Fontana, D., & Slack, I. (1997). *Teaching meditation to children.* London: Element.

Fowler, J. W. (1981). *Stages of faith: The psychology of human development and the quest for meaning.* New York: Harper & Row.

Griffith, J. L., & Griffith, M. E. (2002). *Encountering the sacred in psychotherapy: How to talk with people about their spiritual lives.* New York: Guilford.

Groeschel, B. J. (1983). *Spiritual passage: The psychology of spiritual development.* New York: Crossroad.

Gross, R. M. (1998). *Soaring and settling: Buddhist perspectives on contemporary social and religious issues.* New York: Continuum.

Hammen, C. (1992). The family-environmental context of depression: A perspective on children's risk. In D. Cicchetti & S. Toth (Eds.), *Developmental perspectives on depression* (pp. 251–281). Rochester, NY: University of Rochester Press.

Hart, T. (2003). *The secret spiritual world of children.* Makawao, HI: Inner Ocean.

Hathaway, W. L., Scott, S. Y., & Garver, S. A. (2004). Assessing religious/spiritual functioning: A neglected domain in clinical practice? *Professional Psychology: Research and Practice, 35*(1), 97–104.

Helminiak, D. A. (1987). *Spiritual development: An interdisciplinary study.* Chicago: Loyola University Press.

Jung, C. G. (1960). Synchronicity: An acausal connecting principle. In *The Collected Works of C. G. Jung* (R. F. C. Hull, Trans.). Princeton, NJ: Princeton University Press. (Original work published 1952)

Kabat-Zinn, J. (1994). *Wherever you go, there you are: Mindfulness meditation in everyday life.* New York: Hyperion.

Kabat-Zinn, J. (2000). Indra's net at work: The mainstreaming of Dharma practice in society. In G. Watson, S. Batchelor, & G. Claxton (Eds.), *Psychology of awakening: Buddhism, science, and our day-to-day lives* (pp. 225–249). Boston: Weiser.

Kabat-Zinn, M., & Kabat-Zinn, J. (1997). *Everyday blessings: The inner work of mindful parenting.* New York: Hyperion.

Kegan, R. (1983). *The evolving self: Problem and process in human development.* Cambridge, MA: Harvard University Press.

Kendler, K. S., Gardner, C. O., & Prescott, C. A. (1997). Religion, psychopathology, and substance use and abuse: A multimeasure, genetic-epidemiologic study. *American Journal of Psychiatry, 154*(3), 322–329.

Kessler, R. C., McGonagle, K. A., Zhao, S., Nelson, M., Eshleman, S., Wittchen H.-U., et al. (1994). Lifetime and 12-month prevalence of DSM-III-R psychiatric disorders in the United States: Results from the National Comorbidity Survey. *Archives of General Psychiatry, 51,* 8–19.

Kohlberg, L. (1984). *The psychology of moral development: The nature and validity of moral stages.* San Francisco: Harper & Row.

Kus, R. J. (Ed.). (1995). *Addiction and recovery in gay and lesbian persons.* New York: Haworth.

Leahy, R. L. (2003). *Cognitive therapy techniques: A practitioner's guide.* New York: Guilford.

Linden, W. (1973). Practicing of meditation by school children and their levels of field dependence-independence, test anxiety, and reading achievement. *Journal of Consulting and Clinical Psychology, 41*(1), 139–143.

Miller, J. S. (2005). *A spiritual approach to psychotherapy.* Manuscript submitted for publication.

Miller, L. F., Davies, M., & Greenwald, S. (2000). Religiosity and substance use and abuse among adolescents in the National Comorbidity Survey. *Journal of the American Academy of Child & Adolescent Psychiatry, 39*(9), 1190–1197.

Miller, L. F., & Greenwald, S. (1998, March). *Religion and psychopathology among adolescents in the NCS.* Paper presented at the meeting of the American Psychopathology Association, New York, NY.

Miller, L. F., & Gur, M. (2002). Religiosity, depression, and physical maturation in adolescent girls. *Journal of the American Academy of Child & Adolescent Psychiatry, 41*(2), 206–214.

Miller, L. F., Weissman, M. M., Gur, M., & Greenwald, S. (2002). Adult religiousness and history of childhood depression: Eleven-year follow-up study. *Journal of Nervous and Mental Disease, 190*(2), 86–93.

Oetting, E. R., Donnermeyer, J. F., Trimble, J. E., & Beauvais, F. (1998). Primary socialization theory: Culture, ethnicity, and cultural identification. The links between culture and substance use: IV. *Substance Use & Misuse, 33*(10), 2075–2107.

Reid, E. F. G., Semple, R. J., & Miller, L. F. (in press). Accessing mindfulness in young children: Exploring the five senses. *Journal of Infant, Child, and Adolescent Psychotherapy.*

Reivich, K., & Gillham, J. (2003). Learned optimism: The measurement of explanatory style. In S. J. Lopez & C. R. Snyder (Eds.), *Positive psychological assessment: A handbook of models and measures* (pp. 57–74). Washington, DC: American Psychological Association.

Richards, P. S., & Bergin, A. E. (1997). *A spiritual strategy for counseling and psychotherapy.* Washington, DC: American Psychological Association.

Richards, P. S., & Bergin, A. E. (2000). *Handbook of psychotherapy and religious diversity.* Washington, DC: American Psychological Association.

Richards, P. S., & Potts, W. (1995). Using spiritual interventions in psychotherapy: Practices, successes, failures, and ethical concerns of Mormon psychotherapists. *Professional Psychology: Research and Practice, 26*(2), 163–170.

Rubin, J. B. (1996). *Psychotherapy and Buddhism: Toward an integration.* New York: Plenum.

Schwartz, J. M., & Begley, S. (2002). *The mind and the brain: Neuroplasticity and the power of mental force.* New York: HarperCollins.

Segal, Z. V., Williams, J. M. G., & Teasdale, J. D. (2002). *Mindfulness-based cognitive therapy for depression: A new approach to preventing relapse.* New York: Guilford.

Semple, R. J., Lee, J., & Miller, L. F. (in press). Mindfulness-based cognitive therapy for children. In R. Baer (Ed.), *Mindfulness-based treatment approaches for clinical practitioners.* San Diego, CA: Elsevier.

Semple, R. J., Reid, E. F. G., & Miller, L. (in press). Treating anxiety with mindfulness: An open trial of mindfulness training for anxious children. *Journal of Cognitive Psychotherapy: An International Quarterly.*

Sethi, S., & Seligman, M. E. P. (1994). Optimism and fundamentalism. *Psychological Science, 4*(4), 256–259.

Shafranske, E. P. (Ed.). (1996). *Religion and the clinical practice of psychology.* Washington, DC: American Psychological Association.

Sperry, L. (2001). *Spirituality in clinical practice: Incorporating the spiritual dimension in psychotherapy and counseling.* New York: Brunner-Routledge.

Sperry, L., & Shafranske, E. P. (Eds.). (2004). *Spiritually oriented psychotherapy: Contemporary approaches.* Washington, DC: American Psychological Association.

Stillwell, B. M., Galvin, M., Kopta, S. M., & Padgett, R. J. (1996). Moral valuation: A third domain of conscience functioning. *Journal of the American Academy of Child and Adolescent Psychiatry, 35,* 230–239.

Walsh, F. (Ed.). (1999). *Spiritual resources in family therapy.* New York: Guilford.

Weissman, M. M., Markowitz, J. C., & Klerman, G. L. (2000). *Comprehensive guide to interpersonal psychotherapy.* New York: Basic Books.

Wilber, K. (1999). Spirituality and developmental lines: Are there stages? *Journal of Transpersonal Psychology, 31*(1), 1–10.

30

Bridging the Gap: From Social Science to Congregations, Researchers to Practitioners

Dean Borgman

The situations surrounding young people today demand a handbook such as this one. Quite often my teaching and research are interrupted by calls for help or information. I find myself talking to, or asked about, some young person in crisis. I'm told about dysfunctional schools, social agencies, and families. I'm questioned by confused parents, youth workers without training, or pastors or administrators who have received no education as to how children and young people develop their identities in today's world.

It is not just young people but also families and global societies who are at risk. Globalization, consumerism, and secularism contribute to tensions, and wars are fueled by differences in religious dogmas and styles. East and West, South and North, societies in various stages of development seek different answers to differing questions and needs.

Behind headlines spotlighting world power brokers and extremists are serious thinkers hoping to promote religious and ideological dialogues. Social scientists add to our understanding of human development and dynamics. An underlying assumption of most contributors to this volume is that people of faith can find common ground with secularists while believing in transcendent meaning and power that give spiritual and moral strength to a society and its citizens.

No one would say this handbook has all the answers regarding spiritual development. But it is filled with principles needed to resolve our crises. The contributors explore the science of spiritual development in childhood and adolescence. This chapter considers how theory gets into practice: Why isn't our best research having a greater effect upon the way we are teaching and counseling children and youth—and affecting families? Why aren't congregations having a more profound effect on their children and surrounding communities? How can we get our latest studies and findings "into the trenches"? In some ways we view this chapter as an extension of the discussion offered by Roehlkepartain and Patel (chapter 23, this volume). It will also raise some serious questions about our entire academic enterprise. As does each chapter in this text, this one calls for careful study and concentration.

As part of a larger exploration of the scientific perspectives on spiritual development in childhood and adolescence, this chapter will discuss a more dynamic interaction between theory and practice—keeping the preceding questions in mind.

THE GAP

How can we understand the gap between general theory and local practice, between social science and the congregation, between the academic scholar and the practitioner? Our assumption is that a certain measure of antipathy toward scientific developmental theory exists among practitioners in general, and perhaps among faith-based practitioners especially. Understandably, social scientists, some of whom have been practitioners in the past, may be dismayed when their research and theoretical conclusions are not taken more seriously by those currently working with young people.

Challenges to Practitioners

Lack of interest and attention to research by those working with children and youth can, first of all, be attributed to such basic factors as time and energy. Beset by so many duties and crises, they find it difficult to sit down and study or to go to conferences. If and when they do attend a conference, they may find many of the terms and concepts used puzzling. From their limited reading or discussion, they may feel what they are learning doesn't make that much sense or doesn't really apply to what they are doing in classrooms, youth groups, and perhaps even in counseling.

Antipathy on the part of practitioners may grow out of a perception of conscious or subconscious disdain on the part of academics toward practitioners. Those working with children and youth may also judge that the experts (1) have missed the real issues, (2) may be talking about a different kind of spirituality, or (3) can't possibly understand "our" inner-city neighborhood or third world situation. Those engaged with children or youth may sense that academics are more concerned with head knowledge and tend to bypass crucial matters of the heart and everyday practice.

Practitioners understandably lose sight of the forest as they deal among the trees (specific persons and situations), or even feel caught in a thicket. Some valiant workers in the helping services have studied and forgotten Erikson, Piaget, Kohlberg, and Fowler; others avoided or missed developmental theory altogether. Some were engineering or history students in their academic days now volunteering for a variety of reasons, such as having children of their own.

We must find ways to convince practitioners that *their* research (i.e., their own informal analyses of their situations and efforts) can make their work more effective and satisfying. They need to see how such study can benefit academics—and even stand as correctives to previous limitations of scientific research. Congregations and other organizations need to study their target areas and populations. They can profit from evaluation of their programs. With help, such studies can develop into nonscientific research.

Challenges to Academics

We academicians must admit many difficulties involved in a scientific study of human behavior. General studies may miss crucial nuances; specific studies may fail to grasp the larger picture and immeasurable variables. We get caught in our own disciplines—and even in our own special niches of investigation. Insightful practitioners intuit such limitations. "Researchers have to use controlled or sanitized settings to be scientific," says Rob Zarges of Straight Ahead Ministries, which focuses on juvenile justice. "They miss the unlimited variables that affect a young person's life. For instance, they can attribute something to a mentor that actually comes from a mother" (personal communication, August 2004).[1] Practitioners can see young people more holistically than some researchers.

Moving from opinions to behavior to morals to spirituality poses increasing levels of difficulty for social scientists. A wide range of research techniques and disclaimers is required to get at perplexing problems in and between human beings.

Too often scholarly research, books, and seminars operate from the viewpoint and interests of theoreticians. Even though academicians pay lip service to praxis, they may be trapped in their own contexts and pushed to work for their own and institutional ends. Our presentations and informal conversations reveal our contextual biases to outsiders. If and when youth leaders wander into our academic discussions, there is often a rolling of eyes or tired sighs. It may sound to such practitioners as if the rubber is somehow not meeting their road; there may be, for them, a hollow ivory tower ring to the discourse.

These leaders of children or youth get to know children and youth at a particular stage. They become familiar with a program by watching and imitating others. Their relationships with young people create a good learning environment, and a particular faith tradition is passed on. Too often they fail to observe children at prior stages of development or ponder the fate of their young charges when they pass on to older ages. These volunteers and leaders are busy people who feel the pressures of a packed life. If they are able to read magazines or books about their service, they are usually of the "how to" or "ideas" variety. By this time there is little remembrance of or appeal to theories of growth and faith development.

Most of these practitioners of children's and youth ministries leave the field within five years; many don't last two. Much of their frustration could be relieved by findings of the social sciences and solid theological reflection. But few of them access scientific antidotes for the tendency toward burnout that may have them out of the field in a year or two.

In writing about social science and the local congregation, an academician must move from academia to where the work of faith-based ministry is taking place. In doing this I realize the preceding summary is much too superficial. There are deeper reasons why we social scientists and educators do not get heard at ground level.

Defining Terms

Sometimes, differing worldviews and opinions about the nature of faith and spiritual development separate practitioners from academicians. We need a new and greater facility in "agreeing to disagree" (that is, working across sectarian or ideological boundaries). When relationships are not established between scholars and leaders, when there has not been face-to-face discourse, there are often tendencies for easy stereotypes or underlying fears of who the other is and what the other believes. Our scientific skills and assumptions or our religious values and a particular faith tradition may keep us from seeing values in another perspective. Academicians and practitioners, liberals and conservatives, often don't sense their need for one another.

Cultural Barriers Produce a Gap

There are cultural, semantic, philosophical/ theological, and practical reasons why excellent research and theory often do not reach the streets and organizations. Although we all live in subcultures, we often fail to realize the dynamics of our culture and how others feel and think about it. There are "subcultural" styles around academia, foundations, and research organizations. Youth workers sometimes don't feel at home, even in their own secular or religious institution. When they get together at conferences or network meetings, you can see them seek out comfortable cultural comradeship. Multicultural urban conferences involve greater cultural divisions. Black conventions have a special, dynamic cultural style. As a White presenter one may feel initial suspicion or at least understandable tentativeness. Many youth workers will see us academicians as cultural outsiders.

Cultures communicate with different words and different styles. It is not just the cultural identity of the researcher, but the way she or he talks and explains theory. There is further suspicion regarding the sample. It is at least suspected by some practitioners that the setting for the research and its respondents are mostly White and/or middle class. If the research has turned its sights to Latino or Black urban samplings, there may, on the other hand, be even higher anxiety as to "why you are studying us." We must admit difficulties with our samplings. A significant University of Michigan research project, "Monitoring the Future," has studied decades of American youth.[2] But its results are skewed because it annually measures 50,000 8th graders, 10th graders, and high school seniors. We need this study, but must concede that it depends on students *who will respond* and excludes urban dropouts.

Theological Barriers Produce a Gap

Researchers and practitioners often begin thinking of spiritual development at different places. Spirituality itself may have very different meanings to behavioral scientists and faith-based practitioners. The former are thinking universally; the latter more specifically. Developmentalists generalize patterns of growth; many faith-based practitioners are considering conversions and subsequent spiritual growth.

Let's take a closer look at these philosophical and theological differences. Academicians consider the *stages* put forward by James Fowler, or the *styles* suggested by John H. Westerhoff III, or the *stories* used by Robert Coles (Modica, 1999). Chickering and Reisser (1993) have complemented Erikson's developmental principles as they apply to adolescents and young adults with their suggested "Seven Vectors" of identity development in the college years. Gilligan (1993) and Hess (1997) have offered correctives to male biases in the works of developmental theorists. In addition, there have been cautions from Asian, African American, and other ethnic voices. Other scholars caution that cultural factors are not adequately understood by many developmental researchers at this point.

Even the most critical scholars, however, respect the tenets formulated by Erikson, Piaget, and Kohlberg. They admit to some universal principles of moral and spiritual development— principles not based on the need for some radical "conversion" interruption in the development process.

We can easily miss the fact that some faith-based workers, on the other hand, reject the common framework of developmentalists and replace it with a quite different understanding of spiritual development. For them spiritual and faith development may begin with conversion— or at least openness to the Word. Some faith-based practitioners may feel threatened by a theoretical scheme that sounds secular or liberal. Faith is not for them universal but rather exclusive to the precepts and dynamics of their particular religious tradition. Such disagreements that separate theoreticians and faith-based practitioners may involve both semantic misunderstandings and genuine theological differences.

Human developmentalists and educators sometimes limit their considerations to capacities, whereas practitioners deal with the struggles and actual progress made by children and youth at each stage of spiritual development. An example of work used by practitioners is Dunn (2001), which begins with the day-to-day struggles that characterize life at different stages and leaves consideration of early, middle, and late adolescence to the end—rather than the usual beginning—of the book. And even in those chapters the issues discussed are more social than psychological.

It is important, then, to give fresh attention to definitions that may be taken for granted, as well as to our cultural and theological differences.

CLOSING THE GAP

Rethinking Our Terminology

Thinking about spirituality is beset with several hurdles, one being the many ways in which terms are used. "I'm very spiritual, but I have no use for church or religions," twentysomethings often say, referring to reflective approaches to life and personal inner journeys. Pop culture reviewers may say that a film or a rap song reflects a spiritual quality—an ethereal or meditative mood or a quest for meaning. Finally, spirituality may describe and collect a whole range of issues regarding transcendence, personal faith, and religions. (Thomas Beaudoin's *Virtual Faith* needs a place in our discussion.)

Robert Coles has spent a lifetime investigating and reporting the moral and spiritual life of children and youth. For him spirituality is simply "to wonder about life and try to figure it out" (1995, p. 21). It is striking that this psychiatrist references a point made by Erikson in his *Insight and Responsibility:* "Life's deepest issues are those of conscience, of respect for one's self, of some kind of purpose in life that transcends psychodynamics" (Coles, 1995, p. 11). And again Coles, the psychiatrist, reaffirms for himself: "Our rock-bottom nature, I would argue, is not psychological. It is ultimately spiritual" (1995, p. 20).

Michael Warren, for years a rather radical and esteemed leader in Roman Catholic youth ministry, defines spirituality (especially referring to youthful spirituality) as "a systematic way of attending to the presence of God ... spirituality is a way of walking, a particular way of being in the world" (Warren, 1989, p. 95). Concerned about the demonic forces pushing children and young people toward instant gratification, violence, disconnectedness, and uncertainty, Warren hopes for a spirituality providing "solidarity, unity, and interdependence" (1987, p. 88).

Peter Benson, whose research is a critical component of this book, defines spirituality as "self-transcendence (in which) self becomes embedded in something greater than self, including the sacred (and leading to) connectedness, meaning, purpose, and contribution."[3]

We will use the word *spiritual* here to describe human aspirations or goals that move beyond animal instinct and self-centered concerns to ultimate meaning and sacrificial service for others and the good of the whole. There seems to be general agreement around such an idea of spirituality—as long as we leave room for particular forms of spirituality (Christian, Evangelical, Jewish, Muslim, Buddhist, for instance).

Spiritual propensities and reflection may lead to a faith. Faith can be nonreligious (e.g., scientism or agnosticism), or it can operate within any religion. Faith is seen as genuine when it is not merely inherited or acquired (as by foreclosure; see Borgman, 2003, pp. 37–38; Marcia, 1980) and when it is not just a superficial, cultural overlay. Faith is belief in a body of truths combined with an integration of implied values lived out in a way consistent with those beliefs and values. We speak of faith commitment because it implies believing one thing rather than another—whether broad and universal or narrow and sectarian. When referring to faith, we may be thinking of its personal operation in individual believers or its corporate function in faith communities.

Religions consist of beliefs or doctrines, codes of conduct, and rituals. This delineation parallels the three determinants of any given culture: its geographical location, beliefs or worldviews, and its technology and economy. In premodern times the belief system of a society and its religion were quite similar. Today's pluralistic, secular societies create whole new dynamics and tensions. Scholarly conferences discuss the belief system of a culture *or* the culture of a religion.

Religious Diversity

We have explained some of the gap between those who study spiritual development and those who carry out programs with children or youth in terms of semantic misunderstandings and suspicions of a spiritual threat. Important discussions between those of different faith or philosophical perspectives, as well as between academics and youth workers, often do not take place because of fear and suspicion.

Today's global tensions beg meaningful dialogue among Christians, Muslims, and Jews. Our divisions are not only between religions but also between more liberal and conservative followers of these religions. We need a better definition and understanding of fundamentalism in all three "Western religions" and how conservative or orthodox Jews, Christians, and Muslims are to be distinguished from more extreme fundamentalists.

To this plethora of positions must be added what some are calling the newcomers (though ancient) to the American and European religious scenes: Asian religions, American Indian spirituality, neopaganism, and others. Sometimes bridging the liberal–conservative divide within a particular faith tradition is more difficult than crossing from one religion to another. In some ways conservative Muslims, Jews, and Christians have much in common as they feel threatened by media and education in a pluralistic, secular society. Certain fundamental principles of spirituality and morals are held by all three religions.

Differences in liberal and more conservative understandings of human nature, spiritual needs, and faith development are important to consider. And it is understandable that resistance to government funding may come from religious conservatives as well as from secular humanists. Conservative faith-based congregations and organizations sometimes see possible government funding as a threat to what is distinctive in their faith perspective.

Closer Collaboration

New understandings and attitudes between academicians and practitioners must be practiced in closer collaboration. How can those in the academy and those working with people in congregations be convinced that there is benefit from the extra effort of working together? What do we have to share?

Generally speaking, rarely have organizations and churches brought researchers in to help them evaluate their work. (The few who have should be a separate study that goes far beyond the scope of this chapter.) The challenge, it seems to me, is for both sides of the professional divide to agree that planning, evaluation, and sustainability are interdependent and necessary for any human service organization—faith-based or otherwise. The evaluation process must be user-friendly, positively focused, collaboratively accomplished, and practically useful. Since growth is a basic goal in all human services, human development theory is necessary to this process. We need discussions between practitioners and researchers as to how quantitative and qualitative studies can be framed and used to bring out the best in programs.

Because a majority of faith-based organizations in the United States are Christian, I will continue from that perspective. (We know of strong Jewish philanthropies—educational and camping programs, for instance—and there are dynamic community efforts among Muslims. Hopefully the following discussion will be generally applicable to other religious traditions.)

One way to close the gap between the reliance on academic faith developmentalists versus a distinctive conversion model is to create a matrix from two continuums. Scott Larson, director of Straight Ahead Ministries, has successfully done this. He uses an Eriksonian continuum to measure human growth with another that uses markers of Spiritual Openness, Acceptance, Growth, and Productivity to measure spiritual growth and maturity. The boxes of the consequent matrix help workers understand the needs of the young felons with whom their organization works. Both the young person and the coach can benefit from discussion of the results of this self-administered survey.[4]

The Princeton professor James E. Loder (1998) also helps bridge the gap we are discussing. His work invites more theological consideration into developmental discussion. Loder "acknowledges that psychological stage theories enable us to understand the logic of humans' evolving relationship with the world and with God. At the same time, he demonstrates that the divine spirit has a logic of its own, which is not bound by stages, and which reveals a pattern of ultimate significance in the transient, fleeing moments we call a human life."[5]

Loder takes the position "that a Christian theological interpretation must be allowed to influence our studies of human development" (1998, p. xi). He takes us through the classic stages of human life, showing for each stage how *chronos* (human or earthly time) can be transformed into *kairos* (divine or eternal time). So, we have chapters titled "Infancy in Psychological Perspective: The Emerging Ego," "Infancy in Theological Perspective: The Spirit's Confrontation with Nothingness," "Adolescence in Psychological Perspective: The Five Axes of Youth Identity," and "Adolescence in Theological Perspective: Coming into the Presence of God."

Loder is more intentionally theological than most developmentalists, and although his specific theological ideas may not be embraced by all, he points to a method for bringing together disparate ideas of faith development. And though his theological understanding is specifically Christian, similar theological conceptions of human development could be undertaken from other religious perspectives.

A third and quite different suggestion regarding bridging the gap comes from four symposia held at Boys Town in Nebraska between 1989 and 1993. Presentations given at these gatherings have been recorded in Coles et al. (1995). This third path emphasizes how social scientists and practitioners can be brought together. Along with the academicians, the Reverends Bruce Wall and Buster Soaries represented practitioners in these symposia. It is interesting that their contributions to the resulting book are both narrative and singularly significant—and from a "conversionist" perspective. Both see conversion as a dramatic experience *and* a dynamic process.

Finally, both academicians and practitioners need to be more aware of the social systems surrounding the development of children and youth. Both fail at a holistic and systems thinking approach to family, community, schools, media, and peers. To these must be added the sometimes important institutions of employment and congregation/youth groups. Practitioners need encouragement from researchers as to how to study their target areas and target populations—and how to evaluate their efforts. Academicians can profit from such collaborations with the grass roots and from encouragement to operate in an interdisciplinary manner.

The crucial issue is a methodological one: our need for collaboration between scholars and practitioners. For too long and too many times we have attempted to understand and solve human service and ministry problems in separate camps. Academic work needs practical critique and balance. Practical conferences and books must hear from social scientists. We must not only show up, we need to collaborate.

Many obstacles hinder such collaboration. It is difficult to get all together, and it will call for hard work from all parties. The next section discusses the challenging work ahead.

User-Friendly Assessment Tools

A major way in which developmental scientists can help faith-based programs is to provide them with user-friendly assessment tools. Discussions between the parties will be helpful to both sides. Researchers may be challenged to make greater use of qualitative measures and to make sure their quantitative studies point to goals that are relevant and holistic. Practitioners will see the importance of statistics and understand how anecdotal evidence can help evaluate, plan, and improve; enhance reporting; motivate staff; and lead to better proposals. We must think more intentionally about capacity building in all we do.

The work of Search Institute, especially in the area of assessment, is well known.[6] The popularity and wide use of these tools are attributable to the scientific care with which they have been constructed, the ease with which they can be understood, and the effort made to introduce them to community groups.

Still, few practitioners are familiar with the wide range of assessment tools already developed. Many have inherited some tools their organization has used or neglected for years. Reservations already mentioned may keep them from using such measures and from working with researchers to improve them.

Fitchett (1993) has compiled a guide to spiritual assessment tools. He describes models based on Pruyser, Draper, and Fowler that can be used in congregations, Christian education, youth groups, youth organizations, counseling and retreat centers, and health care centers.

Here is how Fitchett describes the assessment model of Steven S. Ivy. Using Fowler and Kegan, Ivy

> identifies eight styles of consciousness, which are a person's way of meaning-making, action relationship *(pleasure, magical, literal, interpersonal, idealizing, reflective, integrative, and unitive).* A person's way of making meaning or style of consciousness is assessed through two structures, their style of symbolic communication and their style of community. (Fitchett, 1993, p. 14)

Eight categories parallel two styles, and on the bases of this schema Ivy provides sample questions for assessment and tables summarizing their key features along with "general guidelines for pastoral interventions." Fitchett states:

> Ivy believes that assessment begins with conversation, letting the person tell their story in their own words. He describes his model as one of style rather than stages in order to avoid the hierarchical assumptions of the latter, but as a development model the normativeness of the latter is unavoidable. (1993, p. 14)

Fitchett provides us with broad historical background, analysis, and examples in his brief monograph. He helps us see how theory can be made more accessible to many fields of human service.

A more recent book stretches our imagination in making spiritual assessment widely useful to the practitioner. It is David R. Hodge's *Spiritual Assessment* (2003). His introduction gives four reasons for the importance of spiritual assessment to the helping professional. First, people's worldviews are important to them, and for many spirituality is crucial to understanding relationships and their world. We can hardly understand people of different faiths, their attitudes and practices, if we aren't familiar with their spiritual orientation. Second, such assessments give professionals greater respect for client self-determination. According to recent studies, people want to integrate their spiritual values into counseling and their lives. As we try to incorporate people's strengths and assets into the solving of their problems, we find their spirituality to be a central strength. Third, conducting a spiritual assessment focuses attention on a client's strengths rather than weaknesses. Finally, social workers and religious leaders are expected to understand faith diversity and differences in spirituality.

The five assessment tools Hodge describes are unique in that they can serve a variety of constituencies across cultural and personality styles, make use of narrative, drawing, and analytic methods, and form a series that can be connected for fuller interpretation. They are called verbal spiritual history (like "conducting a family history"), spiritual life map (a paper chart), spiritual ecomap ("depicts a client's relationship to various spiritual entities . . . in present environment"), spiritual genogram ("chart the flow of spirituality across at least three generations"), spiritual ecogram ("drawing elements from both spiritual ecomaps and spiritual genograms depicts a person's spirituality in present time and space").

We should notice two goals in all the assessment tools described. They are companion goals. The mentor, coach, or assessor can only succeed in developing spiritual competency in others, as he or she is being spiritually developed. People helping should always be a two-way process. The goal of spiritual competency for practitioners, as Hodge describes it, involves coming to understand our biases, the particular lens through which we view reality, so that we can better understand how those of our own faith group deal with reality. Then we are better able to set aside our lens in order to see reality from the perspectives of those in other groups.

Cooperative Competency Building

As Fitchett and Hodge have interpreted the practical application of renowned spiritual developmental theories to their constituencies,

so we must take the significant material of this handbook and encourage its application wherever children and youth are being served. To do so we must start first, not with theory and academicians, but in places where children and adolescents are educated and served, with the teachers and workers who lead them.

We must find ways to help build competencies at the grass roots, help organizations do their own community research, determine their needs and resources (the assets of their target area and population), understand issues that hinder their efforts, and evaluate their endeavors more effectively. We must decide how this text can be turned into helpful workshops and how it can work for practitioners on the Internet.[7]

Imagine, then, a Head Start program in West Philadelphia or a day care center in Southside Chicago. Whether faith-based or not, administrators and workers need to understand what George Scarlett is saying in chapter 2 about the spirituality of children and his caution that not all spiritual development is good. We need to discuss together the principles and examples given by Tobin Hart (chapter 12, this volume).

Drop-in centers such as the Teen Center in West Springfield, MA, the Net Teen Center in Fairfax County, VA, or Yteens Center in Dayton of Greater Cincinnati all serve hundreds of teenagers a week. Their boards and staff need to consider the context in which teens explore their spirituality as discussed by Richard Lerner and his colleagues (chapter 5, this volume).

Practitioners everywhere are looking for advice in dealing with families, ethnicities, the poor, and at-risk youth. There is help for them throughout this handbook. We must not only encourage, but facilitate, discussions among theorists and practitioners.

CONCLUSIONS

Each chapter of this handbook merits application by faith-based organizations and congregations. We have tried here to suggest ways of relating across academic and cultural borders. We have asked for careful definition of terms, understanding, and respect among different faith perspectives. We have looked at some models for applying theory to practice. And this chapter has urged increased collaborative relationships and efforts.

Real collaboration will demand radical steps to include practitioners in the whole process of understanding human development, producing more effective human services. Such a process will end up drawing clients into the planning and research process. A dynamic triadic collaboration involving researchers, practitioners, and those served by faith-based organizations is the end to which we press. And if we are using the term *faith-based* as more than a buzzword or convenient category, we see our work as proceeding from the larger triad: God's enlightening Spirit, ourselves and our professional niche, and others (other disciplines, organizations, and people).

Certainly our common goals are relevance, professional excellence, contextualization, healing, growth, and community. Our work has been hampered, among other things, by professional ego, institutional turf, as well as value and communication differences between ethnic and class groups. A new and radical spirit of collaboration would bring us together to discuss funding, proposals, hypotheses, research tools, the gathering of data, interpretation of results, and application of findings leading to new research and better practice.

I count myself not as a social scientist but as an educator. The past decades have shown an astounding increase in those who professionally educate and train youth workers and youth ministers. The Association of Youth Ministry Educators (in the United States) and the International Association for the Study of Youth Ministry (international) have both sprung up in the past decade or so and both publish fine journals. I believe we educators could be better links between social scientists and practitioners. We have not taken that challenge seriously enough. A number of professors of youth ministry are producing good studies. But the task of bringing youth workers themselves into the research process remains an important challenge.

Finally, this is not just an academic matter. Those who combine compassion and insight are literally saving young lives. And as we indicated at the beginning of this chapter, the welfare of our society may also be at stake.

Notes

1. See www.straightahead.org for further information about this organization's ministry in juvenile justice.

2. See Monitoring the Future, www.monitoring thefuture.org.

3. Peter Benson's remarks were delivered in a PowerPoint presentation at Tufts University, November 10, 2003, conference titled Spirituality: Its Role in Child and Youth Development. http://www.tucc.tufts.edu/spirituality_conference_info.htm

4. Quick Connect can be ordered through the Straight Ahead Web site (www.straightahead.org). This tool is very reasonably priced and is helpful in any Christian youth ministry.

5. This quotation is taken from the back cover of Loder's book.

6. For further information on Search Institute, go to www.search-institute.org and see Developmental Assets ™ and Sources for Evaluation.

7. See www.centerforyouth.org and the companion Web site www.cys-ministry.org; www.fastennetwork.org, www.youthandreligion.org, and www.search-institute.org, among others.

References

Beaudoin, T. (1998). *Virtual faith: The irreverent spiritual quest of Generation X.* San Francisco: Jossey-Bass.

Borgman, D. (2003). *Hear my story.* Peabody, MA: Hendrickson.

Chickering, A. W., & Reisser, L. (1993). *Education and identity.* San Francisco: Jossey-Bass.

Coles, R., et al. (1995). *The ongoing journey: Awakening spiritual life in at-risk youth.* Boys Town, NE: Boys Town Press.

Dunn, R. R. (2001). *Shaping the spiritual lives of students.* Downers Grove, IL: InterVarsity Press.

Fitchett, G. (1993). *Spiritual assessment in pastoral care: A guide to selected resources.* Decatur, GA: Pastoral Care Publications.

Gilligan, C. (1993*). In a different voice: Psychological theory and women's development.* Cambridge, MA: Harvard University Press.

Hess, C. L. (1997). *Caretakers of our common house: Women's development in communities of faith.* Nashville, TN: Abingdon Press.

Hodge, D. (2003). *Spiritual assessment: Handbook for helping professionals.* Botsford, CT: North American Association of Christians in Social Work.

Loder, J. E. (1998). *The logic of the spirit: Human development in theological perspective.* San Francisco: Jossey-Bass.

Marcia, J. E. (1980). Identity in adolescence. In J. Adelson (Ed.), *Handbook of adolescent psychology* (pp. 159–187). New York: John Wiley.

Modica, J. B. (1999). Stages, styles, or stories? A brief guide to faith development. *Catalyst On-line: Contemporary Evangelical Perspectives for United Methodist Seminarians, 25* (3). Retrieved December 20, 2004, from www.catalystresources.org/issues/253modica.html

Warren, M. (1987). *Youth, gospel, liberation.* San Francisco: Harper & Row.

Warren, M. (1989). *Faith, culture, and the worshipping community.* New York: Paulist Press.

31

INTEGRATING SPIRITUAL DEVELOPMENT INTO CHILD AND YOUTH CARE PROGRAMS AND INSTITUTIONS

DANIEL G. SCOTT

DOUGLAS MAGNUSON

In this chapter we address how a concern for child and youth spiritual development translates into programmatic and institutional practice in professional child and youth care (CYC) work, and we explore the impact of the spirituality of care practice on the spiritual development of children and youth. We bring together conceptions of spirituality and conceptions of practice, addressing the complexity of spirituality in the lives of children in care or in CYC programs, assuming that spiritual development is a part of normative life processes.

Spirituality in child and youth care practice has been perceived to be synonymous with the personal commitment of practitioners or the religious goals or mission statement of care service providers, and there has been little written about practice that takes into account spiritual dimensions. The CYC field has begun to normalize a concern for the spiritual development of children and youth in programmatic and care settings. Two sources of this concern are the UN Convention on the Rights of the Child (1989), several articles of which state that opportunities for the care and nurture of spiritual development are a right of children and youth, and the *North American CYC Professional Competencies* (Mattingly, 2002), a document that identifies spiritual development as part of foundational knowledge for CYC practitioners.

ASSUMPTIONS

In order to locate this chapter in the spectrum of ideas about spiritual development, a number of primary assumptions need to be clarified. First, in keeping with the broader understanding of our field, we are assuming that spirituality is a normative human phenomenon. While there are varying levels of spiritual experience, spirituality is not an accomplishment but rather a central human quality.

Theory about the shape of that spirituality is being debated as researchers have begun to theorize about a second assumption: that children can and do have spiritual experiences, insights, and knowledge without the intervention or assistance of adults. This awareness is supported by research on children's lives from Robinson and Fowler in the 1970s to Coles (1990), Hay and Nye (1998), and Hart (2003). Theories like Hay's "relational consciousness" and Hart's five capacities are built on their studies of and accounts of children's lives. They recognize that children and youth can have primary, unassisted spiritual experiences that are significant in terms of immediate impact and longer term influence. Whether or not these experiences are acknowledged by others or are articulated during childhood, they do impact life-span development, and if retrospective claims are to be accepted (Robinson, 1983; Scott, 2004), they do shape people's lives and their senses of self.

There is a third assumption, with two strands, that is particularly significant in any consideration of programmatic or institutional work with children and youth. First, it is important to note that children's spiritual experiences can occur outside the structures and training of organized religion or they may be filtered through the lens of the religion of a child's family and culture. Children's spiritual experiences are not dependent on instruction or training and can be intense and physically felt. They can include a deep sense of oneness through experiences of light or nature (Hart, 2003; Robinson, 1983; Scott, 2004) or troubling dreams or visionary encounters (Coles, 1991; Hart, 2003; Scott, 2004), experiences of altruism and kindness or compassion (Coles, 1990; Hart, 2003), commitment to another, forgiveness, and so forth. Children who have such experiences may not have accompanying vocabularies to express or articulate their encounters with mystery or the numinous: that which is beyond themselves. As Hay (1998) notes, in order to speak of their experiences they rely on the religious vocabulary provided by their cultures.

The reality of these experiences is instructive for CYC work in both programmatic and institutional settings. In becoming aware of their spiritual potential it is important to remember that, in keeping with the capacity of children to adapt or please their caregivers, they will reflect back what their setting expects. Consequently, the spirituality of their care site and its assumptions about their spiritual development will affect them. Models of care, treatment, intervention, or prevention rarely acknowledge spirituality as part of youth experience. Care and treatment plans do not include spiritual development, so it is important for child and youth care workers to assist their processing of their experiences so that they can integrate them successfully. Their experience may not fit the expectations of their setting: CYC workers in secular settings need to be alert to the danger of denying youths' experience and, in religious settings, cautious not to direct youths' experiences toward specific conclusions.

If one considers the history of aboriginal residential schools in Canada, run by both government and church-based organizations, it is possible to see the unfortunate results of ignoring the spiritual experiences of children that originate from their own culture with its assumptions and beliefs, for example, about the natural spiritual nature of life, and imposing a different spiritual or religious tradition originating in another culture. Severing those children from their own spiritual culture, language, context, and insight had a harsh impact on their sense of self, their resilience, and their future. The damage to family and community life in aboriginal communities has continued for several generations and remains a challenge for communities and for those who provide social services to them.

Usually children and youth are in care programs because of their troubles, and there is a natural tendency to focus on these troubles in organizing a response. Yet the spiritual experience of children and youth should not be ignored or misplaced. Noumenal and transcendent experiences are normative, and they can be an avenue toward overcoming difficulty and away from a preoccupation with or even a tendency to fetishize problems.

There are a number of examples in the literature of programmatic and institutional care settings that assume particular religious or faith-based assumptions for care programs and institutions (Hyland & Herron, 1995; Morgenthaler, 1999; Shelton, 1983). These approaches are dedicated to particular faith-based assumptions and see the care of children and youth as part of their religious obligation and compassion. In addition, there is a vast literature on children and youth programs written for denominational settings and church-based programs that intend to support the religious objectives of those settings and are directed at various forms of religious education and faith development.

In contrast, the second strand of the assumption is that spiritual development is not seen as following the same developmental path or models as faith development, such as those outlined by Fowler (1981) or Grimmitt's (1987) religious education model, which he calls "shared human experience." Spiritual development in children is not determined by participation in a religious community, nor is it dependent on predetermined educational outcomes and instruction. Faith communities and family religious contexts can provide children support for spiritual and religious reflection and do offer interpretations of and vocabulary for children's spiritual experiences. Religious education may provide a form and structure to direct spiritual reflection and nurture spiritual sensitivity, such as the awarenesses identified by Hay or the spiritual capacities named by Hart as normative for children but not a prerequisite for them. These capacities and awarenesses build on the children's own experiences and will develop in any context regardless of instruction. Spiritual development, like other forms of development, happens to all children in all contexts. Faith development and religious education are context specific.

The religious education forms of faith development can be life-giving for children when the spiritual/religious claims made are also congruent with the lived experience of the community. The matter of congruency in children's lives will be taken up in more detail later in this chapter, using Anglin's (2002) important insight about the role of "congruency" in working with children and youth. His recent grounded-theory study of residential care has provided an important theoretical model to look at how care is provided in institutional settings and brings to attention the importance of the maintenance of a congruent, consistent, and coherent context for child and youth care work. The consistency between philosophical or ideological claims and the ways of living and responding in a community has a deep impact on young people's ability to be open and responsive in the context and to absorb and integrate the values espoused. Anglin's model will serve as a theoretical frame of reference that guides this exploration.

Finally, the assumption that spirituality is normative and not dependent on instruction or education means that what we are describing is a kind of philosophical anthropology that includes spirituality as "an account . . . of what it means to be a human being in the social world" (Jacobs, 1996, p. 26) that is independent of the presence of religious ideologies and theologies, ritual practices, codes of belief, and so on (see Ó Murchú, 1998). We attempt here to explicate the implications of this spiritual account for child and youth care practice. Spirituality is a reality of this view of human nature. Specific religious structures may well be attempts to order and describe preoccurring or co-occurring spiritual insight and experience. Spirituality then, is not dependent on religious knowledge or education but may well be shaped by both. Spiritual development can and does exist for children and youth and operates in their lives whether or not it is given attention or care.

Spiritual development may be a more complex, nonlinear process that cannot be easily described in a progressive stage development theory, although some have tried, for example, Fowler (1981) and Conn (1981). Specifically, it is clear that many children have powerful early life experiences that they are separated from or suppress in response to cultural signals. Moreover, spiritual development may include experiences of loss at very early ages and may follow more cyclical patterns of loss and return. The waning of spiritual insight over the years of childhood into adolescence may be a necessary shift of orientation to other developmental tasks that dominate the early years of adult life. In some aboriginal traditions the first 7 to 10 years are identified as the time of spiritual development and the next 7 to 10 years as the time of physical development. Cultural frames of reference become important in understanding how the spiritual lives of children are conceived and the expectations that surround spirituality that children will learn from their context.

CONGRUENCE IN
CHILD AND YOUTH CARE

In a study of group homes, Anglin (2002) identified "congruence" as a central element of successful care for children and youth. Further, he noted that "responding to pain and pain-based behavior is the primary challenge at the level of the carework staff" (p. 55). These two ideas are useful for thinking about spirituality in youth work practice.

Anglin identifies three "major properties" of congruence: "consistency, reciprocity, and coherence" (p. 64):

> Consistency refers to the degree to which the same set of values, principles, processes, or action are demonstrated in practice over time and within and across the various dimensions, levels and domains of group home operation . . . The levels identified include the experiences of youth and families, the behavior of individual staff members, the functioning of a team including the work of the supervisor), the actions of management, and the linkages with outside agencies and professionals. (p. 64)

> Reciprocity as a property of congruence is understood in this context as the degree of mutuality demonstrated in the interactions between persons involved with and within the home. Thus, when interactions are reciprocal, there is a significant degree of commonality between what is intended and what is received in the communication process, as well as an experience of the two-way relationship in the behaviors exhibited. (pp. 64–65)

> Finally, coherence refers to the degree to which all of the behaviors and activities of an individual, a group (or team), the home, or system of care have an overall sense of wholeness and integrity. In a team situation, this coherence is sometimes referred to as cohesiveness. (p. 65)

Congruence is an evaluative and interpretive tool for looking at life in residential settings, although while "the degree of consistency and reciprocity can be examined in relation to individual actions and interactions, coherence can only be determined by stepping back and examining the overall pattern of actions and interactions" (p. 65). In a complex organizational setting like a group home, "there are always competing interests and intentions" and "full congruence (whatever its focus may be) is an ideal state that is never completely achieved" (p. 65).

Congruence has a number of cognates: alignment, balance, and harmony (Anglin, personal communication, 2004). These words have spiritual implications that speak of how the quality of a residence depends on personal integrity. Consistency across levels can include personal integrity, which is then duplicated or expressed in the congruent design of programs, administrative structures, and institutional support.

Congruence requires that there be a higher purpose that all elements of the operation respect and follow. Consistency, reciprocity, and coherence allow for that purpose to be expressed, modeled, and lived out by staff and residents. The "higher" purpose brings things together by offering a significant organizing principle that is beyond the immediate interest of the personnel, the agency, and so on. In offering an evaluative model for assessing residential settings Anglin is also providing a tool to assess the quality of spiritual life possible in an environment. The underlying philosophy and values of a site are being expressed through the consistency, reciprocity, and coherence being enacted by the staff in the delivery of care, and the extent to which this is successful depends on how well spirituality is made congruent throughout all levels of the organization. This is why the idea of spirituality as intent, described earlier, is not adequate. A "faith-based" organization or a religious organization that operates programs may have an altruistic and spiritual intent, but how it carries out that intention at more than just the mission level can be evaluated and examined.

In Anglin's study it was clear that those institutions that worked best had a singular higher purpose: putting the well-being of the child first and organizing administration and procedures toward that end. It is also clear that the central purpose must be other-directed, that is, driven by an ethos of service to the children or youth in care; and all other interests—institutional, procedural, and financial—are second to that. Hidden agendas are easily perceived by children in crisis, because they have developed intense early warning awarenesses for their self-protection. Any hidden desires in interventions may be counterproductive for the children, their families, and the institution. This includes the danger of a secondary religious aim to proselytize, which can fragment and divert efforts away from the best interests of the children or families.

The struggle for congruence is also an inner struggle on the part of staff (Anglin, personal communication, 2004). The work to create a balanced program is paralleled by the work to maintain inner balance. This approach requires an attitude of service, and, as Anglin found, there is a remarkable power in congruence that creates livable space for children in difficulty. A singular congruent focus means that all actions and choices come from the same frame of reference and with the same intent. Such a clear focus may sometimes mean transcending policies for the benefit of the child. Working in this way requires constant attention and struggle. It is worth noting that the practice of attention is a form of spiritual journey when it is acknowledged that the journey is incomplete and in process, that it must be constantly negotiated, that it includes doubt and, at the same time, has the courage to act and risk. The journey being lived by the staff and expressed in the congruence of the site is a model for the child in trouble to use as a way of living to meet and overcome his or her own difficulties and woundedness. The focus on the child is a guiding transcendent principle that can in turn be copied by the child or youth in care.

Spirituality in Practice

The preceding assumptions are important for CYC workers as they alter their approach to children or youth and their families. Every child and youth and every family arrives at our door with a condition of spiritual development whether articulated, acknowledged, or consciously enacted. Similarly, every worker comes with his or her own condition of spiritual development, insight, knowledge, and experience. Any intervention, care interaction, or therapeutic relationship will include aspects of spirituality.

Spirituality is grounded in the lived events of life and in the day-to-day experiences and actions of both CYC workers and their clients and their families. Spirituality is focused not on claims or beliefs but on the enacted concerns and interests of human beings. In CYC residential and programmatic settings, this means that some expression of personal and communal spirituality will be evident in the way life is being lived and the way in which care is delivered. In other words, every person and setting has a set of values, beliefs, principles, and ethics that get expressed in their actions and embodied in their practice. Individual spirituality, then, can be noted in the practices of staff and communal spirituality in the way a residential setting actually operates: what is valued and stressed, the embodied operational principles and policies, and the impact of the embodied ideology on the children or youth in care or in programs.

Consequently, CYC workers will need to develop their awareness of the potential and actual role and benefit of spirituality in their professional settings. It is not only a self-reflective awareness of their own spiritual state that they require but also the capacity to attend to the collective spiritual state of their working environment that is being enacted in both staff relations and relationships with the clients and their families. CYC workers in addition need to be willing to extend their awareness of the spiritual to the spirituality and beliefs of their clients and their families. Childhood and adolescent spiritual experiences can be, if appropriately processed and integrated, sources of strength and resilience for the young. How their experiences are received will play a significant role in how they are integrated and whether they become a resource or an impediment. The assumption is that spirituality is already evident in and being expressed in any care context. Being alert to it and being sensitive to its potential will add to the capacity of programs and care settings to be responsive to clients and participants.

Clients, children, youth, and families come to care programs with cultural and family traditions, histories, and identities that may or may not include an acknowledged religious identity and tradition. Staff and caregivers also bring their own sociocultural location to their therapeutic or care work. Clients and professionals meet in structured settings whose wide range of regulatory and ethical assumptions, locations, and practices may deliberately exclude or include religious practice, discourse, and intentions. In this context it is important to consider how the spirituality of the various players in these care relationships and the spiritual orientation of the site interact and how those interactions might benefit from deliberate attention to spirituality and its role in professional care. CYC professionals need to be alert to both the religious context of the clients' families and the spirituality being expressed by those families and clients in their relationships.

There are different sources of the many ways to consider the role of spirituality in professional practice, and we will now suggest several approaches that might provide a basis for CYC work to take up some of the potential of a heightened spiritual awareness in practice. The first is a set of themes that provide a theoretical/philosophical basis for considering a spirituality for child and youth care practice, and the second will consider the implications of such a spirituality in practice.

THEMES OF SPIRITUALITY IN CHILD AND YOUTH CARE

Gift Giving

> *The gift remains outside, external to, the economy of production and consumption, distribution and exchange. Indeed, the gift remains radically transcendent to the determinations of reciprocity within the economy of goods and services; and insofar as it does impinge upon and interact with this economy. (Schrag, 1997, p. 140)*

The distinction between immanence and transcendence is important to understanding spirituality in child and youth care. Following Schrag, these are two "spheres." That of immanence lies within what he calls the "economy of production . . . and exchange," while transcendence is exemplified by the metaphor of gift giving. These spheres can frame two different ways of thinking about child and youth care.

Some practices of thinking about child and youth care operate from an immanent point of view and within the economy of production and exchange. That is, our goals for young people—healing, behavior change, developmental growth, mastery of social skills, more effective behaviors—are a type of production: We input effort and skill with the expectation of outcomes and a "product." Even humane interpretations of this view of young people as collaborators assume that young people will contribute something—their own effort, their goals, their practice of social skills, their resolution of life issues in the work of producing an acceptable outcome.

Almost every program, intervention, relationship, and setting in work with difficult young people identifies some outcome variable with young people against which the effectiveness of the initiative is measured. And the quality of the program, intervention, relationship, and setting is judged by the relative presence or absence of the outcome variable. But at their core, these measures undermine ethical and spiritual commitment to young people, because they operate at that immanent level of exchange and production.

Imagine a young boy newly admitted to a child and youth care program. From his point of view, he is there for a confusing mixture of reasons: He is a victim of neglect or abuse, and he carries daily the pain of that experience and his abandonment by someone whom he expected to love him; he has been removed from his home, and he feels both relieved to be away from the chaos and fearful of losing his family. Then he encounters a "hothouse" of a program in which he is watched and programmed by staff who have many designed intentions and strategies for intervention in his life. There are suddenly other youth noticing him who may be friendly but may also be occasionally hostile. He may be presented with a long list of behavioral expectations and responsibilities, being taught to him in a highly technical language. The program is a foreign culture, and those around him react in ways that are unexpected and foreign. He realizes that doing what other people want is the agenda of the place, and as long as he does that, he will be rewarded in some way, even though he does not yet feel that the agenda is his own or that the offered rewards are desirable. If he rejects or does not respond to those rewards, he may be punished.

Moreover, he understands clearly that expressing his pain is not usually acceptable, as Anglin (2002) documented, and he may not know socially acceptable ways of doing so. He may even come to understand that admitting he feels pain is unacceptable. He may know that the staff care about him, and he may feel increasingly secure and connected, but in that security he may feel less guarded and more open about his rage and pain. Still, if he shares more of his own turmoil, fear, and pain, aggressive measures may be applied against him to get him to stop, which in turn has consequences for his sense of security.

Specifically, people want things from him, and this wanting is expressed in a program of intervention and instruction. His experience in this setting exemplifies a program guided by "best practices" and operating in the sphere of immanence. He is rewarded for performing, for improving, and for changing, and he is punished—or re-educated—for failure. We input effort toward improving and reforming him, and we expect to be able to see and measure results and outcomes.

This is not an abstract exercise. It is typical, when youth have troubles, for affection to be withdrawn, for youth to be removed from the program and placed somewhere else, for subtle threats of bad outcomes to be insinuated. A climate of despair and frustration permeates any relationship sustained by these practices.

This is easiest to understand in programs where behaviorism is operative, because so much critical literature has been written about it (Kegan, 1982; Kohlberg & Mayer, 1972). These programs, with good intentions, aim to shape the behavior of children and youth toward social expectations, and, to the extent that young people cooperate, they are rewarded with relationships, material objects, privileges, freedoms, and graduation from the program.

But relationships with young people in such systems are contractual, and to the extent that one or the other parties break the contract, the relationship is over. Moreover, the relationship is bounded by the length and terms of the contract. It is a reciprocal agreement between two parties, and the contract can be terminated at any time by either party.

Other sorts of interventions with young people operate similarly, for example, therapeutic counseling, cognitive-developmental reframing, re-education, and skill training. The basic metaphor is exchange and production. Youth in institutions often tell workers how they feel. "You only care about my behaviors—you don't care about me," a girl once told one of the authors. Many youth workers have similar stories. Jackie Thompson (personal communication) said that the prostitutes with whom she worked described residential intervention programs as being like prostitution: "Getting paid for doing what the customer wants."

To attend to young people as spiritual beings requires setting aside the interpretive and diagnostic criteria of the child welfare infrastructure: hydraulic theories of resolution, stimulus–response, and so forth. The difficulties of young people, from a spiritual point of view, have to do with their exploitation and violations of dignity, inadequate love, hatred, transgression, irresponsibility, resentment, and despair. Many young people who require professional care have been violated—physically, sexually, morally, emotionally. Young people who have been exploited, manipulated, and used for the gratification of an adult's pleasure, security, emotional needs, or egocentrism have experienced an ultimate violation, that is, a spiritual violation that in turn operates through the physical, sexual, moral, and emotional actions and expressions of their lives.

To redress the problems from a spiritual point of view, it is necessary to practice gift giving, in the form of a generosity or charity toward young people that does not expect a return on investment, the fulfillment or satisfaction of adults' needs, or a response to adult power. This kind of giving is healing, invoking the possibility of transcending a state of permanent woundedness. The spiritual metaphor of gift giving operates outside this economy of production and exchange: Gift giving, as generous and charitable, does not ask for a return, and does not possess. It is freely given. Care and gifts are not contingent on behavior and on the receiver behaving the way we want them to. They are given independently of circumstances and reward. This charity shows itself in different ways.

First, all youth need care and commitment, but those children and youth who have been damaged by experience especially need it. These youth are familiar with being used by others, and they are acquainted with the social scripts that are invoked when they act on and express their own pain. Thus, charity and kindness must be extended to youth regardless of whether they express appreciation.

Second, staff can absorb the pain, the "acting-out behaviors," the insults, the expressions of anger without retribution or memory. Youth expect others to respond to them in patterned and scripted ways, especially youth who have troubles, and they know well how to invoke those patterns. But in refusing to participate, staff bypass the normal expectations and usual anticipations of youth about what happens to them. Staff can bring into being the unexpected with the possibility of transcendence.

Third, work with youth from a spiritual point of view yields space for mystery and paradox. Normally, interventions with youth aim to manage the environment and youth interactions with it in such a way that behavior is shaped and that youth gradually approximate success. But a spiritual perspective asks us to abandon that carefully managed framework to allow room for the mystery of growth and change. We abandon the notion that we are in control of the change and growth process, and we believe that the practice of spirituality, in this setting, and the practice of commitment will, in the end, invite youth to change. This requires faith in one's principles and values.

The idea here is illustrated by Rousseau's maxim, "Don't save time, lose it." The goal is best achieved by not demanding it.

Suffering

In child and youth care, suffering and pain are pervasive, as Anglin (2002) pointed out:

> The description of the anger and hurt of the young people in some of the homes . . . , the "repercussions" of this hurt and anger, and the busyness of the daily life of staff and residents powerfully conveys a common reality of group home life observed in this study. Despite this ongoing interaction, discussion, or conversation—either between the staff and the residents or even amongst the staff members themselves—was seldom evident concerning the underlying hurt that was being experienced and carried by these young people. The many activities of daily life seemed to disguise and cover over this ever-present and deep-seated pain to the point where one wondered if this "cover up" was an intentional strategy of avoidance. (p. 108)

Taking that suffering seriously is an important spiritual practice. A spiritual interpretation affirms the painfulness of our youth's suffering, affirms the integrity of the feelings of anger, shame, hatred, loneliness, and fear. A youth can be angry, sullen, afraid, without fear of retribution or trite urgings to cheer up. She lives with staff who can also be human, and she knows they are honest about their own doubts and fears. Moreover, she is allowed to learn through and from her suffering, because only in that way, ultimately, can forgiveness and healing occur and the deterministic hold her suffering appears to have on her be loosed and new possibilities imagined.

A spiritual reading of problem behavior, of "acting out," and of anger understands the pain and suffering at its root and responds to the root rather than to the behavior. The young person may learn here that it is possible to be forgiven and that she will not be "mistaken for her mistakes." She is cared for and about, and no one demands that she reciprocate or threatens to remove their care if she does not behave.

Anglin points out that not only are youth in pain, but staff who work with pained youth are also in pain. Some are in pain because of the difficulty of working with these youth. Absorbing the aggression and anger of youth is emotionally exhausting, as is monitoring oneself to prevent reactionary, frustrated, and angry responses. Others are in pain because many staff attracted to this type of work have themselves suffered some kind of trauma. Working with these children recalls their own pain, and their own actions recall for them the social scripts of their own families. These too are acknowledged and their reality accepted. Suffering is a theme of many religious traditions, some of which describe it as a pathway to transcendence—to God. It is not deliberately chosen; it is a fact of life for many, and it has to be faced with courage.

Forgiveness

A third theme is forgiveness. In the context of children's and youths' experience of being wounded or exploited, their pain-based behaviors can include acting out or striking out against those around them (Anglin, 2002), and the responses to their behaviors affect their work of healing and coming to express their pain. Staff in residential and program settings who follow the model of correcting behavior through punishment, service withdrawal, and withholding of privileges do not address the underlying pain. Acts of forgiveness become a second form of generosity and care. The staff takes the first responsibility to alter the relationship, and forgiveness provides the ground for transformation. The responsibility for forgiveness is that of caregivers. When young people express their rage, their fear, and their longings, caregivers forgive, and they do so repeatedly. Forgiveness is healing for the recipient, and the forgiveness exercised by caregivers demonstrates commitment and provides security for youth. Further, it teaches the young person how to forgive and, eventually, to thrive. Youth who have been violated can learn to forgive their violators if their own wounds have been healed. Increasingly, psychologists (see, for example, Friedman, 1999, 2003) have been studying forgiveness in the lives of victims and are finding that when forgiveness is realized, there are powerful effects and transcendent, spiritual consequences for the forgiver.

Both forgiveness and gift giving are freely offered acts that allow one to transcend the past and exercise freedom to choose anew. They contribute to a healing process that addresses the underlying pain in the lives of children and youth who have experienced troubles and difficulty. Their pain is allowed to come to attention and be met with responses that promote transformation and create the possibility of the fourth spiritual theme.

Creation and Rebirth

A fourth theme, creation and rebirth, encompasses the transformative undertaking at the heart of care work and offers the possibility of transcendence to children and youth. The practice of child and youth care is an experience of *re-creation* of program, of setting, of relationship, and of moment. Youth workers make possible new choices—in each moment—of action,

identity, and direction. Children who come with pain-based behaviors will have the space they need to transcend their difficulties in an environment that has put their interests and process in the foreground, where the care they receive is freely given and does not demand change but provides space where change is possible. Anglin (personal communication, February 19, 2004) admitted his surprise at realizing that he had invoked a notion of creation as central in his book and had not thought of it deliberately as a spiritual action. In creating an artificial living environment as the core process of a "good enough" space, a bigger action is enabled that sets the others in motion and mirrors the religious and spiritual tradition of telling founding stories. He noted how often managers told founding stories and the accidents, coincidences, and struggles they went through in founding their site and establishing its central focus. What is being created is a living environment for a child who is already wounded: a life space creation. It is expressed in/as both a program and an institution.

In a space in which creation and creativity are operative and present, the participants/residents begin to reflect back this attitude. Youth are able to see what they need for their own lives. They have opportunities to know, for example, that there are healthy ways to resolve conflict or to live with the hope of possibility. If workers are healthy and carry an inner balance, their ways of being and acting may be models worthy of notice by those in their care. If a child sees a different way of becoming or acting, it may take him or her a long time to process and express the shift in understanding. If years of damage have occurred, it will take more than a few weeks or months to find a way toward normalcy. There is a connection here to the literature on resiliency and how important a different image of acting or being is as a building block to be copied and amplified in a child's life (O'Connell Higgins, 1994). The process of re-creating life begins when the possibility of rebirth is visible and modeled as a way of living.

It is important to grasp that more is at stake than good behavior and appropriate conduct. There is, understandably, much concern in child and youth care programs with teaching young people the right things to do: both in the nonmoral sense of how to act and also in the moral sense of making the right choices and avoiding evil and harm. That this goal is necessary but not sufficient for child and youth care programs is true for reasons of spirituality.

Kierkegaard (cited in Dreyfus, n.d.) described brilliantly what he called the "despair of the ethical," which is, in part, an attempt to fulfill one's life through doing the right thing and through relationships and the group. Ultimately, though, Kierkegaard says, such an attempt leads to despair, because it is a one-dimensional life and the choice of whom to be responsible to is arbitrary. Doing the right thing does not address the urge for significance, the human desire to realize value, or the existential yearning for attention to "ultimate concerns" or to the absolute.

Some young people who are in child and youth care programs instinctively experience the gap between their own quest for significance and purpose and the expectations of the environment in which they live, and for some the inadequacy of those expectations in the face of their own personal crisis may be grounds for a new crisis. Their rebellion and resistance on the basis of this crisis can be mistaken for inability or character deficiencies.

Attention to spirituality focuses on the potential and possibilities for the "pursuit of value" and for "moving beyond oneself" (Conn, 1981, pp. 23, 6) that comes from "sensitive and creative understanding, critical judgment, responsible decision, loyal commitment, and genuine love" (p. 6), motivated by attention to "ultimate concerns." The yearning for significance, and the proper and most meaningful motivation for doing the right thing, are in light of and in response to the aim to realize value in service to something more than the self. It may be a transcendent calling and commitment, an innate sense of vocation to a life task or role (Hillman, 1996), or it may stem from an experience of oneness and connection beyond the self from earlier years (Robinson, 1983; Scott, 2004).

Child and youth care, in addressing spirituality, does more than teach young people what to do and how to do it. We ought to be able to show, through experience, what it is that is worth living for. Each child and youth care program can be interpreted as a time, place, and space that calls—or invites—young people to live fully and to live in service of a higher purpose. The invitations work best when they are concrete. Some programs do this by locating themselves on a farm with access to and responsibility for animals and plants. Some programs have service components or supply jobs. Some provide access to music. Some provide outstanding educational opportunities.

Child and youth care programs look for ways to avoid reinforcing negative identities and fixations on trauma. Being ill can itself become a calling. Concrete opportunities help youth transcend past hurts and invite youth into a present, beyond their troubles, fixations, fears, and anxieties. Moreover, concrete opportunities capitalize on what youth workers do well: organizing the environment so that a fragile person can, over time, develop a new identity, learn from experience, and find hope in present and future opportunities.

And concrete opportunities are most effective when they are congruently structured, focused on a higher purpose that is devoted to the best interests of the children or youth, and built on an attitude of reciprocity and generosity that does not have a secondary outcome-driven focus. The best interest of the child can remain in the foreground when his or her suffering is acknowledged and forgiveness is part of an atmosphere and practice in which care is freely given and the transformational process is consistent with an ethos that displays generosity, patience, forgiveness, and compassion. These programs succeed because they demonstrate the consistency, reciprocity, and coherence Anglin has identified as necessary for congruence. They do what they advocate.

Spirituality and Congruence

Spirituality must be grounded in practice, both in the lives of CYC workers and in the institutional practices of their workplaces. We conclude with a number of specific orientations for a congruent approach to spirituality in child and youth care institutions and programs.

1. The spiritual development of staff is crucial, in that the major mechanism of impact on

young people is the staff's own spiritual insight, sensitivity, and their skillfulness of interpretation, what theologians call "discernment." Forgiveness, for example, requires a mature judgment and willingness to set aside the usual desire for revenge or even for redress. True forgiveness requires staff to avoid developing character judgments, to avoid spreading word of a youth's reputation, to avoid using psychiatric and *Diagnostic and Statistical Manual* labels as character judgments. Linked to the possibility of rebirth, forgiveness also requires staff to be hopeful. It requires reflecting back to young people the persons they can be. It requires allowing for the possibility that the next time will be different and better.

One residential program practices forgiveness by taking youth back over and over and over, even after they run away or commit acts that require temporary removal (Levy, 1996). Moreover, the CYC workers practice forgiveness with a spirit of hope. Each instance is a possibility for renewal, and past efforts do not predetermine the anticipation of success.

2. The maintenance of integrity and the preservation of a program or a site as "whole" are dependent on the focus of its mission. This is the basis of the spirituality of the setting or the community of care. To maintain consistency in approach and program is not a call to rigidity or certainty but is rather the challenge of treating the child consistently while acknowledging that that does not mean treating every child the same but, rather, treating each one in response to needs and circumstances. The higher purpose is the driving force: The best interests of the child require responsiveness and mutuality. Inherent here is a degree of flexibility in care whose outcome is a long-term change in the life of the child or youth. The practice of generosity and forgiveness requires such flexibility. In the context of programs and institutions with congruent practices, Anglin (personal communication, February 19, 2004) described workers whose settings allowed them the freedom to move the containing walls around a child—not physical walls but emotional, psychological ones— moving them closer and tighter when a child is in distress or anxious and further out as a child develops skills and ease in meeting challenges.

This is an example of enacting the sensitivity and discernment described earlier. Part of the work of spiritually sensitive practice is building emotional containers for the pain-based behaviors that can respond to a wide range of behaviors and feelings. Congruence creates a "whole place": Anglin (personal communication, February 19, 2004) reported that children spoke of their deliberate attempts to "break down" foster families or care settings and that in being "unable to break it down" they found livable and safe space in which to engage their pain and seek life. Their struggle could be contained.

3. Spiritual congruence creates a consistency in behaviors and relationships. If the supervisor has the capacity and vision to have faith in staff to act in the service of the singular focus, then staff have an environment in which they also can begin to trust and have faith in the children to do the work they need to do as they are being trusted to do their work. Each function has a role in creating this livable, workable space. Part of making safe space includes giving up control.

Adherence to a higher principle permits an understanding that accepts not staying in control but actually gaining in influence by letting go of control. The more one gives up control, the more responsive others are. If managers give over control to workers, they become more responsive, and this can be duplicated in relationships with clients. Authority is present in this dynamic. It does not have to be proved or defended. The inner confidence that such a stance contains is itself convincing and can be learned by the clients who witness its impact in practice.

4. A congruent life and work space offer the possibility of responsiveness and intervention as action in CYC work where invitation becomes an option. It is when the child or youth invites a worker into their lives that the transformational process begins, because that invitation allows a glimpse at the pain underlying the behavior— the pain being the source that needs care. Successful intervention is really only possible in relationship, and invitation is at the heart of these relationships. It is not the sole responsibility of the worker to reach the child or youth. There is a reciprocal readiness that comes from the child or youth, and it is the exchange of

responses following from the invitation that creates the opening of transformation and rebirth.

In this context it is important to note that a degree of wisdom is required in bringing spirituality to the foreground. A spirituality that is being lived by the staff and echoed in the life of the whole context can be held without comment or instruction until there is an invitation or exploration from the child or youth to engage in that spirituality. Waiting for the invitation is part of the generosity and gift-giving spirituality that must be central in CYC.

5. One of the capacities that must be present in our work with children and youth who are in pain or difficulty is patience. Throughout this discussion we have referred to the importance of the youth being able to see what they need, to have opportunities to know, for example, that there are healthy ways to resolve conflict, or to live with the hope of possibility. If workers are healthy and carry an inner balance, their ways of being and acting may be models worthy of notice by those in their care. A child who sees a different way of becoming or acting may take a long time to process and express the shift in understanding. If years of damage have occurred, it will take more than a few weeks or months to find a way toward normalcy. This requires workers to practice with patience and attentiveness. Rebirth and restoration require resiliency, and resiliency requires a different image of acting or being to use as a building block to be copied and amplified in a child's life (O'Connell Higgins, 1994).

SUMMARY

We are suggesting that CYC programs and institutions require a congruency that includes a practice of spirituality in order for there to be the possibility of spiritual development in the lives of children and youth in care. A spirituality of care that is based on an ethos of gift-giving generosity, the acknowledgment, acceptance, and affirmation of suffering (pain-based behaviors), willing and repetitive forgiveness, and a sense of the possibility for the rebirth and transformation of lives will create a life space for spirituality to be respected and nurtured. The

enactment of this spirituality requires compassion, patience, and commitment to a higher purpose and acts in patience with a tolerance for difficulty and ambiguity in day-to-day interactions with wounded children and youth.

Spirituality, understood as central in practice, has an integrative role. It overarches the design and activities and provides a raison d'être for letting go of other agendas: self-interest and institutional interests. It serves as a focusing lens or a perspective that allows actions and structure to be seen and shaped with the higher purpose in mind. There is a transcendent purpose that integrates all the functions necessary for quality child and youth care.

Finally, an acknowledgment of spirituality in CYC includes an acceptance of the spiritual potential and experience of children and youth. Even those who are most wounded come with a spirituality based on their experience. Their spirituality may be a deep and hidden resource in the midst of their troubles (Seita, Mitchell, & Tobin, 1996), or it may already be damaged and inaccessible to them as a resource for survival and resilience and therefore need care and healing itself. Access to the spiritual potential of children and youth requires environments that accept and model spirituality as a possibility for life.

CYC workers can extend the skills and capacities they have to include an awareness of and alertness to the spirituality in their own lives, in the lives of the children and youth and families they serve, and in their work environment. Spirituality has the potential to be part of a congruent, coherent, and consistent contributor to the well-being and care of children and youth.

REFERENCES

Anglin, J. P. (2002). *Pain, normality, and the struggle for congruence: Reinterpeting residential care for children and youth.* New York: Haworth Press.

Coles, R. (1990). *The spiritual life of children.* Boston: Houghton Mifflin.

Conn, H. E. (1981). *Conscience: Development and self-transcendence.* Birmingham, AL: Religious Education Press.

Dreyfus, H. (n.d.). Kierkegaard on the Internet: Anonymity vs. commitment in the present age.

Retrieved September 22, 2003, from http://socrates.berkeley.edu/~hdreyfus/html/paper_kierkegaard.html

Fowler, J. (1981). *Stages of faith*. New York: Harper & Row.

Freedman, S. (1999). A voice of forgiveness: One incest survivor's experience forgiving her father. *Journal of Family Psychotherapy, 10*(4), 37.

Freedman, S. (2003). The impact of forgiveness on adolescent adjustment to parental divorce. *Journal of Divorce and Remarriage, 39*(1/2), 135–166.

Grimmitt, M. (1987). *Religious education and human development: The relationship between studying religions and personal and social and moral education*. Great Wakering, UK: McCrimmon Publishing.

Hart, T. (2003). *The secret spiritual lives of children*. Makawao, Maui, HI: Inner Ocean Publishing.

Hay, D., with Nye, R. (1998). *The spirit of the child*. London: HarperCollins.

Hillman, J. (1996). *The soul's code: In search of character and calling*. New York: Warner Books.

Hyland, T., & Herron, R. (Eds.). (1995). *The ongoing journey: Awakening spiritual life in at-risk youth*. Boys Town, NE: Boys Town Press.

Jacobs, A. (1996, January/February). The man who heard voices. *Books and Culture*, 24–26.

Kegan, R. (1982). *The evolving self: Problem and process in human development*. Cambridge, MA: Harvard University Press.

Kohlberg, L., & Mayer, R. (1972). Development as the aim of education. *Harvard Educational Review, 42*, 451–496.

Levy, Z. (1996). Conceptual foundations of developmentally oriented residential education: A holistic framework for group care that works. *Residential Treatment for Children and Youth, 13*(3), 69–83.

Mattingly, M. A., with Stuart, C. (2002). Competencies for professional child and youth work practitioners. *Journal of Child and Youth Care Work, 17*, 16–49.

Morgenthaler, S. K. (Ed.). (1999). *Exploring children's spiritual formation: Foundational issues*. River Forest, IL: Pillars Press.

O'Connell Higgins, G. (1994). *Resilient adults: Overcoming a cruel past*. San Francisco: Jossey-Bass.

Ó Murchú, D. (1998). *Reclaiming spirituality*. New York: Crossroad Publishing.

Robinson, E. (1983). *The original vision: A study of the religious experience of childhood*. New York: Seabury Press.

Schrag, C. O. (1997). *The self after postmodernity*. New Haven, CT: Yale University Press.

Scott, D. G. (2004). Retrospective spiritual narratives: Exploring recalled adolescent spiritual experiences. *International Journal of Children's Spirituality, 9*(1), 67–79.

Seita, J., Mitchell, M., & Tobin, C. (1996). *In whose best interest? One child's odyssey, a nation's responsibility*. Elizabethtown, PA: Continental Press.

Shelton, C. M. (1983). *Adolescent spirituality: Pastoral ministry for high school and college youth*. Chicago: Loyola University Press.

United Nations Convention on the Rights of the Child. (1989). Downloadable at http://www.unhchr.ch/html/menu3/b/k2crc.htm

32

BRIDGING TO PUBLIC POLICY AND CIVIL SOCIETY

STEVE HORNBERGER

ROBERTA FURTICK JONES

ROBERT L. MILLER JR.

Although children and adolescents are ultimately the beneficiaries or victims of public policy, social science researchers have only recently suggested a relationship between spirituality, child and adolescent health and well-being, and civil society. Spirituality is rarely included as an important element of public policy needed to create or strengthen civil society.

The current conception of spirituality is insufficient to address an intersection between civil society, child and adolescent development, spirituality, and public policy. It does not address the innate nature of spirituality, nor does it offer strategies and methods to facilitate dialogue and actions between and among different spiritual belief systems, so that spirituality can inform social actions (public policies) for the common good.

Historically, there has been a lack of agreement regarding the suitability of spirituality as a topic for inclusion in various fields of research, for example, social science and medical research. There has been a perception that spirituality and religion are private matters, best left to the individual and other members of one's belief system.

The authors define spirituality as more expansive and inclusive than any one spiritual belief system, spiritual tradition, or relationship with the divine. One need not believe in God or an unseen unifying and organizing energy, or a higher power, to be a good, moral, ethical, human being with clearly defined codes of behavior (toward others and our environment), to have a purpose in life and a yearning for connectedness (Canda, 1999). Spirituality encompasses the fullness of our humanness.

Spirituality is relational and can be understood within the context of one or any combination of four primary relationships: (1) between people and the environment (the land, sea, mountains, sky); (2) between people and others in terms of love and justice (justice without the balancing presence of love can either be harsh or ineffective or unjust); (3) between people and their heritage (ancestry); and (4) between people and the numinous (described as that which affirms connections beyond the physical seeing, touching, measurable environment)

(Waldergrave, Tamasese, Tuhaka, & Campbell, 2003). For purposes of this chapter the term *spiritual belief system* is used to address the breadth, depth, and complexity of these four relationships.

Challenges to examining spirituality in human affairs have abated somewhat. The social and medical sciences have begun to study spirituality as it relates to human affairs. However, understanding the influence of spirituality on public policy has been less well theorized and studied. While discussions of faith-based enterprises have evolved in political, social service, and/or economic debates, these discussions deal mostly with religious institutions, which is outside the scope of this discourse on spirituality.

Acknowledging and infusing this expanded definition of spirituality with the existing developmental tasks of children and adolescents will help them participate and thrive in today's society, while also preparing them to be responsible stewards of tomorrow's society. By appreciating the complexity and diversity of each human being, by providing for equitable opportunities and competencies, thus fostering a sense of belonging and connectedness, we can begin to heal historical oppression and reduce current disparities.

Civil society is understood to be one sector of society, along with polity and economy (Naidoo, 2000; Perlas, 2000; Salamon, Sokolowski, & List, 2003). While each sector has its primary focus—polity, government; economy, business or the market; and civil society, sociocultural issues—these three sectors are interactive, dynamic, and interdependent with one another (Manor, Robinson, & White, 1999; Naidoo, 2000). Civil society is concerned with the social and spiritual capacities (Philippine Agenda 21, 2001) of human development, as well as the well-being and the quality of public life of all human beings, including children and adolescents (e.g., Naidoo, 2000; Novalis Civil Society Initiative, 2001; Salamon et al., 2003). Public policies that recognize the essential nature of spirituality and support the developmental needs of children and adolescents are a means for ensuring the continuity and sustainability of society. As such, they need to express an expanded understanding of humanness; define individual and collective rights and responsibilities; provide for rewards and sanctions; and facilitate achievement of societal goals and aspirations.

As the 21st century begins, the challenge before the adult generation is to balance common human needs with the environmental resources and limitations of nature so as to support social life. The quality of children's and adolescents' lives depends, in part, on their knowledge, as well as their willingness and ability to contribute to the common good of society. The adult generation, which must socialize and care for children and adolescents, bears the responsibility for how well prepared this next generation will be to succeed us, and for the conditions of society and the environment that they will inherit from us.

SPIRITUALITY

Spirituality is related to, though different from, religion. Spirituality is the raw material of all religion, namely, a consciousness of a beyond, a something that, although it is interwoven with this world, is essentially external to the material phenomena of the world (Russell, 1986). Spirituality is the gestalt of the total process of human life and development (Benson, Roehlkepartain, & Rude, 2003; Canda, 1988), with a central feature being an individual's search for a sense of meaning and purpose (Canda & Furman, 1999). This search occurs through relationships with the self, other people, the nonhuman world, and the ground of being (Canda, 1988). Although spirituality may include a relationship with a god (Phelps, 1990), people may engage in spiritual practices or consider themselves spiritual without believing in a deity. The principal characteristics of spirituality are subjectivity and inwardness, as well as an outward, relational quality (Russell, 1986).

The inward dimension of spirituality, which deals with the search for meaning and purpose, signals a particular action. This action is an organizing function often producing a fuller awareness of oneself and a deeper connectivity with one's environment, in an effort to achieve goals such as balance, maturity, wisdom, and peace. The action supporting this effort may also result in greater personal awareness. This action or agency, the belief that one can produce desired effects, is *self-efficacy* (Bandura, 2000). As one's self-efficacy increases, one continues to pursue such awareness as well as have larger and more complex goals and expectations for oneself and others.

In this regard, spirituality provides a framework within which personal effort or power may be conceptualized. The power in spirituality is used as a response to an event or circumstance with the goal of effecting a positive change. Most often people use spirituality to cope with life stressors (Ellis, Campbell, Detwiler-Breidenbach, & Hubbard, 2002), illnesses (Koenig, 2002; Miller, 2000), and psychological distress (Smith, 2003).

When spirituality is specifically understood as a relational construct between individuals and the environment, it may also be conceptualized and used as motivation to serve others. This relational construct of spirituality potentially prompts a helping reaction to attend to the perceived needs of others. While the literature supports the efficacy of personal spirituality on the behalf of others, such as praying for a beneficial outcome for someone else (Palmer, Katerndahl, & Morgan-Kidd, 2004; Tloczynski & Fritzsch, 2002), spirituality is also a motivator to create and achieve a common good (Rost, 2001) in the larger society.

Spirituality and Social Justice

The inward subjectivity as well as the relational quality of spirituality suggests a dynamic tension that includes the inner work of contemplation, reflection, prayer, and meditation, and outer work directed toward the common good (e.g., social action). Praying and meditating for oneself and others and the good of all is one dimension of this phenomenon. The desire for tangible social interaction to effect a change is another dimension of spirituality. This tension gives rise to energy that can drive social justice action. Perry and Rolland (1999) suggest that spirituality engenders therapeutic benefits that social justice activism supports, specifically hope, empowerment, and the healing resulting from equitable, harmonious relations.

Social justice is concerned with the common good, namely, "open opportunities and procedural justice" (Hansson, 2004). Social justice challenges social injustice both locally and globally. Such actions are primarily focused on issues of poverty, unemployment, discrimination, and other forms of inequity.

Service also flows from the relational dimension of spirituality. This service has as its focus the common good of all members of society, as well as the natural resources that support the common good. People who act on this concern engage in social justice to create and ensure opportunities for those members of society who are oppressed and/or marginalized. This view of social justice encourages action that restores equality and human dignity. Any spirituality that does not engage in "work supporting the whole"—namely, "redemptive social consequences" (Trueblood, 1970)—is at risk of being challenged as inconsistent with the common good.

Personal Power

Social justice emphasizes the importance of mutuality and respect for all members of the society. It also assumes individual ownership of responsibility and the recognition of individual power. The relational quality of spirituality is also an opportunity for all human beings to experience an additional dimension of their humanity in order to effect change. Realizing such an opportunity requires intention and action. Inherent in the capacity to bring about change is the exercising of personal power. The French philosopher and commentator Michel Foucault, and the Brazilian educator and commentator Paulo Freire, highlight the recognition of personal power as an opportunity to effect change in support of a sustainable and just society.

Foucault normatively defines power as the ability or capacity to perform or act effectively, conducting a specific activity, a particular faculty or aptitude usually offered in the plural. It is an opportunity for a person, group, or nation to influence the outcome for others. Foucault (Douglas, 1999) suggests that power, in the context of social justice, is not a unitary, centralized force. It is not concentrated in the state or in any single institution. Rather, power is exercised on all levels of society where people relate with each other. Power is always relational: "It is created in the relationships that sustain it" (Weeks, 1981).

Power relationships are fluid. They are not only imposed on people from institutional structures, they also emerge from people who yearn for freedom and justice but who experience inequities due to power imbalances stemming either from their own decisions or from the actions of those who hold more power: the power elites (Sawicki, 1991).

Sawacki (1991) suggests that Foucault's "bottom–up" analysis of power is an attempt to show how power relations, at the microlevel of society, make possible certain global effects of domination, such as class, power, and patriarchy. Foucault makes plain that power cannot be consigned to a single person or institution.

Freire's (1981) work highlights an example of people recognizing power as being available to those who struggle for it. Those whose power has been taken from them are faced with a choice: They can either embrace their oppression or develop an awareness of the "inconsistencies of their environment." He conceptualizes this awareness as *conscientização*. To engage in creative ways to obtain freedom, Freire suggests that people must engage in "radicalization." The more radical a person is, the more fully he or she enters social reality. Thereby knowing social reality better, the person is able to transform it, unafraid to confront, to listen, and to see the world unveiled. People are unafraid to meet or enter into dialogue with each other, and through these interactions change is effected. It is personal power that causes these interactions to take place.

Spirituality provides a context for people to act on their impulse to contribute to the common good. The action driving the impulse is the power of one's belief about the highest good. This power can be used for beneficial, constructive purposes, for example, to assist those in need and to confront those who do not act for the common good. As people become familiar and comfortable with acting in the relational dimension of spirituality, they will have greater capacity to apply power in tangible and intentional ways. Social justice is one result of such action, and it occurs because people engage in behaviors that extend equality.

Individual power is an action that creates opportunity for the common good to be made manifest. Spirituality is a framework that encourages the individual, through concern for others, to engage personal and collective power for actions that promote the common good. Such a vision of the common good, infused with our expanded definition of spirituality, deepens the understanding of child and adolescent development.

CHILD AND ADOLESCENT DEVELOPMENT

How do we assist our children and adolescents to develop into adults who are prepared, willing, and able to engage in actions that promote the common good? How would our understanding of child and adolescent development be broadened if we included our more expansive and inclusive understanding of spirituality as an essential part of human development? How would this understanding of children and adolescents affect how we meet the needs of families, communities, and society?

Stage Theories

There are several ways to think about the development of children. Social science offers what has been the prevailing paradigm for understanding childhood through stage theories. Stage theories present human development as progressive, sequential, and interrelated. Human beings move from birth to childhood, adolescence, adulthood, old age, and death. The developmental process is impacted by the degree to which the individual "successfully" accomplishes the tasks of each developmental stage.

Although stage theories are important to our understanding of child and adolescent development, they do present certain pitfalls: issues of oversimplification, standardization, and difficulty accommodating cultural diversity and individual uniqueness or nonconformity regarding the stated time line or, worse, seeing such nonconformity as aberrant. Stage theories provide an understanding of child and adolescent development; they generally do not, however, adequately address the role of spirituality in child and adolescent development.

Fowler's cognitive-structural faith development theory (1981) and Wilber's transpersonal spectrum model of development (1995, 1996) both suggest that spirituality is fundamental to human development. They state that spiritual development is progressive from the primal trust/fantasy-emotional awareness of infancy to the mythic-literal/symbolic representational thinking of middle childhood to the personalized peer-referenced but conformist perspective of adolescence to the unity of a nondual/universal and inclusive perspective of older adulthood.

Human beings, according to Maslow (Gwynne, 1997), progress from striving to meet basic needs to meeting more complex needs—from physiological needs (air, water, food, sleep, sex) to safety (establishment of stability and consistency, security of self, family, and home), love (belongingness, feeling loved by others), esteem (self-esteem from competence and the esteem that comes from the attention and appreciation of others), and self-actualization (the desire to become more than oneself; to become everything that one has the potential to become; to seek knowledge, peace, aesthetic experiences, self-fulfillment, oneness with God).

The Circle of Courage, developed by Brendtro, Brokenleg, and Van Bockern (1990), is a model of understanding child and adolescent development that is based on the medicine wheel and the Native American (particularly the Sioux Nations') view of life. The medicine wheel is a paradigm for understanding the cycles of life, including human development (e.g., physical, emotional, mental, spiritual). It is believed that each of these four areas of one's life must be intact to have a self-secure, prosocial approach to life. The Circle of Courage presents human development as beginning with an essential sense of *belonging:* feeling valued, important, protected by others, comfortable, and welcomed into a group. Therefore, family and close community are essential to child and adolescent self-esteem. *Mastery,* the second quadrant, speaks to the human need to feel competent, to seek greater skills and knowledge. *Independence,* the next quadrant, speaks to the human need to feel in control of oneself, one's behavior, and one's life. Successful movement through this quadrant leads to autonomy, an acceptance of responsibility for oneself and one's own actions. *Generosity,* the fourth quadrant, addresses the human capacity for empathy toward others, a desire to help others, and true joy in giving.

Maslow's hierarchy of needs and the Circle of Courage are two important ways of understanding children and adolescents because each acknowledges the progressive nature of development. They integrate spiritual development with human development, thereby expanding our understanding of children and adolescents.

Spirituality and Child and Adolescent (Human) Development

During the 1990s, the Decade of the Brain, scientists, social theorists, and educators discovered a closer connection between the functions, physiology, and capacities of the human brain and their relationship to spiritual development. Such research and the discussions it engenders can have significant implications for how we answer the question, "What is the role of spirituality in child and adolescent (human) development?"

The Institute for American Values (along with the Dartmouth Medical School) in 2002 released the report *Hardwired to Connect: The Scientific Case for Authoritative Communities.* This research has linked responses in the brain to activities associated with meditation, prayer, ritual, and religious and spiritual symbols. The executive summary states:

> Much of the first half of this report is a presentation of scientific evidence—largely from the field of neuroscience, which concerns our basic biology and how our brains develop—showing that the human child is "hardwired to connect." We are hardwired for other people and for moral meaning and openness to the transcendent. Meeting these basic needs for connection is essential to health and to human flourishing.

The *Hardwired to Connect* study addresses an American crisis of increasingly high rates of child and adolescent depression, anxiety, attention deficit disorder, conduct disorders, thoughts of suicide, and other serious mental, emotional, and behavioral problems; however, such behaviors and health issues are increasingly international in scope. This is especially true in developing nations as ideals and lifestyles become more like those in the United States. Consequently, the findings of the study are relevant to all children and adolescents. The study also recommends the fostering of authoritative communities (families, neighborhoods, community groups, and religious organizations) to both build and support the spiritual development of the child and adolescent (Institute for American Values, 2002).

Bradford (1995) has stated that in order for a child or young person to experience full quality of life, spirituality in all its aspects must be nurtured and affirmed. He asserts that this need is more pronounced for children or young people who have been marginalized or who have suffered deprivation.

Recent research findings on resilience can also broaden our understanding of the essentialness of spirituality to child and adolescent development. Resilience is described as a set of qualities that fosters successful adaptation and transformation, despite risk and adversity (Bernard, 1991). Another quality of resilience is hope and the awareness that there is something good beyond the current situation that may lack immediate solution. The literature on resilience asserts that we are all born with a capacity for resilience that enables us to develop social competence, problem-solving skills, a critical consciousness, autonomy, and a sense of purpose (Bernard, 1991). Hay (1995), an educational researcher who addresses resilience, describes spiritual development as changes in the child's increased sensitivity to awareness beyond him- or herself, values, and including ideas about good and evil, or what matters, as well as mystery, wonder and awe, and meaning, insight, or connectedness.

Kunjufu (1990) is an educator and sociologist who has examined the impact of racism and oppression on the development of young Black males. He recognizes the relationship between resilience (the ability to survive and thrive against great odds), the innate potential in children for hope and optimism, spiritual development (as we human beings grow more spiritual we become more at one with something greater than ourselves), and the need for and benefit we derive from ritual, specifically rites of passage. Such rituals draw family, friends, and community members into the public acknowledgment of developmental milestones. These rituals focus on child and adolescent developmental capabilities and well-being, becoming stepping-stones to a deeper knowledge of self, others, society, the environment, and the numinous.

The UNICEF Adolescent Project assessed 26 adolescent programs developed in 24 countries (United Nations Children Fund, 2002). The report identified, as others have (Institute for American Values, 2002; Kunjufu 1990; Lerner, Dowling, & Anderson, 2003), the necessity of significant and genuine collaborations: among adolescents (e.g., peer groups); adolescents and program administrators (adolescents must be active participants in program design and implementation—they must feel that their opinions count); adolescents and their families and schools; and programs for adolescents and local government officials. The UNICEF Adolescent Project report provides a good example of the intersection of civil society and child and adolescent development and spirituality, and may suggest a course of action toward sustainable adolescent programs that address the whole child.

It is clear that for children and adolescents to develop in healthy and whole ways, they require nurturance from caring and empathic adults who have high expectations and create real opportunities for children and adolescents to participate meaningfully in society. Such nonacademic care and socialization are best provided by families, neighborhoods, community groups, and religious organizations (Institute for American Values, 2002; Youniss et al., 2002)—the very agencies that form the foundation of civil society.

CIVIL SOCIETY

The Challenge of Spirituality and Civil Society

There are numerous definitions of the term *civil society,* and they are worthy of brief review. From a political and sociological perspective, Manor et al. (1999) articulate the following attributes of a civil society:

The political conception of civil society is rooted in the Anglo-American tradition of liberal-democratic theory, which identifies civic institutions and political activity as an essential component of the emergence of a particular type of political society based on the principles of citizenship, rights, democratic representation and the rule of law. The sociological conception of civil society is that of an intermediate associational realm situated between the state on the one side and the basic building blocks of society on the other (individuals, families and firms), inhabited by social organizations with some degree of autonomy and voluntary participation on the part of their members.

Based upon a consensus-building process, Salamon et al. (2003) describe five features common to civil society entities. They are (1) organized (there is some structure and regularity to their operations, whether or not they are formally constituted or legally registered); (2) private (they are not part of the state apparatus, even though they may receive support from governmental sources); (3) not profit distributing (they are not primarily commercial in purpose and do not distribute profits to directors, stockholders, or managers); (4) self-governing (they have their own mechanisms for internal governance, are able to cease operations on their own authority, and are fundamentally in control of their own affairs); and (5) voluntary (membership or participation in them is not legally required or otherwise compulsory).

In discussing the role of civil society within the larger society, Naidoo (2000) states that its "principal role is in contributing to the creation of a healthy public life as one of several spheres of legitimate societal action . . . to address common problems, advance shared interests, and promote collective aspirations" (p. 4).

Regardless of specific attributes or roles, however, there is a recognition that civil society, polity, and economy together constitute what has been described as a "threefolding of society" (Perlas, 2000). This multisector approach highlights the functional differentiation of these three sectors that are interactive, dynamic, and interdependent of each other. For the purposes of this discussion, civil society "is the key actor in the realm of culture where the central social concern and process is the development of the social and spiritual capacities of human beings in order, among others, to advance the frontiers of knowledge, to achieve clarity and coherence of values, and to advocate the public interest" (Philippine Agenda 21, 2001).

Civil society is, therefore, both a means and a goal by which social and spiritual concerns, our "humanness," are articulated, nurtured, and accomplished. But it is also the agent by which common vision, hopes, and aspirations for the future are born; focus, purpose, and meaning are construed; and decisions are made regarding how to articulate, advocate, and address the current and emerging social and spiritual concerns. Civil society facilitates and draws upon the building of social capital (Briggs, 1997; Coleman, 1990; Putnam, 1993, 1995). The accumulated trust, reciprocity, information, and cooperation of social capital form the basis for social change.

Child and adolescent development takes place within the context of family life and social conditions. Civil society allows for the expression of aspirations, discussions, and consensus to foster a common understanding of our innate humanness and accepted definitions of child and adolescent well-being. Thus, because it focuses on the development of the social and spiritual capacities of human beings, civil society can call on accumulated social, human, and financial capital to promulgate an expanded vision for a sustainable and just society. While polity and economy are essential components of any society, determining in large part the level of societal development and the quality of daily social life, it is civil society that is best able to address concerns of "humanness": questions of who we are, where we are going, how we will achieve such goals, and what the circumstances will be for our children and adolescents.

It is fundamental to acknowledge that the developmental tasks of childhood and adolescence cannot be accomplished by children or adolescents alone. Children or adolescents do not grow into well-functioning, healthy, contributing adults by their own actions alone. The family, immediate community (neighborhood, school), greater community (town, city, village), and the world (our global village) are all agents of socialization. Indeed, such agents significantly affect the life trajectory, the very life chances of each child and adolescent.

All of us have a stake and responsibility in the healthy physical, cognitive, emotional, psychosocial, and spiritual development of children and adolescents, and, by extension, in the foundation of future society. When society fails its youth, it is not just the youth who suffer the consequences. In Abraham Lincoln's widely quoted words:

> A child is a person who is going to carry on what you have started. He is going to sit where you are sitting, and when you are gone, attend to those things which you think are important. You may adopt all the policies you please, but how they are carried out depends on him. He will assume control of your cities, states and nations. He is going to move in and take over your churches, schools, universities, and corporations . . . the fate of humanity is in his hands.

DISCUSSION

This section will further demonstrate the relationship between spirit, child and adolescent development, and civil society, and how each informs and supports public policy. Up to this point we have conceptualized spirituality as larger than any one belief system and valuing all human beings. Because spirituality is hardwired into our biology and, thus, an essential component of human development (inclusive of atheists, agnostics, and existentialists), infusing not only our understanding but also our efforts to promote child and adolescent development with this broader concept of spirituality will enhance the well-being of children and adolescents.

Spirituality is essential to our humanness, and because human beings are the primary actors in civil society, spirituality must be construed as an essential component of civil society. Such an understanding of our commonality was expressed by the Conference of Non-Governmental Organizations (2002):

> [A] global society [is] where there is peace, compassion, love, friendliness, enthusiasm, a feeling of belonging and oneness with all life, as well as commitment, service and responsibility. Such spiritual values are common to all faiths, cultures and traditions, are universal in nature and transcend the boundaries of religion and of nationality. These imperatively need to be reawakened,

nurtured and sustained for the advancement of the world.

Given the pervasive interdependence of technology, environmental issues, and the political and economic sectors, there is a growing awareness that human beings live in a global village, or the global society of the 21st century, which is affected by worldwide natural crises (droughts, earthquakes, hurricanes), free trade agreements, rising oil prices, and other factors that affect many more people's lives than just those in the areas in which they occur. Through technological advances such as the Internet, mass media, and transportation, the distance and time that once separated peoples and nations no longer do so. Developing an awareness of such global dynamics builds upon the values of liberty, human rights, association, common purpose, and community inherent in civil society.

Civil society, which addresses the spiritual needs of its members, is the primary incubator of our humanness. Civil society articulates and acts upon the social and spiritual concerns of human beings and thus offers opportunities to use public policy to achieve and express our ideals for humanity. Therefore, civil society becomes the means by which our common vision and aspirations for the future are born, where focus, purpose, and meaning are construed, and decisions made on how to articulate, advocate for, and address current and emerging social and spiritual concerns.

To further this discussion and address the important question, "What responsibility does society have to nurture children's spiritual development?," we return to stage theory, Maslow's hierarchy of needs, and Brendtro et al.'s Circle of Courage. For instance, the following might occur if society ignores its responsibility to nurture the spiritual development of our children and adolescents. Children with a weak sense of *belonging* may have difficulty forming attachments or may be more prone to choose indiscriminately any group that will accept them (e.g., gangs). Children with an impaired sense of *mastery* may become easily frustrated and give up at the first hint of failure. Children who feel *certain* of failure and are easily frustrated challenge our educational system (they often do not try to succeed), as well as our legal system (anger and challenging behavior are frequent responses to frustration and hopelessness), and become dependent (believing that any effort to succeed will fail). Children who do not achieve a sense of independence (often affirmed by their experience of a society that does not offer enough opportunities) remain dependent and/or develop a sense of entitlement that may cover resentment and anger. When children are not consistently provided with support to access and exercise their innate resilience, they may become depressed and/or externalize feelings of low self-esteem and lack of worth, striking out at society. Those who do not achieve a sense of *generosity* might exhibit a scarcity mentality and become stingy or callous in their interactions with others. Generosity and self-actualization cannot develop if a child's or adolescent's sense of belonging or safety has not been attained.

Engaging in policy examination and development is not new, but examining policy within an expanded definition of spirituality may be. Writers in the social welfare system suggest that policy analysis may be viewed through an analytical paradigm of process, product, and performance (Gilbert & Terrell, 2002). Economists and political scientists have argued for a problem-solving and rational component, rather than chronicling the emergence of various policies (Dror, 1971). This chapter includes a comprehensive analytical model that values inclusivity, mutuality, respect, growth and well-being, and applicability to all people.

The following consensus documents are exemplars of programs and policies that begin to address and bridge the intersection of spirituality, child and adolescent development, civil society, and public policy. They are the UN's Convention on the Rights of the Child (1989) and the Child Welfare League of America's five universal needs for all children (Morgan, Spears, & Kaplan, 2003). From their common vision, the authors suggest several essential elements for child and adolescent development among the analytical criteria used to evaluate policies. Polices that consider the needs of children and adolescents and speak to the common good need to be (1) inclusive of and applicable to all people; (2) respectful of all life; and (3) able to promote and support growth and well-being.

Appealing to and drawing upon the adolescent's natural yearning for something greater than him- or herself therefore becomes an essential component of good public policy, quality programs, and the strengthening of civil society. Not only does such involvement enhance the individual's growth and development, it also increases the human and social capital of civil society and community. Policy makers should base decisions on criteria of effectiveness and efficiency, as well as make policy and programmatic decisions with the additional criterion of equity to redress oppressive conditions and promote social justice.

Social Justice

Given human history, there are past and current oppressions that need to be addressed and reconciled for us to move forward as a global society. The call for social justice has created opportunities for voices that have been silenced to be heard, thereby fostering the social processes necessary to heal wounds and improve societal conditions. In essence, we become better humans through acknowledging truths, strengthening reciprocity, expanding compassion, and developing shared goals for the common good.

If the goal of social justice, through the act of acknowledging and eliminating oppression, is the creation of a sustainable and just society—wherein each person, social group, race, gender, nationality, and spiritual tradition is accepted as a valued member of the human family—then understanding oppression as an opportunity for liberation is an important commitment.

For those who have less power than others in the society, wishing for a change to occur is insufficient. Change requires solidarity, the willingness to use power to bring about greater equity for those who have less. It requires an intentional action for a just distribution of power throughout the society.

True solidarity is found only in the plenitude of the act of love, in its existentiality, in its praxis (practical application or exercise of a branch of learning). It is a farce to affirm that human beings are persons and as persons should be free and yet do nothing tangible to make this affirmation a reality (Freire, 1981). The development of social policies to inform and develop a civil society includes a fundamental recognition of freedom and articulates the collective actions necessary to achieve freedom for all people.

One example of a social justice effort based on the expanded definition of spirituality is the Catholic Campaign for Human Development, sponsored by the U.S. Conference of Catholic Bishops. The campaign has three goals: empowering the poor, educating people about poverty and justice issues, and building solidarity between the poor and nonpoor in order to achieve the campaign's aim of "breaking the cycle of poverty—for a lifetime." A second example is the UN's Millennium Development Goals, ratified by 189 countries at the UN's Millennium Summit, which "agreed to a set of time-bound and measurable goals and targets for combating poverty, hunger, disease (especially child mortality), illiteracy, environmental degradation and discrimination against women" (United Nations Development Programme, n.d.).

Civil Society and Sustainability

. . . the harmonious integration of a sound and viable economy, responsible governance, social cohesion/harmony and ecological integrity to ensure that development is a life-enhancing process. In this context, the ultimate aim of development is human development now and through future generations. (Philippine Agenda 21)

Simply put, sustainable development is the capacity to meet the needs of the present generation without compromising the ability of future generations to meet their own needs. This interdependency between human generations has often been described poetically as "children are our gift to a future we will never know."

The Philippine Agenda 21 (2001) proposes a sustainable human development (SHD) approach on a societal scale. It describes and clarifies the interrelationship of the three sectors, polity, economy, and civil society, through 15 principles:

- Development of full human potential
- Holistic science and appropriate technology
- Cultural, moral, and spiritual sensitivity

- Self-determination
- National sovereignty
- Gender sensitivity
- Peace, order, and national unity
- Social justice, inter- and intragenerational and spatial equity
- Participatory democracy
- Institutional viability
- Viable, sound, and broad-based economic development
- Sustainable population
- Ecological soundness
- Biogeographical equity and community-based resource management
- Global cooperation

Bridging the Gap Between Spirituality, Social Justice, and Sustainability

For therapists to successfully work in poor communities, they have to take the critical context beyond the family into account. Those most in need of the health and welfare resources in most societies and communities are those who experience the most trauma, the greatest stress and as a consequence the most ill-health. They are usually those on low incomes, people in cultures that have been marginalized in the societies in which they live and most frequently women. (Waldegrave, in press)

A policy example that has attempted to bridge the gap between spirituality, civil society, and public policy is the Sustainable Integrated Area Development: Toward a South African Civil Society Agenda 21 (SIAD 21). The Novalis Institute used a consensus approach with all stakeholders to develop the SIAD 21 and is now advocating for its implementation. This document invites civil society not to unite against what is wrong but to work together for what is right. Its stated purpose is the creation of a comprehensive sustainable development plan for South Africa, driven by civil society in which sustainable lifestyles are supported by all dimensions of development, including ecological, economic, governance, social, cultural, and human and spiritual development (Novalis Civil Society Initiative, 2001).

Civil Society, Spirituality, and Workforce Issues

Too often debate centers on whether we should allow spirituality to be part of agency functions, rather than how. Given the history of atrocities and oppression, it is understandable that some would have disdain for the concept. What guidance do we have so that such discourse is not considered proselytizing, self-serving, or ineffectual? It is often incredibly difficult to have discussions about faith and spirituality with like-minded believers, let alone with those from other spiritual traditions.

Spirituality posed a considerable problem for us at the Family Centre. We had formed a cultural partnership of Maori, Pacific Island and Pakeha (European) workers and developed an agency that was determined to honour the cultures, address our colonial history and develop new expressions of equity. Spirituality posed a major problem for us, because in the European world it is largely viewed as a personal matter that has no role in the work place. Whereas for our Maori and Samoan colleagues it was inconceivable to consider health and well-being as ever being disconnected from overt expressions of spirituality. (Waldegrave, 2000)

While there is much interest and growing knowledge in informing professional education and practice with themes of spirituality (Hodge, 2001; Sermabeikian, 1994), social justice (Sheridan, Bullis, Adcock, Berlin, & Miller, 1992; Van Soest, 1995), and sustainable development (Canda, 1999), this issue and related topics such as staff motivation, recruitment, supervision, retention, and appropriateness of skill sets are beyond the scope of this chapter. However, the authors strongly believe that changing professional education, work performance, and organizational culture is necessary to facilitate improvements in how recipients are involved in service design, delivery and evaluation, service outcomes, and therefore the health and well-being of children and adolescents.

The civil society workforce has an important role in working with, and changing, these current circumstances. Beyond the direct provision of services and supports:

Therapists, be they psychologists, social workers, counselors, psychiatrists or nurses, etc., have a critical role in post industrial and largely secular states. They are the predominant professional group who listen to the pain of individuals and families. Therapists, as a professional group, are the most informed "experts" of the collective grounded levels of hurt, sadness and pain in modern countries. Those who live in deep pain are of course the primary "experts" in the sadness and hurt they and their communities experience, but therapists are the professional helpers who continually witness that pain with many individuals and families and across a variety of communities week after week. As such they carry a substantial responsibility to identify, quantify and describe the severity and causes of it. This is ethically essential if they are committed to honouring their client group. They have a responsibility to publish and publicise the causes and outcomes of people's pain in order that they may be addressed in the public debate and impact on policy. Good policy in this sense can address issues of well-being and inclusion in informed and effective ways. (Waldegrave, in press)

Therefore, within human service systems, it is essential to broaden the role definition of staff, both professional and volunteers, to become the "thermometers of pain" in society: to expand the definition from an individualized personal passion or "calling" toward a workforce role expectation that addresses both micro level (person specific) and macro level (social group) issues. Different specializations, disciplines, and organizations will focus more or less narrowly, but there cannot remain the false dichotomy between private pains and public conditions.

The civil society workforce is society's representative, those who experience firsthand the personal suffering of structural inequities and unintended consequences in our societies. For example, their roles are to educate, socialize, provide health care and social services, offer faith-based cultural and recreational services, heal harms, and offer opportunities to succeed. The authors also suggest that their role is to help discover the meaning from the human pain and suffering of their work. Their experience, knowledge, practical wisdom, and suggestions thereby need to inform the goals, public policies, and actions of civil society. Such discourse, and facilitating expression by the voice of those who suffer, would be a viable bridge between the respective sectors of society, and could become an ongoing and valued feedback loop that monitors "how we are doing." The status of child and adolescent health and well-being would then become a "barometer" of a sustainable and just society.

CONCLUSIONS AND FURTHER CONSIDERATIONS

Exploring relationships between matters of the spirit, issues regarding developmental psychology for children and adolescents, political and sociological discussions as they relate to the good of the citizenry and public policy happens more often among people than is reflected in the social science, political, theological, or business literatures. Nonetheless, people are concerned with how local communities can better serve their children as well as improve their own condition. Alternatively, fewer concerned citizens feel equipped to continue the conversation with regard to the recognition of our interdependence with one another on a global scale. Technology has clearly increased awareness of issues around the world, but it has not yet been determined whether global technology has initiated a belief that the average citizen can have an effect on what goes on several time zones away.

An understanding of spirituality that identifies it as essential to the human experience makes it an inherent concern of the development of children and adolescents. Children and adolescents are important members of a just society and in time become leaders. Conceptualizing public policy as both a goal and a means for achieving a desired outcome, though not a novel concept, does help to inform people who are concerned with making a positive difference for the common good. It also provides them with more of an impetus to believe they can effect change. Its potential empowers people to do something that will benefit those who previously seemed out of reach.

Asserting the relational aspect of spirituality has implications for decreasing the distance among people. Allowing civil society to be the incubator, which makes plain the need for people to understand their mutuality and interdependence, is a goal. Crafting policies that allow for the recognition of such truths potentially creates opportunities for further acts of goodwill in the service of the common good. There is much work to be done. There are many issues that are global in nature, yet very local in their consequences. To the extent that a society can nurture its children and adolescents to develop to their maximum potential, that society is better able to explore and normalize expectations of sustainability, justice, and freedom. Understanding spirituality as an inherent component of a civil society is a core feature of new bridges to public policy. It makes plain both the means and the goal, namely, the building and sustaining of an environment for the full participation of all humanity, especially our young people.

What does it mean to be human in the 21st century? Not as an individual, or as a member of a family or cultural group, or even as a citizen of one nation or a believer of a particular spiritual tradition, but rather as a member of the human species, the human family, which in the 21st century lives in an ever present and increasingly global village. How will we define and understand our essential humanness, where each will be acknowledged, respected, and treated with dignity?

Human history is littered with tragedies, horror, and oppression, as well as invention, innovation, and achievement. Yet all of us alive are coexisting, representing generations of different people, cultures, and spiritual traditions, living our lives one generation to the next. However, given the complexity of social, economic, and environmental crises, we are being asked to "become better human beings" and in doing so build a sustainable and just global society. To paraphrase Albert Einstein, the consciousness that creates (or discovers) the problem is not the consciousness that will solve it. We are being asked to broaden our understanding, deepen our compassion, and increase our wisdom.

The challenge for this generation is to grow the consciousness of our common humanness;

our understanding that each of us is more than our spiritual beliefs and practices, our nationality, our accomplishments, or roles in life; that all human beings are interconnected and interdependent in an ever-shrinking global village that is interwoven with nature and the web of life that is the world around us. To acknowledge that human life is a combination of the seen and unseen worlds, the secular and the sacred; to learn how to be better human beings, and thus more spiritual, in order to live with one another on this planet Earth; and to create a sustainable and just society so that all children and adolescents may participate in and contribute to society.

With emerging expansiveness, beyond any specific spiritual belief or tradition, to our essential humanness and beyond like-looking or like-minded, the human family embarks on an inevitable journey into an unknown future. Time, social circumstances, the world, and our very state of being are dynamic, ever moving and always changing. As the elders have said, "You can never step into the same river twice."

REFERENCES

Bandura, A. (2000). Social cognitive theory: An agentic perspective. *Annual Review of Psychology, 52,* 1–26.

Bernard, B. (1991). *Fostering resiliency in kids: Protective factors in the family, school, and community.* San Francisco: Far West Laboratory for Educational Research and Development. (ERIC Document Reproduction Service No. ED335781)

Benson, P. L., Roehlkepartain, E. C., & Rude, S. P. (2003). Spiritual development in childhood and adolescence: Toward a field of inquiry. *Applied Developmental Science, 7,* 205–213.

Bradford, J. (1995). *Caring for the whole child.* London: Children's Society.

Brendtro, L., Brokenleg, M., & Van Bockern, S. (1990). *Reclaiming youth at risk: Our hope for the future.* Bloomington, IN: National Education Service.

Briggs, X. de S. (1997). Social capital and the cities: Advice to change agents. *National Civic Review, 86,* 111–118.

Canda, E. R. (1988). Conceptualizing spirituality for social work: Insights from diverse perspectives. *Social Thought, 14,* 30–46.

Canda, E. (1997). Spirituality. In R. L. Edwards (Ed. in Chief), *Encyclopedia of social work* (19th ed., 1997 Suppl., pp. 299–309). Washington, DC: NASW Press.

Canda, E., & Furman, L. (1999). *Spiritual diversity in social work practice: The heart of helping.* New York: Free Press.

Coleman, J. (1990). *Foundations of social theory.* Cambridge, MA: Harvard University Press.

Conference of Non-Governmental Organizations. (2002, October). *Connexion* (newsletter). Retrieved August 8, 2004, from http://www.ngocongo.org

Douglas, K. B. (1999). *Sexuality and the Black church: A womanist perspective.* Maryknoll, NY: Orbis Books.

Dror, Y. (1971). *Ventures in policy sciences.* New York: Elsevier North Holland.

Ellis, M., Campbell, J., Detwiler-Breidenbach, A., & Hubbard, D. (2002). What do family physicians think about spirituality in clinical practice? *Journal of Family Practice, 51,* 249–254.

Fowler, J. W. (1981). *Stages of faith: The psychology of human development and the quest for meaning.* San Francisco: Harper & Row.

Freire, P. (1981). *Pedagogy of the oppressed.* New York: Seabury Press.

Gilbert, H., & Terrell, P. (2002). *Dimensions of social welfare policy* (5th ed.). Boston: Allyn & Bacon.

Gwynne, R. (1997). *Maslow's hierarchy of needs.* Retrieved May 10, 2004, from http://web.utk.edu/~gwynne/maslow.htm

Hansson, S. O. (2004). What are opportunities and why should they be equal? *Social Choice and Welfare, 22,* 305–316.

Hay, D. (1995). Children and God. *The Tablet, 74,* 1270–1271.

Hodge, D. (2001). Spiritual assessment: Review of major qualitative methods and a new framework for assessing spirituality. *Social Work, 46,* 203–214.

Institute for American Values. (2002). *Hardwired to connect: The scientific case for authoritative communities.* New York: Author. (Executive summary may be downloaded at http://www.americanvalues.org/ExSumm-print.pdf)

Koenig, H. G. (2002). *Spirituality in patient care: Why, how, when, and what.* Philadelphia: Templeton Foundation Press.

Kunjufu, J. (1990). *Countering the conspiracy to destroy Black boys* (Vol. 3). Chicago: African American Images.

Lerner, R. M., Dowling, E. M., & Anderson, P. M. (2003). Positive youth development: Thriving as the basis of personhood and civil society. *Applied Developmental Science, 7,* 172–180.

Manor, J., Robinson, M., & White, G. (1999, August). *Civil society and governance.* Retrieved August 15, 2004, from http://www.ids.ac.uk/ids/civsoc/public.doc

Miller, R. L., Jr. (2000). *The meaning and utility of spirituality in the lives of African American gay men living with AIDS.* Unpublished doctoral dissertation, Columbia University.

Morgan, L. J., Spears, L. S., & Kaplan, C. (2003). *Making children a national priority: A framework for community action.* Executive summary retrieved August 31, 2004, from the Child Welfare League of America Web site: http://www.cwla.org

Naidoo, K. (2000). The promise of civil society. *Asian Review of Public Administration, 12,* 1–9.

Novalis Civil Society Initiative. (2001, June). Sustainable integrated area development: Toward a South African civil society agenda 21. Retrieved August 4, 2004, from http://www.home.mweb.co.za/no/novalis

Palmer, R. F., Katerndahl D., & Morgan-Kidd, J. (2004). A randomized trial of the effects of remote intercessory prayer: Interactions with personal beliefs on problem-specific outcomes and functional status. *Journal of Alternative and Complementary Medicine, 10,* 438–448.

Perlas, N. (2000). *Shaping globalisation: Civil society, cultural life, and threefolding.* Cape Town, South Africa: Novalis Press.

Perry, A., and Rolland, J. (1999). Spirituality expressed in community action and social justice: A therapeutic means to liberation and hope. In F. Walsh (Ed.), *Spiritual resources in family therapy* (pp. 272–292). New York: Guilford.

Phelps, J. (1990). Black spirituality. In R. Maas & G. O'Donnell, O.P. (Eds.), *Spiritual traditions for the contemporary church* (pp. 332–351). Nashville, TN: Abingdon Press.

Philippine Agenda 21. *Principles of unity.* Retrieved May 14, 2004, from http://www.cadi.ph/pa21_principles_of_unity.htm

Putnam, R. (1993). The prosperous community: Social capital and public life. *American Prospect, 13,* 35–42.

Putnam, R. (1995). Bowling alone: America's declining social capital. *Journal of Democracy, 6,* 65–78.

Rost, R. (2001). Intergenerational relationships within the local congregation. *Journal of Religious Gerontology, 13,* 55–68.

Russell, A. (1986). Sociology and the study of spirituality. In C. Jones, G. Wainwright, & E. Yarnold, S.J. (Eds.), *The study of spirituality* (pp. 33–38). New York: Oxford University Press.

Salamon, L. M., Sokolowski, S. W., & List, R. (2003). *Global civil society: An overview.* Baltimore: Johns Hopkins University, Center for Civil Society Studies.

Sawicki, J. (1991). *Disciplining Foucault: Feminism, power and the body.* New York: Routledge.

Seden, J. (2004). *Child of our time: Child spirituality.* Retrieved August 10, 2004, from http://www.open2.net/childofourtime

Sermabeikian, P. (1994). Our clients, ourselves: The spiritual perspective and social work practice. *Social Work, 39,* 178–183.

Sheridan, M. J., Bullis, R. K., Adcock, C. R., Berlin, S. D., & Miller, P. C. (1992). Practitioners' personal and professional attitudes and behaviors toward religion and spirituality: Issues for education and practice. *Journal of Social Work Education, 28,* 190–203.

Smith, P. (2003). Adaptive coping strategies of other mothers: An examination of social support, spirituality, stress and depression. *Dissertation Abstracts International, 64,* 1081A.

Tloczynski, J., & Fritzsch, S. (2002). Intercessory prayer in psychological well-being: Using a multiple-baseline, across-subjects design. *Psychological Report, 91,* 731–741.

Trueblood, E. (1970). *The new man for our time.* New York: Harper & Row.

United Nations Children Fund. (2002). *Working for and with adolescents.* Retrieved August 2, 2004, from http://www.unicef.org/adolescence/working_with_and_for_adolescents.pdf

United Nations Development Programme. (n.d.). *Fast facts: Millennium development goals and the UNDP role.* Retrieved September 17, 2004, from http://www.undp.org

United Nations Development Programme. (2003). *Human development report 2003. Millennium development goals: A compact among nations to end human poverty.* New York: Oxford University Press.

United States Conference of Catholic Bishops. *Catholic Campaign for Human Development.*

Retrieved September 17, 2004, from http://www.nccbuscc.org/cchd/aboutus.htm

Van Soest, D. (1995). Peace and social justice. In R. L. Edwards (Ed. in Chief), *Encyclopedia of social work* (19th ed., Vol. 3, pp. 1810–1817). Washington, DC: NASW Press.

Waldegrave, C. (2000, February). *Grappling with a contemporary and inclusive spirituality.* Keynote speech delivered to the International Narrative Therapy and Community Work Conference, Adelaide, Australia.

Waldegrave, C. (in press). "Just Therapy" in poor communities. *Child Welfare, 84.*

Waldegrave, C., Tamasese, K., Tuhaka, F., & Campbell, W. (2003). *Just Therapy—a journey: A collection of papers from the Just Therapy team, New Zealand.* Adelaide, Australia: Dulwich Centre Publications.

Weeks, J. (1981). *Sex, politics, and society: The regulation of sexuality since 1800.* New York: Longman Group.

Wilber, K. (1995). *Sex, ecology, spirituality: The spirit of evolution.* Boston: Shambhala.

Wilber, K. (1996). *A brief history of everything.* Boston: Shambhala.

Youniss, J., Bales, S., Christman-Bes, V., Diversi, M., McLaughlin, M., & Silbereisen, R. (2002). Youth civic engagement in the twenty-first century. *Journal of Research on Adolescence, 12,* 121–148.

33

CHILDHOOD SPIRITUALITY: STRENGTHENING THE RESEARCH FOUNDATION

DONALD RATCLIFF

REBECCA NYE

Children's spirituality is emerging as an important field of inquiry (Benson, Roehlkepartain, & Rude, 2003), although most of the research in child and adolescent religious and spiritual development actually focuses on adolescents, with particular attention to children only emerging in recent decades. Indeed, the majority of chapters in this handbook look primarily at adolescence. Thus, despite progress, critical issues need to be addressed in order for children's spirituality to be taken seriously within various fields of human development. The present and the past can help frame an adequate agenda for future research that is most likely to advance the discipline toward greater acceptance.

HISTORICAL ROOTS OF CHILDREN'S SPIRITUALITY RESEARCH

Children's spirituality has developed from two prior streams of thought: the idea of an inherent spirituality, primarily reflected in research with adults, and religious concept development

research. Particularly noteworthy in this respect is the theological-anthropological work by Rudolf Otto (1950), Alister Hardy's studies of adult spirituality (1979), and Edward Robinson's study of adult recollections of childhood experiences (1983). The religious concept research, in contrast, involved the study of actual children, yet often built on the stage theories of Jean Piaget, emphasizing children's thinking about religion rather than their spiritual experiences.

Adult and Adult Retrospective Spiritual Experience

The biological correlates of spirituality deserve further study to determine the degree to which spiritual experiences are inherent or the product of specific contextual influences. Although the variety of spiritual experiences possibly suggests that context may be an important influence, the likelihood of a biological foundation to such experiences (Hay & Nye, 1998; Robinson, 1983) provides a basis for the degree of commonality across such experiences,

473

as well as suggesting an evolutionary advantage to spirituality. The latter is more thoroughly developed by Hardy (1966) in his explication of the biology of spirituality, which in turn built on the earlier work of theologians Friedrich Schleiermacher and Rudolf Otto, as well as psychologist William James and sociologist Ernst Troeltsch (Hay & Nye, 1998).

Recent neuropsychological research on the brain tends to confirm this assumption of a biological base to spiritual experiences (see May & Ratcliff, 2004; also see Newberg & Newberg, chapter 13, this volume). Such a biological base makes the likelihood of spiritual experiences from early infancy—perhaps even in utero—plausible. Suggesting a biological basis for spiritual experience does not bifurcate spirituality further from religion, as even the Bible emphasizes repeatedly the object of spiritual experience—not the existence per se of spiritual experience—as distinguishing biblical faith from other faiths.

In light of the emergent and inherent nature of children's spirituality, there is much to be gained by examining the accounts of spiritual experience by children. Otto's (1950) insightful exploration of the "numinous" experience drew from theological explorations of biblical content and Judeo-Christian experience, yet compared them favorably with experiences he documented from a wide variety of other faiths. The value of detailed study within and across multiple religions, both empirically and from historical-theological documents, can enrich the understanding of children's spirituality (Yust, Johnson, Sasso, & Roehlkepartain, in press).

James Fowler's (1981) theory of faith development bridged the gap between adult spiritual experience and religious development research, as it explicated an approach that moved beyond mere structural description (as was the case with Piaget and Kohlberg) to an emphasis on the experience of faith, while leaving the object of faith open. Fowler's stages are not as linear as those of Piaget and Kohlberg, as regression and recapitulation of previous stages were included in the theory (Fowler, 1981, p. 288; also see Fowler & Dell, chapter 3, this volume). Fowler also underscored the importance of narrative in providing content for the experience of faith.

Religious Development Research

The other precursor to children's spirituality research is the work related to religious development. Hundreds of research studies have been conducted worldwide in the area of children's religious development, spanning the 20th century and a variety of faith traditions. However, a disproportionate amount of this research represented Western cultures—primarily the United Kingdom, Europe, the United States, and Scandinavia, in descending order from most to fewest studies—and the majority concentrated on Judeo-Christian beliefs. Much of the research conducted has been sporadic and fragmented; there have been few systematic research programs; and research often has been conducted in comparative ignorance of previous work.

While the earliest religious development theory may well be in the writing of Teresa of Ávila (1577/2004), the earliest published research that could be located was that of Barnes and Boring (1892/2004), which summarized the responses of more than 1,000 children between 6 and 20 years old in California schools. The data included children's compositions on heaven and hell, recollections by adults related to God and religion, conversations between mothers and young children, and discussions between teachers and students. Children described God in anthropomorphic terms. While they often described the omniscience and omnipotence of God, they had more of a struggle with the concept of omnipresence. Heaven was conceived as a perfected earth in the sky, with angels, God, and religious people in white robes. Hell, in contrast, was seen as below the earth, with a stereotypic devil with horns, pitchfork, and pointed tail. While the authors included the ages of children making specific comments, they made no attempt to create a stage theory.

Seventy years later—in 1961, 1962, and 1963—the same journal that published Barnes and Boring, albeit with a name change, featured a series of research studies by David Elkind (later summarized in Elkind, 1978) on how children understood their faith tradition or denomination. Nearly 800 Jewish, Catholic, and Protestant youngsters were interviewed, primarily by Elkind using Jean Piaget's semiclinical interview procedure. As was found in many subsequent studies, the religious concepts followed the same progression as Piaget's theory predicted, with shifts in thinking corresponding to the onset of concrete operations and formal operations stages.

One year after Elkind's third study was published, Ronald Goldman's (1964) controversial study of children's religious thinking was produced. Goldman's work—again using Piaget's procedures for interviewing—confirmed the stage progression found by Elkind and Piaget. What brought on a storm of protest, however, was his conclusion that the lack of formal operational thought prior to about age 13 indicated that theological education should be reserved for teenagers.

Goldman's conclusions were only partially based upon his research; his theology (which emphasized that the Bible should not be interpreted literally but metaphorically) was also a crucial factor in his recommendation not to provide religious education for children. Similarly, in the United States, John Peatling (1973) created and researched a test of religious development that produced lower scores for individuals who took biblical accounts literally (see also Degelman, Mullen, & Mullen, 1984). In both cases, theological assumptions made by researchers affected their recommendations.

Much of the early literature was summarized in a massive volume titled *Research on Religious Development* (Strommen, 1971), as well as Pitts's (1977) early bibliography listing 600 references related to children's religious development. Twenty years later, the most exhaustive survey to date of the work on religious concepts included almost 2,000 studies summarized by Kenneth Hyde (1990). Nearly all of the studies were driven by stage-oriented theory (usually Piaget's), and, as might be expected, they generally revealed stages that strongly resembled Piaget's. Only a handful of studies considered children's experience of religion, and those were primarily surveys that merely asked if such experiences had occurred; children's descriptions of such experiences were noticeably absent. While few researchers cited by Hyde offered the extreme recommendations that Goldman made, a few attempts were made to apply such stage theories to religious education efforts in less extreme and

theologically loaded ways (see, for example, Ratcliff, 1987).

The Emergence of Children's Spirituality Research

Ironically, Hyde's massive review was released the same year that Robert Coles's (1990) groundbreaking work, *The Spiritual Life of Children,* beckoned researchers to follow a different trajectory. Coles shifted the course of research and theory by highlighting the spirituality common to both Christian and other religious groups, and affirmed the possibility of "atheistic spirituality" (not unlike the faith of the unbeliever described by Fowler, 1981). Coles's significant study attracted considerable public attention—particularly in North America, where religious development research had been largely ignored—in part because of his prestige and impeccable record of research related to children in crisis.

What followed Coles's work was a shift in emphasis from religious development to children's spirituality research, the latter often seen as separate from religion altogether. The shift was not as dramatic in the United Kingdom, where there was greater familiarity with spirituality research by Alister Hardy and Edward Robinson. Indeed, religious development research was sometimes found in collections alongside children's spirituality research, such as the research studies in *Research in Religious Education* (Francis, Kay, & Campbell, 1996).

Subsequent milestones in the emerging area of children's spirituality included the founding of a major journal in 1996—*The International Journal of Children's Spirituality*—and the First International Conference on Children's Spirituality held in Chichester, England, in 2000. Although spirituality was separated from children's religious development, the divorce was never complete. Indeed, new rapprochement between religion and spirituality was evidenced by the 2003 Conference on Children's Spirituality: Christian Perspectives held in Chicago and the related book with many of the presentations (Ratcliff, 2004), the newly emerging area of child theology (Bunge, 2001; Miles & Wright, 2003), and the frequent requests by churches for presentations of the second author's research on children's spirituality.

The Scope of Children's Spirituality Research

The extant research on children's spirituality is quite diverse, as the present volume documents, as does an overview of journal articles in this area. For example, an examination of the titles of articles over the first 7 years (1996–2003) of the predominant journal in this area, *The International Journal of Children's Spirituality,* reveals a wide variety of topics, yet also uneven treatment of certain issues.

By far the most common topics were educational and curricular concerns, primarily in public and private schools in the United Kingdom. While numerous studies were conducted in a variety of countries, multicultural issues were the focus of only a handful of studies. Articles related to therapy, dreams, and emotions accounted for about a dozen articles, while another dozen articles were personal reflections of an almost devotional quality. A dozen manuscripts considered childhood sexuality, eight of which were in a special issue on the topic. Stories, writing, and drawing were emphasized in eight articles, while pieces on general theories, morality, and values were slightly less common. Miscellaneous topics that drew one or two articles included holidays, music, gender, the environment, theology, death, the mass media, and drugs. Articles with applications to family and congregational contexts were surprisingly rare.

Many of the articles in the aforementioned journal were research-based; on the other hand, many of the books related to children's spirituality tended to be written at a popular level and the research described is often anecdotal or completely absent (for example, see Fay, 1993; Fitzpatrick, 1991; Myers, 1997; Wolf, 1996). Notable exceptions to this trend are present (such as Morgenthaler, 1999; Reich, Oser, & Scarlett, 1999), but most were popular books consisting almost entirely of opinions and suggestions taken from personal experiences.

Overall, the journal articles and books (even research-based books) often lack concern for methodological rigor. Articles on the distinctive aspects of studying children, and the elusive aspects of measuring and adequately describing spiritual experience, were rare. Mention of the older religious development literature or the adult spiritual experience research is infrequent. Concern for internal and external validity is also missing in most of the research. Even defining spirituality is often overlooked.

These gaps are not too surprising, since many who are concerned with the spirituality of children are in teaching-related professions and often lack sophistication in research methodology. Yet these disparities clearly suggest a need for more work on methodology in the future, if this area of study is to become better established academically.

A VISION FOR CHILDREN'S SPIRITUALITY RESEARCH

As the future of children's spirituality research is considered, it is important to have a vision for what is needed in future research in this area. What specific steps can be taken to bring a marginalized area of study such as children's spirituality into greater prominence? What needs to be done to bring about greater academic respectability and acceptance of children's spirituality and better understanding of their spiritual development and related experiences?

Defining Children's Spirituality and Spiritual Experience

Part of the difficulty in making a case for children's spirituality as a viable area of study is the ambiguity of the phrase. Sometimes researchers and writers talk past one another because this root term is not explicated, and thus the derivative terms *spiritual* and *spirituality* are likewise vague. In sum, it is important to explain the meaning of *spiritual* before significant communication can occur, let alone acceptance by academia.

The working definition suggested by Benson et al. (2003) reveals the difficulties: "Spiritual development is the process of growing the intrinsic human capacity for self-transcendence, in which the self is embedded in something greater than the self, including the sacred" (pp. 205–206). The emphasis on "intrinsic human capacity" highlights the temporal component, while "self-transcendence" and "including the sacred" imply at least the possibility of an alternate spirit realm. Does spiritual development relate to one or both realms?

Crucial to the definition of childhood spirituality is whether it is a global characteristic, involving the totality of the person, or a facet of life (a domain) to be added to existing areas of study. Without question, it can be the latter as a child's spiritual *experience* is clearly distinct from conceptual understandings, physical activity, and social interaction. Yet each of these areas can be affected by, and in turn affect, the child's spiritual experience. In contrast, the child's *spirituality* is more holistic and could encompass all areas of life, including cognitive, physical, and social development. Although the same root word is used, these are two very different ways of looking at the concept—which may, in fact, be two different concepts.

Again, the working definition proposed by Benson and colleagues is instructive: "[Spiritual development] is the developmental 'engine' that propels the search for connectedness, meaning, purpose, and contribution." The latter four qualities can be contrasted with physical development. Yet the four are not separate from cognitive development, since each relies on conceptual development for explanation. At the same time, "connectedness" appears to be related to social development, as may "contribution," but "meaning" and "purpose" may or may not have a social component. In sum, this aspect of the working definition appears to separate children's spiritual development from the other major areas of child development in some respects, yet there is close connection to other areas of child development.

The final part of Benson et al.'s working definition states, "[Spiritual development] is shaped both within and outside of religious traditions, beliefs, and practices." Thus religion and spirituality are understood to have common, overlapping qualities, yet also to be distinct in some ways. This sentence could suggest both of the above connotations of the root term *spirit* and may imply a more global understanding than does the domain of religion, but simultaneous distinction from the topic of religion makes it less than the global term initially implied.

These comments should not be taken as a criticism of the working definition offered, as it is one of the best that has been suggested to date. The point is that it is difficult to clearly identify an area of study that means so many things to different people. More global definitions run the risk of ambiguity, whereas more precise and specific definitions may contribute to obscurity.

Although a clear-cut definition of children's spirituality and their spiritual experiences is considered an important priority for research (Boyatzis & Newman, 2004), it can also be argued that premature closure on such definitions may delimit the issues raised and exclude relevant and important aspects that need to be considered for adequate definitions. Much like grounded theory design in which constructs emerge from analysis, researchers may need to defer precise, uniform, and comprehensive definitions until the wide variety of current definitions has an opportunity to develop an equally wide variety of relevant constructs and related research. At that point, movement toward consensus may be valuable, although it is also possible that a variety of definitions may spawn a wider scope of research studies.

Two opposite dangers need to be highlighted: *uniformity* in definitions (imposed by a consensus of recognized leaders) and *fragmentation,* which makes it difficult to compare one study with another because of different assumptions. Both extremes should be avoided. Creativity may flow freely from diverse perspectives, although a degree of uniformity in definitions may produce a more consistent research agenda. The choice is not between breadth (multiple definitions) and depth (many studies using a single definition), as any single study can reflect greater or lesser depth. In contrast, there is clearly a limit on breadth when a single definition is asserted or imposed—only studies that fit the prescribed definition are likely to be considered appropriate.

Perhaps the best stance, at present, is to consider "working definitions" that may be accepted to a greater or lesser extent by others, such as that proposed by Benson et al. (2003). What is most crucial is that each working definition of spirituality or spiritual experience within a given study be clearly articulated, as well as presuppositions and perspectives implied by the working definition.

Future research, therefore, needs to consider the multiplicity of definitions that have been used in prior research. As part of the philosophical and theoretical base for a given study, researchers can reflect on how the working definition offered interfaces with the specific issues considered in research studies using alternative definitions. Both the limitations and advantages of a given definition can be explored, in comparison with definitions used in other studies. This might prepare the way for some degree of convergence toward working definitions that fit multiple contexts, for a variety of purposes, and for diverse populations.

Focus on Spiritual Experiences

Given the complexity of the definitional issues, it may be useful, at least for the short term, to concentrate on children's spiritual *experiences* rather than spirituality as a whole. For many decades, child development has been dominated by theories that were created by adults using instruments, analyses, and terminology developed by adults. The result is that researchers have generally ignored children's own experiences. Examine the typical developmental psychology textbook: Rarely are children quoted in such textbooks, and when they are, it is usually to provide an example of an adult construct about children. Children's understandings and experiences often are not considered on their own terms, and even rarer are research studies in which children are given the opportunity to analyze their own statements. Furthermore, an emphasis on developmental studies of children's religious experiences is virtually unknown (Boyatzis, in press).

Thus, the emerging emphasis on children's understandings of their experiences—as reflected in child culture theory and similar perspectives (Fine, 1981; McLaren, 1999; Ratcliff, 1995; Sutton-Smith, 1990; Thorne, 1993)—offers a helpful frame for also examining children's spiritual experiences. A concentration on experience moves this area of study beyond religious belief or feeling, yet includes the possibility of studying the structure and content of such experiences, as well as their contextual and cultural adaptations. Spiritual experiences are likely to differ by age and experience, and thus be developmental in nature.

Rigor in Research

It may seem that standardizing definitions in the area should be a priority, but we believe equal priority should be given to methodological rigor and concern for the trustworthiness of data. Academicians are more likely to respect research that is carefully and thoughtfully conducted, with conclusions and applications that flow appropriately from the methodology used, and where there is adequate concern for the validity and reliability of the data.

Boyatzis (in press) recommends longitudinal design, between-group comparisons, and pre-/posttest studies as examples of research that is needed. Multiple measures, using familiar adults to interview children, and interpretive care in the data collection and analysis of children's drawings are also recommended. At a minimum, it seems crucial that there be at least one and preferably several special journal issues on the methodology used in children's spirituality research. Broad summaries of the existing research, with a focus on methodologies used, would help current and potential researchers make use of a greater variety of approaches. More conference sessions, courses in higher education, and publications are needed to address methodological issues that emerge when studying children as well as those inherent in adequately representing spiritual experience.

Although the religious development designs used during the early and mid 20th century tended to favor quantitative methods, there was a major swing to qualitative methodologies in the last decade of that century and into the first decade of the 21st century. The qualitative turn is appropriate for an emerging discipline, particularly as definitions and constructs are still in flux; a blending of qualitative and quantitative procedures, however, would reflect a maturing discipline. Mixed methodologies are likely to better represent both empirical relationships and personal meanings attributed to those relationships by children. Combined qualitative and quantitative studies increase the credibility of research for a wider professional audience. In addition, both longitudinal and cross-sectional research are needed that will provide insights into trajectories of spiritual development across time for individuals, reflecting cohort effects more clearly.

Offering a Unique Perspective or Solutions

It is also important—perhaps even crucial—that the study of children's spirituality contribute conclusions that provide insight and guidance in solving significant problems. For example, issues related to street children, HIV/AIDS and other serious diseases among children in the world, poverty and malnutrition, children engaged in warfare and suffering from war conditions, sexual and physical abuse of children, and other global problems that affect millions of children, need to be addressed in more research related to children's spirituality (see Verma and Sta. Maria, chapter 9, this volume). If the spirituality of children is real and significant, then it should not only be reflected in these kinds of problems, but perhaps the spiritual nature of youngsters may provide clues to understanding and solving such issues.

Children's spirituality in terms of transcendent meaning and purpose is generally assumed to be innate, and if moral foundations and constructive ways of expressing that spirituality are lacking, destructive avenues to spiritual experiences (or perhaps thrills that mimic such experiences) are the likely alternative. For example, Hay and Nye (1998) examined what might be termed "negative spirituality," the response of children and youth to a sense of meaninglessness by resorting to violence, crime, drug abuse, and other aberrant behavior. (Also see Blakeney and Blakeney, chapter 26, this volume.)

Perhaps research into children's spiritual experiences can help provide a fuller explanation for seemingly senseless problem behavior because it is spiritual rather than cognitive in nature. Thus, acceptance and even facilitation of positive spiritual experiences among children might constitute a preventive measure for a wide variety of violent and destructive activities. To the degree that children's spirituality provides new insights into existing unexplained problems in child development, it is likely to be considered a legitimate topic.

Another possibility is to explore the spirituality of children who suffer abuse, including abuse inflicted by clergy (Elizabeth Leonard, personal conversation, November 19, 2004). Not only does the spiritual impact of abuse need to be explicated (Hurley, 2004), but the trajectory or trajectories of spiritual experiences and understandings in the recovery from such abuse also need to be described. This might be a valuable addition to the resilience research (see Crawford, Wright, & Masten, chapter 25, this volume).

Exploring the Universality of Children's Spirituality

Cross-cultural and biological research related to spiritual experiences in general points to the apparent universality of this phenomenon (Hardy, 1979; Hay & Nye, 1998; Robinson, 1983). Hay and Nye (1998) found that children tended to provide acquired religious knowledge when informed that religion or God might be the topics of interviews. When no prior mention was made of these topics, children brought up a surprising amount of spontaneous comments about God and religion (apart from acquired religious knowledge) within the context of discussing their daily lives. This finding points further to the likelihood of the universality of children's spiritual experiences.

Inherent spirituality may be particularly reflected in the unstructured experiences children have, such as on the school playground or with peers in other contexts. Interviews regarding everyday topics and observations of children in typical contexts may reveal an inherent spirituality that has been largely ignored in the past. It may also suggest that general research, particularly qualitative research, might be explored post hoc for evidence of emergent spirituality. It might be asked: When and where is naturally emergent spirituality most likely to surface? What forms does it take in what trajectories of development? And what meanings do children give to these experiences at different points in time? The process by which the meanings of spiritual experiences evolve also deserves research explication.

Diversity and Children's Spirituality

Because of the presumed universality of children's spirituality, spiritual experiences are believed to exist among all ethnic and culture groups, across religions and belief systems, and throughout all of human history. Unlike many issues in child development, spirituality also is an area of common ground for all ages, developmental levels, and intellectual abilities.

Perhaps the most common recommendation in the present volume regarding future research is the pressing need for cross-cultural studies. Kneezel and Emmons (chapter 19, this volume) comment that the research on children's spiritual development may be skewed by the highly individualistic nature of Western society, in which most of the previous research has been conducted, a concern echoed by Donnelly, Matsuba, Hart, and Atkins (chapter 17, this volume). Multiple ethnic groups, socioeconomic influences, political realities, geographical regions, and other ecological influences also need to be included in future research. Contextual influences on spiritual experiences and development should be an important concern in future research (Boyatzis, in press).

How do sex and gender expectations relate to various aspects of children's spirituality? Does location make a significant difference in spiritual experiences, understandings, and associated activities? Does a sense of being marginal to the predominant group in a given social context—or society at large—make a difference in the child's experience of spirituality? Unfortunately, children of color have often been overlooked in the research conducted, with a few notable exceptions (see Crozier & Conde-Frazier, 2004, and Haight, 2002, for example).

Do children with various mental and physical handicaps experience spirituality differently from other children? The field is only beginning to explore the effect of chronic illness on children's spirituality, for example (see Pendleton, Benore, Jonas, Norwood, & Herrmann, 2004). How does a child's spirituality influence well-being and general development, and how, in turn, do these affect the nature and kind of the child's spiritual experiences? How does a thwarted or pathological spirituality (see Wagener and Malony, chapter 10, this volume) influence other areas of life in contrast with a healthy spirituality?

Multiple religious frameworks can enrich the research of children's spiritual development. It may be worthwhile for a religion, and even a faith tradition within a specific religion, to investigate children's spirituality within that specific belief context with considerable depth and in a manner consistent with the doctrine and theology of that faith. When this is done, richly and meaningfully by a variety of faith traditions and religions, there can be more to bring to the table when research is shared. Constructs and even hypotheses that might not surface within one tradition might be developed within another context. For example, what spiritual similarities exist for children from religious backgrounds of Eastern Orthodox mysticism, Jewish Hasidim, Buddhist contemplatives, and the Pentecostal/charismatic Christian tradition? How are the spiritual experiences of such children divergent, and how do those experiences compare with the spiritual experiences of children with atheist, agnostic, and Wiccan/pagan backgrounds? Does religion make a significant difference in children's spirituality, and if so what difference does it make and under what conditions?

This is not to rule out nonfaith traditions, of course, which may also creatively spawn hypotheses and constructs from other working assumptions and beliefs (such as atheism, agnosticism, or indifference to religion). Cross-fertilization of ideas is more likely with such divergent studies, although there should always be a place for studies that cross (or ignore) religious and nonreligious categories.

Examining the Contexts of Children's Spirituality

There is a great need to reflect on how children's spirituality can be expressed, and even encouraged, within those social contexts in which spirituality is most salient, including the home and places of worship. Here the importance of socialization influences must be underscored, as the "nature" aspects of spirituality (it being inherent and universal) interact with the "nurture" of home, congregation, and other socializing institutions.

As Boyatzis, Dollahite, and Marks (chapter 21, this volume) point out, researchers need to explore further the role of the family in spirituality. Under what conditions does family life encourage expressions of children's spirituality, and when does the family suppress spirituality? Similarly, does the place of worship encourage spirituality in children, or does the church, synagogue, mosque, or temple attempt to replace spiritual development with religious information? Does teaching *about* God displace the experience *of* God? Do families and places of worship acknowledge the significant role of spiritual experience in a child's life? What roles do friendship groups, schools, and other organizations play in the encouragement or discouragement of children's spiritual development and experience?

The worship context is most likely to apply to children who affirm or are exposed to religious faith of one kind or another. However, one can also make the case that everyone worships something, whether it be God, nature, possessions, self, or other sources of meaning and transcendence. Existing and innovative methods can be explored in terms of programmatic development and refinement, as well as experiential processes and outcomes by researchers in formal and informal worship contexts.

Similarly, Roehlkepartain and Patel (chapter 23, this volume) suggest a testing of ecological theory in future research of children's spiritual development within the setting of congregations. What is the relationship between various worship practices and spiritual experiences in children? These relationships are likely to vary, depending on the devotion being considered. Yet distinctions and commonalities across religions and between religious and nonreligious expressions of children's spirituality constitute relatively unexamined, but potentially fruitful, areas of inquiry.

CONCLUSIONS

Every new generation must emphasize spirituality as the heart of its task. Each generation of children faces a different world with distinctive issues, norms, and perspectives. A special challenge for the immediate future of research in this area is the innovative nomenclature employed to describe spirituality—terminology can vary significantly from study to study when even the definition of what is being studied is fluid, to say nothing of the proliferation of theories on the subject.

Likewise, every culture must look at the distinctive spirituality concerns that need to be

addressed relevant to the culture's framework. While spiritual experience and development may, indeed, be universal across cultures, the shape of that experience, behavior, and understanding is significantly impacted by the culture and subcultures within which it occurs. Culture-specific research results, theories, and even definitions are thus likely.

Children are more than creatures that will potentially become whole adults; rather they are whole persons as children and should be valued for who they are, not just for what they will become. They are more than bodies and brains to be educated; they are deeply spiritual both in their day-to-day lives as well as in those moments of connectedness to Transcendence that brings meaning, purpose, and relationship with the Otherness that includes faith, belief, and the experience of a spiritual dimension of life.

REFERENCES

Barnes, E., & Boring, O. (2004). Theological life of a California child. In D. Ratcliff (Ed.), *Children's spirituality: Christian perspectives, research, and applications* (pp. 409–417). Eugene, OR: Cascade Books. (Reprinted from *Pedagogical Seminary, 2,* 1892, 442–448.)

Benson, P. L., Roehlkepartain, E. C., & Rude, S. P. (2003). Spiritual development in childhood and adolescence: Toward a field of inquiry. *Applied Developmental Science, 7*(3), 205–213.

Boyatzis, C. (in press). Socialization and cognitive processes in children's religious development: Where we have been, where we must go. In R. F. Paloutzian & C. L. Park (Eds.), *The handbook of the psychology of religion.* New York: Guilford.

Boyatzis, C. J., & Newman, B. T. (2004). How shall we study children's spirituality? In D. Ratcliff (Ed.), *Children's spirituality: Christian perspectives, research, and applications.* Eugene, OR: Cascade.

Bunge, M. J. (2001). *The child in Christian thought.* Grand Rapids, MI: Eerdmans.

Coles, R. (1990). *The spiritual life of children.* Boston: Houghton Mifflin.

Crozier, K., & Conde-Frazier, E. (2004). A narrative of children's spirituality: African American and Latino theological perspectives. In D. Ratcliff (Ed.),

Children's spirituality: Christian perspectives, research, and applications (pp. 284–308). Eugene, OR: Cascade Books.

Degelman, D., Mullen, P., & Mullen, N. (1984). Development of abstract religious thinking: A comparison of Roman Catholic and Nazarene children and adolescents. *Journal of Psychology and Christianity, 3,* 44–49.

Elkind, D. (1978). *The child's reality: Three developmental themes.* Hillsdale, NJ: Erlbaum.

Fay, M. (1993). *Do children need religion?* New York: Pantheon.

Fine, G. A. (1981). Friends, impression management, and preadolescent behavior. In S. R. Asher & J. M. Gottman (Eds.), *The development of children's friendships* (pp. 29–53). Cambridge, UK: Cambridge University Press.

Fitzpatrick, J. G. (1991). *Something more: Nurturing your child's spiritual growth.* New York: Viking.

Fowler, J. W. (1981). *Stages of faith.* New York: HarperCollins.

Francis, L. J., Kay, W. K., & Campbell, W. S. (1996). *Research in religious education.* Macon, GA: Smyth & Helwys.

Goldman, R. (1964). *Religious thinking from childhood to adolescence.* New York: Seabury.

Haight, W. L. (2002). *African American children at church: A sociological perspective.* Cambridge, UK: Cambridge University Press.

Hardy, A. (1966). *The divine flame.* London: Collins.

Hardy, A. (1979). *The spiritual nature of man: A study of contemporary religious experience.* Oxford, UK: Clarendon Press.

Hay, D., & Nye, R. (1998). *The spirit of the child.* London: Fount/HarperCollins.

Hurley, D. L. (2004). Spiritual impact of childhood sexual abuse: Some implications for teacher education. *Journal of Religion and Abuse, 6*(2), 81–101.

Hyde, K. (1990). *Religion in childhood and adolescence.* Birmingham, AL: Religious Education Press.

May, S., & Ratcliff, D. (2004). Brain development and the numinous experiences of children. In D. Ratcliff (Ed.), *Children's spirituality: Christian perspectives, research, and applications* (pp. 149–165). Eugene, OR: Cascade.

McLaren, P. (1999). *Schooling as a ritual performance* (3rd ed.). Lanham, MD: Rowman & Littlefield.

Miles, G., & Wright, J.-J. (2003). *Celebrating children.* Waynesboro, GA: Paternoster Press.

Morgenthaler, S. K. (1999). *Exploring children's spiritual formation: Foundational issues.* River Forest, IL: Pillars Press.

Myers, B. K. (1997). *Young children and spirituality.* New York: Routledge.

Nye, R. (1998). *Psychological perspectives on children's spirituality.* Unpublished doctoral dissertation, University of Nottingham, UK.

Otto, R. (1950). *The idea of the holy: An inquiry into the non-rational factor in the idea of the divine and its relation to the rational* (2nd ed.). New York: Oxford University Press.

Peatling, J. (1973). *The incidence of concrete and abstract religious thinking in the interpretation of three Bible stories by pupils enrolled in grades four through twelve in selected schools in the Episcopal Church in the United States of America.* (Doctoral dissertation, New York University, 1974) (UMI No. 7412859)

Pendleton, S., Benore, E., Jonas, K., Norwood, W., & Herrmann, C. (2004). Spiritual influences in helping children to cope with life stressors. In D. Ratcliff (Ed.), *Children's spirituality: Christian perspectives, research, and applications* (pp. 358–382). Eugene, OR: Cascade Books.

Pitts, P. (1977). *Concept development and the development of the God concept in the child: A bibliography.* Schenectady, NY: Character Research Press.

Ratcliff, D. (1987). Teaching the Bible developmentally. *Christian Education Journal, 7,* 21–32.

Ratcliff, D. (1995). *An elementary school hallway: Social formations and meanings outside the classroom.* Unpublished doctoral dissertation, University of Georgia, Athens, Georgia.

Ratcliff, D. (Ed.). (2004). *Children's spirituality: Christian perspectives, research, and applications.* Eugene, OR: Cascade.

Reich, K. H., Oser, F. K., & Scarlett, W. G. (1999). *Psychological studies on spiritual and religious development.* Scottsdale, AZ: Pabst Science Publishers.

Robinson, E. (1983). *The original vision.* New York: Seabury.

Strommen, M. P. (Ed.). (1971). *Research on religious development.* New York: Hawthorn.

Sutton-Smith, B. (1990). School playground as festival. *Children's Environments Quarterly, 7,* 3–7.

Teresa of Avila. (2004). *The interior castle* (Mirabai Starr, Trans.). East Rutherford, NJ: Riverhead Books. (Original work published 1557)

Thorne, B. (1993). *Gender play: Girls and boys in school*. New Brunswick, NJ: Rutgers University Press.

Wolf, A. D. (1996). *Nurturing the spirit in nonsectarian classrooms*. Hollidaysburg, PA: Parent Child Press.

Yust, K. M., Johnson, A. N., Sasso, S. E., & Roehlkepartain, E. C. (Eds.). (in press). *Nurturing child and adolescent spirituality: Perspectives from the world's religious traditions*. Lanham, MD: Rowman and Littlefield.

34

THE SCIENCE OF CHILD AND ADOLESCENT SPIRITUAL DEVELOPMENT: DEFINITIONAL, THEORETICAL, AND FIELD-BUILDING CHALLENGES

PETER L. BENSON

A s many of the chapters in this volume attest, there is a vibrant community of scholars—in many nations and multiple disciplines—focused on the spiritual development of children and adolescents. Nevertheless, this field of study is still marginalized in the academy.

The explanation for this disparity typically begins with the lament that mainline scholars in many disciplines hold prejudicial views about the significance (or reality of) things religious and/or spiritual. And, in an important but often overlooked analysis in *American Psychologist,* Jones (1994) argues that psychology's refusal to take religion seriously has been due to a prevailing but outdated philosophy of science grounded in positivism. As noted by Browning and Cooper (2004), "Jones believes the dialogue between psychology and religion has frequently been reduced to a monologue in which psychology does all the talking" (p. 246). And in this positivist monologue, psychology fuels an irreconcilable split between science and religion in which science is seen as trading in facts and religion is seen as trading in faith. Fortunately, there are signs that this artificial distinction between faith and fact is eroding.

At the same time, it can be argued that scholarship in child and adolescent spiritual development is in an early stage and not yet ready for "prime time." This chapter evaluates the definitional, theoretical, and research status of the field and offers some ideas for moving the field forward, guided by the hunch that scientific advances will ultimately catch the eye of the academic establishment.

THE DEFINITIONAL CHALLENGE

Part of the difficulty in making a case for spiritual development as a viable area of study is the ambiguity of the term. It is not isomorphic with the term *spirituality*. There are linkages, of course, but they are also as different as cognition is from cognitive development. In the introductory chapter to this volume, the editors review a number of ways in which the concept of spirituality has been defined. And most of this definitional debate has been about how *spirituality* relates to the concepts of religion and religiousness. A number of publications use conceptual and/or quantitative methods to disentangle religion and spirituality (Hill & Hood, 1999; Marler & Hadaway, 2002; Zinnbauer, Pargament, & Scott, 1999). Additionally, many researchers argue that spirituality has multiple domains. For example, Scott (cited in Zinnbauer et al., 1999) analyzed the content of scientific definitions of religiousness and spirituality that had appeared in scientific writings in the past 5 decades. She identified nine content categories in definitions of spirituality: experiences of connectedness or relationship; processes leading to greater connectedness; behavioral responses to something sacred or secular; systems of thought or beliefs; traditional institutional structures; pleasurable states of being; beliefs in the sacred or transcendent; attempts at or capacities for transcendence; and existential questions.

Because of its multidimensionality, spirituality does not fit neatly inside any particular domain of social science. Hill et al. (2000) noted that religion and spirituality inherently involve development, social-psychological phenomena, cognitive phenomena, affective and emotional phenomena, and personality. They suggest that "few phenomena may be as integral across life span development as religious or spiritual concerns" (p. 63). Further, Piedmont (1999) presents evidence that spirituality may be an independent dimension of personality. Thus, a multidisciplinary approach is essential to develop a comprehensive understanding of the domain.

Considerably less scholarly attention has been focused on defining spiritual development. As a developmental concept, what part of human development are we addressing with the adjective *spiritual?* Is it a modifier we use for naming and claiming a heretofore neglected domain or dimension within human development theory and research? Is *spiritual* used to describe the processes by which persons integrate the social, moral, and cognitive dimensions of development? Another possibility, suggested by Scarlett

(chapter 2, this volume), is that the term spiritual might, in some cases, simply rename phenomena such as awe, wonder, or the pursuit of meaning. In our definitional journey, we also have to take seriously the issue of real (or perceived) realities beyond normal, waking consciousness and the extent to which this is central to the process of spiritual development.

The definition of spiritual development posed by Benson, Roehlkepartain, and Rude (2003) was created as a precursor for establishing the parameters for a theoretical approach. Embedded in it are assumptions about three dynamics of human development, each of which needs to be explicated in any theory of human development: (1) the core developmental processes at play that are deemed intrinsic to the nature of human life; (2) the goals or purposes of development; and (3) the contexts that inform how developmental processes play themselves out. First, here is the "working" definition they pose:

> Spiritual development is the process of growing the intrinsic human capacity for self-transcendence, in which the self is embedded in something greater than the self, including the sacred. It is the developmental "engine" that propels the search for connectedness, meaning, purpose and contribution. It is shaped both within and outside of religious traditions, beliefs and practices. (pp. 205–206)

The clauses in this definition can be arrayed as follows, per the three issues posed above:

- The core developmental processes at play: "Spiritual development is the process of growing the intrinsic capacity for self-transcendence, in which the self is embedded in something larger than the self, including the sacred."
- The goals or purposes of development: "connectedness, meaning, purpose and contribution."
- The contexts that inform how such development plays itself out: "It is shaped both within and outside of religious traditions, beliefs and practices."

Further, the definition provides two linkages to the arena of religion and "spirit." The first is in the definition of self-transcendence and the referent to embedding the self in the sacred.

Note, however, that this form of self-transcendence (e.g., placing oneself in the context of God, gods, a chosen people, a divine plan) is assumed to be only one possible variant on the theme of "something greater than the self." Conceivably, other options include embedding the self in non-sacred traditions of thought, ideology, community, or vocation. The second referent is to the role of religious traditions, beliefs, and practices as among the cultural and social contexts that can, but not necessarily, inform how development plays itself out.

Hence, this "working" definition stands solidly on the idea that spiritual development is a universal domain of development that can be dramatically informed by ideas and practices that are theological and/or religious. But, explicit in the definition is the possibility that spiritual development also occurs independent of religion and/or conceptions of sacred, ultimate, or alternative forms of reality.

This exegesis of the definition is made not to justify it but to hold up some of the core issues that need to be explicated in a theory of spiritual development. Definition and theory are, of course, symbiotic. We now turn to the issue of theory, seeking both to expand the range of issues that a theory of spiritual development should address (in addition to the three posed above) and to offer alternate solutions and approaches for making particular theoretical claims.

THE THEORETICAL CHALLENGE

It has often been said that we lack a comprehensive theory about spiritual development and its conceptual sibling, religious development. Nearly all reviews of the literature make this point (Benson, Donahue, & Erickson, 1989; Benson & King, in press; Bridges & Moore, 2002; Donahue and Benson, 1995; Kerestes & Youniss, 2003; Pargament, 2002; Potvin, Hoge, & Nelson, 1976). In spite of this near consensus, there is an upsurge in interest in this domain due in part to a series of reports on positive youth development and prevention that have made their way into public policy discussions (Benson & Pittman, 2001; Bridges & Moore, 2002; Eccles & Gootman, 2002; Resnick et al., 1997).

Each has identified religious engagement as a developmental resource that lessens risk behavior and/or enhances positive outcomes.

This is not to say that the field is devoid of theory. The key issues being raised here are about the need for (1) comprehensive theory; (2) theory that is rooted in, but not exclusive to, human development; and (3) theory that identifies the terrain of life that covers the so-called spiritual dimension (which may or may not overlap with the concept of religion). While the many theories that speak to religious development are germane, each speaks to only part of the conceptual elephant. There are, for example, theoretical approaches to religious experience (Hardy, 1966; Otto, 1917/1950), the development of religious thought (Fowler, 1981; Goldman, 1964), the development of religious judgment (Oser, 1991), the emergence of spirituality in children (Hart, chapter 12, this volume; Hay & Nye, 1998), and the biological basis of spiritual awareness (Hay, Reich, & Utsch, chapter 4, this volume). And new and important work is emerging in two areas: (1) the interplay of culture and person in the development of the spiritual life (Boyer, 2001; Mattis, Ahluwalia, Cowie, & Kirkland-Harris, chapter 20, this volume) and (2) religion as a developmental resource (King & Furrow, 2004; Smith, 2003).

The issue addressed here, then, is how to scope out the parameters for a comprehensive theory of spiritual development. The goal is to posit an architecture for spiritual development theory and to suggest some additional theoretical approaches on which a comprehensive theory could be built.

The Architecture for a Theory of Spiritual Development

As we begin this architectural sketch, several core assumptions (or biases) need to be acknowledged. The first is that a theory of spiritual development must illuminate how the development of persons occurs within multiple systems of developmental influence. Persons are, of course, embedded in culture and social contexts. And the influence we will assume is bidirectional: Persons are both influenced and influence. Second, we assume that persons are active agents in producing their own development.

Central, then, to a theory of spiritual development are conceptions of the developing person, the contexts in which the person is embedded, and the dynamic interaction between the two.

Following Lerner's lead (1984, 1998, 2002, 2003), all of the multiple levels of organizations engaged in human development—from biology and disposition to relationships, social institutions, culture, and history—are fused into an integrated system. Development has to do with changes in the relations among and between these multiple levels of organizations. Consonant with systems thinking in biology, persons—through their dynamic interaction with developmental contexts—experience pattern and order through the process of self-organizing. This key dynamic means that "pattern and order emerge from the interactions of the components of a complex system without explicit instructions, either in the organization itself or from the environment. Self-organization—processes that by their own activities change themselves—is a fundamental property of living things" (Thelen & Smith, 1998, p. 564). At one level, this proposed dynamic interaction of nature and nurture is a dramatic departure from earlier models of human development that created a split between the two (Lorenz, 1965; Skinner, 1938). At another level, however, the concept of self-organization introduces, as Lerner suggested (1976, 2003), a "third source" of development: the organism itself. Schneirla's (1957, 1959) concepts of circular functions and self-stimulation are important illustrations of the organism's centrality and active participation in development.

The person as active agent of her or his own development has not been a common feature of research in spiritual and/or religious development. However, there is a body of literature that points to this phenomenon. In studies of adolescents who share common family, school, and religious community influences, there is still remarkable variability in the content of young people's religious ideation (Benson & Spilka, 1973; Benson, Yeager, Wood, Guerra, & Manno, 1986). The inference in this work is that persons presented with the same religious content show considerable variability in the messages they claim for their own. And the selection is not random. It likely follows dynamic self-organization principles, in which persons select from the information provided them a subset that has psychological and social advantage for prioritized personal goals (Baltes & Baltes, 1990; Baltes, Lindenberger, & Staudinger, 1998). Helpful here also is an adage found in contemporary cultural psychology: Culture and the psyche make each other up in the process of developing what persons know, want, feel, and value (Shweder et al., 1997).

Additionally, a comprehensive theory of spiritual development (like all themes of development) must account for two phenomena. First, it must explain individual variability. Second, it must define what it is about persons that animates the developmental process. We might think of this as the question of what creates the human appetite for the spiritual domain. Putting these two issues together (variability and appetite) reminds us of the useful phrase, "One mind, many mentalities" (Shweder et al., 1997).

In creating an architecture for a theory, there are eight essential "girders" (Figure 34.1). Three of these were enumerated earlier in the discussion of definitions: the core developmental processes at play, the purpose of development, and the contexts that inform development. The eight "girders" will be briefly defined.

Myths, Narratives, and Interpretative Frameworks. The "stuff" of spiritual development, we propose, is the construction of an organizational frame for understanding and explaining "what is good, important, and real." This human "work" can have the self as its primary referent, as is likely in the European and U.S. context. In other social and cultural locations, this "work" may have the collective as its anchor point. There have been many attempts to define this cell in our architectural framework. It is beyond the scope of this chapter to propose a definitive hypothesis. What is claimed, however, is that advancing spiritual development as a central field of inquiry depends heavily on creating compelling (and perhaps competing) understandings of this core dynamic. Some of the many ways of framing this developmental process are listed below. Although not all authors explicitly call these processes of spiritual development, they all resonate with the core

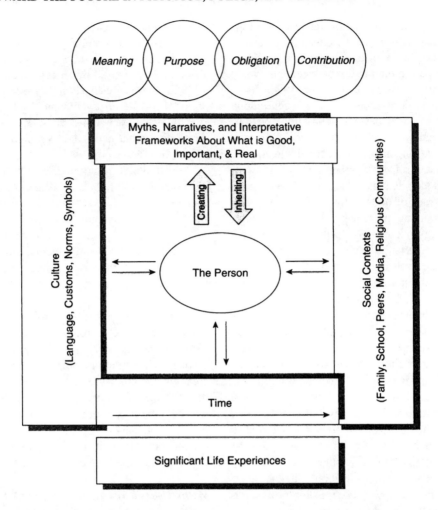

Figure 34.1   Essential Elements in a Comprehensive Theory of Spiritual Development

idea that persons share a developmental press for finding/creating/adapting/discovering/learning a view of self, reality, and the world. So, what are some of the candidates?

- Jones (1994) speaks of content claims that all religions offer. Thinking that these claims can also be understood as depicting some of the territory of myths and narratives more generically (whether one is religious or not), we offer his five as one way of describing the core issues that spiritual development addresses: (a) the nature of the universe; (b) the nature of ultimate reality; (c) the nature of human beings; (d) the place of persons in the universe;

and (e) the nature of morality and what is good or to be valued.

- As noted in the introduction to this volume, Coles (1990) suggests that among the most compelling of human needs is to "gain for ourselves a sense of where we came from and where we are and where we're going" (p. 8).

- Also as noted in the introduction, we can think of spiritual development as the active process of creating a personal narrative, a story of who we are in space and time. Indeed, McAdams (1993) suggests that this narrative creation is a core, essential, and universal dimension of human experience. As already noted, Benson and colleagues (2003) focused on spiritual development as a process of actively constructing a view of the self in the context of self-transcending myths and frames.

- Browning and Cooper (2004) suggest that both traditional religion and modern schools of thought in psychology (e.g., humanistic psychology) "provide concepts and technologies for the ordering of the interior life" (p. 2). We appropriate from this the idea that humans seek an order to the kinds of life issues found in our review of Jones and Coles and that being religious or being Rogerian, Maslowian, or Jungian is a spiritual development pathway. To take this as far as we can, we also suggest that this "work" of ordering, or myth making or self-transcendence, has as many pathways as there are persons, with some creating a spiritual development pathway that either purposefully—or because of lack of exposure—has absolutely nothing to do with symbols emanating from religions or other schools of established thought.

- Finally, it is apparent that most of the approaches we have reviewed are ways of knowing that help individuals value and understand their lives. Each of them accents the individual good more than the social good. If so, what we have is clearly a bias that favors the agentic over the communal. As an antidote, it is possible to reframe the myth-making and interpretive framework goal around themes that are more collectivist. Hence, a theory of spiritual development—if it is to be global in scope—cannot depend only on theory derived from individual human development. The field of cultural psychology (LeVine, 1989; Markus & Kitayama, 1991a, 1991b; Shweder & Sullivan, 1993) provides useful theoretical formulations for the human capacity to create shared meaning, to learn from and promote a symbolic tradition, and to be "active agents in the perpetration of their symbolic inheritance" (Shweder et al., 1997, p. 868).

It is clear that the approaches outlined here lean toward cognitive, consciousness, and theory of mind explanations. There may be other possibilities for framing this part of the theory and that better integrate multiple spheres of development.

The Nature of the Person. The second essential element in a comprehensive theory has to do with the nature of persons (see the oval in Figure 34.1) and what animates the myth-making, narrative-building, and interpretive framing work described above.

It is recommended for future theory construction that the animating forces be placed in human strength rather than in human deficit, as is the case of Freudian psychoanalytic approaches or Ellis's rational-emotive approach to therapy (Ellis, 1955). A number of new approaches to strength-based development could be useful here, including theories focused on thriving and optimal development (Lerner, Alberts, Anderson, & Dowling, chapter 5, this volume), the development of purpose (Damon, Menon, & Bronk, 2003), and positive youth development (Benson, Scales, Hamilton, & Sesma, in press).

Three approaches to the animating process (for being receptive to "inherited" myths and interpretive frames and/or being actively engaged in creating them) have been discussed in this volume. Johnson and Boyatzis (chapter 15, this volume) provide a cognitive-cultural hypothesis based on capacities for cognitive flexibility (Mithen, 1996) and imagination (Harris, 2000). These serve to open the person to the "cognition of more reality," with spiritual development arising from culturally based practices and experiences that "orient to and connect the self with this reality" (p. xx).

Hay et al. (chapter 4, this volume) take us in another direction, holding up natural spiritual awareness as an animating power. They draw on Otto's concepts of the experience of being in the presences of the sacred or the holy (1917/1950), Hardy's account of the evolutionary basis for spiritual awareness (1965, 1966), and the recent positing of relational consciousness (Hay & Nye, 1998). In an important analysis of cultural influence, Hay and colleagues hypothesize that this spiritual spark can be snuffed out by "a socially constructed secularist critique that denies its reality."

Lerner and his colleagues (chapter 5, this volume; see also Lerner, 1984, 1998, 2004) place the animating energy for positive human development in the transactions between person and context. This developmental systems approach to human development accents the influence of plasticity and adaptive human regulation and the potential for successful development when contexts encourage the active engagement of individuals. In this model, spirituality has a direct effect on thriving.

In addition, a particular possibility for integration into theories of the person's role in spiritual development is the narrative-making approach. This life span developmental theory suggests that all persons create identities by fashioning myths "to bring together the different parts of ourselves and our lives into a purposeful and convincing whole" (McAdams, 1993, p. 12). The elements of these myths are the same ones traditional religions speak to, including one's place in the cosmic order. As McAdams suggests, "we do not discover ourselves in myth; we make ourselves through myth" (p. 13). For those scholars interested in the creation of spiritual development theory, this approach gives useful handles for understanding how religious myth becomes organically intertwined with family, community, and cultural sources of "information" about the self; how myths become organized; and how they change across the life span.

The Bidirectional Nature of Influence. This aspect of a comprehensive theory is depicted in Figure 34.1 with the two arrows labeled "Creating" and "Inheriting." It is meant to convey the point made by McAdams: The myths and narratives that organize and give direction to our lives involve a lifelong creative process in which persons actively create (whether the activity is conscious or not) a story, using source material that can come from many institutions and relationships. For some, this source material includes the myths inherited from religious traditions. But, it also includes the myths learned on Grandpa's or Grandma's lap and in the crucible of peer relationships, family, and community. While the source material creates an abundance of texts, the person exercises many creative strategies. These include choosing to abandon some of the inherited texts (as when choosing to move away from one's religion of inheritance; choosing some of the texts and rejecting some of the others; amending the texts or moving toward new communities offering alternative texts). And then there are multiple possibilities for creating new narratives or weaving inherited text and created text together in new ways.

We should also note the other three pairs of bidirectional arrows in the model. These suggest that persons not only are influenced by culture, social contexts, and significant life experiences but also are active players in shaping them. As noted earlier, developmental systems theory posits that development occurs in the transactions between person and context. Consonant with this theory, Bronfenbrenner (1979) put it this way:

> The ecology of human development involves the scientific study of progressive, mutual accommodation between an active, growing human being and the changing properties of the immediate settings in which the developing person lives, as this process is affected by relations between these settings, and by the larger contexts in which the settings are embedded. (p. 21)

In this creative interplay between the person and the myths and texts he or she inherits, a theory of spiritual development should also look for individual differences in the "rules" persons use to create, accept, reject, or modify texts. We think of this as differences in lenses or in organizing frames. What might constitute such frames? One example could be the agentic and communal distinction. We use the distinction here to refer to the accents given to self and community. That is, an agentic approach refers to the degree to which a person seeks to support and reinforce the well-being of the self. A communal approach represents interest in connectedness and interdependence with others. In other words, this distinction is about "me" or "we." The agentic and communal concepts have also been used by Gilligan (1982) in her work on moral development and by McAdams (1993) in his discussion of major themes in personal narratives. Each employed the concepts to contrast power and achievement motives from intimacy motives.

In an interview-based, random sample study of the U.S. Congress, Benson and Williams (1982) coded for agentic and communal themes in responses to open-ended questions about human nature, beliefs about ultimate reality, beliefs about salvation and the paths to salvation, eschatology, theodicy, ethical values, the causes of human behavior, and the dynamics of social change. Three findings are informative: (1) The agentic and communal themes could be tracked with considerable consistency across the domains of the inquiry (e.g., agentic on one domain predicted agentic in many domains); (2) both agentic and communal "types" were clearly evident among members of Congress; and (3) one's location in this typology was dramatically related to voting records in predictable ways; individualism as an organizing frame was strongly associated with individualism in policy choices (e.g., for private ownership, for free enterprise, anti-tax) and a communal worldview connected powerfully to using the resources of government to spread supports and opportunities more equitably (e.g., pro civil liberties, pro hunger relief legislation).

In this study, these individual and communal themes were better predictors of voting than was political party. What we have here, then, is evidence for powerful, behavior-shaping consequences of organizing frames. How these narrative themes emerge is obviously an important research question. McAdams (1993) posits that these kinds of frames emerge in childhood.

The theoretical approach of Baltes and Baltes (1980, 1990; M. M. Baltes, 1987; P. B. Baltes, 1997) may provide a way to understand how persons regulate their interactions with the external world and develop different organizing lenses. The model is called selective optimization with compensation. One hypothesis is that persons select from a range of potential resources a subset that has psychological and social advantage for prioritized personal goals. Selection, then, has to do with both one's preferences and the ecologies one chooses to be the primary crucibles for development. Optimization is "the process of acquiring, refining, coordinating and applying goal-relevant means or resources" toward the selected targets (Lerner, 2002, p. 224). Although Baltes and Baltes were not thinking about spiritual development in these formulations, the principles may have currency in a comprehensive theory.

Time. The box labeled "Time" (in Figure 34.1) can refer to history as well as to a person's life span. Both time-related concepts influence the person, her or his contexts, and the interactions

among them. Elder's life-course theory (1974, 1980, 1999) could be germane to understanding both how persons interact with, learn from, and alter their social contexts and how the narrative-creating work is altered by different points in human history. In his words:

> Human lives are socially embedded in specific historical times and places that shape their content, pattern and direction. As experiments of nature or design, types of historical change are experienced differentially by people of different ages and roles. . . . The change itself affects the developmental trajectory of individuals by altering their life course. (Elder, 1999, p. 969)

Simultaneously, one's location in the life span obviously shapes what one brings to the spiritual development process. Age-related developmental tasks inform goals and priorities and certainly—and dramatically so—what one chooses to select and to optimize. Chapters in this volume, for example, speak to developmental tasks that will inform how one shapes, amends, changes, and chooses major life narratives. These include attachment (Granqvist & Dickie, chapter 14) and identity (Templeton & Eccles, chapter 18).

Significant Life Experiences. The trajectories of development can also be informed by significant life events. A comprehensive theory must reckon with these influences and how they alter the tasks, lenses, perspectives, and energy that shape spiritual narratives. There are several categories of such life events, some representing the tragic side of life, and some representing its generous and healing side. Some experiences known to be or interpreted to be profoundly religious experiences (e.g., glimpses of the divine, encounters with God, mysticism, answers to prayers, conversion) can significantly change how one knows, values, and sees oneself in the grand scheme of things.

Culture and Social Contexts. On the left and the right side of Figure 34.1 are the concepts of culture and social contexts. We would be foolish, of course, to build a theory of spiritual development without acknowledging the embeddedness of persons in both. And in a dynamic theory, we must take into account the multiple and bidirectional interplays. Culture informs the texts that are inherited; the language that shapes one's thinking; the symbols that are accessible; the rituals that command attention and focus the person on culturally sanctioned definitions of person, cosmos, and transcendence; and the degree of normative permission there is for one to consciously and actively engage in one's spiritual development. To add fuel to spiritual development, persons potentially participate in, learn from, respond to, and integrate multiple cultures. There may be national culture and cultures of identity and ideational cultures, each providing scripts and norms shaping the spiritual development process.

Instructive here is recent work on the role of language in shaping functional units of consciousness. Markus and Kitayama (1991a, 1991b) describe the "selfways" dominant in English-speaking, Western societies and those more typical in Japanese, Korean, and Chinese cultures. In the former, language and cultural symbols accent individual agency and independence. In Asian societies, the accent is on the interdependence of individuals:

> Experiencing interdependence entails seeing oneself as part of an encompassing social relationship and recognizing that one's behavior is determined by, contingent on and to a large extent, organized by what the actor perceived to be the thoughts, feelings and actions of others in the relationship. (Markus & Kitayama, 1991a, p. 227)

The implications of such ideational language and symbolic foregrounds for the content, process, and dynamics of spiritual development cannot be underestimated.

Then there is the dynamic interplay of developing persons with multiple social institutions and contexts, including family, school, peer group, media, and religious community. King and Benson (chapter 27, this volume) review some of the literature in this area. Each of these alone or in combination potentially informs the animating process that the person brings to the process, norms that influence the creating and inheriting dynamics, the texts one is exposed to, and the presence (or absence) of significant life events.

Two specific areas of theory development and reason are recommended here. One concerns the role of the media in exposing developing persons to a wide range of ways that people approach and resolve central myth-making issues. Examples include the nature of reality, the origins of life, what is good, and, in more theological language, the concept of theodicy and eschatology. What happens to spiritual development when such exposure is either broad or narrow? And what are the implications of such exposure at different points in the life cycle? Note that it would be difficult to posit how these experiences work without addressing other dynamics represented in Figure 34.1.

As Roehlkepartain and Patel point out (chapter 23, this volume), the role of the social institutions designed to directly nurture the spirit (i.e., mosques, synagogues, congregations, parishes) has not been the focus of deep inquiry. We have a habit of studying frequency of participation but leave aside the compelling questions about congregation in cultural context and the variability in congregational norms and dynamics. Their ecological framework moves us in the right direction.

The Pull of Spiritual Development. At the top of Figure 34.1 are four circles, representing meaning, purpose, obligation, and contribution. The hypothesis here is that there are compelling (and universal) human motivations toward which spiritual development is drawn. To extend this idea, meaning, purpose, obligation (in the sense of one's moral duty), and contribution (knowing and affirming why one matters) *pull* persons into spiritual development (and the road travels through narrative and myth creation) and the animating forces within the person (described in our earlier discussion) *push* the person forward. Hence, spiritual development is energized by both pull and push, and these dynamically intertwined processes are embedded in, responsive to, and emboldened or compromised by society, life experience, and culture.

THE FIELD-BUILDING CHALLENGE

A number of scholars have addressed the issue of building a field of spiritual development that is both rigorous and generates knowledge that becomes central to how the academic establishment thinks about human development (Benson, 2004; Benson et al., 2003; Bridges & Moore, 2002; Hill & Pargament, 2003; King & Boyatzis, 2004). A third potential criterion for effective field building is collaboration with the practice community while simultaneously growing the rigor of theory, measurement, and research. Historically, such practice links occur very late in the process of field formation. It is strongly advocated here that we build "bridges" early and purposefully, and draw in—as co-learners, data interpreters, research agenda consultants, and diffusers of knowledge—those fields of practice that have, or should have, a profound interest in spiritual development. A few include health care, social work, clinical and counseling psychology, family education, youth development, and the many arms of the traditional religious establishment (e.g., seminaries, denominations, religious education). One reason for being inclusive in this way is to address a problem identified by King and Boyatzis (2004):

> We suggest, however, that in our attempt to operationalize our constructs, we must avoid distorting them. Scholars from psychology (Miller & Thoresen, 2003) and comparative religion (Smith, 1963) have warned against objectivist scientists proposing definitions of "spiritual" or "religious" that the spiritual or religious themselves would not recognize as genuine. (pp. 3–4)

The central idea addressed in this chapter is that the first step in advancing the field is to trigger an explosion in theory building, with an eye to constructing frameworks and hypotheses that position spiritual development as a core, central, and universal dimension of human development. In creating these theoretical innovations, it will matter how well we (1) learn from work already under way, including models elaborated by Fowler (1981; Fowler & Dell, chapter 3, this volume), Hay and Nye (1998), and Helminiak (1987); (2) take seriously the immense global diversity of spiritual development pathways and trajectories; (3) incorporate theoretical work in other areas of human development; (4) place spiritual development in a dynamic intersection of

person and context; (5) honor religion while positioning it as "not the only" way in which spiritual development occurs; and (6) use concepts and language that resonate with practitioners.

This is complex but essential work. The architectural features of a theory described in this chapter raise many questions. Perhaps that is how this work is supposed to move. There are several features that are still unsatisfying. The emphasis on narrative, myth, and organizing frames that speak to "where we came from, why we are here, where we are going" is loaded with assumptions that need to be challenged. The emphasis on narrative appears to understate the role of experience and relationship. And the human hungers that "pull" spiritual development are, at this point, proxies for something-to-be-clarified. Two other critiques of the architecture are that it minimizes the role of spiritual practice in spiritual development and that in its portrayal in Figure 34.1, the parts do not adequately move together in a dynamic way. They do, in fact, and this should be made clearer.

Field building will also require theory-driven research and a growing interdisciplinary community of scholars who get hooked on this research agenda. A critical step in the process, of course, is the creation of psychometrically sound measures useful for exploring spiritual development. Several come readily to mind. One would be a process for capturing how individuals create and/or inherit their narratives. Issues include the energy devoted to this work, the sources of the text materials, the levels of coherence across different domains of the narrative, the salience of the narratives, the content of the narratives, and the consequences of the narratives. This battery of measures would make more possible the study of individual differences, patterns, change over time, and cultural and social influences.

It is also suggested that a measure of spiritual thriving would have major advantages. Such a measure would link investigations with a common thread, create interest among practitioners, and potentially bring media attention to this emerging spiritual development field. Although some scholars may think of media attention as interference rather than opportunity, we would offer that such attention is useful for moving ideas into policy deliberations, funding initiatives (both private and governmental), and the world of practice. Buzz is good if theory and research are strong.

The concept of spiritual thriving links to recent theory and research in the fields of youth development and adolescent psychology (Benson, 1997; Lerner et al., chapter 5, this volume; Scales & Benson, 2005; Scales, Benson, Leffert, & Blyth, 2000). It has to do with a process of growth that must be centralized to take seriously each person's developmental contexts and individual strengths, and the relationships among them.

Spiritual thriving suggests vibrancy. It is an active process, not an end point. It suggests moving forward, becoming, learning, fretting and stewing, paying attention, questioning, choosing, wondering, imagining, opening oneself to experience and possibility, and celebrating. It flourishes in community. And it points a person in the direction of generosity and gratitude. Spiritual thriving, we hypothesize, can occur within any stage of cognitive development, at all points in the life span, in all societies, and inside and outside traditional religions. Spiritual thriving can be found in middle schools and universities, in barrios and boardrooms, in seminaries and in seclusion, in Cairo and Cancún. How and why it happens, and how and why it gets compromised, remain mysteries. Mystery may be an interesting part of spiritual development. But, keeping it a mystery in the academy is shortsighted, irresponsible, and compromises our understanding of what it means to be human.

Moving this field forward will require advances in theory and theory-driven research, the collaboration of scholars in many fields, new resources to support the work, and the willingness of the traditional academy to expand its horizons. While one aim is certainly the generation of new knowledge, another is application. For if we know anything, it is that healthy spiritual development is at the heart of individual, societal, and global well-being.

REFERENCES

Baltes, M. M. (1987). Erfolgreiches Altern als Ausdruck von Verhaltenskompetenz und Umweltqualität. In C. Niemitz (Ed.), *Der Mensch im Zusammenspiel von Anlage und Umwelt* (pp. 353–377). Frankfurt: Suhrkamp.

Baltes, P. B. (1997). On the incomplete architecture of human ontogeny: Selection, optimization, and compensation as foundations of developmental theory. *American Psychologist, 52,* 366–380.

Baltes, P. B., & Baltes, M. M. (1980). Plasticity and variability in psychological ageing: Methodological and theoretical issues. In G. E. Gurski (Ed.), *Determining the effects of ageing on the central nervous system* (pp. 41–66). Berlin: Schering.

Baltes, P. B., & Baltes, M. M. (1990). Psychological perspectives on successful aging: The model of selective optimization with compensation. In P. B. Baltes & M. M. Baltes (Eds.), *Successful aging: Perspectives from the behavioral sciences* (pp.1–34). Cambridge, UK: Cambridge University Press.

Baltes, P. B., Lindenberger, U., & Staudinger, U. M. (1998). Life-span theory in developmental psychology. In W. Damon & R. M. Lerner (Eds.), *Handbook of child psychology* (pp. 1029–1143). New York: Wiley.

Benson, P. L. (1997). *All kids are our kids: What communities must do to raise caring and responsible children and adolescents.* San Francisco: Jossey-Bass.

Benson, P. L. (2004). Commentary: Emerging themes in research on adolescent spiritual and religious development. *Applied Developmental Science, 8*(1), 47–50.

Benson, P. L., Donahue, M. J., & Erickson, J. A. (1989). Adolescence and religion: A review of the literature from 1970 to 1986. *Research in the Social Scientific Study of Religion, 1,* 153–181.

Benson, P. L., & King, P. E. (in press). Religion and adolescent development. In H. R. Ebaugh (Ed.), *Handbook of religion and social institutions.* New York: Springer.

Benson, P. L., & Pittman, K. J. (Eds.). (2001). *Trends in youth development: Visions, realities, and challenges.* Norwell, MA: Kluwer Academic.

Benson, P. L., Roehlkepartain, E. C., & Rude, S. P. (2003). Spiritual development in childhood and adolescence: Toward a field of inquiry. *Applied Developmental Science, 7*(3), 205–213.

Benson, P. L., Scales, P. C., Hamilton, S. F., & Sesma, A., Jr. (in press). Positive youth development: Theory, research, and applications. In W. W. Damon & R. M. Lerner (Eds.), *Handbook of child psychology: Vol.1. Theoretical models of human development.* New York: Wiley.

Benson, P. L., & Spilka, B. (1973). God image as a function of self-esteem and locus of control. *Journal for the Scientific Study of Religion, 12,* 297–310.

Benson, P. L., & Williams, D. L. (1982). *Religion on Capitol Hill: Myths and realities.* San Francisco: Harper & Row.

Benson, P. L., Yeager, R. J., Wood, P. K., Guerra, M. J., & Manno, B. V. (1986). *Catholic high schools: Their impact on low-income students.* Washington, DC: National Catholic Educational Association.

Boyer, P. (2001). *Religion explained: The evolutionary origins of religious thought.* London: Random House.

Bridges, L. J., & Moore, K. A. (2002). *Religion and spirituality in childhood and adolescence.* Washington, DC: Child Trends.

Bronfenbrenner, U. (1979). *The ecology of human development: Experiments by nature and design.* Cambridge, MA: Harvard University Press.

Browning, D. S., & Cooper, T. D. (2004). *Religious thought and the modern psychologies* (2nd ed.). Minneapolis, MN: Augsburg Fortress.

Coles, R. (1990). *The spiritual life of children.* Boston: Houghton Mifflin.

Damon, W., Menon, J., & Bronk, K. C. (2003). The development of purpose during adolescence. *Applied Developmental Science, 7*(3), 119–128.

Donahue, M. J., & Benson, P. L. (1995). Religion and the well-being of adolescents. *Journal of Social Issues, 51,* 145–160.

Eccles, J. S., & Gootman, J. A. (2002). *Community programs to promote youth development.* Washington, DC: National Academy Press.

Elder, G. H., Jr. (1974). *Children of the great depression.* Chicago: University of Chicago Press.

Elder, G. H., Jr. (1980). Adolescence in historical perspective. In J. Adelson (Ed.), *Handbook of adolescent psychology* (pp.3–46). New York: Wiley.

Elder, G. H., Jr. (1999). *Children of the great depression: Social change in life experience* (25th anniversary ed.). Boulder, CO: Westview.

Ellis, A. (1955). New approaches to psychotherapy techniques. *Journal of Clinical Psychology, 11,* 207–260.

Fowler, J. W. (1981). *Stages of faith: The psychology of human development and the quest for meaning.* San Francisco: HarperCollins.

Gilligan, C. (1982). *In a different voice: Psychological theory and women's development.* Cambridge, MA: Harvard University Press.

Goldman, R. (1964). *Religious thinking from childhood to adolescence.* London: Routledge and Kegan Paul.

Hardy, A. (1965). *The living stream.* London: Collins.

Hardy, A. (1966). The *divine flame: An essay towards a natural history of religion.* London: Collins.

Harris, P. L. (2000). *The work of the imagination.* Malden, MA: Blackwell.

Hay, D., & Nye, R. (1998). *The spirit in the child.* London: Fount.

Helminiak, D. A. (1987). *Spiritual development.* Chicago: Loyola University Press.

Hill, P. C., & Hood, R. W. (1999). *Measures of religiosity.* Birmingham, AL: Religious Education Press.

Hill, P. C., & Pargament, K. I. (2003). Advances in the conceptualization and measurement of religion and spirituality: Implications for physical and mental health research. *American Psychologist, 58,* 64–74

Hill, P. C., Pargament, K. I., Hood, R. W., McCullough, M. E., Swyers, J. P., Larson, D. B., et al. (2000). Conceptualizing religion and spirituality: Points of commonality, points of departure. *Journal for the Theory of Social Behavior, 30,* 52–77.

Jones, S. L. (1994). A constructive relationship for religion with the science and profession of psychology: Perhaps the boldest model yet. *American Psychologist, 49*(3), 184–199.

Kerestes, M., & Youniss, J. E. (2003). Rediscovering the importance of religion in adolescent development. In R. M. Lerner, F. Jacobs, & D. Wertlieb (Eds.), *Handbook of applied developmental science: Vol. 1. Applying developmental science for youth and families* (pp. 165–184). Thousand Oaks, CA: Sage.

King, P. E., & Boyatzis, C. J. (2004). Exploring adolescent spiritual and religious development: Current and future theoretical and empirical perspectives. *Applied Developmental Science, 8,* 2–6.

King, P. E., & Furrow, J. L. (2004). Religion as a resource for positive youth development: Religion, social capital, and moral outcomes. *Developmental Psychology, 40*(5), 703–713.

Lerner, R. M. (1976). *Concepts and theories of human development.* Reading, MA: Addison-Wesley.

Lerner, R. M. (1984). *On the nature of human plasticity.* Cambridge, UK: Cambridge University Press.

Lerner, R. M. (1998). Theories of human development: Contemporary perspectives. In W. Damon & R. M. Lerner (Eds.), *Handbook of child psychology: Vol. 1. Theoretical models of human development* (5th ed., pp. 1–24). New York: Wiley.

Lerner, R. M. (2002). *Concepts and theories of human development* (3rd ed.). Mahwah, NJ: Erlbaum.

Lerner, R. M. (2003). Developmental assets and asset-building communities: A view of the issues. In R. M. Lerner & P. L. Benson (Eds.), *Developmental assets and asset-building communities: Implications for research, policy, and practice* (pp. 3–18). New York: Kluwer Academic/Plenum.

Lerner, R. M. (2004). *Liberty: Thriving and civic engagement among America's youth.* Thousand Oaks, CA: Sage.

LeVine, R. A. (1989). Cultural environments in child development. In W. Damon (Ed.), *Child development today and tomorrow.* San Francisco: Jossey-Bass.

Lorenz, K. (1965). *Evolution and modification of behavior.* Chicago: University of Chicago Press.

Markus, H. R., & Kitayama, S. (1991a). Cultural variation in the self-concept. In J. Strauss & G. R. Goethals (Eds.), *The self: Interdisciplinary approaches* (pp. 18–48). New York: Springer.

Markus, H. R., & Kitayama, S. (1991b). Culture and the self: Implications for cognition, emotion, and motivation. *Psychological Review, 98,* 224–253.

Marler, P. L., & Hadaway, C. K. (2002). "Being religious" or "being spiritual" in America: A zero-sum proposition. *Journal for the Scientific Study of Religion, 41*(2), 288–300.

McAdams, D. P. (1993). *The stories we live by: Personal myths and the making of the self.* New York: Guilford.

Miller, W. R., & Thoresen, C. E. (2003). Spirituality, religion, and health: An emerging research field. *American Psychologist, 58,* 24–35.

Mithen, S. (1996). *The prehistory of the mind.* London: Thames & Hudson.

Oser, F. K. (1991). The development of religious judgment. In F. K. Oser & W. G. Scarlet (Eds.), *Religious development in childhood and adolescence* (pp. 5–25). San Francisco: Jossey-Bass.

Otto, R. (1950). *The idea of the holy* (2nd ed., J. W. Harvey, Trans.). Oxford, UK: Oxford University Press. (Original work published 1917)

Pargament, K. I. (2002). The bitter and the sweet: An evaluation of the costs and benefits of religiousness. *Psychological Inquiry, 13*(3), 168–181.

Piedmont, R. L. (1999). Does spirituality represent the sixth factor of personality? Spiritual transcendence and the five-factor model. *Journal of Personality, 67,* 985–1013.

Potvin, R. H., Hoge, D. R., & Nelson, H. M. (1976). *Religion and American youth: With emphasis on Catholic adolescents and young adults.* Washington, DC: United States Catholic Conference.

Resnick, M. D., Bearman, P. S., Blum, R. W., Bauman, K. E., Harris, K. M., & Jones, J. (1997). Protecting adolescents from harm: findings from the National Longitudinal Study on Adolescent Health. *Journal of the American Medical Association, 278*(10), 823–832.

Scales, P. C., & Benson, P. L. (2005). Adolescence and thriving. In C. B. Fisher & R. M. Lerner (Eds.), *Encyclopedia of applied developmental science* (pp. 15–19). Thousand Oaks, CA: Sage.

Scales, P. C., Benson, P. L., Leffert, N., & Blyth, D. A. (2000). Contribution of developmental assets to the prediction of thriving among adolescents. *Applied Developmental Science, 4*(1), 27–46.

Schneirla, T. C. (1957). The concept of development in comparative psychology. In D. B. Harris (Ed.), *The concept of development: An issue in the study of human behavior* (pp. 78–108). Minneapolis: University of Minnesota Press.

Schneirla, T. C. (1959). An evolutionary and developmental theory of biphasic processes underlying approach and withdrawal. In M. R. Jones (Ed.), *Nebraska Symposium on Motivation* (pp. 1–42). Lincoln: University of Nebraska Press.

Shweder, R. A., Goodnow, J., Hatano, G., LeVine, R. A., Markus, H., & Miller, P. (1997). The cultural psychology of development: One mind, many mentalities. In W. Damon & R. L. Lerner (Eds.), *Handbook of child psychology: Vol. 1. Theoretical models of human development* (pp. 865–937). New York: Wiley.

Shweder, R. A., & Sullivan, M. (1993). Cultural psychology: Who needs it? *Annual Review of Psychology, 44,* 497–523.

Skinner, B. F. (1938). *The behavior of organisms.* New York: Appleton.

Smith, C. (2003). Theorizing religious effects among American adolescents. *Journal for the Scientific Study of Religion, 42,* 17–30.

Smith, W. C. (1963). *The meaning and end of religion.* New York: Macmillan.

Thelen, E., & Smith, L. B. (1998). Dynamic systems theories. In W. Damon (Series Ed.) & R. M. Lerner (Vol. Ed.), *Handbook on child psychology: Vol. 1. Theoretical models of human development* (5th ed., pp. 563–634). New York: Wiley.

Zinnbauer, B. J., Pargament, K. I., & Scott, A. B. (1999). The emerging meanings of religiousness and spirituality: Problems and prospects. *Journal of Personality, 67,* 889–919.

Author Index

SUBJECT INDEX

ABOUT THE EDITORS

Eugene C. Roehlkepartain is senior adviser in the office of the president, Search Institute, Minneapolis, Minnesota, where he provides leadership for research, publishing, training, and consulting projects that focus on spiritual development, as well as the institute's work with congregations of all faiths. Roehlkepartain has written more than 25 books and reports, and numerous newspaper, magazine, and journal articles on youth development, families and parenting, community building, religious and spiritual development, and related issues. In addition to editing this volume, he is a coeditor of *Nurturing Child and Adolescent Spirituality: Perspectives From the World's Religious Traditions* (2005). He holds a bachelor's degree in journalism and religion from Baylor University in Waco, Texas.

Pamela Ebstyne King serves as research assistant professor of psychology in the Center for Research in Child and Adolescent Development in the School of Psychology at Fuller Theological Seminary in Pasadena, California. Her primary research and teaching interests include positive youth development, spiritual and moral development, and theological perspectives of development. She is particularly interested in enabling thriving through families, congregations, schools, and youth-serving organizations. Ordained in the Presbyterian Church (USA), Dr. King has a background in child, youth, and adult ministry; a master's of divinity; and Ph.D. in family studies from Fuller Theological Seminary. She was a visiting scholar under the Divinity Faculty at Cambridge University and did her postdoctoral work at the Stanford Center on Adolescence. Dr. King is a coauthor of *The Reciprocating Self: Human Development in Theological Perspective* (2005). Her research has been published in *Developmental Psychology, Applied Developmental Science,* the *Journal of Early Adolescence,* and the *Journal of Psychology and Christianity.*

Linda M. Wagener is associate professor of psychology and associate dean of the graduate school of psychology at Fuller Theological Seminary, where she is also codirector of the Center for Research in Child and Adolescent Development. Her research interests include positive youth development, with a particular focus on the spiritual, religious, and moral development of adolescence. Dr. Wagener is currently a principal investigator on an adolescent violence prevention grant from the United States Office of Juvenile Justice and Delinquency Prevention.

Peter L. Benson is president of Search Institute, which provides leadership, knowledge, and resources to promote healthy children, youth, and communities. He has written extensively in adolescent development, altruism, spiritual development, and thriving in adolescence. He serves as principal investigator for Search Institute's initiative on spiritual development in childhood and adolescence. In 1991, he received the William

James Award for career contributions to the psychology of religion from the American Psychological Association. Dr. Benson is the author or editor of numerous books and articles, including *Developmental Assets and Asset-Building Communities, All Kids Are Our Kids: What Communities Must Do to Raise Caring and Responsible Children and Adolescents,* and *Religion on Capitol Hill: Myths and Realities.* He is general editor for the Search Institute Series on Developmentally Attentive Community and Society, published by Springer. He holds a doctorate in experimental social psychology from the University of Denver.

ABOUT THE CONTRIBUTORS

Muninder K. Ahluwalia is assistant professor in the Department of Counseling, Human Development and Educational Leadership in the College of Education and Human Services at Montclair State University in New Jersey. Her research focuses on multicultural counseling competence and identity development of racial and ethnic minorities in the United States. Her recent work addresses relational issues in qualitative research and the role of culture and religion in political contexts in shaping the psychological well-being of Sikh men post-9/11. Her research has been published in journals and texts including the *Journal of Counseling Psychology,* the *Journal of Black Psychology,* and *The Handbook of Counseling Women.*

Amy E. Alberts is a doctoral student in the Eliot-Pearson Department of Child Development at Tufts University, where she is a doctoral research assistant on the 4-H Study of Positive Youth Development and the Research Data Coordinator for the Early Intervention Study at the Brazelton Institute, Children's Hospital, Boston. Her research interests include contextual influences on parenting and adolescent development, outreach scholarship for promoting positive youth development, the family system, and spiritual development.

Hanan A. Alexander heads the Center for Jewish Education and the Department of Overseas Studies at the University of Haifa, where he teaches philosophy of education. He is also a Fellow of the Van Leer Jerusalem Institute and, before moving to Israel with his wife and three children in 1999, was vice president of the University of Judaism in Los Angeles, lecturer in education at UCLA, and editor of the journal *Religious Education.* He has published widely on the philosophy of education and educational policy. His book *Reclaiming Goodness: Education and the Spiritual Quest* (2001) won a National Jewish Book Award, and he recently edited *Ethics and Spirituality in Education: Philosophical, Theological, and Radical Perspectives* (2004).

Pamela M. Anderson is a third-year doctoral student in the Eliot-Pearson Department of Child Development at Tufts University. Pam is a doctoral research assistant on the Overcoming the Odds Study, a longitudinal study that seeks to understand the positive, developmental trajectories of a subset of African American gang and nongang youth in Detroit. Pam's primary research interests involve using applied research to inform programs and policies around the issues of health and well being among adolescents. She is also interested in the development of spirituality, meaning, mattering, and purpose in youth.

Wayne T. Aoki is a clinical psychologist who has served on the faculty of the School of Psychology at Fuller Theological Seminary in Pasadena, California. His research

533

focuses on positive youth development, evaluation of community-based and residential youth programs, and mentoring. Over the past two years he has been part of a team investigating the mediating influence of community assets and youth violence.

Robert Atkins is a nurse and assistant professor in the College of Nursing at Rutgers University in New Jersey. He has a Ph.D. from the Department of Public Health at Temple University in Philadelphia. Over the past five years, he has been involved in research that seeks to investigate the factors that influence the life prospects of urban youth. In collaboration with Daniel Hart, he has coauthored several insightful and highly regarded publications on personality functioning and the civic and moral development of urban youth.

Charles David Blakeney founded and codirected the Institute for Clinical-Developmental Psychology in Berkeley. His domestic policy consulting on children, youth, and families includes two years at the White House. His research and teaching focus on moral disorder, addiction, and recovery. Recent work includes "Leaps of Faith: The Role of Spirituality in Recovering Integrity among Jewish Alcoholics and Drug Addicts" and "Defining Useful Science," an application of the Integrity Scale to evaluating secondary prevention programs. He is currently working on a model of developmental integrity as a research fellow at the Department of Education and Educational Psychology, University of Fribourg, Switzerland. He received a doctorate in education from Harvard University.

Ronnie Frankel Blakeney is visiting professor and research fellow at the University of Fribourg. She received her doctorate at Harvard, was associate professor of ethnic studies at Sonoma State University, and served as codirector of the Institute for Clinical-Developmental Psychology in Berkeley. Her research, consulting, and teaching focus on cross-cultural communication; adolescent development; risk and prevention; and developmental psychopathology. She has consulted internationally on moral psychology and social welfare, including at the White House and the Swiss Federal Office of Public Health. Her current Swiss National Fund project is the intergenerational transmission of values across three generations.

Dean Borgman is professor of youth ministry and holds the Charles E. Culpeper Chair of Youth Ministry at Gordon-Conwell Theological Seminary's urban campus in Boston, Massachusetts. He is also founder and director of the Center for Youth Studies, a national and global network of those interested in research of adolescence and the youth culture. His areas of expertise include urban and cross-cultural youth ministry and the changing youth culture. Among his books are *When Kumbaya Is Not Enough: A Practical Theology for Youth Ministry* and *Hear My Story: Understanding the Cries of Troubled Youth.*

Chris J. Boyatzis is associate professor of psychology at Bucknell University in Lewisburg, Pennsylvania. His primary interest is religious and spiritual development (RSD) processes in the family. He has edited special issues on RSD (March 2003, *Review of Religious Research;* January 2004, *Applied Developmental Science,* coedited with Pamela Ebstyne King). He has authored many chapters and articles on RSD and has papers forthcoming on links between women's and men's religiosity and spirituality in relation to their body image and disordered eating. He organizes a preconference on RSD at the biennial meetings of the Society for Research in Child Development and is involved in religious education at a local and national level.

William M. Bukowski is professor and university research chair in the Department of Psychology and the Centre for Research in Human Development at Concordia

University in Montréal, Québec, Canada. His research program focuses on the features, processes, and effects of children's and adolescents' experiences with their peers.

David Carr is professor of philosophy of education in the University of Edinburgh School of Education. He is author of *Educating the Virtues* (1991), *Professionalism and Ethics in Teaching* (2000), *Making Sense of Education* (2003), and of numerous book chapters and articles in philosophical and educational journals. He is also editor of *Education, Knowledge and Truth* (1998), coeditor (with Jan Steutel) of *Virtue Ethics and Moral Education* (1999) and (with John Haldane) of *Spirituality, Philosophy and Education* (2003).

Robert Coles is the James Agee Professor of Social Ethics at Harvard University and professor of psychiatry and medical humanities at Harvard Medical School. Among his many books is *The Spiritual Life of Children* (Houghton Mifflin, 1990).

Sheri-Ann E. Cowie is a doctoral student in counseling psychology at the Steinhardt School of Education of New York University. She is involved in qualitative and quantitative research on the professional experiences of African American CEOs and mental health professionals, as well as the role of self, other, and divine forgiveness in shaping dispositional optimism and pessimism. Her research interests include the relationship among spirituality, religion, transnational identity and positive psychological development for Jamaicans and other English-speaking West Indians.

Emily Crawford is pursuing her doctorate in clinical psychology at Miami University in Oxford, Ohio. Her research interests focus on the prevention and education of violence against women, in particular, drug-facilitated sexual assault, alcohol use and abuse in college settings, and the interpersonal consequences of childhood abuse experiences and the factors promoting later vulnerability or resilience.

Mary Lynn Dell is associate clinical professor of psychiatry and behavioral sciences and of pediatrics, Children's National Medical Center and George Washington University School of Medicine, Washington, D.C.

Jane R. Dickie is professor of psychology and director of women's studies at Hope College in Holland, Michigan. Her current research interests and publications concern parent–child relationships and children's concepts of God, women's communities and their impact on adult development, relationships between generations of feminists, and children's gendered sense of self and gendered sense of God.

David C. Dollahite is professor of family life at Brigham Young University in Provo, Utah, where he is an Eliza R. Snow University Fellow. He has been a visiting scholar at the University of Massachusetts-Amherst and Dominican University of California. His research interests include religion and family life in Christian, Jewish, and Muslim families, Latter-day Saint (Mormon) family life, and fathering and faith in fathers of children with special needs. He has published approximately 40 scholarly articles and chapters on fathering, faith, and family life, and is editor of *Strengthening Our Families* (2000) and *Helping and Healing Our Families* (2005), both on Latter-day Saint families.

Thomas M. Donnelly is a visiting assistant professor at Rutgers University in Camden, New Jersey. His interests cover a range of areas in cognitive and developmental psychology. At Rutgers, he is working with Daniel Hart, James Youniss, and Robert Atkins in analyzing large national databases to examine civic, moral, and spiritual development. At New York University, Tom is working with Doris Aaronson, studying the reading and mathematical processes and strategies of normal readers, dyslexics, and dyscalculics in college.

Elizabeth M. Dowling is director of research for the ImagineNations Group, based in Pasadena, Maryland. She is responsible for designing and implementing strategies that capture the voices of young people around the world to engage them as critical stakeholders in program and policy development aimed at improving human lives. She received her Ph.D. in 2004 from Tufts University in child development. Elizabeth wrote her dissertation on spiritual and religious development in adolescence, and she has published numerous articles on the topic. She continues to pursue questions of meaning, purpose, and religiosity in her current work with young people around the world.

Jacquelynne S. Eccles is the McKeachie Collegiate Professor of Psychology, Education, and Women's Studies at the University of Michigan. She has conducted research on topics ranging from gender-role socialization and classroom influences on motivation to social development in the family, school, peer, and wider cultural contexts. Her most recent work focuses on (1) ethnicity as a part of the self and as a social category influencing experiences and (2) the relation of self beliefs and identity to the transition from mid to late adolescence and then into adulthood.

Robert A. Emmons is professor of psychology at the University of California, Davis. He is the author of nearly 80 original publications in peer-reviewed journals or chapters in edited volumes, including *The Psychology of Ultimate Concerns: Motivation and Spirituality in Personality* (1999) and *The Psychology of Gratitude* (2004). He is a former associate editor of the *Journal of Personality and Social Psychology* and has served as president of Division 36 (The Psychology of Religion) of the American Psychological Association. His research focuses on personal goals, spirituality, the psychology of gratitude and thankfulness, and subjective well-being.

James W. Fowler is Charles Howard Candler Professor of Human Development, Candler School of Theology, and director of the Center for Ethics in Public Policy and the Professions at Emory University in Atlanta, Georgia

Richard L. Gorsuch is professor of psychology at Fuller Theological Seminary in Pasadena, California, and is best known for his studies in the psychology of religion, substance abuse, social psychology, and statistics. He is the author of *Factor Analysis* (1983) and the developer of the statistical software program Unimult. Dr. Gorsuch is an active member of the Religious Research Association and a fellow of the Society for the Scientific Study of Religion and the American Psychological Association. He has been editor of the *Journal for the Scientific Study of Religion*. His most recent book is *Integrating Psychology and Spirituality.*

Alma Gottlieb is a cultural anthropologist interested in religion, gender, young children, and Africa. She is the author of six books, including *The Afterlife Is Where We Come From: The Culture of Infancy in West Africa* (2004), and coeditor (with Judy DeLoache) of *A World of Babies: Imagined Childcare Guides for Seven Societies* (2000). The memoir she coauthored with Philip Graham, *Parallel Worlds: An Anthropologist and a Writer Encounter Africa* (1993), won the Victor Turner Prize in Ethnographic Writing. Gottlieb has held fellowships from the Guggenheim Foundation, National Endowment for the Humanities, Social Science Research Council, and others. She is professor of anthropology, African studies, and women's studies at the University of Illinois at Urbana–Champaign.

Pehr Granqvist is a postdoc and lecturer in the Department of Psychology, Uppsala University, Sweden. His current research interests include attachment theoretical research on adults and adolescents, developments in attachment methodology, the psychology of religion, and neurotheology. Some of his recent publications concern longitudinal predictions of religious changes in adolescence from attachment and changes in romantic relationship status; a review and meta-analysis of attachment and religious conversions in adults; three experiments addressing the effects on religiousness from subliminal separation primes; and a debate concerning the "depth" approaches in the psychology of religion.

Daniel Hart is professor of psychology and associate dean at Rutgers University in Camden, New Jersey. His research focuses on the development during childhood and adolescence of civic competence, personality, identity, and morality, particularly among urban youth. In one line of investigation, he uses national survey data to characterize the nature and development of civic competence. His second project focuses on the effects of stress on personality regulation. With Robert Atkins, Hart founded the STARR Program, which supports youth development through community service, sports, tutoring, and other activities. He also is cofounder of the Healthy Futures for Camden Youth Project, which seeks to increase enrollment among Camden's families in New Jersey's subsidized health insurance program for low-income families.

Tobin Hart is a father, author, psychologist, and speaker. He serves as professor of psychology at the State University of West Georgia. He is cofounder and chair of the ChildSpirit Institute, a nonprofit educational and research hub exploring and nurturing the spirituality of children and adults (www.childspirit.net). His work examines consciousness, spirituality, psychotherapy, and education. His latest books are *From Information to Transformation: Education for the Evolution of Consciousness* (2001) and *The Secret Spiritual World of Children* (2003).

David Hay is a zoologist who worked for several years at the Religious Experience Research Unit set up in Oxford by the zoologist Sir Alister Hardy in 1969. After Hardy's death in 1985, Hay became director of the unit. Subsequently, he was appointed reader in spiritual education at Nottingham University, a post from which he retired in 2000. Currently he holds the posts of honorary senior research fellow in the Department of Divinity and Religious Studies in the University of Aberdeen and visiting professor in the Institute for the Study of Religion in the University of Krakow in Poland.

Steve Hornberger, M.S.W., has more than 25 years' experience in human services and community building as a social worker, grassroots activist, educator, consultant, and administrator. In his current position as founding director of the Behavioral Health Division for the Child Welfare League of America, Mr. Hornberger is responsible for identifying and creating evidence-based innovations to strengthen services and supports in the areas of alcohol and other drugs, mental health, and child welfare. He also teaches graduate-level courses in spirituality and social work. In March 2005, he coedited the special edition of *Child Welfare* on "Community Building and 21st Century Child Welfare Practice." Mr. Hornberger is particularly interested in the expansion of the role of consumers in the design, delivery, and evaluation of services; the collaboration and integration of formal and informal systems of care; and the expansion of the role of civil society in fostering community life.

Heidi Ihrke is a Ph.D. student in the Clinical Psychology Program at Bowling Green State University. Her research interests pertain to the psychology of religion with regard to family life and applied therapeutic techniques, specifically, religious appraisals of parental divorce, sanctification of marriage, and the integration of psychospiritual interventions into clinical practice.

Carl N. Johnson is chair of the Psychology in Education Department in the School of Education at the University of Pittsburgh. His research interests include children's mental, supernatural, and metaphysical ideas. With Karl S. Rosengren and Paul L. Harris, he coedited *Imagining the Impossible: Magical, Scientific, and Religious Thinking in Children* (2000), which includes his review of the development of metaphysical thinking. He is a member of the international advisory aboard of the new *Journal of Cognition and Culture.*

Roberta Furtick Jones has a master's in social work from New York University. She has worked with senior citizens, children, and families in a variety of social service venues. She is a practicing family therapist, has provided clinical training and supervision to social workers, and was the director of a family counseling center in Brooklyn, New York. Ms. Jones has also presented at conferences on spirituality and social work. Her practice and research interests include making spirituality an accessible resource to the helping professions and the healthy development of urban boys of African descent.

Julie Dombrowski Keith received her master's degree from the Maxwell School of Citizenship and Public Affairs at Syracuse University. She has worked on studies of depression in young adults as well as in senior citizens, teenage childbearing, positive measures of adolescent well-being, and child care analysis. Beyond those topics, her research interests lie in education, development, family strengths, and the intersection of race/ethnicity and socioeconomic status in everyday life.

Brien Kelley is a doctoral student in clinical psychology at Teachers College, Columbia University, New York. His interests include positive emotions and mental health, Buddhist contributions to psychotherapies, and spiritual development in adolescence. He is coauthor, with Lisa Miller, of a chapter in *The Handbook of the Psychology of Religion* (forthcoming).

Aria M. Kirkland-Harris is an undergraduate psychology and political science major at Columbia University. She is involved in qualitative and quantitative research on rejection sensitivity in race-based relations involving African Americans and Latino youth and the professional experiences of African American CEOs and mental health professionals.

Teresa T. Kneezel is a psychology graduate student at the University of California, Davis, and holds a bachelor's degree in psychology and religion from the University of Rochester. Primarily interested in religious motivation, personality integration, and well-being, she is currently examining the effects of approach–avoidance motivation in spiritual and sanctified goals on an individual's well-being. Kneezel has presented her work at the International Positive Psychology Symposium and the International Conference on Self-Determination Theory.

Richard M. Lerner is the Bergstrom Chair in Applied Developmental Science and the director of the Institute for Applied Research in Youth Development in the Eliot-Pearson Department of Child Development at Tufts University. Dr. Lerner is the author or editor of 59 books and more than 400 scholarly articles and chapters. He edited volume 1, *Theoretical Models of Human Development,* for the fifth edition of the *Handbook of Child Psychology.* He is the founding editor of the *Journal of Research on Adolescence* and of *Applied Developmental Science.* He is known for his theory of, and research about, relations between life span human development and contextual or ecological change.

Laura H. Lippman is area director for data and measurement and senior research associate at Child Trends in Washington, D.C., where she directs a variety of projects related to indicators of child and family well-being, early childhood, education, positive development, and international comparisons. Her recent publications include *What Do Children Need to Flourish? Conceptualizing and Measuring Indicators of Positive Development* (coedited with Kristin A. Moore) and "The Measurement of Family Religiosity and Spirituality" with Erik Michelsen and Eugene C. Roehlekepartain. Ms. Lippman was the lead staff person for the Federal Interagency Forum on Child and Family Statistics in developing the first official government monitoring report on child well-being, *America's Children: Key National Indicators of Well-Being.*

Douglas Magnuson is assistant professor of youth and human services at the University of Northern Iowa, where he teaches courses in youth work and youth development in the undergraduate and graduate programs. He is also the project manager for the National Study of Campus Ministries. His research interests are evaluation theory, moral development in youth organizations, and youth work practice models. For the past three years he has evaluated after-school programs, and he is writing a book about the experience. Dr. Magnuson is editor of the journal *Child & Youth Services* and coeditor of the journal *Child and Youth Care Forum.*

Annette Mahoney is an associate professor at Bowling Green State University and a licensed, practicing clinical psychologist. Dr. Mahoney's primary research interests pertain to the psychology of religion, particularly with regard to family life. Her recent publications focus on the sanctification of marriage, parenting, family relationships, major life strivings, one's body, and premarital sexuality, as well as the psychological impact of perceiving negative life events as desecrations and sacred losses. Other research interests are links between marriage, parenting and child behavior problems, and physical aggression in families.

H. Newton Malony is senior professor of psychology in the Graduate School of Psychology at Fuller Theological Seminary. A prodigious scholar, Dr. Malony's most recent publications include *Living with Paradox: Religious Leadership and the Genius of Double Vision* (1998). He has published broadly in the areas of the psychology of religion, religious intolerance, transactional analysis, and the integration of psychology and religion. A licensed psychologist and ordained United Methodist minister, Dr. Malony has also maintained professional involvement in the American Psychological Association, the California Psychological Association, the Society for the Scientific Study of Religion, and the American College of Forensic Examiners.

Loren Marks is assistant professor of family, child, and consumer sciences in the School of Human Ecology at Louisiana State University. In collaboration with David Dollahite, he has conducted extensive qualitative research with more than 100 Christian, Jewish, Mormon, and Muslim families from around the United States and has authored or coauthored approximately 20 articles or chapters addressing religion in connection with parenting, marriage, and individual development.

Ann S. Masten is Distinguished McKnight University Professor at the University of Minnesota. In 1986, she joined the faculty of the Institute of Child Development at Minnesota, later heading this department from 1996 to 2005. Her research is focused on risk, competence, and resilience in development, with the ultimate goal of reducing the burden and promoting better life chances for children threatened by family adversities, war, terrorism, homelessness, and other hazardous conditions. Dr. Masten is currently president of Division 7 (developmental) of the American Psychological Association.

M. Kyle Matsuba is an assistant professor at the University of Northern British Columbia, Canada. He received his doctorate from the University of British Columbia in developmental psychology working with Lawrence Walker. Dr. Matsuba's research has focused on moral development and personality, psychosocial impact of technology, and assessing at-risk youth postintervention. In addition, he continues to work with Drs. Donnelly, Atkins, and Hart, studying the antecedents and consequences of volunteer work.

Jacqueline S. Mattis is associate professor of applied psychology in the Steinhardt School of Education of New York University. Her research focuses on the meanings and functions of religion and spirituality for African Americans, the factors that inform African American religious and spiritual involvement, and the impact of religious and spiritual ideologies and practices on such positive psychological outcomes as altruism, volunteerism, forgiveness, and optimism. Her research has been published in numerous journals and texts, including the *Journal of Community Psychology,* the *Journal of Adult Development,* and *Personality and Individual Differences.*

Lisa Miller is associate professor of psychology and education at Teachers College, Columbia University, New York. Dr. Miller's research and clinical orientation focus on spiritual experience and development throughout the life span, with a particular focus on childhood, adolescence, and parenthood. Recently she has contributed to *The Handbook of the Psychology of Religion* (forthcoming), *Casebook for a Spiritual Strategy in Counseling and Psychotherapy* (2004), and *Spiritually Oriented Psychotherapy* (2005); she also was involved with the production of *Series IV (spirituality): Spiritual Awareness Psychotherapy,* a DVD released by the American Psychological Association.

Robert L. Miller Jr. explores the intersection of spirituality, social welfare, and public health. He has examined spirituality in the lives of African Americans affected by AIDS, including gay men and women over 50, as well as clergy and pastoral responses to AIDS. He also studies community health collaboration efforts between federally qualified health centers and urban churches. His recent publications include *An Appointment with God: AIDS, Place and Spirituality; The Church and Gay Men: A Spiritual Opportunity in the Wake of the Clergy Sexual Crisis; Look What God Can Do: African American Gay Men, AIDS and Spirituality;* and *Spirituality and Professional Social Work: Implications for Practice, Research and Education.* Dr. Miller is an assistant professor in social work at the University of Albany, State University of New York.

Andrew B. Newberg, M.D., is assistant professor of radiology and psychiatry at the University of Pennsylvania Health System in Philadelphia. His primary research area is functional neuroimaging with a focus on religious and spiritual phenomena. He is coauthor of *Why God Won't Go Away: Brain Science and the Biology of Belief* (Ballantine).

Stephanie K. Newberg, M.Ed., LCSW, is assistant director of Center City and Wynnewood Offices, and senior staff therapist for the Council for Relationships in Philadelphia. Her clinical and research interests include adolescent psychology and the relationship between psychology and religion.

Rebecca Nye was the primary researcher for and coauthor, along with David Hay, of a study that became the groundbreaking book *The Spirit of the Child* (1998), one of the most frequently cited research studies in the children's spirituality movement. She is now the coordinator of a major children's spirituality research initiative at Cambridge University and is widely sought as a conference speaker. She is currently the research coordinator for the Godly Play approach to children's spirituality. She is the mother of three children, the third born as this book was being written.

Doug Oman is adjunct assistant professor in the Maternal Child Health Program, School of Public Health, University of California, Berkeley. His research focuses on spirituality, religion, and health. He has studied psychological processes through which religion and spirituality are transmitted, how mortality is affected by religious involvement, and how health professionals can benefit from receiving training in a comprehensive nonsectarian spiritual tool kit. He is author (with Carl E. Thoresen) of "Spiritual Modeling: A Key to Spiritual and Religious Growth?" (2003) and (with J. D. Driskill) of "Holy Name Repetition as a Spiritual Exercise and Therapeutic Technique" (2003).

Eboo Patel is the founder and executive director of the Interfaith Youth Core, a Chicago-based nonprofit that brings young people from different faith communities together to do service projects. He is also adjunct professor at Chicago Theological Seminary and president of the board of *CrossCurrents* magazine. Dr. Patel's research interests include religion in the contemporary world, progressive Islam, interfaith work, religious movements, and the religious identity of youth. He is coeditor (with Patrice Brodeur) of *Building the Interfaith Youth Movement* (forthcoming) and special editor of the spring 2005 issue of *CrossCurrents* magazine on contemporary issues in interfaith work.

Sara Pendleton, M.D., is an assistant professor at Wayne State University and an acade-· mic general pediatrician at Children's Hospital of Michigan in Detroit. Dr. Pendleton currently conducts both qualitative and quantitative research on the role of religion and spirituality in coping with chronic childhood illness and the roles and boundaries of religion and spirituality in the physician–patient interaction. Her future research goals include creating valid and reliable measures of religiousness/spirituality in children to foster better understanding of the role that religiousness/spirituality plays in illness and health.

Donald Ratcliff has spent more than a quarter of a century studying the religious concepts of children, as well as the latent emergent spirituality of children in natural settings. He has edited several graduate-level textbooks on religious education, including one on preschoolers, another on school-aged children, and a third on adolescents. He teaches at Vanguard University in Costa Mesa, California, and is the father of three children, including two boys in their twenties and one teenage daughter. He was the senior editor of *Children's Spirituality: Christian Perspectives, Research, and Applications* (2004).

K. Helmut Reich is a former physicist who since 1984 has worked at the School of Education in the University of Fribourg, Switzerland. His main research interests are cognitive and religious development as well as the relation between science and religion and theology. In 1994 Dr. Reich was appointed professor at the (nonresidential) Stratford University International at Richmond (British Columbia) and Evanston (Wyoming) School of Consciousness Studies and Wisdom Traditions. Reich holds doctoral degrees in electrical engineering, physics, and theology. In 1997 he received the William James Award of the American Psychological Association, Division 36 (Psychology of Religion).

Kevin S. Reimer is associate professor of psychology in the Department of Graduate Psychology at Azusa Pacific University in Southern California. He is also a Templeton fellow in science and religion at the University of Oxford. Reimer earned his Ph.D. in marriage and family studies from the Graduate School of Psychology, Fuller Theological Seminary, in 2001, receiving the David Allan Hubbard Achievement Award for academic excellence. He was a postdoctoral fellow with Lawrence J. Walker at the University of British Columbia. Reimer's research program focuses on the psychology of morality, altruism, and spirituality using discourse process analysis to explore symbolic representation in social systems. He has received research grants from the John

Fetzer Institute and the John Templeton Foundation, and is ordained in the Presbyterian Church (USA).

W. George Scarlett is an assistant professor of child development and deputy chair in the Eliot-Pearson Department of Child Development at Tufts University. His current research interests are reflected in his most recent writings, which include *Trouble in the Classroom: Managing the Behavior Problems of Young Children* (1998), *Children's Play* (2004, coauthored with S. Nadeau, D. Salonius-Pasternak, and I. Ponte), and the first ever chapter on religious and spiritual development in R. M. Lerner and W. Damon (eds.), *Handbook of Child Psychology* (2005)

Kelly Dean Schwartz is assistant professor in the Department of Behavioural Science at Nazarene University College in Calgary, Alberta, Canada. His research interests are the social-developmental factors related to child and adolescent development (e.g., parents, peers, music), family and ecological systems theories, identity and positive youth development, and spirituality and religiosity across the life span.

Daniel G. Scott is assistant professor and graduate adviser in the School of Child and Youth Care of the University of Victoria, and was recently awarded the 2004 Faculty of Human and Social Development Award for Teaching Excellence. His current research includes a participatory research project with a group of women who are exploring the spirituality expressed in their own adolescent diaries and journals. His recent publications include: "Retrospective Spiritual Narratives: Exploring Recalled Childhood and Adolescent Spiritual Experiences" (2004) and "Spirituality in Child and Youth Care: Considering Spiritual Development and 'Relational Consciousness'" (2003).

Madelene Sta. Maria is a professor in the Department of Psychology at De La Salle University in Manila, Philippines. She obtained her doctorate in psychology at the University of Cologne, Germany. Her research has focused on the organization of adolescent life in culture and society, on cultural psychological bases of peaceful and conflictual interactions, and on culture and emotions.

Janice L. Templeton is a doctoral candidate in the Combined Program in Education and Psychology at the University of Michigan. Broadly defined, her research interests focus on positive youth development and on spiritual development from a life-span perspective. More specifically, her interests include (1) the development of personal and collective spirituality identities and their function in individual experience; (2) the relation of spiritual identities to beliefs, values, and life goals; and (3) individual, social and environmental well-being outcomes associated with spiritual identities.

Carl E. Thoresen is professor emeritus in the School of Education and Departments of Psychology and Psychiatry and Behavioral Sciences at Stanford University. His initial research focused on the psychology of behavioral self-management in adolescents and adults. In the 1980s he conducted with others the first studies on changing Type A behavior and reducing coronary disease morbidity and mortality. Active in the emergence of behavioral medicine, he currently is studying the effects of spiritual practices on health, disease, and well-being.

Michael Utsch has completed academic studies in theology and psychology. In his doctoral dissertation, he developed a synopsis of different psychological approaches to religiousness, focusing on their anthropological presuppositions. He was trained in Adlerian psychotherapy and maintains a small private practice. After working in different clinical settings, since 1997 he has collaborated with the Protestant Center for Worldviews in Berlin, which provides information on new religious and ideological movements.

Suman Verma is chair of the Department of Child Development, Government Home Science College, Chandigarh, India. Her research and published works are in the areas of life experiences of street and working children, time use, leisure, adolescent family life, school stress, abuse, and life skills training.

Donald Walker is a recent graduate of the Graduate School of Psychology at Fuller Theological Seminary. His research interests focus on the integration of religious and spiritual interventions in psychotherapy with children, adolescents, and their families. He has published most recently in *Counseling and Values*.

Lawrence J. Walker is professor of psychology and director of the graduate program at the University of British Columbia in Vancouver, Canada. Dr. Walker's program of research focuses on the psychology of moral development, including such topics as gender and cultural differences, family and peer contexts, developmental mechanisms, models of stage transition, moral personality and character, and moral exemplarity. He has been elected a fellow of both the Canadian and the American Psychological Associations; and has served as president of the Association for Moral Education, chair of the board of Carey Theological College, and a member of the editorial board for several psychology journals. He currently serves as associate editor for the *Merrill-Palmer Quarterly*.

Margaret O'Dougherty Wright, Ph.D., is an associate professor of psychology at Miami University in Oxford, Ohio. Her research focuses on the long-term consequences of trauma across the life span, with a particular emphasis on risks emanating from the family such as sexual, physical, and psychological abuse. She has examined protective factors that might mediate the relationship between childhood trauma and later resilience, including social support, spirituality, coping, and meaning-making strategies. She has also examined ways in which childhood trauma may be linked to further trauma exposure across the life span, with a focus on revictimization and intergenerational transmission of child maltreatment.

CPSIA information can be obtained at www.ICGtesting.com
Printed in the USA
LVOW11*1146130114

369206LV00007B/36/P